# Business Ethics

## Ethical Decision Making and Cases

# Business Ethics

## Ethical Decision Making and Cases

### Sixth Edition

**O. C. FERRELL**
Colorado State University

**JOHN FRAEDRICH**
Southern Illinois University
at Carbondale

**LINDA FERRELL**
University of Wyoming

**Houghton Mifflin Company**  *Boston   New York*

*V.P., Editor-in-Chief:* George T. Hoffman
*Associate Sponsoring Editor:* Joanne Dauksewicz
*Senior Project Editor:* Fred Burns
*Editorial Assistant:* Lisa Goodman
*Senior Production/ Design Coordinator:* Sarah Ambrose
*Manufacturing Manager:* Florence Cadran
*Senior Marketing Manager:* Steven W. Mikels

Cover image: © White Packert/Getty Images

Printed in the U.S.A.

Library of Congress Control Number: 2003114145

ISBN: 0-618-39573-3

4 5 6 7 8 9—MP—08 07 06 05

# Brief Contents

# Contents

## PART THREE    Implementing Business Ethics in a Global Economy . . . . . . . . . . . . . . . . .165

## PART FOUR   Cases . . . . . . . . . . . . . . . . . . . . . . . . . .247

*This book is dedicated to:*

My son James Collins Ferrell

*O. C. Ferrell*

---

My wife Debbie and my children Anna, Jacob, Joseph, Joshua, and Lael as well as my parents Gerhard and Bernice.

*John Fraedrich*

---

My parents Norlan and Phyllis Nafziger

*Linda Ferrell*

# Preface

Business Ethics continues to advance as one of the most widely adopted business ethics texts available today. Using a managerial framework, we explain how ethics can be integrated into strategic business decisions. This framework provides *an overview of the concepts, processes, and best practices* associated with successful business ethics programs. Some approaches to business ethics are excellent for exercises in intellectual reasoning but do not deal with the actual ethical decision-making situations that people in business organizations face. Our approach prepares students for ethical dilemmas they will face in their business careers.

The dramatic increase in business ethics concerns over the last three years resulted from numerous scandals and loss of confidence in Corporate America. The Sixth Edition has been revised to reflect these events by providing up-to-date examples and cases. Business ethics issues that have become extremely relevant include concern for stakeholders, corporate governance, accounting ethics, and some stakeholders' desire for more regulation in business. Business schools are being asked to do a better job in teaching business ethics to help prepare future managers to be more responsible and more responsive to stakeholder concerns. More corporations are developing ethics programs and making ethics a higher priority than in previous years.

We have been careful in this revision to provide the most up-to-date knowledge while retaining the strengths that have made this text so successful. This book has been successful because *it addresses the complex environment of ethical decision making in organizations and real-life issues.* Every individual has unique personal values, and every organization has its own set of values and ethical policies. Business ethics must consider the organizational culture and interdependent relationships between the individual and other significant persons involved in organizational decision making. Without effective guidance, a businessperson cannot make ethical decisions while facing organizational pressures and day-to-day challenges in the competitive environment.

By focusing on the issues and organizational environments, this book provides students the opportunity to see the roles and responsibilities they may face as they advance in the workplace. Our primary goal—as always—is to enhance the awareness and the decision-making skills students will need to make business ethics decisions that contribute to responsible business conduct. By focusing on the concerns and issues of today's challenging business environment, we demonstrate that studying business ethics provides vital knowledge that contributes to overall business success.

## Philosophy of This Text

Business ethics in organizations requires values-based leadership from top management, purposeful actions that include planning and implementation of standards of appropriate conduct, as well as openness and continuous effort to improve the organization's ethical performance. Although personal values are important in ethical decision making, they are just one of the components that guide the decisions, actions, and policies of organizations. The burden of ethical behavior relates to the organization's values and traditions, not just to the individuals who make the decisions and carry them out. A firm's ability to plan and implement ethical business standards depends in part on structuring resources and activities to achieve ethical objectives in an effective and efficient manner.

The purpose of this book is to help students improve their ability to make ethical decisions in business by providing them with a framework that they can use to identify, analyze, and resolve ethical issues in business decision making. Individual values and ethics are important in this process. By studying business ethics, students begin to understand how to cope with conflicts between their personal values and those of the organization.

Many ethical decisions in business are close calls. It often takes years of experience in a particular industry to know what is acceptable. We do not, in this book, provide ethical answers but instead attempt to prepare students to make informed ethical decisions. First, we do not moralize by indicating what to do in a specific situation. Second, although we provide an overview of moral philosophies and decision-making processes, we do not prescribe any one philosophy or process as best or most ethical. Third, by itself, this book will not make students more ethical nor will it tell them how to judge the ethical behavior of others. Rather, its goal is to help students understand and use their current values and convictions in making business decisions and to encourage everyone to think about the effects of their decisions on business and society.

Many people believe that business ethics cannot be taught. Although we do not claim to teach ethics, we suggest that by studying business ethics a person can improve ethical decision making by identifying ethical issues and recognizing the approaches available to resolve them. An organization's reward system can reinforce appropriate behavior and help shape attitudes and beliefs about important issues. For example, the success of some campaigns to end racial or gender discrimination in the workplace provides evidence that attitudes and behavior can be changed with new information, awareness, and shared values.

It is important to recognize the relationship between personal morals and ethical business decisions. While business ethics reflects acceptable conduct based on the social, cultural, political, and legal environment at a point in time, personal morals reflect deeper and more enduring philosophies about life. Whereas virtues linked to the high moral ground of truthfulness, honesty, fairness, and openness are often assumed to be self-evident and easy to apply, business decisions involve complex managerial and social considerations. Some business ethics perspectives assume that ethics training is for people who have unacceptable personal moral development, but that is not necessarily the case. Because organizations are culturally diverse and personal values must be respected, a collective agreement on organizational ethics is as vital as other managerial decisions.

## Complete Content Coverage

In writing *Business Ethics,* Sixth Edition, we have strived to be as informative, complete, accessible, and up to date as possible. Instead of focusing on one area of ethics, such as moral philosophy or codes of ethics, we provide balanced coverage of all areas relevant to the current development and practice of ethical decision making. In short, we have tried to keep pace with new developments and current thinking in teaching and practices. The corporate responsibility issues that resulted in the passage of the Sarbanes-Oxley Act of 2002 are appropriately addressed. General issues such as conflicts of interest, honesty, truthful communications, and legal compliance are addressed to provide an understanding of appropriate conduct. Specific ethical issues including accounting fraud, Internet privacy, discrimination, falsification of information, and other issues that may cause social or environmental damage are covered through dilemmas, examples, and cases. Additionally, we have added a new chapter on implementing and auditing ethics and social initiatives to reflect managerial desires for performance measurement tools and stakeholder demands for greater transparency.

## Organization of the Text

The first half of the text consists of ten chapters, which provide a framework to identify, analyze, and understand how businesspeople make ethical decisions and deal with ethical issues. Several enhancements have been made to chapter content for this edition. Some of the most important are listed below.

Part One, "An Overview of Business Ethics," includes three chapters that help provide a broader context for the study of business ethics. Chapter 1, "The Importance of Business Ethics," has been revised with many new examples and survey results to describe issues and concerns important to business ethics. A new section on the benefits of business ethics has been integrated into this chapter, while the section on the development of business ethics has been updated. Chapter 2, "Emerging Business Ethics Issues," has been significantly reorganized and updated with new examples and issues. This chapter also includes an introduction to the Sarbanes-Oxley Act, which resulted from a number of much publicized ethics scandals and may have a significant impact on corporate activities. Chapter 3, "Ethics As a Dimension of Social Responsibility," has been reorganized and revised with new examples that provide an understanding of economic, competitive, legal, and philanthropic issues, and place business ethics issues into a broader context.

Part Two, "The Ethical Decision-Making Process," consists of four chapters providing extensive coverage of the various factors that influence ethical decision making in business. These factors are brought together in a useful framework in Chapter 4, "Understanding Ethical Decision Making and Corporate Governance," which has been revised and updated to reflect current research and understanding of ethical decision making. This chapter also includes an overview of corporate governance and how governance systems can influence ethical conduct in business organizations. Chapter 5, "Individual Factors: Moral Philosophies and Cognitive Moral Development," has been reorganized and revised to explore the role of moral philosophies and cognitive moral development as individual factors in the ethical decision-making process. Chapter 6, "Organizational Factors: Corporate Culture," examines the role of corporate culture and ethical climate in ethical decision making. This chapter also looks at how leadership, organizational structure, and group dimensions can influence corporate culture and ethical decisions. Chapter 7, "Organizational Factors: Structure, Relationships, and Conflicts," considers additional organizational influences on business decisions, such as role relationships, differential association, and other organizational pressures, as well as whistle-blowing.

Part Three, "Implementing Business Ethics in a Global Economy," looks at specific measures that companies can take to build an effective ethics program, as well as how these programs may be affected by global issues. Chapter 8, "Developing an Effective Ethics Program," has been refined and updated with corporate best practices for developing effective ethics programs. Chapter 9, "Implementing and Auditing Ethics Programs," is a brand new chapter that offers a framework for auditing ethics initiatives as well as the importance of doing so. Such audits can help companies pinpoint problem areas, measure their progress in improving conduct, and even provide a "debriefing" opportunity after a crisis. Finally, Chapter 10, "Business Ethics in a Global Economy," contains new examples of international business ethics issues, conflicts, and cooperative efforts to establish universal standards of conduct.

Part Four consists of eighteen cases that bring reality into the learning process. Nine of these cases are new to the Sixth Edition, while the remaining eight have been revised and updated. The companies and situations portrayed in these cases are real; names and other facts are not disguised; and all cases include developments up to 2003. By reading and analyzing these cases, students can gain insight into ethical decisions and the realities of making decisions in complex situations.

Two appendixes provide additional real-world examples and practice in identifying and weighing ethical issues. These appendixes include company codes of ethics, as well as the Caux Round Table Business Principles of Ethics. We provide several codes of ethics that provide good examples of comprehensive codes that are being implemented today.

Like the previous edition, the Sixth Edition provides three behavioral simulation role-play cases developed for use in the business ethics course. The role-play cases and implementation methods can be found in the *Instructor's Resource Manual with Test Bank* and on the Web site. Role-play cases may be used as a culminating experience to help students integrate concepts covered in the text. Alternatively, the cases may be used as an ongoing exercise to provide students with extensive opportunities for interacting and making ethical decisions.

Role-play cases simulate a complex, realistic, and timely business ethics situation. Students form teams and make decisions based on an assigned role. The role-play case complements and enhances traditional approaches to business learning experiences because it (1) gives students the opportunity to practice making decisions that have business ethics consequences; (2) re-creates the power, pressures, and information that affect decision making at various levels of management; (3) provides students with a team-based experience that enriches their skills and understanding of group processes and dynamics; and (4) uses a feedback period to allow for the exploration of complex and controversial issues in business ethics decision making. The role-play can be used with classes of any size.

## Business Ethics Learning Center Web Site

The Web site developed for the Sixth Edition provides up-to-date examples, issues, and interactive learning devices to assist students in improving their decision-making skills. "The Business Ethics Learning Center" has been created to take advantage of information available on the Internet while providing new interactive skill-building exercises that can help students practice ethical decision making. The site contains links to companies and organizations highlighted in each chapter; Internet exercises; ACE (ACyber Evaluation) interactive quizzes, which help students master chapter content through multiple-choice questions; links to association, industry, and company codes of conduct; case Web site linkages; company and organizational examples; and academic resources, including links to business ethics centers throughout the world and the opportunity to sign up for weekly abstracts of relevant *Wall Street Journal* articles. Four Ethical Leadership Challenge scenarios are available for each chapter. Training devices, including Lockheed Martin's Gray Matters ethics game, are also available online. In addition, students have access to their own set of PowerPoint slides to help them review and master the text material.

**To acccess the text's Web site**

- **Go to** *http://college.hmco.com*
- **Select "Instructors" or "Students"**
- **Select "Go to Your Discipline" and then "Business"**
- **Select Ferrell/Fraedrich/Ferrell,** *Business Ethics* **from the Textbook Sites menus**

## Effective Tools for Teaching and Learning

Many tools are available in this text to help both students and instructors in the quest to improve students' ability to make ethical business decisions. Each chapter opens with an outline and a list of learning objectives. Immediately following is "An Ethical Dilemma" that should provoke discussion about ethical issues related to the chapter. The short vignette describes a hypothetical incident involving an ethical conflict. Questions at the end of the "Ethical Dilemma" section focus discussion on how the dilemma could be resolved. At the end of each chapter there is a chapter summary and an important terms list, both of which are handy tools for review. Also included at the end of each chapter is a "Real-Life Situation" section. The vignette describes a realistic drama that helps students experience the process of ethical decision making. The "Real-Life Situation" minicases presented in this text are hypothetical; any resemblance to real persons, companies, or situations is coincidental. Keep in mind that there are no right or wrong solutions to the minicases. The ethical dilemmas and real-life situations provide an opportunity for students to use concepts in the chapter to resolve ethical issues. Each chapter concludes with a series of questions that allow students to test their E.Q. (Ethics Quotient).

In Part Four, following each real-world case are questions to guide students in recognizing and resolving ethical issues. For some cases, students can conduct additional research to determine recent developments, since many ethical issues in companies take years to resolve. Students can also study the codes of ethics in Appendixes A and B to determine ethical issues that companies attempt to resolve.

The *Instructor's Resource Manual with Test Bank* contains a wealth of information. Teaching notes for every chapter include a brief chapter summary, detailed lecture outline, and notes for using the "Ethical Dilemma" and "Real-Life Situation" sections. Detailed case notes point out the key issues involved and offer suggested answers to the questions. A separate section provides guidelines for using case analysis in teaching business ethics. Detailed notes are provided to guide the instructor in analyzing or grading the cases. Simulation role-play cases, as well as implementation suggestions, are included. A test bank provides multiple-choice and essay questions for every chapter in the text. A computerized version of the test bank is also available. Instructor-only PowerPoint slides are available on the password-protected portion of the Web site. Finally, a selection of video segments is available to help bring real-world examples and skill-building scenarios into the classroom.

## Acknowledgments

A number of individuals provided reviews and suggestions that helped to improve this text. We sincerely appreciate their time and effort.

Suzanne Allen
*Walsh University*

Carolyn Ashe
*University of Houston–Downtown*

Laura Barelman
*Wayne State College*

Russell Bedard
*Eastern Nazarene College*

B. Barbara Boerner
*Brevard College*

Greg Buntz
*University of the Pacific*

Julie Campbell
*Adams State College*

Peggy Cunningham
*Queen's University*

Carla Dando
*Idaho State University*

James E. Donovan
*Detroit College of Business*

A. Charles Drubel
*Muskingum College*

Philip F. Esler
*University of St. Andrews*

Joseph M. Foster
*Indiana Vocational Technical College–Evansville*

Terry Gable
*Truman State University*

Robert Giacalone
*University of Richmond*

Suresh Gopalan
*West Texas A&M University*

Charles E. Harris, Jr.
*Texas A&M University*

Kenneth A. Heischmidt
*Southeast Missouri State University*

Neil Herndon
*University of Missouri-Columbia*

Walter Hill
*Green River Community College*

Jack Hires
*Valparaiso University*

David Jacobs
*American University*

R.J. Johansen
*Montana State University–Bozeman*

Edward Kimman
*Vrije Universiteit*

Nick Lockard
*Texas Lutheran College*

Terry Loe
*Kennesaw State University*

Nick Maddox
*Stetson University*

Debbie Thorne McAlister
*Texas State University—San Marcos*

Isabelle Maignan
*Vrije Universiteit*

Phylis Mansfield
*Pennsylvania State University-Erie*

Randy McLeod
*Harding University*

Lester Myers
*University of San Francisco*

Patrick E. Murphy
*University of Notre Dame*

Cynthia Nicola
*Carlow College*

Carol Nielsen
*Bemidji State University*

Cynthia A. M. Simerly
*Lakeland Community College*

Filiz Tabak
*Towson University*

Wanda V. Turner
*Ferris State College*

Jim Weber
*Duquesne University*

Ed Weiss
*National-Louis University*

Jan Zahrly
*University of North Dakota*

The authors wish to acknowledge the many people who assisted us in writing this book. We are deeply grateful to Gwyneth V. Walters for helping us organize and manage the revision process and for preparing the *Instructor's Resource Manual with Test Bank*. We are also indebted to Barbara Gilmer for her contributions to previous editions of this text. Debbie Thorne McAlister, Texas State University—San Marcos, provided advice and guidance on the text and cases. Heather Stein, Linda Frazier-Mullin, and Neil Herndon assisted in preparing and updating the cases in this edition. Finally, we express appreciation to the administration and to our colleagues at Colorado State University, Southern Illinois University at Carbondale, and the University of Wyoming for their support.

We invite your comments, questions, or criticisms. We want to do our best to provide teaching materials that enhance the study of business ethics. Your suggestions will be sincerely appreciated.

O. C. FERRELL
JOHN FRAEDRICH
LINDA FERRELL

# Business Ethics

Ethical Decision Making and Cases

# Part One

# An Overview
# of Business
# Ethics

**Chapter**

# 1

# The Importance of Business Ethics

## An Ethical Dilemma*

John Peters had just arrived at the main offices of Dryer & Sons (D&S) from Midwest State University. A medium-size company, D&S manufactured components for several of the major defense contractors in the United States. Recently, D&S had started a specialized software division and had hired John as a salesperson for both the company's hardware and software.

A diligent student at Midwest State, John had earned degrees in engineering and management information systems (MIS). His minor was in marketing—specifically, sales. Because of his education as well as other activities, John was not only comfortable discussing numbers with engineers, but also had the people skills to convey complex solutions in understandable terms. This was one of the main reasons Al Dryer had hired him. "You've got charisma, John, and you know your way around computers," Dryer explained.

D&S was established during World War II and had manufactured parts for military aircraft. During the Korean War and then the Vietnam War, D&S had become a stable subcontractor for specialized parts for aircraft and missiles. When Al Dryer and his father started the business, Al was the salesperson for the company. In time, D&S had grown to employ several hundred workers and five salespeople; John was the sixth salesperson.

During his first few months at the company, John got his bearings in the defense industry. For example, when Ed, his trainer, would take procurement people out to lunch, everyone would put money into a snifter at the table. The money collected was usually much less than the bill, and Ed would make up the difference. Golf was a skill that Ed required John to learn because often "that's where deals are really transacted." Again, Ed would indirectly pick up the golfing bill, which sometimes totaled several hundred dollars.

Another of Ed's requirements was that John read the Procurement Integrity Section of the Office of Federal Procurement Policy Act and the Federal Acquisition Regulation, which implements the act. In addition, John had to read the Certificate of Procurement Integrity, which procurement agents had to sign. As John read the documents, he noted the statement in Section 27(a)(2), forbidding agents to "offer, give, or promise to offer or give, directly or indirectly, any money, gratuity, or other thing of value to any procurement official of such agency; or (3) solicit or obtain, directly or indirectly, from any officer or employee of such agency, prior to the award of a contract any proprietary or source selection information regarding such procurement."

"Doesn't this relate to what we're doing, Ed?" John asked.

"Yes and no, my boy, yes and no," was Ed's only answer.

One Monday, when Ed and John had returned from sales calls in St. Louis and Washington, D.C., Ed called John into his office and said: "John, you don't have the right numbers down for our expenses. You're 15 percent short because you forgot all of your tips." As John looked at his list of expenses, he realized that Ed was right, yet there was no item on his expense report for such things. "Ed, where do I put the extra expenses? There's no line on the forms for this." "Just add it into the cost of things as I've done," replied Ed, showing John his expense report. As John looked at Ed's report, he noticed some numbers that seemed quite large. "Why don't we mention this problem to Mr. Dryer so that accounting can put the extra lines on the reports?" John suggested. "Because this is the way we do things around here, and they don't like changes to the system. We have a saying in the company that a blind eye goes a long way to getting business done," Ed lectured John. John didn't quite grasp the problem and did as he was told.

On another trip John learned the differences between working directly with the federal government procurement people and the companies with which D&S subcontracted. For example, certain conversations of the large defense contractors were relayed to D&S, and then Ed and John would visit certain governmental agencies and relay that information. In one case Ed and John were told to relay a very large offer to an official who was entering the private sector the next year. In addition, Ed and John were used to obtaining information on requests for proposals, as well as other competitive information, from procurement agents. When John asked Ed about this, Ed said: "John, in order to excel in this business you need to be an expert on knowing exactly where things become legal and illegal. Trust me, I've been doing this for fifteen years, and I've never had a problem. Why do you think I'm your trainer?"

John started reviewing more government documents and asking the other salespeople about Ed. Two replied that Ed was a smart operator and knew the ropes better than anyone at the company. The other two salespeople had a different story to tell. One asked, "Has he tried to explain away his padding of the expense reports to you yet?" "But I thought that's what everyone does!" John exclaimed. "Ed has been doing business with the Feds and the large defense companies for so long that he sometimes doesn't realize that the rules have changed. He's been lucky that he hasn't been caught. Watch your step, John, or you'll find yourself with dirty hands and nowhere to clean them," the second salesperson said.

At the end of another trip to Washington, D.C.,

Ed called John into his office. "John, your numbers don't add up," he pointed out. "Didn't I tell you to add at least 15 percent to your totals for tips and miscellaneous items? Let's get with it. Do you want to be in training forever? You know that I have to sign off before you can go it alone, and I want to make sure you understand the ropes. Just between you and me, I think Dryer is finally going to make a vice president slot, which should go to me because of my seniority. So hurry up and learn this stuff because you're my last trainee. Now just sign the document with these revised numbers on them."

What should John do?

## Questions ■ Exercises

1. What is Ed's ethical dilemma?
2. What are the ethical and legal considerations for John at D&S?
3. Identify the ethical conflict in this situation.
4. Discuss the implications of each decision John has made and will make.

\* This case is strictly hypothetical; any resemblance to real persons, companies, or situations is coincidental.

The ability to recognize and deal with complex business ethics issues has become a significant priority in twenty-first century companies. In recent years, a number of well-publicized scandals resulted in public outrage about deception and fraud in business and a demand for improved business ethics and greater corporate responsibility. The publicity and debate surrounding highly visible legal and ethical lapses at a number of well-known firms, including Enron, WorldCom, Arthur Andersen LLP, and Tyco, highlight the need for businesses to integrate ethics and responsibility into all business decisions. A survey concluded that 57 percent of the general public feels that the values and standards of business leaders and executives have declined in the last twenty years.[1] Another poll found that two-thirds of surveyed respondents believe that "recent economic events have created a crisis of confidence and trust in the way we do business in America."[2] Largely in response to this crisis, business decisions and activities have come under greater scrutiny by many different constituents, including consumers, employees, investors, government regulators, and special-interest groups. Additionally, new legislation and regulations designed to encourage higher ethical standards in business have been put in place.

The field of business ethics deals with questions about whether specific business practices are acceptable. For example, should a salesperson omit facts about a product's poor safety record in a sales presentation to a client? Should an accountant report inaccuracies he or she discovered in an audit of a client, knowing the auditing company will probably be fired by the client for doing so? Should an automobile tire manufacturer intentionally conceal safety concerns to avoid a massive and costly tire recall? Regardless of their legality, the actions taken in such situations will certainly be judged by others as right or wrong, ethical or unethical. By its very nature, the field of business ethics is controversial, and there is no universally accepted approach for resolving its issues.

Before we get started, it is important to state our philosophies regarding this book. First, we do not moralize by telling you what is right or wrong in a specific situation. Second, although we provide an overview of group and individual decision-making processes, we do not prescribe any one philosophy or process as best or most ethical. Third, by itself, this book will not make you more ethical, nor will it tell you how to judge the ethical behavior of others. Rather, its goal is to help you understand and use your current values and convictions when making business decisions so that you think about the effects of those decisions on business and society. To this end, we aim to help you learn to recognize and resolve ethical issues within business organizations. The framework we develop in this book therefore focuses on how organizational ethical decisions are made and on ways companies can improve their ethical conduct.

In this chapter, we first develop a definition of business ethics and discuss why it has become an important topic in business education. We also discuss why studying business ethics can be beneficial. Next, we examine the evolution of business ethics in North America. Then we explore the performance benefits of ethical decision making for businesses. Finally, we provide a brief overview of the framework we use for examining business ethics in this text.

## Business Ethics Defined

The term *ethics* has many nuances. It has been defined as "inquiry into the nature and grounds of morality where the term morality is taken to mean moral judgments, standards and rules of conduct."[3] Ethics has also been called the study and philosophy of human conduct, with an emphasis on determining right and wrong. *The American Heritage Dictionary* offers these definitions of ethics: "The study of the general nature of morals and of specific moral choices; moral philosophy; and the rules or standards governing the conduct of the members of a profession."[4] One difference between an ordinary decision and an ethical one lies in "the point where the accepted rules no longer serve, and the decision maker is faced with the responsibility for weighing values and reaching a judgment in a situation which is not quite the same as any he or she has faced before."[5] Another difference relates to the amount of emphasis decision makers place on their own values and accepted practices within their company. Consequently, values and judgments play a critical role when we make ethical decisions.

Building on these definitions, we can begin to develop a concept of business ethics. Most people would agree that high ethical standards require both businesses and individuals to conform to sound moral principles. However, some special aspects must be considered when applying ethics to business. First, to survive, businesses must earn a profit. If profits are realized through misconduct, however, the life of the organization may be shortened. Many firms, including Arthur Andersen, Enron, Kmart, and Sunbeam, that made headlines due to wrongdoing and scandal ultimately went bankrupt or failed because of the legal and financial repercussions of their misconduct. Second, businesses must balance their desires for profits against the needs and desires of society. Maintaining this balance often requires compromises or tradeoffs. To address these unique aspects of the business world, society has developed rules—both legal and implicit—to guide businesses in their efforts to earn profits in ways that do not harm individuals or society as a whole.

Most definitions of business ethics relate to rules, standards, and moral principles regarding what is right or wrong in specific situations. For our purposes and in simple terms, **business ethics** comprises the principles and standards that guide behavior in the world of business. Whether a specific action is right or wrong, ethical or unethical, is often determined by investors, employees, customers, interest groups, the legal system, and the community. Although these groups are not necessarily "right," their judgments influence society's acceptance or rejection of a business and its activities.

## Why Study Business Ethics?

### A Crisis in Business Ethics

As we've already mentioned, ethical misconduct has become a major concern in business today. The Ethics Resource Center conducted the National Business Ethics Survey (NBES) of fifteen hundred U.S. employees to gather reliable data on key ethics and compliance outcomes and to help identify and better understand the ethics issues that are important to employees. The NBES found that observed misconduct is higher in large organizations—those with more than five hundred employees—than in smaller ones and that there are differences in observed misconduct across employment sectors—for-profit, government, and nonprofit (Figure 1–1).[6]

Accounting fraud, insider trading of stocks and bonds, falsifying documents, deceptive advertising, defective products, bribery, and employee theft are all problems cited as evidence of declining ethical standards. For example, the U.S. Justice Department is investigating whether Metabolife International made false statements to the Food and Drug Administration about side effects associated with its popular herbal weight-loss supplement. The supplement contains ephedra, which has been linked to adverse effects such as high blood pressure, seizures, and heart attacks, as well as unsubstantiated reports of seventy deaths.[7] Martha Stewart was investigated for insider trading after she sold nearly four thousand shares of ImClone Systems stock prior to the company's announcement that regulators had rejected its application for a cancer-fighting drug. The firm's CEO, Samuel Waksal, pleaded guilty of attempting to sell his own shares in advance of the announcement and was sentenced to seven years in prison. Although Stewart pleaded not guilty to charges of securities fraud and obstruction of justice, she resigned as CEO of her company, Martha Stewart Living Omnimedia, and was forced to give up her seat on the board of the New York Stock Exchange. Moreover, shares of the stock of her company plummeted after the stock sale scandal was exposed.[8] After HealthSouth Corporation was investigated for allegedly inflating earnings by $2.5 billion, eleven former employees, including all the firm's former chief financial officers, pleaded guilty to fraud charges.[9] Such highly

| FIGURE 1–1 | Observed Misconduct by Employment Sector |

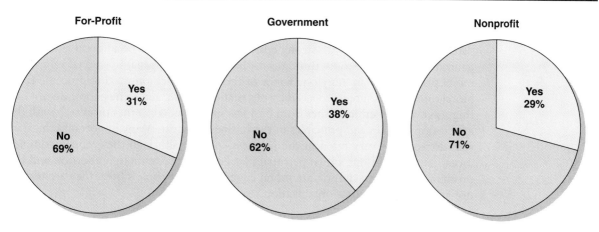

Have you observed misconduct in the workplace?

Source: The Ethics Resource Center, *2000 National Business Ethics Survey: How Employees Perceive Ethics at Work* (Washington, D.C.: Ethics Resource Center, 2000), p. 28. Reprinted with permission.

publicized cases strengthen the perception that ethical standards in business need to be raised.

In government, several politicians and some high-ranking officials have had to resign in disgrace over ethical indiscretions. For example, James Traficant of Ohio was expelled from Congress and sent to jail after being convicted of accepting bribes while serving in the U.S. House of Representatives.[10] Several scientists have been accused of falsifying research data, which could invalidate later research based on their data and jeopardize trust in all scientific research. Bell Labs, for example, fired a scientist for falsifying experiments on superconductivity and molecular electronics and for misrepresenting data in scientific publications. Jan Hendrik Schon's work on creating tiny, powerful microprocessors seemed poised to significantly advance microprocessor technology and potentially bring yet another Nobel prize in physics to the award-winning laboratory, a subsidiary of Lucent Technologies.[11] Even sports can be subject to ethical lapses. For example, Chicago Cubs player Sammy Sosa accepted a seven-game suspension for using a corked bat, although he claimed it was an accident. Additionally, several colleges and universities have been put on probation and in some cases given the "death penalty"—complete suspension of their athletic programs—for illegally recruiting or paying players.

Whether made in science, politics, or business, most decisions are judged as either right or wrong, ethical or unethical. Regardless of what an individual believes about a particular action, if society judges it to be unethical or wrong, whether correctly or not, that judgment directly affects the organization's ability to achieve its business goals. For this reason alone, it is important to understand business ethics and recognize ethical issues.

## The Reasons for Studying Business Ethics

Studying business ethics is valuable for several reasons. Business ethics is not merely an extension of an individual's own personal ethics. Many people believe that if a company hires good people with strong ethical values, then it will be a "good citizen" organization. But as we show throughout this text, an individual's personal values and moral philosophies are only one factor in the ethical decision-making process. True, moral rules can be applied to a variety of situations in life, and some people do not distinguish everyday ethical issues from business ones. Our concern, however, is with the application of rules and principles in the business context. Many important ethical issues do not arise very often in the business context, although they remain complex moral dilemmas in one's own personal life. For example, although abortion and the possibility of human cloning are moral issues in many people's lives, they are usually not an issue in a business organization.

Professionals in any field, including business, must deal with individuals' personal moral dilemmas as these issues affect everyone's ability to function on the job. Normally, a business does not establish rules or policies on personal ethical issues such as sex or the use of alcohol outside the workplace; indeed, in some cases, such policies would be illegal. Only when a person's preferences or values influence his or her performance on the job do an individual's ethics play a major role in the evaluation of business decisions.

Just being a good person and, in your own view, having sound personal ethics may not be sufficient to enable you to handle the ethical issues that arise in a business organization. It is important to recognize the relationship between legal and ethical decisions. While abstract virtues linked to the high moral ground of truthfulness, honesty, fairness, and openness are often assumed to be self-evident and accepted by all employees, business strategy decisions involve complex and detailed discussions. For example, there is considerable debate over what constitutes antitrust, deceptive advertising, and violations of the Foreign Corrupt Practices Act. A high level of personal moral development may not prevent an individual from violating the law in a complicated organizational context, where even experienced lawyers debate the exact meaning of the law. Some approaches to business ethics assume that ethics training is for people whose personal moral development is unacceptable, but that is not necessarily the case. Because organizations are culturally diverse and personal values must be respected, ensuring collective agreement on organizational ethics (that is, codes reasonably capable of preventing misconduct) is as vital as any other effort an organization's management may undertake.

Many people who have limited business experience suddenly find themselves making decisions about product quality, advertising, pricing, sales techniques, hiring practices, and pollution control. The values they learned from family, religion, and school may not provide specific guidelines for these complex business decisions. In other words, a person's experiences and decisions at home, in school, and in the community may be quite different from his or her experiences and decisions at work. Many business ethics decisions are close calls. Years of experience in a particular industry may be required to know what is acceptable. Consider the challenge faced by Harry Kraemer, the CEO of Baxter International, after 53 dialysis patients died during treatment in the United States, Spain, and five other countries. The dialysis filters used in each of the cases had come from a single lot manufactured by Althin Medical AB, a firm that Baxter had acquired the previous year. After investigating, Kraemer took responsibility, apologized, recalled all of Althin's dialysis filters, and ultimately decided to shut down Althin's operations, actions that cost Baxter $189 million. Kraemer later asked the company's board of directors to reduce his bonus because of the deaths. Kraemer could have made different decisions, but he put the situation in a broader context: "We have this situation. The financial people will assess the potential financial impact. The legal people will do the same. But at the end of the day, if we think it's a problem that a Baxter product was involved in the deaths of 53 people, then those other issues become pretty easy. If we don't do the right thing, then we won't be around to address those other issues."[12]

Studying business ethics will help you begin to identify ethical issues when they arise and recognize the approaches available for resolving them. You will also learn more about the ethical decision-making process and about ways to promote ethical behavior within your organization. By studying business ethics you may begin to understand how to cope with conflicts between your own personal values and those of the organization in which you work.

## The Development of Business Ethics

The study of business ethics in North America has evolved through five distinct stages—(1) before 1960, (2) the 1960s, (3) the 1970s, (4) the 1980s, and (5) the 1990s—and continues to evolve in the twenty-first century.

### Before 1960: Ethics in Business

Prior to 1960 the United States went through several agonizing phases of questioning the concept of capitalism. In the 1920s the Progressive Movement attempted to provide citizens with a "living wage," defined as income sufficient for education, recreation, health, and retirement. Businesses were asked to check unwarranted price increases and any other practices that would hurt a family's "living wage." In the 1930s came the New Deal, which specifically blamed business for the country's economic woes. Business was asked to work more closely with the government to raise family income. By the 1950s the New Deal had evolved into the Fair Deal by President Harry S Truman; this program defined such matters as civil rights and environmental responsibility as ethical issues that businesses had to address.

Until 1960, ethical issues related to business were often discussed within the domain of theology or philosophy. Individual moral issues related to business were addressed in churches, synagogues, and mosques. Religious leaders raised questions about fair wages, labor practices, and the morality of capitalism. For example, Catholic social ethics, which were expressed in a series of papal encyclicals, included concern for morality in business, workers' rights, and living wages; for humanistic values rather than materialistic ones; and for improving the conditions of the poor. Some Catholic colleges and universities began to offer courses in social ethics. Protestants also developed ethics courses in their seminaries and schools of theology and addressed issues concerning morality and ethics in business. The Protestant work ethic encouraged individuals to be frugal, work hard, and attain success in the capitalistic system. Such religious traditions provided a foundation for the future field of business ethics. Each religion applied its moral concepts not only to business but also to government, politics, the family, personal life, and all other aspects of life.

### The 1960s: The Rise of Social Issues in Business

During the 1960s American society turned to causes. An antibusiness attitude developed as many critics attacked the vested interests that controlled the economic and political sides of society—the so-called military-industrial complex. The 1960s saw the decay of inner cities and the growth of ecological problems, such as pollution and the disposal of toxic and nuclear wastes. This period also witnessed the rise of consumerism—activities undertaken by independent individuals, groups, and organizations to protect their rights as consumers. In 1962 President John F. Kennedy delivered a "Special Message on Protecting the Consumer Interest," in which he outlined four basic consumer rights: the right to safety, the right to be informed, the right to choose, and the right to be heard. These came to be known as the **Consumers' Bill of Rights.**

The modern consumer movement is generally considered to have begun in 1965 with the publication of Ralph Nader's *Unsafe at Any Speed,* which criticized the auto industry as a whole, and General Motors Corporation (GM) in particular, for putting profit and style ahead of lives and safety. GM's Corvair was the main target of Nader's criticism. His consumer protection organization, popularly known as Nader's Raiders, fought successfully for legislation that required automobile makers to equip cars with safety belts, padded dashboards, stronger door latches, head restraints, shatterproof windshields, and collapsible steering columns. Consumer activists also helped secure passage of several consumer protection laws, such as the Wholesome Meat Act of 1967, the Radiation Control for Health and Safety Act of 1968, the Clean Water Act of 1972, and the Toxic Substance Act of 1976.[13]

After Kennedy came President Lyndon B. Johnson and the Great Society, which extended national capitalism and told the business community that the U.S. government's responsibility was to provide the citizen with some degree of economic stability, equality, and social justice. Activities that could destabilize the economy or discriminate against any class of citizens began to be viewed as unethical and unlawful.

### The 1970s: Business Ethics As an Emerging Field

Business ethics began to develop as a field of study in the 1970s. Theologians and philosophers had laid the groundwork by suggesting that certain principles could be applied to business activities. Using this foundation, business professors began to teach and write about corporate **social responsibility,** an organization's obligation to maximize its positive impact on stakeholders and to minimize its negative impact. Philosophers increased their involvement, applying ethical theory and philosophical analysis to structure the discipline of business ethics. Companies became more concerned with their public images, and, as social demands grew, many businesses realized that they had to address ethical issues more directly. The Nixon administration's Watergate scandal focused public interest on the importance of ethics in government.

Conferences were held to discuss the social responsibilities and ethical issues of business. Centers dealing with issues of business ethics were established. Interdisciplinary meetings brought business professors, theologians, philosophers, and businesspeople together. President Jimmy Carter attempted to focus on personal and administrative efforts to uphold ethical principles in government. The Foreign Corrupt Practices Act was passed during his administration, making it illegal for U.S. businesses to bribe government officials of other countries.

By the end of the 1970s a number of major ethical issues had emerged, such as bribery, deceptive advertising, price collusion, product safety, and the environment. *Business ethics* became a common expression and was no longer considered an oxymoron. Academic researchers sought to identify ethical issues and describe how businesspeople might choose to act in particular situations. However, only limited efforts were made to describe how the ethical decision-making process worked and to identify the many variables that influence this process in organizations.

## The 1980s: Consolidation

In the 1980s business academics and practitioners acknowledged business ethics as a field of study. A growing and varied group of institutions with diverse interests promoted its study. Business ethics organizations grew to include thousands of members. Five hundred courses in business ethics were offered at colleges across the country, with more than forty thousand students enrolled. Centers for business ethics provided publications, courses, conferences, and seminars. Business ethics was also a prominent concern within leading companies, such as General Electric, Chase Manhattan, General Motors, Atlantic Richfield, Caterpillar, and S. C. Johnson & Son, Inc. Many of these firms established ethics and social policy committees to address ethical issues.

In the 1980s the **Defense Industry Initiative on Business Ethics and Conduct** (DII) was developed to guide corporate support for ethical conduct. In 1986 eighteen defense contractors drafted principles for guiding business ethics and conduct.[14] The organization has since grown to nearly fifty members. This effort established a method for discussing best practices and working tactics to link organizational practice and policy to successful ethical compliance. The Defense Industry Initiative includes six principles. First, DII supports codes of conduct and their widespread distribution. These codes of conduct must be understandable and provide details on more substantive areas. Second, member companies are expected to provide ethics training for their employees as well as continuous support between training periods. Third, defense contractors must create an open atmosphere in which employees feel comfortable reporting violations without fear of retribution. Fourth, companies need to perform extensive internal audits and develop effective internal reporting and voluntary disclosure plans. Fifth, DII insists that member companies preserve the integrity of the defense industry. Finally, member companies must adopt a philosophy of public accountability.[15]

The 1980s ushered in the Reagan/Bush eras, with the accompanying belief that self-regulation, rather than regulation by government, was in the public's interest. Many tariffs and trade barriers were lifted, and businesses merged and divested within an increasingly global atmosphere. Thus, while business schools were offering courses in business ethics, the rules of business were changing at a phenomenal rate because of less regulation. Corporations that once were nationally based began operating internationally and found themselves mired in value structures where accepted rules of business behavior no longer applied.

## The 1990s: Institutionalization of Business Ethics

The administration of President Bill Clinton continued to support self-regulation and free trade. However, it also took unprecedented government action to deal with health-related social issues, such as teenage smoking. Its proposals included restricting cigarette advertising, banning vending machine sales, and ending the use of cigarette logos in connection with sports events.[16] Clinton also appointed Arthur Levitt as chairman of the Securities and Exchange Commission in 1993. Levitt unsuccessfully pushed for many reforms that could have prevented the accounting ethics scandals exemplified by Enron and WorldCom.[17]

The **Federal Sentencing Guidelines for Organizations** (FSGO), approved by Congress in November 1991, set the tone for organizational ethical compliance programs in the 1990s. The guidelines, which were based on the six principles of the Defense Industry Initiative,[18] broke new ground by codifying into law incentives to reward organizations for taking action to prevent misconduct, such as developing effective internal legal and ethical compliance programs.[19] Provisions in the guidelines mitigate penalties for businesses that strive to root out misconduct and establish high ethical and legal standards.[20] On the other hand, under FSGO, if a company lacks an effective ethical compliance program and its employees violate the law, it can incur severe penalties. The guidelines focus on firms taking action to prevent and detect business misconduct in cooperation with government regulation. At the heart of the FSGO is the carrot-and-stick approach: by taking preventive action against misconduct, a company may avoid onerous penalties should a violation occur. A mechanical approach using legalistic logic will not suffice to avert serious penalties. The company must develop corporate values, enforce its own code of ethics, and strive to prevent misconduct.

## The Twenty-First Century: A New Focus on Business Ethics

Although business ethics appeared to become more institutionalized in the 1990s, new evidence emerged in the early 2000s that more than a few business executives and managers had not fully embraced the public's desire for high ethical standards. For example, Dennis Kozlowski, former CEO of Tyco, was indicted on 38 counts of misappropriating $170 million of Tyco funds and netting $430 million from improper sales of stock. Kozlowski, who pleaded not guilty to the charges, allegedly used the funds to purchase many personal luxuries, including a $15 million vintage yacht and a $3.9 million Renoir painting and to throw a $2 million party for his wife's birthday.[21] Arthur Andersen, a "Big 5" accounting firm, was convicted of obstructing justice after shredding documents related to its role as Enron's auditor.[22] The reputation of the once venerable accounting firm disappeared over night, along with most of its clients, and the firm ultimately went out of business. In addition to problems with its auditing of Enron, Arthur Andersen also faced questions surrounding its audits of other companies that were charged with employing questionable accounting practices, including Halliburton, WorldCom, Global Crossing, Dynegy, Qwest, and Sunbeam.[23] These accounting scandals made it evident that falsifying financial reports and reaping questionable benefits had become part of the culture of many companies.

Such abuses increased public and political demands to improve ethical standards in business. A survey by ABC News and the *Washington Post* found that 75 percent of the public has only limited confidence in large corporations, and 63 percent believe that corporate regulation "is necessary to protect the public."[24] To address the loss of confidence in financial reporting and corporate ethics, Congress in 2002 passed the **Sarbanes-Oxley Act,** the most far-reaching change in organizational control and accounting regulations since the Securities and Exchange Act of 1934. The new law made securities fraud a criminal offense and stiffened penalties for corporate fraud. It also created an accounting oversight board that requires corporations to establish codes of ethics for financial reporting and to develop greater transparency in financial reports to investors and other interested parties. Additionally, the law requires top executives to sign off on their firms' financial reports, and they risk fines and long jail sentences if they misrepresent their companies' financial position. The legislation further requires company executives to disclose stock sales immediately and prohibits companies from giving loans to top managers.[25]

The current trend is away from legally based ethical initiatives in organizations to cultural or integrity-based initiatives that make ethics a part of core organizational values. To develop more ethical organizational climates, many businesses are communicating core values to their employees by creating ethics programs and appointing ethics officers to oversee them. The New York Stock Exchange, for example, requires all member companies to have codes of ethics. Many firms now have ethics officers, and some firms, including UPS, Raytheon, and Baxter International, take ethics seriously enough to have their ethics officers report directly to senior management or boards of directors. The growth of the Ethics Officer Association (EOA) to 850 members, representing 420 companies, highlights the increasing importance of this position in business today. The organization is considering launching an ethics certification program for potential officers.[26]

Globally, businesses are working more closely together to establish standards of acceptable behavior. We are already seeing collaborative efforts by a range of organizations to establish goals and mandate minimum levels of ethical behavior, from the European Union, the North American Free Trade Agreement (NAFTA), the Common Market of the Southern Cone (MERCOSUR), and the World Trade Organization (WTO) to, more recently, the Council on Economic Priorities' Social Accountability 8000 (SA 8000), the Ethical Trading Initiative, and the U.S. Apparel Industry Partnership. Some companies will not do business with organizations that do not support and abide by these standards. The development of global codes of ethics, such as the Caux Round Table, highlights common ethical concerns for global firms. The Caux Round Table (reprinted in Appendix B) is a group of businesses, political leaders, and concerned interest groups that desire responsible behavior in the global community.

## The Benefits of Business Ethics

The field of business ethics continues to change rapidly as more firms recognize the benefits of improving ethical conduct and the link between business ethics and financial

---

FIGURE 1–2   **The Role of Organizational Ethics in Performance**

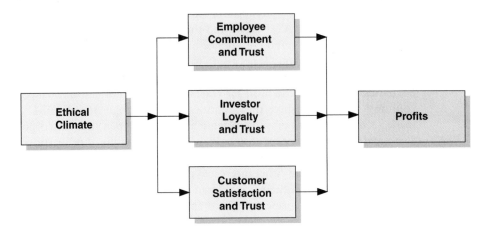

performance. Both research and examples from the business world demonstrate that building an ethical reputation among employees, customers, and the general public pays off. Figure 1–2 provides an overview of the relationship between business ethics and organizational performance. Although we believe there are many practical benefits to being ethical, many businesspeople make decisions because they believe a particular course of action is simply the right thing to do as a responsible member of society. For example, after a small Massachusetts textile plant owned by Malden Mills burned to the ground, Malden Mills' CEO, Aaron Feuerstein, could have opted to close the plant in favor of moving the work to an overseas facility with lower wages, just as many of his competitors had already done. However, he recognized the negative impact that such a decision would have had on the plant's employees as well as the community. Thus, he chose not only to rebuild the plant, but also to continue to pay its three thousand workers for ninety days while the plant was being rebuilt.[27]

Among the rewards for being more ethical and socially responsible in business are increased efficiency in daily operations, greater employee commitment, increased investor willingness to entrust funds, improved customer trust and satisfaction, and better financial performance. The reputation of a company has a major effect on its relationships with employees, investors, customers, and many other parties.

## Ethics Contributes to Employee Commitment

Employee commitment comes from employees who believe their future is tied to that of the organization and their willingness to make personal sacrifices for the organization.[28] The more a company is dedicated to taking care of its employees, the more likely it is that the employees will take care of the organization. Figure 1–3 shows the importance of ethics to employees' commitment to the organization. Issues that may foster the development of an ethical climate for employees include a safe work environment, competitive salaries, and the fulfillment of all contractual obligations toward employees. Social programs that may improve the ethical climate range from work-family

**FIGURE 1–3** Importance of Ethics in Continuing to Work for Employer

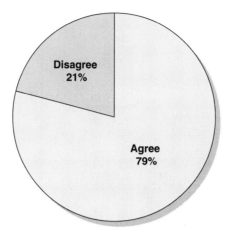

Disagree
21%

Agree
79%

Ethics is important in my
continuing to work here.

Source: Ethics Resource Center, *2000 National Business Ethics Survey: How Employees Perceive Ethics at Work* (Washington, D.C.: 2000), p. 67. Reprinted with permission.

programs and stock ownership plans to community service. Home Depot associates, for example, participate in disaster relief efforts after hurricanes and tornadoes by rebuilding roofs, repairing water damage, planting trees, and clearing roads in their communities. Because employees spend a considerable amount of their waking time at work, a commitment by the organization to goodwill and respect for its employees usually increases the employees' loyalty to the organization and their support of its objectives.

Employees' perception that their firm has an ethical environment leads to performance-enhancing outcomes within the organization.[29] For the sake of both productivity and teamwork, it is essential that employees both within and between departments throughout the organization share a common vision of trust. The influence of higher levels of trust is greatest on relationships within departments or work groups, but trust is a significant factor in relationships between departments as well. Consequently, programs that create a work environment that is trustworthy make individuals more willing to rely and act on the decisions and actions of their coworkers. In such a work environment, employees can reasonably expect to be treated with full respect and consideration by their coworkers and superiors. Trusting relationships between upper management and managers and their subordinates contribute to greater decision-making efficiencies. One survey found that when employees see values such as honesty, respect, and trust applied frequently in the workplace, they feel less pressure to compromise ethical standards, observe less misconduct, are more satisfied with their organizations overall, and feel more valued as employees.[30] Figure 1–4 shows employee satisfaction percentages when honesty, respect, and trust are applied.

FIGURE 1–4 **Employee Satisfaction by Values Applied in the Workplace**

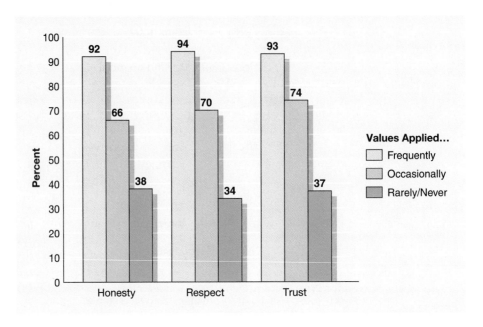

Source: Ethics Resource Center, *2000 National Business Ethics Survey: How Employees Perceive Ethics at Work* (Washington, D.C.: 2000), p. 85. Reprinted with permission.

The ethical climate of a company seems to matter to employees. According to a report on employee loyalty and work practices, companies viewed as highly ethical by their employees were six times more likely to keep their workers.[31] Also, employees who view their company as having a strong community involvement feel more loyal to their employers and feel positive about themselves.

### Ethics Contributes to Investor Loyalty

Employee commitment also helps a firm's reputation among other constituents. Companies perceived by their employees as having a high degree of honesty and integrity had an average three-year total return to shareholders of 101 percent, whereas companies perceived as having a low degree of honesty and integrity had a three-year total return to shareholders of just 69 percent.[32] Investors today are increasingly concerned about the ethics, social responsibility, and reputation of companies in which they invest, and various socially responsible mutual funds and asset management firms can help investors purchase stock in ethical companies. Investors are also recognizing that an ethical climate provides a foundation for efficiency, productivity, and profits. On the other hand, investors know too that negative publicity, lawsuits, and fines can lower stock prices, diminish customer loyalty, and threaten a company's long-term viability. Many companies accused of misconduct, including Global Crossing, Adelphia,

FreddieMac, and HealthSouth, have experienced dramatic declines in the value of their stock when concerned investors divested their stocks and bonds.

To be successful, relationships with investors must rest on dependability, trust, and commitment. Investors look at the bottom line for profits or the potential for increased stock prices or dividends. But they also look for any potential flaws in the company's performance, conduct, and financial reports. Thus, many executives spend considerable time communicating with investors about their firms' reputation and financial performance and trying to attract them to the company's stock. The issue of drawing and keeping investors is a critical one for CEOs, as roughly 50 percent of investors sell their stock in companies within one year, and the average household replaces 80 percent of its common stock portfolio each year.[33] Therefore, gaining investors' trust and confidence is vital to sustaining the financial stability of the firm.

## Ethics Contributes to Customer Satisfaction

It is generally accepted that customer satisfaction is one of the most important factors in successful business strategy. Although a company must continue to develop, alter, and adapt products to keep pace with customers' changing desires and preferences, it must also seek to develop long-term relationships with customers. For most businesses, both repeat purchases and an enduring relationship of mutual respect and cooperation with their customers are essential for success. By focusing on customer satisfaction, a company continually deepens the customer's dependence on the company, and as the customer's confidence grows, the firm gains a better understanding of how to serve the customer so the relationship may endure. Successful businesses provide an opportunity for customer feedback, which can engage the customer in cooperative problem solving. As is often pointed out, a happy customer will come back, but a disgruntled customer will tell others about his or her dissatisfaction with a company and discourage friends from dealing with it.

The public's trust is essential to maintaining a good long-term relationship between a business and consumers. The Millennium Poll of twenty-five thousand citizens in twenty-three countries found that almost 60 percent of people focus on social responsibility ahead of brand reputation or financial factors when forming impressions of companies.[34] For example, after the *Exxon Valdez* oil spill, special-interest groups and individual citizens boycotted the company. Before Chicken of the Sea and many of its competitors adopted dolphin-friendly nets to catch tuna, many consumers refused to buy tuna. Moreover, consumers may avoid the products of companies that are perceived as treating their employees unfairly. Companies that subcontract manufacturing operations abroad have had to confront the ethical issues associated with supporting facilities that abuse or underpay their work force—sometimes called "sweatshops." The Gap, the number-one U.S. clothing chain, and Nike, the world's largest maker of athletic shoes, suspended orders at June Textiles Co., a Cambodian garment factory, after learning that the British Broadcasting Corporation planned to air a program alleging use of child labor at the factory.[35] New industry codes of conduct, such as SA 8000, mentioned earlier, have been established to help companies identify and address these ethical issues. When consumers learn about abuses in subcontracting, they may boycott the companies' products.

When an organization has a strong ethical environment, it usually focuses on the core value of placing customers' interests first.[36] Putting customers first does not mean that the interests of employees, investors, and local communities should be ignored, however. An ethical climate that focuses on customers incorporates the interests of all employees, suppliers, and other interested parties in decisions and actions. Employees working in an ethical environment support and contribute to the process of understanding customers' demands and concerns. Ethical conduct toward customers builds a strong competitive position that has been shown to affect business performance and product innovation positively.[37]

## Ethics Contributes to Profits

A company cannot nurture and develop an ethical climate unless it has achieved adequate financial performance in terms of profits. Businesses with greater resources—regardless of their staff size—have the means to practice social responsibility while serving their customers, valuing their employees, and establishing trust with the public. Many studies have found a positive relationship between corporate social responsibility and business performance.[38] Companies convicted of misconduct experience a significantly lower return on assets and on sales than firms that have not faced such charges. Research indicates that the negative effect on return on sales does not appear until the third year following the conviction, and multiple convictions are more harmful than a single one.[39]

There are many examples of companies that have experienced significant performance declines after the disclosure of their failure to act responsibly toward various stakeholders. For example, Columbia/HCA experienced serious declines in stock prices and earnings after the revelation that it was systematically overcharging the government for Medicare services. Employees and customers also lodged complaints against the hospital chain for putting profits ahead of their interests. Employees alleged that they were forced to do jobs beyond their abilities, and many patients accused the company of charging them for services they did not need or transferring them to other facilities if there were questions about their ability to pay. Once Columbia/HCA's misconduct became public knowledge, its reputation was damaged within a few months.[40] Sears suffered when its automotive repair shops sold customers parts they didn't really need.[41] Beech-Nut lost customers after selling juice that was labeled as 100 percent pure but actually contained the chemical equivalent of apple juice.[42] Every day, business newspapers and magazines offer new examples of the consequences of business misconduct. It is also worth noting, however, that most of these companies have learned from their mistakes and recovered after they implemented programs to improve ethical and legal conduct. For example, Columbia/HCA, now renamed HCA—The Healthcare Company, has become a role model for organizational ethics programs in the health care industry. The company's code of ethics is featured in Appendix A.

There is ample evidence that being ethical pays off with better performance. As indicated earlier, companies that are perceived by their employees as having a high degree of honesty and integrity had a much higher average total return to shareholders than did companies perceived as having a low degree of honesty and integrity.[43] A study of the five hundred largest public corporations in the United States found that those that commit to ethical behavior or emphasize compliance with their code of conduct have better financial performance.[44] These results provide strong evidence that corporate concern for ethical conduct is becoming a part of strategic planning toward obtaining the outcome of higher profitability. Rather than being just a compliance program, ethics is becoming one of the management issues within the effort to achieve competitive advantage.

## Our Framework for Studying Business Ethics

We have developed a framework for this text to help you understand how people make ethical decisions and deal with ethical issues. Table 1–1 summarizes each element in the framework and describes where each topic is discussed in this book.

In Part One of this book, we provide an overview of business ethics. Chapter 1 defines the term *business ethics* and explores its growing importance. In Chapter 2, we explore a number of emerging issues as defined by various stakeholder groups. In Chapter 3, we examine ethics as a dimension of social responsibility.

Part Two focuses on the decision-making process that may be used to make ethical and unethical decisions. In Chapter 4, we describe the basic factors of the decision-making process and study how corporate governance mechanisms affect this process. Chapter 5 explores individual factors that may influence ethical decisions in business, including moral philosophies and cognitive moral development. In Chapter 6, we focus on the role of corporate, or organizational, culture in ethical decision making. Chapter 7 examines additional organizational factors in the decision-making process, including organizational structure, relationships, and conflict.

In Part Three, we explore issues associated with implementing business ethics into strategic planning in North America as well as abroad. Chapter 8 discusses the development of an effective ethics program. In Chapter 9, we examine issues related to implementing and auditing ethics programs. And finally, Chapter 10 considers ethical issues in a global context.

We hope that this framework will help you to develop a balanced understanding of the various perspectives and alternatives available to you when making ethical business decisions. Regardless of your own personal values, the more you know about how individuals make decisions, the better prepared you will be to cope with difficult ethical decisions. Such knowledge will help you improve and control the ethical decision-making environment in which you work.

It is your job to make the final decision in an ethical situation that affects you. Sometimes that decision may be right; sometimes it may be wrong. It is always easy to look back with hindsight and know what one should have done in a particular situation. At the time, however, the choices might not have been so clear. To give you practice making ethical decisions, Part Four of this book contains a number of cases. In addition, each chapter begins with a vignette and ends with a minicase that involves ethical problems. We hope they will give you a better sense of the challenges of making ethical decisions in the real business world.

| TABLE 1–1 | Our Framework for Studying Business Ethics |

| CHAPTER | HIGHLIGHTS |
|---|---|
| 1. The Importance of Business Ethics | ■ Definitions<br>■ Reasons for studying business ethics<br>■ History<br>■ Benefits of business ethics |
| 2. Emerging Business Ethics Issues | ■ Stakeholder relationships<br>■ Current ethical issues, including honesty and fairness, conflicts of interest, fraud, discrimination, and information technology |
| 3. Ethics As a Dimension of Social Responsibility | ■ Economic issues<br>■ Competitive issues<br>■ Legal and regulatory issues<br>■ Philanthropic issues |
| 4. Understanding Ethical Decision Making and Corporate Governance | ■ Ethical issue intensity<br>■ Individual factors in decision making<br>■ Organizational factors in decision making<br>■ Opportunity in decision making<br>■ Business ethics evaluations and intentions<br>■ Corporate governance |
| 5. Individual Factors: Moral Philosophies and Cognitive Moral Development | ■ Moral philosophies, including teleological, deontological, relativist, virtue ethics, and justice philosophies<br>■ Stages of cognitive moral development |
| 6. Organizational Factors: Corporate Culture | ■ Organizational culture<br>■ Leadership dimensions<br>■ Organizational structure<br>■ Group dimensions<br>■ Organizational issues in decision making |
| 7. Organizational Factors: Relationships and Conflicts | ■ Variations in employee conduct<br>■ Role dimensions<br>■ Whistle-blowing<br>■ Opportunity<br>■ Conflict |
| 8. Developing an Effective Ethics Program | ■ Ethics programs<br>■ Codes of ethics<br>■ Program responsibility<br>■ Communication of ethical standards<br>■ Systems to monitor and enforce ethical standards<br>■ Continuous improvement of ethics programs |
| 9. Implementing and Auditing Ethics Programs | ■ Implementation<br>■ Ethics audits |
| 10. Business Ethics in a Global Economy | ■ Ethical perceptions<br>■ Culture and cultural relations<br>■ Multinational corporations<br>■ Universal ethics<br>■ Global ethics issues |

## Summary

This chapter provides an overview of the field of business ethics and introduces the framework hich business ethics will be discussed throughout this text. Business ethics comprises principles and standards that guide behavior in the world of business. Whether a specific action is right or wrong, ethical or unethical, is often determined by investors, employees, customers, interest groups, the legal system, and the community.

Studying business ethics is important for many reasons. Recent incidents of unethical activity in business underscore the widespread need for a better understanding of the factors that contribute to ethical and unethical decisions. Individuals' personal moral philosophies and decision-making experience may not be sufficient to guide them in the business world. Studying business ethics will help you begin to identify ethical issues and recognize the approaches available to resolve them.

The study of business ethics evolved through five distinct stages. Before 1960, business ethics issues were discussed primarily from a religious perspective. The 1960s saw the emergence of many social issues involving business and the idea of social conscience as well as a rise in consumerism, which culminated with Kennedy's Consumers' Bill of Rights. Business ethics began to develop as an independent field of study in the 1970s, with academics and practitioners exploring ethical issues and attempting to understand how individuals and organizations make ethical decisions. These experts began to teach and write about the idea of corporate social responsibility, an organization's obligation to maximize its positive impact on stakeholders and to minimize its negative impact. In the 1980s centers of business ethics provided publications, courses, conferences, and seminars, while many companies established ethics committees and social policy committees. The Defense Industry Initiative on Business Ethics and Conduct was developed to guide corporate support for ethical conduct; its principles had a major impact on corporate ethics.

However, less government regulation and an increase in businesses with international operations raised new ethical issues. In the 1990s government continued to support self-regulation. The Federal Sentencing Guidelines for Organizations set the tone for organizational ethics programs by providing incentives for companies to take action to prevent organizational misconduct. The twenty-first century ushered in a new set of ethics scandals, suggesting that many companies had not fully embraced the public's desire for higher ethical standards. The Sarbanes-Oxley Act therefore stiffened penalties for corporate fraud and established an accounting oversight board. The current trend is away from legally based ethical initiatives in organizations toward cultural or integrity-based initiatives that make ethics a part of core organizational values.

Research and anecdotes demonstrate that building an ethical reputation among employees, customers, and the general public provides benefits that include increased efficiency in daily operations, greater employee commitment, increased investor willingness to entrust funds, improved customer trust and satisfaction, and better financial performance. The reputation of a company has a major effect on its relationships with employees, investors, customers, and many other parties, and thus has the potential to affect its bottom line.

Finally, this text introduces a framework for studying business ethics. Each chapter of this book addresses some aspect of business ethics and decision making within a business context. The major concerns are ethical issues in business; social responsibility; ethical decision-making processes; moral philosophies and cognitive moral development; organizational culture; organizational relationships and conflicts; developing an effective ethics program; implementing and auditing the ethics program; and global business ethics.

| Important Terms for Review | | |
| --- | --- | --- |
| business ethics | | Federal Sentencing Guidelines for |
| consumers' bill of rights | | Organizations |
| social responsibility | | Sarbanes-Oxley Act |
| Defense Industry Initiative on Business Ethics and Conduct | | |

# A Real-Life Situation*

Frank Garcia was just starting out as a salesman with Acme Corporation. Acme's corporate culture was top-down, or hierarchical. Because of the competitive nature of the medical-supplies industry, few mistakes were tolerated. Otis Hillman was a buyer for Thermocare, a national hospital chain. Frank's first meeting with Otis was a success, resulting in a $500,000 contract. This sale represented a significant increase for Acme and an additional $1,000 bonus for Frank.

Some months later Frank called on Thermocare, seeking to increase the contract by $500,000. "Otis, I think you'll need the additional inventory. It looks as if you didn't have enough at the end of last quarter," said Frank. "You may be right. Business has picked up. Maybe it's because of your product, but then again, maybe not. It's still not clear to me whether Acme is the best for us. Speaking of which, I heard that you have season tickets to the Cubs!" replied Otis. "I've always wanted to see Sammy Sosa hit a homer!"

Frank thought for a moment and said, "Otis, I know that part of your increases are due to our quality products. How about we discuss this over a ball game?" "Well, OK," Otis agreed. By the seventh-inning stretch, Frank had convinced Otis that the additional inventory was needed and offered to give Thermocare a pair of season tickets. When Frank's boss, Amber, heard of the sale, she was very pleased. "Frank, this is great. We've been trying to get Thermocare's business for a long time. You seem to have connected with their buyer." As a result of the Thermocare account, Frank received another large bonus check and a letter of achievement from the vice president of marketing.

Two quarters later Frank had become one of the top producers in the division. At the beginning of the quarter Frank had run the numbers on Thermocare's account and found that business was booming. The numbers showed that Otis's business could probably handle an additional $750,000 worth of goods without hurting return on assets. As Frank went over the figures with Otis, Otis's response was, "You know, Frank, I've really enjoyed the season tickets, but this is a big increase." As the conversation meandered, Frank soon found out that Otis and his wife had never been to Cancun, Mexico. Frank had never been in a situation like this before, so he excused himself to another room and called Amber about what he was thinking of doing. "Are you kidding!" responded Amber. "Why are you even calling me on this? I'll find the money somewhere to pay for it." "Is this OK with Acme?" asked Frank. "You let me worry about that," Amber told him. When Frank suggested that Otis and his wife be his guests in Cancun, the conversation seemed to go smoothly. In Cancun, Otis decided to purchase the additional goods, for which Frank received another bonus increase and another positive letter from headquarters.

Some time later Amber announced to her division that they would be taking all of their best clients to Las Vegas for a thank-you party. One of those invited was Thermocare. When they arrived, Amber gave each person $500 and said, "I want you to know that Acme is very grateful for the business that you have provided us. As a result of your understanding the qualitative differences of our products, we have doubled our production facilities. This trip and everything that goes with it for the next few days is our small way of saying thank you. Every one of you has your salesperson here. If there is anything that you need, please let them know and we'll try to accommodate you. Have a good time!"

That night Otis had seen Frank at dinner and suggested to him that he was interested in attending an "adult entertainment" club. When Frank came to Amber about this, she said, "Is he asking you to go with him?" "No, Amber, not me!" "Well, then, if he's not asking you to go, I don't understand why you're talking to me. Didn't I say we'd take care of their needs?" "But what will Acme say if this gets out?" asked Frank. "Don't worry; it won't," said Amber.

---

## Questions ▪ Exercises

1. What are the potential ethical issues faced by the Acme Corporation?
2. What should Acme do if there is a desire to make ethics a part of its core organizational values?
3. Identify the ethical issues of which Frank needs to be aware.
4. Discuss the advantages and disadvantages of each decision Frank could make.

\* This case is strictly hypothetical; any resemblance to real persons, companies, or situations is coincidental.

---

## Check Your EQ

Check your E.Q., or Ethics Quotient, by completing the following. Assess your performance to evaluate your overall understanding of the chapter material.

1. Business ethics focuses mostly on personal ethical issues.    Yes   No
2. Business ethics deals with right or wrong behavior within a particular organization.    Yes   No
3. The 1990s could be characterized as the period when ethics programs were greatly influenced by government legislation.    Yes   No
4. Business ethics contributes to investor loyalty.    Yes   No
5. The trend is away from cultural or ethically based initiatives to legal initiatives in organizations.    Yes   No

ANSWERS: 1. No. Business ethics focuses on organizational concerns (legal and ethical—employees, customers, suppliers, society). 2. Yes. That stems from the basic definition. 3. Yes. The impact of the Federal Sentencing Guidelines for Organizations means the 1990s are seen as the period in which business ethics were institutionalized. 4. Yes. Many studies have shown that trust and ethical conduct contribute to investor loyalty. 5. NO. Many businesses are communicating their core values to their employees by creating ethics programs and appointing ethics officers to oversee them.

# Emerging Business Ethics Issues

# An Ethical Dilemma*

Carla knew something was wrong when Jack got back to his desk. He had been with Aker & Aker Accounting (A&A) for seventeen years, starting there right after graduation and progressing through the ranks. Jack was a strong supporter of the company, and that was why Carla had been assigned to him. Carla had been with A&A for two years. She had graduated in the top 10 percent of her class and passed the CPA exam on the first try. She had chosen A&A over one of the "Big 5" firms because A&A was the biggest and best firm in Smallville, Ohio, where her husband, Frank, managed a locally owned machine tools company. She and Frank had just purchased a new home when things started to turn strange with Jack, her boss.

"What's the matter, Jack?" Carla asked.

"Well, you'll hear about it sooner or later. I've been denied a partner's position. Can you imagine that? I have been working sixty- and seventy-hour weeks for the last ten years, and all that management can say to me is 'not at this time'," complained Jack.

Carla asked, "So what else did they say?"

Jack turned red and blurted out, "They said maybe in a few more years. I've done all that they've asked me to do. I've sacrificed a lot, and now they say a few more years. It's not fair."

"What are you going to do?" Carla asked.

"I don't know," Jack said. "I just don't know."

Six months later, Carla noticed that Jack was behaving oddly. He came in late and left early. One Sunday Carla went into the office for some files and found Jack copying some of the software A&A used in auditing and consulting. A couple of weeks later, at a dinner party, Carla overheard a conversation about Jack doing consulting work for some small firms. Monday morning, she asked him if what she had heard was true.

Jack responded, "Yes, Carla, it's true. I have a few clients that I do work for on occasion."

"Don't you think there's a conflict of interest between you and A&A?" asked Carla.

"No," said Jack. "You see, these clients are not technically within the market area of A&A. Besides, I was counting on that promotion to help pay some extra bills. My oldest son decided to go to a private university, which is an extra $25,000 each year. Plus our medical plan at A&A doesn't cover some of my medical problems. And you don't want to know the cost. The only way I can afford to pay for these things is to do some extra work on the side."

"But what if A&A finds out?" Carla asked. "Won't they terminate you?"

"I don't want to think about that. Besides, if they don't find out for another six months, I may be able to start my own company."

"How?" asked Carla.

"Don't be naive, Carla. You came in that Sunday. You know." Carla realized that Jack had been using A&A software for his own gain. "That's stealing!" she said.

"Stealing?" Jack's voice grew calm. "Like when you use the office phones for personal long-distance calls? Like when you decided to volunteer to help out your church and copied all those things for them on the company machine? If I'm stealing, you're a thief as well. But let's not get into this discussion. I'm not hurting A&A and, who knows, maybe within the next year I'll become a partner and can quit my night job."

Carla backed off from the discussion and said nothing more. She couldn't afford to antagonize her boss and risk bad performance ratings. She and Frank had bills, too. She also knew that she wouldn't be able to get another job at the same pay if she quit. Moving to another town was not an option because of Frank's business. She had no physical evidence to take to the partners, which meant that it would be her word against Jack's, and he had seventeen years of experience with the company.

## Questions ■ Exercises

1. Identify the ethical issues in this case.
2. Assume you are Carla. Discuss your options and what the consequences of each option might be.
3. Assume you are Jack. Discuss your options.
4. Discuss any additional information you feel you might need before making your decision.

* This case is strictly hypothetical; any resemblance to real persons, companies, or situations is coincidental.

A s we mentioned in Chapter 1, employees, consumers, and shareholders, as well as suppliers, special-interest groups, government agencies, and the community and society as a whole all ultimately determine whether specific business actions and decisions are perceived as ethical or unethical. Additionally, these groups often raise ethical issues when they exert pressure on businesses to make decisions that serve their particular agendas. For example, corporate shareholders often demand that managers make decisions that boost short-term earnings, thus maintaining or increasing the value of the shares of stock they own in that firm. Such pressure may have led managers at Bristol-Myers Squibb to inflate sales by nearly $1 billion by offering incentives to wholesalers to place orders earlier so the pharmaceutical firm could meet its revenue targets for that year. Although the company has denied wrongdoing, the Securities and Exchange Commission is investigating its pricing practices.[1]

People make ethical decisions only when they recognize that a particular issue or situation has an ethical component. Thus, a first step toward understanding business ethics is to develop ethical-issue awareness. Ethical issues typically arise because of conflicts among individuals' personal moral philosophies and values, the values and culture of the organizations in which they work, and those of the society in which they live. The business environment presents many potential ethical conflicts. A company's efforts to achieve its organizational objectives may collide with its employees' endeavors to fulfill their own personal goals. Similarly, consumers' desires for safe and quality products may conflict with a manufacturer's need to earn adequate profits. The ambition of top executives to secure sizable increases in compensation may conflict with stockholders' desires to control costs and increase the value of the corporation. A manager's wish to hire specific employees that he or she likes may be at odds with the organization's intent to hire the best-qualified candidates as well as with society's aim to offer equal opportunity to minority-group members and women. Characteristics of the job and of the culture of the organization and society in which one does business can also create ethical issues. Gaining familiarity with the ethical issues that frequently arise in the business world will help you identify and resolve them when they occur.

In this chapter we consider some of the ethical issues that are emerging in business today, how these issues arise from the demands of specific stakeholder groups, and how corporate governance systems can guide firms in making ethical decisions. In the first half of the chapter, we focus on the concept of stakeholders and examine the growing importance of these groups in business today. The second half of the chapter explores a number of emerging ethical issues, including issues associated with honesty and fairness, conflicts of interest, fairness, fraud, and information technology.

## Stakeholders Define Ethical Issues in Business

In a business context, customers, investors and shareholders, employees, suppliers, government agencies, communities, and many others who have a "stake" or claim in some aspect of a company's products, operations, markets, industry, and outcomes are known as **stakeholders.** These groups are influenced by business, but they also have the ability to affect businesses. The relationship between companies and their stakeholders can therefore be viewed as a two-way street.[2] The recent ethics crisis in

Corporate America has demonstrated how employees and investors can suffer dire consequences as a result of unethical corporate practices. For example, after a major accounting scandal resulted in the collapse of Enron, many employees lost their jobs, Enron retirees and those near retirement age saw their pension funds essentially erased, and Enron investors lost billions of dollars after the company's stock price plummeted.[3] New reforms to improve corporate accountability and transparency also suggest that other stakeholders—including banks, attorneys, or public accounting firms—can play a major role in fostering responsible decision making.[4]

Stakeholders apply their values and standards to many diverse issues, such as working conditions, consumer rights, environmental conservation, product safety, and proper information disclosure. These issues may or may not directly affect an individual stakeholder's own welfare. We can assess the level of social responsibility an organization bears by scrutinizing its effects on the issues of concern to its stakeholders. Table 2–1 provides examples of common stakeholder issues along with indicators of businesses' impacts on those issues.[5]

Stakeholders provide resources that are more or less critical to a firm's long-term success. These resources may be both tangible and intangible. Shareholders, for example, supply capital; suppliers offer material resources or intangible knowledge; employees and managers grant expertise, leadership, and commitment; customers generate revenue and provide loyalty and positive word-of-mouth promotion; local communities provide infrastructure; and the media transmits positive corporate images. When individual stakeholders share similar expectations about desirable business conduct, they may choose to establish or join formal communities that are dedicated to better defining and advocating these values and expectations. Stakeholders' ability to withdraw—or to threaten to withdraw—these needed resources gives them power over businesses.[6]

## *Identifying Stakeholders*

We can identify two different types of stakeholders. **Primary stakeholders** are those whose continued association is absolutely necessary for a firm's survival; these include employees, customers, investors, and shareholders, as well as the governments and communities that provide necessary infrastructure. **Secondary stakeholders** do not typically engage in transactions with a company and thus are not essential for its survival; these include the media, trade associations, and special-interest groups. Both primary and secondary stakeholders embrace specific values and standards that dictate what constitutes acceptable or unacceptable corporate behaviors. It is important for managers to recognize that while primary groups may present more day-to-day concerns, secondary groups cannot be ignored or given less consideration in the ethical decision-making process.[7]

Historically, businesspeople viewed the principal objective of business as maximizing profit, which resulted in the belief that business is accountable primarily to investors and to others involved in the market and economic aspects of the company. In the latter half of the twentieth century, however, perceptions of business accountability shifted toward a broader view of the role and responsibilities of business in society. Theodore Levitt, a renowned business professor, once wrote that while profits are required for business just like eating is required for living, profit is not the purpose of

| TABLE 2–1 | Examples of Stakeholder Issues and Associated Measures of Corporate Impacts |
| --- | --- |

| STAKEHOLDER GROUPS AND ISSUES | POTENTIAL INDICATORS OF CORPORATE IMPACT ON THESE ISSUES |
| --- | --- |
| **Employees** | |
| 1. Compensation and benefits | 1. Ratio of lowest wage to national legal minimum or to local cost of living |
| 2. Training and development | 2. Changes in average years of training of employees |
| 3. Employee diversity | 3. Percentages of employees from different genders and races |
| 4. Occupational health and safety | 4. Standard injury rates and absentee rates |
| 5. Communications with management | 5. Availability of open-door policies or ombudsmen |
| **Customers** | |
| 1. Product safety and quality | 1. Number of product recalls over time |
| 2. Management of customer complaints | 2. Number of customer complaints and availability of procedures to answer them |
| 3. Services to disabled customers | 3. Availability and nature of measures taken to ensure services to disabled customers |
| **Investors** | |
| 1. Transparency of shareholder communications | 1. Availability of procedures to inform shareholders about corporate activities |
| 2. Shareholder rights | 2. Frequency and type of litigation involving violations of shareholder rights |
| **Suppliers** | |
| 1. Encouraging suppliers in developing countries | 1. Prices offered to suppliers in developed countries in comparison to other suppliers |
| 2. Encouraging minority suppliers | 2. Percentage of minority suppliers |
| **Community** | |
| 1. Public health and safety protection | 1. Availability of emergency response plan |
| 2. Conservation of energy and materials | 2. Data on reduction of waste produced and comparison to industry |
| 3. Donations and support of local organizations | 3. Annual employee time spent in community service |

| TABLE 2–1 | Examples of Stakeholder Issues and Associated Measures of Corporate Impacts (*cont'd.*) |
|---|---|

| Environmental Groups | |
|---|---|
| 1. Minimizing the use of energy | 1. Amount of electricity purchased; percentage of "green" electricity |
| 2. Minimizing emissions and waste | 2. Type, amount, and designation of waste generated |
| 3. Minimizing adverse environmental effects of goods and services | 3. Percentage of product weight reclaimed after use |

Source: Isabelle Maignan, O. C. Ferrell, and Linda Ferrell, "Managing Corporate Social Responsibility: How to Nurture Stakeholders' Confidence," working paper, Colorado State University, 2003, pp. 3–5. Reprinted with permission.

business any more than eating is the purpose of life.[8] Norman Bowie, a well-published philosopher, extended Levitt's sentiment by noting that a sole focus on profit can create an unfavorable paradox that causes a firm to fail to achieve its objective. Bowie contends that when a business also cares about the well-being of other constituencies, it earns trust and cooperation that ultimately reduce costs and increase productivity.[9] On the other hand, in response to the business ethics scandals at the turn of the twenty-first century, Nobel laureate economist Milton Friedman suggested that although those individuals guilty of wrongdoing should be held accountable, the market rather than new laws and regulations should deter firms from and punish them for further wrongdoing.[10] Thus, Friedman would diminish the role of stakeholders such as the government and employees in requiring that businesses demonstrate responsible and ethical behavior.

Figure 2–1 offers a conceptualization of the relationship between businesses and stakeholders. In this **stakeholder interaction model,** there are two-way relationships between the firm and a host of stakeholders. In addition to the fundamental input of investors, employees, and suppliers, this approach recognizes other stakeholders and explicitly acknowledges the two-way dialog and effects that exist with a firm's internal and external environment.

## A Stakeholder Orientation

The degree to which a firm understands and addresses stakeholder demands can be referred to as a stakeholder orientation. This orientation comprises three sets of activities: (1) the organizationwide generation of data about stakeholder groups and assessment of the firm's effects on these groups, (2) the distribution of this information throughout the firm, and (3) the organization's responsiveness as a whole to this intelligence.[11]

Generating data about stakeholders begins with identifying the stakeholders that are relevant to the firm. Relevant stakeholder communities should be analyzed on the basis of the power each enjoys as well as by the ties between them. Next, the firm should characterize the concerns about the business's conduct that each relevant stakeholder group shares. This information can be derived from formal research, including surveys, focus groups, Internet searches, or press reviews. For instance, Ford Motor Company obtains input on social and environmental responsibility issues from

| FIGURE 2–1 | Interactions Between a Company and Its Primary and Secondary Stakeholders |
|---|---|

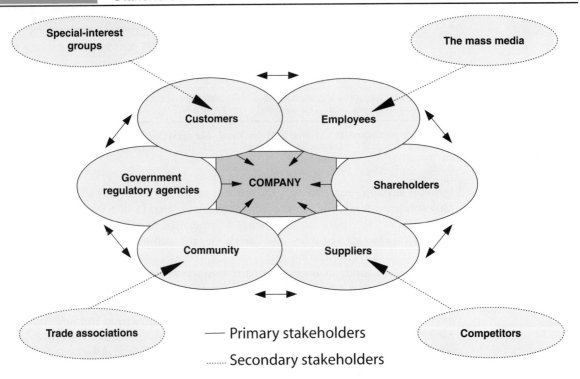

Source: Adapted from Isabelle Maignan, O. C. Ferrell, and Linda Ferrell, "Managing Corporate Social Responsibility: How to Nurture Stakeholders' Confidence," working paper, Colorado State University, 2003, p. 29. Used with permission.

company representatives, suppliers, customers, and community leaders. Shell has an online discussion forum where Web site visitors are invited to express their opinions on the company's activities and their implications. This information can also be generated informally by employees and managers as they carry out their daily activities. For example, purchasing managers know about suppliers' demands, public relations executives about the media, legal counselors about the regulatory environment, financial executives about investors, sales representatives about customers, and human resources advisers about employees. Finally, the company should evaluate its impact on the issues that are important to the various stakeholders it has identified.[12]

Given the variety of the employees involved in the generation of information about stakeholders, it is essential that this intelligence be circulated throughout the firm. This requires that the firm facilitate the communication of information about the nature of relevant stakeholder communities, stakeholder issues, and the current impact of the firm on these issues to all members of the organization. The dissemination of stakeholder intelligence can be organized formally through activities such as newsletters and internal information forums.[13]

A stakeholder orientation is not complete unless it includes activities that actually address stakeholder issues. The responsiveness of the organization as a whole to stakeholder intelligence consists of the initiatives the firm adopts to ensure that it abides by or exceeds stakeholder expectations and has a positive impact on stakeholder issues. Such activities are likely to be specific to a particular stakeholder group (e.g., family-friendly work schedules) or to a particular stakeholder issue (e.g., pollution-reduction programs). Noticeably, these responsiveness processes may involve the participation of the concerned stakeholder groups. Mattel, for example, includes special-interest groups and university representatives in its programs to curtail child labor.[14]

A stakeholder orientation can be viewed as a continuum in that firms are likely to adopt the concept to varying degrees. To gauge a given firm's stakeholder orientation, it is necessary to evaluate the extent to which the firm adopts behaviors that typify both the generation of stakeholder intelligence and the dissemination and responsiveness to it. A given organization may generate and disseminate more intelligence about certain stakeholder communities than about others and may respond to that intelligence differently.[15]

## Ethical Issues in Business

As mentioned earlier, stakeholders define a business's ethical issues. An **ethical issue** is a problem, situation, or opportunity that requires an individual, group, or organization to choose among several actions that must be evaluated as right or wrong, ethical or unethical. A constructive next step toward identifying and resolving ethical issues is to classify the issues that are relevant to most business organizations. In this section we classify ethical issues in relation to honesty and fairness, conflict of interest, fraud, discrimination, and information technology. Although not all-inclusive or mutually exclusive, these classifications provide an overview of some of the major ethical issues that business decision makers face.

### Honesty and Fairness

**Honesty** refers to truthfulness, integrity, and trustworthiness; **fairness** is the quality of being just, equitable, and impartial. Honesty and fairness relate to the general moral attributes of decision makers. At a minimum, businesspeople are expected to follow all applicable laws and regulations. In addition, they should not knowingly harm customers, clients, employees, or even other competitors through deception, misrepresentation, or coercion. Although businesspeople often act in their own economic self-interest, ethical business relations should be grounded on fairness, justice, and trust. Buyers should be able to trust sellers; lenders should be able to trust borrowers. Failure to live up to these expectations or to abide by laws and standards destroys trust and makes it difficult, if not impossible, to continue business exchanges.[16]

Ideas of fairness are sometimes shaped by vested interests. One or both parties in the relationship may view an action as unfair or unethical because the outcome was less beneficial than expected. Fuji and Kodak, for example, have waged a long legal battle against Jazz Photo Corporation and other firms that recycle disposable cameras by patching them with electrical tape, inserting new film, putting new sleeves on them, and reselling them for much less than Fuji and Kodak's new disposable cameras. Beyond the fact that many consumers may not realize that these "single-use" cameras have been used as many as seven times, Fuji contends that these disposable camera reloaders are violating its patents on disposable cameras. A federal jury sided with Fuji and ordered Jazz Photo to pay the Japanese firm $25 million in damages for lost profits and royalties.[17]

Issues related to fairness and honesty also arise because business is sometimes regarded as a "game" governed by its own rules rather than those of society. Author Eric Beversluis suggests that unfairness is a problem because people often reason along these lines:

1. Business relationships are a subset of human relationships that are governed by their own rules, which, in a market society, involve competition, profit maximization, and personal advancement within the organization.
2. Business can therefore be considered a game people play, comparable in certain respects to competitive sports such as basketball or boxing.
3. Ordinary rules and morality do not hold in games like basketball or boxing. (What if a basketball player did unto others as he would have them do unto him? What if a boxer decided it was wrong to try to injure another person?)
4. Logically, then, if business is a game like basketball or boxing, ordinary ethical rules do not apply.[18]

This type of reasoning leads many people to conclude that anything is fair in sports, war, and business. Indeed, several books have compared business to warfare—for example, *The Guerrilla Marketing Handbook* and *Sun Tsu: The Art of War for Managers*. The common theme is that surprise attacks, guerrilla warfare, and other warlike tactics are necessary to win the battle for consumers' dollars. This business-as-war mentality may foster the idea that fairness and honesty are not necessary in business. An intensely competitive environment creates the potential for companies to engage in questionable conduct. For example, as competition in the market for beer intensified, Miller, Coors, and Anheuser Busch increasingly offered products and advertising that tried to appeal to younger consumers by featuring extreme behavior, even though marketing to minors under the age of twenty-one is illegal.

Many argue, however, that business is not a game like basketball or boxing. Because people are not economically self-sufficient, they cannot withdraw from the game of business. Therefore, business ethics must not only make clear what rules apply in the "game" of business but must also develop rules appropriate to the nonvoluntary character of everyone's participation in it.[19]

## Conflicts of Interest

A **conflict of interest** exists when an individual must choose whether to advance his or her own interests, those of the organization, or those of some other group. For example, federal investigators are looking into whether a $1 million donation by Citigroup to the 92nd St. Y nursery school represents a conflict of interest. Jack Grubman, an analyst for Salomon Smith Barney, upgraded his rating for AT&T stock after Sanford Weill, CEO of Citigroup (the parent company of Salomon Smith Barney), agreed to use his influence to help Grubman's twins gain admission to the elite Manhattan nursery school. Grubman has denied elevating his rating for AT&T's stock for a quid pro quo, but his children were enrolled.[20] If Grubman placed his family's interests ahead of his company's and the investors who paid his company for impartial advice, then those stakeholders are likely to consider his action a conflict of interest.

To avoid conflicts of interest, employees must be able to separate their private interests from their business dealings. Organizations, too, must avoid potential conflicts of interest when providing goods or services. For example, Arthur Andersen LLP served as outside auditor for Waste Management, Inc., while it was also providing consulting services to the firm. This situation led the Securities and Exchange Commission to investigate charges that the consulting fees Arthur Andersen received may have compromised the independence of its auditing of Waste Management's books. The accounting firm eventually agreed to pay $7 million to settle the case and later paid $100 million to settle a lawsuit brought against the firm by Waste Management shareholders. Within a year, Arthur Andersen was forced to pay out millions of dollars to settle similar federal charges and shareholder lawsuits surrounding accounting irregularities at Sunbeam and Qwest Communications, while investigations of its auditing of other highly visible firms continued.[21]

In many developed countries, it is generally recognized that employees should not accept bribes, personal payments, gifts, or special favors from people who hope to influence the outcome of a decision. However, as discussed later in this text, bribery is an accepted way of doing business in many countries. Bribes have been associated with the downfall of many managers, legislators, and government officials. One source estimates that some $80 billion is paid out worldwide in the form of bribes or some other payoff every year.[22] When a government official accepts a bribe, it is usually from a business that seeks some favor—perhaps a chance to influence legislation that affects it. Giving bribes to legislators or public officials, then, is a business ethics issue.

## Fraud

When an individual engages in deceptive practices to advance his or her own interests over those of his or her organization or some other group, charges of fraud may result. In general, **fraud** is any purposeful communication that deceives, manipulates, or conceals facts in order to create a false impression. It is considered a crime, and convictions may result in fines, imprisonment, or both. Fraud costs U.S. organizations more than $400 billion a year; the average company loses about 6 percent of total revenues to fraud and abuses committed by its own employees.[23] Among the most common fraudulent activities employees report about their coworkers are stealing office supplies or shoplifting, claiming to have worked extra hours, and stealing money or products.[24] In recent years, accounting fraud has become a major ethical issue, but as we will see fraud may also relate to marketing and consumer issues.

*Accounting Fraud* One area in which fraud has become a major issue is accounting. A corporation's financial reports provide important information on which investors and others base decisions that may involve millions of dollars. If those documents contain inaccurate information, whether intentionally or not, lawsuits and criminal penalties may result. AOL, for example, is under investigation for improperly reporting $49 million in advertising and commerce revenues.[25] Such scrutiny of financial reporting increased dramatically in the wake of the accounting scandals in the early 2000s. As a result of the negative publicity surrounding the allegations of accounting fraud at a number of companies, many firms were forced to take a second look at their financial documents. More than a few chose to restate their earnings to avoid being drawn into the scandal.[26] For example, Qwest Communications, which provides local and long-distance telephone service, announced that it overstated revenue by $1.9 billion during 2000 and was forced to restate about $1.5 billion in earnings for that year.[27]

Ethical issues also exist with regard to the accounting services provided to individuals, particularly tax-shelter advice. For example, when Henry Camferdam and his partners sold their computer business for $70 million, accountants at Ernst & Young LLP advised them to enter into a very complex tax-shelter arrangement to minimize the amount of taxes they would have to pay on their profits from the sale. When an Internal Revenue Service audit several years later determined that the partners owed potentially $20 million in back taxes, penalties, and interest, they filed a lawsuit against Ernst & Young, accusing the accounting firm of capitalizing on its position as a trusted adviser to entice them into engaging in an illegal "tax sham." Although Ernst & Young contends the partners' suit has no merit, the lawsuit is but one of many that have been brought by individual tax payers against accounting firms that advised them to enter questionable and complicated schemes for sheltering income from taxation.[28]

The field of accounting has changed dramatically over the last decade. The profession used to have a club-type mentality: those who became certified public accountants (CPAs) were not concerned about competition. Now CPAs advertise their skills and short-term results in an environment in which competition has increased and overall billable hours have significantly decreased because of technological innovations. Additionally, accountants are now permitted to charge performance-based fees rather than hourly rates. This rule change encouraged some large accounting firms to promote tax-avoidance strategies for high-income individuals because the firms can charge 10 to 40 percent of the amount of taxes saved.[29] Pressures on accountants include the following: time, reduced fees, client requests to alter opinions concerning financial conditions or lower tax payments, and increased competition. Other issues that accountants face daily involve compliance with complex rules and regulations, data overload, contingent fees, and commissions. An accountant's life is filled with rules and data that have to be interpreted correctly. Because of such pressures, and the ethical predicaments they spawn, problems within the accounting industry are on the rise.

As a result, accountants must abide by a strict code of ethics, which defines their responsibilities to their clients and the public interest. The code also discusses the concepts of integrity, objectivity, independence, and due care. Despite the standards the code provides, the accounting industry has been the source of numerous fraud investigations in recent years. Congress passed the Sarbanes-Oxley Act in 2002 to address many of the issues that could create conflicts of interest for accounting firms auditing public corporations. The law generally prohibits accounting firms from providing both auditing and consulting services to the same firm. Additionally, the law specifies that corporate boards of directors must include outside directors with financial knowledge on the company's audit committee.

*Marketing Fraud*  Marketing—the process of creating, distributing, promoting, and pricing products—is another area in business that generates potential ethical issues. Marketing communications that are false or misleading can destroy customers' trust in a company. Lying, a major ethical issue involving communications, may be a significant problem. In both external and internal communications, it causes ethical predicaments because it destroys trust. For example, two former executives of World-Com—chief financial officer Scott Sullivan and controller David Myers—were arrested and charged with concealing $3.8 billion in expenses as well as lying to investors and regulators to hide their deception.[30]

False or deceptive advertising is a key issue in marketing communications. Abuses in advertising can range from exaggerated claims and concealed facts to outright lying. Exaggerated claims are those that cannot be substantiated, as when a commercial states that a certain product is superior to any other on the market. For example, the FTC filed formal complaints against Stock Value 1 Inc. and Comstar Communications Inc. for making unsubstantiated claims that their radiation-protection patches block the electromagnetic energy emitted by cellular telephones. The FTC's complaint charged that the companies "made false statements that their products had been scientifically 'proven' and tested" when in fact that was not the case.[31]

Another form of advertising abuse involves making ambiguous statements in which the words are so weak or general that the viewer, reader, or listener must infer the advertiser's intended message. These "weasel" words are inherently vague and enable the advertiser to deny any intent to deceive. The verb *help* is a good example (as in expressions such as "helps prevent," "helps fight," "helps make you feel").[32] Consumers may view such advertisements as unethical because they fail to communicate all the information needed to make a good purchasing decision or because they deceive the consumer outright.

Labeling issues are even murkier. For example, Mott's, Inc., the nation's leading producer of applesauce and apple juice, agreed to revise the labels of some of its fruit products after New York's attorney general claimed they were misleading consumers. The products—often made by blending apple juice with enough grape juice or cherry juice to make the designated flavor—had labels with the words "100% Juice" and a picture of grapes or cherries and the fruits' names in large lettering underneath. The attorney general argued that placing the fruits' name under "100% Juice" could lead consumers to assume that the products were 100 percent grape juice or cherry juice. Mott's admitted no wrongdoing but agreed to pay $177,500 to cover the investigation costs and to institute a minor change to the labels in question.[33]

In the telephone industry, AT&T sued Business Discount Plan (BDP), accusing it of using fraud and deception to routinely "slam" customers to its telecommunication service. Slamming refers to changing a customer's phone service without authorization. AT&T charged that BDP gave the impression that it was affiliated with AT&T. As part of the settlement, BDP had to send letters to consumers telling them that BDP was not affiliated with AT&T.[34] Such misleading behavior creates ethical issues because the communicated messages do not include all the information consumers need to make good purchasing decisions. They frustrate and anger customers, who feel that they have been deceived. In addition, they damage the seller's credibility and reputation.

Advertising and direct sales communication can also mislead by concealing the facts within the message. For instance, a salesperson anxious to sell a medical insurance policy might list a large number of illnesses covered by the policy but fail to mention that it does not cover some commonly covered illnesses. Indeed, the fastest-growing area of fraudulent activity is in direct marketing, which employs the telephone and nonpersonal media to communicate information to customers, who then purchase products via mail, telephone, or the Internet. In 2000, consumers reported losses of $138 million resulting from fraud to the Federal Trade Commission. In 2001, the FTC received an estimated twenty-five thousand complaints about Internet fraud alone.[35]

*Consumer Fraud*  Of course, companies and their employees do not hold a monopoly on fraud. Consumers have also been known to attempt to deceive businesses for their own gain. Shoplifting, for example, accounts for nearly 32 percent of the losses of the 118 largest U.S. retail chains, although this figure is still far outweighed by the nearly 49 percent of losses perpetrated by store employees, according to the National Retail Security Survey. Together with vendor fraud and administrative error, these losses cost U.S. retailers more than $31 billion a year.[36] Among others, actress Winona Ryder was convicted of shoplifting in 2002.[37]

Consumers engage in many other forms of fraud against businesses, including price-tag switching, item switching, lying to obtain age-related and other discounts, and taking advantage of generous return policies by returning used items, especially clothing that has been worn (with the price tags carefully concealed, but not removed). Such behavior by consumers hurts retail stores as well as other consumers who, for example, unwittingly purchase new clothing that has actually been worn.[38]

## Discrimination

Although a person's racial and sexual prejudices belong to the domain of individual ethics, racial and sexual **discrimination** in the workplace creates ethical issues within the business world. Once dominated by white men, the U.S. work force today includes significantly more women, African Americans, Hispanics, and other minorities, as well as disabled and older workers. Experts project that within the next fifty years, Hispanics will represent 24 percent of the population, while African Americans and Asians/Pacific Islanders will comprise 13 percent and 9 percent, respectively.[39] These groups have traditionally faced discrimination and higher unemployment rates and been denied opportunities to assume leadership roles in corporate America.

Indeed, race, gender, and age discrimination are a major source of ethical and legal debate in the workplace. Between seventy-five thousand and eighty thousand charges of discrimination are filed annually with the Equal Employment Opportunity Commission (EEOC).[40] Sexual harassment filings with the EEOC average about sixteen thousand per year.[41] Salomon Smith Barney was ordered to pay $3.2 billion to a female broker as part of a class-action lawsuit. The broker alleged that men in her branch office made sex-related insults and lewd comments to her, brought in female strippers, watched pornographic videos in a sales manager's office, and engaged in simulated phone sex on an office speaker-phone during work hours.[42]

Discrimination remains a significant ethical issue in business despite nearly forty years of legislation to outlaw it. For instance, the Age Discrimination in Employment Act specifically outlaws hiring practices that discriminate against people between the ages of forty-nine and sixty-nine, as well as those that require employees to retire before the age of seventy. Despite this legislation, charges of age discrimination persist in the workplace. For example, Woolworth's, now known as Foot Locker Specialty, paid $3.5 million to settle charges that it systematically laid off workers over age forty in order to reduce costs, although the company denied any wrongdoing.[43] A survey by the American Association for Retired Persons (AARP), an advocacy organization for people fifty and older, highlighted how little most companies value older workers. When AARP mailed invitations to ten thousand companies for a chance to compete for a listing in *Modern Maturity* magazine as one of the "best employers for workers over 50," it received just fourteen applications. Given that nearly 20 percent of the nation's workers will be fifty-five years old or over by 2015, many companies need to change their approach toward older workers.[44]

To help build work forces that reflect their customer base, many companies have initiated **affirmative action programs**, which involve efforts to recruit, hire, train, and promote qualified individuals from groups that have traditionally been discriminated against on the basis of race, gender, or other characteristics. Such initiatives may be imposed by federal law on an employer that contracts or subcontracts for business with the federal government; as part of a settlement agreement with a state or federal agency; or by court order.[45] For example, Safeway, a chain of supermarkets, established a program to expand opportunities for women in middle- and upper-level management after settling a sex-discrimination lawsuit.[46] However, many companies voluntarily implement affirmative action plans in order to build a more diverse work force.[47] For example, a Chicago real estate developer decided to help employers identify available female workers by launching the Female Employment Initiative, an outreach program designed to create opportunities for women in the construction industry through training programs, counseling and information services, and referral listings.[48]

Although many people believe that affirmative action requires that quotas be used to govern employment decisions, it is important to note that two decades of Supreme Court rulings have made it clear that affirmative action does *not* permit or require quotas, reverse discrimination, or favorable treatment of unqualified women or minorities. To ensure that affirmative action programs are fair, the Supreme Court has established a number of standards to guide their implementation: (1) there must be a strong reason for developing an affirmative action program; (2) affirmative action programs must apply only to qualified candidates; and (3) affirmative action programs must be limited and temporary and therefore cannot include "rigid and inflexible quotas."[49]

Discrimination can also be an ethical issue in business when companies use race or other personal factors to discriminate against specific groups of customers. Many companies, particularly in the insurance industry, have been accused of using race to deny service or charge higher prices to certain ethnic groups. Ford Motor Credit Company, the nation's largest automobile finance firm, was accused in a lawsuit of charging African-American car buyers higher interest rates for auto loans than white customers with similar credit histories. The suit, filed by four African Americans who insist they were overcharged, alleges that the company empowers dealers to inflate loan costs to buyers they think will pay higher rates. Ford denied the allegations.[50]

## Information Technology

The final category of ethical issues relates to **technology** and the numerous advances made in Internet and other forms of electronic communications in the last few years. As the number of people who use the Internet increases, the areas of concern related to its use increase as well. Some issues that must be addressed by businesses include the monitoring of employees' use of available technology, consumer privacy, site development and online marketing, and legal protection of intellectual properties, such as music, books, and movies.

A challenge for companies today is meeting their business needs while protecting employees' desires for privacy. There are few legal protections of an employee's right to privacy, and businesses therefore have much flexibility in establishing policies regarding employees' privacy while they are on company property and using company equipment. The increased use of electronic communications in the workplace and technological advances that permit employee monitoring and surveillance provide companies with new opportunities to obtain data about employees. According to Michael Hoffman, a leading business ethics consultant, "fifty percent, and probably more, of America's companies conduct random e-mail surveillance, and most don't warn employees they are going to do it."[51] One survey of employees found that most assume that their use of technology at work will be monitored, and a large majority approved of most monitoring methods (see Figure 2–2).[52] Concerns about employee privacy extend to Europe as well. In Finland, an executive vice president and several employees of Sonera Corp. were arrested as part of an investigation into whether the

---

**FIGURE 2–2** **Percentage of Employees Who Approve of Certain Monitoring Methods**

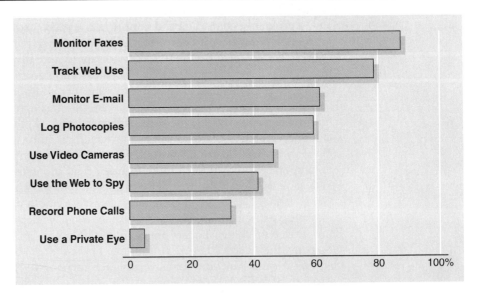

Source: John Galvin, "The New Business Ethics," SmartBusinessMag.com, June 2000, p. 97. Reprinted from Ziff Davis Smart Business, June 2000, with permission. Copyright © 2001 Ziff Davis Media, Inc. All Rights Reserved.

wireless telecommunications company violated the privacy of its workers by monitoring their call records, a serious offense in Finland. The investigation was launched after a local newspaper reported that Sonera was tracing employees' phone calls in order to identify who may have leaked information about the company to the media. The company has denied the accusations.[53]

Clearly conveying the organization's policy on workplace privacy should reduce the opportunity for employee lawsuits and the resulting costs of such actions. However, if a company fails to monitor employees' use of e-mail and the Internet, the costs can be huge. For example, Chevron Corp. agreed to pay $2.2 million to employees who claimed that unmonitored sexually harassing e-mail created a threatening environment for them.[54] Instituting practices that show respect for employee privacy but do not abdicate the employer's responsibility should help create a climate of trust that promotes opportunities for resolving employee–employer disputes without lawsuits.

There is ample evidence that people use their companies' technology for personal business while they are at work. A survey of twelve hundred employees by Vault.com found that 47 percent spend at least half an hour a day surfing non-work-related Web sites for personal reasons.[55] Electronic monitoring allows a company to determine whether productivity is being reduced because employees are spending too much time on personal Web activities. Knowing this can then enable the company to take steps to remedy the situation. Internet filtering companies, such as Cyber Patrol, Surfcontrol, Surfwatch, and WebSense, provide products that block employee access to Web sites deemed distracting or objectionable. WebSense launched AfterWork.com, a personal home page for each employee at a company that allows employees to visit non-work-related Web sites during breaks and lunch as well as before and after work hours.[56] One survey of Internet-related employee behaviors found that 58 percent of employees rated using company resources for personal Web surfing an "extremely serious" or "very serious" business ethics violation.[57] Table 2–2 provides more of the survey results.

| TABLE 2–2 | Employee Internet-Related Behavior Rated As "Extremely Serious" or "Very Serious" Business Ethics Violations |

| BEHAVIOR | EMPLOYEE OPINION | EMPLOYER OPINION |
| --- | --- | --- |
| E-mail harassment of another employee | 91% | 94% |
| Circulating pornography through company e-mail | 85% | 93% |
| Using company resources for personal Web surfing | 58% | 56% |
| Using company resources and time for personal e-mail | 45% | 50% |

Source: "Ethical Issues in the Employer–Employee Relationship," Society of Financial Service Professionals, www.financialpro.org/press/Ethics/es2000/Ethics_Survey_2000_Report_FINAL.cfm (accessed Feb. 6, 2003). Reprinted with permission from the Society of Financial Service Professionals ethics survey "Ethical Issues in the Employer–Employee Relationship" (www.financialpro.org). Copyright © 2000 by the Society of Financial Service Professionals, 270 S. Bryn Mawr Avenue, Bryn Mawr, PA 19010. Distribution prohibited without publisher's written permission.

The second ethical issue created by advances in technology relates to consumer privacy. There are two dimensions to this issue: consumer awareness of information collection and a growing lack of consumer control over how companies use the personal information they collect. Online purchases and even random Web surfing can be tracked without a consumer's knowledge. A survey by the Progress and Freedom Foundation found that 96 percent of popular commercial Web sites collect personally identifying information from visitors.[58] For example, www.edu.com is a site through which registered college students can make online purchases with a student discount. The site collects personal information on all users and even contacts their colleges to verify that they are actually enrolled. The company then passes collected information to its partners—computer makers (such as Apple Computer, Inc.) and credit card issuers (such as AT&T and Citibank)—in exchange for the right to sell those companies' products at a discount. The firm says it does not sell names or specific individual information but rather data on the kinds of products students would like to see, hobbies in which they are involved, and features they would like to see on particular sites.[59]

A U.S. Department of Commerce study on e-commerce and privacy found that 81 percent of Internet users and 79 percent of consumers who buy products and services over the Web were concerned about online threats to privacy.[60] Another survey found that 38 percent of respondents felt that it is never ethical to track customers' Web activities, and 64 percent said they don't trust Web sites that do.[61] These concerns have led some companies to cut back on the amount of information they collect: 84 percent of the sites surveyed by the Progress and Freedom Foundation indicated that they are collecting less data than before.[62] Companies are also working to find ways to improve consumers' trust in their Web sites. For example, an increasing number of Web sites display an online seal from BBBOnline, available only to sites that subscribe to certain standards. Another seal is available through TRUSTe, a nonprofit global initiative, that certifies those Web sites that adhere to its principles. Visit *e-businessethics.com* for more on Internet privacy.

A third ethical issue related to technology involves the legal protection of intellectual properties, such as music, books, and movies. Laws such as the Copyright Act of 1976, the Digital Millennium Copyright Act, and the Digital Theft Deterrence and Copyright Damages Improvement Act of 1999 were designed to protect the creators of intellectual property. However, with the advance of technology, ethical issues still abound for Web sites. For example, Napster.com allowed individuals to download copyrighted music for personal use without providing compensation to the artists until it was sued for copyright infringement.

A decision by the federal Copyright Office helped lay the groundwork for intellectual property rules in a digital world. The office decided to allow just two exemptions to the federal law that makes it illegal for Web users to hack through barriers that copyright holders erect around material released on line, such as books, films, and music. The first exemption was for software that blocks users from finding obscene or controversial material on the Web, and the second was for people who want to bypass malfunctioning security features of software or other copyrighted goods they have purchased. This decision reflects the fact that copyright owners are being favored in digital copyright issues.[63] There have been many lawsuits related to this issue, and some have had costly results. MP3.com paid Universal Music Group $53.4 million to end its dispute with major record labels over copyright infringement.[64]

## Recognizing an Ethical Issue

Although we have described a number of relationships and situations that may generate ethical issues, in practice it can be difficult to recognize specific ethical issues. Failure to acknowledge ethical issues is a great danger in any organization, particularly if business is treated as a "game" in which ordinary rules of fairness do not apply. Sometimes people who take this view do things that are not only unethical but also illegal so they can maximize their own position or boost the profits or goals of their organization. However, just because an unsettled situation or activity is an ethical issue does not mean the behavior is necessarily unethical. An ethical issue is simply a situation, a problem, or even an opportunity that requires thought, discussion, or investigation to determine the moral impact of the decision. Because the business world is dynamic, new ethical issues are emerging all the time.

One way to determine whether a specific behavior or situation has an ethical component is to ask other individuals in the business how they feel about it and whether they approve. Another way is to determine whether the organization has adopted specific policies on the activity. An activity approved of by most members of an organization, if it is also customary in the industry, is probably ethical. An issue, activity, or situation that can withstand open discussion between many stakeholders, both in and outside the organization, and survive untarnished probably does not pose ethical problems. For instance, when engineers and designers at Ford Motor Co. discussed what type of gas-tank protection should be used in its Pinto automobile, they reached consensus within the organization, but they did not take into account the interests of various external stakeholders, such as the public's desire for maximum safety. Consequently, even though they might have believed the issue had no ethical dimension, Ford erred in not opening up the issue to public scrutiny. (As it turned out, the type of gas-tank protection used in the Pinto resulted in several fires and deaths when the cars suffered rear-end collisions.) Years later, another controversy developed when Ford Explorer sport utility vehicles (SUVs) equipped with Firestone Wilderness AT tires were associated with many rollover accidents and deaths. Although Ford denied responsibility for the accidents, statistics found that Ford Explorers with Firestone tires rolled over more frequently than other SUVs with those tires.[65] In these cases, greater openness in communications with stakeholders was needed to inform the public of relevant dangers.

Once an individual recognizes that an ethical issue exists and can openly discuss it and ask for guidance and the opinions of others, he or she is ready to enter the ethical decision-making process, which we will examine in Chapter 4.

## Summary

Customers, investors and shareholders, employees, suppliers, government agencies, communities, and many others who have a "stake" or claim in some aspect of a company's products, operations, markets, industry, and outcomes are known as stakeholders. They are both influenced by and have the ability to affect businesses. Stakeholders provide both tangible and intangible resources that are more or less critical to a firm's

long-term success, and their ability to withdraw—or to threaten to withdraw—these resources gives them power.

Primary stakeholders are those whose continued association is absolutely necessary for a firm's survival; while secondary stakeholders do not typically engage in transactions with a company and thus are not essential for its survival. The stakeholder interaction model suggests that there are two-way relationships between the firm and a host of stakeholders. The degree to which a firm understands and addresses stakeholder demands can be expressed as a "stakeholder orientation," which comprises three sets of activities: (1) the generation of data across the firm about its stakeholder groups and the assessment of the firm's effects on these groups, (2) the distribution of this information throughout the firm, and (3) the responsiveness of every level of the firm to this intelligence. A stakeholder orientation can be viewed as a continuum in that firms are likely to adopt the concept to varying degrees.

An ethical issue is a problem, situation, or opportunity that requires an individual or organization to choose among several actions that must be evaluated as right or wrong, ethical or unethical. Ethical issues typically arise because of conflicts between individuals' personal moral philosophies and values and the values and attitudes of the organizations in which they work and the society in which they live.

This book classifies ethical issues into five categories: honesty and fairness, conflict of interest, fraud, discrimination, and technology. Honesty refers to truthfulness, integrity, and trustworthiness; fairness is the quality of being just, equitable, and impartial. Issues related to fairness and honesty often arise in business because many participants believe that business is a game governed by its own rules rather than those of society. A conflict of interest exists when an individual must choose between advancing his or her own personal interests and those of the organization or some other group. Fraud is any purposeful communication that deceives, manipulates, or conceals facts in order to create a false impression. In accounting, fraud may create ethical issues related to how a company reports its financial position to interested stakeholders. In marketing, fraud generally relates to false or deceptive marketing communications. Consumers may also defraud businesses. Although a person's racial and sexual prejudices are an individual ethical concern, racial and sexual discrimination in the workplace creates ethical issues in the business world. Ethical issues related to technology have increased with advances in technology. Among the most challenging are employee privacy, consumer privacy, and the protection of intellectual property.

A good rule of thumb is that an activity that is approved of by most members of an organization and is customary in the industry is probably ethical. An issue, activity, or situation that can withstand open discussion and survive untarnished probably poses no ethical problem. Once an individual recognizes that an ethical issue exists and can openly discuss it and ask for guidance and the opinions of others, he or she enters the ethical decision-making process.

| **Important Terms for Review** | stakeholders | fairness |
|---|---|---|
| | primary stakeholders | conflict of interest |
| | secondary stakeholders | fraud |
| | stakeholder interaction model | discrimination |
| | ethical issue | affirmative action programs |
| | honesty | technology |

## A Real-Life Situation*

Joseph Freberg had been with Alcon for eighteen months. He had begun his career right out of college with a firm in the Southeast called Cala Industrial, which specialized in air compressors. Because of his work with Cala, he had been lured away to Alcon, in Omaha, as a sales manager. Joseph's first six months had been hard. Working with salespeople older than he, trying to get a handle on his people's sales territories, and settling into the corporate culture of a new firm took sixteen-hour days, six days a week. During those six months he also bought a house, and his fiancée furnished it. Ellen had stepped right in and decided almost everything, from the color of the rugs to the style of the curtains.

Ellen had taken a brokerage job with Trout Brothers and seemed to be working even more hours than Joseph. But the long days were paying off. Ellen was now starting to handle some large accounts and was being noticed by the "right" crowd in the wealthier Omaha areas.

Costs for the new home had exceeded their anticipated spending limit, and the plans for their wedding seemed to be getting larger and larger. In addition, Ellen was commuting from her apartment to the new home and then to her job, and the commute killed her car. As a result, she decided to lease something that exuded success. "Ellen, don't you think a Mercedes is a little out of our range? What are the payments?" inquired Joseph. "Don't worry, darling. When my clients see me in this—as well as when we start entertaining at the new house once we're married—the payments on the car will seem small compared with the money I'll be making," Ellen mused as she ran her fingers through Joseph's hair and gave him a peck on the cheek. By the time of the wedding and honeymoon, Joseph and Ellen's bank statement looked like a bullfighter's cape—red. "Don't worry, Joseph, everything will turn out okay. You've got a good job. I've got a good job. We're young and have drive. Things will straighten out after a while," said Ellen as she eyed a Rolex in a store window.

After the wedding, things did settle down—to a hectic pace, given their two careers and their two sets of parents two thousand miles in either direction. Joseph had realized that Alcon was a paternal type of organization, with good benefits and tremendous growth potential. He had identified who to be friends with and who to stay away from in the company. His salespeople seemed to tolerate him, sometimes calling him "Little Joe" or "Joey" because of his age, and his salespeople were producing—slowly climbing up the sales ladder to the number-one spot in the company.

While doing some regular checkup work on sales personnel, Joseph found out that Carl had been giving kickbacks to some of his buyers. Carl's sales volume accounted for a substantial amount of the company's existing clientele sales, and he had been a trainer for the company for several years. Carl also happened to be the vice president's son-in-law. Joseph started to check on the other reps more closely and discovered that, although Carl seemed to be the biggest offender, three of his ten people were doing the same thing. The next day Joseph looked up Alcon's policy handbook and found this statement: "Our company stands for doing the right thing at all times and giving our customers the best product for the best prices." There was no specific mention of kickbacks, but everyone knew that kickbacks ultimately reduce fair competition, which eventually leads to reduced quality and increased prices for customers. By talking to a few of the old-timers at Alcon, Joseph learned that there had been sporadic enforcement of the "no kickback" policy. It seemed that when times were good it became unacceptable and when times were bad it slipped into the acceptable range. And then there was his boss, Kathryn, the vice president. Joseph knew that Kathryn had a tendency to shoot the bearer of bad news. He remembered a story he had heard about a sales manager coming in to see Kathryn to explain an error in a bid that one of his salespeople had made. Kathryn called in the entire sales staff and fired the salesman on the spot. Then, smiling, she told the sales manager: "This was your second mistake, so I hope that you can get a good recommendation from personnel. You have two weeks to find employment elsewhere." From then on, the office staff had a nickname for Kathryn—Jaws.

Trying to solve the problem he was facing, Joseph broached the subject of kickbacks at his monthly meeting with Carl. Carl responded, "You've been in this business long enough to know that this happens all the time. I see nothing wrong with this practice if it increases sales. Besides, I take the money out of

my commission. You know that right now I'm trying to pay off some big medical bills. I've also gotten tacit clearance from above, but I wouldn't mention that if I were you." Joseph knew that the chain-of-command structure in the company made it very dangerous to go directly to a vice president with this type of information.

As Joseph was pondering whether to do nothing, bring the matter into the open and state that it was wrong and that such practices were against policy, or talk to Kathryn about the situation, his cell phone rang. It was Ellen. "Honey, guess what just happened. Kathryn, your boss, has decided to use me as her new broker. Isn't that fantastic!"

What should Joseph do?

## Questions ■ Exercises

1. What are Joseph's ethical problems?
2. Assume you are Joseph and discuss your options.
3. What other information do you feel you need before making your decision?
4. Discuss in which business areas the ethical problems lie.

* This case is strictly hypothetical; any resemblance to real persons, companies, or situations is coincidental.

---

## Check Your EQ

Check your E.Q., or Ethics Quotient, by completing the following. Assess your performance to evaluate your overall understanding of the chapter material.

| | | |
|---|---|---|
| 1. Stakeholders provide resources that are more or less critical to a firm's long-term success. | Yes | No |
| 2. Key ethical issues in an organization relate to fraud, discrimination, honesty and fairness, conflicts of interest, and technology. | Yes | No |
| 3. Three primary stakeholders are customers, special-interest groups, and the media. | Yes | No |
| 4. Fraud occurs when a false impression exists, which conceals facts. | Yes | No |
| 5. If an activity is approved by most members of an organization and it is also customary in the industry, it is probably ethical. | Yes | No |

ANSWERS: 1. Yes. These resources are both tangible and intangible. 2. Yes. See pages 31–41 regarding these key ethical issues and their implications for the organization. 3. No. Although customers are primary stakeholders, special-interest groups are usually considered secondary stakeholders. 4. No. Fraud must be purposeful, rather than accidental, and exists when deception and manipulation of facts are concealed to create a false impression that causes harm. 5. Yes. An activity that is generally regarded as ethical and survives open discussion inside and outside the organization is usually acceptable.

# Ethics As a Dimension of Social Responsibility

## CHAPTER OBJECTIVES

- To distinguish between the complementary concepts of social responsibility and business ethics
- To explore economic issues in social responsibility
- To examine competitive issues in social responsibility
- To explore the legal and regulatory environment of social responsibility
- To discuss the philanthropic dimension of social responsibility
- To appreciate business ethics as a dimension of social responsibility

## CHAPTER OUTLINE

## An Ethical Dilemma*

Myron had just graduated from West Coast University with both chemistry/pharmacy and business degrees and was excited to work for Producto International (PI). He loved having the opportunity to discover medicinal products around the world. His wife, Quan, was also enthusiastic about her job as an import-export agent for a subsidiary of PI.

Producto International was the industry leader, with headquarters in Paris. Worldwide, hundreds of small firms were competing with PI; however, only six had equivalent magnitude. These six had cornered 75 percent of world sales. So many interrelationships had developed that competition had become "managed." However, this did not constitute any illegal form of monopolistic behavior as defined by the European Union.

Myron's first assignment was in India and concerned exporting betel nuts to South and perhaps North America. It is estimated that more than 20 million people chew betel nuts in India alone. The betel nut is one of the world's most popular plants, and its leaf is used as a paper for rolling tobacco. The betel nut is also mashed or powdered with other ingredients and rolled up in a leaf and sold as candy. Myron quickly found that regular use of the betel nut will, in time, stain the mouth, gums, and teeth a deep red, which in Asia is a positive quality. As Myron was learning more about the betel nut, he came across the following report from the People's Republic of China: "Studies show that the chewing of the spiced betel nut can lead to oral cancer. According to research, 88 percent of China's oral cancer patients are betel nut chewers. Also, people who chew betel nuts and smoke are 90 times more likely to develop oral cancer than nonusers." Myron found that the betel nut primarily affects the central nervous system. It increases respiration while decreasing the work load on the heart (a mild high). Myron also found that demand for it was starting to emerge in the United States as well as in other developed countries.

While Myron was working on the betel nut, David, Myron's boss, also wanted him to work on introducing khat (pronounced "cot") into Asia. Khat is a natural stimulant from a plant grown in East Africa and southern Arabia. Fresh khat leaves, which are typically chewed like tobacco, produce a mild cocaine- or amphetamine-like euphoria. However, its effect is much less intense than that produced by either of those substances, with no reports of a rush sensation or paranoia, for example. Chewing khat produces a strong aroma and generates intense thirst. Casual users claim that khat lifts spirits, sharpens thinking, and, when its effects wear off, generates mild lapses into depression similar to those observed among cocaine users. The body appears to have a physical intolerance to khat due in part to limitations in how much can be ingested by chewing. As a result, reports suggest that there are no physical symptoms accompanying withdrawal. Advocates of khat use claim that it eases symptoms of diabetes, asthma, and disorders of the stomach and the intestinal tract. Opponents claim that khat damages health, suppresses appetite, and prevents sleep. In the United States, khat has been classified as a schedule IV substance by the Drug Enforcement Agency (DEA): freshly picked khat leaves (i.e., within forty-eight hours of harvest) are classified as a schedule I narcotic, the most restrictive category used by the DEA.

After doing his research, Myron delivered his report to David and said, "I really think that, given the right marketing to some of the big pharmaceutical companies, we should have two huge revenue makers."

"That's great, Myron, but the pharmaceutical market is only secondary to our primary market—the two billion consumers to whom we can introduce these products."

"What do you mean, David?" Myron asked.

"I mean these products are grown legally around the world, and the countries that we are targeting have no restrictions on these substances," David explained. "Why not tailor the delivery of the product by country? For example, we find out which flavors people want the betel nut in, in North and South America or the Middle East. The packaging will have to change by country as well as branding. Pricing strategies will need to be developed relative to our branding decisions, and of course quantity usages will have to be calculated. For example, single, multiple, supervalue sizes, etc., need to be explored. The same can be done for khat." David added, "Because of your research and your business background, I'm putting you on the marketing team for both. Of course, this means that you're going to have to be promoted and at least for a while live in Hong Kong. I know Quan will be excited. In fact, I told her the news this morning that she would be working on the same project in Hong Kong. Producto International tries to be sensitive to the dual-career family problems that can occur. Plus you'll be closer to relatives. I told Quan that with living allowances and all of the other things that go with international placement, you two should almost triple your salaries! You don't have to thank me, Myron. You've worked hard on these projects and now you deserve to have some of the benefits."

Myron went back to his office to think about his and Quan's future. He had heard of another employee who had rejected a similar offer, and that person's career had languished at PI. Eventually, that individual left the industry, never to be heard from again.

## Questions ■ Exercises

1. Identify the social responsibility issues in this scenario.
2. Discuss the advantages and disadvantages of each decision Myron could make.
3. Discuss the issue of marketing products that are legal but have addictive properties associated with them.

* This case is strictly hypothetical; any resemblance to real persons, companies, or situations is coincidental.

---

The concepts of ethics and social responsibility are often used interchangeably, although each has a distinct meaning. In Chapter 1, we defined the term *social responsibility* as an organization's obligation to maximize its positive impact on stakeholders and to minimize its negative impact. PNC Financial Services Group, for example, contributes $20 million in grants and corporate sponsorships to arts, community improvement, and educational causes. The company also supports employees with flexible work schedules and backup and holiday daycare, as well as a free daycare center for new parents. For its operations and technology center in Pittsburgh, the company built the nation's largest "green building" conforming to environmental guidelines on site planning, energy efficiency, water conservation, material conservation, and indoor environmental quality. It also built several "green" bank branches in New Jersey.[1] Like PNC, many businesses have tried to determine what relationships, obligations, and duties are appropriate between the organization and various stakeholders. Social responsibility can be viewed as a contract with society, whereas business ethics involves carefully thought-out rules or heuristics of business conduct that guide decision making.

There are four levels of social responsibility—economic, legal, ethical, and philanthropic—and they can be viewed as steps (see Figure 3–1).[2] At the most basic level, companies have an economic responsibility to be profitable so they can provide a return on investment to their owners and investors, create jobs for the community, and contribute goods and services to the economy. Of course, marketers are also expected to obey all laws and regulations. Business ethics, as previously defined, comprises principles and standards that guide behavior in the world of business. Finally, philanthropic responsibility refers to activities that are not required of businesses but that promote human welfare or goodwill. Ethics, then, is one dimension of social responsibility.

FIGURE 3–1   ## Steps of Social Responsibility

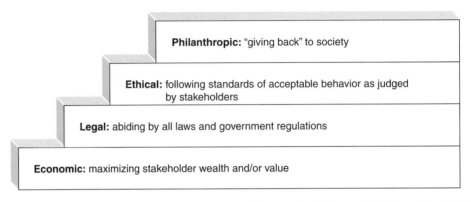

Source: Adapted from Archie B. Carroll, "The Pyramid of Corporate Social Responsibility: Toward the Moral Management of Organizational Stakeholders," *Business Horizons* (July-Aug. 1991): 42, Figure 3.

The term **corporate citizenship** is often used to express the extent to which businesses strategically meet the economic, legal, ethical, and philanthropic responsibilities placed on them by their various stakeholders.[3] It includes the activities and organizational processes adopted by businesses to meet their social responsibilities. A firm's commitment to corporate citizenship indicates a strategic focus on fulfilling the social responsibilities its stakeholders expect of it. Corporate citizenship involves *acting* on the firm's commitment to the corporate citizenship philosophy and measuring the extent to which it follows through by actually implementing citizenship initiatives. For example, Herman Miller, Inc., a multinational provider of office, residential, and health care furniture and services, has crafted a statement it calls the *Blueprint for Corporate Community* (see Figure 3–2). This statement sets forth Herman Miller's corporate citizenship philosophy—its commitment to being a different kind of company in the way it fulfills its responsibilities to customers, shareholders, employees, the community, and the natural environment.[4] Because this statement affects all Herman Miller's stakeholders and applies directly to all operations, products, markets, and business relationships, it demonstrates the company's strategic focus on corporate citizenship. Herman Miller's philosophy and actions have regularly landed the company on *Business Ethics* magazine's annual list of "Best Corporate Citizens" (see Table 3–1).

In this chapter, we examine a number of social responsibility issues, beginning with the foundation for all business activities—economic issues. Companies that fail to respond to these issues cannot survive for the long term. Next we explore issues related to how businesses compete. We also take a detailed look at the legal and regulatory environment of business, another dimension of social responsibility. By fulfilling their philanthropic responsibilities, firms contribute financial and human resources to the community and society that improve the quality of life. Finally, we consider how business ethics relates to social responsibility. Each of these categories of social responsibility and citizenship issues create challenges and opportunities for business decision makers.

| FIGURE 3–2 | Herman Miller, Inc.'s Blueprint for Corporate Community |

---

## — HERMAN MILLER, INC. —

**Herman Miller, Inc.,** is more than just a legal entity. It combines the talents, hopes, and dreams of thousands of people. At its best, it is a high-performance, values-driven community of people tied together by a common purpose. **Herman Miller** has always stood apart from the crowd because of what we believe, and we have always believed that what we stand for matters. Our strategies will change as the needs of our business change. Our core values will not. We build our business on them. How well we live up to these values will determine whether we are to be trusted by others.

*What we believe in:*

**Making a meaningful contribution to our customers**

**Cultivating community, participation, and people development**

**Creating economic value for shareholders and employee-owners**

**Responding to change through design and innovation**

**Living with integrity and respecting the environment**

Source: Herman Miller, www.hermanmiller.com/CDA/category/aboutus/0,1243,c13,00.html (accessed January 13, 2003). Reprinted with permission from Herman Miller, Inc.'s Blueprint for Corporate Community.

## Economic Issues

During the 1990s, the U.S. economy, along with the stock markets, grew dramatically. By 2000 the value of most companies had reached their highest levels ever. These heady years helped investors reap strong returns on their investments and gave CEOs the opportunity to take care of their employees and respond favorably to many other stakeholders. Enron, for example, made it onto a list of the one hundred best companies to work for in America three years in a row; it also received six environmental awards in 2000. During this time, the energy company developed strong policies on environmental climate change, human rights, and anti-corruption, and put together a statement of values emphasizing "communication, respect, and integrity."[5] Enron's chief financial officer was featured in the business press as a role model for corporate America. In 2001, however, the stock market crashed, heralding an economic downturn. Many companies, including some renowned for employee-friendly practices and no-layoff policies, began letting go tens of thousands of employees. Some took money from "over-funded" pension plans to prop up their bottom lines. Other firms moved to Bermuda and other countries to avoid paying taxes. Enron, as we saw in Chapter 1, collapsed after irregularities in its accounting practices came to

| TABLE 3–1 | The Top Twenty Best Corporate Citizens | | |
|-----------|------------------------|-------|----------|
| RANK | COMPANY | RANK | COMPANY |
| 1. | General Mills | 11. | AT&T |
| 2. | Cummins Inc. | 12. | Fannie Mae |
| 3. | Intel | 13. | Bank of America |
| 4. | Procter & Gamble | 14. | Motorola |
| 5. | IBM | 15. | Herman Miller |
| 6. | Hewlett-Packard | 16. | Expedia |
| 7. | Avon Products | 17. | Autodesk |
| 8. | Green Mountain Coffee Roasters | 18. | Cisco Systems |
| 9. | John Nuveen | 19. | Wild Oats Markets |
| 10. | St. Paul | 20. | Deluxe |

Source: Peter Asmus, with Sandra Waddock and Samuel Graves, "100 Best Corporate Citizens of 2003," Business Ethics, Spring 2003, p. 8. Reprinted with permission from Business Ethics, P.O. Box 8439, Minneapolis, MN 55408, 612/879-0695.

light; the company eventually laid off thousands of employees. They lost not only their jobs, but also their retirement pensions, which were heavily invested in the company's own stock. Many investors lost millions of dollars as the company's stock cratered.[6]

The economy is affected by the way companies relate to shareholders and other investors, employees, customers, competitors, the community, and even the natural environment. When economic downturns or poor decisions lead companies to lay off employees, communities often suffer as they attempt to absorb the displaced employees. Customers may experience diminished levels of service because there are fewer experienced employees. Stock prices often decline when layoffs are announced, which affects the value of stockholders' investment portfolios. Moreover, stressed-out employees facing demands to reduce expenses may make poor decisions that affect product quality, customer service, employee rights, and the natural environment. Thus, economic responsibilities require finding a balance between society's demand for social responsibility and investors' desire for profits.[7]

When people talk about the "economy," they generally mean cyclical conditions such as inflation, recession, and employment rates as well as how these conditions affect their ability to obtain the resources they need or desire. **Inflation** refers to an increase in the overall level of prices over an extended time; while a **recession** is characterized by rising unemployment, falling prices, restriction of credit, low output and investment, and many bankruptcies. The economy is in constant flux, and these business cycles influence the quality of life and the decisions of both consumers and companies. Occasionally, these decisions can harm stakeholders. For example, businesses typically deal with inflation by increasing prices or reducing the size or quality of goods sold. In an inflationary environment, opportunities may develop to implement exploitive pricing or to manipulate packaging and labels so consumers continue to believe they are purchasing the same amount of product for the same price. For example, Russia is the main source of palladium, which auto makers have begun using in catalytic converters because it costs less than platinum. As manufacturers around the world retooled for palladium, the Russian government increased the price from $100 per ounce to $800 per ounce.[8] This increase forced auto makers to raise prices, making it more difficult for consumers to purchase a new vehicle. To address the rising price of one resource, auto makers had fewer resources available to focus on automobile safety or the natural environment. Consumers who believe that prices will continue to rise are likely to borrow more, which, in turn, increases the demand for credit and raises interest rates. Unless the government steps in to manipulate the money supply, this situation can result in a spiral of rising prices. However, if improperly managed, this effort may lead to a recession in which too many jobs are lost and economic growth stagnates. Unemployment, low wages, and continued recession can harm the welfare of citizens.

The economy is also driven by **supply**—the amount of goods available at a given price at any time—and **demand**—how many consumers desire the available goods. Indeed, these two concepts are the building blocks of economics. However, when a company uses deception or manipulates a product's supply and demand, stakeholders can be harmed. For example, Eckerd's, a subsidiary of J.C. Penney, has been accused of charging customers for medicines they did not receive, using a practice known in the pharmaceutical industry as "rounding up." In one case, a patient paid $57.29 to purchase 3 milliliters of prescription eye drops at Eckerd's but actually received only 2.5 milliliters. A $100 million lawsuit has been filed against the pharmacy chain.[9] Many people believe that such overcharging has become rampant in the health care industry. The reasons relate to supply and demand along with the patchwork of rules and regulations that govern private insurance companies, health management organizations (HMOs), preferred provider organizations (PPOs), Medicare, and Medicaid. In the United States, those who have private insurance overpay because others only pay a set amount. As a result, inexpensive medical items can become very pricey as companies attempt to recoup their expenses. Consider the patient who stayed at Duke University Medical Center for thirty-four days and received a final bill for $5.2 million. One item, a syringe, was priced at $7,000.[10]

An organization's sense of economic responsibility is especially significant for employees because it raises such issues as equal job opportunities, workplace diversity, job safety, health, and employee privacy. In the United States, the concept of employment-at-will gives companies the right to terminate an employee without just cause and has been used to hire and determine when to terminate employees. Many companies have "downsized" and laid off millions of employees in the most recent economic downturn. The resulting rise in unemployment puts a drain on the economy as well as the personal hardships and suffering it creates for the unemployed. A *Business Week*/Harris poll found that almost two-thirds of respondents believe that job security for employees in big companies is poor (29 percent) or only fair (36 percent).[11]

Because local governments often maintain close ties with business and even offer companies incentives to locate in their areas, citizens may believe that businesses have a social responsibility to the community. Social responsibility issues often center on differences in how this obligation is interpreted. In an effort to offset hostile feelings between business and community governments and to protect workers, Congress has enacted legislation that requires companies to give sixty day's notice for all plant closings.

## Competitive Issues

The issues surrounding the impact of competition on business's social responsibility arise from the rivalry among businesses for customers and profits. When businesses compete unfairly, legal and social responsibility issues can result. Intense competition sometimes makes managers feel that their company's very survival is threatened. In these situations, managers may begin to see unacceptable alternatives as acceptable, and they may begin engaging in questionable practices to ensure the survival of their organizations. For example, Aventis SA and Andrx Corp agreed to pay $80 million to settle charges that Aventis had paid Andrx nearly $100 million not to market a cheaper, generic version of Cardizem CD, a blood-pressure medication. Although both companies denied conspiring to manipulate the supply of the drug, they were also sued by pharmaceutical wholesalers over the same practice. Aventis claimed the agreement was necessary to protect its patent.[12] Because medications are necessary to so many people, ethical and social issues arise when a lower-price drug that should be available is not.

Size frequently gives some companies an advantage over others. For example, large firms can often generate economies of scale (e.g., by forcing their suppliers to lower their prices) that allow them to put smaller firms out of business. Consequently, small companies and even whole communities may resist the efforts of firms like Wal-Mart, Home Depot, and Best Buy to open stores in their vicinity. These firms' sheer size enables them to operate at such low costs that small, local firms often cannot compete. In Austin, Texas, for example, many consumers threatened to boycott a new development that would have featured a Borders Books and Music superstore because it would have competed with popular locally owned book and music stores across the street from the new development.[13] Borders eventually withdrew from the project, citing "economic reasons."

Some companies' competitive strategies may focus on weakening or destroying a competitor, which can harm competition and ultimately reduce consumer choice. For example, Clear Channel Communications, which owns more than 10 percent of the nation's radio stations, was summoned before a U.S. Senate hearing to answer charges that it was using unfair competitive tactics. Small radio station owners and musicians charged that Clear Channel forces musicians to offer "payola" to promoters to get their songs played on the company's stations. They also charged that Clear Channel's ownership of so many stations in certain large markets represents a monopoly that limits consumer access to new music. Other critics accused the conglomerate of "blackballing" artists and promoters who refuse to use Clear Channel stations to promote their songs and concerts. Musician Don Henley argued that the firm's domination of the airwaves in some large cities has transformed the radio dial from a place where consumers had great choice in music to one where "everyone gets the same McDonald's hamburger." The Senate was considering whether to allow the modification of current regulations on the number of stations that one company can own in certain markets and strengthen punishment for anticompetitive tactics in radio and television. Despite the issues raised during the hearing, the Federal Communications Commission further relaxed regulations to permit companies to operate even more media outlets within a single market.[14]

Other examples of anticompetitive strategies include sustained price cuts, discriminatory pricing, and price wars. The primary objective of U.S. antitrust laws is to distinguish competitive strategies that enhance consumer welfare from those that reduce it. The difficulty of this task lies in determining whether the intent of a company's pricing policy is to weaken or even destroy a competitor.[15] For example, concerns about anticompetitive behavior emerged in the software industry when the Department of Justice investigated Microsoft. Ken Wasch, president of the Software Publishers Association, stated: "Justice clearly recognizes that the restoration of a level playing field in the computer software and technology industries is critical for ensuring consumer choice and ongoing innovation."[16] Microsoft's competitors complained that the company's practice of bundling its Internet Explorer Web browser into its Windows operating system stifled consumers' choice as to which Internet browser they would utilize. They also claimed that Microsoft's virtual monopoly on the market for operating system software reduced consumer choice and stifled innovation in the software industry.[17] After a year-long process, Microsoft settled the charges with the Justice Department and nine states. The company later settled a suit brought by the state of California, agreeing to repay consumers $1 billion in the form of vouchers.[18]

Intense competition may also lead companies to resort to corporate espionage. *Fortune* 1000 companies lose an estimated $100 billion annually from the theft of corporate trade secrets, although determining an accurate amount is difficult because most companies do not report such losses for fear that the publicity will harm their stock price or encourage further break-ins. Espionage may be carried out by outsiders or by employees—executives, programmers, network or computer auditors, engineers, or janitors who have legitimate reasons to access facilities, data, computers or networks. They may utilize a variety of techniques for obtaining valuable information. "Hacking," or breaking into computer networks, is considered one of the top three methods for obtaining trade secrets. Hacking sometimes involves "social engineering," in which a person is manipulated into revealing valuable information or even his or her password in order to gain access to the firm's computer network.[19] A relatively new method of espionage is "whacking," or eavesdropping on wireless networks. Once tapped into a wireless network, an intruder can access anything on both wired and wireless networks because the data sent over networks is usually unencrypted.[20] Corporate spies can also eavesdrop on phone transmissions via a digital recording device that monitors fax line transmissions. Some spies go "Dumpster diving," which is perfectly legal: Once trash is discarded onto a public street or alley, it is considered fair game.[21]

## Legal and Regulatory Issues

Laws and regulations are established by governments to set minimum standards for responsible behavior—society's codification of what is right and wrong. Laws regulating business conduct are passed because certain stakeholders believe that business cannot be trusted to do what is right in certain areas, such as consumer safety and environmental protection. Because public policy is dynamic and often changes in response to business abuses and consumer demands for safety and equality, many laws have been passed to resolve specific problems and issues. But the opinions of society, as expressed in legislation, can change over time, and different courts or state legislatures may take diverging views. For example, the thrust of most business legislation can be summed up as follows: any practice is permitted that does not substantially lessen or reduce competition or harm consumers or society. Courts differ, however, in their interpretations of what constitutes a "substantial" reduction of competition. Laws can help businesspeople determine what society believes at a certain point in time, but what is legally wrong today may be perceived as acceptable tomorrow, and vice versa. Still, personal views on legal issues may vary tremendously.

Laws are categorized as either civil or criminal. **Civil law** defines the rights and duties of individuals and organizations (including businesses). **Criminal law** not only prohibits specific actions—such as fraud, theft, or securities trading violations—but also imposes fines or imprisonment as punishment for breaking the law. The primary difference between criminal and civil law is that criminal laws are enforced by the state or nation, whereas civil laws are enforced by individuals (generally, in court). Criminal and civil laws are derived from four sources: the Constitution (constitutional law), precedents established by judges (common law), federal and state laws or statutes (statutory law), and federal and state administrative agencies (administrative law). Federal administrative agencies established by Congress control and influence business by enforcing laws and regulations to encourage competition and to protect consumers, workers, and the environment.

The primary method of resolving conflicts and serious business ethics disputes is through lawsuits, in which one individual or organization uses civil laws to take another individual or organization to court. For example, Shirley Slesinger Lasswell, whose late husband acquired the rights to Winnie the Pooh and his friends from creator A. A. Milne in 1930, filed a lawsuit against the Walt Disney Company over merchandising rights to the beloved character. Although Lasswell granted rights to use the character to Walt Disney, she contends that the company cheated her and her family out of millions of dollars in royalties on video sales for two decades. Disney contends that video sales were not specified in its agreement with Lasswell and has declined to pay her a percentage of those sales.[22]

The role of laws is not so much to distinguish what is ethical or unethical as to determine the appropriateness of specific activities or situations. In other words, laws establish the basic ground rules for responsible business activities. Most of the laws and regulations that govern business activities fall into one of five groups: (1) regulation of competition, (2) protection of consumers, (3) promotion of equity and safety, (4) protection of the natural environment, and (5) incentives to encourage organizational compliance programs to deter misconduct.

## Laws Regulating Competition

Laws have been passed to prevent the establishment of monopolies, inequitable pricing practices, and other practices that reduce or restrict competition among businesses. These laws are sometimes called **procompetitive legislation** because they were enacted to encourage competition and prevent activities that restrain trade (see Table 3–2). The Sherman Antitrust Act of 1890, for example, prohibits organizations from holding monopolies in their industry, and the Robinson-Patman Act of 1936 bans price discrimination between retailers and wholesalers.

| TABLE 3–2 | Laws Regulating Competition |
|---|---|
| Sherman Antitrust Act, 1890 | Prohibits monopolies |
| Clayton Act, 1914 | Prohibits price discrimination, exclusive dealing, and other efforts to restrict competition |
| Federal Trade Commission Act, 1914 | Created the Federal Trade Commission (FTC) to help enforce antitrust laws |
| Robinson-Patman Act, 1936 | Bans price discrimination between retailers and wholesalers |
| Wheeler-Lea Act, 1938 | Prohibits unfair and deceptive acts regardless of whether competition is injured |
| McCarran-Ferguson Act, 1944 | Exempts the insurance industry from antitrust laws |
| Lanham Act, 1946 | Protects and regulates brand names, brand marks, trade names, and trademarks |
| Celler-Kefauver Act, 1950 | Prohibits one corporation from controlling another where the effect is to lessen competition |
| Consumer Goods Pricing Act, 1975 | Prohibits price maintenance agreements among manufacturers and resellers in interstate commerce |
| FTC Improvement Act, 1975 | Gives the FTC more power to prohibit unfair industry practices |
| Antitrust Improvements Act, 1976 | Strengthens earlier antitrust laws—Justice Department has more investigative authority |
| Trademark Counterfeiting Act, 1980 | Provides penalties for individuals dealing in counterfeit goods |
| Trademark Law Revision Act, 1988 | Amends the Lanham Act to allow brands not yet introduced to be protected through patent and trademark registration |
| Federal Trademark Dilution Act, 1995 | Gives trademark owners the right to protect trademarks and requires them to relinquish those that match or parallel existing trademarks |
| Digital Millenium Copyright Act, 1998 | Refines copyright laws to protect digital versions of copyrighted materials, including music and movies |

In law, however, there are always exceptions. Under the McCarran–Ferguson Act of 1944, for example, Congress exempted the insurance industry from the Sherman Antitrust Act and other antitrust laws. Insurance companies were allowed to join together and set insurance premiums at specific industrywide levels. However, this legal "permission" could still be viewed as irresponsible and unethical if it neutralizes competition and if prices no longer reflect the true costs of insurance protection. This illustrates the point that what is legal is not always considered ethical by some interest groups.

| TABLE 3–3 | Laws Protecting Consumers | |
|---|---|
| Pure Food and Drug Act, 1906 | Prohibits adulteration and mislabeling of foods and drugs sold in interstate commerce |
| Wool Products Labeling Act, 1939 | Prohibits mislabeling of wool products |
| Fur Products Labeling Act, 1951 | Requires proper identification of the fur content of all products |
| Federal Hazardous Substances Labeling Act, 1960 | Controls the labeling of hazardous substances for household use |
| Truth in Lending Act, 1968 | Requires full disclosure of credit terms to purchasers |
| Consumer Product Safety Act, 1972 | Created the Consumer Product Safety Commission to establish safety standards and regulations for consumer products |
| Fair Credit Billing Act, 1974 | Requires accurate, up-to-date consumer credit records |
| Magnuson-Moss Warranty Act, 1975 | Established standards for consumer product warranties |
| Energy Policy and Conservation Act, 1975 | Requires auto dealers to have "gas mileage guides" in their showrooms |
| Consumer Goods Pricing Act, 1975 | Prohibits price maintenance agreements |
| Consumer Leasing Act, 1976 | Requires accurate disclosure of leasing terms to consumers |
| Fair Debt Collection Practices Act, 1978 | Defines permissible debt collection practices |
| Toy Safety Act, 1984 | Gives the government the power to recall dangerous toys quickly |
| Nutritional Labeling and Education Act, 1990 | Prohibits exaggerated health claims and requires all processed foods to have labels showing nutritional information |
| Telephone Consumer Protection Act, 1991 | Establishes procedures for avoiding unwanted telephone solicitations |
| Children's Online Privacy Protection Act, 1998 | Requires the FTC to formulate rules for collecting online information from children under age thirteen |

## Laws Protecting Consumers

Laws that protect consumers require businesses to provide accurate information about products and services and to follow safety standards (see Table 3–3). The first **consumer protection law** was passed in 1906, partly in response to a novel by Upton Sinclair. *The Jungle* describes, among other things, the atrocities and unsanitary conditions of the meat-packing industry in turn-of-the-century Chicago. The outraged public response to this book and other exposés of the industry resulted in the passage of the Pure Food and Drug Act. Likewise, Ralph Nader had a tremendous impact on consumer protection laws with his book *Unsafe at Any Speed*. His critique and attack of General Motors' Corvair had far-reaching effects on autos and other consumer products. Other consumer protection laws emerged from similar processes.

In recent years, large groups of people with specific vulnerabilities have been granted special levels of legal protection relative to the general population. For example, the legal status of children and the elderly, defined according to age-related criteria, has received greater attention. American society has responded to research and documentation showing that young consumers and senior citizens encounter difficulties in the acquisition, consumption, and disposition of products. Special legal protection provided to vulnerable consumers is considered to be in the public interest.[23] For example, the Children's Online Privacy Protection Act (COPPA) requires commercial Internet sites to carry privacy policy statements, obtain parental consent before soliciting information from children under the age of thirteen, and provide an opportunity to remove any information provided by children using such sites. As a result, Zeeks.com, a children's Web site, discontinued its chat area, free e-mail system, and other features because the cost of obtaining parents' permission was prohibitive.[24] Critics of COPPA argue that children age thirteen and older should not be treated as adults on the Web. In a study of children ages ten to seventeen, nearly half indicated that they would give their name, address, and other demographic information in exchange for a gift worth $100 or more. In addition, about half of the teens surveyed would provide information on family cars and their parents' favorite stores in exchange for a free gift. More than 20 percent would reveal their parents' number of sick days, alcohol consumption, weekend hobbies, church attendance—and whether they speed when driving.[25]

The role of the Federal Trade Commission's Bureau of Consumer Protection is to protect consumers against unfair, deceptive, or fraudulent practices. The bureau, which enforces a variety of consumer protection laws, is divided into five divisions. The Division of Enforcement monitors compliance with and investigates violations of laws, including unfulfilled holiday delivery promises by online shopping sites, employment opportunities fraud, scholarship scams, misleading advertising for health care products, and more.

### Laws Promoting Equity and Safety

Laws promoting equity in the workplace were passed during the 1960s and 1970s to protect the rights of minorities, women, older persons, and persons with disabilities; other legislation has sought to protect the safety of all workers (see Table 3–4). Of these laws, probably the most important to business is Title VII of the Civil Rights Act, originally passed in 1964 and amended several times since. Title VII specifically prohibits discrimination in employment on the basis of race, sex, religion, color, or national origin. The Civil Rights Act also created the Equal Employment Opportunity Commission (EEOC) to help enforce the provisions of Title VII. Among other things, the EEOC helps businesses design affirmative action programs. These programs aim to increase job opportunities for women and minorities by analyzing the present pool of employees, identifying areas where women and minorities are underrepresented, and establishing specific hiring and promotion goals, along with target dates for meeting those goals.

Other legislation addresses more specific employment practices. The Equal Pay Act of 1963 mandates that women and men who do equal work must receive equal pay. Wage differences are allowed only if they can be attributed to seniority, performance, or qualifications. The Americans with Disabilities Act of 1990 prohibits discrimination against people with disabilities. Despite these laws, inequities in the workplace

| TABLE 3–4 | **Laws Promoting Equity and Safety** | |
|---|---|---|
| Equal Pay Act of 1963 | Prohibits discrimination in pay on the basis of sex |
| Equal Pay Act of 1963 (amended) | Prohibits sex-based discrimination in the rate of pay to men and women working in the same or similar jobs |
| Title VII of the Civil Rights Act of 1964 (amended in 1972) | Prohibits discrimination in employment on the basis of race, color, sex, religion, or national origin |
| Age Discrimination in Employment Act, 1967 | Prohibits discrimination in employment against persons between the ages of 40 and 70 |
| Occupational Safety and Health Act, 1970 | Designed to ensure healthful and safe working conditions for all employees |
| Vocational Rehabilitation Act, 1973 | Prohibits discrimination in employment because of physical or mental handicaps |
| Vietnam Era Veterans Readjustment Act, 1974 | Prohibits discrimination against disabled veterans and Vietnam War veterans |
| Pension Reform Act, 1974 | Designed to prevent abuses in employee retirement, profit-sharing, thrift, and savings plans |
| Equal Credit Opportunity Act, 1974 | Prohibits discrimination in credit on the basis of sex or marital status |
| Pregnancy Discrimination Act, 1978 | Prohibits discrimination on the basis of pregnancy, childbirth, or related medical conditions |
| Immigration Reform and Control Act, 1986 | Prohibits employers from knowingly hiring a person who is an unauthorized alien |
| Americans with Disabilities Act, 1990 | Prohibits discrimination against people with disabilities and requires that they be given the same opportunities as people without disabilities |

still exist. According to a report from the Bureau of Labor Statistics, women earn, on average, seventy-six cents for every dollar earned by men. The disparity in wages is even higher for African-American, Hispanic, and older women.[26] Figure 3–3 shows the median weekly income of full-time males and females by age group.

Congress has also passed laws that seek to improve safety in the workplace. By far the most significant of these is the Occupational Safety and Health Act of 1970, which mandates that employers provide safe and healthy working conditions for all workers. The Occupational Safety and Health Administration (OSHA), which enforces the act, makes regular surprise inspections to ensure that businesses maintain safe working environments.

Even with the passage and enforcement of safety laws, many employees still work in unhealthy or dangerous environments. Safety experts suspect that companies underreport industrial accidents to avoid state and federal inspection and regulation. The current emphasis on increased productivity has been cited as the main reason for the growing number of such accidents. Competitive pressures are also believed to lie behind the increases in manufacturing injuries. Greater turnover in organizations due to downsizing means that employees may have more responsibilities and less experience in their current positions, thus increasing the potential for accidents. They may

**FIGURE 3–3**  **Median Weekly Income of Full-Time Male and Female Workers**

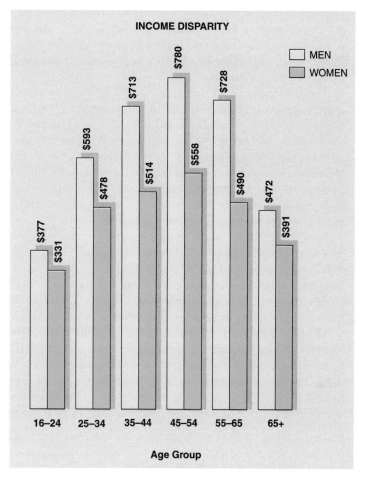

Source: "Bureau of Labor Statistics," *USA Today,* March 10, 2000, p. A1.

also be required to work longer hours, perhaps in violation of the law. Wal-Mart, for example, was found guilty of illegally requiring some employees to work unpaid overtime in Oregon stores. More than four hundred employees sued the discount retailer because they say they were reprimanded for claiming overtime hours and felt pressured to comply with managers' request to clean stores "off the clock." They also claim that the company deleted some of their hours from time-keeping records. The company faces thirty-nine similar lawsuits from employees in thirty states.[27]

## Laws Protecting the Environment

Environmental protection laws have been enacted largely in response to concerns over business's impact on the environment, which began to emerge in the 1960s. Many people have questioned the cost-benefit analyses often used in making business decisions. Such analyses try to take into account all factors in a situation, represent them with dollar figures, calculate the costs and benefits of the proposed action, and determine whether an action's benefits outweigh its costs. The problem, however, is that it is difficult to arrive at an accurate monetary valuation of environmental damage or physical pain and injury. In addition, people outside the business world often perceive such analyses as inhumane.

The Environmental Protection Agency (EPA) was created in 1970 to coordinate environmental agencies involved in enforcing the nation's environmental laws. The major area of environmental concern relates to air, water, and land pollution. Large corporations are being encouraged to establish pollution-control mechanisms and other policies favorable to the environment. Otherwise, these companies could deplete resources and damage the health and welfare of society by focusing only on their own economic interests. For example, 3M voluntarily stopped making Scotchguard, a successful product for forty years with $300 million in sales, after tests showed that it did not decompose in the environment.[28]

Increases in toxic waste in the air and water, as well as noise pollution, have prompted the passage of a number of laws (Table 3–5). Many environmental protection laws have resulted in the elimination or modification of goods and services. For instance, leaded gasoline was phased out during the 1990s by the EPA because catalytic converters, which reduce pollution caused by automobile emissions and are required by law on most vehicles, do not work properly with leaded gasolines.

The harmful effects of toxic waste on water life and on leisure industries such as resorts and fishing have raised concerns about proper disposal of these wastes. Few disposal sites meet EPA standards, so businesses must decide what to do with their waste until disposal sites become available. Some firms have solved this problem by illegal or unethical measures: dumping toxic wastes along highways, improperly burying drums containing toxic chemicals, and discarding hazardous waste at sea. For example, a

| TABLE 3–5 | Laws Protecting the Environment |
|---|---|
| Clean Air Act, 1970 | Established air-quality standards; requires approved state plans for implementation of the standards |
| National Environmental Policy Act, 1970 | Established broad policy goals for all federal agencies; created the Council on Environmental Quality as a monitoring agency |
| Coastal Zone Management Act, 1972 | Provides financial resources to the states to protect coastal zones from overpopulation |
| Federal Water Pollution Control Act, 1972 | Designed to prevent, reduce, or eliminate water pollution |
| Noise Pollution Control Act, 1972 | Designed to control the noise emission of certain manufactured items |
| Toxic Substances Control Act, 1976 | Requires testing and restricts use of certain chemical substances, to protect human health and the environment |

five-year investigation found that ships owned by Royal Caribbean Cruises Ltd. used "secret bypass pipes" to dump waste oil and hazardous materials overboard, often at night. Justice Department officials accused the company of dumping to save the expense of properly disposing waste at the same time that the cruise line was promoting itself as environmentally friendly. The company ultimately pleaded guilty to twenty-one felony counts, paid $27 million in fines, spent as much as $90,000 per vessel to install new oily water treatment systems, and placed an environmental officer on board each vessel.[29] Congress regularly evaluates legislation to increase the penalties for disposing of toxic wastes in this way. Disposal issues remain controversial because, although everyone acknowledges that the wastes must go somewhere, no community wants them dumped in its own backyard.

One solid waste problem is the result of rapid innovations in computer hardware, which render machines obsolete after just eighteen months. By 2005, 350 million computers will have reached obsolescence, and at least 55 million are expected to end up in landfills.[30] Computers contain such toxic substances as lead, mercury, and polyvinyl chloride, which can leach into the soil and contaminate groundwater when disposed of improperly. Dell Computer has come under increasing criticism from environmental groups for failing to adopt a leadership role in reducing the use of toxic materials in the manufacture of computers and in recycling used computers parts. The company has also encountered criticism for using prison labor to handle the recycling it does do. Several states are considering legislation that would require computers to be recycled at the same levels as in Europe.[31]

## Laws That Encourage Ethical Conduct

Violations of the law usually begin when businesspeople stretch the limits of ethical standards, as defined by company or industry codes of conduct, and then choose to engage in schemes that knowingly or unwittingly violate the law. In recent years, new laws and regulations have been passed to discourage such decisions—and to foster programs designed to improve business ethics and social responsibility. The most important of these are the Federal Sentencing Guidelines for Organizations and the Sarbanes-Oxley Act.

*The Federal Sentencing Guidelines for Organizations* As mentioned in Chapter 1, Congress passed the Federal Sentencing Guidelines for Organizations (FSGO) in 1991 to create an incentive for organizations to develop and implement programs designed to foster ethical and legal compliance. These guidelines, which were developed by the United States Sentencing Commission, apply to all felonies and Class A misdemeanors committed by employees in association with their work. As an incentive, organizations that have demonstrated "due diligence" in developing effective compliance programs that discourage unethical and illegal conduct may be subject to reduced organizational penalties if an employee commits a crime.[32] Overall, the government philosophy is that legal violations can be prevented through organizational values and a commitment to ethical conduct.

The commission delineated seven steps that companies must implement to demonstrate due diligence. First, a firm must develop and disseminate a code of conduct that communicates required standards and identifies key risk areas for the organization.

Second, high-ranking personnel in the organization who are known to abide by the legal and ethical standards of the industry (such as an ethics officer, vice president of human resources, general counsel, and so forth) must have oversight over the program. Third, no one with a known propensity to engage in misconduct should be put in a position of authority. Fourth, a communications system for disseminating standards and procedures (ethics training) must also be put into place. Fifth, organizational communications should include a way for employees to report misconduct without fearing retaliation, such as an anonymous toll-free hot line or an ombudsman. Monitoring and auditing systems designed to detect misconduct are also required. Sixth, if misconduct is detected, then the firm must take appropriate and fair disciplinary action. Individuals both directly and indirectly responsible for the offense should be disciplined. In addition, the sanctions should be appropriate for the offense. Finally—seventh—after misconduct has been discovered, the organization must take steps to prevent similar offenses in the future. This usually involves making modifications to the ethical compliance program, additional employee training, and issuing communications about specific types of conduct. The government expects these seven steps for compliance programs to undergo continuous improvement and refinement.[33]

These steps are based on the commission's determination to emphasize compliance programs and to provide guidance for both organizations and courts regarding program effectiveness. Organizations have flexibility as to the type of program they develop; the seven steps are not a checklist requiring that legal procedures be followed to gain certification of an effective program. The program must be capable of reducing the opportunity that employees have to engage in misconduct.

*The Sarbanes-Oxley Act* In 2002, largely in response to widespread corporate accounting scandals, Congress passed the Sarbanes-Oxley Act to establish a system of federal oversight of corporate accounting practices. In addition to making fraudulent financial reporting a criminal offense and strengthening penalties for corporate fraud, the law requires corporations to establish codes of ethics for financial reporting and to develop greater transparency in financial reporting to investors and other stakeholders.[34]

Supported by both Republicans and Democrats, the Sarbanes-Oxley Act was enacted to restore stakeholder confidence after accounting fraud at Enron, WorldCom, and hundreds of other companies resulted in investors and employees losing much of their savings. During the resulting investigations, the public learned that hundreds of corporations had not reported their financial results accurately. Many stakeholders came to believe that accounting firms, lawyers, top executives, and boards of directors had developed a culture of deception to ensure investor approval and gain competitive advantage. Many boards failed to provide appropriate oversight of the decisions of their companies' top officers. At Adelphia Communications, for example, the Rigas family amassed $3.1 billion in off-balance-sheet loans backed by the company. Dennis Kozlowski, CEO of Tyco, was accused of improperly using corporate funds for personal use as well as fraudulent accounting practices.[35] At Kmart, CEO Charles Conaway allegedly hired unqualified executives and consultants for excessive fees. Kmart's board also approved $24 million in loans to various executives, just a month before the retailer filed for Chapter 11 bankruptcy protection. Conaway and the other executives have since left the company or were fired. Loans of this type are now illegal under Sarbanes-Oxley.[36]

As a result of public outrage over the accounting scandals, the Sarbanes-Oxley Act garnered nearly unanimous support not only in Congress, but also by government regulatory agencies, the president, and the general public. When President George W. Bush signed the Sarbanes-Oxley Act into law, he emphasized the need for new standards of ethical behavior in business, particularly among the top managers and boards of directors responsible for overseeing business decisions and activities.

At the heart of the Sarbanes-Oxley Act is the newly created Public Company Accounting Oversight Board, which monitors accounting firms that audit public corporations and establishes standards and rules for auditors in accounting firms. The law gave the board investigatory and disciplinary power over auditors as well as securities analysts who issue reports about corporate performance and health. The law attempts to eliminate conflicts of interest by prohibiting accounting firms from providing both auditing and consulting services to the same client companies without special permission from the client firm's audit committee; it also places limits on the length of time lead auditors can serve a particular client. Table 3–6 summarizes the significant provisions of the new law.

The Sarbanes-Oxley Act requires corporations to take greater responsibility for their decisions and to provide leadership based on ethical principles. For instance, the

| TABLE 3–6 | Major Provisions of the Sarbanes-Oxley Act |
|---|---|
| | 1. Requires the establishment of a Public Company Accounting Oversight Board in charge of regulations administered by the Securities and Exchange Commission. |
| | 2. Requires CEOs and CFOs to certify that their companies' financial statements are true and without misleading statements. |
| | 3. Requires that corporate board of directors' audit committees consist of independent members who have no material interests in the company. |
| | 4. Prohibits corporations from making or offering loans to officers and board members. |
| | 5. Requires codes of ethics for senior financial officers; code must be registered with the SEC. |
| | 6. Prohibits accounting firms from providing both auditing and consulting services to the same client without the approval of the client firm's audit committee. |
| | 7. Requires company attorneys to report wrongdoing to top managers and, if necessary, to the board of directors; if managers and directors fail to respond to reports of wrongdoing, the attorney should stop representing the company. |
| | 8. Mandates "whistle-blower protection" for persons who disclose wrongdoing to authorities. |
| | 9. Requires financial securities analysts to certify that their recommendations are based on objective reports. |
| | 10. Requires mutual fund managers to disclose how they vote shareholder proxies, giving investors information about how their shares influence decisions. |
| | 11. Establishes a ten-year penalty for mail/wire fraud. |
| | 12. Prohibits the two senior auditors from working on a corporation's account for more than five years; other auditors are prohibited from working on an account for more than seven years. In other words, accounting firms must rotate individual auditors from one account to another from time to time. |

law requires top managers to certify that their firms' financial reports are complete and accurate, making CEOs and CFOs personally accountable for the credibility and accuracy of their companies' financial statements. Similar provisions are required of corporate boards of directors, especially audit committees, and senior financial officers are now subject to a code of ethics that addresses their specific areas of risk. Additionally, the law modifies the attorney-client relationship to require lawyers to report wrongdoing to top managers and/or the board of directors. It also provides protection for "whistle-blowing" employees who might report illegal activity to authorities. These provisions provide internal controls to make managers aware of and responsible for legal and ethical problems. Table 3–7 summarizes the benefits of the legislation.

On the other hand, the Sarbanes-Oxley Act has raised a number of concerns. The complex law may impose burdensome requirements on executives; the first installment of rules and regulations already runs to more than three thousand pages. Some people also believe that a new law will not be sufficient to stop those executives who want to lie, steal, manipulate, or deceive. They believe that a deep commitment to managerial integrity, rather than additional rules and regulations, are the key to solving the current crisis in business.[37] Additionally, the new act has caused many firms to restate their financial reports to avoid penalties. Of the 17,000 public companies in the United States, 330 restated their earnings in 2002, up 22 percent from the previous year.[38]

## Philanthropic Issues

Philanthropic issues are another dimension of social responsibility and relate to business's contributions to the local community and society. Philanthropy provides four major benefits to society. First, it improves the quality of life and helps make communities places where people want to do business, raise families, and enjoy life. Thus, improving the quality of life in a community makes it easier to attract and retain employees and customers. Second, philanthropy reduces government involvement by providing help to people with legitimate needs. Third, philanthropy develops staff leadership skills. Many firms, for example, use campaigns by the United Way and other community service organizations as leadership- and skill-building exercises for their employees. Finally, philanthropy builds staff morale. Employees who volunteer typically feel better about themselves, their company, and their community, and higher morale improves a firm's bottom line.[39]

| TABLE 3–7 | Benefits of the Sarbanes-Oxley Act |
|---|---|
| 1. | Greater accountability of top managers and boards of directors to employees, investors, communities, and society. |
| 2. | Renewed investor confidence. |
| 3. | Clear explanations by CEOs as to why their compensation package is in the best interest of the company; the loss of some traditional senior management perks, such as company loans; greater disclosures by executives about their own stock trades. |
| 4. | Greater protection of employee retirement plans. |
| 5. | Improved information from stock analysts and rating agencies. |
| 6. | Greater penalties for and accountability of senior managers, auditors, and board members. |

## *Quality-of-Life Issues*

People want much more than just the bare necessities—shelter, clothing, and food—to sustain life. Food must not only provide the nutrients necessary for life and good health but also be conveniently available. Consumers want their food free from toxic chemicals, and they want food producers to avoid polluting the natural environment or harming endangered wildlife. For example, some environmentally minded consumers stopped buying shrimp to protest Gulf Coast shrimpers' refusal to use devices that would allow endangered sea turtles to escape drowning in their nets. Society also expects adequate supplies of low-cost healthy grains and livestock. Thus, it expects farmers to produce pest-free and disease-free products without using chemicals that are harmful to consumers or to the laborers who get agricultural products to market.

The public also wants sophisticated medical services that prolong life and make it more enjoyable. Diseases such as meningitis, malaria, elephantiasis, hepatitis B, AIDS, influenza, and polio cause death, yet the poor in less-developed countries typically cannot afford medicines to treat these diseases. As a result, vaccine manufacturers, including Merck & Company, American Home Products, SmithKline Beecham, and Aventis Pharma AG, have pledged millions in free drugs that will help the Global Alliance for Vaccines and Immunization, a Geneva nonprofit organization that has been supported by a $750 million donation from the Bill and Melinda Gates Foundation.[40] Additionally, Merck discovered that one of its products was effective against the parasite that causes river blindness in the tropical river valleys of Africa, Central and Latin America, and the Middle East. Since Merck initiated a program to donate Mectizan, it has distributed more than 700 million tablets, and the program now reaches 30 million people at risk for river blindness in thirty countries annually.[41]

Additionally, people want communication systems that permit them to talk to anyone anywhere in the world and thus disseminate information rapidly. However, most people do not want the widespread availability of information to infringe on their privacy. Cisco Systems, Inc., a global leader in computer networking, has responded to communication issues by donating technological assistance to many nonprofit organizations, empowering them to use the Internet to deliver community services that focus on education and meet basic human needs. Cisco technology grants have facilitated the delivery of services to homeless shelters, job-training programs, mentorship and role-model programs for youth development, food banks, and national services programs.[42]

Consumers also want rapid, convenient, and efficient transportation to take them wherever and whenever they want to go. They also want clean air, but automobiles are the number-one source of air pollution. As a result, the automobile industry is facing increasing pressure to develop inexpensive, fuel-efficient automobiles that do not contribute to air pollution problems. Toyota, for example, introduced the Prius, a hybrid vehicle that uses electric motors to augment its internal combustion engines, improving its fuel efficiency without a reduction in power. Ford, General Motors, and Dodge planned to introduce competing hybrid vehicles in 2004.[43] Auto makers are also exploring other alternatives, such as fuel cells, to power vehicles in ways that do less harm to the natural environment than internal combustion engines.

People want a high quality of life. They do not want to spend all their waking hours working. They seek leisure time for recreation, entertainment, and relaxation in a pleasant environment. Quality of life is enhanced by leisure time, clean air and water, unlittered earth, conservation of wildlife and natural resources, and security from radiation and poisonous substances. Thus, society expects businesses to modify their manufacturing processes to reduce pollutants and wastes. Herman Miller, guided by its Blueprint for Corporate Community, has received numerous accolades for its efforts to do just that. For example, the firm's office chairs now contain as much as 77 percent recycled material, and the firm has ceased using woods not harvested from sustained-yield forests. The company has also revised manufacturing processes to minimize waste and the use of water and electricity.[44]

## Philanthropic Contributions

The most common way that businesses demonstrate philanthropy is through donations to local and national charitable organizations. Corporations gave more than $12 billion to environmental and social causes in 2002.[45] IBM, for example, contributed $126 million in cash and resources, primarily to educational causes.[46] Indeed, many companies have become concerned about the quality of education in the United States, after realizing that the current pool of prospective employees lacks many basic work skills. Recognizing that today's students are tomorrow's employees and customers, firms such as Kroger, Campbell Soup Co., Eastman Kodak, American Express, Apple Computer, Xerox, and Coca-Cola have donated money, equipment, and employee time to help improve schools in their communities and throughout the nation. Hewlett-Packard's Diversity in Education Initiative focuses on math and science in four minority communities and works with students from elementary school to the university level. The program provides hands-on science kits to elementary and middle schools and gives forty high school students (ten from each community) annual $3,000 college scholarships. A mentor is assigned to each of the students, who are given a paid summer internship at Hewlett-Packard and taught how to conduct a job search.[47]

Organizations are also interested in supporting the arts. Many aspects of the arts—museums, civic centers, and symphony orchestras—would not exist without individual and corporate help. AT&T, for example, supports theater arts through its AT&T: OnStage program. In sixteen years, the program has sponsored eighty-four works at fifty-six U.S., Canadian, and British theaters. The company extended the program with AT&T: FirstStage to bring art to children through grants to playwrights.[48] Some companies seeking to do good through philanthropy link gifts to marketing activities.

## Strategic Philanthropy

Tying philanthropic giving to overall strategy and objectives is also known as **strategic philanthropy.** Strategic philanthropy is the synergistic and mutually beneficial use of an organization's core competencies and resources to deal with key stakeholders so as to bring about organizational and societal benefits. For example, last year Hewlett-Packard (HP) donated $54 million in cash and equipment to nonprofit agencies and educational institutions worldwide. HP focuses its philanthropic efforts on programs that promote educational opportunities for people in underserved communities around the world.[49] Founder's Week, McDonald's annual celebration of company founder Ray Kroc's birthday, focuses on giving back to local communities. Last year, McDonald's employees nationwide participated in twenty-five thousand hours of community service, including tutoring children, painting classrooms, planting trees and shrubs, constructing homes with Habitat for Humanity, and assisting families and children at Ronald McDonald Houses across the country.[50] Both Hewlett-Packard and McDonald's realize the benefits of supporting causes that are of interest to their target market.

## Ethics as a Force in Social Responsibility

From the perspective of social responsibility, business ethics embodies standards, norms, and expectations that reflect a concern of major stakeholders, including consumers, employees, shareholders, suppliers, competitors, and the community. In other words, these stakeholders have concerns about what is fair, just, or in keeping with respect for or protection of stakeholders' rights.

Many businesspeople and scholars have questioned the role of ethics and social responsibility in business. Legal and economic responsibilities are generally accepted as the most important determinants of performance: "If this is well done," say classical theorists, "profits are maximized more or less continuously and firms carry out their major responsibilities to society."[51] Some economists believe that if companies address economic and legal issues, they are satisfying the demands of society and that trying to anticipate and meet additional needs would be almost impossible. Milton Friedman has been quoted as saying that "the basic mission of business [is] thus to produce goods and services at a profit, and in doing this, business [is] making its maximum contribution to society and, in fact, being socially responsible."[52] On the other hand, there is much evidence that social responsibility, including business ethics, is associated with increased profits. For example, one survey indicates that three out of four consumers refuse to buy from certain businesses, and a business's conduct was considered an important reason to avoid a business.[53] An important academic study found that there is a direct relationship between social responsibility and profitability. The study also found that social responsibility contributes to employee commitment and customer loyalty—vital concerns of any firm trying to increase profits.[54]

It should be obvious from this discussion that ethics and social responsibility cannot be just a reactive approach to issues as they arise. Only if firms make ethical concerns a part of their foundation and incorporate ethics in their business strategy can social responsibility as a concept be embedded in daily decision making. A description of corporate ethical responsibility should include rights and duties, consequences and values, all of which refer to specific strategic decisions.[55] The ethical component of business strategy should be capable of providing an assessment of top-management, work-group, and individual behavior as it relates to ethical decisions.

## Summary

Although the concepts of business ethics and social responsibility are often used interchangeably, the two terms have distinct meanings. Social responsibility in business refers to an organization's obligation to maximize its positive impact and minimize its negative impact on society. There are four levels of social responsibility—economic, legal, ethical, and philanthropic—and they can be viewed as a pyramid. The term

*corporate citizenship* is often used to communicate the extent to which businesses strategically meet the economic, legal, ethical, and philanthropic responsibilities placed on them by their various stakeholders.

The economy is affected by the way companies relate to shareholders and other investors, employees, customers, competitors, the community, and even the natural environment. When people talk about the "economy," they generally mean cyclical conditions such as inflation, recession, and employment rates or economic concepts such as supply and demand. The economic aspects of social responsibility relate to how businesses use resources and respond to changes in business cycles. An organization's sense of economic responsibility is especially significant for employees because it raises such issues as equal job opportunities, workplace diversity, job safety, health, and employee privacy.

The ethical aspects of business competition arise from the rivalry among businesses for customers and profits. When businesses do not compete fairly or do not use legal and socially accepted methods of gaining advantage, stakeholders, especially other competitors, may be harmed. In particular, size may grant some firms an advantage over others that they may exploit to the detriment not only of competing firms, but also consumers and communities.

Laws and regulations are established by governments to set minimum standards for responsible behavior—society's codification of what is right and wrong. Civil and criminal laws regulating business conduct are passed because society—including consumers, interest groups, competitors, and legislators—believes that business must comply with society's standards. Such laws regulate competition, protect consumers, promote safety and equity and in the workplace, protect the environment, and provide incentives for preventing misconduct.

Philanthropic issues touch on businesses' social responsibility insofar as businesses contribute to the local community and to society. Philanthropy provides four major benefits to society: improving the quality of life, reducing government involvement, developing staff leadership skills, and building staff morale. Companies contribute significant amounts of money to education, the arts, environmental causes, and the disadvantaged by supporting local and national charitable organizations. Strategic philanthropy involves linking core business competencies to societal and community needs.

From a social responsibility perspective, business ethics embodies standards, norms, and expectations that reflect a concern of major stakeholders, including consumers, employees, shareholders, suppliers, competitors, and the community. Only if firms include ethical concerns in their foundational values and incorporate ethics in their business strategy can social responsibility as a value be embedded in daily decision making.

| Important Terms for Review | | |
| --- | --- | --- |
| | corporate citizenship | civil law |
| | inflation | criminal law |
| | recession | procompetitive legislation |
| | supply | consumer protection laws |
| | demand | strategic philanthropy |

## A Real-Life Situation*

Albert Chen was sweating profusely in his Jaguar on the expressway as he thought about his options and the fact that Christmas and the Chinese New Year were at hand. He and his wife, Mary, who were on their way to meet Albert's parents at New York's John F. Kennedy Airport, seemed to be looking up from an abyss, with no daylight to be seen. Several visits and phone calls from various people had engulfed both him and Mary.

He had graduated with honors in finance and had married Mary in his senior year. They had both obtained prestigious brokerage jobs in the New York area, and both had been working killer hours to develop their accounts. Listening to other brokers, both had learned that there were some added expenses to their professions. For example, they were told that brokers need to "look" and "act" successful. So Albert and Mary bought the appropriate clothes and cars, joined the right clubs, and ate at the right restaurants with the right people. They also took the advice of others, which was to identify the "players" of large corporations at parties and take mental notes. "You'd be surprised at what information you hear with a little alcohol in these people," said one broker. Both started using this strategy, and five months later their clients began to see significant profits in their portfolios.

Their good luck even came from strange places. For example, Albert had an uncle whose work as a janitor gave him access to many law offices that had information on a number of companies, especially those about to file for bankruptcy. Mary and Albert were able to use information provided by this uncle to benefit their clients' portfolios. The uncle even had some of his friends use Albert. To Albert's surprise, his uncle's friends often had nest eggs in excess of $200,000. Because some of these friends were quite elderly, Albert was given permission to buy and sell nonrisky stocks at will.

As both of them were earning good salaries, the Chens soon managed to invest in the market themselves, and their investments included stock in the company for which Mary's father worked. After eighteen months, Albert decided to jump ship and start working for Jarvis, Sunni, Lamar & Morten (JSL&M). JSL&M's reputation was that of a fast mover in the business. "We go up to the line and then measure how wide the line is so that we know how far we can go into it," was a common remark at the brokerage firm.

About six months ago, Mary's father, who was with a major health care company, commented that the management team was running the company into the ground. "If only someone could buy the company and put in a good management team," he mused. After the conversation, Mary investigated the company and discovered that the stock was grossly undervalued. She made a few phone calls and found a company that was interested in doing a hostile takeover. Mary also learned from her father that if a new management were acceptable to the union, the union would do everything in its power to oust the old management—by striking, if necessary—and welcome the new one. As things started to materialize, Mary told several of her best clients, who in turn did very well on the stock. This increased her status in the firm, which kept drawing bigger clients.

Albert soon became a player in initial public stock offerings (IPOs) of new companies. Occasionally, when Albert saw a very hot IPO, he would talk to some of his best venture-capital friends, who then bought the IPOs and gained some very good returns. This strategy helped attract some larger players in the market. By this point in his young career, Albert had made a great many friends.

One of those friends was Barry, who worked on the stock floor. As they were talking, Barry mentioned that if Albert wanted to, he, as a favor, when placing orders to buy shares, would occasionally put Albert's or Mary's trade before the client order.

The first sign of trouble came when Mary told Albert about what was happening at her office. "I'm getting e-mail from some of the brokers with off-color jokes and even some nude photos of women and men. I just don't care for it."

"So what are you doing about it?" Albert asked.

"Well, I've just started not even opening my messages if they come from these people," Mary replied.

"What about messages that request that you send them on? What do you do with those?" queried Albert.

"I just e-mail them along without looking at them," was her response.

"This isn't good, Mary. A couple of analysts were just fired for doing that at a big firm last week," said Albert.

Several weeks later the people who were sending Mary the obnoxious messages were fired. Mary was also asked to see the head of her division. When she came to his office, he said, "Please shut the door, Mary. I have some bad news. I know that you weren't involved with what was happening with the e-mail scandal; however, you did forward messages that contained such material. As a result, I have no alternative but to give you your two weeks' notice. I know this is unfair, but I have my orders. Because of this mess, the SEC [Securities and Exchange Commission] wants to check all your trades for the last eight months. It seems to be a formality, but it will take time, and as you well know, the chances of going to another firm with that hanging over your head are slim. I'm sorry that it's only two months until the holidays." That night Mary fell into a depression.

To exacerbate the situation, Albert's parents were flying in from the People's Republic of China. They were not happy with Albert's marriage to a Caucasian, but they had consoled themselves that Mary had a good job. They had also said that if things should go badly for them in New York, they could always come to the parents' retirement home in Taiwan. However, the idea of leaving the United States, attempting to learn Mandarin, and raising children in an unfamiliar culture did not appeal to Mary.

Albert was also having some problems. As their income was cut in half, Albert tried to make up for the loss by trading in some high-risk markets, such as commodities and precious metals. However, many of these investments turned sour, and he found himself buying and selling more and more to pull his own portfolio, as well as those of his clients, into the black. He was getting worried because some of his uncle's friends' portfolios were losing significant value. Other matters, however, were causing him even more anxiety. The previous week Barry had called him, asking for some inside information on several companies that he was working with for an IPO. Albert knew that this could be construed as insider information and had said no. Today, Barry called again and said, "Look, Al, I've been doing you favors for a while. I need to score big because of the holidays. You probably don't know, but what I've been doing for you could be construed as spinning, which is not looked upon favorably. I'm not asking for the IPO information—I'm demanding it. Is that clear enough for you, Al? E-mail it over by tomorrow morning." Then Barry hung up. An hour later Albert's supervisor came in and said, "Al, I need a favor from you. I want you to buy some stock for me and a few friends. When it goes to $112, I want you to sell it. We'll pay the taxes and give you a little bonus for Christmas as well. I want you to buy tomorrow as soon as the market opens. Here are the account numbers for the transaction. I must run. See you tomorrow."

## Questions ▪ Exercises

1. Identify the ethical and legal issues of which Albert needs to be aware.
2. Discuss the advantages and disadvantages of each decision Albert could make and has made.
3. Identify the pressures that have brought about these issues.

* This case is strictly hypothetical; any resemblance to real persons, companies, or situations is coincidental.

# Check Your EQ

Check your E.Q., or Ethics Quotient, by completing the following. Assess your performance to evaluate your overall understanding of the chapter material.

1. Social responsibility in business refers to maximizing the visibility of social involvement.  Yes  No

2. The primary method for resolving business ethics disputes is through the criminal court system.  Yes  No

3. The Federal Sentencing Guidelines for Organizations provide an incentive for organizations to conscientiously develop and implement ethics programs.  Yes  No

4. The Sarbanes-Oxley Act encourages CEOs and CFOs to report their financial statements accurately.  Yes  No

5. Strategic philanthropy represents a new direction in corporate giving that maximizes the benefit to societal or community needs and relates to business objectives.  Yes  No

ANSWERS: 1. No. Social responsibility refers to an organization's obligation to maximize its positive impact on society and minimize its negative impact. 2. No. Lawsuits and civil litigation are the primary way in which business ethics disputes are resolved. 3. Yes. Well-designed ethics and compliance programs can minimize legal liability when organizational misconduct is detected. 4. No. The Sarbanes-Oxley Act *requires* CEOs and CFOs to accurately report their financial statements to a federal oversight committee; they must sign the document and are held personally liable for any inaccuracies. 5. Yes. Strategic philanthropy helps both society and the organization.

# The Ethical Decision-Making Process

# Understanding Ethical Decision Making and Corporate Governance

## An Ethical Dilemma*

Bill Church was in a bind. A recent graduate of a prestigious business school, he had taken a job in the auditing division of Greenspan & Co., a fast-growing leader in the accounting industry. Greenspan relocated Bill, his wife, and their one-year-old daughter from the Midwest to the East Coast. On arriving, they bought their first home and a second car. Bill was told that the company had big plans for him. Thus, he did not worry about being financially overextended.

Several months into the job, Bill found that he was working late into the night to complete his auditing assignments. He realized that the company did not want its clients billed for excessive hours and that he needed to become more efficient if he wanted to move up in the company. He asked one of his friends, Ann, how she managed to be so efficient in auditing client records.

Ann quietly explained: "Bill, there are times when being efficient isn't enough. You need to do what is required to get ahead. The partners just want results—they don't care how you get them."

"I don't understand," said Bill.

"Look," Ann explained, "I had the same problem you have a few years ago, but Mr. Reed [the manager of the auditing department] explained that everyone eats time so that the group shows top results and looks good. And when the group looks good, everyone in it looks good. No one cares if a little time gets lost in the shuffle."

Bill realized that "eating time" meant not reporting all the hours required to complete a project. He also remembered one of Reed's classic catchphrases, "results, results, results." He thanked Ann for her input and went back to work. Bill thought of going over Reed's head and asking for advice from the division manager, but he had met her only once and did not know anything about her.

### Questions ▪ Exercises

1. What should Bill do? Describe the process through which Bill might attempt to resolve his dilemma.
2. Consider the impact of this company's approach on young accountants. Why could working long hours be an ethical problem?

* This case is strictly hypothetical; any resemblance to real persons, companies, or situations is coincidental.

To improve ethical decision making in business, one must first understand how individuals make ethical decisions in an organizational environment. Too often it is assumed that individuals in organizations make ethical decisions in the same way they make ethical decisions at home, in their family or their personal lives. Within the context of an organizational work group, however, few individuals have the freedom to decide ethical issues independently of organizational pressures.

This chapter summarizes our current knowledge of ethical decision making in business and provides insights into the role corporate governance plays in structuring ethical decision making in organizations. Although it is impossible to describe exactly how any one individual or work group might make ethical decisions, we can offer generalizations about average or typical behavior patterns within organizations. These generalizations are based on many studies and at least six ethical decision models that have been widely accepted by academics and practitioners.[1] Based on these models, we present a framework for understanding ethical decision making in the context of business organizations. This framework integrates concepts from philosophy, psychology, and sociology, as well as business. Finally, we present an overview of how our framework for ethical decision making relates to corporate governance.

## A Framework for Ethical Decision Making in Business

As Figure 4–1 shows, our model of the ethical decision-making process in business includes ethical issue intensity, individual factors such as individual moral philosophy, organizational factors such as corporate culture, and opportunity. These factors are interrelated and all influence the evaluations of and intentions behind decisions that produce ethical or unethical behavior. We will take a closer look at specific individual and organizational factors in Chapters 5, 6, and 7.

### Ethical Issue Intensity

The first step in ethical decision making is to recognize that an ethical issue requires an individual or work group to choose among several actions that various stakeholders inside or outside of the firm will ultimately evaluate as right or wrong. The intensity of an ethical issue relates to its perceived importance to the decision maker.[2] **Ethical issue intensity,** then, can be defined as the relevance or importance of an ethical issue in the eyes of the individual, work group, and/or organization. It is personal and temporal in character to accommodate values, beliefs, needs, perceptions, the special characteristics of the situation, and the personal pressures prevailing at a particular place and time.[3] For example, many of the Enron employees and managers who were aware of the firm's use of off-balance sheet partnerships—which turned out to be the major cause of the energy firm's collapse—were advised that these partnerships were legal, so they did not perceive them as an ethical issue. Although such partnerships were in fact legal at that time, the way some Enron officials designed them and the methods they used to provide collateral for them (i.e., Enron stock) created a Ponzi-like scheme that brought about the collapse of the company.[4] (In a Ponzi, or

---

**FIGURE 4–1**    **Framework for Understanding Ethical Decision Making in Business**

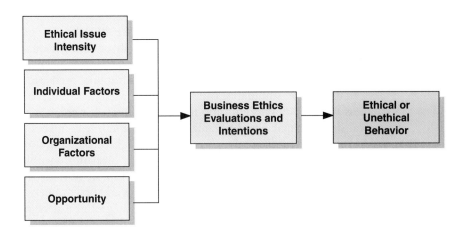

pyramid, scheme, funds from new investors are used to generate money to pay "returns" to earlier investors; without continually adding new investors, the scheme eventually collapses.[5]) Thus, ethical issue intensity involves individuals' cognitive state of concern about an issue, which indicates their involvement in making choices.

Ethical issue intensity reflects the ethical sensitivity of the individual or work group that faces the ethical decision-making process. Research suggests that individuals are subject to six "spheres of influence" when confronted with ethical choices—the workplace, family, religion, legal system, community, and profession—and that the level of importance of each of these influences will vary depending on how important the decision maker perceives the issue to be.[6] Additionally, the individual's sense of the situation's moral intensity increases the individual's perceptiveness regarding ethical problems, which in turn reduce his or her intention to act unethically.[7] All the other factors in Figure 4–1, including individual factors, organizational factors, and intentions, determine why ethical issues are perceived differently by different individuals.[8] For example, the study mentioned earlier found that, on average, women have more ethical intentions than men.[9] Unless individuals in an organization share some common concerns about ethical issues, the stage is set for ethical conflict. The perception of ethical issue intensity can be influenced by management, which can use rewards and punishments, corporate policies, and corporate values to sensitize employees. In other words, managers can affect the degree to which employees perceive the importance of an ethical issue through positive and/or negative incentives.[10]

For some employees, ethical issues may not reach the critical awareness level if managers fail to identify and educate employees about specific problem areas. Organizations that consist of employees with diverse values and backgrounds must train them in the way the firm wants specific ethical issues handled. Identifying the ethical issues that employees might encounter is a significant step toward developing their ability to make ethical decisions. Many ethical issues are identified by industry groups or through general information available to a firm.

Companies must assess areas of ethical and legal risk that are, in reality, ethical issues. Issues that are communicated as being high in ethical importance could trigger increases in employees' ethical issue intensity. The perceived importance of an ethical issue has been found to have a strong impact on both employees' ethical judgment and their behavioral intention. The more likely individuals are to perceive an ethical issue as important, the less likely they are to engage in questionable or unethical behavior.[11] Therefore, ethical issue intensity should be considered a key factor in the ethical decision process.

## Individual Factors

When people need to resolve ethical issues in their daily lives, they often base their decisions on their own values and principles of right or wrong. People generally learn these values and principles through the socialization process with family members, social groups, church, and in their formal education. The actions of specific individuals in scandal-plagued companies such as Enron, WorldCom, Halliburton, Qwest, Arthur Andersen, and Adelphia often raise questions about those individuals' personal character and integrity. They appear to operate in their own self-interest or in total disregard of the law and interests of society. At Adelphia Communications, for example, the Rigas family members who founded the firm allegedly spent corporate funds on themselves, purchasing luxuries such as a $12.8 million golf course and using $250 million to comply with margin calls on their own personal stock holdings. They then allegedly covered their actions by falsifying the firm's financial reports. Three family members and two other company executives have been arrested and charged with multiple fraud violations.[12]

In the workplace, personal ethical issues typically involve honesty, conflicts of interest, discrimination, nepotism, and theft of organizational resources. For example, as shown in Figure 4–2, many individuals make personal phone calls on company time. Most employees limit personal calls to a few minutes, and most companies probably overlook these as reasonable. Some employees, however, make personal calls in excess of thirty minutes, which companies are likely to view as an excessive use of company time for personal reasons. The decision to use company time to make a personal phone call is an example of a personal ethical decision. It illustrates the fine line between what may be acceptable or unacceptable in a business environment. It also reflects how well an individual will assume responsibilities in the work environment. Often this decision will depend on company policy and the corporate environment.

The way the public perceives individual ethics generally varies according to the profession in question. A recent survey, which asked the public to rate the honesty and ethics of twenty-one professions, found that telemarketers, car salespersons, advertising practitioners, stock brokers, and real estate brokers are perceived as having the lowest ethics. Specific factors that affect individuals—including personal moral philosophies and their stage of cognitive development—can help organizations understand, predict, and control the actions of individual employees, managers, and directors in businesses. We will take a detailed look at specific individual factors in Chapter 5.

---

**FIGURE 4–2**  **Personal Telephone Calls at Work**

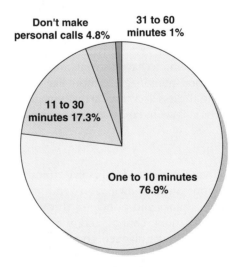

Personal Calls on the Job
Time that workers spend on personal phone calls a day

Source: At-A-Glance survey of 1,385 office workers. Margin of error + –2.7 percentage points.

## Organizational Factors

Although people can and do make individual ethical choices in business situations, no one operates in vacuum.[13] Indeed, research has established that in the workplace, the organization's values often have greater influence on decisions than do a person's own values.[14] Ethical choices in business are most often made jointly, in work groups and committees, or in conversations and discussions with coworkers. Employees approach ethical issues not only on the basis of what they learned from their own backgrounds but also on the basis of what they learn from others in the organization. The outcome of this learning process depends on the strength of each person's personal values, opportunities to behave unethically, and exposure to others who behave ethically or unethically. Although people outside the organization, such as family members and friends, also influence decision makers, an organization's culture and structure operate through the relationships of its members to influence their ethical decisions.

*Corporate Culture* A **corporate culture** can be defined as a set of values, beliefs, goals, norms, and ways of solving problems that members (employees) of an organization share. As time passes, stakeholders come to view the company or organization as a living organism, with a mind and will of its own. The Walt Disney Company, for example, requires all new employees to take a course in the traditions and history of Disneyland and Walt Disney, including its ethical dimensions. The corporate culture at American Express Company stresses that employees help customers out of difficult situations whenever possible. This attitude is reinforced through numerous company legends of employees who have gone above and beyond the call of duty to help customers. This strong tradition of customer loyalty thus might encourage an American Express employee to take unorthodox steps to help a customer who encounters a problem while traveling overseas. Employees learn that they can take some risks in helping customers. Such strong traditions and values have become a driving force in many companies, including McDonald's, IBM, Procter & Gamble, Southwest Airlines, and Hershey Foods. Saturn is a division of General Motors, but it has developed its own corporate culture, including values related to product quality, customer service, and fairness in pricing.

An important component of corporate, or organizational, culture is the company's ethical climate. Whereas corporate culture involves values and rules that prescribe a wide range of behavior for organizational members, the ethical climate reflects whether the firm also has an ethical conscience. Thus, the **ethical climate** of a corporation's culture can be thought of as the character or decision processes employees use to determine whether their responses to ethical issues are right or wrong.[15] Ethical climate is a function of many factors, including corporate policies on ethics, top management's leadership on ethical issues, the influence of coworkers, and the opportunity for unethical behavior. Within the organization as a whole, subclimates can develop within individual departments or workgroups, but they are influenced by the strength of the firm's overall ethical climate, as well as the function of the department and the stakeholders it serves.[16]

The more ethical employees perceive an organization's culture to be, the less likely they are to make unethical decisions. Corporate culture and ethical climate are closely associated with the idea that "significant others" within the organization (see the next section) help to determine ethical decisions within that organization. Research also indicates that the ethical values embodied in an organization's culture are positively related to employees' commitment to the firm and their sense that they fit into the company. These findings suggest that companies should develop and promote ethical values to enhance employees' experiences in the workplace.[17] We will take a more detailed look at the role of corporate culture in ethical decision making in Chapter 6.

*Significant Others* Those who have influence in a work group, including peers, managers, coworkers, and subordinates, are referred to as **significant others.** They help workers on a daily basis with unfamiliar tasks and provide advice and information in both formal and informal ways. Coworkers, for instance, can offer help in the comments they make in discussions over lunch or when the boss is away. Likewise, a manager may provide directives about certain types of activities that employees perform on the job. Indeed, an employee's supervisor can play a central role in helping employees develop and fit in socially in the workplace.[18] Numerous studies conducted over the years confirm that significant others within an organization have more impact on a worker's decisions on a daily basis than any other factor.[19]

Obedience to authority is another aspect of the influence significant others exercise. Obedience to authority helps to explain why many employees resolve business ethics issues by simply following the directives of a superior. In organizations that emphasize respect for superiors, for example, employees may feel that they are expected to carry out orders by a supervisor even if those orders are contrary to the employees' sense of right and wrong. Later, if the employee's decision is judged to have been wrong, he or she is likely to say, "I was only carrying out orders" or "My boss told me to do it this way."

In Chapter 7, we take a closer look at how significant others in organizations influence employees' decision-making process through role interaction and conflict.

## Opportunity

**Opportunity** describes the conditions in an organization that limit or permit ethical or unethical behavior. Opportunity results from conditions that either provide rewards, whether internal or external, or fail to erect barriers against unethical behavior. Examples of internal rewards include feelings of goodness and personal worth generated by performing altruistic acts. External rewards refer to what an individual expects to receive from others in the social environment. Rewards are external to the individual to the degree that they bring social approval, status, and esteem.

An example of a condition that fails to erect barriers against unethical behavior is a company policy that does not punish employees who accept large gifts from clients. The absence of punishment essentially provides an opportunity for unethical behavior because it allows individuals to engage in such behavior without fear of consequences. The prospect of a reward for unethical behavior can also create an opportunity for questionable decisions. For example, a salesperson who is given public recognition and a large bonus for making a valuable sale that he or she obtained through unethical tactics will probably be motivated to use such tactics in the future, even if such behavior goes against the salesperson's personal value system.

Opportunity relates to individuals' immediate job context—where they work, whom they work with, and the nature of the work. The **immediate job context** includes the motivational carrots and sticks that superiors use to influence employee behavior. Pay raises, bonuses, and public recognition are carrots, or positive reinforcers, whereas demotions, firings, reprimands, and pay penalties act as sticks, the negative reinforcers.

The opportunity employees have for unethical behavior in an organization can be eliminated through formal codes, policies, and rules that are adequately enforced by management. For example, financial companies, such as banks, savings and loan associations, and securities companies, have developed elaborate sets of rules and procedures to avoid the opportunity for individual employees to manipulate or take advantage of their trusted position. In banks, one such rule requires most employees to take a vacation and stay out of the bank a certain number of days every year so they cannot be physically present to cover up embezzlement or other diversion of funds. This rule prevents the opportunity for inappropriate conduct. As another example, DoubleClick Inc., an Internet advertising company, was criticized for its plans to combine the records of people's Web-surfing habits with a consumer database that contained names, addresses, and other personal information—thus creating a considerable opportunity for inappropriate conduct. These plans were abandoned, however, and to eliminate future opportunity for inappropriate conduct, DoubleClick appointed an independent panel that reviews new products and services for their potential threat to Web users' privacy.[20]

The opportunity for unethical behavior cannot be eliminated without aggressive enforcement of codes and rules. A national jewelry store chain president explained to the authors of this text how he dealt with a jewelry buyer in one of his stores who had taken a bribe from a supplier. There was an explicit company policy against taking incentive payments in order to deal with a specific supplier. When the president of the firm learned that one of his buyers had taken a bribe, he immediately traveled to that buyer's office and terminated his employment. He then traveled to the supplier (manufacturer) selling jewelry to his stores and terminated his relationship with the firm. The message was clear: taking a bribe is not acceptable for the store's buyers, and salespeople from supplying companies could cost their firm significant sales by offering bribes. This type of policy enforcement illustrates how the opportunity to commit unethical acts can be eliminated.

## Business Ethics Evaluations and Intentions

Ethical dilemmas involve problem-solving situations in which decision rules are often vague or in conflict. The results of an ethical decision are often uncertain; no one can always tell us whether we have made the right decision. There are no magic formulas, nor is there computer software that ethical dilemmas can be plugged into for a solution. Even if they mean well, most businesspeople will make ethical mistakes. Thus, there is no substitute for critical thinking and the ability to take responsibility for our own decisions.

An individual's intentions and the final decision regarding what action he or she will take are the last steps in the ethical decision-making process. When the individual's intentions and behavior are inconsistent with his or her ethical judgment, the person may feel guilty. For example, when an advertising account executive is asked by her client to create an advertisement that she perceives as misleading she has two alternatives: to comply or to refuse. If she refuses, she stands to lose business from that client and possibly her job. Other factors, such as pressure from the client, the need to keep her job to pay her debts and living expenses, and the possibility of a raise if she develops the advertisement successfully, may influence her resolution of this ethical dilemma. Because of these other factors, she may decide to act unethically and develop the advertisement even though she believes it to be inaccurate. Because her actions are inconsistent with her ethical judgment, she will probably feel guilty about her decision.

## Corporate Governance as a Dimension of Ethical Decision Making[21]

To remove the opportunity for employees to make unethical decisions, most companies have developed formal systems of accountability, oversight, and control—known as **corporate governance.** *Accountability* refers to how closely workplace decisions are aligned with a firm's stated strategic direction and its compliance with ethical and legal considerations. *Oversight* provides a system of checks and balances that limit employees' and managers' opportunities to deviate from policies and strategies and that prevent unethical and illegal activities. *Control* is the process of auditing and improving organizational decisions and actions. A clear delineation of accountability helps employees, customers, investors, government regulators, and other stakeholders understand why and how the organization chooses and achieves its goals. Even if a company has adopted a consensus approach for decision making, there should be oversight and authority for delegating tasks, making difficult and sometimes controversial decisions, balancing power throughout the firm, and maintaining ethical compliance. Governance also provides mechanisms for identifying risks and for planning for recovery when mistakes or problems occur.

All the elements of our framework for ethical decision making in business (Figure 4–1) relate to corporate governance. The individual factors we discussed earlier in the chapter relate to the personal ethical decisions that interface with the corporation's governance structure. Corporate governance is also part of a firm's corporate culture. A governance system that does not provide checks and balances creates opportunities for top managers to put their own self-interests before those of important stakeholders. Consider the accounting scandal at Adelphia Communications mentioned earlier. Founders John J. Rigas, Timothy J. Rigas, and Michael J. Rigas were able to defraud Adelphia's stockholders out of billions of dollars by falsifying the firm's financial reports because its corporate governance systems failed to prevent this type of fraud.[22]

Concerns about the need for greater corporate governance are not limited to the United States. Reforms in governance structures and issues are occurring all over the world.[23] In many nations, companies are being pressured to implement stronger corporate governance mechanisms by international investors, by the process of becoming privatized after years of unaccountability as state companies, or by the desire to imitate successful governance movements in the United States, Japan, and the European Union.[24]

Table 4–1 lists examples of major corporate governance issues. These issues normally involve strategic-level decisions and actions taken by boards of directors, business owners, top executives, and other managers with high levels of authority and

| TABLE 4–1 | Corporate Governance Issues |
|---|---|
| Shareholder rights | |
| Executive compensation | |
| Composition and structure of the board of directors | |
| Auditing and control | |
| Risk management | |
| CEO selection and termination decisions | |
| Integrity of financial reporting | |
| Stakeholder participation and input into decisions | |
| Compliance with corporate governance reform | |
| Role of the CEO in board decisions | |
| Organizational ethics programs | |

accountability. Although these people have often been relatively free from scrutiny, changes in technology, consumer activism, government attention, recent ethical scandals, and other factors have brought new attention to such issues as transparency, executive pay, risk and control, resource accountability, strategic direction, stockholder rights, and other decisions made for the organization.

## Views of Corporate Governance

To better understand the role of corporate governance in business today, it is important to consider how it relates to fundamental beliefs about the purpose of business. Some organizations take the view that as long as they are maximizing stockholder wealth and profitability, they are fulfilling their core responsibilities. Other firms, however, believe that a business is an important member, even citizen, of society and therefore must assume broad responsibilities that include complying with social norms and expectations. From these assumptions, we can derive two major approaches to corporate governance: the shareholder model and the stakeholder model.[25]

The **shareholder model of corporate governance** is founded in classic economic precepts, including the goal of maximizing wealth for investors and owners. For publicly traded firms, corporate governance focuses on developing and improving the formal system for maintaining performance accountability between top management and the firms' shareholders.[26] Thus, a shareholder orientation should drive a firm's decisions toward serving the best interests of investors. Underlying these decisions is a classic agency problem, where ownership (i.e., investors) and control (i.e., managers) are separate. Managers act as agents for investors, whose primary goal is increasing the value of the stock they own. However, investors and managers are distinct parties with unique insights, goals, and values with respect to the business. Managers, for example, may have motivations beyond stockholder value, such as market share, personal compensation, or attachment to particular products and projects. For example, U.S. Bancorp Piper Jeffray paid $32.5 million in fines and other penalties for failing to provide independent research to its client investors and for misconduct in allocating initial public offerings of stock. Because the mid-sized brokerage firm served as the investment banker for the initial public offerings, some stakeholders believe the firm had a conflict of interest when selling those same stocks to its customers.[27] Because of these potential differences, corporate governance mechanisms are needed to align investor and management interests. The shareholder model has been criticized for its somewhat singular purpose and focus, because there are other ways of "investing" in a business. Suppliers, creditors, customers, employees, business partners, the community, and others also invest their resources into the success of the firm.[28]

The **stakeholder model of corporate governance** adopts a broader view of the purpose of business. Although a company has a responsibility for economic success and viability to satisfy its stockholders, it also must answer to other stakeholders, including employees, suppliers, government regulators, communities, and special interest groups with which it interacts. Due to limited resources, companies must determine which of their stakeholders are primary. Once the primary groups have been identified, managers must then implement the appropriate corporate governance mechanisms to promote the development of long-term relationships.[29] This approach entails creating governance systems that consider stakeholder welfare in tandem with corporate needs and interests.

Although these two approaches seem to represent the ends of a continuum, the reality is that the shareholder model is a more restrictive precursor to the stakeholder orientation. Many businesses have evolved into the stakeholder model as a result of government initiatives, consumer activism, industry activity, and other external forces.

## Elements of Corporate Governance Related to Ethical Decision Making

Two major elements of corporate governance that relate to ethical decision making are the role of the board of directors and executive compensation.

*Boards of Directors* For public corporations, boards of directors hold the ultimate responsibility for their firms' success or failure, as well as for the ethics of their actions. The members of a company's board of directors assume legal responsibility for the firm's resources and decisions, and they appoint its top executive officers. Board members have a fiduciary duty, meaning they have assumed a position of trust and confidence that entails certain responsibilities, including acting in the best interests of those they serve. Thus, board membership is not intended as a vehicle for personal financial gain; rather, it provides the intangible benefit of ensuring the success of both the organization and people involved in the fiduciary arrangement. The role and expectations of boards of directors assumed greater significance after the accounting scandals of the early 2000s motivated many shareholders and other stakeholders to demand greater accountability from boards.[30] For example, after $9 billion in accounting irregularities led WorldCom to declare the largest ever bankruptcy, the company replaced the board members who had failed to prevent the accounting scandal. The firm also fired many managers.[31]

The traditional approach to directorship assumed that board members managed the corporation's business. Research and practical observation have shown that boards of directors rarely, if ever, perform the management function.[32] First, boards meet only a few times a year, which precludes them from managing effectively. In addition, the complexity of modern organizations mandates full attention on a daily basis. Thus, today boards of directors are concerned primarily with monitoring the decisions made by executives on behalf of the company. This includes choosing top executives, assessing their performance, helping to set strategic direction, and ensuring that oversight, control, and accountability mechanisms are in place. In sum, board members assume ultimate authority for their organization's effectiveness and subsequent performance.

Just as improved ethical decision making requires more of employees and executives, so too are boards of directors feeling greater demands for accountability and transparency. In the past, board members were often retired company executives or friends of current executives, but the trend today is toward "outside directors" who had little vested interest in the firm before assuming the director role. Inside directors are corporate officers, consultants, major shareholders, or others who benefit directly from the success of the organization. Directors today are increasingly chosen for their expertise, competence, and ability to bring diverse perspectives to strategic discussions. Outside directors are also thought to bring more independence to the monitoring function because they are not bound by past allegiances, friendships, a current role in the company, or some other issue that may create a conflict of interest.

Many of the corporate scandals uncovered in recent years might have been prevented if each of the companies' boards of directors had been better qualified, more knowledgeable, and less biased. A survey by *USA Today* found that corporate boards have considerable overlap. More than one thousand corporate board members sit on four or more company boards, and of the nearly two thousand boards of directors in the United States, more than twenty-two thousand of their members are linked to boards of more than one company. For example, of the one thousand largest companies, one-fifth share at least one board member with another top 1,000 firm.[33] This overlap creates the opportunity for conflicts of interest in decision making and limits the independence of individual boards of directors. For example, the telecommunication firm Verizon, which shares four board members with prescription drug producer Wyeth, recently withdrew from the nonprofit organization Business for Affordable Medicine, which Wyeth had criticized for its stance on bringing generic drugs to market sooner.[34] In some cases, individuals have earned placement on multiple boards of directors because they have gained a reputation for going along with top management. This may foster a corporate culture that limits outside oversight of top managers' decisions.

Board independence has become so desirable that it is one of the criteria, along with board quality, shareholder accountability, and corporate performance, that *Business Week* magazine uses to assess the quality of corporate boards of directors. Table 4–2 shows the ten best and ten worst boards as evaluated by leading Wall Street investors and governance experts for *Business Week*. Several factors about the best boards of directors stand out. These boards are generally more independent and have greater accountability to shareholders than in other corporations. Their directors often own company stock, which makes them more sympathetic to shareholder concerns. Moreover, these directors often take a more active role than directors of other firms. For example, Home Depot, which has just two insiders on its twelve-member board, requires directors to visit twenty stores a year. This gives them a stronger sense of what is going on within the company, as well as the opportunity to address issues before they become problems.[35]

| TABLE 4–2 | *Business Week*'s Best and Worst Corporate Boards of Directors |
|-----------|----------------------------------------------------------------|

| BEST BOARDS | WORST BOARDS |
|-------------|--------------|
| Company | Company |
| 3M | Apple |
| Apria Healthcare | Conseco |
| Colgate-Palmolive | Dillard's |
| General Electric | Gap |
| Home Depot | Kmart |
| Intel | Qwest |
| Johnson & Johnson | Tyson Foods |
| Medtronic | Xerox |
| Pfizer | |
| Texas Instruments | |

Source: "The Best and Worst Boards," *Business Week*, Oct. 7, 2002, pp. 106–107. Reprinted by special permission. Copyright © 2002 by The McGraw-Hill Companies, Inc.

*Executive Compensation*   One of the biggest issues that corporate boards of directors face is executive compensation. In fact, most boards spend more time deciding how much to compensate top executives than they do ensuring the integrity of the company's financial reporting systems.[36] How executives are compensated for their leadership, organizational service, and performance has become a controversial topic. Indeed, 73 percent of respondents in a *Business Week*/Harris poll indicated they believe that top officers of large U.S. companies receive too much compensation, while only 21 percent reported executive compensation as "just about the right amount."[37] Many executives have received large compensation and bonus packages regardless of the success of their companies. Raytheon CEO Daniel P. Burnham, for example, received a $900,000 bonus even though his company lost $181 million in one quarter and its stock plummeted from $76 to $20 a share.[38] In some cases, large firms have paid dearly to send underperforming CEOs packing. Conseco, Inc.'s Stephen Hilbert, for example, got a $72.4 million severance package. In the seven years prior to his departure, Hilbert made $457 million, including salary, bonuses, free shares of stock, and gains from exercising stock options.[39]

Many people believe that no executive is worth millions of dollars in annual salary and stock options, even if he or she has brought great financial return to investors. Their concerns often center on the relationship between the highest-paid executives and median employee wages in the company. If this ratio is perceived as too large, then critics believe that either employees are not being compensated fairly or high executive salaries represent an improper use of company resources. According to a recent report by United for a Fair Economy, the average executive now earns 419 times the average blue-collar worker. Because of this enormous difference, the business press is now usually careful to support high levels of executive compensation only when it is directly linked to strong company performance. Although the issue of executive compensation has received much attention in the media of late, some business owners have long recognized its potential ill effects. In the early twentieth century, for example, capitalist J. P. Morgan implemented a policy that limited the pay of top managers in businesses he owned to no more than twenty times the pay of any other employee.[40]

Other people argue that because executives assume so much risk on behalf of the company, they deserve the rewards that follow from strong company performance. In addition, many executives' personal and professional lives meld to the point that they are "on call" twenty-four hours a day. Because not everyone has the skill, experience, and desire to become an executive, with the accompanying pressure and responsibility, market forces dictate a high level of compensation. When the pool of qualified individuals is limited, many corporate board members feel that offering large compensation packages is the only way to attract and retain top executives and so ensure that their firms are not left without strong leadership. In an era when top executives are increasingly willing to "jump ship" to other firms that offer higher pay, potentially lucrative stock options, bonuses, and other benefits, such thinking is not without merit.[41] The average salary, benefits, and options package for chief executives of major corporations in the United States in 2001 was $11 million.[42] The ethics crisis of the early 2000s led more than one CEO to return millions of dollars in compensation in response to stockholder anger over performance. For example, Dollar General CEO Cal Turner Jr. returned $6.8 million that he earned as a result of financial results that the company later was forced to restate.[43]

Executive compensation is a difficult but important issue for boards of directors and other stakeholders to consider because it receives much attention in the media, sparks shareholder concern, and is hotly debated in discussions of corporate governance. One area for board members to consider is the extent to which executive compensation is linked to company performance. Plans that base compensation on the achievement of several performance goals, including profits and revenues, are intended to align the interests of owners with management. Another issue is whether performance-linked compensation encourages executives to focus on short-term performance at the expense of long-term growth.[44] Shareholders today, however, may be growing more concerned about transparency than short-term performance and executive compensation. A recent study determined that companies which divulge more details about their corporate governance practices generate higher shareholder returns than less transparent companies.[45]

## Using the Ethical Decision-Making Framework to Improve Ethical Decisions

The ethical decision-making framework presented in this chapter cannot tell you if a business decision is ethical or unethical. It bears repeating that it is impossible to tell you what is right or wrong; instead, we are attempting to prepare you to make informed ethical decisions. Although this chapter does not moralize by telling you what to do in a specific situation, it does provide an overview of typical decision-making processes and factors that influence ethical decisions. The framework is not a guide for how to make decisions but is intended to provide you with insights and knowledge about typical ethical decision-making processes in business organizations.

Because it is impossible to agree on normative judgments about what is ethical, business ethics scholars developing descriptive models have instead focused on regularities in decision making and the various phenomena that interact in a dynamic environment to produce predictable behavioral patterns. Furthermore, it is unlikely that an organization's ethical problems will be solved strictly by having a thorough knowledge about how ethical decisions are made. By its very nature, business ethics involves value judgments and collective agreement about acceptable patterns of behavior.

We propose that gaining an understanding of typical ethical decision making in business organizations will reveal several ways that such decision making could be improved. With more knowledge about how the decision process works, you will be better prepared to critically analyze ethical dilemmas and to provide ethical leadership regardless of your role in the organization. One important conclusion that should be taken from our framework is that ethical decision making within an organization does not rely strictly on the personal values and morals of individuals. Organizations take on a culture of their own, which when combined with corporate governance mechanisms, may have a significant influence on business ethics.

## Summary

The key components of the ethical decision-making framework provided in this chapter include ethical issue intensity, individual factors, organizational factors, and opportunity. These factors are interrelated and influence business ethics evaluations and intentions, which result in ethical or unethical behavior.

The first step in ethical decision making is to recognize that an ethical issue requires that an individual or work group choose among several actions that will ultimately be evaluated as ethical or unethical by various stakeholders. Ethical issue intensity is the perceived relevance or importance of an ethical issue to the individual or work group. It reflects the ethical sensitivity of the individual or work group that triggers the ethical decision process. All the other factors in our ethical decision-making framework influence this sensitivity, thus determining why ethical issues are often perceived differently by different individuals.

People who face ethical issues often base their decisions on their own values and principles of right or wrong. These values and principles are learned through the socialization process with family members, social groups, church, and formal education. Individual factors that influence decision making include personal moral philosophies and the individual's stage of cognitive development.

In the workplace, an organization's values often have greater influence on individual's decisions than that person's own values. Decisions in business are most often made jointly, in work groups and committees, or in conversations and discussions with coworkers. Organizational culture and structure operate through the individual relationships of the organization's members to influence those members' ethical decisions. A corporate culture can be defined as a set of values, beliefs, goals, norms, and ways of solving problems that members (employees) of an organization share. Corporate culture involves norms that prescribe a wide range of behavior for the organization's members. The ethical climate of an organization indicates whether it has an ethical conscience. Significant others—including peers, managers, coworkers, and subordinates—who influence the work group have more daily impact on an employee's decisions than any other factor in the decision-making framework. Obedience to authority may explain why many business ethics issues are resolved simply by following the directives of a superior.

Ethical opportunity results from conditions that either provide rewards, whether internal or external, or limit barriers to ethical or unethical behavior. Included in opportunity is a person's immediate job context, which includes the motivational techniques superiors use to influence employee behavior. The opportunity employees have for unethical behavior in an organization can be eliminated through formal codes, policies, and rules that are adequately enforced by management.

Ethical dilemmas arise in problem-solving situations in which decision rules are often vague or in conflict. There is no substitute for the employee's own critical thinking and ability to accept responsibility for his or her decision.

To control opportunities for unethical decisions, most companies have developed formal corporate governance systems of accountability, oversight, and control of organizational decisions and resources. All the elements of the decision-making framework in this chapter relate to corporate governance.

There are two perceptions of corporate governance, which can be viewed as a continuum. The shareholder model is founded in classic economic precepts, including the maximization of wealth for investors and owners. The stakeholder model adopts a broader view of the purpose of business that includes satisfying the concerns of other stakeholders, from employees, suppliers, and government regulators to communities and special-interest groups.

Two major elements of corporate governance that relate to ethical decision making are the role of the board of directors and executive compensation. The members of a public corporation's board of directors assume legal responsibility for the firm's resources and decisions. Important issues related to corporate boards of directors include accountability, transparency, and independence. Boards of directors are also responsible for appointing and setting the compensation for top executive officers, a controversial topic. Concerns about executive pay may center on the often disproportionate relationship between the highest-paid executives and median employee wages in the company.

The ethical decision-making framework provided in this chapter is not a guide for making decisions. It is intended to provide insights and knowledge about typical ethical decision-making processes in business organizations. Ethical decision making within organizations does not rely strictly on the personal values and morals of employees. Organizations have a culture of their own, which when combined with corporate governance mechanisms, may significantly influence business ethics.

| Important Terms for Review | | |
| --- | --- | --- |
| | ethical issue intensity | corporate governance |
| | corporate culture | shareholder model of corporate |
| | ethical climate | governance |
| | significant others | stakeholder model of corporate |
| | opportunity | governance |
| | immediate job context | |

## A Real-Life Situation*

Kent was getting pressure from his boss, parents, and wife about the marketing campaign for Broadway Corporation's new video game called "Lucky." He had been working for Broadway for about two years, and the Lucky game was his first big project. After Kent and his wife, Amy, had graduated from the same college, they decided to go back to their hometown of Las Cruces, New Mexico, near the Mexican border. Kent's father knew the president of Broadway, which enabled Kent to get a job in its marketing department. Broadway is a medium-size company with about five hundred employees, making it one of the largest employers in Las Cruces. Broadway develops, manufactures, and markets video arcade games.

Within the video arcade industry, competition is fierce. Games typically have a life cycle of only eighteen to twenty-four months. One of the key strategies in the industry is providing unique, visually stimulating games by using color graphics technology, fast action, and participant interaction. The target markets for Broadway's video products are children aged five to twelve and teenagers aged thirteen to nineteen. Males constitute 75 percent of the market.

When Kent first started with Broadway, his task was to conduct market research on the types of games players desired. His research showed that the market wanted more action (violence), quicker graphics, multiple levels of difficulty, and sound. Further research showed that certain tones and types of sound were more pleasing than others. As part of his research, Kent also observed people in video arcades, where he found that many became hypnotized by a game and would quickly put in quarters when told to do so. Research suggested that many target consumers exhibited the same symptoms as compulsive gamblers. Kent's research results were very well received by the company, which developed several new games using his information. The new games were instant hits with the market.

In his continuing research, Kent had found that the consumer's level of intensity increased as the game's intensity level increased. Several reports later, Kent suggested that target consumers might be willing, at strategic periods in a video game, to insert multiple coins. For example, a player who wanted to move to a higher level of difficulty would have to insert two coins; to play the final level, three coins would have to be inserted. When the idea was tested, Kent found it did increase game productivity.

Kent had also noticed that video games that gave positive reinforcements to the consumer, such as audio cues, were played much more frequently than others. He reported his findings to Brad, Broadway's president, who asked Kent to apply the information to the development of new games. Kent suggested having the machines give candy to the game players when they attained specific goals. For the teen market, the company modified the idea: the machines would give back coins at certain levels during the game. Players could then use the coins at strategic levels to play a "slot-type" chance opening of the next level. By inserting an element of chance, these games generated more coin input than output, and game productivity increased dramatically. These innovations were quite successful, giving Broadway a larger share of the market and Kent a promotion to product manager.

Kent's newest assignment was the Lucky game— a fast-action scenario in which the goal was to destroy the enemy before being destroyed. Kent expanded on the slot-type game for the older market, with two additions. First, the game employed virtual reality technology, which gives the player the sensation of actually being in the game. Second, keeping in mind that most of the teenage consumers were male, Kent incorporated a female character who, at each level, removed a piece of her clothing and taunted the player. A win at the highest level left her nude. Test market results suggested that the two additions increased profitability per game dramatically.

Several weeks later, Brad asked about the Lucky project. "I think we've got a real problem, Brad," Kent told him. "Maybe the nudity is a bad idea.

Some people will be really upset about it." Brad was very displeased with Kent's response.

Word got around fast that the Lucky project had stalled. During dinner with his parents, Kent mentioned the Lucky project, and his dad said something that affected Kent. "You know, son, the Lucky project will bring in a great deal of revenue for Broadway, and jobs are at stake. Some of your coworkers are upset with your stand on this project. I'm not telling you what to do, but there's more at stake here than just a video game."

The next day Kent had a meeting with Brad about Lucky. "Well," Brad asked, "what have you decided?"

Kent answered, "I don't think we should go with the nudity idea."

Brad answered, "You know, Kent, you're right. The U.S. market just isn't ready to see full nudity as well as graphic violence in arcades in their local malls. That's why I've contacted an Internet provider who will take our game and put it on the Net as an adult product. I've also checked out the foreign markets and found that we can sell the machines to the Mexican market if we tone down the violence. The Tai-

wanese joint venture group has okayed the version we have now, but they would like you to develop something that is more graphic in both areas. You see, they already have similar versions of this type of game now, and their market is ready to go to the next level. I see the Internet market as secondary because we can't get the virtual reality equipment and software into an Internet mode. Maybe when PCs get faster we'll be able to tap into it at that level, but not now. So, Kent, do you understand what you need to be doing on Lucky?"

## Questions ■ Exercises

1. What are the ethical and legal issues?
2. What are Kent's options?
3. Discuss the acceptability and commercial use of sex, violence, and gambling in the United States.
4. Are marketing sex, violence, and gambling acceptable in other countries if they fit their culture?

\* This case is strictly hypothetical; any resemblance to real persons, companies, or situations is coincidental.

---

## Check Your EQ

Check your E.Q., or Ethics Quotient, by completing the following. Assess your performance to evaluate your overall understanding of the chapter material.

1. The first step in ethical decision making is to understand the individual factors that influence the process.                                    Yes    No
2. Opportunity describes the conditions within an organization that limit or permit ethical or unethical behavior.                                    Yes    No
3. Corporate governance is not necessary if the firm adopts a consensus for decision making.                                    Yes    No
4. The most significant influence on ethical behavior in the organization is the opportunity to engage in (un)ethical behavior.                                    Yes    No
5. Obedience to authority relates to the influence of organizational culture.                                    Yes    No

ANSWERS 1. No. The first step is to become more aware that an ethical issue exists and to consider its relevance to the individual or work group. 2. Yes. Opportunity results from conditions that provide rewards or fail to erect barriers against unethical behavior. 3. No. Corporate governance is necessary to plan for and avoid risk, regardless of the decision-making approach. 4. No. Significant others have more impact on ethical decisions within an organization. 5. No. Obedience to authority relates to the influence of significant others and supervisors.

# 5

# Individual Factors: Moral Philosophies and Cognitive Moral Development

## CHAPTER OBJECTIVES

- To understand how moral philosophies influence individual and group ethical decision making in business

- To compare and contrast teleological, deontological, and relativist perspectives of moral philosophy

- To consider virtue ethics as a philosophy for understanding business ethics

- To discuss the impact of philosophies of justice on business ethics

- To understand that people may change their moral philosophy in different situations

- To recognize the stages of cognitive moral development and understand how to apply them

## CHAPTER OUTLINE

**Moral Philosophy Defined**

**Moral Philosophy Perspectives**
Teleology
Deontology
The Relativist Perspective
Virtue Ethics
Justice
Applying Moral Philosophy to Ethical Decision Making

**Cognitive Moral Development**

## An Ethical Dilemma*

One of the problems Lael Matthews has had to deal with in trying to climb the corporate ladder is the "glass ceiling" faced by minorities and women. In her current position, she must decide which of three managers to promote. Her superior has informed her that making the wrong decision would not be good, either internally or externally. These are the candidates:

Liz (African American, 34, divorced, one child) graduated in the lower half of her college class (Northwest State). She has been with the company for four years and in the industry for eight years, with mediocre performance ratings but a high energy level. She has had some difficulties in managing her staff. Her child has had medical problems, and so higher pay would be helpful. If promoted, Liz would be the first African-American female manager at this level. Lael has known Liz only a short time, but they seem to have hit it off. In fact, Lael once baby-sat Liz's daughter, Janeen, in an emergency. The downside to promoting Liz, though, might be a perception that Lael is playing favorites.

Roy (white, 57, married, three children) graduated from a private university in the top half of his class. Roy has been with the company for twenty years and in the industry for thirty. He has always been a steady performer, with mostly average ratings. The reason Roy has been passed over before was his refusal to relocate, but that is no longer a problem. Roy's energy level is average to low; however, he has produced many of the company's top sales performers in the past. This promotion would be his last before retirement, and many in the company feel he has earned it. In fact, one senior manager stopped Lael in the hall and said, "You know, Lael, Roy has been with us for a long time. He has done many good things for the company, sacrificing not only himself but also his family. I really hope that you can see your way to promoting him. It would be a favor to me that I wouldn't forget."

Quang Yeh (female, Asian, 27, single) graduated from State University in the top 3 percent of her class and has been with the company for three years. She is known for putting in sixty-hour weeks and for her very meticulous management style, which has generated some criticism from her sales staff. The last area she managed showed record increases, despite the loss of some older accounts that for some reason did not like dealing with Quang. Moreover, Quang sued her previous employer for discrimination and won. A comment that Lael had heard from that company was that Quang was intense and that nothing would stop her from reaching her goals. As Lael was going over some of her notes, another upper-management individual came to her office and said, "You know, Lael, Quang is engaged to my son. I've looked over her personnel files and she looks very good. She looks like a rising star, which would indicate that she should be promoted as quickly as possible. I realize that you're not in my division, but the way people get transferred, you never know. I would really like to see Quang get this promotion."

Finally, Lael's immediate supervisor came to her to talk about Liz. "You know, Lael, Liz is one of a very few people in the company who is both an African-American female and qualified for this position. I've been going over the company's hiring and promotion figures, and it would be very advantageous for me personally and for the company to promote her. I've also spoken to public relations, and they believe that this would be a tremendous boost for the company."

As Lael pondered her decision, she mentally went through each candidate's records and found that each had advantages and disadvantages. While she was considering her problem, the phone rang. It was Liz, sounding frantic. "Lael, I'm sorry to disturb you at this late hour but I need you to come to the hospital. Janeen [Liz's daughter] has been in an accident, and I don't know who to turn to. Can you come?" "Yes, I'm on my way," Lael responded. When Lael got to the hospital, she found that Janeen's injuries were fairly serious and that Liz would have to miss some work to help with the recuperation process. Lael also realized that this accident would create a financial problem for Liz, which a promotion could help solve.

The next day seemed very long and was punctuated by the announcement that Roy's son was getting married to the vice president's daughter. The wedding would be in June, and it sounded as though it would be a company affair. By 4:30 that afternoon Lael had gone through four aspirins and two antacids. Her decision was due in two days.

What should she do?

## Questions ■ Exercises

1. Discuss the advantages and disadvantages of each candidate.
2. What are the ethical and legal considerations for Lael?
3. Identify the pressures that have made her promotion decision an ethical and legal issue.
4. Discuss the implications of each decision Lael could make.

\* This case is strictly hypothetical; any resemblance to real persons, companies, or situations is coincidental.

 s mentioned in Chapter 4, individual values, such as honesty, trustworthiness, and integrity, are learned from parents, teachers, religious leaders, and society. As we mature, we combine these values into moral philosophies that define what is "good" or "moral" when evaluating the world as a whole. These value sets help to explain why a person believes that one action is right whereas another is wrong, and people often cite these philosophies to justify decisions or explain actions. To understand how people make ethical decisions, it is therefore useful to have a grasp of the major types of moral philosophies, as well as the stages of cognitive development through which people progress in developing these moral philosophies.

In this chapter we explore several aspects of moral philosophy. First, we define moral philosophy and discuss how it applies to business. Next, we describe two broad classifications of moral philosophy: teleology and deontology. Then we consider the relativist perspective from which many ethical or unethical decisions are made in everyday life. We also discuss virtue ethics and how it can be applied to today's multinational business environment. Next, we introduce a concept called cognitive moral development and discuss how this might explain variations in employee conduct.

## Moral Philosophy Defined

When people talk about philosophy, they usually mean the system of values by which they live. **Moral philosophy** refers in particular to the principles or rules that people use to decide what is right or wrong. For example, a production manager may be guided by a general philosophy of management that emphasizes encouraging workers to know as much as possible about the product they are manufacturing. Moral philosophy comes into play when the manager must make decisions such as whether to notify employees in advance of upcoming layoffs. Although workers would prefer advance warning, giving it might adversely affect production quality and quantity. Such decisions require a person to evaluate the "rightness," or morality, of choices in terms of his or her own principles and values.

Moral philosophies present guidelines for "determining how conflicts in human interests are to be settled and for optimizing mutual benefit of people living together in groups."[1] They guide businesspeople as they formulate business strategies and resolve specific ethical issues. However, there is no single moral philosophy that everyone accepts. Some managers, for example, view profit as the ultimate goal of an enterprise and therefore may not be concerned about the impact of their firms' decisions on society. As we have seen, the economist Milton Friedman supports this viewpoint, contending that the market will reward or punish companies for unethical conduct without the need for government regulation.[2] The emergence of capitalism as the dominant and most widely accepted economic system has created market-driven societies around the world. However, economic systems not only allocate resources and products within a society, but also affect individuals and society as a whole. Thus, the success of an economic system depends both on its philosophical framework and on individuals within the system who maintain moral philosophies that bring people together in a cooperative, efficient, and productive marketplace. There is a long Western tradition, going back to Aristotle, of questioning whether a market economy and individual moral behavior are compatible. In reality, individuals in today's society exist within the framework of social, political, and economic institutions.

Moral philosophies are ideal moral perspectives that provide individuals with abstract principles for guiding their social existence. For example, individuals' decisions to recycle waste or to purchase or sell recycled or recyclable products are influenced by moral philosophies and attitudes toward recycling.[3] Thus, it is often difficult to implement an individual moral philosophy within the complex environment of a business organization. On the other hand, the functioning of our economic system depends on individuals coming together and sharing philosophies that create the moral values, trust, and expectations that allow the system to work. Most employees within a business organization do not think about what particular moral philosophy they are using when they are confronted with an ethical issue. Individuals learn decision-making approaches or philosophies through their cultural and social development.

## Moral Philosophy Perspectives

There are many moral philosophies, and each one is complex. Because a detailed study of all moral philosophies is beyond the scope of this book, we will limit our discussion to those that are most applicable to the study of business ethics. Our approach will focus on the most basic concepts needed to help you understand the ethical decision-making process in business. We will not prescribe the use of any particular moral philosophy, for there is no one "correct" way to resolve ethical issues in business.

To help you understand how the moral philosophies discussed in this chapter may be applied in decision making, we will use a hypothetical situation as an illustration. Suppose that Sam Colt, a sales representative, is preparing a sales presentation for his firm, Midwest Hardware, which manufactures nuts and bolts. Sam hopes to obtain a large sale from a construction firm that is building a bridge across the Mississippi River near St. Louis. The bolts manufactured by Midwest Hardware have a 3 percent defect rate, which, although acceptable in the industry, makes them unsuitable for use in certain types of projects, such as those that may be subject to sudden, severe stress. The new bridge will be located near the New Madrid Fault line, the source of the United States' greatest earthquake, in 1811. The epicenter of that earthquake, which caused extensive damage and altered the flow of the Mississippi, is less than two hundred miles from the

| TABLE 5-1 | A Comparison of the Philosophies Used in Business Decisions |
|---|---|
| Teleology | Stipulates that acts are morally right or acceptable if they produce some desired result, such as realization of self-interest or utility |
| *Egoism* | Defines right or acceptable actions as those that maximize a particular person's self-interest as defined by the individual |
| *Utilitarianism* | Defines right or acceptable actions as those that maximize total utility, or the greatest good for the greatest number of people |
| Deontology | Focuses on the preservation of individual rights and on the intentions associated with a particular behavior rather than on its consequences |
| Relativist | Evaluates ethicalness subjectively on the basis of individual and group experiences |
| Virtue ethics | Assumes that what is moral in a given situation is not only what conventional morality requires, but also what the mature person with a "good" moral character would deem appropriate |
| Justice | Evaluates ethicalness on the basis of fairness: distributive, procedural, and interactional |

new bridge site. Earthquake experts believe there is a 50 percent chance that an earthquake with a magnitude greater than seven on the Richter scale will occur somewhere along the New Madrid Fault by the year 2015. Bridge construction in the area is not regulated by earthquake codes, however. If Sam wins the sale, he will earn a commission of $25,000 on top of his regular salary. But if he tells the contractor about the defect rate, Midwest may lose the sale to a competitor that markets bolts with a lower defect rate. Thus, Sam's ethical issue is whether to point out to the bridge contractor that, in the event of an earthquake, some Midwest bolts could fail, which could possibly result in the collapse of the bridge and catastrophe for anyone driving across it.

We will come back to this illustration as we discuss particular moral philosophies, asking how Sam Colt might use each philosophy to resolve his ethical issue. We will not judge the quality of Sam's decision, and we will not advocate any one moral philosophy. In fact, this illustration and Sam's decision rationales are necessarily simplistic as well as hypothetical. In reality, the decision maker would probably have many more factors to consider in making his or her choice, and thus might reach a different decision. With that note of caution, we will introduce several types of moral philosophy: teleology, deontology, the relativist perspective, virtue ethics, and justice (see Table 5–1).

## *Teleology*

**Teleology** (from the Greek word for "end" or "purpose") refers to moral philosophies in which an act is considered morally right or acceptable if it produces some desired result, such as pleasure, knowledge, career growth, the realization of self-interest, utility, wealth, or even celebrity. In other words, teleological philosophies assess the moral worth of a behavior by looking at its consequences, and thus moral philosophers to-day often refer to these theories as **consequentialism.** Two important teleological philosophies that often guide decision making in individual business decisions are egoism and utilitarianism.

*Egoism* **Egoism** defines right or acceptable behavior in terms of its consequences for the individual. Egoists believe that they should make decisions that maximize their own self-interest, which is defined differently by each individual. Depending on the egoist, self-interest may be construed as physical well-being, power, pleasure, fame, a satisfying career, a good family life, wealth, or something else. In an ethical decision-making situation, an egoist will probably choose the alternative that contributes most to his or her self-interest. The egoist's creed can be generally stated as "Do the act that promotes the greatest good for oneself." Many believe that egoists are inherently unethical, that egoistic people and companies are short-term oriented and will take advantage of any opportunity or consumer. For example, some telemarketers demon-strate this negative tendency when they prey on elderly consumers who may be vul-nerable because of loneliness or fear of losing their financial independence. Thousands of senior citizens fall victim to fraudulent telemarketers every year. In many cases, they lose all of their savings and sometimes their homes.

An extreme form of egoism is **hedonism,** which defines right or acceptable behav-ior as that which maximizes personal pleasure. Moral philosophers describe those who believe that more pleasure is better as *quantitative hedonists* and those who believe that it is possible to get too much of a good thing (pleasure) as *qualitative hedonism.* Those who believe that pleasure is just one aspect of "the good life" are classified as non-hedonists or *pluralists.* Pluralists may view many things, including education, knowledge, and helping others, as contributing to their own self-interest.

However, there is also enlightened egoism. **Enlightened egoists** take a long-range perspective and allow for the well-being of others, although their own self-interest re-mains paramount. Enlightened egoists may, for example, abide by professional codes of ethics, control pollution, avoid cheating on taxes, help create jobs, and support community projects. Yet they do so not because these actions benefit others, but be-cause they help achieve some ultimate goal for the egoist, such as advancement within the firm. An enlightened egoist might call management's attention to a coworker who is cheating customers, but only to safeguard the company's reputation and thus the egoist's own job security. Many securities companies dismissed analysts after it became public that they were issuing misleading, or even false, stock ratings. Jack Grubman, for example, hyped telecommunications stocks such as WorldCom even after it be-came public that the stocks were poor investments. Salomon Smith Barney fired Grubman after his actions were publicly questioned.[4]

When businesses donate money, resources, or time to specific causes and institu-tions, their motives may not be purely altruistic either. For example, International Busi-ness Machines (IBM) has a policy of donating or reducing the cost of computers to educational institutions. The company receives tax breaks for donations of equipment, which reduce the costs of its philanthropy. In addition, IBM hopes to build future sales by placing its products on campus. When students enter the work force, they may re-quest the IBM products with which they have become familiar. Although the com-pany's actions benefit society in general, in the long run they also benefit IBM.

We now return to the hypothetical case of the salesperson who must decide whether to warn the bridge contractor that 3 percent of Midwest Hardware's bolts are likely to be defective. If Sam Colt is an egoist, he will probably choose the alternative that maximizes his own self-interest. If he defines self-interest as personal wealth, his personal moral philosophy may lead him to value a $25,000 commission more than a chance to reduce the risk of a bridge collapse. As a result, an egoist Colt might well resolve his ethical dilemma by keeping quiet about the bolts' defect rate, hoping to win the sale and the $25,000 commission. He might rationalize that there is a slim chance of an earthquake and that bolts would not be a factor in a major earthquake. Besides, no one would know that defective bolts could cause the bridge to collapse.

*Utilitarianism* Like egoism, **utilitarianism** is concerned with consequences, but the utilitarian seeks the greatest good for the greatest number of people. Utilitarians believe that they should make decisions that result in the greatest total *utility*, that is, achieve the greatest benefit for all those affected by a decision.

Utilitarian decision making relies on a systematic comparison of the costs and benefits to all affected parties. Using such a cost-benefit analysis, a utilitarian decision maker calculates the utility of the consequences of all possible alternatives and then selects the one that results in the greatest benefit. For example, the Supreme Court has ruled that supervisors are responsible for the sexual misconduct of employees, even if the employers knew nothing about the behavior. Thus, it has established a strict standard for harassment on the job. One of the justices indicated in the ruling that the employer's burden to prevent harassment is "one of the costs of doing business."[5] Apparently, the court has decided that the greatest utility to society will result from forcing businesses to prevent harassment.

In evaluating an action's consequences, many utilitarians consider the effects on animals as well as on human beings. This perspective is especially significant in the controversy surrounding the use of animals for research purposes by cosmetics and pharmaceutical companies. Animal rights groups have protested that such testing is unethical because it harms and even kills the animals, depriving them of their rights. Researchers for pharmaceutical and cosmetics manufacturers, however, defend animal testing on utilitarian grounds. The consequences of the research (new or improved drugs to treat disease, safer cosmetics) create more benefit for society, they argue, than would be achieved by halting the research to preserve the animals' rights. Nonetheless, many cosmetics firms have responded to the controversy by agreeing to stop animal research.

Now suppose that Sam Colt, the bolt salesperson, is a utilitarian. Before making his decision, he would conduct a cost-benefit analysis to assess which alternative would create the greatest utility. On the one hand, building the bridge would improve roadways and allow more people to cross the Mississippi River to reach jobs in St. Louis. The project would create hundreds of jobs, enhance the local economy, and unite communities on both sides of the river. Additionally, it would increase the revenues of Midwest Hardware, allowing the firm to invest more in research to lower the defect rate of bolts it produced in the future. On the other hand, a bridge collapse could kill or injure as many as one hundred people. But the bolts have only a 3 percent defect rate; there is only a 50 percent probability of an earthquake *somewhere* along the fault line; and there might be only a few cars on the bridge at the time of a disaster.

After analyzing the costs and benefits of the situation, Sam might rationalize that building the bridge with his company's bolts would create more utility (jobs, unity, economic growth, company growth) than would result from telling the bridge contractor that the bolts might fail in an earthquake. If so, the utilitarian Sam would probably not call the bridge contractor's attention to the defect rate.

Utilitarians use various criteria to judge the morality of an action. Some utilitarian philosophers have argued that general rules should be followed to decide which action is best.[6] These *rule utilitarians* determine behavior on the basis of principles, or rules, designed to promote the greatest utility, rather than on an examination of each particular situation. One such rule might be "bribery is wrong." If people felt free to offer bribes whenever they might be useful, the world would become chaotic; therefore, a rule prohibiting bribery would increase utility. A rule utilitarian would not bribe an official, even to preserve workers' jobs, but would adhere strictly to the rule. Rule utilitarians do not automatically accept conventional moral rules, however. If an alternative rule would promote greater utility, they would advocate changing it.

Other utilitarian philosophers have argued that the rightness of each individual action must be evaluated to determine whether it produces the greatest utility for the greatest number of people.[7] These *act utilitarians* examine the specific action itself, rather than the general rules governing the action, to assess whether it will result in the greatest utility. Rules, such as "bribery is wrong," serve only as general guidelines for act utilitarians. They would agree that bribery is generally wrong, not because there is anything inherently wrong with bribery, but because the total amount of utility decreases when one person's interests are placed ahead of those of society.[8] In a particular case, however, an act utilitarian might argue that bribery is acceptable. For example, a sales manager might believe that her firm will not win a construction contract unless a local government official gets a bribe; moreover, if the firm does not obtain the contract, it will have to lay off one hundred workers. The manager might therefore argue that bribery is justified because saving a hundred jobs creates more utility than obeying a law. Another example may be found in the actions of John Rigas, the billionaire founder of the Adelphia Communications. In his hometown, Rigas was viewed as a hero because he helped fund everything from hospitals to roads and gave loans to local people in need. In one instance, he flew a resident's daughter, who was dying of cancer, from Pennsylvania to Denver to see a faith healer. However, Rigas took Adelphia—and himself—into bankruptcy because of questionable accounting practices and improper use of $3 billion in company funds for loans to himself and family members. When these actions became public, Adelphia's stock plummeted to 13 cents a share from a high of $86.56.[9]

### Deontology

**Deontology** (from the Greek word for "ethics") refers to moral philosophies that focus on the rights of individuals and on the intentions associated with a particular behavior rather than on its consequences. Fundamental to deontological theory is the idea that equal respect must be given to all persons. Unlike utilitarians, deontologists argue that there are some things that we should *not* do, even to maximize utility. For example, deontologists would consider it wrong to kill an innocent person or commit a serious injustice against a person, no matter how much greater social utility might result from doing so, because such an action would infringe on that person's rights as an individual. The utilitarian, however, might consider as acceptable an action that resulted in a person's death if that action created some greater benefit.

Deontological philosophies regard certain behaviors as inherently right, and the determination of this rightness focuses on the individual actor, not society. Thus, these perspectives are sometimes referred to as **nonconsequentialism,** or the ethics of *respect for persons.*

Contemporary deontology has been greatly influenced by the German philosopher Immanuel Kant, who developed the so-called categorical imperative: "Act as if the maxim of thy action were to become by thy will a universal law of nature."[10] Simply put, if you feel comfortable allowing everyone in the world to see you commit an act and if your rationale for acting in a particular manner is suitable to become a universal principle guiding behavior, then committing that act is ethical. For example, if a person borrows money, promising to return it but with no intention of keeping that promise, he or she cannot "universalize" that act. If everyone were to borrow money without the intention of returning it, no one would take such promises seriously and all lending would cease.[11] Therefore, the rationale for the action would not be a suitable universal principle, and the act cannot be considered ethical.

The term *nature* is crucial for deontologists. In general, deontologists regard the nature of moral principles as permanent and stable, and they believe that compliance with these principles defines ethicalness. Deontologists believe that individuals have certain absolute rights:

- Freedom of conscience
- Freedom of consent
- Freedom of privacy
- Freedom of speech
- Due process[12]

To decide whether a behavior is ethical, deontologists look for conformity to moral principles. For example, if a manufacturing worker becomes ill or dies as a result of conditions in the workplace, a deontologist might argue that the company must modify its production processes to correct the condition, no matter what the cost—even if it means bankrupting the company and thus causing all workers to lose their jobs. In contrast, a utilitarian would analyze all the costs and benefits of modifying production processes and make a decision on that basis. This example is greatly oversimplified, of course, but it helps clarify the difference between teleology and deontology. In short, teleological philosophies consider the *ends* associated with an action whereas deontological philosophies consider the *means.*

Returning again to our bolt salesman, let us consider a deontological Sam Colt. He would probably feel obliged to tell the bridge contractor about the defect rate because of the potential loss of life that might result from an earthquake-caused bridge collapse. Even though constructing the bridge would benefit residents and earn the salesman a substantial commission, the failure of the bolts during an earthquake would infringe on the rights of any person crossing the bridge at the time of the collapse. Thus, the deontological Colt would probably inform the bridge contractor of the defect rate and point out the earthquake risk, even though doing so could mean losing the sale.

As with utilitarianism, deontologists may be divided into those who focus on moral rules and those who focus on the nature of the acts themselves. So-called *rule deontologists* believe that conformity to general moral principles determines ethicalness. Deontological philosophies use reason and logic to formulate rules for behavior. Examples include Kant's categorical imperative and the Golden Rule of Judeo-Christian tradition: Do unto others as you would have them do unto you. Such rules, or principles, guiding ethical behavior override the imperatives that emerge from a specific context. One could argue that Jeffery Wigand—who exposed the underside of the tobacco industry when he blew the whistle on his employer, Brown & Williamson Tobacco—was such a rule deontologist. Although it cost him both financially and socially, Wigand testified to Congress about the realities of marketing cigarettes and their effects on society.[13]

The basic rights of the individual, coupled with rules of conduct, constitute rule deontology. For example, a video store owner accused of distributing obscene materials could argue from a rule deontological perspective that the basic right to freedom of speech overrides the other indecency or pornography aspects of his business. Indeed, the free speech argument has held up in many courts. Kant and rule deontologists would support a process of discovery to identify the moral issues relevant to a firm's mission and objectives. Then, would follow a process of justifying that mission or those objectives based on rules.[14]

*Act deontologists,* in contrast, hold that actions are the proper basis on which to judge morality or ethicalness. Act deontology requires that a person use equity, fairness, and impartiality when making and enforcing decisions.[15] For act deontologists, as for act utilitarians, rules serve only as guidelines, with past experiences weighing more heavily than rules within the decision-making process. In effect, act deontologists suggest that people simply *know* that certain acts are right or wrong, regardless of the consequences or any appeal to deontological rules. In addition, act deontologists regard the particular act or moment in time as taking precedence over any rule. For example, many people view data collection by Internet sites as a violation of personal privacy in itself. Regardless of any Web site's stated rules or policies, many Internet users want to be left alone unless they provide permission to be tracked while online.[16]

As we have seen, ethical issues can be evaluated from many different perspectives. Each type of philosophy discussed here would have a distinct basis for deciding whether a particular action is right or wrong. Adherents of different personal moral philosophies may disagree in their evaluations of a given action, yet all are behaving ethically, *by their own standards*. All would agree that there is no one "right" way to make ethical decisions and no best moral philosophy except their own. The relativist perspective may be helpful in understanding how people make such decisions in practice.

## The Relativist Perspective

From the **relativist perspective,** definitions of ethical behavior are derived subjectively from the experiences of individuals and groups. Relativists use themselves or the people around them as their basis for defining ethical standards.

The relativist observes the actions of members of some relevant group and attempts to determine that group's consensus on a given behavior. A positive consensus signifies that the group considers the action to be right or ethical. Such judgments may not remain valid forever. As circumstances evolve or the makeup of the group changes, a formerly accepted behavior may come to be viewed as wrong or unethical, or vice versa. Within the accounting profession, for example, it was traditionally considered unethical to advertise. However, advertising has been gaining acceptance among accountants. This shift in ethical views may have come about by the steady increase in the number of accountants, which has resulted in greater competition. Moreover, the federal government investigated the restrictions that accounting groups placed on their members and concluded that they inhibited free competition. Consequently, an informal consensus has emerged in the accounting industry that advertising is now acceptable.

In the case of the Midwest Hardware salesperson, if he were a relativist he would attempt to determine the group consensus before deciding whether to tell his prospective customer about the bolts' defect rate. That is, Sam Colt would look at both his own company's policy and at general industry practice. He might also informally survey his colleagues and superiors as well as consulting industry trade journals and codes of ethics. Such investigations would help him determine the group consensus, which should reflect a variety of moral philosophies. If Sam learns that general company policy, as well as industry practice, is to discuss defect rates with those customers for whom faulty bolts may cause serious problems, he may infer that there is a consensus on the matter. As a relativist, he would probably then inform the bridge contractor that some of the bolts may fail, perhaps leading to a bridge collapse in the event of an earthquake. Conversely, if Sam determines that the normal practice in his company and the industry is to not inform customers about defect rates, he would probably not raise the subject with the bridge contractor.

Relativism acknowledges that we live in a society in which people have many different views and many different bases from which to justify decisions as right or wrong. The relativist looks to the interacting group and tries to determine probable solutions based on group consensus. When formulating business strategies and plans, for example, a relativist would try to anticipate the conflicts that could arise between the different philosophies held by members of the organization, its suppliers, its customers, and the community at large.

## Virtue Ethics

A moral virtue represents an acquired disposition that is valued as a part of an individual's character. As an individual develops socially, he or she may become disposed to behave habitually in the same way and with reasons, feelings, and desires that are characteristic of what may be considered a morally concerned person.[17] A person who has the character trait of honesty will be disposed to tell the truth because it is considered to be right and comfortable. This individual will always try to tell the truth because of its importance in human communication. A virtue is considered praiseworthy because it is an achievement that an individual develops through practice and commitment.[18]

This philosophy, termed **virtue ethics,** posits that what is moral in a given situation is not only what conventional morality or moral rules (current societal definitions), however justified, require, but also what the mature person with a "good" moral character would deem appropriate. Virtue ethics assumes that what current societal moral rules require may indeed be the moral minimum for the beginning of virtue. Many who believe in virtue ethics assume that a series of transcendental constants permeates the moral equation. These constants are defined as timeless, without cultural specificity. Furthermore, virtue can be enhanced by belief, knowledge, and subsequent behavior.

The viability of our political, social, and economic systems depends on the presence of certain virtues among the citizenry that are vital for the proper functioning of a market economy.[19] Indeed, virtue theory could be thought of as a dynamic theory of how to conduct business activities. Which virtues to pursue would depend on the employee's position in the firm as well as the type of organization. Specific virtues, such as truthfulness, provide sensitivity to circumstances and opportunities as well as clarity of purpose.[20]

The virtue ethicist believes that to have a successful market economy, society must be capable of carving out sanctuaries, such as family, school, church, and community, where virtues can be nurtured. These virtues can play a role in the functioning of an individualistic, contractual economy. Virtues such as truth, trust, tolerance, and restraint create obligations that make social cooperation possible. The operation of a market economy based on virtues provides a traditional existence where individuals in the economic system have powerful inducements to conform to prevailing standards of behavior. While some philosophers think that virtues may be weakened by the operation of the market, virtue ethicists believe that institutions and society must maintain a balance and constantly add to their stock of virtues.[21] Some of the virtues that could lubricate a market economy are listed in Table 5–2. The list is not comprehensive, but it provides examples of the types of virtues that support the business environment.

The elements of virtue important to business transactions have been defined as trust, self-control, empathy, fairness, and truthfulness. Attributes in contrast to virtue would include lying, cheating, fraud, and corruption. In their broadest sense, these terms appear to be accepted within all cultures. The problem of virtue ethics comes in its implementation within and between cultures. Those who practice virtue ethics go beyond social norms. For example, if a company tacitly approves of corruption, the employee who adheres to the virtues of trust and truthfulness would consider it wrong to sell unneeded repair parts despite the organization's approval of such acts. Some employees might call this truthful employee highly ethical and, in order to rationalize their own behavior, judge his or her ethics as going beyond what is required by their job or society. They might argue that virtue is an unattainable goal and thus one should not be obliged to live up to its standards. However, to those who espouse virtue ethics, this relativistic argument is meaningless, for they believe in the universal reality of the elements of virtue.

If our salesman Sam Colt were a virtue ethicist, he would consider the elements of virtue and then tell the prospective customer about the defect rate and about his concerns regarding the bridge and the risk of injury, death, and destruction. He would not resort to puffery to explain the product or its risks and, indeed, he might suggest alternative products or companies that would lower the probability of the bridge collapsing.

## *Justice*

Justice as it is applied in business ethics involves evaluations of fairness or the disposition to deal with perceived injustices of others. Justice is fair treatment and due

| TABLE 5–2 | Virtues That Support Business Transactions |
| --- | --- |
| Trust | The predisposition to place confidence in the behavior of others while taking the risk that the expected behavior will not be performed. Trust eliminates the need for and associated cost of monitoring compliance with agreements, contracts, and reciprocal agreements. There is the expectation that a promise or agreement can be relied on. |
| Self-control | The disposition to pass up an immediate advantage or gratification. It indicates the ability to avoid exploiting a known opportunity for self-interest. The tradeoff is between short-term self-interest and long-term benefits. |
| Empathy | The ability to share the feelings or emotions of others. It promotes civility because success in the market depends on the courteous treatment of people who have the option of going to competitors. The ability to anticipate needs and satisfy customers and employees contributes to a firm's economic success. |
| Fairness | The disposition to deal equitably with the perceived injustices of others. Fairness often relates to doing the right thing with respect to small matters in order to cultivate a long-term business relationship. |
| Truthfulness | The disposition to provide the facts or correct information as known to the individual. Telling the truth involves avoiding deception and contributes to trust in business relationships. |
| Learning | The disposition to constantly acquire knowledge internal and external to the firm, whether of an industry, culture, or other societies. Learning involves gaining knowledge to make better, more informed decisions. |
| Gratitude | A sign of maturity that is the beginning of civility and decency. The recognition that people do not succeed alone. |
| Civility | The disposition or essence of courtesy, politeness, respect, and consideration for others. Civility relates to the process of doing business in a culturally correct way, thus decreasing communication errors and increasing trust. |
| Moral Leadership | Strength of character, peace of mind and heart, and happiness in life. Those in leadership positions who follow a consistent pattern of behavior based on virtues. |

Source: Adapted from Ian Maitland, "Virtuous Markets: The Market As School of the Virtues," *Business Ethics Quarterly*, Jan. 1997, p. 97; and Gordon B. Hinckley, *Standing for Something: 10 Neglected Virtues That Will Heal Our Hearts and Homes* (New York: Three Rivers Press, 2001).

reward in accordance with ethical or legal standards. In business, this means that the decision rules used by an individual to determine the justice of a situation could be based on the perceived rights of individuals and on the intentions of the people involved in a given business interaction. For that reason, justice is more likely to be based on deontological moral philosophies than on teleology or utilitarianism. In other words, justice deals more with the issue of what individuals feel they are due based on their rights and performance in the workplace. For example, the U.S. Equal Employment Opportunity Commission exists to help employees who suspect they have been unjustly discriminated against in the workplace.

Three types of justice provide a framework for evaluating the fairness of different situations (see Table 5–3). **Distributive justice** is based on the evaluation of the outcomes or results of the business relationship. If some employees feel that they are paid less than their coworkers for the same work, they have concerns about distributive justice. Distributive justice is difficult to develop when one member of the business exchange intends to take advantage of the relationship.

**Procedural justice** is based on the processes and activities that produce the outcome or results. Evaluations of performance that are not consistently developed and applied can lead to problems with procedural justice. For instance, employees' concerns about inequitable compensation would relate to their perception that the processes of fairness or justice in their company were inconsistent. A climate that emphasizes procedural justice is expected to positively influence employees' attitudes and behaviors toward work-group cohesion. The visibility of supervisors and the work-group's perceptions of its own cohesiveness are products of a climate of procedural justice.[22] When there is strong employee support for decisions, decision makers, organizations, or outcomes, procedural justice is less important to the individual. In contrast, when employees' support for decisions, decision makers, organizations, or outcomes is not very strong, then procedural justice becomes more important.[23] For example, Wainwright Bank and Trust Corporation in Boston has made a commitment to promoting justice to all stakeholders by providing a "sense of inclusion and diversity that extends from the boardroom to the mail room."[24] The bank, in other words, uses methods of procedural justice to establish positive stakeholder relationships by promoting understanding and inclusion in the decision-making process.

**Interactional justice** is based on evaluating the communication processes used in the business relationship. Because interactional justice is linked to fairness in communication,

| TABLE 5–3 | Types of Justice | |
|---|---|---|
| **JUSTICE TYPE** | | **EVALUATIONS OF FAIRNESS** |
| **Distributive justice:** based on the evaluation of outcomes or results of the business relationship | | Benefits derived<br>Equity in rewards |
| **Procedural justice:** based on the processes and activities that produce the outcome or results | | Decision-making process<br>Level of access, openness, and participation |
| **Interactional justice:** based on an evaluation of the communication process used in the business relationship | | Accuracy of information<br>Truthfulness, respect, and courtesy in the process |

it often involves the individual's relationship with the business organization through the accuracy of the information the organization provides. Employees can also be guilty in interactional justice disputes. For example, many employees admit that they stay home when they are not really sick if they feel they can "get away with it." Such workplace absenteeism costs businesses millions of dollars each year. Being untruthful about the reasons for missing work is an example of an interactional justice issue.

All three types of justice—distributive, procedural, and interactional—could be used to evaluate a single business situation and the fairness of the organization involved. In the example of Sam Colt, Sam's decision to implement a justice perspective would be identical to using a deontological moral philosophy. That is, he would feel obligated to tell all affected parties about the bolt defect rate and the possible consequences. In general, justice evaluations result in restitution seeking, relationship building, and evaluations of fairness in business relationships.

### Applying Moral Philosophy to Ethical Decision Making

There is strong evidence that individuals use different moral philosophies depending on whether they are making a personal decision outside the work environment or making a work-related decision on the job.[25] Two possible reasons may explain this. First, in the business arena some goals and pressures for success differ from the goals and pressures in a person's nonwork life. As a result, an employee might view a specific action as "good" in the business sector but "unacceptable" in the nonwork environment. The second reason people change moral philosophies could be their firm's corporate culture. Consider that when a child enters school, he or she learns certain rules such as to raise your hand or to ask permission to use a certain toy. So it is with a new employee. Rules, personalities, and historical precedence exert pressure on the person to conform to the new firm's culture. As this occurs, the individual's moral philosophy can change to be compatible with the work environment. The employee may alter some or all of the values within his or her moral philosophy as he or she shifts into the firm's different moral philosophy.

The concept of a moral philosophy is not exact. For that reason, moral philosophies must be assessed on a continuum rather than as static entities. Simply put, when examining moral philosophies, we must remember that each philosophy states an ideal perspective and that most individuals seem to shift to other moral philosophies as they interpret ethical dilemmas. In other words, implementing moral philosophies from an individual perspective is not an exact science. It requires individuals to take their own accepted value system and attempt to apply it to real-world situations. Individuals make judgments about what they believe to be right or wrong, but in their business lives they make decisions that may be based, not on perceived right or wrong, but on producing the greatest benefits with the least harm. Such decisions should respect fundamental moral rights as well as perspectives on fairness, justice, and the common good.

The virtue approach to business ethics, as discussed earlier, assumes that there are certain ideals and values that everyone should strive for in order to achieve the maximum welfare and happiness of society.[26] Aspects of these ideals and values are expressed through individuals' specific moral philosophies. Every day in the workplace, employees must decide what is right or wrong and act accordingly. At the same time, as members of large organizations they cannot simply enforce their own personal perspective, especially if they adhere narrowly to a single moral philosophy. Because individuals cannot control most of the decisions in their work environment, though they are always responsible for their own actions they rarely have the power (especially in entry level and middle management ranks) to impose their own personal moral perspective on others.

Sometimes a company makes decisions that could be questionable according to individual customers' and employees' values and moral philosophies. For example, AT&T Corp. now offers a hard-core adult movie channel through its cable unit. The significant profits that AT&T can make from sexually explicit movies may satisfy some stakeholders, but others may reject or question the decision.[27] A company's core values will determine how decisions that bring moral philosophies into conflict are made. Most businesses have developed a mission statement, a corporate culture, and a set of core values that express how they want to relate to their stakeholders, including customers, employees, the legal system, and society.

Problems arise when employees encounter ethical situations that they cannot resolve. Sometimes gaining a better understanding of the basic premise of their decision rationale can help them choose the "right" solution. For instance, to decide whether they should offer bribes to customers to secure a large contract, salespeople need to understand their own personal moral philosophy as well as their firm's core values. If complying with company policy or legal requirements is an important motivation to the individual, he or she is less likely to offer a bribe. On the other hand, if the salesperson's ultimate goal is a "successful" career and if offering a bribe seems likely to result in a promotion, then bribery might not be inconsistent with that person's moral philosophy of acceptable business behavior. He or she may rationalize that bribery is necessary to be competitive "because everyone else does it" even though bribery is illegal under U.S. law.

## Cognitive Moral Development

Many people believe that individuals advance through stages of moral development as their knowledge and socialization continue over time. In this section, we examine a well-accepted model that describes this cognitive moral development process—that is, the stages through which people progress in their development of moral thought. Most of the models developed to explain, predict, and control individuals' ethical behavior within business organizations propose that cognitive moral processing is a crucial element in ethical decision making. Cognitive moral processing is based on a body of literature in psychology that focuses on studying children and their cognitive development.[28] Psychologist Lawrence Kohlberg developed the six-stage model of cognitive development described in the following pages (though not specifically for a business context).[29] According to **Kohlberg's model of cognitive moral development,** people make different decisions in similar ethical situations because they are in different stages of six cognitive moral development stages:

1. *The stage of punishment and obedience.* An individual in Kohlberg's first stage defines *right* as literal obedience to rules and authority. A person in this stage will respond to rules and labels of "good" and "bad" in terms of the physical power of those who determine such rules. Right and wrong are not associated

with any higher order or philosophy but rather with a person who has power. Stage one is usually associated with small children, but signs of stage-one development are also evident in adult behavior. For example, some companies forbid their buyers to accept gifts from salespeople. A buyer in stage one might justify a refusal to accept gifts from salespeople by referring to the company's rule that defines accepting gifts as an unethical practice, or the buyer may accept the gift if he or she believes that there is no chance of being caught and punished.

2. *The stage of individual instrumental purpose and exchange.* An individual in stage two defines *right* as that which serves his or her own needs. In this stage, the individual no longer makes moral decisions solely on the basis of specific rules or authority figures; he or she now evaluates behavior on the basis of its fairness to him or her. For example, a sales representative in stage two doing business for the first time in a foreign country may be expected by custom to give customers "gifts." Although gift giving may be against company policy in the United States, the salesperson may decide that certain company rules designed for operating in the United States do not apply overseas. In the culture of some foreign countries, gifts may be considered part of a person's pay. So, in this instance, not giving a gift might put the salesperson at a disadvantage. Some refer to stage two as the stage of reciprocity because, from a practical standpoint, ethical decisions are based on an agreement that "you scratch my back and I'll scratch yours" instead of on principles of loyalty, gratitude, or justice.

3. *The stage of mutual interpersonal expectations, relationships, and conformity.* An individual in stage three emphasizes others rather than him- or herself. Although ethical motivation is still derived from obedience to rules, the individual considers the well-being of others. A production manager in this stage might obey upper management's order to speed up an assembly line if he or she believed that this would generate more profit for the company and thus save employee jobs. This manager not only considers his or her own well-being in deciding to follow the order, but also tries to put him- or herself in upper management's and fellow employees' shoes. Thus, stage three differs from stage two in that fairness to others is one of the individual's ethical motives.

4. *The stage of social system and conscience maintenance.* An individual in stage four determines what is right by considering his or her duty to society, not just to other specific people. Duty, respect for authority, and maintaining the social order become the focal points. For example, some managers consider it a duty to society to protect privacy and therefore refrain from monitoring employee conversations.

5. *The stage of prior rights, social contract, or utility.* In stage five, an individual is concerned with upholding the basic rights, values, and legal contracts of society. Individuals in this stage feel a sense of obligation or commitment, a "social contract," to other groups and recognize that in some cases legal and moral points of view may conflict. To reduce such conflict, stage-five individuals base their decisions on a rational calculation of overall utilities. The president of a firm may decide to establish an ethics program because it will provide a buffer against legal problems and the firm will be perceived as a responsible contributor to society.

6. *The stage of universal ethical principles.* A person in this stage believes that right is determined by universal ethical principles that everyone should follow. Stage-six individuals believe that there are inalienable rights, which are universal in nature and consequence. These rights, laws, or social agreements are valid not because of a particular society's laws or customs, but because they rest on the premise of universality. Justice and equality are examples of principles that are deemed universal in nature. A person in this stage may be more concerned with social ethical issues and thus not rely on the business organization for ethical direction. For example, a businessperson at this stage might argue for discontinuing a product that has caused death and injury because the inalienable right to life makes killing wrong, regardless of the reason. Therefore, company profits would not be a justification for the continued sale of the product.[30]

Kohlberg's six stages can be reduced to three different levels of ethical concern. Initially, a person is concerned with his or her own immediate interests and with external rewards and punishments. At the second level, an individual equates *right* with conformance to the expectations of good behavior of the larger society or some significant reference group. Finally, at the third, or "principled," level, an individual sees beyond the norms, laws, and authority of groups or individuals. Employees at this level make ethical decisions regardless of negative external pressures. However, research has shown that most workers' abilities to identify and resolve moral dilemmas do not reside at this third level and that their motives are often a mixture of selflessness, self-interest, and selfishness. These findings suggest that an organization's formal structure plays an important role in affecting workers' ethical behavior.[31] Kohlberg's model implies that a person's level of moral development influences his or her perception of and response to an ethical issue.

Kohlberg's model suggests that people continue to change their decision priorities after their formative years. According to his model, as people progress through the stages of moral development, and with time, education, and experience, they may change their values and ethical behavior. In the context of business, an individual's moral development can be influenced by corporate culture, especially ethics training. Ethics training and education have been shown to improve managers' moral development scores.[32] Because of corporate reform, most employees in *Fortune* 1000 companies today receive some type of ethics training. One poll found that 54 percent of the employees surveyed indicated that ethics training was frequently useful in guiding their work-related decisions and conduct.[33] However, another study found that the value of compulsory ethics education as a way to improve the moral reasoning of real estate salespeople was highly questionable.[34] On the other hand, a Gallup poll about the integrity of various professions found that real-estate professionals were ranked as having high or very high honesty and ethics by just 19 percent of the public. In this respect, they ranked among the five lowest professional groups.[35]

Experience in resolving moral conflicts accelerates an individual's progress in moral development. A manager who relies on a specific set of values or rules may eventually come across a situation to which the rules do not apply. For example, suppose Sarah is a manager whose policy is to fire any employee whose productivity declines for four consecutive months. Sarah has an employee, George, whose productivity has suffered because of depression, but George's coworkers tell Sarah that George will recover and soon be a top performer again. Because of the circumstances and the perceived value of the employee, Sarah may bend the rule and keep George. Managers in the highest stages of the moral development process seem to be more democratic than autocratic. They are likely to be more aware of the ethical views of the other people involved in an ethical decision-making situation.

The theory of cognitive moral development provides encouragement that individuals in a company can change or improve their moral development. The study of moral philosophies supports management's development of employees' moral principles through applicable strategies. These strategies and principles make it possible to systematically analyze, criticize, and guide employees' business decisions. They can also be helpful in identifying the morally significant factors in a given workplace decision-making situation.[36] On the other hand, as we have seen, the work environment and the influence of coworkers appear to have the greatest influence on individual's ethical decision making. Therefore, the best way to improve employees' business ethics is to provide training for cognitive moral development and moral philosophy.

## Summary

Moral philosophy refers to the set of principles or rules that people use to decide what is right or wrong. These principles or rules present guidelines for resolving conflicts and for optimizing the mutual benefit of people living in groups. Businesspeople are guided by moral philosophies as they formulate business strategies and resolve specific ethical issues.

Teleological, or consequentialist, philosophies stipulate that acts are morally right or acceptable if they produce some desired result, such as realization of self-interest or utility. Egoism defines right or acceptable behavior in terms of the consequences for the individual. In an ethical decision-making situation, the egoist will choose the alternative that contributes most to his or her own self-interest. Egoism can be further classified into hedonism and enlightened egoism. Utilitarianism is concerned with maximizing total utility, or providing the greatest benefit for the greatest number of people. In making ethical decisions, utilitarians often conduct a cost-benefit analysis, which considers the costs and benefits to all affected parties. Rule utilitarians determine behavior on the basis of rules designed to promote the greatest utility rather than by examining particular situations. Act utilitarians examine the action itself, rather than the rules governing the action, to determine whether it will result in the greatest utility.

Deontological, or nonconsequentialist, philosophies focus on the rights of individuals and on the intentions behind an individual's particular behavior rather than on its consequences. In general, deontologists regard the nature of moral principles as permanent and stable, and they believe that compliance with these principles defines ethicalness. Deontologists believe that individuals have certain absolute rights that must be respected. Rule deontologists believe that conformity to general moral principles determines ethicalness. Act deontologists hold that actions are the proper basis on which to judge morality or ethicalness and that rules serve only as guidelines.

According to the relativist perspective, definitions of ethical behavior are derived subjectively from the experiences of individuals and groups. The relativist observes behavior within a relevant group and attempts to determine what consensus group members have reached on the issue in question.

Virtue ethics posits that what is moral in a given situation is not only what is required by conventional morality or current social definitions, however justified, but also what a person with a "good" moral character would deem appropriate. Those who profess virtue ethics do not believe that the end justifies the means in any situation.

Ideas of justice as applied in business relate to evaluations of fairness. Justice is fair treatment and due reward in accordance with ethical or legal standards. Distributive justice is based on the evaluation of the outcome or results of a business relationship. Procedural justice is based on the processes and activities that produce the outcomes or results. Interactional justice is based on an evaluation of the communication process in business.

The concept of a moral philosophy is not exact; moral philosophies can only be assessed on a continuum. Individuals use different moral philosophies depending on whether they are making a personal decision or a workplace decision.

According to Kohlberg's model of cognitive moral development, individuals make different decisions in similar ethical situations because they are in different stages of moral development. In Kohlberg's model people progress through six stages of moral development: (1) the stage of punishment and obedience; (2) the stage of individual instrumental purpose and exchange; (3) the stage of mutual interpersonal expectations, relationships, and conformity; (4) the stage of social system and conscience maintenance; (5) the stage of prior rights, social contract, or utility; or (6) the stage of universal ethical principles. Kohlberg's six stages can be further reduced to three levels of ethical concern: immediate self-interest, social expectations, and general ethical principles. This model may help explain why some people change their beliefs or moral values.

| Important Terms for Review | | |
|---|---|---|
| | moral philosophy | nonconsequentialism |
| | teleology | relativist perspective |
| | consequentialism | virtue ethics |
| | egoism | distributive justice |
| | hedonism | procedural justice |
| | enlightened egoists | interactional justice |
| | utilitarianism | Kohlberg's model of cognitive moral |
| | deontology | development |

## A Real-Life Situation*

Twenty-eight-year-old Elaine Hunt, who is married and has one child, has been with United Banc Corp. (UBC) for several years. During that time she has seen it grow from a relatively small to a medium-size company with domestic and international customers. Elaine's husband, Dennis, has been involved in the import-export business.

The situation that precipitated their current problem began six months ago. Elaine had just been promoted to senior financial manager, which put her in charge of ten branch-office loan managers, each of whom had five loan officers who reported to him or her. For the most part, the branch loan officers would go through the numbers of their loan people, as well as sign off on loans under $250,000. But recently this limit had been increased to $500,000. For any loan over this amount and up to $40 million Elaine had to sign off. For larger loans, a vice president would have to be involved.

Recently, Graphco, Inc. requested a $10 million loan, which Elaine had been hesitant to approve. Graphco was a subsidiary of a tobacco firm embroiled in litigation concerning the promotion of its products to children. When reviewing the numbers, Elaine could not find any glaring problems, yet she had decided against the loan even when Graphco had offered to pay an additional interest point. Some at UBC applauded her moral stance while others did not, arguing that it was not a good "financial business decision." The next prospective loan was for a Canadian company that was doing business in Cuba, exporting cigars. Elaine cited the U.S. policy against Cuba as the reason for not approving that loan. "The Helms-Burton Amendment gives us clear guidance as to what we shouldn't be doing with Cuba," she said to others in the company, even though the loan was to a Canadian firm. The third loan application she was unwilling to approve had come from Electrode International, which sought $50 million. The numbers had been marginal, but the sticking point for Elaine was Electrode's unusually high profits during the last two years. During dinner with Dennis, she had learned about a meeting in Zurich during which Electrode and others had allegedly fixed the prices on their products. Because only a handful of companies manufactured these particular products, the price increases were very successful. When Elaine suggested denying the loan on the basis of this information, she was overruled. At the same time, a company in Brazil was asking for an agricultural loan to harvest parts of the rain forest. The Brazilian company was willing to pay almost two points over the going rate for a $40 million loan. Because of her stand on environmental issues, Elaine rejected this application as well. The company obtained the loan from one of UBC's competitors.

Recently, Elaine's husband's decision making had fallen short of his superior's expectations. First, there was the problem of an American firm wanting to export nicotine and caffeine patches to Southeast Asia. With new research showing both these drugs to be more problematic than previously thought, the manufacturing firm had decided to attempt a rapid-penetration marketing strategy—that is, to price the products very low or at cost in order to gain market share and then over time slightly increase the margin. With two billion potential customers, a 1 cent markup could result in millions of dollars in profits. Dennis had rejected the deal, and the firm had gone to another company. One person in Dennis's division had said, "Do you realize that you had the perfect product—one that was low cost and both physically and psychologically addictive? You could have serviced that one account for years and would have had enough for early retirement. Are you nuts for turning it down?!"

Soon afterward an area financial bank manager wanted Elaine to sign off on a revolving loan for ABCO. ABCO's debt/equity ratio had increased significantly and did not conform to company regulations. However, Elaine was the one who had written the standards for UBC. Some in the company felt that Elaine was not quite up with the times. For example, several very good bank staff members had left in the past year because they found her regulations too provincial for the emerging global marketplace. As Elaine reviewed ABCO's credit report, she found many danger signals; however, the loan was relatively large, $30 million, and the company had been in a credit sales slump. As she questioned ABCO, Elaine learned that the loan was to develop a new business venture within the People's Republic of China, which rumor had it was also working with the Democratic People's Republic of Korea. The biotech venture was for fetal tissue research and harvesting. Recently, attention had focused on the economic benefits of such tissue in helping a host of ailments. Anticipated global market sales for such products were being estimated at $10 billion for the next decade. ABCO was also willing to go almost two points above the standard interest equation for such a revolving loan. Elaine realized that if she signed off on this sale, it would signal an end to her standards. However, if she did not and ABCO went to another company for the loan and paid off the debt, she would have made a gross error and everyone in the company would know it.

As she was wrestling with this problem, Dennis's commissions began to slip, putting a crimp in their cash-flow projections. If things did not turn around quickly for Dennis, they could lose their new home, get behind in other payments, and reduce the number of educational options for their child. Elaine had also had a frank discussion with senior management about her loan standards as well as her stand on tobacco, which had lost UBC precious income. The response was, "Elaine, we applaud your moral outrage about such products, but your morals are negatively impacting the bottom line. We can't have that all the time."

## Questions ■ Exercises

1. Discuss the advantages and disadvantages of each decision Elaine has made.
2. What are the ethical and legal considerations facing Elaine, Dennis, and UBC?
3. Discuss the moral philosophies that may be relevant to this situation.
4. Discuss the implications of each decision Elaine could make.

* This case is strictly hypothetical; any resemblance to real persons, companies, or situations is coincidental.

# 6

# Organizational Factors: Corporate Culture

## An Ethical Dilemma*

Dawn Prarie had been with PCA Health Care Hospitals for three years and had been promoted to marketing director in the Miami area. She had a staff of ten and a fairly healthy budget. Dawn's job was to attract more patients into the HMO while helping to keep costs down. At a meeting with Dawn, Nancy Belle, the vice president, had explained the ramifications of the Balanced Budget Act and how it was affecting all HMOs. "Being here in Miami does not help our division," she told Dawn. "Because of this Balanced Budget Act, we have been losing money on many of our elderly patients. For example, we used to receive $600 or more a month, per patient, from Medicare, but now our minimum reimbursement is just $367 a month! I need solutions, and that's where you come in. By the end of the month I want a list of things that will help us show a profit. Anything less than a positive balance sheet will be unacceptable."

It was obvious that Nancy was serious about cutting costs and increasing revenues within the elderly market. That's why Dawn had been promoted to marketing director. The first thing Dawn did after the meeting with Nancy was to fire four key people. She then gave their duties to six who were at lower salaries and put the hospital staff on notice that changes would be occurring at the hospital over the next several months. In about three weeks Dawn presented Nancy with an extensive list of ideas. It included these suggestions:

1. Trimming some prescription drug benefits
2. Reducing redundant tests for terminal patients
3. Hiring physician assistants to see patients but billing patients at the physician rate
4. Allowing physicians to buy shares in PCA, thus providing an incentive for bringing in more patients
5. Sterilizing and reusing cardiac catheters
6. Instituting a one-vendor policy on hospital products to gain quantity discounts
7. Prescreening "insurance" patients for probability of payment

Dawn's assistants felt that some of the hospital staff could be more aggressive in the marketing area. They urged using more promotional materials, offering incentives for physicians who suggested PCA or required their patients to be hospitalized, and prescreening potential clients into categories. "You see," said Ron, one of Dawn's staff, "we feel that there are four types of elderly patients. There are the healthy elderly, whose life expectancies are ten or more years. There are the fragile elderly, with life expectancies of two to seven years. Then there are the demented and dying elderly, who usually have one to three years. Finally, we have the high-cost/uninsured elderly. Patients who are designated healthy would get the most care, including mammograms, prostate-cancer screening, and cholesterol checks. Patients in the other categories would get less."

As she implemented some of the recommendations on Dawn's list, Nancy also launched an aggressive plan to destabilize the nurses' union. As a result, many nurses began a work slowdown and were filing internal petitions to upper management. Headquarters told Nancy to give the nurses and other hospital staff as much overtime as they wanted but not to hire anyone new. One floor manager suggested splitting up the staff into work teams, with built-in incentives for those who worked smarter and/or faster. Nancy approved the plan, and in three months productivity jumped 50 percent, with many of the hospital workers making more money. The downside for Nancy was an increase in worker-related accidents.

When Dawn toured the hospital around this time, she found that some of the most productive workers were using substandard procedures and poorly made products. One nurse said, "Yes, the surgical gloves are somewhat of a problem, but we were told that the quality met the minimum requirements and so we have to use them." Dawn brought this to Nancy's attention, whereupon Nancy drafted the following memo:

ATTENTION HOSPITAL STAFF

It has come to management's attention that minor injuries to staff and patients are on the rise. Please review the Occupational Safety and Health Administration guidelines, as well as the standard procedures handbook, to make sure you are in compliance. I also want to thank all those teams that have been keeping costs down. We have finally gone into the plus side as far as profitability. Hang on and we'll be able to stabilize the hospital to make it a better place to care for patients and to work.

At Nancy's latest meeting with Dawn, she told Dawn: "We've decided on your staff's segmentation strategy for the elderly market. We want you to develop a questionnaire to prescreen incoming HMO patients, as well as existing clients, into one of the four categories so we can tag their charts and alert the HMO physicians to the new protocols. Also, since the recommendations we've put into practice have worked so well, we've decided to use the rest of your suggestions. The implementation phase will start next month. I want you, Dawn, to be the lead person in developing a long-term strategy to break the unions in the hospital. Do whatever it takes. We just need to do more with less. I'm firm on this—so you're either on board or you're not. Which is it going to be?"

## Questions ■ Exercises

1. Discuss PCA Health Care Hospitals' corporate culture and its ethical implications.
2. What factors are affecting Dawn's options?
3. Discuss the issue of for-profit versus nonprofit health care facilities.
4. If you were Dawn, what information would you like to have to make your decisions?

* This case is strictly hypothetical; any resemblance to real persons, companies, or situations is coincidental.

Organizations are much more than structures in which we work. Although they are not alive, we attribute human characteristics to them. When times are good, we say the company is "well"; when times are not so good, we may try to "save" the company. Understandably, people have feelings toward the place that provides them with income and benefits; challenge, satisfaction, and self-esteem; and often lifelong friendships. In fact, excluding the time spent sleeping, we spend almost 50 percent of our lives in this second home with our second "family." It is important, then, to examine how the culture and structure of these organizations influence the ethical decisions made within them.

In the decision-making framework described in Chapter 4, we introduced the idea that organizational factors such as corporate culture and interpersonal relationships influence the ethical decision-making process. In this chapter, we take a closer look at corporate culture and the way a company's values and traditions can affect employees' ethical behavior. We also discuss the role of leadership in influencing ethical behavior within the organization. Next we describe two organizational structures and examine how they may influence ethical decisions. Then we consider the impact of groups within organizations. Finally, we examine the implications of organizational relationships for ethical decisions.

## The Role of Corporate Culture in Ethical Decision Making

Chapter 4 defined the term *corporate culture* as a set of values, beliefs, goals, norms, and ways of solving problems shared by the members (employees) of an organization. Corporate culture can be created by a founder and his or her values and expectations, as in the case of McDonald's. The fast-food giant's support of and reputation for quality, service, cleanliness, and value derive from founder Ray Kroc. In recent years, however, these values may not have been implemented as well, as McDonald's customer satisfaction scores are declining.[1] Corporate culture includes the behavioral patterns, concepts, values, ceremonies, and rituals that take place in the organization.[2] It gives the members of the organization meaning as well as the internal rules of behavior.[3] When these values, beliefs, customs, rules, and ceremonies are accepted, shared, and circulated throughout the organization, they represent its culture. All organizations, not just corporations, have some sort of culture, and thus we use the terms *organizational culture* and *corporate culture* interchangeably.

Although organizational culture is a broad and widely used concept, the term has a multitude of definitions, none of which has achieved universal acceptance. These range from highly specific to generically broad. For example, *culture* has been defined as "the way we do things around here,"[4] "the collective programming of the mind,"[5] and "the social fiber that holds the organization together."[6] Culture is also viewed as "the shared beliefs top managers in a company have about how they should manage themselves and other employees, and how they should conduct their business(es)."[7] Mutual of Omaha defines corporate culture as the "personality of the organization, the shared beliefs that determine how its people behave and solve business problems."[8] Mutual of Omaha executives believe that its corporate culture provides the foundation for the company's work and objectives, and the company has adopted a set of core values called "Values for Success" (see Table 6–1). The company believes

| TABLE 6-1 | Mutual of Omaha's "Values for Success" |
|---|---|

*Openness and Trust*—We encourage an open sharing of ideas and information, displaying a fundamental respect for each other as well as our cultural diversity.

*Teamwork (Win/Win)*—We work together to find solutions that carry positive results for others as well as ourselves, creating an environment that brings out the best in everyone.

*Accountability/Ownership*—We take ownership and accept accountability for achieving end results, and empower team members to do the same.

*Sense of Urgency*—We set priorities and handle all tasks and assignments in a timely manner.

*Honesty and Integrity*—We are honest and ethical with others, maintaining the highest standards of personal and professional conduct.

*Customer-focus*—We never lose sight of our customers, and constantly challenge ourselves to meet their requirements even better.

*Innovation and Risk*—We question "the old way of doing things" and take prudent risks that can lead to innovative performance and process improvements.

*Caring/Attentive (Be Here Now)*—We take time to clear our minds to focus on the present moment, listening to our teammates and customers, and caring enough to hear their concerns.

*Leadership*—We provide direction, purpose, support, encouragement, and recognition to achieve our vision, meet our objectives and our values.

*Personal and Professional Growth*—We challenge ourselves and look for ways to be even more effective as a team and as individuals.

Source: "Transforming Our Culture: The Values for Success," Mutual of Omaha, www.careerlink.org/emp/mut/corp.htm (accessed Feb. 19, 2003). Reprinted with permission.

that these values form the foundation for a corporate culture that will help the organization realize its vision and achieve its goals.

A company's history and unwritten rules are a part of its culture. Thus, for many years IBM salespeople adhered to a series of unwritten standards for dealing with clients. The history or stories passed down from generation to generation within an organization are like the traditions that are propagated within society. Henry Ford, the founder of Ford Motor Co., left a legacy that emphasized the importance of the individual employee and the natural environment. Just as Henry Ford pioneered the then-unheard-of high wage of $5 a day in the early years of the twentieth century, current chairman William Clay Ford Jr. continues to affirm that employees represent the only sustainable advantage of a company. William Ford has maintained his grandfather's legacy by taking a leadership role in improving vehicle fuel efficiency while reducing emissions. He has pushed the company to conserve energy at facilities around the world and to modernize the firm's historic Rouge manufacturing plant in Dearborn, Michigan, into "a global model of lean and sustainable manufacturing."[9]

Some cultures are so strong that to outsiders they come to represent the character of the entire organization. For example, Levi Strauss, Ben & Jerry's Homemade (the ice cream company), and Hershey Foods are widely perceived as casual organizations with strong ethical cultures, whereas Lockheed Martin, Procter & Gamble, and Texas Instruments are perceived as more formal, ethical ones. The culture of an organization may be explicitly articulated or left unspoken.

Explicit statements of values, beliefs, and customs usually come from upper management. Memos, written codes of conduct, handbooks, manuals, forms, and ceremonies are all formal expressions of an organization's culture. Many of these statements can be found on company Web sites, like Mutual of Omaha's values for success.

Corporate culture is often expressed informally—for example, through comments, both direct and indirect, that communicate the wishes of management. In some companies, shared values are expressed through informal dress codes, working late, and participation in extracurricular activities. Corporate culture can even be expressed through gestures, looks, labels, promotions, and legends (or the lack of these). For example, production workers at some companies have been asked to wear stickers on their hardhats to promote team building and group cohesiveness. On one offshore oil rig, workers' hardhats sport the sticker "Start to understand me," with a pattern of colored dots that communicate to coworkers something of the personality under the hat.[10] This sensitivity training is intended to help workers understand one another and to create trust, respect, and understanding among employees. Even such subtle expressions of organizational values, such as the use of slogans and stickers in the workplace, indicate behavior expectations to employees.

### Ethical Framework and Audit for Corporate Culture

Corporate culture has been conceptualized in many ways. Authors N. K. Sethia and M. A. Von Glinow have proposed two basic dimensions to describe an organization's culture: concern for people—the organization's efforts to care for its employees' well-being; and concern for performance—the organization's efforts to focus on output and employee productivity. A two-by-two matrix represents the four general types of organizational cultures (see Figure 6–1).[11]

FIGURE 6–1 **A Framework of Organizational Culture Typologies**

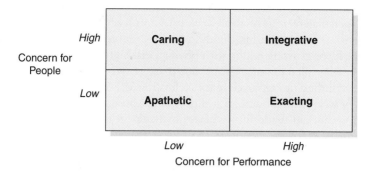

Source: *Gaining Control of the Corporate Culture,* by N. K. Sethia and M. A. von Glinow, 1985, Jossey-Bass, Inc. This material is used by permission of John Wiley & Sons, Inc.

As Figure 6–1 shows, the four organizational cultures can be classified as apathetic, caring, exacting, and integrative. The apathetic culture shows minimal concern for either people or performance. In this culture, individuals focus on their own self-interests. Apathetic tendencies can occur in almost any organization. For example, IBM announced a switch from defined-benefits pensions to cash-balance plans, which meant pension cuts of up to 50 percent for older employees. After a massive uproar from angry employees and a letter from ten members of Congress urging the Internal Revenue Service to investigate the company, IBM officials agreed to allow thirty-five thousand employees to choose either plan. However, there were still significant losses for fifteen thousand employees. In all, 325 companies have adopted cash-balance plans, but more than 75 percent of them have allowed senior workers to keep their old plan.[12] Simple gestures of gratitude, such as anniversary watches, rings, dinners, or birthday cards for family members, are being dropped. Many companies view long-serving employees as deadwood and do not take into account past performance. This attitude demonstrates the companies' apathetic culture.

The caring culture exhibits high concern for people but minimal concern for performance issues. From an ethical standpoint, the caring culture seems to be very appealing. Southwest Airlines, for example, has a long-standing reputation of concern for its employees. CEO Herb Kelleher is the purveyor of wit, wisdom, and continuity in Southwest's culture. Employees "love the company" because they believe it cares for and is concerned about them. Employee loyalty and commitment at Southwest are very high. Kelleher has been known to go into the cargo hold of a plane attired in a dress and feather boa to assist employees with baggage. Southwest feels that if employees are well cared for, then customers will be taken care of and the competition will be surpassed. Customers must indeed feel that they are being taken care of because Southwest received the fewest customer complaints for twelve years in a row, as reported in the Department of Transportation's *Air Travel Consumer Report.*[13]

In contrast, the exacting culture shows little concern for people but a high concern for performance; it focuses on the interests of the organization. United Parcel Service

(UPS) has always been very exacting. It knows precisely how many workers it needs to deliver its ten million packages a day. To combat the uncaring, unsympathetic attitude of many of its managers, UPS developed a community service program for its upper managers. The four-week program has the managers work with nonprofit organizations involved in building houses, mentoring young men, boxing food for the needy, or assisting adults with physical disabilities. After assisting disabled residents at a center called Orange Grove, one manager vowed to be more sympathetic to and understanding of employee requests for time off to handle family matters. Another manager who helped build an addition on a house for a family of seven indicated that the program had made him a better manager, forcing him to take a harder look at the struggles of people in the workplace. UPS has invested more than $500,000 a year in sending managers through the program. More than twelve hundred have participated since its inception.[14]

The integrative culture combines high concern for people and for performance. An organization becomes integrative when superiors recognize that employees are more than interchangeable parts—that employees have an ineffable quality that helps the firm meet its performance criteria. Many companies—among them MasterCard International and Visa International—have such cultures. That does not mean, however, that they are impervious to ethical problems. For example, Visa and MasterCard may have to pay out $500 million to settle a lawsuit over foreign-exchange conversion fees. Customers accused the two credit card firms of failing to adequately disclose these fees and contended that they didn't find out they had been paying the fees until months or even years after making their overseas purchases.[15]

Companies can classify their corporate culture and identify its specific values, norms, beliefs, and customs by conducting a cultural audit. A cultural audit is an assessment of the organization's values. It is usually conducted by outside consultants but may be performed internally as well. Table 6–2 illustrates some of the issues that an ethics audit of a corporate culture should address. These issues can help identify a corporate culture that creates ethical conflict.

## Ethics As a Component of Corporate Culture

As indicated in the framework presented in Chapter 4, corporate culture is a significant factor in ethical decision making. If a firm's culture encourages or rewards unethical behavior, its employees may well act unethically. If the culture dictates hiring people who have specific, similar values, and if those values are perceived as unethical by society, society will view the organization and its members as unethical. Such a pattern often occurs in certain areas of marketing. For instance, salespeople may be seen as unethical because they sometimes use aggressive selling tactics to get customers to buy things they do not need or want. If a company's primary objective is to make as much profit as possible, through whatever means, its culture may foster behavior that conflicts with stakeholders' ethical values. For example, twelve investment banking firms, including Citigroup and Salomon Smith Barney, have paid more than $1.4 billion to settle charges of conflicts of interest between their investment banking and stock analysis services. According to the charges, analysts at these firms inflated their assessment of stocks for which their companies also served as investment bankers in order to increase sales of those stocks. Investors who bought the stocks based on the

| TABLE 6-2 | Organizational Culture Ethics Audit |
| --- | --- |

Answer YES or NO for each of the following questions:*

| | | | |
| --- | --- | --- | --- |
| YES | NO | 1. | Has the founder or top management of the company left an ethical legacy to the organization? |
| YES | NO | 2. | Does the company have methods for detecting ethical concerns within the organization and outside it? |
| YES | NO | 3. | Is there a shared value system and understanding of what constitutes appropriate behavior within the organization? |
| YES | NO | 4. | Are stories and myths embedded in daily conversations about appropriate ethical conduct when confronting ethical situations? |
| YES | NO | 5. | Are codes of ethics or ethical policies communicated to employees? |
| YES | NO | 6. | Are there ethical rules or procedures in training manuals or other company publications? |
| YES | NO | 7. | Are there penalties, that are publicly discussed, for ethical transgressions? |
| YES | NO | 8. | Are there rewards for good ethical decisions even if they don't always result in a profit? |
| YES | NO | 9. | Does the company recognize the importance of creating a culture that is concerned about people and their self-development as members of the business? |
| YES | NO | 10. | Does the company have a value system of fair play and honesty toward customers? |
| YES | NO | 11. | Do employees treat each other with respect, honesty, and fairness? |
| YES | NO | 12. | Do employees spend their time working in a cohesive way on what is valued by the organization? |
| YES | NO | 13. | Are there ethically based beliefs and values about how to succeed in the company? |
| YES | NO | 14. | Are there heroes or stars in the organization who communicate a common understanding about what positive ethical values are important? |
| YES | NO | 15. | Are there day-to-day rituals or behavior patterns that create direction and prevent confusion or mixed signals on ethics matters? |
| YES | NO | 16. | Is the firm more focused on the long run than on the short run? |
| YES | NO | 17. | Are employees satisfied or happy, and is employee turnover low? |
| YES | NO | 18. | Do the dress, speech, and physical work setting prevent an environment of fragmentation or inconsistency about what is right? |
| YES | NO | 19. | Are emotional outbursts about role conflict and ambiguity very rare? |
| YES | NO | 20. | Has discrimination and/or sexual harassment been eliminated? |
| YES | NO | 21. | Is there an absence of open hostility and severe conflict? |
| YES | NO | 22. | Do people act on the job in a way that is consistent with what they say is ethical? |
| YES | NO | 23. | Is the firm more externally focused on customers, the environment, and the welfare of society than on its own profits? |

| | | | |
|---|---|---|---|
| **TABLE 6–2** | | **Organizational Culture Ethics Audit (continued)** | |

| | | | |
|---|---|---|---|
| YES | NO | 24. | Is there open communication between superiors and subordinates on ethical dilemmas? |
| YES | NO | 25. | Have employees ever received advice on how to improve ethical behavior or been disciplined for committing unethical acts? |

\* Add the number of yes answers. The greater the number of yes answers, the less ethical conflict is likely in your organization.

analysts' recommendations lost billions of dollars.[16] Though these investors were key stakeholders in these firms, their interests may have been ignored by these firms in their efforts to boost profits.

On the other hand, if the organization values ethical behaviors it will reward them. At Starbucks, for example, desired behaviors and goals are clearly articulated by management through the firm's mission statement and guiding principles. The coffee retailer states that its mission is both to "establish Starbucks as the premier purveyor of the finest coffee in the world while maintaining our uncompromising principles while we grow" and to commit "to a role of environmental leadership in all facets of our business."[17] This strong corporate culture may help explain the company's reputation for corporate citizenship, which is reflected in its position on such lists as *Fortune*'s "America's Most Admired Companies" and *Business Ethics*' "100 Best Corporate Citizens."[18]

An organization's failure to monitor or manage its culture may foster questionable behavior. At Credit Suisse First Boston (CSFB), for example, a manager allegedly directed some of his employees to delete certain documents that may have related to a class-action lawsuit. The suit, filed against fifty-five securities firms as well as three hundred companies they represented, charged that the securities firms, including CSFB, manipulated the companies' stock prices, causing investors to overpay for the firms' stocks. The officer faces federal obstruction-of-justice charges.[19]

Management's sense of the organization's culture may be quite different from the values and ethical beliefs that are actually guiding the firm's employees. Ethical issues may arise because of conflicts between the cultural values perceived by management and those actually at work in the organization. For example, managers may believe that the culture encourages respect for peers and subordinates. On the basis of the rewards or sanctions associated with various behaviors, however, the firm's employees may believe that the company encourages competition among organizational members. A competitive orientation may result in a less ethical corporate culture. On the other hand, employees appreciate working in an environment that is designed to enhance workplace experiences through goals that encompass more than just maximizing profits.[20] Thus, it is very important for top managers both to determine what the organization's culture is and to monitor its values, traditions, and beliefs to ensure that they represent the desired culture. However, the rewards and punishments imposed by an organization need to be consistent with the actual corporate culture. As two business ethics experts have observed, "Employees will value and use as guidelines those activities for which they will be rewarded. When a behavior that is rewarded comes into conflict with an unstated and unmonitored ethical value, usually the rewarded behavior wins out."[21]

## The Role of Leadership in a Corporate Culture

Top managers provide a blueprint for what a firm's corporate culture should be.[22] If these leaders fail to express desired behaviors and goals, a corporate culture will evolve on its own but will still reflect the goals and values of the company. **Leadership,** the ability or authority to guide and direct others toward achievement of a goal, has a significant impact on ethical decision making because leaders have the power to motivate others and enforce the organization's rules and policies as well as their own viewpoints. Leaders are key to influencing an organization's corporate culture and ethical posture. However, one poll found that less than half (47 percent) of employees in large (twenty-five hundred employees or more) organizations think their senior leadership is highly ethical.[23] Figure 6–2 shows the survey results.

Although we often think of CEOs and other top managers as the most important leaders in an organization, the corporate governance reforms discussed in Chapter 4 make it clear that a firm's board of directors is also an important leadership component. Indeed, directors have a legal obligation to manage companies "for the best interests of the corporation." To determine what is in the best interest of the firm, directors can consider the effects that a decision may have not only on shareholders

| FIGURE 6–2 | **What Employees in Small, Medium, and Large Organizations Think About the Ethics of Their Organizations** |

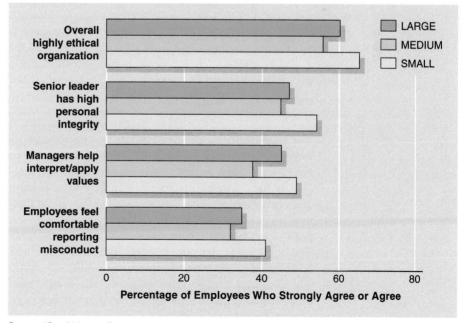

Source: "Small Virtues: Entrepreneurs Are More Ethical." Reprinted from *Business Week,* May 8, 2000 by special permission. Copyright © 2000 by the McGraw-Hill Companies, Inc.

and employees, but also on other important stakeholders.[24] Therefore, when we discuss leadership, we include the corporate directors as well as top executives.

In the long run, if stakeholders are not reasonably satisfied with a company's leader, he or she will not retain a leadership position. A leader must not only have his or her followers' respect but must also provide a standard of ethical conduct to them. Sunbeam, for example, fired CEO Al Dunlap after the Securities and Exchange Commission (SEC) initiated an investigation into whether the firm had fraudulently manipulated its financial reports. Dunlap, nicknamed "Chainsaw Al" for his track record of aggressive downsizing, wrote a book entitled *Mean Business,* which took a somewhat questionable approach to achieving organizational profitability.[25] He ultimately paid $500,000 to settle the SEC's charges that he had defrauded investors by inflating the small-appliance maker's sales. He also paid $15 million to shareholders who filed a class-action suit on similar charges.[26]

## Leadership Styles Influence Ethical Decisions

Leadership styles influence many aspects of organizational behavior, including employees' acceptance of and adherence to organizational norms and values. Styles that focus on building strong organizational values among employees contribute to shared standards of conduct. They also influence the organization's transmittal and monitoring of values, norms, and codes of ethics.[27] In short, the leadership style of an organization influences how its employees act. For example, the management philosophy of Mike Armstrong, former CEO of AT&T, is characterized by the observations of its labs chief David Nagel: "Most bosses hate conflict. Mike is delighted when he sees us getting at each other." Armstrong has been characterized as scary, demanding, a taskmaster, and a maniac—in an affectionate way. The fast-paced, intensely competitive telecommunications industry requires a "nontraditional" leadership style to achieve success.[28] Studying a firm's leadership styles and attitudes can also help pinpoint where future ethical issues may arise. Even for actions that may be against the law, employees often look to their organizational leaders to determine how to resolve the issue.

Six leadership styles that are based on emotional intelligence—the ability to manage ourselves and our relationships effectively—have been identified by Daniel Goleman.

1. The coercive leader demands instantaneous obedience and focuses on achievement, initiative, and self-control. Although this style can be very effective during times of crisis or during a turnaround, it otherwise creates a negative climate for organizational performance.
2. The authoritative leader—considered to be one of the most effective styles—inspires employees to follow a vision, facilitates change, and creates a strongly positive performance climate.
3. The affiliative leader values people, their emotions, and their needs and relies on friendship and trust to promote flexibility, innovation, and risk taking.
4. The democratic leader relies on participation and teamwork to reach collaborative decisions. This style focuses on communication and creates a positive climate for achieving results.

5. The pacesetting leader can create a negative climate because of the high standards he or she sets. This style works best for attaining quick results from highly motivated individuals who value achievement and take the initiative.
6. The coaching leader builds a positive climate by developing skills to foster long-term success, delegates responsibility, and is skillful in issuing challenging assignments.

The most successful leaders do not rely on one style but alter their techniques based on the characteristics of the situation. Different styles can be effective in developing an ethical climate depending on the leader's assessment of risks and desire to achieve a positive climate for organizational performance.[29]

Another way to consider leadership styles is to classify them as transactional or transformational. **Transactional leaders** attempt to create employee satisfaction through negotiating, or "bartering," for desired behaviors or levels of performance. **Transformational leaders** strive to raise employees' level of commitment and to foster trust and motivation.[30] Both transformational and transactional leaders can positively influence the organizational culture.

Transformational leaders communicate a sense of mission, stimulate new ways of thinking, and enhance as well as generate new learning experiences. They consider employee needs and aspirations in conjunction with organizational needs. They also build commitment and respect for values that provide agreement on how to deal with ethical issues. Thus, transformational leaders strive to promote activities and behavior through a shared vision and common learning experience. As a result, they have a stronger influence on coworker support for ethical decisions and building an ethical culture than do transactional leaders. Transformational ethical leadership is best suited for organizations that have higher levels of ethical commitment among employees and strong stakeholder support for an ethical climate. A number of industry trade associations, including the American Institute of Certified Public Accountants, Defense Industry Initiative on Business Ethics and Conduct, Ethics Officer Association, and Mortgage Bankers Association of America, are helping companies provide transformational leadership.[31]

In contrast, transactional leaders focus on ensuring that required conduct and procedures are implemented. Their negotiations to achieve desired outcomes result in a dynamic relationship with subordinates in which reactions, conflict, and crisis influence the relationship more than ethical concerns. Transactional leaders produce employees who achieve a negotiated level of performance, including compliance with ethical and legal standards. As long as employees and leaders both find this exchange mutually rewarding, the relationship is likely to be successful. However, transactional leadership is best suited for rapidly changing situations, including those that require responses to ethical problems or issues. When Michael Capellas took over as CEO and chairman of WorldCom, he used transactional leadership to change the firm's culture and ethical conduct after an accounting scandal had forced the company into bankruptcy proceedings. Capellas sought to restore WorldCom's credibility in the marketplace by bringing in a new board of directors, creating a corporate ethics office, enhancing the code of ethics, and launching new employee financial-reporting and ethics-training initiatives.[32]

## The Power of Leaders Influences Ethical Decisions

A second dimension of leadership is power and influence. Power refers to the influence that leaders and managers have over the behavior and decisions of subordinates. An individual has power over others when his or her presence causes them to behave differently. Exerting power is one way to influence the ethical decision-making framework we described in Chapter 4 (especially significant others and opportunity).

The status and power of leaders is directly related to the amount of pressure they can exert on employees to conform to their expectations. A superior in an authority position can put strong pressure on employees to comply, even when their personal ethical values conflict with the superior's wishes. For example, a manager might say to a subordinate, "I want the confidential data about our competitor's sales on my desk by Monday morning, and I don't care how you get it." A subordinate who values his or her job or who does not realize the ethical questions involved may feel pressure to do something unethical to obtain the data.

There are five power bases from which one person may influence another: (1) reward power, (2) coercive power, (3) legitimate power, (4) expert power, and (5) referent power.[33] These five bases of power can be used to motivate individuals either ethically or unethically.

*Reward Power* **Reward power** refers to a person's ability to influence the behavior of others by offering them something desirable. Typical rewards might be money, status, or promotion. Consider, for example, a retail salesperson who has two watches (a Timex and a Casio) for sale. Let us assume that the Timex is of higher quality than the Casio but is priced about the same. In the absence of any form of reward power, the salesperson would logically attempt to sell the Timex watch. However, if Casio gave him an extra 10 percent commission, he would probably focus his efforts on selling the Casio watch. This "carrot dangling" has been shown to be very effective in getting people to change their behavior in the long run. In the short run, however, it is not as effective as coercive power.

*Coercive Power* **Coercive power** is essentially the opposite of reward power. Instead of rewarding a person for doing something, coercive power penalizes actions or behavior. As an example, suppose a valuable client asks an industrial salesperson for a bribe and insinuates that he will take his business elsewhere if his demands are not met. Although the salesperson believes bribery is unethical, she has been told by her boss that she must keep the client happy or lose her chance at promotion. The boss is imposing a negative sanction if certain actions are not performed.

Coercive power relies on fear to change behavior. For this reason, it has been found to be more effective in changing behavior in the short run than in the long run. Coercion is often employed in situations where there is an extreme imbalance in power. However, people who are continually subjected to coercion may seek a counterbalance by aligning themselves with other, more powerful persons or by simply leaving the organization. In firms that use coercive power, relationships usually break down in the long run. Power is an ethical issue not only for individuals but also for work groups that establish policy for large corporations.

*Legitimate Power* **Legitimate power** stems from the belief that a certain person has the right to exert influence and that certain others have an obligation to accept it. The titles and positions of authority that organizations bestow on individuals appeal to this traditional view of power. Many people readily acquiesce to those who wield legitimate power, sometimes committing acts that are contrary to their beliefs and values.

Such staunch loyalty to authority figures can also be seen in corporations that have strong charismatic leaders and centralized structures. In business, if a superior tells an employee to increase sales "no matter what it takes" and that employee has a strong affiliation to legitimate power, the employee may try anything to fulfill that order.

*Expert Power* **Expert power** is derived from a person's knowledge (or the perception that the person possesses knowledge). Expert power usually stems from a superior's credibility with subordinates. Credibility, and thus expert power, is positively related to the number of years a person has worked in a firm or industry, the person's education, or the honors he or she has received for performance. Expert power can also be conferred on a person by others who perceive him or her to be an expert on a specific topic. A relatively low-level secretary may have expert power because he or she knows specific details about how the business operates.

Expert power may cause ethical problems when it is used to manipulate others or to gain an unfair advantage. Physicians, lawyers, or consultants can take unfair advantage of unknowing clients, for example. Accounting firms may gain extra income by ignoring concerns about the accuracy of financial data they are provided in an audit.

*Referent Power* **Referent power** may exist when one person perceives that his or her goals or objectives are similar to another's. The second person may attempt to influence the first to take actions that will lead both to achieve their objectives. Because they share the same objective, the person influenced by the other will perceive the other's use of referent power as beneficial. For this power relationship to be effective, however, some sort of empathy must exist between the individuals. Identification with others helps to boost the decision maker's confidence when making a decision, thus increasing his or her referent power.

Consider the following situation: Lisa Jones, a manager in the accounting department of a manufacturing firm, has asked Michael Wong, a salesperson, to speed up the delivery of sales contracts, which usually take about one month to process after a deal is reached. Michael protests that he is not to blame for the slow process. Rather than threaten to slow delivery of Michael's commission checks (coercive power), Lisa makes use of referent power. She invites Michael to lunch, and they discuss some of their work concerns, including the problem of slow-moving documentation. They agree that if document processing cannot be speeded up, both will be hurt. Lisa then suggests that Michael start faxing contracts instead of mailing them. He agrees to give it a try, and within several weeks the contracts are moving faster. Lisa's job is made easier, and Michael gets his commission checks a little sooner.

The five bases of power are not mutually exclusive. People typically use several power bases to effect change in others. Although power in itself is neither ethical nor unethical, its use can raise ethical issues. Sometimes a leader uses power to manipulate a situation or a person's values in a way that creates a conflict with the person's value structure. For example, a manager who forces an employee to choose between staying home with his sick child and keeping his job is using coercive power, which creates a direct conflict with the employee's values.

## Motivating Ethical Behavior

A leader's ability to motivate subordinates plays a key role in maintaining an ethical organization. **Motivation** is a force within the individual that focuses his or her behavior toward achieving a goal. To create motivation, an organization offers incentives to encourage employees to work toward organizational objectives. Understanding motivation is important to the effective management of people, and it also helps to explain their ethical behavior. For example, a person who aspires to higher positions in an organization may sabotage a coworker's project so as to make that person look bad. This unethical behavior is directly related to the first employee's ambition (motivation) to rise in the organization.

As businesspeople move into middle management and beyond, higher-order needs (social, esteem, and recognition) tend to become more important than lower-order needs (salary, safety, and job security).[34] Research has shown that an individual's career stage, age, organization size, and geographic location affect the relative priority he or she gives to satisfying respect, self-esteem, and basic physiological needs.

From an ethics perspective, needs or goals may change as a person progresses through the ranks of the company. This shift may cause or help solve problems depending on that person's current ethical status relative to the company or society. For example, junior executives might inflate purchase or sales orders, overbill time worked on projects, or accept cash gratuities if they are worried about providing for their families' basic physical necessities. As they continue up the ladder and are able to fulfill these needs, such concerns may become less important. Consequently, these managers may go back to obeying company policy or culture and be more concerned with internal recognition and achievement than their families' physical needs.

An individual's hierarchy of needs may influence his or her motivation and ethical behavior. After basic needs such as food, working conditions (existence needs), and survival are satisfied, relatedness needs and growth needs become important. **Relatedness needs** are satisfied by social and interpersonal relationships, and **growth needs** are satisfied by creative or productive activities.[35] Consider what happens when a new employee, Jill Taylor, joins a company. At first Jill is concerned about working conditions, pay, and security (existence needs). After some time on the job, she feels she has satisfied these needs and begins to focus on developing good interpersonal relations with coworkers. When these relatedness needs have been satisfied, Jill wants to advance to a more challenging job. However, she learns that a higher-level job would require her to travel a lot. She greatly values her family life and feels that travel and nights away from home would not be good for her. She decides, therefore, not to work toward a promotion (resulting in a "need frustration"). Instead, she decides to focus on furthering good interpersonal relations with her coworkers. This is termed "frustration-regression" because, to reduce her anxiety, Jill is now focusing on an area (interpersonal relations) not related to her main problem: the need for a more challenging job. In this example, Jill's need for promotion has been modified by her values. To feel productive, she attempts to fill her needs by going back to an earlier stage in her hierarchy of needs. Whatever her present job is, Jill would continue to emphasize high performance in it. But this regression creates frustration that may lead Jill to seek other employment.

Examining the role motivation plays in ethics offers a way to relate business ethics to the broader social context in which workers live and the deeper moral assumptions on which society depends. Workers are individuals, and they will be motivated by a variety of personal interests. While we keep emphasizing that managers are positioned to exert pressure and force individuals' compliance on ethically related issues, we also acknowledge that an individual's personal ethics and needs will significantly affect his or her ethical decisions.

## Organizational Structure and Business Ethics

An organization's structure is important to the study of business ethics because the various roles and job descriptions that comprise that structure may create opportunities for unethical behavior.[36] The structure of organizations can be described in many ways. For simplicity's sake, we will discuss two broad categories of organizational structures—centralized and decentralized. Note that these are not mutually exclusive structures; in the real world, organizational structures exist on a continuum. Table 6–3 compares some strengths and weaknesses of centralized and decentralized structures.

In a **centralized organization,** decision-making authority is concentrated in the hands of top-level managers, and little authority is delegated to lower levels. Responsibility, both internal and external, rests with top-level managers. This structure is especially suited for organizations that make high-risk decisions and whose lower-level managers are not highly skilled in decision making. It is also suitable for organizations in which production processes are routine and efficiency is of primary importance.

**TABLE 6–3** | **Structural Comparison of Organizational Types**

| CHARACTERISTIC | EMPHASIS | |
| --- | --- | --- |
| | Decentralized | Centralized |
| Hierarchy of authority | Decentralized | Centralized |
| Flexibility | High | Low |
| Adaptability | High | Low |
| Problem recognition | High | Low |
| Implementation | Low | High |
| Dealing with changes in environmental complexity | Good | Poor |
| Rules and procedures | Few and informal | Many and formal |
| Division of labor | Ambiguous | Clear-cut |
| Span of control | Few employees | Many employees |
| Use of managerial techniques | Minimal | Extensive |
| Coordination and control | Informal and personal | Formal and impersonal |

These organizations are usually extremely bureaucratic, and the division of labor is typically very well defined. Each worker knows his or her job and what is specifically expected, and each has a clear understanding of how to carry out assigned tasks. Centralized organizations stress formal rules, policies, and procedures, backed up with elaborate control systems. Their codes of ethics may specify the techniques to be used for decision making. General Motors, the Internal Revenue Service, and the U.S. Army are examples of centralized organizations.

Because of their top-down approach and the distance between employee and decision maker, centralized organizational structures can lead to unethical acts. If the centralized organization is very bureaucratic, some employees may behave according to "the letter of the law" rather than the spirit. For example, a centralized organization can have a policy about bribes that does not include wording about donating to a client's favorite charity before or after a sale. Such donations or gifts can, in some cases, be construed as a tacit bribe because the employee buyer could be swayed by the donation, or gift, to act in a less than favorable way or not to act in the best interests of his or her firm.

Other ethical concerns may arise in centralized structures because they typically have very little upward communication. Top-level managers may not be aware of problems and unethical activity. Some companies' use of sweatshop labor may be one manifestation of this lack of upward communication. Sweatshops produce products such as garments by employing laborers, sometimes forced immigrant labor, who often work twelve- to sixteen-hour shifts for little or no pay. Many illegal immigrants in Europe become indentured slaves or earn little more than the food they eat. By outsourcing production to such sweatshops, small and mid-size suppliers are able to offer products to retailers that beat or match the lowest global market prices. Many of these products end up in leading retailers' stores because their suppliers' top managers claim they were not aware of how their products were made.[37]

Another ethical issue that may arise in centralized organizations is blame-shifting, or "scapegoating." People may try to transfer blame for their actions to others who are not responsible. The specialization and significant division of labor in centralized organizations can also create ethical problems. Employees may not understand how their actions can affect the overall organization because they work on one piece of a much larger puzzle. This lack of connectedness can lead employees to engage in unethical behavior because they fail to understand the overall ramifications of their behavior.

In a **decentralized organization,** decision-making authority is delegated as far down the chain of command as possible. Such organizations have relatively few formal rules, and coordination and control are usually informal and personal. They focus instead on increasing the flow of information. As a result, one of the main strengths of decentralized organizations is their adaptability and early recognition of external change. With greater flexibility, managers can react quickly to changes in their ethical environment. A parallel weakness of decentralized organizations is the difficulty they have in responding quickly to changes in policy and procedures established by top management. In addition, independent profit centers within a decentralized organization may deviate from organizational objectives. Other decentralized firms may look no further than the local community for their ethical standards. For example, if a firm that produces toxic wastes leaves decisions on disposal to lower-level operating units, the managers of those units may feel that they have solved their waste-disposal

| TABLE 6–4 | **Examples of Centralized and Decentralized Corporate Cultures** |

| COMPANY | ORGANIZATIONAL CULTURE | CHARACTERIZED BY |
|---|---|---|
| Nike | Decentralized | Creativity, freedom, informality |
| Southwest Airlines | Decentralized | Fun, teamwork orientation, loyalty |
| General Motors | Centralized | Unions, adherence to task assignments, structured |
| Microsoft | Decentralized | Creative, investigative, fast-paced |
| Procter & Gamble | Centralized | Experienced, dependable, a rich history and tradition of products, powerful |

problem as long as they find a way to dump wastes outside their immediate community. Table 6–4 gives examples of centralized versus decentralized organizations and describes their corporate culture.

Due to the strict formalization and implementation of ethics policies and procedures in centralized organizations, they tend to be more ethical in their practices than decentralized organizations. Centralized organizations may also exert more influence on their employees because they have a central core of policies and codes of ethical conduct. Decentralized organizations give employees extensive decision-making autonomy because management empowers the employees. However, it is also true that decentralized organizations may be able to avoid ethical dilemmas by tailoring their decisions to the specific situations, laws, and values of a particular community. If widely shared values are in place in decentralized organizations, there may be no need for excessive compliance programs. However, different units in the company may evolve diverse value systems and approaches to ethical decision making. For example, a high-tech defense firm like Lockheed Martin, which employs more than two hundred thousand people, might have to cope with many different decisions on the same ethical issue if it did not have a centralized ethics program.

Unethical behavior is possible in either centralized or decentralized structures when specific corporate cultures permit or encourage workers to deviate from accepted standards or ignore corporate legal and ethical responsibilities. Centralized firms may have a more difficult time uprooting unethical activity than decentralized organizations. The latter may have a more fluid history, in which changes affect only a small portion of the company. Often, when a centralized firm uncovers unethical activity and it appears to be pervasive, the leadership is removed so the old unethical culture can be uprooted and replaced it with a more ethical one. For example, Mitsubishi Motors proposed sweeping management changes after it was discovered that a cover-up of auto defects had been going on for at least twenty years.[38]

Some centralized organizations are seeking to restructure to become more decentralized, flexible, and adaptive to the needs of employees and customers. For example, Coco-Cola's chairman Doug Daft announced plans to meet with top management to discuss the company's new decentralized corporate structure and more caring posture. According to a company spokesman, "we're moving away from globalization to 'multi-localization.'"[39] Decentralized decisions about ethics and social responsibility allow regional or local operators to set policy and establish conduct requirements.

## Group Dimensions of Organizational Structure and Culture

When discussing corporate culture, we tend to focus on the organization as a whole. But corporate values, beliefs, patterns, and rules are often expressed through smaller groups within the organization. Moreover, individual groups within organizations often adopt their own rules and values. We will therefore look next at several types of groups as well as the conflicts that can occur between the norms of these groups and individuals.

### Types of Groups

Two main categories of groups affect ethical behavior in business. A **formal group** is defined as an assembly of individuals that has an organized structure accepted explicitly by the group. An **informal group** is defined as two or more individuals with a common interest but without an explicit organizational structure.

*Formal Groups* Formal groups can be divided into committees and work groups and teams.

#### Committees

A committee is a formal group of individuals assigned to a specific task. Often a single manager could not complete the task, or management may believe that a committee can better represent different constituencies and improve the coordination and implementation of decisions. Committees may meet regularly to review performance, develop plans, or make decisions about personnel. Most formal committees in organizations operate on an ongoing basis, but their membership may change over time. A committee is an excellent example of a situation in which coworkers and significant others within the organization can influence ethical decisions. Committee decisions are to some extent legitimized because of agreement or majority rule. In this respect, minority views on issues such as ethics can be pushed aside through the majority's authority. Committees bring diverse personal moral values into the ethical decision-making process, which may expand the number of alternatives considered. The main disadvantage of committees is that they typically take longer to reach a decision than an individual would. Committee decisions are also generally more conservative than those made by individuals and may be based on unnecessary compromise rather than on identifying the best alternative. Also inherent in the committee structure is a lack of individual responsibility. Because of the diverse composition of the group, members may not be committed or willing to assume responsibility for the "group" decision.

Although many organizations have financial, diversity, personnel, or social responsibility committees, only a very few organizations have committees that are devoted exclusively to ethics. An ethics committee might raise ethical concerns, resolve ethical dilemmas in the organization, and create or update the company's code of ethics. Motorola, for example, maintains a Business Ethics Compliance Committee, which interprets, classifies, communicates, and enforces the company's code and ethics initiatives. An ethics committee can gather information on functional areas of the business and examine manufacturing practices, personnel policies, dealings with suppliers, financial reporting, and sales techniques to find out whether the company's practices are ethical.

Though much of a corporation's culture operates informally, an ethics committee would be a highly formalized approach for dealing with ethical issues.

Ethics committees can be misused if they are established for the purpose of legitimizing management's ethical standards on some issue. For example, ethics committees may be quickly assembled for political purposes, that is, to make a symbolic decision on some event that has occurred within the company. If the CEO or manager in charge selects committee members who will produce a predetermined outcome, the ethics committee may not help the organization resolve its ethical issues in the long run.

Ethics committee members may also fail to understand their role or function. If they attempt to apply their own personal ethics to complex business issues, resolving ethical issues may be difficult. Because most people's personal ethical perspectives differ, the committee may experience conflict. Even if the committee members reach a consensus, they may enforce their personal beliefs rather than the organization's standards on certain ethical issues.

Ethics committees should be organized around professional, business-related issues that occur internally. In general, the ethics committee should formulate policy, develop ethical standards, and then assess the organization's compliance with these requirements. Ethics committees should be aware of their industries' codes of ethics, community standards, and the organizational culture in which they work. Although ethics committees do not always succeed, they can provide one of the best organizational approaches to resolving internal ethical issues fairly. As one of many examples in the corporate world, Sunstrand Corporation, a *Fortune* 500 company, has established employee-managed ethics committees at each of its facilities to stimulate employees' "ownership" of their ethical conduct and to distribute accountability throughout the organization.[40]

### *Work Groups and Teams*

Work groups are used to subdivide duties within specific functional areas of a company. For example, on an automotive assembly line, one work group might install the seats and interior design elements of the vehicle while another group installs all the dashboard instruments. This enables production supervisors to specialize in a specific area and provide expert advice to work groups.

Whereas work groups operate within a single functional area, teams bring together the functional expertise of employees from several different areas of the organization—for example, finance, marketing, and production—on a single project, such as developing a new product. Many manufacturing firms, including General Motors, Westinghouse, and Procter & Gamble, are using the team concept to improve participative management. Ethical conflicts may arise because team members come from different functional areas. Each member of the team has a particular role to play and has probably had limited interaction with other members of the team. Members may have encountered different ethical issues in their own functional areas and may therefore bring different viewpoints when the team faces an ethical issue. For example, a production quality-control employee might believe that side-impact air bags should be standard equipment on all automobiles for safety reasons. A marketing member of the team may reply that the cost of adding the air bags would force the company to raise prices beyond the reach of some consumers. The production employee might then argue that it is unethical for an automobile maker to fail to include a safety feature that could save hundreds of lives. Such conflicts often occur when members of different organizational groups must interact. However, airing viewpoints representative of all the functional areas helps to provide more options from which to choose.

Work groups and teams provide the organizational structure for group decision making. One of the reasons individuals cannot implement their personal ethical beliefs in organizations is that so many decisions are reached collectively by work groups. However, persons who have legitimate power are in a position to influence ethics-related activities. The work group and team often sanction certain activities as ethical or define others as unethical.

*Informal Groups* In addition to the groups that businesses formally organize and recognize—such as committees, work groups, and teams—most organizations have a number of informal groups. These groups are usually composed of individuals, often from the same department, who have similar interests and band together for companionship or for purposes that may or may not be relevant to the goals of the organization. For example, four or five people who have similar tastes in outdoor activities and music may discuss their interests while working, and they may meet outside work for dinner, concerts, sports events, or other activities. Other informal groups may evolve to form a union, improve working conditions or benefits, get a manager fired, or protest work practices they view as unfair. Informal groups may generate disagreement and conflict, or they may enhance morale and job satisfaction.

Informal groups help to develop informal channels of communication, sometimes called the "grapevine," which are important in every organization. Informal communication flows up, down, diagonally, and horizontally, not necessarily following the communication lines on a company's organization chart. Information passed along the grapevine may relate to the job, the organization, or an ethical issue, or it may simply be gossip and rumors. The grapevine can act as an early warning system for employees. If employees learn informally that their company may be sold or that a particular action will be condemned as unethical by top management or the community, they have time to think about what they will do. Since gossip is not uncommon in an organization, the information passed along the grapevine is not always accurate. Managers who understand how the grapevine works can use it to reinforce acceptable values and beliefs.

The grapevine is also an important source of information for individuals to assess ethical behavior within their organization. One way an employee can determine acceptable behavior is to ask friends and peers in informal groups about the consequences of certain actions, such as lying to a customer about a product safety issue. The corporate culture may provide employees with a general understanding of the patterns and rules that govern behavior, but informal groups make this culture come alive and provide direction for employees' daily choices. For example, if a new employee learns anecdotally through the grapevine that the organization does not punish ethical violations, he or she may seize the next opportunity for unethical behavior if it accomplishes the organization's objectives. In this case, the grapevine has clearly communicated that the organization rewards those who break the ethical rules to achieve desirable objectives.

## Group Norms

**Group norms** are standards of behavior that groups expect of their members. Just as corporate culture establishes behavior guidelines for an organization's members, so group norms help define acceptable and unacceptable behavior within a group. In particular, group norms define the limit allowed on deviations from group expectations.

Most work organizations, for example, develop norms that govern groups' rates of production and communication with management, as well as providing a general understanding of behavior considered right or wrong, ethical or unethical, within the group. For example, an employee who reports to a supervisor that a coworker has covered up a serious production error may be punished by other group members for this breach of confidence. Other members of the group may glare at the informant, who has violated a group norm, and refuse to talk to or sit by him or her.

Norms have the power to enforce a strong degree of conformity among group members. At the same time, norms define the different roles for various positions within the organization. Thus, a low-ranking member of a group may be expected to carry out an unpleasant task, such as accepting responsibility for someone else's ethical mistake.

Sometimes group norms conflict with the values and rules prescribed by the organization's culture. For example, the organization may value hard work done quickly, and management may use rewards and punishments to encourage this culture. In a particular informal group, however, norms may encourage doing only enough work to meet quotas and avoid drawing management's attention. Issues of equity may arise in this situation if other groups believe they are unfairly forced to work harder to make up for the underperforming group. These other employees may complain to management or to the offending group. If they believe management is not taking corrective action, they, too, may slow down and do only enough work to get by, thus hurting the whole organization's productivity. For this reason, management must carefully monitor not only the corporate culture but also the norms of all the various groups within the organization. Sanctions may be necessary to bring in line a group whose norms deviate sharply from the overall culture.

## Can People Control Their Own Actions Within an Organizational Culture?

Many people find it hard to believe that an organization's culture can exert so strong an influence on individuals' behavior within the organization. In our society, we want to believe that individuals control their own destiny. A popular way of viewing business ethics is therefore to see it as a reflection of the alternative moral philosophies that individuals use to resolve their personal moral dilemmas. As this chapter has shown, however, ethical decisions within organizations are often made by committees and formal and informal groups, not by individuals. Decisions related to financial reporting, advertising, product design, sales practices, and pollution-control issues are often beyond the influence of individuals alone. In addition, these decisions are frequently based on business rather than personal goals.

Most new employees in highly bureaucratic organizations have almost no input into the basic operating rules and procedures for getting things done. Along with learning sales tactics and accounting procedures, employees may be taught to ignore a design flaw in a product that could be dangerous to users. Although many personal ethics issues may seem straightforward and easy to resolve, individuals entering business will usually need several years of experience within a specific industry to understand how to resolve ethical close calls. For example, what constitutes false claims about a product? When Kellogg Co. introduced Heartwise cereal, the Federal Trade Commission insisted that the name be changed to Fiberwise because there was no conclusive evidence that the cereal benefited the heart. The branding of the cereal was a complex decision that required the judgment of many professional people on the cereal's benefits. And some professional health experts do, in fact, believe that a high-fiber diet is related to good health, including a strong heart. There is no way to avoid such ethical problems. The only thing that is certain is that one person's opinion is usually not sufficient. Group decisions are used when complex issues must be resolved.

It is not our purpose to suggest that you ought to go along with management or the group on business ethics issues. Honesty and open discussion of ethical issues are important to successful ethical decision making. We believe that most companies and businesspeople try to make ethical decisions. However, because there is so much difference between individuals, ethical conflict is inevitable.

Regardless of how a person or organization views the acceptability of a particular activity, if society judges it to be wrong or unethical, then this larger view directly affects the organization's ability to achieve its goals. Not all activities deemed unethical by society are illegal. But if public opinion decries or consumers protest against a particular activity, the result may be legislation that restricts or bans a specific business practice. For instance, concern about teen smoking prompted the government to regulate the placement of cigarette advertising and curb the use of characters and approaches designed to appeal to children. Public concern and outrage at the growth in cigarette smoking among minors spurred much of this intervention. Besieged by mounting negative opinion, numerous class-action lawsuits, and a landmark settlement with forty-six states, Philip Morris USA, producer of the world's best-selling cigarette, was forced to modify its marketing strategies, in particular to avoid marketing its products to minors. The company now uses the Internet, TV commercials, school publications, and print ads to encourage teenagers not to smoke. The company has spent $300 million on youth smoking prevention efforts.[41]

If a person believes that his or her personal ethics severely conflict with the ethics of the work group and of superiors in an organization, that individual's only alternative may be to leave the organization. In the highly competitive employment market of the twenty-first century, quitting a job because of an ethical conflict requires courage and, possibly, the ability to survive without a job. Obviously, there are no easy answers for resolving ethical conflicts between the organization and the individual. Our goal is not to tell you what you should do. But we do believe that the more you know about how ethical decision making occurs within organizations, the more opportunity you will have to influence decisions positively and resolve ethical conflict more effectively.

## Summary

Corporate culture refers to the set of values, beliefs, goals, norms, and ways of solving problems that the members (employees) of an organization share. These shared values may be formally expressed or unspoken. Corporate cultures can be classified in several ways, and a cultural audit can be conducted to identify an organization's culture. If an organization's culture rewards unethical behavior, people within the company are more likely to act unethically. A company's failure to monitor or manage its culture may foster questionable behavior.

Leadership—the ability or authority to guide others toward achieving goals—has a significant impact on the ethical decision-making process because leaders have the power to motivate others and enforce both the organization's rules and policies and their own viewpoints. A leader must not only gain the respect of his or her followers but also provide a standard of ethical conduct. Six leadership styles based on emotional intelligence have been identified: coercive, authoritative, affiliative, democratic, pacesetting, and coaching. Leadership styles may also be classified as transactional or transformational. Leaders exert power to influence the behaviors and decisions of subordinates. There are five power bases from which a leader may influence ethical behavior: reward power, coercive power, legitimate power, expert power, and referent power. Leaders also attempt to motivate subordinates; motivation is an internal force that focuses an individual's behavior toward achieving a goal. It can be created by the incentives that an organization offers employees.

The structure of an organization may create opportunities to engage in unethical behavior. In a centralized organization, decision-making authority is concentrated in the hands of top managers, and little authority is delegated to lower levels. In a decentralized organization, decision-making authority is delegated as far down the chain of command as possible. Centralized organizations tend to be more ethical than decentralized ones because they enforce more rigid controls, such as codes of ethics and corporate policies on ethical practices. However, unethical conduct can occur in both types of structures.

In addition to the values and customs that represent the culture of an organization, individual groups within the organization often adopt their own rules and values, and even create subcultures. The main types of groups are formal groups—which include committees, work groups, and teams—and informal groups. Informal groups often feed an informal channel of communication called the "grapevine." Group norms are standards of behavior that groups expect of their members. They help define acceptable and unacceptable behavior within a group and especially define the limits on deviating from group expectations. Sometimes group norms conflict with the values and rules prescribed by the organization's culture.

Sometimes an employee's own personal ethical standards conflict with what is expected of them as members of an organization and its corporate culture. This is especially true given that an organization's ethical decisions are often resolved by committees, formal groups, and informal groups rather than by individuals. When such ethical conflict is severe, the individual may have to decide whether to leave the organization.

| Important Terms for Review | | |
| --- | --- | --- |
| leadership | motivation |
| transactional leadership | relatedness needs |
| transformational leadership | growth needs |
| reward power | centralized organization |
| coercive power | decentralized organization |
| legitimate power | formal group |
| expert power | informal group |
| referent power | group norms |

## A Real-Life Situation*

As Gerard sat down in his expensive new chair, he was worried. What had he gotten himself into? How could things have gone so wrong so fast? It was as if he'd been walking and some truck had blindsided him. Gerard had been with Trawlers Accounting, a medium-size firm, for several years. His wife, Vicky, had a job in the pharmaceutical industry, and their first child was due any day now. The doctor had told her that she would need to stop work early because hers was a high-risk pregnancy. So three months before her due date, she asked and received a four-month leave of absence. This was great, but the leave was without pay. Luckily, Gerard had received a promotion and now headed a department.

Some interesting activities were going on in the accounting industry. For example, Gerard's superior had decided that all CPAs would take exams to become registered investment advisers. The rationale for such a new development was simple. The firm could use its relationships with clients to increase investment revenues. Because of the long-term nature of these relationships with many firms and individuals as well as the implicit sense of honesty that CPAs must bring to their jobs, clients understood that a violation of so high a trust was unlikely—or so Gerard's boss argued. Many of the people in Gerard's department didn't like this new policy; however, some who had passed the exams increased their pay by 15 percent. During lunch, one of Gerard's financial friends engaged him heatedly. "What you're doing, Gerard, is called unfair competition," the friend accused him. "For example, your CPAs have exclusive access to confidential client taxpayer information, which could give you insight into people's financial needs. Besides, you could easily direct clients to mutual funds that you already own in order to keep your own personal investments afloat. Also, if your people start chasing commissions and fees on mutual funds that go bad, your credibility will become suspect and you won't be trusted. Plus, your people will now have to keep abreast of financial, as well as tax and accounting changes."

When Gerard got to his office, he found that some of his people had been recommending a group of mutual funds that Trawlers had been auditing. Then someone from another of his company's accounting clients, CENA Mutual Funds, telephoned. "What's the idea of having your people suggest PPI Mutual Funds when they are in direct competition with us?" the caller yelled. "We pay you at lot, Gerard, to do our accounting procedures, and that's how you reward us? I want to know by the end of the day if you are going to continue to push our competitor's product. I don't have to tell you that this will directly affect your department and you. Also, things like this get around the business circles, if you know what I mean." With these words, the caller hung up on Gerard.

## Questions ▪ Exercises

1. Identify any ethical and legal issues of which Gerard needs to be aware.
2. Discuss the advantages and disadvantages of each decision Gerard has made and could make.
3. Discuss the issue of accounting firms going into the financial services market.
4. Discuss the type of groups that are influencing Gerard.

* This case is strictly hypothetical; any resemblance to real persons, companies, or situations is coincidental.

# Check Your EQ

Check your E.Q., or ethics quotient, by completing the following. Assess your performance to evaluate your overall understanding of the chapter material.

1. Decentralized organizations tend to put the blame for unethical behavior on lower-level personnel.  Yes  No

2. Decentralized organizations give employees extensive decision-making autonomy.  Yes  No

3. Organizational culture provides rules for behaving within the organization.  Yes  No

4. An integrative culture shows high concern for performance and little concern for people.  Yes  No

5. Coercive power works in the same manner as reward power.  Yes  No

ANSWERS: 1. No. That's more likely to occur in centralized organizations. 2. Yes. This is known as empowerment. 3. Yes. Values, beliefs, customs, and ceremonies represent what is acceptable and unacceptable in the organization. 4. No. That's an exacting culture. An integrative culture combines high concern for people and production. 5. No. Coercive power is the opposite of reward power. One offers rewards and the other punishment to encourage appropriate behavior.

# Organizational Factors: Relationships and Conflicts

## An Ethical Dilemma*

At twenty-six, Debbie Richardson was in her fourth year at Lamb Consulting. In that time, she had progressed from an assistant to a project manager for one of the smaller divisions within the company. Debbie had worked forty-plus hours a week for the past three years to get ahead. If no major problems arise in the next several years, top management intends to give her the nod up the ladder as senior project manager. Within the select group of twenty-five project managers, there is only one other woman, Jessica Smart.

Rumor has it that Jessica had been promoted for a variety of unknown reasons. For example, her first boss had promoted her quickly and then divorced his wife, fueling expectations that he would wed Jessica. When the rumor got to top management, Jessica's coworkers assumed that she would be fired. After all, the company's founder felt that extracurricular romances were not consistent with business and blamed women for them. Jessica's next superior fell victim to a well-orchestrated plot that showed flaws in his management style. Everyone assumed that his replacement would be someone other than Jessica; however, she received the promotion. The next step after senior project manager is director, and the directors' group has been nicknamed the "Teflon twelve."

Lamb Consulting has been in business for forty years. It started out as a one-man operation in the form of Zedikia Lamb. Over the years, the company has grown to more than a thousand employees, yet it still bears Lamb's imprint. As a result, most senior managers are high on control and low on tolerance. If something goes wrong, the general view is that the Teflon twelve will find an underling responsible and fire him or her. The company is top-down and uncaring in every sense of the word. Lamb himself hands out projects to the twelve directors, who distribute the best to their favorite senior project managers, who in turn give the best ones to their favorites. People stay with Lamb because he pays well, and the consulting industry knows that if you can make it at his firm for two years, you are well trained to take on other opportunities.

As Debbie got back to her office, she could feel the headache start at the base of her neck and tighten all the way to her temples, accompanied by nausea. She was ill and also angry at the predicament that Susan Gatewick had handed her. Susan, a bright and intelligent project manager, had come to the firm right out of college and was now in her third year at the firm under Bob Hachet. Concerning her boss, Susan had recently confided in Debbie:

> In the beginning, when I first came to Lamb, I didn't think anything of it. Bob would come into my office and tell me what a great job I was doing. We started going out to lunch, but the talk wasn't about work. It was about our personal lives. He would tell me how beautiful I looked and I would reciprocate. Then sometimes he'd give me neck rubs, and we'd talk about his struggles at home. We've gone out occasionally for drinks with coworkers, other times alone, but last month it just started to change. When we were having lunch, he put his hand on my knee. I didn't say anything, but it just kinda unnerved me.
>
> Later in the week, he gave me a little kiss on the cheek and then hugged me. But last week, well, let's just say he's putting his hands all over me. When I mentioned to him that I just wasn't comfortable with what was happening, he looked confused and then got angry! What am I going to do? I need this job, Debbie, and besides the pay is great, with a good future. If I stick it out, he'll probably get promoted, or better yet, I will and then the problem goes away for me. But what should I do in the meantime, Debbie?

Debbie sighed and told Susan that, as a member of management, she was obliged to report what Susan had told her to top management. The company's code of conduct specifically states: "Any member of management hearing in the first person of any remarks, actions, or physical activities that could be construed as sexual harassment or contributing to a hostile work environment must report such information to the proper authorities or be subject to penalties, sanctions, dismissal, and/or go without legal representation afforded by Lamb in any civil or criminal suit developed by such information."

"What are you saying, Debbie?! That you're going to make a formal report about this? I can't believe you would do such a thing. You know Bob will hold a grudge. He's like that. You remember when you two were both at the same place in the organization and he made that accounting error and you brought it to the attention of the owner. Remember how for more than a year he tried to get back at you: the backbiting, the undermining of some of your decisions, the innuendoes. And now you're going to make it public that he's been putting his hands on me? Do you realize that if he gets promoted my career is over? And what happens when I try to apply to another firm? Even though it's not true, they'll say, 'Didn't she cry sexual harassment at her last place of employment?'"

On reflection, Debbie realized that she had heard of some companies in the industry that avoided hiring women to reduce the possibility of ever having a sexual harassment problem. Others seemed afraid to hire more female employees because of the uncertainty about what was permissible and what wasn't. As one executive told Debbie, "We [men] just don't know anymore where the line is. The courts tell us when we step over it, but it's too late then. Frankly, there are real differences between how men and women perceive things. I've got some friends who

thought their behavior was OK, but then some woman cried sexual harassment and there was nothing they could do once they'd been accused. Men have become frightened of women, and so many are hiring only men."

As Debbie pondered this, she couldn't help wondering what Bob and her own superior, Jessica, would do. At first she thought that Jessica might be sensitive to Susan's predicament; however, Jessica had dealt harshly with the last known similar complaint by a woman, as well as with those who had brought it to her attention. Debbie also didn't know whether Jessica wanted her promoted. Someone had once said to Debbie, "Jessica is a political animal. The terms *right* and *wrong* are meaningless to her."

Later that day, Debbie bumped into Bob, who hinted that someone was making waves and that he was going to talk to Jessica about the individual. "And if you want to step up to the plate for this person, know that I'll drag you down as well," he added.

What should Debbie do?

---

### Questions ■ Exercises

1. Determine the ethical and legal issue(s), if any.
2. Discuss each individual's options.
3. What are the risks for each individual?
4. Evaluate the company's corporate culture and ethical compliance efforts.

* This case is strictly hypothetical; any resemblance to real persons, companies, or situations is coincidental.

---

Businesspeople learn ethical or unethical behavior not only from society and culture, but also from people with whom they associate in their work groups and in the business organization as a whole. The outcome of this learning process depends on the strength of individuals' personal values, opportunity, and their exposure to others who behave ethically or unethically. Members of organizations usually make ethical decisions jointly with the significant others they associate with in informal groups as well as in formal relationships within the work environment. As we have seen, the term *significant others* is used here to include superiors, peers, and subordinates in the organization who influence the ethical decision-making process. Although persons outside the organization, such as family members and friends, also influence decision makers, we focus here on the influence of significant others within the organization.

In this chapter we discuss how organizational structure and culture operate through significant others in the ethical decision-making process. We begin by examining interpersonal relationships in organizations. We also look at the responsibility of the corporation in these relationships and the ways that employee conduct, role relationships, differential association, whistle-blowing, and organizational pressures relate to ethical decisions in the workplace. We also explore the role of opportunity and conflict in organizational ethical decision making. Finally, we begin to consider ways to improve ethical decision making in business.

## Interpersonal Relationships in Organizations

Organizations consist of individuals and groups of people working together to achieve one or more objectives. If a company has a mission statement that indicates respect for the well-being of stakeholders and states an objective of contributing to society, then managers and employees should work together to their mutual advantage. The mission of Merck & Co., Inc., for example, is "to provide society with superior products and services by developing innovations and solutions that improve the quality of life and satisfy customer needs, and to provide employees with meaningful work and advancement opportunities, and investors with a superior rate of return."[1] Many companies now publicize their mission statements on their Web sites.

One of the biggest challenges for business managers is to get diverse people to work together efficiently and ethically while coordinating their skills. Relationships among individuals and within groups are an important part of the proper functioning of a business organization. In fact, interpersonal relations play a key role in business ethics. To understand how interpersonal relations influence decisions about ethical issues, we first consider both the corporation's responsibility as a moral agent and the idea of variation in employee conduct. Next, we examine the role relationships within the organization, which include socialization, role-sets, and role stress; differential association; whistle-blowing; and organizational pressures.

### The Responsibility of the Corporation As a Moral Agent

Increasingly, corporations are viewed not merely as profit-making entities but also as moral agents that are accountable for their conduct to their employees, investors, suppliers, and customers. Companies are more than the sum of their parts or participants. Because corporations are chartered as citizens of a state and/or nation, they generally have the same rights and responsibilities as individuals. Through legislation and court precedents, society holds companies accountable for the conduct of their employees as well as for their decisions and the consequences of those decisions. Arthur Andersen, for example, no longer exists because its clients lost confidence in the accounting firm due to charges of accounting fraud and obstruction of justice.[2]

As mentioned, companies can be viewed as moral agents that are required to obey the laws and regulations that define acceptable business conduct. However, it is important to acknowledge that they are not human beings who can think through moral issues. Because companies are not human, laws and regulations are necessary to provide formal structural restraints and guidance on ethical issues. Although individuals may attempt to abide by their own values and moral philosophy, as employees they are supposed to act in the company's best interests. Thus, the individual as a moral agent has a moral obligation beyond that of the corporation because it is the individual, not the company, who can think responsibly through complex ethical issues.[3]

Though obviously not a person, a corporation can be considered a societal moral agent that is created to perform specific functions in society and is therefore responsible to society for its actions. Because corporations have the characteristics of agents, responsibility for ethical behavior is assigned to them as legal entities as well as to individuals or work groups they employ.[4] As such, companies may be punished for wrongdoing and rewarded for good business ethics. New Belgium Brewing Company (Fort Collins, Colorado), for example, has won numerous awards for ethics and social responsibility, including an Environmental Excellence Award from *Business Ethics* magazine. Other recent recipients of *Business Ethics* awards include White Dog Cafe (Philadelphia, Pennsylvania) and Fastener Industries (Berea, Ohio), all small businesses.[5]

One major misunderstanding in studying business ethics is to assume that a coherent ethical corporate culture will evolve through individual and interpersonal relationships. Because ethics is often viewed as an individual matter, many reason that the best way to develop an ethical corporate culture is to provide character education to employees or to hire individuals with good character and sensitize them to ethical issues. This assumes that ethical conduct will develop through companywide agreement and consensus. Although these assumptions are laudable and have some truth, the companies that are responsible for most of the economic activity in the world employ thousands of culturally diverse individuals who will never reach agreement on all ethical issues. Many ethical business issues are complex close calls, and the only way to ensure consistent decisions that represent the interests of all stakeholders is to require ethical policies. This chapter provides support for the belief that implementing a centralized corporate ethics program can provide a cohesive, internally consistent set of statements and policies representing the corporation as a moral agent.

## Variation in Employee Conduct

Although the corporation is required to take responsibility for conducting its business ethically, a substantial amount of research indicates that there are significant differences in the values and philosophies that influence how the individuals that comprise corporations make ethical decisions.[6] In other words, because people are culturally diverse and have different values, they interpret situations differently and will vary in the ethical decisions they make on the same ethical issue.

Table 7–1 shows that approximately 10 percent of employees say they take advantage of situations to further their own personal interests. These individuals are more likely to manipulate, cheat, or be self-serving when the benefits gained from doing so are greater than the penalties for the misconduct. Such employees may choose to make personal long-distance telephone calls from work if the only penalty they may suffer if caught is having to pay for their calls. The lower the risk of being caught, therefore, the higher is the likelihood that the 10 percent most likely to take advantage will be involved in unethical activities.

As Table 7–1 shows, another 40 percent of workers go along with the work group on most matters. These employees are most concerned about the social implications of their actions and want to fit into the organization. Although they have their own

| TABLE 7–1 | Variation in Employee Conduct |
| --- | --- |

| 10 PERCENT | 40 PERCENT | 40 PERCENT | 10 PERCENT |
| --- | --- | --- | --- |
| Follow their own values and beliefs; believe that their values are superior to those of others in the company | Always try to follow company policies | Go along with the work group | Take advantage of situations if<br>- the penalty is less than the benefit<br>- the risk of being caught is low |

These percentages are based on a number of studies in the popular press and data gathered by the authors. These percentages are not exact and represent a general typology that may vary by organization.
Source: Copyright © 1999 O. C. Ferrell.

personal opinions, they are easily influenced by what people around them are doing. These individuals may know that using work telephones for personal long-distance calls is improper, yet they view it as acceptable because their coworkers do it. These employees rationalize their action by saying that personal telephone use must be one of the benefits of working at their particular business, and it must be acceptable because the company does not enforce a policy precluding the behavior. Coupled with this philosophy is the belief that no one will get into trouble for doing what everybody else is doing, for there is safety in numbers.

Table 7–1 also indicates that about 40 percent of a company's employees always try to follow company policies and rules. These workers not only have a strong grasp of their corporate culture's definition of acceptable behavior, but they also attempt to comply with codes of ethics, ethics training, and other communications about appropriate conduct. If the company has a policy prohibiting personal long-distance telephone calls from work, these employees probably would observe it. However, they likely would not speak out about the 40 percent who choose to go along with the work group, for these employees prefer to focus on their jobs and steer clear of any organizational misconduct. If the company fails to communicate standards of appropriate behavior, members of this group will devise their own.

According to Table 7–1, the final 10 percent of employees try to maintain formal ethical standards that focus on rights, duties, and rules. They embrace values that assert certain inalienable rights and actions, which they perceive to be always ethically correct. In general, members of this group believe that their values are right and superior to the values of others in the company, or even to the company's value system, when an ethical conflict arises. These individuals have a tendency to report the misconduct of others or to speak out when they view activities within the company as unethical. Consequently, members of this group would probably report colleagues who make personal long-distance calls at work.

The significance of this variation in the way individuals behave ethically is simply this: employees use different approaches when making ethical decisions. Because of the probability that a large percentage of any work group will either take advantage of a situation or at least go along with the work group, it is vital that companies provide communication and control mechanisms to maintain an ethical climate. Companies that fail to monitor activities and enforce ethics policies provide a low-risk environment for those employees who are inclined to take advantage of situations to accomplish their personal, and sometimes unethical, objectives.

Good business practice and concern for the law requires organizations to recognize this variation in employees' desire to be ethical. The percentages cited above are only estimates, and the actual percentages of each type of employee may vary widely across organizations based on individuals and corporate culture. The specific percentages are less important than the fact that our research has identified these variations as existing within most organizations. Organizations should focus particular attention on managers who oversee the day-to-day operations of employees within the company. They should also provide training and communication to ensure that the business operates ethically; that it does not become the victim of fraud or theft; and that employees, customers, and other stakeholders are not abused through the misconduct of people who have a pattern of unethical behavior.

As we have seen throughout this book, many examples can be cited of employees and managers who have no concern for ethical conduct but are nonetheless hired and placed in positions of trust. Some corporations continue to support executives who ignore environmental concerns, poor working conditions, or defective products, or who engage in accounting fraud. Executives who can get results, regardless of the consequences, are often admired and lauded, especially in the business press. When their unethical or even illegal actions become public knowledge, however, they risk more than the loss of their positions. Consider former Tyco chief financial officer (CFO) Mark Swartz, who was indicted for failing to report a $12.5 million bonus on his tax return. Swartz, along with former Tyco CEO Dennis Kozlowski, also faces fines and jail time if he is convicted of criminal charges that he and Kozlowski stole $600 million from Tyco through unauthorized pay and fraudulent stock sales.[7]

## Role Relationships

Much like a part in a movie, a **role** is a part that a person plays in an organization. All the roles that a person plays in a company constitute his or her position, and, together, they prescribe the behavior that others expect of someone in that position. Consider the position of supermarket cashier. The cashier's role involves scanning goods and receiving payment for them. The cashier is expected to behave professionally and courteously while assisting customers for the benefit of the supermarket. However, another role the cashier may play is as a member of a store committee on minimizing coupon fraud at the checkout or ensuring that each product is registered at the appropriate price. Each person in an organization has a specialized role or set of tasks or roles in helping the organization achieve its goals. Some work on the assembly line; some do clerical work; some make marketing and accounting decisions. Other members, such as foremen or department heads, have broader tasks, for example, to keep all the groups in the organization working toward the common goal.

The work group potentially has the greatest effect on daily ethical decisions. Within the work group, conflicts between employees over roles and expected behavior may directly or indirectly influence how much unethical behavior occurs. For example, it is possible that an otherwise honest cashier may be informally expected to overcharge a few customers to make up for undercharging mistakes. The more conflict there is within the organization, the less the work group will be perceived as ethical.[8] For this reason, it is vital that organizations support the ethics of the work group.

*Socialization* **Socialization** refers to the process through which a person learns the values and behavior patterns considered appropriate by an organization or group. New employees learn through socialization how to act in their roles, including what is acceptable ethical behavior. However, they may also be socialized to accept unethical practices, such as when Merrill Lynch stock analysts urged investors to buy Internet stocks that were in fact poorly rated so they could generate large fees on these new offerings—which Merrill Lynch had underwritten. The company eventually paid $100 million to settle the charges and agreed to strengthen barriers between its stock research and investment-banking divisions to avoid potential conflicts of interest.[9]

Through socialization, employees are taught how to behave in accordance with their roles. For example, new employees are usually socialized to accept the principle of accountability—that they are answerable to a superior or to peers for the outcome of a project. The socialization process is a powerful influence on ethical behavior. Ethical issues such as lying, cheating, paying bribes, and overcharging clients may be defined through socialization of organizational values and norms. Even if an individual disagrees with the values and norms of the organization, it may be difficult for him or her to refuse to go along with the decisions and actions of others, especially superiors. According to professor Linda Trevino, "Most people will try to do what they're being asked to do because they want the company to succeed and they want to feel good about achieving their goals."[10]

*Role-Sets* A **role-set** is the total of all role relationships in which a person is involved as a result of his or her position in an organization. For example, an account executive in an advertising agency has relationships with immediate superiors, upper-level managers, peers (other account executives), advertising copywriters and artists, and employees and managers from other departments, as well as with clients and media personnel. He or she has a different role relationship with each of these persons by virtue of holding the account executive's position. A role-set, then, explains all of the position's role relationships with others, including their location, authority, perceived beliefs, and behaviors. Understanding a person's role-set may help predict his or her ethical behavior.

Persons in the same department are socialized within the same immediate organizational context and often share the same specialization and knowledge base. Even when they work in different departments, members of the same organization tend to resemble each other more than they do people who are not members of the organization. The boundaries between (and within) departments and organizations limit the individual's knowledge of attitudes and behaviors beyond his or her immediate group. As a result, others outside the individual's group probably differ in orientation, goals, and interests. The greater the distance between the decision maker and a coworker, the less likely the other is to influence ethical behavior. For example, if there are four layers of management between a decision maker and the regional vice president, the vice president may have only marginal influence on the decision maker. With fewer layers of management between them, the vice president's influence would be greater. Of course, some high-ranking managers may have so much charisma and personal visibility that their suggestions, ideas, and value system may be adopted throughout the organization.

Within an organization, peers and top managers are likely to have a major influence on the ethical decisions of individual employees. In fact, the actions of peers and top managers are better predictors of an individual's unethical behavior than that individual's own personal belief system or opportunity for engaging in unethical behavior.[11] Figure 7–1 illustrates this relationship.

This does not mean, however, that individuals are not responsible for the consequences of their behavior. Sometimes the consequences of any group member's ethical actions are not that easy for one individual to see. Ethical decisions do not just happen in the group; obviously, they are made through human choice. Personal values do play a role in the final decision, but on business matters, group decisions are often used to resolve ethical dilemmas. Indeed, experts say that people may find it easier to justify their unethical behavior when they are members of groups or to violate their own personal ethical code on behalf of their coworkers or employer. In such cases, they may view an ethically difficult situation as "a pair of mutual favors" that benefit two parties while forgetting about other stakeholders such as investors, consumers, or suppliers, who might be harmed in the process.[12]

Higher levels of trust should be evident in work environments where coworkers consider the rights and interests of others in making decisions that affect them. Figure 7–2 indicates that the majority of employees in the National Business Ethics Survey (NBES) felt that the values of honesty, respect, and trust are applied frequently in the workplace.[13] The relationship between ethical behavior and trust is intuitively attractive, but there is also research that supports this link. Many studies have found that an ethical organizational climate has a positive impact on trust.[14] For example, when a firm establishes a quota system that requires employees to sell a specific number of products per day or week regardless of the what customers need, trust among that firm's employees deteriorates. The quota system may create internal competition for customers and cause employees to engage in unethical activities to make the quota.

Trust starts at the individual level with employees who are trustworthy. Then, at the organizational level, employees need to trust each other, transforming the work group into a unified team with a shared vision.[15] Manipulative tactics to get workers to perform at a desired level damage the ethical climate. With a quota system that is almost impossible to meet, there could be infighting, divisive politics, and misconduct—especially misconduct directed at customers—to accomplish corporate objectives.

| FIGURE 7–1 | Significant Others Are the Most Influential Factor in Organizations' Ethical Decision Making |

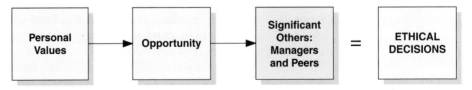

**FIGURE 7–2**    Values Applied in the Workplace

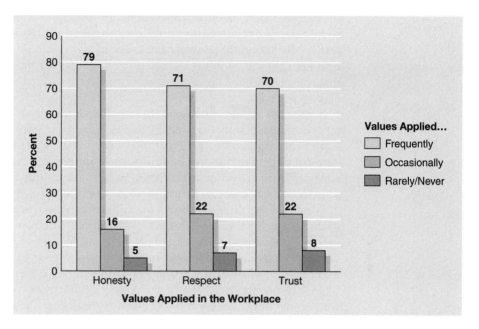

Source: The Ethics Resource Center, *2000 National Business Ethics Survey: How Employees Perceive Ethics at Work* (Washington, D.C.: Ethics Resource Center, 2000), Figure 6.1, p. 55. Reprinted by permission.

Employees can be influenced by significant others and by the role supervisors play in supporting an ethical work environment. This statement can be alarming to those who feel that one's personal ethics should be a major consideration when occupying business roles. Conflicts between what superiors ask you to do and your personal ethics create many ethical dilemmas, as well as opportunities to improve business ethics. Because our findings show that managers often go along with peers or superiors on ethical issues does not mean we are suggesting that you ought to behave this way as well.

Managers in supervisory positions should take responsibility for the actions of their subordinates, including unethical behavior. This means developing an ethical work environment. However, a manager may be unable to influence the rogue employee who wants to take advantage of opportunities for misconduct. These employees must be dealt with or they may spoil the work environment for everyone. Managers need to get closer to their employees to develop a successful ethical environment. Openness, trust, and friendship are often cited as the key factors in building positive interpersonal relationships. These factors also seem important to the communication of ethical values and the encouragement of responsible conduct.[16] The building blocks of trust include clear communication, consistency of message and action, and a willingness to address difficult questions. Conversely, enemies of trust include inconsistent standards, incompetence, and supporting false feedback.[17]

*Role Stress* Stress on the job has been found to be a major factor influencing unethical behavior.[18] As an indication of its prevalence and seriousness, a recent survey showed that 21 percent of the responding firms offered stress-reduction programs and 8 percent offered massage therapy to employees.[19] **Role stress** is the strain, conflict, or disruption that results from a lack of agreement on certain job-related activities. The role that an individual plays in a business, and the specific tasks that go with that role, can potentially create conflict that has a direct bearing on ethical decision-making behavior.

Some tasks require a decision maker to make many more tradeoffs and face many more ethical dilemmas than others. Salespeople, for example, are often confronted by customers who state or imply that they will purchase a product if they are given extra personal incentives that may be against company policy—that is, a bribe. Similarly, accountants who are auditing a company may be called aside and asked not to report information in a way that might disclose discrepancies. A personnel manager may discriminate against a minority. Marketing managers face many ethical dilemmas when making advertising decisions. For example, a dramatic commercial for Nuveen Investments shown during a recent Super Bowl led some people to believe that actor Christopher Reeve could walk again. In the computer-engineered ad, Reeve, who was paralyzed in a horse-riding accident, was shown rising from a chair and walking to a stage. The executive director of the National Spinal Cord Injury Association felt the commercial might have given too much hope to paralyzed people. He said, "When you go out with an advertisement like that, you tread a very, very narrow line between trying to be creative . . . and being misleading."[20] Because there is little doubt that ethical decision making is stressful for decision makers who face conflict, role-stress situations tend to increase the likelihood of unethical behavior.

## Differential Association

**Differential association** refers to the idea that people learn ethical or unethical behavior while interacting with others who are part of their role-sets or belong to other intimate personal groups.[21] The learning process is more likely to result in unethical behavior if the individual associates primarily with persons who behave unethically. Associating with others who are unethical, combined with the opportunity to act unethically, is a major influence on ethical decision making, as described in the decision-making framework in Chapter 4.[22]

Consider two cashiers working different shifts at the same supermarket. Kevin, who works in the evenings, has seen his cashier friends take money from the bag containing the soft-drink machine change, which is collected every afternoon but not counted until closing time. Although Kevin personally believes that stealing is wrong, he has often heard his friends rationalize that the company owes them free beverages while they work. During his break one evening, Kevin discovers that he has no money to buy a soda. Because he has seen his friends take money from the bag and has heard them justify the practice, Kevin does not feel guilty about taking four quarters. However, Sally, who works the day shift, has never seen her friends take money from the bag. When she discovers that she does not have enough money to purchase a beverage for her break, it does not occur to her to take money from the change bag. Instead, she borrows from a friend. Although both Sally and Kevin view stealing as wrong, Kevin has associated with others who say the practice is justified. When the opportunity arose, Kevin used his friends' rationalization to justify his theft.

A variety of studies have supported the notion that such differential association influences ethical decision making. In particular, superiors have a strong influence on the ethics of their subordinates. Consider the actions of Mark Hernandez, who worked at NASA's Michoud Assembly Facility applying insulating foam to the space shuttles' external fuel tanks. Within a few weeks on the job, coworkers taught him to repair scratches in the insulation without reporting the repairs. Supervisors encouraged the workers not to bother filling out the required paperwork on the repairs so they could meet the space shuttle program's tight production schedules. After the shuttle Columbia broke up on re-entry, killing all seven astronauts on board, investigators focused on whether a piece of foam falling off a fuel tank during lift-off may have irreparably damaged the shuttle. The final determination of the cause of the disaster may require years of investigation.[23]

Several research studies have found that employees, especially young managers, tend to go along with their superiors' moral judgments to demonstrate loyalty.[24] Hopefully, we have made it clear that *how* people typically make ethical decisions is not necessarily the way they *should* make ethical decisions. But we believe you will be able to improve your own ethical decision making once you understand the potential influence of your interaction with others in your intimate work groups.

## Whistle-Blowing

Interpersonal conflict ensues when employees think they know the right course of action in a situation, yet their work group or company promotes or requires a different, unethical decision. In such cases, employees may choose to follow their own values and refuse to participate in the unethical or illegal conduct. If they conclude that they cannot discuss what they are doing or what should be done with their coworkers or immediate supervisors, these employees may go outside the organization to publicize and correct the unethical situation. **Whistle-blowing** means exposing an employer's wrongdoing to outsiders, such as the media or government regulatory agencies.

Whistle-blowers have provided pivotal evidence documenting corporate malfeasance at a number of companies. The importance of their role was highlighted when *Time* magazine named three whistle-blowers as its 2002 "Persons of the Year": Sherron Watkins of Enron, Cynthia Cooper of WorldCom, and Coleen Rowley of the FBI. Watkins, an Enron vice president, warned Kenneth Lay, the firm's CEO, that the company was using improper accounting procedures. "I am incredibly nervous that we will implode in a wave of accounting scandals," she told him, and the energy firm did exactly that within a few short months. Soon after, Watkins testified before Congress that Enron had concealed billions of dollars in debt through a complex scheme of off-balance-sheet partnerships.[25]

Historically, the fortunes of whistle-blowers have not been as positive: most were labeled traitors, and many lost their jobs. A study of three hundred whistle-blowers by researchers at the University of Pennsylvania found that 69 percent lost their jobs or were forced to retire after exposing their companies' misdeeds.[26] Ted Beatty, for example, worked for Houston-based Dynegy. After he was passed over for promotion, he began collecting information on Dynegy's complex energy trades. When Beatty gave the information to the Securities and Exchange Commission, an investment fund, and the media, it led to the resignation of the firm's top officers. Beatty did not benefit financially from blowing the whistle on Dynegy. In fact, he has been unable to find another job, had his home broken into, and received numerous threats.[27] Although most whistle-blowers do not receive positive recognition for pointing out corporate misconduct, some have turned to the courts and obtained substantial settlements. For example, the whistle-blowers who exposed Medicare fraud at SmithKline Beecham were awarded $52 million. In subsequent appeals, however, they learned that they might not be entitled to the full amount because it was unclear whether they were solely responsible for uncovering the abuses.[28] Table 7–2 provides a checklist of questions an employee should ask before blowing the whistle.

If whistle-blowers present an accurate picture of organizational misconduct, they should not fear for their jobs. Indeed, the Sarbanes-Oxley Act makes it illegal to "discharge, demote, suspend, threaten, harass, or in any manner discriminate against" a whistle-blower and sets penalties of up to ten years in jail for executives who retaliate against whistle-blowers. The law also requires publicly traded companies to implement an anonymous reporting mechanism that allows employees to question actions that they believe may indicate securities fraud.[29] Additionally, the Federal Sentencing Guidelines for Organizations provides rewards for companies that systematically detect and address unethical or illegal activities. Even before the passage of the Sarbanes-Oxley Act, an increasing number of companies were setting up anonymous reporting services, normally toll-free numbers, through which employees can report suspected violations or seek input on how to proceed when encountering ambiguous situations. These reporting services are perceived to be most effective when they are managed by an outside organization that specializes in maintaining ethics hot lines. Duke Energy, for example, employs an outside organization to run its toll-free ethics hot line A survey of U.S. workers by Ernst and Young found that the most preferred method of reporting fraud to management was by anonymous phone call (30 percent), followed by confidential (but not anonymous) hot line (27 percent), anonymous letter (20 percent), and anonymous use of the company Web site (16 percent).[30]

## *Organizational Pressures*

Because an organization's success is determined by its employees' everyday performance in achieving company goals, pressure to achieve these goals can sometimes create ethical issues. Middle managers, for example, may be subject to particularly intense pressure to perform and increase profits. Internal organizational pressure stemming

| TABLE 7–2 | Questions to Ask Before Blowing the Whistle |
| --- | --- |
| 1. | Is this the only method to resolve my concerns? |
| 2. | Do I have the appropriate documentation and evidence to prove my case? |
| 3. | What is my motivation for expressing concern over employee or company activities? |
| 4. | Am I prepared to deal with the matter on both a personal and professional level? |

Source: Adapted from Paula Dwyer and Dan Carney, with Amy Borrus, Lorraine Woellert, and Christopher Palmeri, "Year of the Whistleblower," *Business Week,* Dec. 16, 2002, p. 108.

from role-set relationships, role stress, and differential association is a major predictor of unethical behavior. Although individuals can overcome this pressure and act ethically, they may risk losing their jobs in the process.

It is very difficult to know when to report a coworker who is apparently committing unethical or illegal acts. As mentioned in the previous section, more companies are setting up anonymous hot lines and encouraging employees to use them to report misconduct. But having recourse to a mechanical process such as a hot line does not solve the problem of when to report a colleague. The NBES found that only 57 percent of the employees who had observed misconduct reported it to management or another appropriate person. The survey also concluded that senior and middle managers were more likely to report observed misconduct than other employee groups and that professional and technical employees' reporting of misconduct was more than thirty percentage points below that of senior managers. Though 84 percent of employees felt they could report misconduct without negative consequences, the key reasons given by those who declined to report misconduct were the belief that nothing would be done and fear of retaliation.[31] Even when an organization agrees with the employees who report misconduct and takes action, those employees may not be satisfied with the organization's response. Nearly half of all employees in the NBES who said they had reported misconduct were dissatisfied with the response of their organizations.[32]

As we have seen, top managers and superiors play crucial roles in developing the environment that influences ethical decisions. Most experts agree that the chief executive officer and other executive managers set the ethical tone for the entire organization.[33] Lower-level managers take their cues from the top, yet their personal value systems also have an influence on the business. This interplay between corporate culture and executive leadership helps determine the firm's ethical value system.

Let us now take a closer look at the ways opportunity and conflict influence ethical decision making.

## The Role of Opportunity and Conflict

Opportunity and conflict—which we discussed in presenting our framework for understanding ethical decision making in Chapter 4—both play important roles in influencing the ethical decision making in interpersonal relationships. For instance, while low-cost labor in developing countries represents a business opportunity, it conflicts with paying low wages to workers. Activists have alleged that some clothing sold at Wal-Mart is sewn at Korean-owned factories in Honduras, where the base wage of forty-three cents an hour enables the factory employees to meet just 54 percent of the cost of survival.[34] Workers there have never heard of the Wal-Mart Code of Conduct and probably have no idea that the clothes end up at Wal-Mart. On the other hand, Wal-Mart was ranked as the "most admired company" by *Fortune* magazine in 2003.[35] This suggests that American society believes that the social and economic benefits Wal-Mart provides outweigh any questionable behavior. This example illustrates how both opportunity and conflict can exist at the individual, organizational, and social levels.

## Opportunity Creates Ethical Dilemmas

As mentioned in Chapter 4, opportunity is a set of conditions that limit unfavorable behavior or reward favorable behavior. The rewards may be internal: the feelings of goodness and self-worth one experiences after doing something beneficial without expecting anything in return. For example, if a factory worker reports to management that another employee is drinking or using drugs on the job, this draws attention to the coworker's problem and may reduce danger to others as well as help a peer with a substance-abuse issue. The reality is that 10 percent of employees in the NBES reported observing the abuse of alcohol or drugs on the job.[36] The rewards that opportunity provides may also be external—such as a raise or praise for a job well done. A salesperson who refuses a bribe, for instance, may be praised by superiors for appropriate behavior.

A person who behaves unethically and is rewarded (or not punished) for the behavior is likely to continue to act unethically, whereas a person who is punished (or not rewarded) for behaving unethically is less likely to repeat the behavior. Thus, an accountant who receives a raise after knowingly preparing financial documents that are not completely accurate is being rewarded for unethical behavior and may continue to use such tactics in the future. Over the past decade accountants working for Enron, Global Crossing, Halliburton, and many other firms used aggressive tactics to make financial reports appear rosier than they really were.[37] When they were rewarded, rather than punished, for their willingness to go along with questionable practices, they continued the behavior. Barbara Toffler, an ethics consultant and professor, learned firsthand how difficult it can be to follow one's own moral compass when she worked as a consultant at Arthur Andersen creating ethics programs for Andersen clients (the firm itself had no internal ethics program). After charging a client $1 million for developing an ethics program that should have cost $500,000, the praise Toffler earned from Andersen "was the only day in four years that I felt truly valued by Arthur Andersen." Despite her expertise, she learned that "unethical or illegal behavior happens when decent people are put under the unbearable pressure to do their jobs and meet ambitious goals without the resources to get the job done right."[38]

On the other hand, both customers and society at large often punish transgressions. For example, although e-mail users complain about unwanted direct-marketing e-mail (commonly called spam), direct-marketing e-mails can be effective if the privacy of others is respected. Amazon.com personalizes its e-mails to deliver information to customers about books, music, and other products of specific interest to them. Many companies refuse to use the opportunity e-mail affords to communicate with their customers because of rising fears about Internet privacy issues, which could result in restrictive legislation.[39] To balance this opportunity and potential conflict, most firms must develop an ethics policy on e-mail communication with employees and customers to control how this opportunity, created by technology, can be managed to develop competitive advantages.

When an opportunity is discovered, an ethical dilemma often arises as to whether to exploit it. For many businesses, opportunity means the chance to market a product that will earn large profits and benefit customers and other stakeholders, perhaps even save lives. Ethical issues may arise, however, when businesses hurry those products to the marketplace without adequate testing or with dangerous flaws. Because of the magnitude of an opportunity, some companies may knowingly either bring a product to market prematurely or modify other products to existing markets. In rare cases is the company's original intent to defraud. Consider the case of Richard F. Norris, who brought people to his offices by offering salaried jobs. However, he then had them sign contracts that obligated them to buy and sell large quantities of a diet supplement. Norris sued those who failed to sell the product or tried to return it.[40]

Opportunity also comes from knowledge. The two most common types of misconduct observed in the NBES were lying to employees, customers, vendors, or the public or withholding needed information from them.[41] A person who has an information base, expertise, or information about competition has the opportunity to exploit this knowledge. An individual can be a source of information because he or she is familiar with the organization. Individuals who have been employed by one organization for many years become "gatekeepers" of its culture, unwritten traditions, and rules. They help socialize newer employees to abide by the rules and norms of the company's internal and external ways of doing business. They may function as mentors or supervise managers in training. Like drill sergeants in the army, these trainers mold the new recruits into what the company wants. This can contribute to either ethical or unethical conduct.

Trainers and mentors influence a new employee's decision process in two ways. First, by providing information, the trainer can determine whether the new employee will identify a certain kind of situation as posing an ethical choice. In the NBES, 21 percent of employees observed other employees misreport their actual time or hours worked, and 12 percent observed falsification of records and reports.[42] As mentioned earlier, some employees at NASA's Michoud Assembly Facility were taught by coworkers to repair scratches in the shuttles' external fuel tank insulation without reporting the repairs, although they were required to do so.[43] Such attitudes are influenced in part by those who trained the employees. Second, by virtue of their title and its associated power, trainers can lead new employees to replace their own value systems with those of the trainer and the organization. Opportunity is lost or gained by the way trainers of new employees use their knowledge base.

Persons outside the organization can also have an impact on opportunity. Thus, financial auditors, though external to the organization, encounter many ethically laden situations because of the nature of their profession. The primary responsibility of an auditor is to determine the financial soundness of an organization by reviewing accounting data and presenting these data objectively. Opportunity for ethical conflict exists because the auditor is hired and paid by the company requesting the audit. What happens if the company screens potential auditors until it finds one that will provide a favorable statement? The auditor's credibility as an impartial reporter then comes into question because of the selection process. The auditor is under implicit pressure to give a positive judgment. The opportunity to become involved in potentially unethical situations results from the status the independent auditor is given. It is an opportunity a number of auditing firms have exploited in recent years. Research suggests that an organization's ethical culture and orientation can affect the ethical judgment of accountants in the United States, namely, by using more codes of conduct to restrict unethical opportunities.[44]

## Conflict Resolution

Opportunity sometimes leads to or results from conflict between the values of the decision maker and those of coworkers, the organization, or society. **Conflict** occurs when it is not clear which goals or values take precedence—those of the individual, the organization, or society. When individuals must choose between two equally good goals, particularly if one may result in more positive rewards than the other, they experience conflict. A choice between two bad alternatives can also cause conflict. As noted earlier, conflict can occur along several dimensions: personal, organizational, and societal.

Personal–organizational conflict occurs when a person's individual values and methods for reaching a desired goal differ from those of the organization or a group within the organization. For example, suppose that a convenience store manager has strong views against distributing magazines such as *Playboy, Hustler,* and *Penthouse,* but the company's policy is to sell these products. In this case, the organizational philosophy conflicts directly with the individual's personal philosophy. The manager has two options: to comply with the company's policy or to refuse to sell the magazines. Conceivably, refusal could mean getting fired. On the other hand, it would also elicit the feelings of self-esteem that come from acting in accordance with one's own values. Complying with company policy would maintain the individual's employment and income status, but at the price of sacrificing his or her personal values.

Employees often find themselves in such conflict situations, especially before they have been fully socialized into the organization. Many people try so hard to land their first job that they fail to consider the corporate values that will govern on-the-job decisions. For example, a person may not share the values that are characteristic of other members of his or her profession. Attitudes and values related to drinking, gambling, sex, and religion are personal moral issues. A person who believes drinking is wrong, for example, might feel uncomfortable working in an organization in which some after-hours business is conducted over drinks in a nearby bar. In such a situation, the new employee typically decides either to adjust to the work environment or to find a job in a more compatible organization. Those who choose to fight the system usually fail because they lack the power and support to change the company's values. Also, there is the question of whose values are right.

Personal–societal conflict occurs when an individual's values deviate from those of society. Societal values are often codified as laws and regulations established by federal and local governments. Values, such as the desire for clean air and water, can be translated into regulations on behavior. An ethical conflict may arise when different communities impose divergent regulations or values. Alcohol consumption, certain types of entertainment, and Sunday business activities are other examples of behaviors treated differently by different communities.

When society believes that a particular activity is unethical although currently legal, new laws may be enacted to help define the minimum level of ethical behavior. In the realm of business, this pattern began as early as the railroad monopolies of the 1800s, which prompted passage of the Sherman Antitrust Act. In the early twentieth century, society responded to Upton Sinclair's novel *The Jungle* by raising standards for food processing. More recently, legislation has been passed to regulate the use of the Internet to protect children and to require greater accountability in financial reporting.

Because the United States is a pluralistic democracy, personal–societal conflicts will continue to evolve and be redefined.

When the norms and values of a business contravene those of society in general, organizational–societal conflict occurs. The marketing of new products often brings business into conflict with society, especially when the products have moral overtones for certain groups. Many groups, for example, question advertising violent entertainment products inappropriately. For example, the Federal Trade Commission (FTC) determined that "the vast majority of the best-selling restricted movies, music, and video games were deliberately marketed for children as young as 12." To validate its claims, the FTC cited internal industry memos, including one about an R-rated film that said that the studio's promotional "goal was to find the elusive teen target audience and make sure everyone between the ages of twelve and eighteen was exposed to the film." Another memo about a mature-rated video game described its "primary" audience as "males 12–17."[45] Some retailers have pledged to increase their enforcement of rating codes. Kmart, for example, announced that it would stop selling M-rated games to anyone under seventeen by using a bar-code scanner to prompt cashiers to ask for identification from youths. Wal-Mart adopted a similar policy, while other stores, including Sears, opted to stop selling the M-rated games altogether.[46]

Advertising products may also result in conflict when society believes that advertising wrongly appeals to certain groups. In recent years, many consumer groups have expressed concerns about alcohol and cigarette advertising that appeals to teenagers and young college students not legally allowed to use these products.

We do not want to leave the impression that the only way for a company to prevent unethical behavior is to eliminate opportunity. Conflict can be a positive circumstance when it provides a firm with the occasion to resolve an ethical dilemma through discussion and debate. Sometimes only through recognizing a conflict can an ethical decision be made. The relationships in business are based on trust and responsible behavior. Just as the majority of people who go into retail stores do not try to shoplift at each opportunity, so most businesspeople do not try to take advantage of every opportunity for unethical behavior. Differences in personal character may have a major impact on whether an individual becomes opportunistic and attempts to take advantage of situations, regardless of the circumstances. Because there are variations in employees' ethical conduct in every organization, companies must develop policies and codes to prevent improper behavior and encourage employees to support an ethical work environment.

## Improving Ethical Decision Making in Business

As we have emphasized, personal values, significant others, and opportunity all affect ethical behavior. One study of the values of corporate managers concluded that personal values are involved in ethical decisions but are not the central component that guides an organization's decisions, actions, and policies. This same study found that personal values make up only one part of an organization's total value system.[47] Ethical behavior depends on the organization's values and traditions, opportunity and conflict resolution, and the personal values of the individuals who actually make the decisions. Some people, for instance, will not consider working for a company unless it maintains a certain level of ethical values. A high standard of ethics will not necessarily motivate such employees to work harder, but it may keep them from changing their own values or being swayed by peers (significant others) or money (opportunity). The corporation can be deemed a moral agent that has a responsibility to maintain core values and a set of checks and balances to encourage ethical behavior.

Consequently, ethical behavior may be a function of several different dimensions of an organization's system: the corporate culture, significant others, and the personal value preferences of the organization's groups and individual members. This may explain why Michelle Marie Valencia allegedly manipulated natural gas price indexes. In addition to being fired, the Dynegy gas trader faces the prospect of $2.75 million in fines and thirty-five years in prison if convicted of federal criminal-fraud charges. Dynegy itself paid $5 million to settle charges by the Commodity Futures Trading Commission that its traders had manipulated indexes for their own financial benefit.[48] The individual member of an organization assumes some measure of ethical responsibility by agreeing in general to abide by the organization's rules and standard operating procedures. Significant others help in the socialization process that transforms the employee from an outsider into an insider. This process produces cohesiveness in the organization, with members demonstrating loyalty, support, and trust.

If managers and coworkers can provide direction and encourage ethical decision making, significant others become a force in helping individuals make better ethical decisions. When workers have greater participation in the design and implementation of assignments, conflict within work groups is reduced and ethical behavior may increase.

Businesses with an organizational culture that results in managers and employees acting contrary to their individual ethics need to understand the costs of unethical behavior. Some employees succumb to organizational pressures rather than follow their own values, rationalizing their decisions by maintaining that they are simply agents of the corporation. According to Gene R. Laczniak and Patrick E. Murphy, this rationalization has several weaknesses, including the following:

1. People who work in business organizations can never fully abdicate their personal ethical responsibility when making business decisions. Claiming to be an agent of the business organization is not accepted as a legal excuse and is even less defensible from an ethical perspective.
2. It is difficult to determine what is in the best interest of the business organization. Short-term profits earned through unethical behavior may not be in a company's long-run interest.
3. Employees of a business have a responsibility to parties other than the organization itself. When making ethical decisions, they must consider stakeholders who can be affected by the firm.[49]

Understanding the influence of interpersonal relationships within the organization provides insights into the ethical decision-making process. For business-related decisions, significant others have been found to be the most influential variable affecting ethical decisions. In extreme situations—for instance, if asked to break into a competitor's office to obtain trade secrets—employees may abide by their own personal value systems. But in most day-to-day matters, the employee tends to go along with the group on decisions that the employee believes are not of major importance and that appear to be defined and controlled by the work group. Hence, understanding how corporate culture and coworkers influence the ethical decision-making process will help to explain why unethical decisions are made in business.

## Summary

Significant others include superiors, peers, and subordinates within the organization who influence the ethical decision-making process. Relationships among these individuals and within groups are an important part of the functioning of a business organization and strongly influence ethical behavior.

The corporation can be viewed as a moral agent that is accountable for its ethical conduct. Although a corporation is not a person who can think through ethical issues, it can be considered a moral agent and therefore is responsible to society for its decisions. Because the corporation has the characteristics of an agent, business ethics and social responsibility obligations are assigned to it as an entity as well as to the individuals or work groups it employs.

Research indicates that the ways in which individuals make ethical decisions varies considerably. Approximately 10 percent of employees may take advantage of opportunities to be unethical to further their own personal interests. About 40 percent of workers go along with the work group on most matters, while another 40 percent try to follow company policies and rules. The final 10 percent of employees believe that their value system is superior to that of their coworkers and the organization.

A role is the part that a particular person plays in an organization; it refers both to that person's position and the behavior others expect from someone holding that position. Socialization is the process through which a person learns the values and appropriate behavior patterns of an organization or group as well as the behaviors expected of his or her role within the organization. Ethical issues such as lying, cheating, and paying bribes may be defined through the socialization process. A role-set is the total of all role relationships a person is involved because of his or her position in an organization. Role stress refers to the strain, conflict, or disruption that results from a lack of agreement on certain job-related activities. The role that an individual plays within a business, including the various tasks that have the potential to create conflict, may have a direct bearing on his or her ethical decision-making behavior.

Differential association refers to the idea that people learn ethical or unethical behavior while interacting with those who are part of their role-sets or other intimate personal groups. This social learning process encourages ethical or unethical behavior, depending on the behavior of the person's associates.

Conflict may occur when employees think they know the right course of action, yet their work group or company promotes or requires unethical decisions. In such cases, they may choose to refuse to participate in unethical or illegal conduct or even go outside the organization to publicize and correct a harmful situation. Whistle-blowing involves exposing an employer's wrongdoing to outsiders, such as the media or government regulatory agencies.

Pressure to perform and increase profits stems from role-set relationships, role stress, and differential association. It is a major predictor of unethical behavior. The roles that top management and superiors play are extremely important in developing the environment that influences employees' ethical decisions.

Both opportunity and conflict affect ethical decision making in interpersonal relations. Opportunity is a set of conditions that limit unfavorable behavior or reward favorable behavior. Rewards may be internal or external. An unethical individual who is rewarded or not punished is likely to continue to act unethically, whereas a person who is punished or not rewarded for behaving unethically is less likely to repeat the behavior. An individual who has an information base, expertise, or information about competition has the opportunity to exploit this knowledge unethically.

Conflict occurs when there is a question as to which goals or values take precedence in a situation: those of the individual, the organization, or society. A personal–organizational conflict arises when an individual's philosophies or methods for reaching a desired goal differ from those of the organization. Such situations occur frequently, especially for new employees who have not yet been socialized into the organization. Persons whose values do not coincide with those of others in their profession may fight or leave the organization. Personal–societal conflict develops when an individual's values differ from those of society. When society feels that a particular activity is unethical yet legal, new laws may be enacted to help redefine the minimum level of ethical behavior. Organizational–societal conflict occurs when the norms and values of the organization are opposed to those of society in general. The marketing of new products often brings business into conflict with society, especially when those products raise moral issues for certain groups.

Ethical behavior can be a function of several dimensions of an organization's system: its corporate culture, its significant others, and the personal value preferences of its groups and individual members. Significant others have been found to be the most influential variable affecting ethical decisions in business-related matters. Some employees may rationalize their decisions by maintaining that they are simply agents of the corporation. This is not acceptable as a legal excuse and is even less defensible from an ethical perspective.

| Important Terms for Review | | |
|---|---|---|
| | role | differential association |
| | socialization | whistle-blowing |
| | role-set | conflict |
| | role stress | |

# A Real-Life Situation*

Gordon McGinnis, assistant dean and director of student activities at Mountain State University, had vehemently banned credit card solicitations on campus during his five-year tenure. To him, it was a matter of acting in the best interests of Mountain State's thirty thousand full-time students, 95 percent of whom are between seventeen and twenty-two years old. Over the years a number of credit card companies and banks had approached him, offering deals to market their cards on campus that would generate good income for the university. Typically, the companies and banks would propose marketing their cards at kiosks located at special school events, by inserting credit card applications when purchases from the school bookstore were bagged, by posting "take-one" applications around campus, and/or by pitching the credit cards at sign-up tables during freshman orientation. However, Gordon had always stood his ground and turned the credit card companies and banks down.

However, he learned through the grapevine that credit card hawkers frequently appeared in dormitories and high-traffic campus locations unannounced and without permission, trying to entice students to sign up with items such as free T-shirts, Frisbees, music CDs, chances to win airline tickets—even promises of an easy way to pay for spring break vacations. Several times student organization members had been directly approached by the marketers, who asked them to encourage classmates to sign up for the cards in return for up to $3,000 a year. Even though the student leaders assured Gordon that students could sign up for a card just to get the goodies and then destroy the card, Gordon always held his ground.

Gordon's rationale for reducing the prevalence of credit cards on campus was simple—students were, in effect, throwing away their credit ratings by getting into debt in exchange for a few trinkets. He had heard stories from his colleagues at other colleges of students cutting back on classes or dropping out to earn money to pay off debt. And bad credit histories often hurt students seeking their first jobs, especially since many of them had both student loan and credit card debt. Gordon had even heard tales of students using their credit line to gamble online. From his personal discussions with students, he also knew that many were unprepared to manage their finances. Some did not know how to use credit or even balance a checkbook.

Gordon was not alone in his discomfort with the marketing of credit cards to college students. Lawmakers in several states have tried to ban card marketers from colleges altogether, and increasingly schools have been actively restricting or banning certain credit card marketers from campus. Consumer advocates who see campuses as the financial world's version of crack houses, complete with professional dealers who hook students with easy doses of credit, have blasted credit card companies. Credit-hungry students are often a card issuer's best customers, despite the fact that most have no credit history or even a job. Students are often loyal to their first credit card throughout adulthood. And once a bank secures a captive student audience, it can cross-promote other products, such as first mortgages, car loans, and—in Gordon's view, a sinister twist—even debt-consolidation loans to help students repay credit card debt.

Despite his successes in keeping the credit card hawkers at bay, Gordon was given a new challenge recently when he received a phone call from Elsie Lombardi, the university's treasurer and vice president for finance. "I was just made an offer I don't think we can refuse," began Elsie. "Highland Bank Corporation's credit-card division wants us to enter into an exclusive affinity-marketing credit card program with them. They'll pay us $5 million over the next three years to allow them to be the only bank card issuer allowed to market on campus at sports events, in the student union building, and in the university bookstore, plus through student and alumni mailing lists. The card will be adorned with Mountain State's picture and logo, which will make cardholders feel more loyal to the school—for users it will be like being part of a club. They'll also give the university one-half of a percent of every transaction charge, which they estimate will amount to about $1.5 million annually. If you accept this deal, I'm prepared to turn over to your student activities division half of the revenues we make on these charges. And they'll give us $6 for each new account that's opened. What could be easier money?"

"While quite a few of our student organizations are operating in the hole and we could really use the money, I'm afraid I'll have to say 'no,' Elsie," replied Gordon. "I'm philosophically opposed to marketing credit cards on campus."

"I didn't know you were a philosopher," quipped Elsie. "What's your problem? You know the financial crisis the university is in due to dwindling state fiscal support. Plus, doing an exclusive deal with Highland will mean getting other credit card issuers off campus and give us total control. Students won't have to worry about shopping around for the best deal. They're giving our students a good one at an interest rate of prime plus 3.9 percent, where most competitors offer prime plus 6 to 8 percent. They also offer no annual fee and have no requirement for actually using the card. The credit limit will be only $2,500. It's a win–win proposition."

"No. You win, and I win, but our students lose," insisted Gordon. "Remember, very few of our students have taken a course in personal finance. The bank will tell the students that 'there's no cost to you,' but there's the hidden cost of high interest payments on unpaid balances, the possibility of high debt upon graduation, and ruined credit ratings in some cases."

"Those are the extreme cases," retorted Elsie. "Highland assures me that, although many students lack credit experience, most use credit responsibly and handle credit cards as well or better than most adults. It's a service our students want in a world where, like it or not, plastic is very important. Having a credit card helps students establish a credit history; assists them in meeting emergency needs such as a sudden trip home; makes paying for things like gas, food, rent, and books more convenient; and empowers them to become more financially responsible. Also, those who pay off their balances each month get the benefit of a short-term, interest-free loan. And Highland pointed out that almost two-thirds of the nation's parents think their children should have a credit card by age eighteen, mainly because it's a convenience for them since they don't

need to continually send their kids money. I'll tell you what, Gordon. I'll let Student Activities have all the new-account payments of $6 as well as three-fifths of the revenue from transactions. Why don't you sleep on it and get back to me tomorrow?"

"I suppose I can do that," Gordon reluctantly agreed. He decided to seek the advice of Alan Whitehead, assistant director of student activities.

"I think we should take Ms. Lombardi up on her generous offer," opined Alan. "Even if our students graduate with average debts of around $1,000, given their likely earning power upon graduation, such levels of debt are easily recoverable, and the bank knows that. They aren't in the business of issuing credit to those who can't pay. And Highland is right—college students who qualify for credit are no different from nonstudent customers. At the end of the day, the responsibility is with the cardholder."

"Unfortunately, a lot of students, as well as adults, just aren't responsible," insisted Gordon. "Even for adults, credit cards foster bad habits. People think that because they have a $1,500 limit they can buy something that costs $1,500 and take their time paying it off, rather than saving until they have $1,500."

"Stop exaggerating," exclaimed Alan. "I think students can grasp the principle of debt. You're being nannyish. Credit card issuers will get their offer in students' faces one way or another. They won't be stopped by your righteous efforts. We tell our eighteen-year-olds that they're ready for the work force or college and that they can vote and even fight a war. Many work full or part time. Some are raising families. How can we tell them they can't manage their own credit card? Let's get with the program and get a piece of the action."

Gordon went back to his office, his head swimming. He thought that maybe Alan had some valid points. Maybe he was being too paternalistic. And, speaking of parents, didn't they have some responsibility for their kids' spending? Shouldn't they think twice before allowing their youngsters to have credit cards with a $2,500 spending limit? The banks are responding to demand, most students are fairly responsible, and anyway, it's the bank that is taking the risk of higher levels of default. After all, the relatively high rates of interest are justified since credit card debt is a pretty high-risk, unsecured type of loan.

Then he had an idea. Perhaps he could use some of the funds that Student Activities would get to institute a financial-education program on campus to help students understand the responsibility of owning and using a credit card. In fact, he had heard that some of the big banks and credit card companies had accepted the responsibility for providing personal finance guidance for students through posters on campus, "credit awareness" brochures, interactive online game shows, and even seminars on financial management. Perhaps Mountain State and Highland could be partners in a program to deliver financial information and education to students.

## Questions ■ Exercises

1. Summarize the pros and cons of marketing credit cards to college students mentioned in this situation. Can you think of other reasons for and against marketing credit cards to college students?

2. Does Mountain State University have a responsibility as a moral agent to students in this case? Why or why not?

3. Discuss the organizational relationships that Gordon should consider as he makes his decision.

4. What are the decision alternatives Gordon faces? Which alternative is most ethical, will help build the most trust, and will enhance the university's reputation among Mountain State's stakeholders?

* This real-life situation was prepared by Geoffrey P. Lantos, Stonehill College, and is strictly hypothetical; any resemblance to real persons, companies, or situations is coincidental. The author thanks Michael Durkin, assistant dean and director of student activities at Stonehill College for his input.

# Check Your EQ

Check your E.Q., or Ethics Quotient, by completing the following. Assess your performance to evaluate your overall understanding of the chapter material.

1. Roughly 40 percent of employees will take advantage of a situation to further their personal interests.  Yes  No

2. Socialization refers to the process in which a person learns the values and behaviors considered appropriate by an organization.  Yes  No

3. Differential association means that people learn ethical behavior from their personal upbringing and socialization.  Yes  No

4. Whistle-blowers often retain their positions and continue to advance within the organization.  Yes  No

5. A person who behaves unethically and is rewarded is likely to continue to act unethically.  Yes  No

ANSWERS: 1. No. Ten percent of employees take advantage of a situation if the penalty is less than the benefit and they are at low risk of being caught. 2. Yes. Socialization teaches employees how to behave with respect to their roles within the organization. 3. No. Differential association relates to the idea that individuals in an organization learn ethical and unethical behavior while interacting with other employees who are part of their role-sets. 4. No. Whistle-blowers often lose their jobs. 5. Yes. If no punishment occurs for unethical behavior or the behavior is rewarded, it is likely to continue.

Part **Three**

# Implementing Business Ethics in a Global Economy

# Developing an Effective Ethics Program

## An Ethical Dilemma*

Victoria was starting to wonder about the implications of her actions, as well as her company's strategy. She had begun working for Koke International (KI) after graduating from Pacific West University with degrees in both finance and marketing. KI was the leader in franchised home repair outlets in the United States. In twenty-five years KI had grown from several stores in the Pacific Northwest to two hundred and fifty over much of the United States and Canada. Koke International came to dominate the markets it entered by undercutting local competitors on price and quality. The lower prices were easy to charge because KI received large quantity discounts from its vendors. The franchise concept also helped create another barrier to entry for KI's competitors. By expanding rapidly, KI was able to spread the costs of marketing to many more stores, giving it still another differential advantage. This active nourishment of its brand image coupled with some technological advances such as just-in-time inventory, electronic scanners, and electronic market niching had sent KI's stock soaring. As a result, it had a 50 percent share of the market. Koke International had done such an excellent job of positioning itself in its field that articles in major business newspapers were calling it "the Microsoft of home improvements." The view was that "KI is going to continue to be a very profitable endeavor, with less expected direct competition in a slow-growth, high-margin market for the future."

Wendy, Victoria's boss, had brought her in on KI's next potential conquest: the New England states of Maine, Vermont, New Hampshire, Connecticut, and Massachusetts.

"This is the last big potential market," Wendy said at a planning session with her senior staff. "I want you to realize that when we launch into these states we're going to have to be ruthless. I'd like your suggestions as to how we're going to eliminate the competition."

One person spoke up: "We first need to recognize that there are only five major players (multiple-store chains), with Home Designs being the largest."

"The top corporate people want us to attack Maine, New Hampshire, and Vermont first and then make a secondary attack on the other two states," interjected Victoria.

"Our buildings are four months from completion," Wendy pointed out, "and the media blitz is due to start one month prior to the twenty-store grand opening. With that much exposed capital from our franchises, we need to make sure everything goes well. Vicky, have you completed your price analysis of all of the surrounding home repair stores?"

"Yes, and you're not going to like the news," Victoria replied. "Many of the stores are going to be extremely competitive relative to our normal pricing. In a few cases they seem to have an edge."

Wendy turned to Ed. "Ed, how much cash flow/reserves have you been able to calculate from the five players?"

"Well, Wendy, it looks like if we slash our prices for about six months to a year, we could drive all but Home Designs into near bankruptcy, providing that our promotional campaign doesn't have a misstep."

"What about personnel, Frank?" Wendy cut in. "Have you done the usual research to see about hiring away the five players' key personnel?"

"Yes, but many won't go unless they get a 50 percent raise, which is way out of line with our other stores."

At this point, Wendy slammed her fist on the table and shouted, "I'm tired of hearing negative reports! It's our job to drive out the competition, so I want solutions!"

There was a long silence in the room. Wendy was noted for her quick temper and her quick firings when things didn't go as planned. She had been the first woman to make it this high in the company, and it wasn't the result of being overly pleasant.

"So this is what we're going to do," Wendy said softly. "Frank, you're going to hire those key people at a 50 percent increase. You're going to keep the unions away from the rest of the people. In eighteen months, when these overpriced employees have trained the others, we'll find some way of getting rid of them. Ed, you're going to lean on the players' bankers. See if we do business with them as well. See what other information you can squeeze out of them. Victoria, since you're the newest, I'm putting you in charge of breaking the pricing problem. I want you to come up with a unique pricing strategy for each of the twenty stores that will consistently undercut the competition for the next eighteen months, even if we have to lose money on everything in the stores! The franchisees will go with this once we explain the payout."

One of the newer staff asked, "If we're successful, doesn't that make us a monopoly in the area? Don't we have to worry about antitrust issues?"

Wendy raised her eyebrow a little and said, "We don't mention the word *monopoly* around here as if it were wrong. It took the Feds decades to break up AT&T. Microsoft was next on their list, and now it's MasterCard. We're in retail. No one has ever had problems with the Feds in this industry. By the time they deal with what we're doing, we will all be retired."

## Questions ■ Exercises

1. Identify the issues of which Victoria needs to be aware.
2. Discuss the implications of each decision Wendy made.
3. Discuss the issue of monopolies and whether they are right or wrong.

\* This case is strictly hypothetical; any resemblance to real persons, companies, or situations is coincidental.

Programs that are designed to foster ethical decision making in business are controversial today because much unethical and illegal business conduct has continued to occur, even in organizations that have adopted such programs. Enron, for example, had a code of ethics and was a member of the Better Business Bureau, yet the company was ruined by unethical activities and corporate scandal. Many business leaders believe that ethics initiatives should arise naturally from a company's corporate culture and that hiring good employees will limit unethical conduct. Moreover, many business executives and board members often do not understand how organizational ethics can be systematically implemented. We believe, however, that a customized ethical program will help many businesses provide guidance so that employees from diverse backgrounds will understand what behaviors are acceptable (or unacceptable) within the organization. In business, many ethical issues are complex and require that organizations reach a consensus on appropriate action. Top executives and boards of directors must provide the leadership and a system to resolve these issues.

Business ethics programs have the potential to help top managers establish an ethical culture and eliminate the opportunity for unethical conduct. This chapter therefore provides a framework for developing an ethics program that is consistent with research, best practices, the decision-making process described in Chapter 4, as well as the Federal Sentencing Guidelines for Organizations (FSGO) and the Sarbanes-Oxley Act. These legislative reforms require both executives and boards of directors to assume responsibility and ensure that ethical standards are properly implemented on a daily basis.

In this chapter, we first provide an overview of why businesses need to develop an organizational ethics program. Next, we consider the factors that must be part of such a program: a code of conduct; an ethics officer and the appropriate delegation of authority; an effective ethics training program; a system for monitoring and supporting ethical compliance; and continual efforts to improve the ethical program. Finally, we consider common mistakes made in designing and implementing ethics programs.

## *The Need for Organizational Ethics Programs*

To understand why companies need to develop ethics programs, consider the following exercise and judge whether each of the described actions is unethical or illegal:

1. You want to skip work to go to a baseball game but you need a doctor's excuse, so you make up some symptoms so your insurance company pays for the doctor's visit. (unethical, illegal)
2. While having a latte at Starbucks, you run into an acquaintance who works as a salesperson at a competing firm. You wind up chatting about future product prices. When you get back to your office, you tell your supervisor what you heard. (unethical, illegal)
3. You get fired from your company but before leaving to take a position with another company, you take a confidential list of client names and telephone numbers that you compiled for your former employer. (unethical, illegal)
4. You receive a loan from your parents to make the down payment on your first home but when describing the source of the down payment on the mortgage application, you characterize it as a gift. (unethical, illegal)
5. Your manager asks you to book some sales revenue from the next quarter into this quarters' sales report to help reach target sales figures. You agree to do so. (unethical, illegal)

You probably labeled one or more of these five scenarios as unethical rather than illegal. The reality is that all of them are illegal. You may have chosen incorrectly because it is nearly impossible to know every detail of the highly complex laws relevant to these situations. Consider that there are ten thousand laws and regulations associated with the processing and selling of a single hamburger. Unless you are a lawyer who specializes in a particular area, it is difficult to know every law associated with your job. However, you can become more sensitized to what might be unethical or in this case illegal. One reason why ethics programs are required in one form or another is to help sensitize employees to the potential legal and ethical issues within their work environments.

As we have mentioned throughout this book, recent ethics scandals in U.S. business have destroyed trust in top management and significantly lowered the public's trust of business. As a result, the chairman of the Securities and Exchange Commission issued a challenge for "American organizations to behave more ethically than the law requires to help restore investors' trust."[1] A survey by Golin/Harris International found that 82 percent of the public believes that the crisis of trust in America will stay the same or worsen, and two-thirds hold CEOs personally accountable for restoring trust and confidence in business. The survey respondents were asked to make recommendations that they considered essential or important to establishing and maintaining trust.[2] Table 8–1 lists some of their responses. These results signify that the public is looking for clear, creative, and constructive leadership from CEOs—leadership that demonstrates that trust is a management priority.

Understanding the factors that influence the ethical decision-making process, as discussed in Chapter 4, can help companies encourage ethical behavior and discourage undesirable conduct. Fostering ethical decision making within an organization

| TABLE 8–1 | Top Recommendations to CEOs for Rebuilding Trust and Confidence |
| --- | --- |

| RECOMMENDATION | PERCENTAGE RECOMMENDING |
| --- | --- |
| Make customers the top priority | 91% |
| Assume personal responsibility and accountability | 90% |
| Communicate openly and frequently | 89% |
| Handle crises better and more honestly | 87% |
| Stick to code of business ethics no matter what | 85% |

Source: "62% of Americans Tell CEOs 'You're Not Doing Enough to Restore Trust and Confidence in American Business," Golin/Harris International, press release, June 20, 2002 www.golinharris.com/news/releases.asp?ID=3788.

requires terminating unethical persons and improving the firm's ethical standards. Consider the "bad apple–bad barrel" analogy. Some people are simply "bad apples" who will always do things in their own self-interest regardless of their organization's goals or accepted standards of conduct. Eliminating such bad apples through screening techniques and enforcement of the firm's ethical standards can help improve the firm's overall behavior.[3] For example, ClearOne Communications Inc. fired its CEO and CFO after they were named as defendants in a complaint filed by the Securities and Exchange Commission. The SEC alleged that they directed sales personnel to push extra products on customers in addition to their orders so as to inflate sales and earnings.[4] In this case, the CEO and CFO not only allegedly directed employees to act unethically, but also contributed to an unethical corporate culture.

Organizations also can become "bad barrels," not because the individuals within them are bad, but because the pressures to succeed create opportunities that reward unethical decisions. In the case of such bad barrels, the firms must redesign their image and culture to conform to industry and social standards of acceptable behavior.[5] Most companies attempt to improve ethical decision making by establishing and implementing a strategic approach to improving their organization's ethics. Companies as diverse as Texas Instruments, Starbucks, Ford Motor Company, and Johnson & Johnson have adopted a strategic approach to organizational ethics but also continuously monitor their programs and make improvements when problems occur.

To promote legal and ethical conduct, an organization should develop an organizational ethics program by establishing, communicating, and monitoring the ethical values and legal requirements that characterize its history, culture, industry, and operating environment. Without such programs and uniform standards and policies of conduct, it is difficult for employees to determine what behaviors are acceptable within a company. As discussed in Chapters 6 and 7, in the absence of such programs and standards, employees generally will make decisions based on their observations of how their coworkers and superiors behave. A strong ethics program includes a written code of conduct, an ethics officer to oversee the program, careful delegation of authority, formal ethics training, and rigorous auditing, monitoring, enforcement, and revision of program standards. Without a strong program, problems likely will occur. Such is the case in Latin America where a survey by a Latin American business magazine found that Argentine businesses have the greatest number of ethical problems. In Latin America there is no method, rule, or corporate internal policy that controls in absolute terms what business managers plan, execute, or do, and only 26 percent of all executives follow the values of the founder or owner of the business in which they are employed.[6]

Although there are no universal standards that can be applied to organizational ethics programs, most companies develop codes, values, or policies to provide guidance on business conduct. However, it would be naïve to think that simply having a code of ethics will solve all the ethical dilemmas a company might face.[7] Indeed, most of the companies that have experienced ethical and legal difficulties in recent years have had formal ethics codes and programs. The problem is that top managers have not integrated these codes, values, and standards into their firms' corporate culture, where they can provide effective guidance for daily decision making. Tyco, for example, had an ethics program and was a member of the Ethics Officer Association. However, it was never active in that organization, and its top managers were involved in misconduct that sacrificed public confidence in the company. CEO Dennis Kozlowski allegedly used millions of dollars of company funds for personal use and was indicted for criminal tax avoidance schemes.[8] If a company's leadership fails to provide the vision and support needed for ethical conduct, then an ethics program will not be effective. Ethics is not something to be delegated to lower-level employees while top managers break the rules.

To satisfy the public's escalating demands for ethical decision making, companies need to develop plans and structures for addressing ethical considerations. Some directions for improving ethics have been mandated through regulations, but companies must be willing to have in place a system for implementing values and ethics that exceeds the minimum requirements.

## An Effective Ethics Program

Throughout this book, we have emphasized that ethical issues are at the forefront of organizational concerns as managers and employees face increasingly complex decisions. These decisions are often made in a group environment comprising different value systems, competitive pressures, and political concerns that contribute to the opportunity for misconduct. In a national survey by KPMG, 76 percent of the nearly twenty-four hundred workers surveyed indicated that they had observed violations of the law or of company standards in the previous twelve months.[9] When opportunity to engage in unethical conduct abounds, companies are vulnerable to both ethical problems and legal violations if their employees do not know how to make the right decisions.

A company must have an effective ethics program to ensure that all employees understand its values and comply with the policies and codes of conduct that create its ethical climate. Because we come from diverse business, educational, and family backgrounds, it cannot be assumed that we know how to behave appropriately when we enter a new organization or job. At the pharmaceutical company Merck, for example, all employees are expected to uphold the organization's corporate code of conduct. Merck's sixty thousand employees participate in an interactive ethical business practices program that exposes them to real-life situations they might encounter.

According to Merck's chief ethics officer, "we want employees to know how Merck's values apply to their day-to-day activities so that they can adhere to these standards and model these values whenever and wherever they conduct Merck business."[10]

## An Ethics Program Can Help a Company Avoid Legal Problems

As mentioned in Chapter 4, some corporate cultures provide opportunities for or reward unethical conduct because their management lacks concern or the company has failed to comply with the minimum requirements of the Federal Sentencing Guidelines for Organizations (see Table 8–2). In such cases, the company may face penalties and the loss of public confidence if one of its employees breaks the law. The guidelines encourage companies to assess their key risk areas and to customize a compliance program that will address these risks and satisfy key effectiveness criteria. The guidelines also hold companies responsible for the misconduct of their employees. The KPMG organizational survey found that 61 percent of those surveyed felt that their company would not discipline workers guilty of an ethical infraction, and 38 percent said that management would authorize illegal or unethical conduct to meet business goals.[11]

At the heart of the Federal Sentencing Guidelines for Organizations is a carrot-and-stick philosophy. Companies that act to prevent misconduct by establishing and enforcing ethical and legal compliance programs may receive a "carrot" and avoid penalties should a violation occur. The ultimate "stick" is the possibility of being fined or put on probation if convicted of a crime. Organizational probation involves using consultants on site to observe and monitor a company's legal compliance efforts as well as to report the company's progress toward avoiding misconduct to the U.S. Sentencing Commission. Table 8–3 shows the fines that have been imposed on sentenced organizations for leading offenses, including antitrust violations and fraud. Thus, the government now views corporations as moral agents that are responsible for the conduct of their employees.

The Federal Sentencing Guidelines for Organizations also require federal judges to increase fines for organizations that continually tolerate misconduct and to reduce or eliminate fines for firms with extensive compliance programs that are making due diligence attempts to abide by legal and ethical standards. Until the guidelines were for-

---

| **TABLE 8–2** | **Minimum Requirements for Ethical Compliance Programs** |
| --- | --- |

1. Standards and procedures, such as codes of ethics, that are reasonably capable of detecting and preventing misconduct
2. High-level personnel who are responsible for ethics compliance programs
3. No substantial discretionary authority given to individuals with a propensity for misconduct
4. Standards and procedures communicated effectively via ethics training programs
5. Establishment of systems to monitor, audit, and report misconduct
6. Consistent enforcement of standards, codes, and punishment
7. Continuous improvement of the ethical compliance program

Source: Adapted from U.S. Sentencing Commission, *Federal Sentencing Guidelines Manual* (St. Paul, Minn.: West Publishing, 1994), Chapter 8.

| TABLE 8–3 | **Mean and Median Fines Imposed on Sentenced Organizations in Five Offense Categories** |
|---|---|

**CASES WITH FINE IMPOSED**

| Offense | Total Number of Cases | Cases with Fine Imposed | | |
|---|---|---|---|---|
| | | Number | Mean Fine | Median Fine |
| Antitrust | 16 | 12 | $20,980,184 | $3,999,744 |
| Fraud | 72 | 50 | 1,900,357 | 107,496 |
| Tax | 7 | 7 | 1,416,802 | 240,000 |
| Environmental—water | 31 | 29 | 744,863 | 100,000 |
| Environmental—hazardous toxic pollutants | 14 | 12 | 568,299 | 25,000 |

Source: U.S. Sentencing Commission, *2001 Sourcebook of Federal Sentencing Statistics,* Table 52 www.ussc.gov/ANNRPT/2001/SBTOC01.htm (accessed Feb. 26, 2003).

mulated, courts were inconsistent in holding corporations responsible for employee misconduct. There was no incentive to build effective programs to encourage employees to make ethical and legal decisions. Now companies earn credit for creating ethics programs that meet a rigorous standard. The effectiveness of a program is determined by its design and implementation: it must deal effectively with the risk associated with a particular business and has to become part of the corporate culture.

An ethics program can help a firm avoid civil liability, but the company still bears the burden of proving that it has an effective program. A program developed in the absence of misconduct will be much more effective than one imposed as a reaction to scandal or prosecution. A legal test of a company's ethics program is possible when an individual employee is charged with misconduct. The court system or the U.S. Sentencing Commission evaluates the organization's responsibility for the individual's behavior during the process of an investigation. If the courts find that the company contributed to the misconduct or failed to show due diligence in preventing misconduct, then the firm may be convicted and sentenced.

The Sarbanes-Oxley Act of 2002, as discussed in Chapter 3, established new requirements for corporate governance to prevent fraudulent behavior in business. The heart of this act is an accounting oversight board that establishes financial reporting requirements, including instituting a code of conduct for senior financial officers. This legislation covers many issues related to corporate governance, including the role of board members relative to the oversight of ethics programs. It also requires public corporations to file their code of ethics with the accounting oversight board or explain why they do not have a code of ethics.

## *Values Versus Compliance Programs*

No matter what their goals, ethics programs are developed as organizational control systems the aim of which is to create predictability in employee behavior. Two types of control systems can be created. A **compliance orientation** creates order by requiring that employees identify with and commit to specific required conduct. It uses legal terms, statutes, and contracts that teach employees the rules and penalties for noncompliance. The other type of system is a **values orientation,** which strives to develop shared values. Although penalties are attached, the focus is more on an abstract core of ideals such as respect and responsibility. Instead of relying on coercion, the company's values are seen as something to which people willingly aspire.[12]

Research into compliance- and values-based approaches reveals that both types of programs can interact or work toward the same end but that a values orientation can better help explain and influence employees. Values-based programs increase employees' awareness of ethics at work, their integrity, their willingness to deliver bad news to supervisors, and the perception that better decisions are made. Compliance-based programs are linked to employees' awareness of ethical issues at work, their perception that decision making is better because of the program, and that the employees have explicit knowledge of rules and expectations that makes decision making easier. In the final analysis, both orientations can be used to help employees and managers; however, it appears that a values-based program may be better for companies in the long run.

## Codes Of Conduct

Most companies begin the process of establishing organizational ethics programs by developing **codes of conduct,** which are formal statements that describe what an organization expects of its employees. Such statements may take three different forms: a code of ethics, a code of conduct, and a statement of values. A **code of ethics** is the most comprehensive and consists of general statements, sometimes altruistic or inspirational, that serve as principles and the basis for rules of conduct. A code of ethics generally specifies methods for reporting violations, disciplinary action for violations, and a structure of due process. A code of conduct is a written document that may contain some inspiration statements but usually specifies acceptable or unacceptable types of behavior. A code of conduct is more akin to a regulatory set of rules and as such, tends to elicit less debate about specific actions. One problem with codes of conduct is that they tend to be developed without broad-based participation from stakeholders.[13] The final type of ethical statement is a **statement of values,** which serves the general public and also addresses distinct groups such as stakeholders. Values statements are conceived by management and are fully developed with input from all stakeholders. Despite our distinctions, it is important to recognize that these terms are often used interchangeably. According to an Ethics Resource Center survey, 79 percent of employees surveyed reported that their firm has written standards of ethical business conduct such as codes of ethics or conduct, policy statements on ethics, or guidelines on proper business conduct.[14]

Regardless of the degree of comprehensiveness, a code of ethics should reflect upper managers' desire for compliance with the values, rules, and policies that support an ethical climate. The development of a code of ethics should involve the president, board of directors, and chief executive officers who will be implementing the code. Legal staff should also be called on to ensure that the code has correctly assessed key areas of risk and that it provides buffers for potential legal problems. A code of ethics that does not address specific high-risk activities within the scope of daily operations is inadequate for maintaining standards that can prevent misconduct. Table 8–4 shows factors to consider when developing and implementing a code of ethics.

These codes may address a variety of situations, from internal operations to sales presentations and financial disclosure practices. Research has found that corporate codes of ethics often contain about six core values or principles in addition to more detailed descriptions and examples of appropriate conduct.[15] The six values that have been suggested as being desirable for codes of ethics include: (1) trustworthiness, (2) respect, (3) responsibility, (4) fairness, (5) caring, and (6) citizenship.[16] These values will not be effective without distribution, training, and the support of top management in making these values a part of the corporate culture. Employees need specific examples of how these values can be implemented.

Codes of conduct will not resolve every ethical issue encountered in daily operations, but they help employees and managers deal with ethical dilemmas by prescribing or limiting specific activities. Many companies have a code of ethics, but it is not communicated effectively. A code that is placed on a Web site or in a training manual is useless if it is not reinforced every day. By communicating to employees both what is expected of them and what punishments they face if they violate the rules, codes of conduct curtail opportunities for unethical behavior and thereby improve ethical decision making. Fidelity Investment's code of ethics, for example, specifies that the sanctions for violating its code range from cautions and warnings to dismissal and criminal prosecution.[17] Codes of conduct do not have to be so detailed that they take into account every situation, but they should provide guidelines and principles that are capable of helping employees achieve organizational ethical objectives and addressing risks in an accepted way.

In the United States, Texas Instruments (TI) has gained recognition as having one of the nation's leading ethics programs. The company has won three major ethics awards: the David C. Lincoln Award for Ethics and Excellence in Business, the American Business Ethics Award, and the Bentley College Center for Business Ethics Award. Seventy-three percent of TI's employees feel that the company is very serious about ethics and integrity.[18] For this reason, it is worthwhile to take a close look at how TI has implemented its ethics program.

| TABLE 8–4 | Developing and Implementing a Code of Ethics |
| --- | --- |
| 1. | Consider areas of risk and state the values as well as conduct necessary to comply with laws and regulations. Values are an important buffer in preventing serious misconduct. |
| 2. | Identify values that specifically address current ethical issues. |
| 3. | Consider values that link the organization to a stakeholder orientation. Attempt to find overlaps in organizational and stakeholder values. |
| 4. | Make the code understandable by providing examples that reflect values. |
| 5. | Communicate the code frequently and in language that employees can understand. |
| 6. | Revise the code every year with input from organizational members and stakeholders. |

## Texas Instruments' Code of Ethics

A large multinational firm, Texas Instruments (TI) manufactures computers, calculators, and other high-technology products. Its code of ethics resembles that of many organizations. It addresses issues relating to policies and procedures; government laws and regulations; relationships with customers, suppliers, and competitors; accepting gifts, travel, and entertainment; political contributions; expense reporting; business payments; conflicts of interest; investing in TI stock; handling proprietary information and trade secrets; using TI employees and assets to perform personal work; relationships with government officials and agencies; and enforcing the code. TI's code emphasizes that ethical behavior is critical to maintaining long-term success and that each individual is responsible for upholding the integrity of the company:

> Our reputation at TI depends upon all of the decisions we make and all the actions we take personally each day. Our values define how we will evaluate our decisions and actions . . . and how we will conduct our business. We are working in a difficult and demanding, ever-changing business environment. Together we are building a work environment on the foundation of integrity, innovation, and commitment. Together we are moving our company into a new century . . . one good decision at a time. We are prepared to make the tough decisions or take the critical actions . . . and do it right. Our high standards have rewarded us with an enviable reputation in today's marketplace . . . a reputation of integrity, honesty, and trustworthiness. That strong ethical reputation is a vital asset . . . and each of us shares a personal responsibility to protect, to preserve, and to enhance it. Our reputation is a strong but silent partner in all business relationships. By understanding and applying the values presented on the following pages, each of us can say to ourselves and to others, "TI is a good company, and one reason is that I am part of it." Know what's right. Value what's right. Do what's right.[19]

Like most codes of ethics, TI's requires employees to obey the law. In many instances, however, TI expects its employees to abide by ethical standards that are more demanding than the law. For example, although some local laws permit companies to contribute to political candidates or elected officials, TI's code states that "no company funds may be used for making political contributions of any kind to any political candidate or holder of any office of any government—national, state or local. This is so even where permitted by local law." TI also goes beyond the federal law prohibiting discrimination against minorities and expects its employees to treat all fellow workers with dignity and respect: "The hours we spend at work are more satisfying and rewarding when we demonstrate respect for all associates regardless of gender, age, creed, racial background, religion, handicap, national origin, or status in TI's organization."

Texas Instruments' code of ethics is not just lip service paid to social concerns about business ethics; the company enforces the code through audits and disciplinary action where necessary. TI's corporate internal audit function measures several aspects of business ethics, including compliance with policies, procedures, and regulations; the economical and efficient use of resources; and the internal controls of management systems. In addition, the code states that "any employee who violates TI's ethical standards is subject to disciplinary action which can include oral reprimand, written reprimand, probation, suspension, or immediate termination." The TI Ethics Committee, established in 1987, oversees all the activities of the ethics office. The committee consists of five high-level TI managers, who review and approve policy, procedures, and publications; monitor compliance initiatives; review any major ethical issues; and approve appropriate corrective actions.

To ensure that its employees understand the nature of business ethics and the ethical standards they are expected to follow, TI has three key publications: *Standard Policies and Procedures, The TI Commitment,* and *The Value and Ethics of TI.* Employees are also provided with a mini-pamphlet containing an "ethics quick test" to help them when they have doubts about the ethics of specific situations and behaviors:

- Is the action legal?
- Does it comply with our values?
- If you do it, will you feel bad?
- How will it look in the newspaper?
- If you know it's wrong, don't do it!
- If you're not sure, ask.
- Keep asking until you get an answer.

TI also provides a toll-free number (1-800-33-ETHIC) for employees to call, anonymously, to report incidents of unethical behavior or simply to ask questions.[20]

The extent of TI's commitment to its employees is further evidenced by the programs and support it offers them:

- "Open door" policy for all managers (any level)
- No retaliation, retribution, discrimination, or harassment
- Required sexual harassment training
- Required forty hours of ethics training per year
- Educational support from external sources
- Promotion from within
- Community involvement support
- Career development networks

Texas Instruments explicitly states what it expects of its employees and what behaviors are unacceptable. By enforcing the codes wholeheartedly, TI has taken logical steps to safeguard its excellent reputation for ethical and responsible behavior. When such standards of behavior are not made explicit, employees sometimes base ethical decisions on their observations of the behavior of peers and management. The use of rewards and punishments to enforce codes and policies enables TI to control the opportunities employees have to behave unethically and to increase employees' acceptance of ethical standards.

## Ethics Officers

Organizational ethics programs also must have oversight by high-ranking persons known to respect legal and ethical standards. These individuals—often referred to as **ethics officers**—are responsible for managing their organizations' ethics and legal compliance programs. They are usually responsible for assessing the needs and risks that an organizationwide ethics program must address, developing and distributing a code of conduct or ethics, conducting training programs for employees, establishing and maintaining a confidential service to answer employees' questions about ethical issues, making sure that the company is in compliance with government regulation, monitoring and auditing ethical conduct, taking action on possible violations of the company's code, and reviewing and updating the code. Ethics officers are also responsible for knowing thousands of pages of relevant regulations as well as communicating and reinforcing values that build an ethical organizational culture. According to the Ethics Resource Center Survey, 50 percent of respondents reported that their firm has a designated office, person, or telephone line where they can get advice about ethical issues.[21]

The Ethics Officer Association (EOA) has approximately 900 members, who are at the front lines of managing ethics programs.[22] Ethics officers often move into their position from other jobs in their company rather than having formal ethics training. One-third of EOA members have law degrees, one-fourth have financial backgrounds, and in some cases, they moved up through their companies' ranks and were selected because of their knowledge of the company and their ability to communicate and develop training programs. The financial reporting requirements of the Sarbanes-Oxley Act put more pressure on ethics officers to monitor financial reporting and the reporting of sales and inventory movements to prevent fraud in booking revenue and profits.[23]

In most firms, ethics officers do not report directly to the board of directors, although that will likely change over the next few years. At Sun Microsystems, the ethics officer already reports to the board of directors, and employees can report concerns to someone outside the firm. If their concerns have merit, the outside help center can report directly to the appropriate board committee, which can request a full investigation. A Conference Board survey of one hundred senior ethics officers revealed that 60 percent indicated that their own board of directors is not sufficiently engaged in ethics issues. Fifty-seven percent said they have never engaged their board of directors in ethics training.[24]

The European equivalent of the U.S. Ethics Officer Association has been set up as a debating and training forum for those responsible for managing company ethics. The Ethics Practitioner Forum has attracted interest from ethics officers in Spain, France, Germany, the Netherlands, Belgium, Denmark, Norway, Italy, and the United Kingdom. Initially, the Forum will consist of a series of small national groups that will share information and best practices on a Web site and meet annually.[25]

## Ethics Training and Communication

A major step in developing an effective ethics program is implementing a training program and communication system to communicate and educate employees about the firm's ethical standards. According to the Ethics Resource Center survey, 55 percent of respondents employed by for-profit organizations reported that their firm provides ethics training.[26] Figure 8–1 indicates that a significant number of employees report that they frequently find such training useful. Training can educate employees about the firm's policies and expectations, as well as relevant laws and regulations and general social standards. Training programs can make employees aware of available re-

| FIGURE 8-1 | Usefulness of Ethics Training |

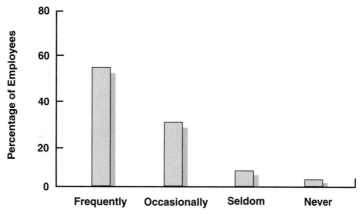

Source: Copyright © 2003, Ethics Resource Center. Used with permission of the Ethics Resource Center, 1747 Pennsylvania Avenue, N.W., Suite 400, Washington, D.C. 20006, www.ethics.org.

sources, support systems, and designated personnel who can assist them with ethical and legal advice. They can also empower employees to ask tough questions and make ethical decisions. Many companies are now incorporating ethics training into their employee and management development training efforts. At HCA—The Healthcare Company, for example, two hours of orientation training on the company's code of conduct is required for each employee within thirty days of employment, and a code of conduct refresher course is conducted for all employees annually.[27]

As we emphasized in Chapters 6 and 7, ethical decision making is influenced by organizational culture, by coworkers and supervisors, and by the opportunities available to engage in unethical behavior.[28] Ethics training can affect all three types of influence. Full awareness of the philosophy of management, rules, and procedures can strengthen both the organizational culture and the ethical stance of peers and supervisors. Such awareness, too, arms employees against opportunities for unethical behavior and lessens the likelihood of misconduct. Thus, the existence and enforcement of company rules and procedures limit unethical practices in the organization. If adequately and thoughtfully designed, ethics training can ensure that everyone in the organization (1) recognizes situations that might require ethical decision making; (2) understands the values and culture of the organization; and (3) is able to evaluate the impact of ethical decisions on the company in the light of its value structure.[29]

If ethics training is to be effective, it must start with a foundation, a code of ethics, a procedure for airing ethical concerns, line and staff involvements, and executive priorities on ethics that are communicated to employees. Managers from every department must be involved in the development of an ethics training program. Training and communication initiatives should reflect the unique characteristics of an organization: its size, culture, values, management style, and employee base. It is important for the ethics program to differentiate between personal and organizational ethics. Discussions in ethical training programs sometimes break down into personal opinions about what should or should not be done in particular situations. To be successful, business ethics programs should educate employees about formal ethical frameworks and models for analyzing business ethics issues. Then employees can base ethical decisions on their knowledge of choices rather than on emotions.

Some of the goals of an ethics training program might be to improve employees' understanding of ethical issues and their ability to identify them; to inform employees of related procedures and rules; and to identify the contact person who could help them resolve ethical problems. In keeping with these goals, the purpose of the Boeing Corporation's "Boeing Ethics and Business Conduct" program is as follows:

- Communicate Boeing's values and standards of ethical business conduct to employees.
- Inform employees of company policies and procedures regarding ethical business conduct.
- Establish processes to help employees obtain guidance and resolve questions regarding compliance with the company's standards of conduct and values.
- Establish criteria for ethics education and awareness programs and for coordinating compliance oversight activities.[30]

Boeing also asks employees to take ethics refresher training each year. On the company's "Ethics Challenge" Web page, employees (as well as the general public) can select from a variety of ethical dilemma scenarios, discuss them with their peers, and select from several potential answers. After clicking on the answer they think is most ethically correct, employees get feedback: the company's own opinion of the correct response and its rationale for it.

Indeed, most experts agree that one of the most effective methods of ethics training is exercise in resolving ethical dilemmas that relate to actual situations employees may face in their jobs. Lockheed Martin, for example, developed a training game called "Gray Matters" that includes dilemmas that can be resolved in teams. Each team member can offer his or her perspective, thereby helping other team members understand the ramifications of a decision for coworkers and the organization.

A relatively new training device is the behavioral simulation, which gives participants a short, hypothetical ethical-issue situation to review. Each participant is assigned a role within a hypothetical organization and is provided with varying levels of information about the scenario. Participants then must interact to develop recommended courses of action representing short-term, mid-term, and long-term considerations. Such simulations recreate the complexities of organizational relationships as well as the realities of having to address difficult situations with incomplete information. They help participants gain awareness of the ethical, legal, and social dimensions of business decision making; develop analytical skills for resolving ethical issues; and gain exposure to the complexity of ethical decision making in organizations. Research indicates that "the simulation not only instructs on the importance of ethics but on the processes for managing ethical concerns and conflict."[31]

Top executives must communicate with managers at the operations level (in production, sales, and finance, for instance) and enforce overall ethical standards within the organization. Table 8–5 lists the factors crucial to successful ethics training. It is most important to help employees identify ethical issues and give them the means to address and resolve such issues in ambiguous situations. In addition, employees should

| TABLE 8–5 | Keys to Successful Ethics Training |
|---|---|

1. Help employees identify the ethical dimensions of a business decision.

2. Give employees a means to address ethical issues.

3. Help employees understand the ambiguity inherent in ethical situations.

4. Make employees aware that their actions define the company's ethical posture both internally and externally.

5. Provide direction for employees to find managers or others who can help them resolve ethical conflicts.

6. Eliminate the belief that unethical behavior is *ever* justifiable by stressing that

- stretching the ethical boundaries results in unethical behavior.

- whether discovered or not, an unethical act is just that.

- an unethical act is *never* in the best interests of the company.

- the firm is held responsible for the misconduct of its members.

Source: Adapted from Walter W. Manley II, *The Handbook of Good Business Practice,* 1992, p. 87. Reprinted by permission of International Thomson Publishing Ltd.

be offered direction in how to seek assistance from managers, the ethics officer, or other designated personnel when resolving ethical problems.

Although training and communication should reinforce values and provide employees with opportunities to learn about rules, they represent just one part of an effective ethics program. Moreover, ethics training will be ineffective if conducted solely because it is required or because it is something that competing firms are doing. The majority of ethics officers surveyed by the Conference Board said that even ethics training would not have prevented the collapse of Enron due to accounting improprieties.[32] Enron executives knew they had the support of Arthur Andersen, the firm's auditing and accounting consulting partner, as well as that of law firms, investment analysts, and in some cases, government regulators. Enron's top managers therefore probably thought that their efforts to hide debt in off-balance-sheet partnerships would not be exposed.

In the Conference Board survey 56 percent of ethics officers responded that they do not survey their employees to assess the effectiveness of their ethics programs, and 54 percent do not have ethics measurements as part of their performance appraisal systems.[33] Both of these activities could help determine the effectiveness of a firm's ethics training. If ethical performance is not a part of regular performance appraisals, this sends the message that ethics is not an important component of decision making. For ethics training to make a difference, employees must understand why it is conducted, how it fits into the organization, and what their own role in implementing it is.

## Systems to Monitor and Enforce Ethical Standards

An effective ethics program employs a variety of resources to monitor ethical conduct and measure the program's effectiveness. Compliance with the company's ethical code and standards can be assessed by observing employees, internal audits, surveys, reporting systems, and investigations. An external audit and review of company activities may sometimes be helpful in developing benchmarks of compliance. We examine the process of ethical auditing in Chapter 9.

To determine whether a person is performing his or her job adequately and ethically, observers might focus on how the employee handles an ethically charged situation. For example, many businesses employ role-playing exercises in training salespeople and managers. Ethical issues can be introduced into the discussion, and the results can be videotaped so that both participants and their superiors can evaluate the outcome of the ethical dilemma.

Questionnaires can serve as benchmarks in an ongoing assessment of ethical performance by surveying employees' ethical perceptions of their company, their superiors, their coworkers, and themselves, as well as gaining their ratings of ethical or unethical practices within the firm and industry. Then, if unethical conduct appears to be increasing, management will have a better understanding of what types of unethical practices may be occurring and why. A change in the company's ethics training may then be necessary.

The existence of an internal system by which employees can report misconduct is especially useful for monitoring and evaluating ethical performance. Many companies have set up ethics assistance lines—often called help lines—or help desks to offer support and give employees an opportunity to ask questions or report ethical concerns. A survey of *Fortune* 500 companies indicates that 90 percent offer toll-free help lines. It is interesting to note that Kenneth Lay, who was often a featured ethics speaker at conferences, did not offer employees at Enron a help line when he was Enron's CEO. Enron's auditor, Arthur Andersen, also had no help line.[34]

Although there is always some concern that employees may misreport a situation or abuse a help line to retaliate against a coworker, help lines have become widespread, and employees do utilize them. An easy-to-use help line or desk can serve as a safety net that increases the chance of detecting and responding to unethical conduct in a timely manner. Help lines serve as a central contact point where critical comments, dilemmas, and advice can be assigned to the person most appropriate for handling a specific case.[35] Sears offers two help lines so that its 330,000 employees can ask questions about how to interpret company policy as well as specific work-related issues. Most of these calls are directed to a human resources manager and five associates who are trained in negotiation, conflict resolution, and investigation. About half of the issues raised on company help lines relate to human resource issues and complaints such as coworker abuse, the failure of managers to intervene in such abuse, and inappropriate language. Lubrizol, a company of forty-five hundred employees, offers a help line, conducts employee surveys, and has employees rate their managers on ethical performance. Its ethical issues have ranged from an employee who used the corporation to advance a personal business to human resource-related issues such as sexual harassment.[36]

If a company is not making progress toward creating and maintaining an ethical culture, it needs to determine why and take corrective action, either by enforcing current standards more strictly or by setting higher standards. Corrective action may involve rewarding employees who comply with company policies and standards and punishing those who do not. When employees abide by organizational standards, their efforts should be acknowledged through public recognition, or even through bonuses, raises, or some other means. On the other hand, when employees violate organizational standards, they must be reprimanded, transferred, docked, suspended, or even fired. If the firm fails to take corrective action against unethical or illegal behavior, the inappropriate behavior is likely to continue. In the National Business Ethics Survey, two in five employees who reported misconduct were dissatisfied with their organization's response, suggesting that such corrective action is often not taken.[37]

Consistent enforcement and necessary disciplinary action are essential to a functional ethics or compliance program. The ethics officer is usually responsible for implementing all disciplinary actions for violations of the firm's ethical standards. Many companies are including ethical compliance in employee performance appraisals. During performance appraisals, employees may be asked to sign an acknowledgment that they have read the company's current ethical guidelines. The company must also promptly investigate any known or suspected misconduct. The appropriate company official, usually the ethics officer, needs to make a recommendation to senior management on how to deal with a particular ethical infraction. In some cases, a company may be required to report substantiated misconduct to a designated government or regulatory agency so as to receive credit. Under the Federal Sentencing Guidelines for Organizations, such credit for having an effective compliance program can reduce fines.[38]

Efforts to deter unethical behavior are important for companies' long-term relationships with their employees, customers, and community. If the code of ethics is aggressively enforced and becomes part of the corporate culture, it can effectively improve ethical behavior within the organization. If a code is not properly enforced, it becomes mere window dressing and will accomplish little toward improving ethical behavior and decisions.

## Continuous Improvement of the Ethics Program

Improving the system that encourages employees to make more ethical decisions differs little from implementing any other type of business strategy. Implementation requires designing activities to achieve organizational objectives using available resources and given existing constraints. Implementation translates a plan for action into operational terms and establishes a means by which an organization's ethical performance will be monitored, controlled, and improved.

A firm's ability to plan and implement ethical business standards depends in part on how it structures resources and activities to achieve its ethical objectives. Starbucks', for example, communicates its corporate values—what it stands for and what its people believe in—in its values statement (see Table 8–6), which specifies how the business should be run. People's attitudes and behavior must be guided by a shared commitment to the business rather than mere obedience to traditional managerial authority. Encouraging diversity of perspectives, disagreement, and the empowerment of people helps to align the company's leadership with its employees.

If a company determines that its performance has been less than satisfactory ethically, executives may want to reorganize how certain kinds of decisions are made. For

| TABLE 8–6 | Starbucks' Environmental Mission Statement |
|---|---|

Starbucks is committed to a role of environmental leadership in all facets of our business. We fulfill this mission by a commitment to:

- Understanding of environmental issues and sharing information with our partners.

- Developing innovative and flexible solutions to bring about change.

- Striving to buy, sell and use environmentally friendly products.

- Recognizing that fiscal responsibility is essential to our environmental future.

- Instilling environmental responsibility as a corporate value.

- Measuring and monitoring our progress for each project.

- Encouraging all partners to share in our mission.

Source: http://www.starbucks.com/aboutus/environment.asp. Reprinted with permission.

example, a decentralized organization may need to centralize key decisions, at least for a time, so that upper managers can ensure that the decisions are ethical. Centralization may reduce the opportunities lower-level managers and employees have to make unethical decisions. Executives can then focus on initiatives for improving the corporate culture and infuse more ethical values throughout the firm by rewarding positive behavior and sanctioning negative behavior. In other companies, decentralizing important decisions may be a better way to attack ethical problems, so that lower-level managers, familiar with the forces of the local business environment and local culture and values, can make more decisions. Whether the ethics function is centralized or decentralized, the key need is to delegate authority in such a way that the organization can achieve ethical performance.

## Common Mistakes in Designing and Implementing an Ethics Program

Many business leaders recognize that they need to have an ethics program, but few take the time to answer fundamental questions about the goals of such programs. As mentioned previously, some of the most common program objectives are to deter and detect unethical behavior as well as violations of the law; to gain competitive advantages through improved relationships with customers, suppliers, and employees; and, especially for multinational corporations, to link employees through a unifying and shared corporate culture. Failure to understand and appreciate these goals is the first mistake many firms make when designing ethics programs.

A second mistake is not setting realistic and measurable program objectives. Once a consensus on objectives is reached, companies should solicit input through interviews, focus groups, and survey instruments. Finding out what employees might do in a particular situation and why can help companies better understand how to correct unethical or illegal behavior either reactively or proactively. Research suggests that employees and senior managers often know that they are doing something unethical but are able to rationalize their behavior as being "for the good of the company." As a result, ethics program objectives should contain some elements that are measurable.[39]

The third mistake is senior management's failure to take ownership of the ethics program. Maintaining an ethical culture may be impossible if chief executive officers do not support an ethical climate. In recent years, many firms, particularly in the telecommunications industry, have falsified revenue reports by recording sales that never took place, shipping products before customers agreed to delivery, or recording all revenue from long-term contracts up front instead of over the life of the contracts in order to keep earnings high and boost their stock prices. In a number of cases, top executives encouraged such fraud because they held stock options or other bonus packages tied to the company's performance. Thus, reporting higher revenues ensured that they earned larger payoffs. Of the most highly visible accounting fraud cases brought by the Securities and Exchange Commission (SEC), more than half involved falsifying revenue records. For example, the SEC, along with the Department of Justice and a congressional committee, investigated whether Qwest improperly recorded revenues from the sale of fiber-optic capacity as immediate gains even though most of the deals involved long-term leases.[40] If top managers behave unethically, creating and enforcing an ethical climate will be difficult, if not impossible.

The fourth mistake is developing program materials that do not address the needs of the average employee. Many compliance programs are designed by lawyers to ensure that the company is legally protected. These programs usually yield complex "legalese" that few within the organization can understand. To avoid this problem, ethics programs—including codes of conduct and training materials—should include feedback from employees from across the firm, not just the legal department. Including a question-and-answer section in the program, referencing additional resources for guidance on key ethical issues, and using checklists, illustrations, and even cartoons can help make program materials more user friendly.

The fifth common mistake made in implementing ethics programs is transferring an "American" program to a firm's international operations. In multinational firms, executives should involve overseas personnel as early as possible in the process. This can be done by developing an inventory of common global management practices and processes and examining the corporation's standards of conduct in this international context.

A final common mistake is designing an ethics program that is little more than a series of lectures. In such cases, participants typically recall less than 15 percent the day after the lecture. A more practical solution is to allow employees to practice the skills they learn through case studies or small group exercises.

A firm cannot succeed solely by taking a legalistic approach to ethics and compliance with sentencing guidelines. Top managers must seek to develop high ethical standards that serve as a barrier to illegal conduct. Although an ethics program should help reduce the possibility of penalties and negative public reaction to misconduct, a company must want to be a good corporate citizen and recognize the importance of ethics to success in business. Table 8–7 summarizes the steps executives should take to demonstrate that they understand the importance of ethics in doing business.

| TABLE 8-7 | The Role of Leadership in Developing an Ethics Program |
|---|---|

| | |
|---|---|
| 1. | Conduct a rigorous self-assessment of the firm's values and its existing ethics and compliance program. |
| 2. | Maintain commitment from top managers. |
| 3. | Publish, post, and make codes of ethics available and understandable. |
| 4. | Communicate ethical standards through multiple channels (paper documents, Web pages, etc.). |
| 5. | Provide timely training to reinforce knowledge. |
| 6. | Provide confidential resources to whom employees can go for advice or to report their concerns. |
| 7. | Ensure consistent implementation. |
| 8. | Respond and enforce consistently, promptly, and fairly |
| 9. | Monitor and assess using appropriate methods. |
| 10. | Revise and reform to ensure continuous improvement. |

Source: Adapted from Jane E. Dubinsky, "Business Ethics: A Set of Practical Tools," *Internal Auditing,* July/Aug. 2002.

## Summary

ACE

business.college.hmco.com/students

Ethics programs help sensitize employees to potential legal and ethical issues within their work environments. To promote ethical and legal conduct, organizations should develop ethics programs by establishing, communicating, and monitoring ethical values and legal requirements that characterize the firms' history, culture, industry, and operating environment. Without such programs and such uniform standards and policies of conduct, it is difficult for employees to determine what behaviors a company deems acceptable.

A company must have an effective ethics program to ensure that employees understand its values and comply with its policies and codes of conduct. An ethics program should help reduce the possibility of legally enforced penalties and negative public reaction to misconduct. The main objective of the Federal Sentencing Guidelines for Organizations is to encourage companies to assess risk, then self-monitor and aggressively work to deter unethical acts and punish unethical employees. Ethics programs are developed as organizational control systems to create predictability in employee behavior. These control systems may have a compliance orientation—which uses legal terms, statutes, and contracts that teach employees the rules and the penalties for noncompliance—or a values orientation—which consists of developing shared values.

Most companies begin the process of establishing organizational ethics programs by developing codes of conduct, which are formal statements that describe what an organization expects of its employees. Variations of codes of conduct include the code of ethics and the statement of values. A code of ethics must be developed as part of senior management's desire to ensure that the company complies with values, rules, and policies that support an ethical climate. Without uniform policies and standards, employees will have difficulty determining what is acceptable behavior in the company.

An ethical compliance program can be significantly enhanced by having a high-level manager or committee who is responsible for its administration and oversight. Such ethics officers are usually responsible for assessing the needs of and risks to be addressed in an organizationwide ethics program, developing and distributing a code of conduct or ethics, conducting training programs for employees, establishing and maintaining a confidential service to answer questions about ethical issues, making sure the company is complying with government regulation, monitoring and auditing ethical conduct, taking action on possible violations of the company's code, and reviewing and updating the code.

Successful ethics training is important in helping employees identify ethical issues and in providing them with the means to address and resolve such issues. Training can educate employees about the firm's policies and expectations, available resources, support systems, and designated ethics personnel, as well as about relevant laws and regulations and general social standards. Top executives must communicate with managers at the operations level and enforce overall ethical standards within the organization.

An effective ethics program employs a variety of resources to monitor ethical conduct and measure the program's effectiveness. Compliance with the company's ethical code and standards can be assessed through observing employees, performing internal audits and surveys, instituting reporting systems, and conducting investigations, as well as by external audits and review, as needed. Corrective action involves rewarding employees who comply with company policies and standards and punishing those who do not. Consistent enforcement and disciplinary action are necessary for a functioning ethical compliance program.

Ethical compliance can be ensured by designing activities that achieve organizational objectives, using available resources and given existing constraints. A firm's ability to plan and implement ethical business standards depends in part on its ability to structure resources and activities to achieve its ethical objectives effectively and efficiently.

In implementing ethics and compliance programs, many firms make some common mistakes, including failing to answer fundamental questions about the goals of such programs; not setting realistic and measurable program objectives; failing to have its senior management take ownership of the ethics program; developing program materials that do not address the needs of the average employee; transferring an "American" program to a firm's international operations; and designing an ethics program that is little more than a series of lectures. Although an ethics program should help reduce the possibility of penalties and negative public reaction to misconduct, a company must want to be a good corporate citizen and recognize the importance of ethics to successful business activities.

| Important Terms for Review | | |
| --- | --- | --- |
| compliance orientation | code of ethics | |
| values orientation | statement of values | |
| code of conduct | ethics officers | |

# A Real-Life Situation*

Jim, now in his fourth year with Cinco, was made a plant manager three months ago after completing the company's management-training program. Cinco Corporation owns pulp-processing plants that produce various grades of paper from fast-growing, genetically altered trees. Jim's plant, the smallest and oldest of Cinco's, is located in upstate New York, near a small town. It employs between 100 and 175 workers, mostly from the nearby town. In fact, the plant boasts about employees whose fathers and grandfathers have also worked there. Every year Cinco holds a Fourth of July picnic for the entire town.

Cinco's policy is to give each manager a free hand in dealing with employees, the community, and the plant itself. Its main measure of performance is the bottom line, and the employees are keenly aware of this fact.

Like all pulp-processing plants, Cinco is located near a river. Because of the plant's age, much of its equipment is outdated. Consequently, it takes more time and money to produce paper at Jim's plant than at Cinco's newer plants. Cinco has a long-standing policy of breaking in new managers at this plant to see if they can manage a work force and a mill efficiently and effectively. The tradition is that a manager who does well with the upstate New York plant will be transferred to a larger, more modern one. As a result, the plant's workers have had to deal with many managers and have become hardened and insensitive to change. In addition, most of the workers are older and more experienced than their managers, including Jim.

In his brief tenure as plant manager, Jim learned much from his workers about the business. Jim's secretary, Ramona, made sure that reports were prepared correctly, that bills were paid, and that Jim learned how to perform his tasks. Ramona had been with the plant for so long that she had become a permanent fixture. Jim's three foremen were all in their late forties and kept things running smoothly. Jim's wife, Elaine, was having a difficult time adjusting to upstate New York. Speaking with other managers' wives, she learned that the "prison sentence," as she called it, typically lasted no longer than two years. She had a large calendar in the kitchen and crossed off each day they were there.

One morning as Jim came into the office, Ramona didn't seem her usual stoic self. "What's up?" Jim asked her. "You need to call the EPA," she replied. "It's not real important. Ralph Hoad said he wanted you to call him." When Jim made the call, Ralph told him the mill's waste disposal into the river exceeded Environmental Protection Agency (EPA) guidelines, and he would stop by next week to discuss the situation. Jim hung up the phone and asked Ramona for the water sample results for the last six months upstream, downstream, and at the plant. After inspecting the data and comparing them with EPA standards, he found no violations of any kind. He then ordered more tests to verify the original data. The next day Jim compared the previous day's tests with the last six months' worth of data and still found no significant differences and no EPA violations. As he continued to look at the data, however, something stood out on the printouts that he hadn't noticed before. All the tests had been done on the first or second shifts. Jim called the foremen of the two shifts to his office and asked if they knew what was going on. Both men were extremely evasive in their answers and referred him to the third-shift foreman. When Jim phoned him, he, too, was evasive and said not to worry—that Ralph would explain it to him.

That night Jim decided to make a spot inspection of the mill and test the wastewater. When he arrived at the river, he knew by the smell that something was very wrong. Jim immediately went back to the mill and demanded to know what was happening. Chuck, the third-shift foreman, took Jim down to the lowest level of the plant. In one of the many rooms stood four large storage tanks. Chuck explained to Jim that when the pressure gauge reached a certain level, a third-shift worker opened the valve and allowed the waste to mix with everything else. "You see," Chuck told Jim, "the mill was never modernized to meet EPA standards, so we have to divert the bad waste here; twice a week it goes into the river." "Who knows about this?" asked Jim. "Everyone who needs to," answered Chuck.

When Jim got home, he told Elaine about the situation. Elaine's reaction was, "Does this mean we're stuck here? Because if we are, I don't know what I'll do!" Jim knew that all the managers before him must have had the same problem. He also knew that there would be no budget for installing EPA-approved equipment for at least another two years. The next morning Jim checked the EPA reports and was puzzled to find that the mill had always been in compliance. There should have been warning notices and fines affixed, but he found nothing. That afternoon Ralph Hoad stopped by. Ralph talked about the weather, hunting, fishing, and then he said, "Jim, I realize you're new. I apologize for not coming sooner, but I saw no reason to because your predecessor had taken care of me until this month." "What do you mean?" Jim asked. "Ramona will fill you in. There's nothing to worry about. I know no one in town wants to see the mill close down, and I don't want it to either. There are lots of memories in this old place. I'll stop by to see you in another couple of months." With that, Ralph left.

Jim asked Ramona about what Ralph had said. She showed him a miscellaneous expense of $100 a month in the ledgers. "We do this every month,"

she told him. "How long has this been going on?" asked Jim. "Since the new EPA rules," Ramona replied. She went on to clarify Jim's alternatives. Either he could continue paying Ralph, which didn't amount to much, or he could refuse to, which would mean paying EPA fines and a potential shutdown of the plant. As Ramona put it, "Headquarters only cares about the bottom line. Now, unless you want to live here the rest of your life, the first alternative is the best for your career. The last manager who bucked the system lost his job. The rule in this industry is that if you can't manage Cinco's upstate New York plant, you can't manage. That's the way it is."

## Questions ■ Exercises

1. Identify the ethical and legal issues of which Jim needs to be aware.
2. Discuss the advantages and disadvantages of each decision Jim could make.
3. Identify the pressures that have brought about the ethical and legal issues.
4. What is Jim's power structure and leadership position at the plant?

\* This case is strictly hypothetical; any resemblance to real persons, companies, or situations is coincidental.

---

**Check Your EQ**

Check your E.Q., or Ethics Quotient, by completing the following. Assess your performance to evaluate your overall understanding of the chapter material.

| | | | |
|---|---|---|---|
| 1. | A compliance program can be deemed effective if it addresses the seven minimum requirements for ethical compliance programs. | Yes | No |
| 2. | The accountability and responsibility for appropriate business conduct rest with top management. | Yes | No |
| 3. | Ethical compliance can be measured by observing employees as well as through investigating and reporting mechanisms. | Yes | No |
| 4. | The key goal of ethics training is to help employees identify ethical issues. | Yes | No |
| 5. | An ethical compliance audit is designed to determine the effectiveness of ethics initiatives. | Yes | No |

ANSWERS: 1. No. An effective compliance program has the seven elements of a compliance program in place and goes beyond those minimum requirements to determine what will work in a particular organization. 2. Yes. Executives in the organization determine the culture and initiatives that support ethical behavior. 3. Yes. Sometimes external monitoring is necessary, but internal monitoring and evaluation are the norm. 4. No. It is much more than that—it involves not only recognition, but also an understanding of the values, culture, and rules in the organization as well as the impact of ethical decisions on the company. 5. Yes. It helps in establishing the code and in making program improvements.

# Implementing and Auditing Ethics Programs

## An Ethical Dilemma*

Chantal has been with Butterfly Industries for thirteen years. She started out as an assistant buyer and was later promoted to buyer. At one point, she married her boss, Juan, but they divorced several years later. After Juan left, Chantal threw herself into her work, and within a few years she had moved into the corporate offices, but with only Whiskers, a black-and-white cat, to cheer her progress up the corporate ladder.

During Chantal's tenure, Butterfly Industries grew from fewer than five hundred employees to more than thirty-five thousand. The company expanded all over the world and opened offices on every continent; it had nearly exclusive arrangements with suppliers from six different countries. Such rapid growth eroded the freedoms of a small firm, in which one could do anything one wanted. So many employees—with different cultures, languages, time zones, varied clients—from so many countries, each with its own political realities, made corporate life much more complicated. To Chantal, it seemed that the firm had grown at a whirlwind pace, and sometimes she thought that whirlwind had become an ugly black cloud. She had heard, for example, that some of Butterfly's suppliers in Puerto Rico mistreated their workers. In other foreign locations, Butterfly's products were bringing changes to the environment, as well as to local culture and gender roles. Because these workers tended to be women, children were being left to fend for themselves. In some Latin American countries, husbands were angry because their wives earned more than they did. And, then there were the rumors that retailers in some countries were selling Butterfly products without adequate service or, worse, diluting the products and selling them as "full strength." After Butterfly went public, Chantal's sense of a foreboding whirlwind grew darker as headquarters' employees scrambled to satisfy shareholders' demands for specific information about products, projected earnings, employee benefit policies, and equal employment opportunity records. Chantal was also troubled that so many of the corporate people were men; only she and one other woman were directly involved in the inner workings of the increasingly complex firm.

Six months ago, Chantal began hearing that some plant employees were suffering pay cuts while others weren't. In some cases, employees who had been working for Butterfly for fifteen years had been cut to thirty-six-hour work weeks, losing their full-time benefits. She began to notice political alliances being erected between marketing, finance, manufacturing, and corporate headquarters. Because each plant operated as an independent profit-making entity, each was guarded in its communication with other plants, knowing that if it could increase its profits it could also increase overall pay.

Chantal was not the only to recognize that Butterfly needed guidance in a variety of areas, but no one had stepped forward. Then a month ago, Butterfly's president, Jermaine, asked Chantal to lunch. This was not unusual, but the conversation soon took a significant twist that Chantal was unprepared for. "Chantal, you've been with the company for thirteen years now, right?" asked Jermaine.

"Yes, that's about right," Chantal answered.

"You know as well as anyone that I haven't kept pace with the growth," Jermaine continued with a mixture of sadness and determination. "When I founded this company, I could tell a few staffers to check out an idea and several weeks later we'd talk about whether it would work. There was a time when I knew every employee, and even their families, but not anymore. Chantal, I think Butterfly has outgrown my style of management. What this company needs is a comprehensive set of rules and guidelines for every part of the company. I need to delegate more. That's why I wanted to talk to you."

Chantal, noticing her mouth was open, closed it and asked, "Jermaine, what are you saying to me?"

"Chantal, I've always been impressed with your work ethic and your sense of values. You know this company and its culture so well. I know you've heard some of the same rumors, so we both know that all is not well at Butterfly. What I'd like is for you to become the head of Butterfly's new ethics committee. Of course, you know that we don't have an ethics committee, so that's where you come in."

"Me!?" Chantal asked with surprise.

"Yes, you. If you're willing, I want you to create this entity and run it so that we all can be proud of Butterfly again. So that people inside and outside the company know that we stand for what is right. You will be promoted to vice president, your salary will be doubled, and you can select your own team. Chantal, this is your chance to really make a huge difference. What's your answer?" asked Jermaine.

Chantal hesitated for a moment and then said, "Yes."

"Great! I knew I could count on you. The first thing I need is a proposed outline of the responsibilities of the new ethics committee, enforcement procedures—the works—and I want it in two weeks along with a list of people for the committee."

That night, as she stroked Whiskers, Chantal began to plan.

---

## Questions ■ Exercises

1. Prioritize the issues that Butterfly needs to address. How can an ethics program address these issues?
2. Develop an outline of who should be on the new ethics committee and describe what the committee's first steps should be toward implementing an effective ethics program.
3. Should the new ethics committee commission an ethics audit? If yes, when should this audit be conducted? If no, why not?

* This case is strictly hypothetical; any resemblance to real persons, companies, or situations is coincidental.

---

In Chapter 8, we introduced the idea of ethics programs as a way for organizations to improve ethical decision making and conduct in business. To properly implement these programs and ensure their effectiveness, companies need to measure their impact. Increasingly, companies are applying the principles of financial auditing to ascertain whether their ethics codes, policies, and corporate values are having a positive impact on the firm's ethical conduct. These audits can help companies identify risks, noncompliance with laws and company policies, and areas that need improvement. An audit should provide a systematic and objective survey of the firm's ethical climate and values.

In this chapter, we examine the concept of an ethics audit as a way to implement an effective ethics program. We begin by defining the term *ethics audit* and exploring its relationship to a social responsibility audit. Next, we examine the benefits and limitations of this implementation tool, especially with regard to avoiding a management crisis. We then detail our framework for the steps of an ethics audit, including securing the commitment of directors and top managers; establishing a committee to oversee the audit; defining the scope of the audit process; reviewing the firm's mission, values, goals, and policies and defining ethical priorities; collecting and analyzing relevant information; verifying the results; and reporting them. Finally, we consider the strategic importance of ethics auditing.

## The Ethics Audit

An **ethics audit** is a systematic evaluation of an organization's ethics program and performance to determine whether it is effective. A major component of the ethics program we described in Chapter 8, the ethics audit includes "regular, complete, and documented measurements of compliance with the company's published policies and procedures."[1] As such, the audit provides an opportunity to measure conformity to the firm's desired ethical standards. An audit can even be a precursor to setting up an ethics program in that it identifies the firm's current ethical standards and policies and risk areas so that an ethics program can effectively address problem areas. Although few companies have so far conducted ethics audits, recent legislation will encourage greater ethics auditing as companies attempt to demonstrate to various stakeholders that they are abiding by the law and have established programs to improve ethical decision making.

The concept of ethics auditing emerged from the movement to audit and report on companies' broader social responsibility initiatives, particularly with regard to the natural environment. An increasing number of companies are auditing their social responsibility programs and reporting the results so as to document their efforts to be more responsible to various interested stakeholder groups. **Social auditing** is the process of assessing and reporting a business's performance in fulfilling the economic, legal, ethical, and philanthropic responsibilities expected of it by its stakeholders.[2] Social reports often discuss issues related to a firm's performance in the four dimensions of social responsibility as well as to specific social responsibility and ethical issues, such as staff issues, community economic development, volunteerism, and environmental impact.[3] In contrast, ethics audits focus on more narrow issues related to assessing and reporting on a firm's performance in terms of ethical and legal conduct. However, an ethics audit can be a component of a social audit, and, indeed, many companies include ethical issues in their social audits. British Petroleum, for example, includes ethical performance in its "Environmental and Social Report."[4]

Regardless of the breadth of the audit, ethics auditing is a tool that companies can employ to identify and measure their ethical commitment to stakeholders. Employees, customers, investors, suppliers, community members, activists, the media, and regulators are increasingly demanding that companies be ethical and accountable for their conduct. In response, businesses are working to incorporate accountability into their actions, from long-term planning, everyday decision making, and rethinking processes for corporate governance and financial reporting to hiring, retaining, and promoting employees and building relationships with customers. The ethics audit provides an objective method for demonstrating a company's commitment to improving strategic planning, including its compliance with legal and ethical standards and social responsibility. The auditing process is important to business because it can improve a firm's performance and effectiveness, increase its attractiveness to investors, improve its relationships with stakeholders, identify potential risks, and decrease the risk of misconduct and adverse publicity that could harm its reputation.[5]

Ethics auditing is similar to financial auditing in that it employs similar procedures and processes to create a system of integrity that includes objective reporting. Like an accounting audit, an ethics audit may be conducted by someone with expertise from outside the organization. Although the standards used in financial auditing can be adapted to provide an objective foundation for ethics reporting, there are significant differences between the two audit types. Whereas financial auditing focuses on all systems related to money flow and on financial assessments of value for tax purposes and managerial accountability, ethics auditing deals with the internal and broad external impact of the organization's ethical performance. Another significant difference is that ethics auditing is a voluntary process, whereas financial audits are required of public companies that issue securities. Because ethics and social audits are voluntary, there are few standards that a company can apply with regard to reporting frequency, disclosure requirements, and remedial actions that it should take in response to results. This may change as more companies build ethics programs in the current environment—where regulatory agencies support giving boards of directors oversight of corporate ethics. For boards to track the effectiveness of ethics programs, audits will be required.

## Benefits of Ethics Auditing

There are many reasons why companies choose to understand, report on, and improve their ethical conduct. Recent accounting scandals and legal and ethical transgressions have encouraged companies to better account for their actions in a wide range of areas, including corporate governance, ethics programs, customer relationships, employee relations, environmental policies, and community involvement. Bristol-Myers Squibb, for example, saw its stock value halved after it was forced to restate its revenues and profits because of improperly recorded sales. Moreover, after the company filed new patents and lawsuits to forestall competition from generic versions of some of its best-selling medications, it faced lawsuits claiming antitrust violations.[6] At one extreme, a company may want to achieve the most ethical performance possible, whereas another firm may use an ethics audit merely to project a good image to hide its corrupt culture. Still other companies may see the auditing process as a key component of improving the organization. Thus, the real reasons why companies exceed the ethical reporting standards prescribed by law actually lie along a vast spectrum.[7] For example, it is common for firms to conduct audits of business practices with legal ramifications, such as employee safety, environmental impact, and financial reporting. Although these practices are important to a firm's ethics and social responsibility, they are also legally required and thus constitute the minimum level of commitment. However, because stakeholders are now demanding increased transparency and are taking a more active role through external organizations that represent their interests, government regulators are calling on companies to improve their ethical conduct and make more decisions based on principles rather than laws alone.

The auditing process can highlight trends, improve organizational learning, and facilitate communication and working relationships.[8] As such, auditing provides benefits for both organizations and their stakeholders. Auditing can help companies assess the effectiveness of their programs and policies, which often improves their operating efficiencies and reduces costs. Information from audits and reports can also help identify priorities among various activities so the company can ensure that it is achieving the greatest possible impact with available resources.[9] The process of ethics auditing can also help an organization identify potential risks and liabilities and improve its compliance with the law. Furthermore, the audit report may help to document the firm's compliance with legal requirements as well as to demonstrate its progress in areas where it previously failed to comply, such as by describing the systems it is implementing to reduce the likelihood of a recurrence of misconduct.[10]

For organizations, one of the greatest benefits of the auditing process is improved relationships with stakeholders who desire greater transparency. Many stakeholders have become wary of corporate public relations campaigns. Verbal assurances by corporate management are no longer sufficient to gain the trust of stakeholders. Consider that former Enron CEO Ken Lay often spoke to stakeholders about the importance of ethics, yet Enron demonstrated little concern for ethics when it concealed millions of dollars in debt in off-balance-sheet partnerships. When companies and their employees, suppliers, and investors trust each other, the costs of monitoring and managing these relationships are lower. Companies experience less conflict with these stakeholders, which results in a heightened capacity for innovation and relationship building.

As a result, shareholders and investors have welcomed the increased disclosure that comes with corporate accountability. A growing number of investors are considering nonfinancial measures—such as the existence of ethics programs, legal compliance, board diversity and independence, and other corporate governance issues such as CEO compensation—when they analyze the quality of current and potential investments. Research suggests that investors may be willing to pay higher prices for the stock of companies they deem to be accountable.[11] Consider that the "most admired companies" in the United States—Wal-Mart, Southwest Airlines, Berkshire Hathaway, Dell Computer, and General Electric—have generally avoided major ethical problems.[12] However, even these companies have experienced some legal issues or had their ethics questioned. Wal-Mart, for example, has been accused of treating its men and women employees differently and faces a class-action discrimination suit from as many as five hundred thousand female employees who say the giant retailer paid them lower wages and salaries than it did men in comparable positions. Pre-trial proceedings uncovered discrepancies not only between the pay of men and women, but also in the fact that men dominate higher-paying store manager positions while women occupy more than 90 percent of cashier jobs, most of which pay about $14,000 a year. Wal-Mart faces fines and penalties in the millions of dollars if found guilty of sexual discrimination.[13] Such problems could have been uncovered and addressed with a regular ethics audit.

Regular audits permit shareholders and investors to judge whether a firm is achieving the goals it has established and whether it abides by the values it has specified as important. Moreover, it permits stakeholders to influence the organization's behavior.[14] Increasingly, a broad range of stakeholder groups are seeking specific, often quantifiable, information from companies. These stakeholders expect companies to take a deeper look at the nature of their operations and to publicly disclose both their progress and problems in addressing these issues. Some investors are using their rights as stockholders to encourage companies to modify their plans and policies to address specific ethical issues. At Tyco, for example, shareholders voted to eliminate some executive benefits after a scandal involving unauthorized pay and fraudulent stock sales.[15]

## Ethical Crisis Management and Recovery

A significant benefit of ethics auditing is that it may help prevent public relations crises resulting from ethical or legal misconduct, crises that can potentially be more devastating than traditional natural disasters or technological disruptions. Just as companies develop *crisis management* plans to respond to and recover from natural disasters, they should also prepare for ethical disasters, which can result not only in substantial legal and financial costs, but also disrupt routine operations, paralyze employees and reduce productivity, destroy organizational reputation, and erode stakeholder confidence. Ethical and legal crises have resulted in the demise of a number of well-known companies, including Enron and Arthur Andersen. Many other companies—Colombia/HCA, Firestone, Waste Management, Sunbeam, WorldCom, Rite Aid, Mitsubishi Motors, Xerox, Daiwa Bank of Japan, Archer Daniels Midland, and Microsoft, to name but a few—survived ethical and legal crises. However, they paid a high price not only financially but also in terms of compromised reputation and declining stakeholder trust. Consider that Qwest spent $7 million a month in 2003 on outside legal counsel to defend itself against allegations of accounting irregularities and fraud.[16] One study found that publicity about unethical corporate behavior lowers stock prices for at least six months.[17] A poll by Harris Interactive found many scandal-plagued firms at the bottom of its annual survey of perceived corporate reputation, including Enron, Global Crossing, WorldCom, Andersen Worldwide, and Adelphia. The most recent survey, which ranks companies according to respondents' ratings of companies on twenty attributes, also found that public perceptions of trust had declined considerably because of the accounting scandals of the early twenty-first century. Joy Sever, a Harris vice president, reported that "The scandals cost many companies their emotional appeal, the strongest driver of reputation."[18]

Despite the high costs of misconduct, a PricewaterhouseCoopers survey indicates that U.S. companies are failing to identify and manage ethical, social, economic, and environmental issues of concern. Although most companies recognize that these issues have the potential to harm their reputations and threaten their relationships with customers, suppliers, and other stakeholders, few are taking steps to identify, evaluate, and respond to them.[19] Table 9–1 indicates areas of concern that some companies consider in contingency planning for crisis management. Ethics audits could help more companies identify potential risks and liabilities so they can implement plans to eliminate or reduce them before they reach crisis dimensions.

Ethical misconduct can be caused by organizational members who engage in questionable or even illegal conduct. These rogue employees can threaten the overall integrity of the organization. Top leaders in particular can magnify ethical misconduct

**TABLE 9–1** ## Ethical Misconduct Readiness/Preparedness

| ETHICAL MISCONDUCT DISASTER READINESS | COMPANIES READINESS, RATED LOW TO NONE |
|---|---|
| Ethnic/sexual harassment | 35% |
| Regulatory violations | 39% |
| Criminal conduct | 36% |
| Fraud | 37% |
| Unethical behavior | 36% |
| Unlawful discrimination | 35% |
| Falsifying records | 39% |
| Criminal charges | 41% |
| Deceiving customers | 42% |
| Public relations disaster | 44% |
| Bribery | 45% |

Source: Robert C. Chandler and J. D. Wallace, Pepperdine University Ethical Misconduct Disaster Recovery Preparedness Survey, conducted at DRJ Spring World 2001, San Diego, California.

to disastrous dimensions. For example, the stock of Martha Stewart Living Omnimedia crashed after CEO and founder Martha Stewart was investigated for alleged illegal insider trading. Other examples of organizational disaster resulting from individual misconduct include Rigas family members at Adelphia Communications, Andrew Fastow at Enron, and Dennis Kozlowski at Tyco.[20] An ethics audit can discover rogue employees who are violating the firm's ethical standards and policies or laws and regulations.

Ethical disasters follow recognizable phases of escalation, from ethical issue recognition and the decision to act unethically to the organization's discovery of and response to the act. Appropriate anticipation of and intervention during these can stave off organizational disaster. Such contingency planning assesses risks, plans for these potential occurrences, and provides ready tools for responding to ethical crises. The process of ethical disaster recovery planning involves assessing the organization's values, developing an ethics program, performing an ethics audit, and developing contingency plans for potential ethical disasters. The ethics audit itself provides the key link to preventing ethical disasters.

## Risks and Requirements in Ethics Auditing

Although ethics audits provide many benefits for individual companies and their stakeholders, they do have the potential to create risks. For example, a firm may uncover a serious ethical problem that it would prefer not to disclose until it can remedy the situation. It may find that one or more of its stakeholders' criticisms cannot be dismissed or easily addressed. Occasionally, the process of conducting an ethics audit may foster stakeholder dissatisfaction rather than stifle it. Moreover, the auditing process imposes burdens (especially with regard to recordkeeping) and costs for firms that undertake it. Finally, the process of auditing and reporting a firm's ethics programs is no guarantee that it will avoid challenges related to its efforts.[21] In addition, because this type of auditing is relatively new, there are few common standards to judge disclosure and effectiveness or to make comparisons.[22]

Being viewed by the public as needing to be audited can motivate companies to conduct one so they can signal their intention to respond to concerns.[23] Companies in the public eye because of questionable conduct or legal violations, such as Qwest Communications, Xerox, Sunbeam, Bristol-Meyers, and WorldCom, should conduct an ethics audit to demonstrate their visible commitment to improving decision making and business conduct.

Although ethics and social responsibility are defined and perceived differently by various stakeholders, a core of minimum standards for ethical performance is evolving. These standards represent a fundamental step toward the development of minimum ethics requirements that are specific, measurable, achievable, and meaningful to the business's impact on communities, employees, consumers, the environment, and economic systems. These standards help companies set measurable and achievable targets for improvement and form an objective foundation for reporting the firm's efforts to all direct stakeholders. There may still be disagreements on key issues and standards, but through these standards progress should be made.[24] Both the Federal Sentencing Guidelines for Organizations' seven steps for effective ethical compliance, as discussed in Chapters 3 and 8, and the Sarbanes-Oxley Act provide standards that organizations can use in ethics auditing.

## The Auditing Process[25]

Many questions should be addressed when conducting an audit, such as how broad the audit should be, what standards of performance should be applied, how often the audit should be conducted, whether and how the audit's results should be reported to stakeholders, and what actions should be taken in response to audit results. Thus, corporate approaches to ethics audits are as varied as organizations' approaches to ethics programs and responses to improve social responsibility.

It is our belief that an ethics audit should be unique to each company, reflecting its size, industry, corporate culture, and identified risks, as well as the regulatory environment in which it operates. Thus, an ethics audit for a bank will differ from one for an automobile manufacturer or a food processor. Each has different regulatory concerns and unique risks stemming from the nature of its business. For this reason, we have mapped out a framework (see Table 9–2) that is somewhat generic and that most companies can therefore expand on when conducting their own ethics audit. The steps in our framework can also be applied to a broader social audit that includes specific ethical issues as well as other economic, legal, and philanthropic concerns of interest to various stakeholders. As with any new initiative, companies may choose to begin their effort with a smaller, less-formal audit and then work up to a more comprehensive social audit. For example, a firm may choose to focus on primary stakeholders in its initial audit year and then expand to secondary groups in subsequent audits. Additionally, companies with fewer resources may wish to use the judging criteria from the Better Business Bureau's International Torch Award for Marketplace Ethics (Table 9–3) as benchmarks for their informal self-audits.

---

| **TABLE 9–2** | **Framework for an Ethics Audit** |
| --- | --- |

- Secure commitment of top managers and board of directors.
- Establish a committee to oversee the ethics audit.
- Define the scope of the audit process, including subject matter areas important to the ethics audit.
- Review the organization's mission, policies, goals, and objectives and define its ethical priorities.
- Collect and analyze relevant information in each designated subject matter area.
- Have the results verified by an independent agent.
- Report the findings to the audit committee and, if approved, to managers and stakeholders.

---

Sources: These steps are compatible with the social auditing methods prescribed by Warren Dow and Roy Crowe, *What Social Auditing Can Do for Voluntary Organizations* (Vancouver: Volunteer Vancouver, July 1999); "Accountability," Business for Social Responsibility, www.bsr.org/BSRResources/WhitePaperDetail.cfm?DocumentID=259 (accessed Feb. 13, 2003); Sandra Waddock and Neil Smith, "Corporate Responsibility Audits: Doing Well by Doing Good," *Sloan Management Review*, 41 (Winter 2000): 79.

| TABLE 9–3 | Judging Criteria for the Better Business Bureau's International Torch Award for Marketplace Ethics |
|---|---|

Candidates for this annual award are judged against the following criteria:

- High ethical standards of behavior toward customers, suppliers, shareholders, employees, and the communities in which they do business
- Demonstrated ethical practices surrounding their buyer/seller relationships
- Long-standing history of and reputation for ethical practices in the marketplace
- Marketing, advertising, communications, and sales practices that truly represent what the company is offering in the marketplace
- Acknowledgment of company's ethical marketplace practices by industry peers in the communities where they do business
- Management practices and policies that give long-term value to shareholders, customers, employees, vendors, and surrounding communities
- Training programs that assist employees in carrying out established ethics policies

Source: "International Torch Award Judging Criteria," Better Business Bureau, www.bbb.org/torchaward/judgetorch.asp (accessed Mar. 17, 2003). Copyright © 1995, 1998, 2000 Council of Better Business Bureaus, Inc. Reproduction of a single copy for educational purposes is permitted. For additional copies, contact the Council of Better Business Bureaus.

Our framework encompasses a wide range of business responsibilities and relationships. The audit entails an individualized process and outcomes for a particular firm, as it requires the careful consideration of the unique issues that face a particular organization. For example, the auditing process at Kellogg Company includes the following:

> The Social Responsibility Committee of the Board of Directors shall identify, evaluate and monitor the social, political, environmental, occupational safety and health trends, issues, and concerns, domestic and foreign, which affect or could affect the Company's business or performance.
>
> The Committee shall make recommendations to assist in the formulation and adoption of policies, programs and practices concerning the matters set forth above including, but not limited to, environmental protection, employee and community health and safety, ethical business conduct, consumer affairs, alcohol and drug abuse, equal opportunity matters, and government relations, and shall monitor the Company's charitable contributions.[26]

Thus, although this chapter presents a structure and recommendations for both general social and ethics-specific audits, there is no generic approach that will satisfy every firm's circumstances. Nevertheless, the benefits and limitations that companies derive from auditing are relatively consistent.

### Secure Commitment of Top Managers and Board of Directors

The first step in conducting any audit is securing the commitment of the firm's top management and, if it is a public corporation, its board of directors. Indeed, the push for an ethics audit may come directly from the board of directors in response to specific stakeholder concerns or in response to corporate governance reforms related to the Sarbanes-Oxley Act of 2002, which suggests that boards of directors should provide oversight for *all* auditing activities. In addition, court decisions related to the Federal Sentencing Guidelines for Organizations hold board members responsible for the ethical and legal compliance programs of the firms they oversee. New rules and regulations associated with the Sarbanes-Oxley Act require that boards include members who are knowledgeable and qualified to oversee accounting and other types of audits to ensure that these reports are accurate and include all material information. While a board's financial audit committee will examine ethical standards throughout the organization as they relate to financial matters, it will also deal with the implementation of codes of ethics for top financial officers. Many of those issues relate to corporate governance issues such as compensation, stock options, and conflicts of interest. An ethics audit can demonstrate that a firm has taken steps to prevent misconduct, which can be useful in cases where civil lawsuits blame the firm and its directors for the actions of a rogue employee.

Pressure for an audit can also come from top managers who are looking for ways to track and improve ethical performance and perhaps give their firm an advantage over competitors that are facing questions about their ethical conduct. Additionally, under the Sarbanes-Oxley Act, CEOs and CFOs may be criminally prosecuted if they knowingly certify misleading financial statements. They may request an ethics audit as a tool to help improve their confidence in their firm's reporting processes. Some companies have established a high-level ethics office in conjunction with an ethics program, and the ethics officer may campaign for an ethics audit as a way to measure the effectiveness of the firm's ethics program. Regardless of where the impetus for an audit comes from, its success hinges on the full support of top management, particularly the CEO and the board of directors. Without this support, an ethics audit will not improve the ethics program and corporate culture.

## Establish a Committee to Oversee the Ethics Audit

The next step in our framework is to establish a committee or team to oversee the audit process. Ideally, the board of directors' financial audit committee would oversee the ethics audit, but this is not the case in most companies. In most firms, social and ethics auditing is conducted by managers or ethics officers, who do not always report to the board of directors. In any case, this team should include members who are knowledgeable about the nature and role of ethics audits and come from various departments within the firm. It may recruit individuals from within the firm or hire outside consultants to coordinate the audit and report the results directly to the board of directors. For example, the Chris Hani Baragwanath Hospital, the largest public hospital in the world, commissioned the Ethics Institute of South Africa to conduct an ethics audit.[27] As with the financial audit, an external auditor should not have other consulting or conflict-of-interest relationships with top managers or board members. Based on the best practices of corporate governance, audits should also be monitored by an independent board of directors' committee, as recommended by the Sarbanes-Oxley Act.

## Define the Scope of the Audit Process

The ethics audit committee should establish the scope of the audit and monitor its progress to ensure that it stays on track. The scope of an audit depends on the type of business, the risks faced by the firm, and the opportunities available to manage ethics. This step includes defining the key subject matter or risk areas that are important to the ethics audit (e.g., environment, discrimination, product liability, employee rights, privacy, fraud, financial reporting, legal compliance) as well as the bases on which they should be assessed. Assessments can be made on the basis of direct consultation, observation, surveys, or focus groups.[28] Table 9–4 lists some sample subject matter areas and the audit items for each.

## Review Organizational Mission, Values, Goals, and Policies and Define Ethical Priorities

Because ethics audits generally involve comparing an organization's ethical performance to its goals, values, and policies, the audit process should include a review of the current mission statement and strategic objectives. The company's overall mission may incorporate ethics objectives, but these may also be found in separate documents, including those that focus on social responsibility. For example, the firm's ethics statement or statement of values may offer guidance for managing transactions and human relationships that support the firm's reputation, thereby fostering confidence from the firm's external stakeholders.[29] Niagara Mohawk, for example, specifies five core values in its ethics program: management by fact, respect for people, focus on the customer, continuous improvement, and ethical behavior.[30]

This review step should examine all formal documents that make explicit commitments to ethical, legal, or social responsibility, as well as less-formal documents, including marketing materials, workplace policies, and ethics policies and standards for suppliers or vendors. This review may reveal a need to create additional statements to fill the identified gaps or to create a new comprehensive mission statement or ethical policy that addresses any deficiencies.[31]

It is also important to examine all of the firm's policies and practices with respect to the specific areas covered by the audit. For example, in an audit whose scope includes discrimination issues, this review step would consider the company's goals and objectives regarding discrimination, its policies on discrimination, the means available for communicating these policies, and the effectiveness of this communication. This assessment should also look at whether and how managers are rewarded for meeting their goals and the systems employees have available to give and receive feedback. An effective ethics audit should review all these systems and assess their strengths and weaknesses.[32]

Concurrent with this step in the auditing process, the firm should define its ethical priorities. Determining these priorities is a balancing act, as it can be difficult to identify the needs and assess the priorities of each stakeholder. Because there may be no legal requirements for ethical priorities, it is up to management's strategic planning processes to determine appropriate standards, principles, and duties as well as the action required to deal with ethics issues. It is very important in this stage to articulate these priorities and

| TABLE 9–4 | The Ethics Audit |
|---|---|

| | | | **ORGANIZATIONAL ISSUES*** |
|---|---|---|---|
| YES | NO | 1. | Does the company have a code of ethics that is reasonably capable of preventing misconduct? |
| YES | NO | 2. | Does the board of directors participate in the development and evaluation of the ethics program? |
| YES | NO | 3. | Is there a person with high managerial authority responsible for the ethics program? |
| YES | NO | 4. | Are there mechanisms in place to avoid delegating authority to individuals with a propensity for misconduct? |
| YES | NO | 5. | Does the organization effectively communicate standards and procedures to its employees via ethics training programs? |
| YES | NO | 6. | Does the organization communicate its ethical standards to suppliers, customers, and significant others that have a relationship with the organization? |
| YES | NO | 7. | Do the company's manuals and written documents guiding operations contain ethics messages about appropriate behavior? |
| YES | NO | 8. | Is there formal or informal communication within the organization about procedures and activities that are considered acceptable ethical behavior? |
| YES | NO | 9. | Does top management have a mechanism to detect ethical issues relating to employees, customers, the community, and society? |
| YES | NO | 10. | Is there a system for employees to report unethical behavior? |
| YES | NO | 11. | Is there consistent enforcement of standards and punishments in the organization? |
| YES | NO | 12. | Is there a committee, department, team, or group that deals with ethical issues in the organization? |
| YES | NO | 13. | Does the organization make a continuous effort to improve its ethical compliance program? |
| YES | NO | 14. | Does the firm perform an ethics audit? |

*A high number of Yes answers indicates that ethical control mechanisms and procedures are in place within the organization.

| | | | **EXAMPLES OF SPECIFIC ISSUES THAT COULD BE MONITORED IN AN ETHICS AUDIT**** |
|---|---|---|---|
| YES | NO | 1. | Are there any systems and operational procedures to safeguard individual employees' ethical behavior? |
| YES | NO | 2. | Is it necessary for employees to break the company's ethical rules in order to get the job done? |
| YES | NO | 3. | Is there an environment of deception, repression, and cover-ups concerning events that would embarrass the company? |
| YES | NO | 4. | Are there any participatory management practices that allow ethical issues to be discussed? |
| YES | NO | 5. | Are compensation systems totally dependent on performance? |
| YES | NO | 6. | Is there sexual harassment? |
| YES | NO | 7. | Is there any form of discrimination—race, sex, or age—in hiring, promotion, or compensation? |

| | | | |
|---|---|---|---|
| **TABLE 9–4** | | **The Ethics Audit** *(continued)* | |

**EXAMPLES OF SPECIFIC ISSUES THAT COULD BE MONITORED IN AN ETHICS AUDIT\*\***

| | | | |
|---|---|---|---|
| YES | NO | 8. | Are the only standards about environmental impact those that are legally required? |
| YES | NO | 9. | Do the firm's activities show any concern for the ethical value systems of the community? |
| YES | NO | 10. | Are there deceptive and misleading messages in promotion? |
| YES | NO | 11. | Are products described in misleading or negative ways or without communicating their limitations to customers? |
| YES | NO | 12. | Are the documents and copyrighted materials of other companies used in unauthorized ways? |
| YES | NO | 13. | Are expense accounts inflated? |
| YES | NO | 14. | Are customers overcharged? |
| YES | NO | 15. | Is there unauthorized copying of computer software? |

\*\*The number of Yes answers indicates the number of possible ethical issues to address.

values as a set of parameters or performance indicators that can be objectively and quantitatively assessed. Because the ethics audit is a structured report that offers quantitative and descriptive assessments, actions should be measurable by quantitative indicators. However, it is sometimes not possible to go beyond description.[33]

At some point, the firm must demonstrate action-oriented responsiveness to those ethics issues it has given top priority. HCA—The Healthcare Company, for example, has developed a comprehensive corporate ethics and compliance program in response to its past ethical and legal problems. HCA's program requires not only that standards of compliance and ethical conduct be articulated, but also that a system be implemented for auditing performance "in areas of compliance risk to ensure that established policies and procedures are being followed and are effective."[34]

### Collect and Analyze Relevant Information

The next step in our ethical audit framework is to identify the tools or methods for measuring the firm's progress in improving employees' ethical decisions and conduct. In this step, the firm should collect relevant information for each designated subject matter area. To understand employee issues, for example, the auditing committee will work with the firm's human resources department to gather employee survey information and other statistics and feedback. A thorough ethics audit will review all relevant reports, including external documents sent to government agencies and others. The information collected in this measurement step will help determine baseline levels of compliance as well as the internal and external expectations of the company. This step will also identify where the company has, or has not, met its commitments, including those dictated by its mission statement and other policy documents. The documents reviewed in this process will vary from company to company, depending on the firm's size, the nature of its business, and the scope of the audit process.[35] For example, Ford Motor Company launched a formal inquiry to determine whether president and CEO Nick Scheele violated company purchasing policies when he ordered that all of Ford's advertising and marketing business be directed toward WPP Group PLC, a London-based advertising firm that already handles much of the auto maker's advertising and for which Scheele's son works. Ford has a specific purchasing policy governing single-source contracts.[36] This inquiry would gather relevant information related to the subject of conflicts of interest and purchasing policies.

Some techniques for collecting evidence might involve examining both internal and external documents, observing the data-collection process (such as by consulting with stakeholders), and confirming information in the organization's accounting records. Auditors may also employ ratio analysis of relevant indicators to identify any inconsistencies or unexpected patterns. The importance of objective measurement is the key consideration of the ethics auditor.[37]

Because integrating stakeholder feedback in the ethics audit process is so crucial, these stakeholders must first be defined and then interviewed during the data-collection stage. For most companies, stakeholders include employees, customers, investors, suppliers, community groups, regulators, nongovernment organizations, and the media. Both social and ethics audits typically interview and conduct focus groups with these stakeholders to gain an understanding of how they perceive the company. For example, the Chris Hani Baragwanath Hospital (CHBH) in Johannesburg, South Africa, conducted an ethics audit that included focus groups with the hospital's management, doctors, nurses, related health professionals, support staff, and patients. Using the trends uncovered in these focus groups, CHBH then developed a questionnaire for an ethics survey, which it administered to a larger group of individual stakeholders.[38] The more stakeholders auditors include in this measurement stage, the more time and resources the audit will consume. However, a larger sample of stakeholders may yield a more useful variety of opinions about the company. In multinational corporations, a decision must also be made whether to include in the audit only the main office or headquarters region or all facilities around the globe.[39]

Because employees carry out a business's operations, including its ethics initiatives, understanding employee issues is vital to a successful audit. Useful indicators for assessing employee issues include staff turnover and employee satisfaction. High turnover rates could indicate poor working conditions, an unethical climate, inadequate compensation, or general employee dissatisfaction. Companies can analyze these factors to determine key areas for improvement.[40] Questionnaires that survey employees' ethical perception of their company, their superiors, coworkers, and themselves, as well as ratings of ethical or unethical practices within the firm and industry can serve as benchmarks in an ongoing assessment of ethical performance. Then, if unethical behavior is perceived to increase, management will better understand what types of unethical practices may be occurring and why. For example, the Chris Hani Baragwanath Hospital ethics survey asked employees about many issues, including organizational culture and values, their physical workplace, human resources issues, misconduct, standards of patient care, and problems and sources of stress.[41] Most organizations recognize that employees will behave in ways that lead to recognition and rewards and avoid behavior that results in punishment. Thus, companies can design and implement human resources policies and procedures for recruiting, hiring, promoting, compensating, and rewarding employees that encourage ethical behavior.[42]

Customers are another primary stakeholder group because their patronage and loyalty determines the company's financial success. Providing meaningful feedback is critical to creating and maintaining customer satisfaction. Through surveys and customer-initiated communication systems such as response cards, e-mail, and toll-free telephone systems, an organization can monitor and respond to customer issues and its perceived social performance. Sears, for example, surveyed more than two million customers to investigate their attitudes toward products, advertising, and the social performance of the company.

A growing number of investors are seeking to include in their investment portfolios the stocks of companies that conduct ethics and social audits. They are becoming more aware of the financial benefits that can stem from socially responsible management systems—as well as the negative consequences of a lack of responsibility. For example, after the Securities and Exchange Commission filed civil fraud charges against HealthSouth Corporation for overstating its earnings by $2.5 billion over a three-and-a-half-year period, the company's stock price plummeted 44 percent. The suit also accused the company of overstating assets by $800 million and its chief executive officer, Richard Scrushy, of instructing staff to inflate earnings to meet estimates. An internal audit later identified $3 billion in fraudulent or improper accounting entries. The SEC suit sparked additional lawsuits against the company by its shareholders.[43] Thus, even the hint of wrongdoing can affect a company's relations with investors. Additionally, many investors simply do not want to invest in companies that engage in certain business practices, such as cigarette production, or that fail to provide adequate working conditions, such as sweatshops. It is therefore critical that companies understand the issues of this very important group of stakeholders and what they expect from corporations they have invested in, both financially and socially.

Organizations can obtain feedback from stakeholders through standardized surveys, interviews, and focus groups. Companies can also encourage stakeholder exchanges by inviting specific groups together for discussions. Such meetings also may include an office or facility tour or a field trip by company representatives to sites in the community. Regardless of how companies collect information about stakeholders' views, the primary objective is to generate a variety of opinions about how the company is perceived and whether it is fulfilling stakeholders' expectations.[44]

Once these data have been collected, the firm should then compare its internal perceptions to those discovered during the stakeholder assessment stage and summarize these findings. During this phase, the audit committee should draw some conclusions about the information it obtained in the previous stages. These conclusions may involve descriptive assessments of the findings, such as the costs and benefits of the company's ethics program, the strengths and weaknesses of the firm's policies and practices, feedback from stakeholders, and issues that should be addressed in future audits. In some cases, it may be appropriate to weigh the findings against standards identified earlier, both quantitatively and qualitatively.[45]

Data analysis should also include an examination of how other organizations in the industry are performing in the designated subject matter areas. For example, the audit committee can investigate the successes of some other "benchmark" firm that is considered the best in a particular area and compare the auditing company's performance to it. Some common examples of the benchmark information available from most corporate ethics audits are employee or customer satisfaction, how the company is perceived by community groups, and the impact of the company's philanthropy. For example, the Ethics Officer Association (EOA) conducts research on legal and ethical issues in the workplace. These studies allow EOA members to compare their responses to the aggregate results obtained through the study.[46] Such comparisons can help the audit committee identify best practices for a particular industry or establish a baseline for minimum requirements for ethics. It is important to note that a wide variety of standards are emerging that apply to ethics accountability. The aim of these standards is to create a tool for benchmarking and a framework for businesses to follow.[47]

### Verify the Results

The next step is to have the results of the data analysis verified by an independent party, such as a social/ethics audit consultant, a financial accounting firm that offers social auditing services (e.g., KPMG), or a nonprofit special-interest group with auditing experience (e.g., the New Economics Foundation). Business for Social Responsibility, a nonprofit organization supporting social responsibility initiatives and reporting, has defined verification as an independent assessment of the quality, accuracy, and completeness of a company's social report. Independent verification offers a measure of assurance that the company has reported its ethical performance fairly and honestly, as well as providing an assessment of its social and environmental reporting systems.[48] As such, verification by an independent party gives stakeholders confidence in a company's ethics or social audit and lends the audit report credibility and objectivity.[49] British Petroleum, for example, had its "Environmental and Social Report," which includes ethical performance issues, verified by the accounting firm Ernst & Young.[50] However, a survey conducted by one of the Big Four accounting firms found that only a few social reports contained any form of external verification. This lack of third-party assurance may have contributed to the criticism that social and ethics auditing and reporting has more to do with public relations than genuine change. However, the number of outside verified reports is increasing.[51]

Although the independent validation of ethics audits is not required, an increasing number of companies are choosing to do so, much as they have their financial reports certified by a reputable auditing firm. Many public policy experts believe that an independent, objective audit can be provided only if the auditor has played no role in the reporting process—in other words, consulting and auditing should be distinctly separate roles. The Sarbanes-Oxley Act essentially legalized this belief.

The process of verifying the results of an audit should involve standard procedures that control the reliability and validity of the information. As with a financial audit, auditors can apply substantive tests to detect material misstatements in the audit data and analysis. The tests commonly used in financial audits—confirmation, observation, tracing, vouching, analytical procedures, inquiry, recomputing—can be used in ethics and social audits as well. For example, positive confirmations can be requested from the participants of a stakeholder focus group to affirm that the reported results are consistent with what the focus group believes it found. Likewise, an ethics auditor can actually observe a company's procedures for handling ethical disputes to verify statements made in the report. And, just as a financial auditor traces from the supporting documents to the financial statements to test their completeness, an ethics auditor or verifier may examine employee complaints about an ethics issue to attest whether the reporting of such complaints was complete. An auditor can also employ analytical procedures by examining plausible relationships, such as the prior year's employee turnover ratio or the related ratio commonly reported within the industry. With the reporting firm's permission, an auditor can contact the company's legal counsel to inquire about pending litigation that may shed light on ethical and legal issues currently facing the firm.[52]

Additionally, a financial auditor may be asked to provide a letter to the company's board of directors and senior managers to highlight inconsistencies in the reporting process. The auditor may request that management reply to particular points in the letter to indicate the actions it intends to take to address problems or weaknesses. The financial auditor is required to report to the board of directors' financial audit committee (or equivalent) any significant adjustments or difficulties encountered during the audit and any disagreements with management. Therefore, ethics auditors should be required to report to the company's audit committee the same issues that a financial auditor would report.[53]

## Report the Findings

The final step in our framework is issuing the ethics audit report. This involves reporting the audit findings through a formal report to the relevant internal parties—namely, the board of directors and top executives—and, if approved, to external stakeholders. Although some companies prefer not to release the results of their auditing efforts to the public, more companies are choosing to make their reports available to a broad group of stakeholders. Some companies, including U.K.-based Co-operative Bank, integrate the results of the social audit with their annual report of financial documents and other important information. Many other companies, including The Body Shop, Johnson & Johnson, Shell, British Petroleum, and VanCity, also make their audit reports available on their corporate Web sites.[54]

Based on the guidelines established by the Global Reporting Initiative and Accountability, the report should spell out the purpose and scope of the audit, the methods used in the audit process (evidence gathering and evaluation), the role of the (preferably independent) auditor, any auditing guidelines followed by the auditor, and any reporting guidelines followed by the company.[55] The ethics audit of Johannesburg's Chris Hani Baragwanath Hospital follows these guidelines.[56]

As mentioned earlier, ethics audits may resemble financial audits, but they take quite different forms. In a financial audit, the Statement of Auditing Standards dictates literally every word found in a financial audit report in terms of content and placement. Based on the auditor's findings, the report issued can take one of the following four forms, among other variations. An unqualified opinion states that the financial statements are fairly stated, while a qualified opinion asserts that although the auditor believes the financial statements are fairly stated, an unqualified opinion is not possible because of limitations placed on the auditor or minor issues involving disclosure or accounting principles. An adverse opinion states that the financial statements are not fairly stated, and, finally, a disclaimer of opinion qualifies that the auditor didn't have full access to records or discovered a conflict of interest. The technical difference between these various opinions has enormous consequences to the company.

## Strategic Importance of Ethics Auditing

Although the concept of auditing implies an official examination of ethical performance, many organizations audit their performance informally. Any attempt to verify outcomes and to compare them with standards can be considered an auditing activity. Many smaller firms probably would not use the word *audit*, but they do perform auditing activities.

The ethics audit, like the financial audit, should be conducted regularly rather than in response to problems involving or questions about a firm's priorities and conduct. In other words, the ethics audit is not a control process to be used during a crisis, although it can pinpoint potential problem areas and generate solutions in a crisis situation. As mentioned earlier, an audit may be comprehensive and encompass all of the ethics and social responsibility areas of a business, or it can be specific and focus on one or two areas. One specialized audit could be an environmental-impact audit in which specific environmental issues, such as proper waste disposal, are analyzed. According to the KPMG International Survey of Corporate Sustainability Reporting, 45 percent of the top 250 companies in the Global *Fortune* 500 issued environmental, social, or sustainability reports, up from 35 percent just three years before.[57] Examples of other specialized audits include diversity, employee benefits, and conflicts of interest. Table 9–5 lists some issues related to quality and effectiveness in auditing.

Ethics audits can present several problems. They can be expensive and time consuming, and selecting the auditors may be difficult if objective, qualified personnel are

---

**TABLE 9–5** **Quality and Effectiveness in Ethics Auditing**

- Inclusivity means that the audit process must include the views of all the principal stakeholders, not just the "noisy" stakeholders. Therefore, the assessment is based on many different views rather than just one.
- Comparability is the ability to compare the organization's performance from one audit period to another.
- Completeness means that no area of the company is excluded from the audit. This eliminates any "choice" selection of the best areas of the company, and it gives a more accurate and honest view.
- Evolution is what the company goes through when it fully commits to the audit.
- Management policies and systems are needed to ensure that the process of auditing is done in a controlled way.
- The information obtained from the audit must be disclosed if it is to be truly effective. The question of how many people the information should be disclosed to is continually debated.
- Continuous improvement ensures that the audit process is not only retrospective, but also uncovers areas needing change and improvement.

Source: "How to Do It," in *Business Corporate Accountability: The Emerging Practices in Social and Ethical Accounting, Auditing, and Reporting,* ed. Simon Zadek, Peter Pruzan, and Richard Evans (London: Earthscan Publications, Ltd., 1997), pp. 35–49.

not available. Employees sometimes fear comprehensive evaluations, especially by outsiders, and in such cases ethics audits can be extremely disruptive.

Despite these problems, however, auditing ethical performance can generate many benefits, as we have seen throughout this chapter. The ethics audit provides an assessment of a company's overall ethical performance as compared to its core values, ethics policy, internal operating practices, management systems, and, most important, key stakeholders' expectations.[58] As such, ethics and social audit reports are a useful management tool for helping companies identify and define their impact and facilitate important improvements.[59] This assessment can be used to reallocate resources and activities as well as focus on new opportunities. The audit process can also help companies fulfill their mission statements in ways that boost profits and reduce risks.[60] More specifically, a company may seek continual improvement in its employment practices, customer and community relations, and the ethical soundness of its general business practices.[61] Thus, the audit can pinpoint areas where improving operating practices can improve both bottom-line profits and stakeholder relationships.[62]

Most managers view profitability and ethics and social responsibility as a trade-off. This "either/or" mindset prevents them from taking a more proactive "both/and" approach.[63] However, the auditing process can demonstrate the positive impact of ethical conduct and social responsibility initiatives on the firm's bottom line, convincing managers—and other primary stakeholders—of the value of adopting more ethical and socially responsible business practices.[64]

## Summary

An ethics audit is a systematic evaluation of an organization's ethics program and/or performance to determine its effectiveness. Such audits provide an opportunity to measure conformity to the firm's desired ethical standards. The concept of ethics auditing has emerged from the movement toward auditing and reporting on companies' broader social responsibility initiatives. Social auditing is the process of assessing and reporting a business's performance in fulfilling the economic, legal, ethical, and philanthropic social responsibilities expected of it by its stakeholders. An ethics audit may be conducted as a component of a social audit. Auditing is a tool that companies can employ to identify and measure their ethical commitment to stakeholders and to demonstrate their commitment to improving strategic planning, including their compliance with legal, ethical, and social responsibility standards.

The auditing process can highlight trends, improve organizational learning, and facilitate communication and working relationships. It can help companies assess the effectiveness of programs and policies, identify potential risks and liabilities, improve compliance with the law, and demonstrate progress in areas of previous noncompliance. One of the greatest benefits for businesses is improved relationships with stakeholders. A significant benefit of ethics auditing is that it may help prevent the public relations crises associated with ethical or legal misconduct. Although ethics audits provide many benefits for companies and their stakeholders, they do have the potential to create risks. In particular, the process of auditing cannot guarantee that the firm will not face challenges. Additionally, there are few common standards for judging disclosure and effectiveness or for making comparisons.

An ethics audit should be unique to each company based on its size, industry, corporate culture, identified risks, and the regulatory environment in which it operates. The chapter offered a framework for conducting an ethics audit that can also be used for a broader social audit.

The first step in conducting an audit is securing the commitment of the firm's top management and/or its board of directors. The push for an ethics audit may come directly from the board of directors in response to specific stakeholder concerns or corporate governance reforms, or from top managers looking for ways to track and improve ethical performance. The audit's success hinges on the full support of top management.

The second step is establishing a committee or team to oversee the audit process. Ideally, the board of directors' financial audit committee would oversee the ethics audit, but in most firms auditing is conducted by managers or ethics officers. This committee will recruit an individual from within the firm or hire an outside consultant to coordinate the audit and report the results.

The third step is establishing the scope of the audit, which depends on the type of business, the risks faced by the firm, and available opportunities to manage ethics. This step includes defining the key subject matter or risk areas that are important to the ethics audit.

The fourth step should include a review of the firm's mission, values, goals, and policies. This step should include an examination of both formal documents that make explicit commitments with regard to ethical, legal, or social responsibility and less-formal documents, including marketing materials, workplace policies, and ethics policies and standards for suppliers or vendors. During this step, the firm should define its ethical priorities and articulate them as a set of parameters or performance indicators that can be objectively and quantitatively assessed.

The fifth step is identifying the tools or methods that can be employed to measure the firm's progress and then collecting and analyzing the relevant information. Some evidence collection techniques might involve examining both internal and external documents, observing the data-collection process (such as stakeholder consultation), and confirming the information in the organization's accounting records. During this step, a company's stakeholders need to be defined and interviewed to understand how they perceive the company. This can be accomplished through standardized surveys, interviews, and focus groups. Once these data have been collected, they should be analyzed and summarized. Analysis should include an examination of how other organizations in the industry are performing in the designated subject matter areas.

The sixth step is having the results of the data analysis verified by an independent party, such as a social/ethics audit consultant, a financial accounting firm that offers social auditing services, or a nonprofit special-interest group with auditing experience. Verification is an independent assessment of the quality, accuracy, and completeness of a company's audit process . Such verification gives stakeholders confidence in a company's ethics audit and lends the audit report credibility and objectivity. The process of verifying the results of an audit should employ standard procedures that control the reliability and validity of the information.

The final step in the audit process is reporting the audit findings to the board of directors and top executives and, if approved, to external stakeholders. The report should spell out the purpose and scope of the audit, the methods used in the audit process (evidence gathering and evaluation), the role of the (preferably independent) auditor, any auditing guidelines followed by the auditor, and any reporting guidelines followed by the company.

Although the concept of auditing implies an official examination of ethical performance, many organizations audit informally. The ethics audit should be conducted regularly. Although social auditing may present problems, it can generate many benefits. Through the auditing process, a firm can demonstrate the positive impact of ethical conduct and social responsibility initiatives on its bottom line, which may convince stakeholders of the value of adopting more ethical and socially responsible business practices.

| Important Terms for Review | ethics audit<br>social audit |
| --- | --- |

## A Real-Life Situation*

As Jerry looked around at the other members of the board, he wondered if it was too late to resign. How could he have been stupid enough to be dragged into this ethics audit quagmire! It had started innocently enough. With the passing of the Sarbanes-Oxley Act, everyone was aware of the consequences of accounting problems and their potential negative impact on a company, its board members, and its employees. So when Jerry's friend John, the president of Soumey Corporation, had asked him to be on the company's board of directors, Jerry had checked the company out. Not that he didn't trust John; he just felt that he should never take unnecessary chances. But when Jerry's investigation of Soumey Corp. uncovered nothing unusual, he accepted the board position.

Soumey's board of directors included John Jacobs, Soumey's president; Alan Kerns, a retired Soumey executive; Alice Finkelstein, a retired executive from a similar company; Latisha Timme, a consultant within the industry; and Jerry. With Jerry on board, one of the board's first tasks was to conduct an ethics audit. The directors decided to contract the task to Teico, Inron, and Wurrel, an accounting firm highly recommended by Timme. A few months later, Teico, Inron, and Wurrel filed its final report of the audit with the board. The report indicated that, with a few exceptions, Soumey was doing a good job of monitoring ethical issues. Among the recommendations the report offered were that the company should appoint a person with high managerial authority to be responsible for its ethical compliance program, that it establish a confidential hot line for employees who had ethical or legal concerns, and that it create an ethics committee to address ethical issues in the organization.

At the next board meeting, John suggested that Alan be the ethics compliance officer because he lived close to the main offices and had time to do it. Alan quickly agreed, provided there was substantial remuneration for his time, which John affirmed. Jerry asked a few questions, like whether Alan had sufficient managerial authority. Alice responded, "Jerry, this industry is rather small with only a few large players, Soumey being one of them. Trust me when I say that Alan, as a retired president of the company, will definitely have the respect of the employees." Jerry had no more questions, and Alan became Soumey's new compliance officer. The confidential hot line was quickly installed, and announcements about its existence were widely distributed around the various offices and plant buildings to ensure it reached all of the firm's several thousand employees. The board also discussed Teico, Inron, and Wurrel's final suggestion for an ethics committee, and all but Jerry agreed that the board could handle that task as well. Jerry pointed out, "I don't think this is wise, John. This is a conflict of interest for you, isn't it?" After a moment of hesitation, John replied, "You're right, Jerry, it is a conflict of interest that I be on the ethics committee." After another bit of silence, John suggested, "Wouldn't you agree that I should not be on the committee, Alan, Alice, and Latisha?" They all discussed the matter and agreed that Jerry's suggestion made perfect sense.

Time passed and the board held its quarterly meetings. Nothing unusual was brought up, just the same old issues that any publicly held company must deal with relative to shareholders, lawyers, regulators, and the public. Alan had suggested that the ethics compliance committee meet twice a year so he could fill everyone in on what was happening. At these meetings, Alan would usually report the number of calls to the hot line, the status of complaints, and whether there were any serious allegations such as sexual harassment or any reported forms of race, sex, or age discrimination in hiring personnel.

After two years of quarterly board meetings and semiannual ethics meetings, Jerry suggested to Alan that they conduct another ethics audit. "Why would we want to do that, Jerry? Things are going smoothly with the approach we're taking. Why have another outside audit? Do you think that we're doing a bad job!?" Jerry hedged, "I'm not saying that, Alan. What I'm saying is that we may need to have an outside audit just to make sure everything looks good to the public. Why don't we discuss this with Latisha and Alice this week?" he asked. Alan agreed. When the ethics committee met that week, it was obvious to Jerry that Alan had spoken to Alice and Latisha about their meeting, so he wasn't surprised when the committee decided another audit would diminish the confidence in Alan's performance as ethics compliance officer. Several weeks later, John sent all the board members a letter announcing an increase in their pay as board directors as well as doubling their

pay as ethics committee members. The letter stated, "Soumey Corporation has decided that your service to the company has been exemplary both as board members and as an ethics committee."

In Jerry's third year on the board of directors, he was finally able to attend Soumey's annual company picnic with his wife and children. They arrived late after all of the introductions, and everyone was already in the generous buffet line. As a result, no one really knew who he was. The kids were having fun, and Jerry and his wife Rosa were too. However, after a while Jerry began to overhear some interesting comments. In one conversation, a production worker spoke about a toxic spill that had occurred because of the lack of safeguards. He told his companion, "Yeah, I know it was pretty messy but only a few of my crew were hurt." His friend asked, "Did they or you report it to management?" He exclaimed, "Are you kidding, my guys don't want to lose their bonuses. Remember what happened to Bob's crew when the same thing happened and some of his guys complained. They had them filling out paperwork for a whole day, and the next week they were assigned a project with no incentives. They lost 40 percent of what they had been making with all the overtime and performance-based stuff. The guys and I agreed not to report it for those reasons." Jerry couldn't help interrupting, "So why didn't the company fix the problem after it happened the first time?" One of the men asked, "Are you new here?" "Yeah, been here only a few weeks," Jerry lied. The production worker answered, "You want to boost your pay, right? So you cut a few corners to get by."

Later that evening after Jerry and his family returned home, Rosa told him about a conversation she had overheard. "These women were talking about how unfair it is that most of the incentive-based pay seems to go to men with families. One woman said that she heard of a man over fifty-five who should have gotten a promotion but was turned down because his supervisor was told not to give it to him. Rumor was that this guy had bucked the last president of Soumey, and this was his payback. Jerry, you should have heard what they say about Alan, that he's like Santa Claus and the Grinch. You never see him, and if you do it's not a pleasant experience. One woman told me that when she was working for him, he use to be a little too friendly. She said that's why no one really uses the ethics hot line for certain issues: they know that the fox is guarding the hen house." A little later, one of Jerry's sons bounced into the room and asked him a question about the picnic. "Dad, how come all the Spanish workers are on the night shift? It really makes it hard for a couple of my friends to get their parents to drop them off for soccer."

The picnic had opened Jerry's eyes about an uglier side of Soumey. At the next board meeting, he indirectly addressed some of the problems he had noticed. But John responded, "We're going into a recession, and we have to cut a few corners to keep our dividends up to the market's expectations. Timme has been watching and consulting me on the best way to keep ahead of the pack on this." Latisha and Alice both commented, "Thank goodness we have a large Spanish work force to offset some price increases. They're hard workers and don't complain." "You're absolutely right," said Alan. "We don't have the EPA, OSHA, or other agencies on our backs because these people know how to work and keep quiet. If some federal agencies do start to poke around, I have some contingency plans to prevent any type of ethical disaster."

That evening Jerry and Rosa were talking about the situation. He told Rosa, "I think Soumey has some potentially ethical issues that need to be addressed, but what can I do?" "Well," sighed Rosa,

"We've lived in this town for a long time. We know the families that are on the board. They're good people. However, there's one thing you didn't hear at that picnic because of your lack of Spanish. I've told you that it's important to learn it, even if it's just for my family. A few of the people I overheard were talking about how the hot line isn't really anonymous. That's just not right, Jerry. You need to do something even if it does mean losing the extra income." Rosa's points struck a nerve because Jerry knew they were a little overextended financially. "I'll see what I can do," he told her. Still, she warned him, "That's good, honey, but remember I don't want you to make too many waves. We still have to live here, and you know we can't swing a dead cat and not hit one of the people at Soumey."

## Questions ■ Exercises

1. What areas of its ethics audit should Soumey change?
2. Does Jerry have a legal duty to report any of the items that he has heard to an outside authority?
3. Discuss the makeup of Soumey's board of directors. Is it ethical?
4. Is Jerry liable for the problems associated with Soumey over the last three years? Explain why or why not.

* This case is strictly hypothetical; any resemblance to real persons, companies, or situations is coincidental.

# Business Ethics in a Global Economy

## CHAPTER OBJECTIVES

- To understand the role of culture as a factor in business ethics
- To discuss cultural relativism as a framework for global business ethics
- To explore global values
- To assess the role of multinational corporations in business ethics
- To gain awareness of a number of ethical issues around the globe

## CHAPTER OUTLINE

**Ethical Perceptions and International Business**
Culture As a Factor in Business
Adapting Ethical Systems to a Global Framework

**Global Values**

**The Multinational Corporation**

**Ethical Issues Around the Globe**
Sexual and Racial Discrimination
Human Rights
Price Discrimination
Bribery
Harmful Products
Pollution and the Natural Environment
Telecommunications Issues
Intellectual Property Protection
World Trade Organization

## An Ethical Dilemma*

At the Dun and Ready (D&R) Company, Sid was responsible for monitoring the Japanese stock market to determine patterns and identify stocks that could become active. One of ten company representatives in Japan, Sid, who was of Japanese decent and fluent in the language, had been assigned to Tokyo. Being relatively new to the firm, he was told to gather information for his boss, Glenna. Glenna had been with D&R for ten years, but because of the cultural barriers she was not enthusiastic about her Tokyo assignment. Glenna encouraged Sid to get to know the Japanese brokers, traders, and other key people in the business, and thanks to his background, he found that he blended easily into the culture.

In Japan, ceremony and giving favors is a way of life. Sid learned that by observing Japanese customs and perfecting his Japanese he not only became an information resource on the Japanese stock market and its players for his company, but also a resource for the Japanese who wanted to invest in the U.S. market. He found that the locals would talk to him about important investments rather than coming into the office to see Glenna.

Among Sid's duties was taking key customers to bars, restaurants, and vacation spots for entertainment. One day a government official in the group Sid was entertaining hinted that he and the others would like to play golf on some famous U.S. courses. Sid understood what the government official wanted and relayed the request to Glenna, who told him that granting a favor of this kind would normally be against policy, but since such favors seemed to be the custom in Japan, they could do some "creative bookkeeping." "When in Rome, right, Sid?" was Glenna's response to the whole situation. By pulling some strings, Glenna managed to have these officials play at ten of the most exclusive U.S. golf courses. Later, several officials passed the word to people in Japan's elite financial circle about Sid's helpfulness.

Six months later Glenna was transferred back to the States. Rumor had it that expenses were too high and revenue too low. Her replacement, Ron,

didn't like being sent to Japan either. In his very first week on the job, he told the staff that he would shorten his tour in Tokyo by slashing expenses and increasing productivity. Ron was a "by-the-book" person. Unfortunately, company rules had not caught up with the realities of cultural differences. After two months with Ron, seven of the original ten company representatives had quit or been fired.

Sid was barely surviving. Then one of his contacts in the government repaid a favor by recommending several stocks to buy and sell. The information paid off, and Sid gained some breathing room from Ron. Around the same time, some of Sid's Japanese clients lost a considerable amount of money in the U.S. markets and wanted a "discount"—the term used for the practice in some large Japanese brokerage houses of informally paying off part of their best clients' losses. When Glenna was still in Tokyo, she had dipped into the company's assets several times to fund such discounts. Because everything required Ron's approval, Sid and his colleagues believed that this practice would not be tolerated. However, late one afternoon Sid and a few others provided the proper forms, and Ron signed them without realizing what he had done.

Several months passed, and the three survivors had resorted to lowering their expenses by using their own funds. This, in turn, led to Sid churning some of his accounts—that is, he bought and sold stocks for the express purpose of increasing his own revenues. Churning was tolerated in Japan, along with other practices that would be deemed questionable in the United States. Ron was oblivious to what Sid was doing because his focus was on reducing expenses.

In the previous month a group of important D&R clients had given a party for a few of their favorite brokers at one of their local haunts. After the customary toasts and small talk, it was suggested to Sid that a Japanese cartel might be interested in D&R. Sid was cautious, and nothing else was mentioned. Several weeks later at another party, Sid and the two remaining D&R people had been told that a takeover was imminent. But to make the takeover painless, the cartel needed certain sensitive information. Sid's reward for providing it would be a high position in the new, reorganized company and a "wink/nod" agreement that he could go anywhere in the world for his next assignment.

That week Ron had announced that headquarters was pleased with the productivity of the Tokyo group. "It's only a matter of time before I get transferred out, and I want out of Tokyo," he told them. The office knew that if Ron was successful, his next position would be that of vice president. He also informed the group that corporate representatives would be coming to Tokyo the following week. "It seems that they've heard rumors of a possible hostile takeover attempt on D&R from someone in Japan, and they want us to check it out," Ron said, adding with a tight smile, "There will be some changes next week." Sid suspected that this meant there would be even fewer people working even harder. It might also mean, however, that someone knew that Sid and the two representatives had been talking to the wrong people, as defined by D&R. Or maybe one of

the three had sold out the other two. If Sid was to gather the information sought by the cartel, he would have to act quickly.

---

## Questions ■ Exercises

1. What are the ethical issues here?
2. What moral philosophies were Sid, Glenna, and Ron using?
3. What are some control options that D&R could have introduced to create a more ethical climate?
4. Discuss the advantages and disadvantages of each decision Sid could make.
5. Identify the pressures that have caused the ethical issues to develop.
6. Discuss Sid's power structure and leadership position at D&R and what it might be at the new D&R.

\* This case is strictly hypothetical; any resemblance to real persons, companies, or situations is coincidental.

---

A dvances in communication, technology, and transportation have minimized the world's borders, creating a new global economy. More countries are attempting to industrialize and compete internationally. Because of these trends, more companies are doing business outside their home countries. These transactions across national boundaries define global business. Global business brings together people from countries that have different cultures, values, laws, and ethical standards. Thus, the international businessperson must not only understand the values, culture, and ethical standards of his or her own country but also be sensitive to those of other countries. In addition, although about 90 percent of American companies have a written code of ethics, surveys indicate that ethical codes are found less frequently outside the United States. For example, 51 percent of German firms, 41 percent of British firms, and 30 percent of French firms surveyed had ethics codes in place.[1]

In this chapter, we explore the ethical complexities and challenges facing businesses that operate internationally. We first consider the different perceptions worldwide of corporate ethics, cultural differences, and cultural relativism. We also discuss a global framework for ethical principles. Then we examine multinational corporations and the ethical problems they face. Finally, we highlight some of the major global ethical issues. As before, we do not offer absolute answers to the ethical issues. Our goal is to help you understand how international business activities can create ethical conflict and to help you improve your ethical decision-making ability.

## Ethical Perceptions And International Business

When businesspeople travel, they sometimes perceive that other business cultures have different modes of operation. Research reveals that there is at least the perception in the United States that American companies are different from those in other countries. This implied perspective of ethical superiority—"us" versus "them"—is also common in other countries. Table 10–1 indicates the countries that businesspeople, risk analysts, and the general public perceived as the most and least corrupt. In business, the idea that "we" differ from "them" is called the **self-reference criterion (SRC)**.

The SRC is the unconscious reference to one's own cultural values, experiences, and knowledge. When confronted with a situation, we react on the basis of knowledge we have accumulated over a lifetime, which is usually grounded in our culture of origin. Our reactions are based on meanings, values, and symbols that relate to our culture but may not have the same relevance to people of other cultures. In the United States, for example, **dumping**—the practice of charging high prices for products sold in domestic markets while selling the same products in foreign markets at low prices, often below the costs of exporting them—is viewed negatively, and the United States has a number of anti-dumping laws. The U.S. Congress recently passed the Byrd Amendment, which allows U.S. Customs to distribute money generated from foreign companies accused of dumping products to U.S. firms harmed by the dumping. However, the World Trade Organization (WTO) has ruled that this distribution of funds to U.S. firms violates its international trade rules and regulations. The

**TABLE 10–1**     **Perceptions of Countries as Least/Most Corrupt**

| LEAST CORRUPT | MOST CORRUPT |
| --- | --- |
| 1. Finland (1)* | 1. Bangladesh (1) |
| 2.** Denmark (2) | 2. Nigeria (2) |
| 2. New Zealand (3) | 3. Paraguay (—) |
| 4. Iceland (4) | 3. Madagascar (—) |
| 5. Singapore (4) | 3. Angola (—) |
| 5. Sweden (6) | 6. Kenya (5) |
| 7. Canada (7) | 6. Indonesia (3) |
| 7. Luxembourg (9) | 8. Azerbaijan (5) |
| 7. Netherlands (8) | 9. Uganda (3) |
| 10. United Kingdom (13) | 9. Moldova (—) |

*Numbers in parentheses indicate country's previous rank. A dash within the parentheses indicates that the country was not in the previous survey ranking. **The same number ranking indicates a tie (for example, Denmark and New Zealand tied for second). Note: The United States ranked as the sixteenth least corrupt country in both the 2001 and 2002 surveys.

Source: "Corrupt Political Elites and Unscrupulous Investors Kill Sustainable Growth in its Tracks, Highlights New Index," Transparency International, press release, Aug. 28, 2002, www.transparency.org/pressreleases_archive/2002/2002.08.28.cpi.en.html; " New Index Highlights Worldwide Corruption Crisis, Says Transparency International," Transparency International, press release, June 27, 2001, www.transparency.org/cpi/2001/cpi2001.html. Courtesy of Transparency International.

WTO has recommended that the United States repeal the Byrd Amendment, but the U.S. has officially rejected this recommendation. Although the United States is a member of the WTO, in this case, it has rejected its rules or culture.[2]

## Culture As a Factor in Business

One of the most difficult concepts to understand and apply to the global business environment is culture. Because customs, values, and ethical standards vary from person to person, company to company, and even society to society, ethical issues that arise from international business activities often differ significantly from those that evolve from domestic business activities. Distinctively international issues are often related to differences in cultures. Thus, it is important to define and explore the concept of culture as it relates to the global setting.

**Culture** is everything in our surroundings that is made by people—both tangible items and intangible concepts and values. Language, religion, law, politics, technology, education, social organization, general values, and ethical standards are all included in this definition. Each nation has a distinctive culture and, consequently, distinctive beliefs about what business activities are acceptable or unethical. Distinct subcultures can also be found within many nations. Thus, when transacting international business, individuals encounter values, beliefs, and ideas that may diverge from their own because of cultural differences. In this chapter you can test your own "cultural IQ."

Cultural differences include differences in speech. Problems of translation often make it difficult for businesspeople to express exactly what they mean. For example, when Bacardi created a fruity drink for the French market, it attempted to market the beverage in both France and Germany under the name Pavian. Unfortunately, "Pavian" translates as "baboon" in German. Even within the same language, words can mean different things in different countries. In Puerto Rico, for example, Tropicana brand orange juice was advertised as "Jugo de China," where "China" translates as "orange." But these same Spanish ads did not go over well with the Cuban population in Miami, Florida, for whom "Jugo de China" literally means "Chinese juice."[3]

Although blunders in communication may have their humorous side, they frequently offend or anger others, derail important business transactions, and even damage international business relations. When Touchstone Pictures, a subsidiary of Walt Disney, released the films *Father of the Bride, Part II; In the Army Now; Aladdin: The Return of Jafar; Kazaam;* and *GI Jane,* the International Arab League accused Disney of presenting a distorted image of Arabs. Although Disney generates a large portion of revenue from foreign distributions and activities, it failed to find success with these films in Islamic and Arab countries.[4]

Cultural differences in body language can also lead to misunderstandings. Body language is the nonverbal, usually unconscious communication we make through our gestures, posture, and facial expressions. Americans, for instance, nod their heads up and down to indicate "yes," but in Albania, an up-and-down nod means "no," while in Britain, it indicates only that the person has heard, not that he or she agrees. Pointing an index finger, a commonplace gesture among Americans, is considered quite rude in Asia and Africa. Personal space—the distance at which one person feels comfortable when talking with another—also varies from culture to culture. American and British businesspeople prefer a larger space than do South American, Greek, and Japanese. This difference can make people from different countries ill at ease with each other in their negotiations.

Perceptions of time may likewise differ from country to country. Americans value promptness, but businesspeople from other lands approach punctuality in a more relaxed manner. An American firm lost a contract in Greece after it tried to impose its customs on the local negotiators by setting time limits for meetings. Greeks deem such limits insulting and lacking in finesse.[5] Americans, on the other hand, may view the failure to meet on time as a sign that contractual obligations won't be met on a timely basis, thus increasing the potential cultural misperceptions.

When firms transfer personnel, cultural variations can turn into liabilities. Consequently, large corporations spend thousands of dollars to ensure that the employees they send abroad are culturally prepared. Eastman Chemical Company, for example, has devised a preparation program so effective that 99 percent of participating employees successfully complete their term in a foreign country. Eastman's program provides cultural orientation for the entire family, not just the employee, and includes language training, a house-hunting trip, and counseling to prepare the family for life in a new culture.[6]

The seemingly innocuous customs of one country can be offensive or even dangerous in others. For example, employees of a California construction company presented green baseball caps to top Taiwanese company executives at a meeting. To traditional Taiwanese, however, green caps symbolize adultery. Unwittingly, the Americans had accused their associates of having unfaithful wives.[7] Table 10–2 lists acceptable standards of gift giving in selected areas of the world.

Divergent religious values can also create ethical issues in international business. For instance, before a British fast-food hamburger chain entered the Indian market, its market research identified an issue. The ruling class in India is predominately Hindu, and its members abstain from eating beef for religious reasons. Although other Indian religions have no taboos regarding the consumption of beef, the British firm decided not to use beef for its burgers to avoid giving offense. Some companies are not always so considerate of other cultures' values and mores, however. When Walt Disney opened EuroDisney near Paris, there was a backlash of anti-Americanism. The French viewed the company as preaching American cultural values, and responded with protests, rallies, and boycotts.

One of the critical ethical issues linked to cultural differences is the question of whose values and ethical standards take precedence during international negotiations and business transactions. When conducting business outside their own country, should businesspeople impose their own values, ethical standards, and even laws on members of other cultures? Or should they adapt to the values, ethical standards, and laws of the country in which they are doing business? As with many ethical issues, there are no easy answers to these questions.

## Adapting Ethical Systems to a Global Framework

"When in Rome, do as the Romans do" or "You must adapt to the cultural practices of the country you are in" are rationalizations businesspeople sometimes offer for straying from their own ethical values when doing business abroad. By defending the payment of bribes or "greasing the wheels of business" and other questionable

| TABLE 10–2 | Acceptable Standards of Gift Giving in Selected Countries |
|---|---|

### Japan

- Consult the staff in better department stores in Japan to find an appropriate gift in a particular situation.
- Always wrap gifts, but never in white, which is associated with funerals.
- Give and receive gifts with both hands and a slight bow.

### China

- Present a reasonably priced gift only when negotiations are complete or nearly so.
- Give gifts to everyone involved, with each gift's value based on the recipient's rank.
- Do not give gifts involving amounts of four because the number is associated with death in some areas.
- Wrapping in red symbolizes good luck, but red ink is taboo because it implies the severing of a relationship.
- If Chinese people decline your gift, you should do the same if offered one by them.

### Singapore

- Gift giving is not a common practice, and corruption is not tolerated.
- If necessary, give only inexpensive, token gifts, such as pens or other items with a company logo.

### India

- Graft is widespread.
- Although illegal, bribes are often solicited at each bureaucratic level.
- Rely on the advice of local associates because some Indian businesspeople may expect expensive gifts while others may be offended.

Source: Tibbett L. Speer, "Avoid Gift Blunders in Asian Locales," *USA Today,* Apr. 25, 2000, www.usatoday.com/life/ travel/business/1999/t0316bt2.htm.

practices in this fashion, they are resorting to **cultural relativism:** the concept that morality varies from one culture to another and that business practices are therefore differentially defined as right or wrong by particular cultures. For example, Exxon-Mobil Corporation and Royal Dutch/Shell Group have invested heavily in developing the oil reserves of Sakhalin Island, a Russian territory north of Japan. The companies have invested $22 billion in oil and gas drilling equipment not only because there may as much as thirteen billion barrels of oil in its waters but also because Russia's environmental rules are almost nonexistent and seldom enforced. However, the seismic blasting and toxic mud associated with developing the area's oil fields are hazardous to the endangered Western Pacific grey whale. If a spill or other accident were to occur, the nearest cleanup equipment is fifty miles away, making it impractical to save salmon and other animal species from harm.[8] Although the Russian gov-

| FIGURE 10–1 | Matrix for Global Relativists When Making Cross-Cultural Ethics Decisions (Quadrants relate to the perceived ethicalness for global relativists doing business abroad.) |
|---|---|

**Home Country Perceptions**

|  |  | Ethical | Unethical |
|---|---|---|---|
| **Foreign Country Perceptions** | **Ethical** | Ethical | Ethical |
|  | **Unethical** | Ethical | Unethical |

ernment and people who live in the area are happy for the jobs, in this case the multinational investment group seems to be applying Russian cultural values toward the natural environment rather than the more stringent ones of their own countries.

As with most philosophies, cultural relativists fall along a continuum. Some profess the belief that only one culture defines ethical behavior for the whole globe, without exceptions. For the business relativist, for example, there may be no relevant ethical standards but the one of the culture in which his or her current transaction is taking place. Such individuals may adjust to the ethics of a particular foreign culture or use their own culture as a defense of something unethical as perceived in the foreign country. The disadvantage is that they may be in conflict with their own individual moral standards and perhaps with their own culture's values and legal system. Figure 10–1 shows a two-by-two matrix that many relativists may use to make multicultural decisions.

As business becomes more global and multinational corporations proliferate, the chances of ethical conflict increase. There is a growing need for companies to adopt an international ethics code. Figure 10–2 details an International Code of Ethics for Canadian businesses. The code had thirteen signatories, including ALCAN Aluminum and Canadian Occidental Petroleum.

## Global Values

Many theorists have tried to establish a set of global or universal ethical standards. Table 10–3 lists six books and documents that suggest that there is a pattern of shared values—such as truthfulness, integrity, fairness, and equality—across the globe. When applied to global business, these values suggest a universal set of ethics. The Caux Round Table in Switzerland, in collaboration with business leaders in other European countries, Japan, and the United States, has created an international ethics code

**FIGURE 10-2**   International Code of Ethics for Canadian Business

## INTERNATIONAL CODE OF ETHICS FOR CANADIAN BUSINESS

### PRINCIPLES

A.  Concerning Community Participation and Environmental Protection, we will:

- strive within our sphere of influence to ensure a fair share of benefits to stakeholders impacted by our activities.
- ensure meaningful and transparent consultation with all stakeholders and attempt to integrate our corporate activities with local communities as good corporate citizens.
- ensure our activities are consistent with sound environmental management and conservation practices.
- provide meaningful opportunities for technology, training and capacity building within the host nation.

B.  Concerning Human Rights, we will:

- support and promote the protection of international human rights within our sphere of influence.
- not be complicit in human rights abuses.

C.  Concerning Business Conduct, we will:

- not make illegal and improper payments and bribes and will refrain from participating in any corrupt business practices.
- comply with all application laws and conduct business activities in a transparent fashion.
- ensure contractor's, supplier's and agent's activities are consistent with these principles.

D. Concerning Employees Rights and Health and Safety, we will:

- ensure health and safety of workers is protected.
- strive for social justice and promote freedom of association and expression in the workplace.
- ensure consistency with universally accepted labour standards, including those related to exploitation of child labour.

### APPLICATION

The signators of this document are committed to implementation with their individual firms through the development of operational codes and practices that are consistent with the vision, beliefs, values and principles contained herein.

| FIGURE 10–2 | International Code of Ethics for Canadian Business |

### INTERNATIONAL CODE OF ETHICS FOR CANADIAN BUSINESS

#### VISION

Canadian business has a global presence that is recognized by all stakeholders as economically rewarding to all parties, acknowledged as being ethically, socially and environmentally responsible, welcomed by the communities in which we operate, and that facilitates economic, human resource and community development within a stable operating environment.

#### BELIEFS

We believe that:
- we can make a difference within our sphere of influence (our stakeholders).
- business should take a leadership role through establishment of ethical business principles.
- national governments have the prerogative to conduct their own government and legal affairs in accordance with their sovereign rights.
- all governments should comply with international treaties and other agreements that they have committed to, including the areas of human rights and social justice.
- while reflecting cultural diversity and differences, we should do business throughout the world consistent with the way we do business in Canada.
- the business sector should show ethical leadership.
- we can facilitate the achievement of wealth generation and a fair sharing of economic benefits.
- our principles will assist in improving relations between the Canadian and host governments.
- open, honest and transparent relationships are critical to our success.
- local communities need to be involved in decision-making for issues that affect them.
- multistakeholder processes need to be initiated to seek effective solutions.
- confrontation should be tempered by diplomacy.
- wealth maximization for all stakeholders will be enhanced by resolution of outstanding human rights and social justice issues.
- doing business with other countries is good for Canada, and vice versa.

#### VALUES

We value:
- human rights and social justice.
- wealth maximization for all stakeholders.
- operation of a free market economy.
- a business environment that mitigates against bribery and corruption.
- public accountability by governments.
- equality of opportunity.
- a defined code of ethics and business practice.
- protection of environmental quality and sound environmental stewardship.
- community benefits.
- good relationships with all stakeholders.
- stability and continuous improvement within our operating environment.

Source: Errol Mendes, Human Rights Research and Education Center, University of Ottawa. Reprinted by permission.

| TABLE 10–3 | Global Management Ethics |
|---|---|

| 1993 Parliament of the World's Religions *The Declaration of a Global Ethic* | *State of California Handbook on . . . Moral and Civic Education . . .* | Michael Josephson *Character Counts, Ethics: Easier Said Than Done* |
|---|---|---|
| Nonviolence (love) | Morality | Trustworthiness |
| Respect for life | Truth | Honesty |
| Commitment | Justice | Integrity |
| Solidarity | Patriotism | Promise keeping |
| Truthfulness | Self-esteem | Loyalty |
| Tolerance | Integrity | Respect for others |
| Equal rights | Empathy | Responsibility |
| Sexual morality | Exemplary conduct | Fairness |
| | Reliability | Caring |
| | Respect for family, property, law | Citizenship |
| William J. Bennett *The Book of Virtues* | Thomas Donaldson *Fundamental International Rights* | Rushworth W. Kidder *Shared Values for a Troubled World* |
| Self-discipline | Physical movement | Love |
| Compassion | Property, ownership | Truthfulness |
| Responsibility | No torture | Fairness |
| Friendship | Fair trial | Freedom |
| Work | Nondiscrimination | Unity |
| Courage | Physical security | Tolerance |
| Perseverance | Speech and association | Responsibility |
| Honesty | Minimal education | Respect for life |
| Loyalty | Political participation | |
| Faith | Subsistence | |

*Source:* "Global Management Ethics," from Andrew Sikula, *Applied Management Ethics,* 1996, p. 127. Used by permission of the author, Andrew Sikula.

(reprinted in Appendix B). The shared values assume that we all have basic rights and responsibilities that must be adhered to when doing business.

If there is a universal set of ethics, why then do businesspeople have trouble understanding what is ethical or unethical? The answer lies partly in how these basic rights and responsibilities are operationalized or implemented. When someone from another culture mentions words such as *integrity* or *democracy,* most listeners feel reassured because these are familiar concepts. However, differences surface when someone from another culture explains what these concepts mean from the perspective of his or her culture. Consider that honesty is valued in both Japan and the United States. Part of honesty is operationalized by trust. In Japan's banking industry, businesspeople demonstrated that trust by hiring retired Japanese bureaucrats to become auditors, directors, executives, and presidents—a practice known as *amakudari,* or "descent from heaven." Because these men were so trusted, bankers felt that nothing bad or unethical could happen to the banks. However, because the regulators implicitly trusted their former superiors, the relationship between regulated and regulator became fuzzy. In the United States, businesspeople may trust former superiors, but they also believe that there should be a separation between those who regulate and those who are regulated.[9]

Although honesty, charity, virtue, and doing good to others may be universally desirable qualities, differences in implementing them can raise ethical issues. To address such problems, General Motors Corp., Procter & Gamble, the Shell Group, and about thirty other companies agreed to abide by the Global Sullivan Principles (see Table 10–4). These principles seek to encourage social responsibility around the world, though some of these companies have not implemented these principles.[10] In addition, fifty of the world's largest corporations have signed the UN Global Compact, the purpose of which is to support free trade unions, abolish child labor, and protect the natural environment. Signatory companies are required to post an annual update on their progress in these areas and are expected to cooperate with UN agencies on social projects in the developing countries in which they operate.[11]

A major challenge to businesses operating in global markets is how to accommodate inconsistencies in ethics and regulations and how to be proactive in developing responsible conduct. A review of regulatory efforts in some world regions shows that international consensus exists on approaches to encouraging ethical conduct in business organizations. The concern is not only to develop legal limitations for behavior but also to develop incentives for self-regulation and ethical conduct that are acceptable in a global business environment. The challenge is not only enforcing ethical conduct but also developing organizational value systems that promote an ethical business environment. Identifying ethical issues and implementing codes of conduct that incorporate both legal and ethical concerns comprise the best approach for preventing violations and avoiding civil litigation. Companies and trade associations need to assess how to better develop the programs and determine the management practices that will result in excellent legal and ethical performance. Also key to improving global ethical and legal performance is determining the relationship between national differences in individuals' moral philosophies and the corporate core values in management systems.[12]

## The Multinational Corporation

**Multinational corporations (MNCs)** are public companies that operate on a global scale without significant ties to any one nation or region. MNCs represent the highest level of international business commitment and are characterized by a global strategy of focusing on opportunities throughout the world. Examples of multinational corporations include Shell Oil, Nike, Monsanto, and Cisco Systems. Some of these firms have grown so large that they generate higher revenues than the gross domestic product (GDP) of some of the countries in which they do business, as shown in Table 10–5. (Gross domestic product refers to the sum of all the goods and services produced in a country during one year.). Consider Jack Welch, the former CEO of General Electric

## TABLE 10–4 The Global Sullivan Principles

As a company which endorses the Global Sullivan Principles we will respect the law, and as a responsible member of society we will apply these Principles with integrity consistent with the legitimate role of business. We will develop and implement company policies, procedures, training and internal reporting structures to ensure commitment to these principles throughout our organization. We believe the application of these Principles will achieve greater tolerance and better understanding among peoples, and advance the culture of peace.

Accordingly, we will:

- Express our support for universal human rights and, particularly, those of our employees, the communities within which we operate, and parties with whom we do business.
- Promote equal opportunity for our employees at all levels of the company with respect to issues such as color, race, gender, age, ethnicity or religious beliefs, and operate without unacceptable worker treatment such as the exploitation of children, physical punishment, female abuse, involuntary servitude, or other forms of abuse.
- Respect our employees' voluntary freedom of association.
- Compensate our employees to enable them to meet at least their basic needs and provide the opportunity to improve their skill and capability in order to raise their social and economic opportunities.
- Provide a safe and healthy workplace; protect human health and the environment; and promote sustainable development.
- Promote fair competition including respect for intellectual and other property rights, and not offer, pay or accept bribes.
- Work with government and communities in which we do business to improve the quality of life in those communities—their educational, cultural, economic and social well-being—and seek to provide training and opportunities for workers from disadvantaged backgrounds.
- Promote the application of these principles by those with whom we do business.
- We will be transparent in our implementation of these principles and provide information which demonstrates publicly our commitment to them.

Source: Reprinted from *Ethikos: Examining Ethical and Compliance Issues in Business* (Mamaroneck, N.Y.).

Corporation, whose total personal assets are estimated to be about $456.2 million. To put this in a global perspective, Welch's wealth represents about half the GDP of Monaco and nearly the total GDP of Grenada.[13]

Because of their size and financial power, multinational corporations have been the subject of much ethical criticism, and their impact on the countries in which they do business has been hotly debated. Both American and European labor unions argue that it is unfair for MNCs to transfer jobs overseas, where wage rates are lower. Other critics have charged that multinationals use labor-saving devices that increase unemployment in the countries where they manufacture. MNCs have also been accused of increasing the gap between rich and poor nations and of misusing and misallocating scarce resources. Their size and financial clout enable MNCs to control money sup-

| TABLE 10–5 | Comparison of World's Largest Corporations Revenues to Countries' Gross Domestic Product |
| --- | --- |

| COUNTRY/COMPANY | GDP/REVENUES (IN BILLIONS OF DOLLARS) |
| --- | --- |
| United States | 10,820 |
| China | 5,560 |
| Japan | 3,450 |
| India | 2,660 |
| France | 1,540 |
| United Kingdom | 1,470 |
| Italy | 1,402 |
| Brazil | 1,340 |
| Russia | 1,200 |
| Mexico | 920 |
| Canada | 875 |
| South Korea | 865 |
| Spain | 828 |
| Indonesia | 687 |
| Australia | 466 |
| Argentina | 453 |
| Turkey | 443 |
| Iran | 426 |
| Netherlands | 413 |
| South Africa | 412 |
| Thailand | 410 |
| Taiwan | 386 |
| Poland | 340 |
| Philippines | 335 |
| Pakistan | 299 |
| Belgium | 268 |
| Egypt | 258 |
| Saudi Arabia | 241 |
| Bangladesh | 230 |
| Sweden | 228 |
| Switzerland | 226 |
| Colombia | 225 |
| Austria | 220 |
| WAL-MART STORES (US) | 220 |
| Ukraine | 205 |
| Greece | 201 |
| Malaysia | 200 |

| TABLE 10–5 | Comparison of World's Largest Corporations Revenues to Countries' Gross Domestic Product (continued) |
|---|---|

| COUNTRY/COMPANY | GDP/REVENUES (IN BILLIONS OF DOLLARS) |
|---|---|
| EXXONMOBIL (US) | 192 |
| Portugal | 182 |
| Hong Kong | 180 |
| GENERAL MOTORS (US) | 177 |
| Algeria | 177 |
| BP (BRITAIN) | 174 |
| FORD MOTOR (US) | 162 |
| Czech Republic | 156 |
| Denmark | 156 |
| Chile | 153 |
| Romania | 153 |

All other countries in the world are below $150 billion.

Source: Adapted from "The World's Largest Corporations," *Fortune,* July 22, 2002, pp. F–1–F–11; CIA, "Field Listing," Feb. 13, 2003, *The World Fact Book 2002,* www.cia.gov/cia/publications/factbook/fields/2116.

plies, employment, and even the economic well-being of less-developed countries. In some instances, MNCs have controlled entire cultures and countries. For example, a Los Angeles judge recently ruled that Unocal may be liable for the conduct of the government of Myanmar (formerly known as Burma). Documents presented in court contend that forced labor was commonly used in Myanmar to build Unocal projects and that workers' refusal to work resulted in their imprisonment and/or execution at the hands of the Myanmar army. Unocal's financial size and determination to complete certain projects at any cost compelled the Myanmar government to sanction the use of forced labor.[14]

Critics believe that the size and power of multinationals create ethical issues involving the exploitation of both natural and human resources. One question is whether MNCs should be able to pay a low price for the right to remove minerals, timber, oil, and other natural resources and then sell products made from those resources for a much higher price. In many instances, only a small fraction of the ultimate sale price of such resources comes back to benefit the country of origin. This complaint led many oil-producing countries to form the Organization of Petroleum Exporting Countries (OPEC) in the 1960s to gain control over the revenues from oil produced in those lands.

Critics also accuse MNCs of exploiting the labor markets of host countries. Although some MNCs have been accused of paying inadequate wages, the ethical issue of fair wages is a complicated one. Sometimes MNCs pay higher wages than local employers can afford to match; then local businesses complain that the most productive and skilled workers go to work for multinationals. Measures have been taken to curtail such practices. For example, many MNCs are trying to help organize labor unions and establish minimum-wage laws. In addition, host governments have levied import taxes that increase the price MNCs charge for their products and reduce their profits. Import taxes are meant to favor local industry as sources of supply for an MNC manufacturing in the host country. If such a tax raises the MNC's costs, it might lead the MNC to charge higher prices or accept lower profits, but such effects are not the fundamental goal of the law. Host governments have also imposed export taxes on MNCs to force them to share more of their profits.

The activities of multinational corporations may also raise issues of unfair competition. Because of their diversified nature, MNCs can borrow money from local capital resources in such volume that little is left for local firms. MNCs have also been accused of failing to carry an appropriate share of the cost of social development. They frequently apply advanced, high-productivity technologies that local companies cannot afford or cannot implement because they lack qualified workers. The MNCs thus become more productive and can afford to pay higher wages to workers. Because of their technology, however, they require fewer employees than the local firms would hire to produce the same product. And, given their economies of scale, MNCs can also negotiate lower tax rates. By manipulating transfer payments among their affiliates, they may pay little tax anywhere. All these special advantages explain why some claim that MNCs compete unfairly. For example, many heavy-equipment companies in the United States try to sell construction equipment to foreign companies that build major roads, dams, and utility complexes. They argue that this equipment will make it possible to complete these projects sooner, thus benefiting the country. Some less-developed countries counter that such equipment purchases actually remove hard currency from their economies and increase unemployment. Certain nations, such as India, therefore believe that it is better in the long run to hire laborers to do construction work than to buy a piece of heavy equipment. The country keeps its hard currency in its economy and creates new jobs, which increases the quality of life more than does having a project completed sooner.

Although it is unethical or illegal conduct by multinational corporations that grabs world headlines, some MNCs also strive to be good global citizens with strong ethical values. Texas Instruments (TI), for example, has adopted a three-level global approach to ethical integrity that asks: (1) "Are we complying with all legal requirements on a local level?" (2) "Are there business practices or requirements at the local level which impact how we interact with co-workers in other parts of the world?" and (3) "Do some of our practices need to be adapted based on the local laws and customs of a specific locale? On what basis do we define our universal standards that apply to TI employees everywhere?" TI generally follows conservative rules regarding the giving and receiving of gifts. However, what may be considered an excessive gift in the United States may be viewed differently according to the local customs of other parts of the world. TI used to define gift limits in terms of U.S. dollars, but now it just specifies that gift-giving should not be used in a way that exerts undue pressure to win business or implies a quid pro quo.[15]

Many companies, including Coca-Cola, Du Pont, Hewlett-Packard, Levi Strauss & Co., Texaco, and Wal-Mart, endorse following responsible business practices abroad. These companies support a globally based resource system called Business for Social Responsibility (BSR). BSR tracks emerging issues and trends, provides information on corporate leadership and best practices, conducts educational workshops and training, and assists organizations in developing practical business ethics tools. It addresses such issues as community investment, corporate social responsibility, the environment, governance, and accountability. BSR has also established formal partnerships with other organizations that focus on corporate responsibility in Brazil, Israel, the United Kingdom, Chile, and Panama.[16]

Although multinational corporations are not inherently unethical, their size and power often seem threatening to less-developed countries. The ethical problems that MNCs face arise from the opposing points of view inherent in multicultural situations. Differences in cultural perspectives may be as important as differences in economic interests. Because of their size and power, multinational corporations must therefore take extra care to make ethical decisions that not only achieve their own objectives but also benefit the countries where they manufacture or market their products. Even premier MNCs sometimes find themselves in ethical conflict—and face liability as a result. After investigating the tires on Ford automobiles that were involved in sixty-two accidents and more than forty deaths in Venezuela, the Venezuelan attorney general determined that the incidents could lead to fines against or even criminal prosecution of the tires' manufacturer, Bridgestone/Firestone, Inc., and Ford. Ford reportedly had requested that Bridgestone/Firestone insert an extra nylon layer between the tires' steel belt and tread (cap ply) to accommodate the hotter, more humid, and more demanding driving conditions in Venezuela. When Firestone's Venezuelan plant began producing the tires for Ford, however, the Venezuelan plant "inadvertently began marketing tires without a cap ply" as tires that had the extra nylon layer for an unspecified time. Because of the string of accidents in Venezuela, tire safety has become a major issue in the United Sates and the European Union (EU), where many accidents and deaths occurred in Ford sport utility vehicles equipped with Firestone tires. The resulting international scandal brought about the resignation of Bridgestone's U.S. CEO as well as the dissolution of a seventy-year-long agreement between Ford and Bridgestone. Ford has since switched to Michelin tires on all of its Explorers. Other tire suppliers, including Goodyear, are increasing the amount of testing they do for all tires that go to Ford.[17]

## Ethical Issues Around the Globe

Now we turn our attention to some common global ethical issues that arise when companies transact business internationally. These include sexual and racial discrimination, human rights concerns, price discrimination, bribery, harmful products, pollution, telecommunications issues, and intellectual property issues. Several organizations have been established to provide guidance on such international business issues. This list of issues is certainly not exhaustive, but provides a sample of the complexity of ethical decision making in the global arena.

### Sexual and Racial Discrimination

Various U.S. and European laws prohibit businesses from discriminating on the basis of sex, race, religion, or disabilities in their hiring, firing, and promotion decisions. However, the problem of discrimination is still a reality in the world. In the United Kingdom, East Indians have traditionally been relegated to the lowest-paying, least desired jobs. In Germany, the government will not grant citizenship to Turkish workers who have been living there for decades or even to second-generation Turkish-German residents. Australian aborigines have long been the victims of social and economic discrimination. In many Southeast Asian and Far Eastern countries, employees from particular ethnic backgrounds may not be promoted. In Japan, for example, there appears to be a glass ceiling for Japanese-Koreans. In Russia, job advertisements frequently specify the age and gender of prospective employees. Female entrepreneurs in Russia face endless bureaucracy, problems obtaining credit, and a tangled legal system. One woman business owner was jailed for ten days with no charges filed, evidence brought, or, after she was released, apologies offered.[18]

Businesswomen remain a rarity in many Middle Eastern nations. In some Middle Eastern countries, women are required to wear special clothing and cover their faces; in public, they may be physically separated from men. Because these countries prescribe only nonbusiness roles for women, companies negotiating with Middle Eastern firms have encountered problems when they use women sales representatives. Indeed, a Middle Eastern company may simply refuse to negotiate with saleswomen or may take an unfavorable view of the foreign organizations that employ them. The ethical issue in such cases is whether foreign businesses should respect Middle Eastern values and send only men to negotiate sales transactions, thus denying women employees the opportunity to further their careers and contribute to organizational objectives. The alternative would be for these firms to try to maintain their own ideas of social equality, knowing that the women sales representatives will probably be unsuccessful because of the cultural norms in those societies.

By acknowledging and attempting to curb discrimination, businesses around the world can realize specific benefits. Reducing discrimination helps to decrease employee turnover because people who believe they are hired, promoted, and treated according to their skills and abilities rather than their personal characteristics or beliefs are more likely to remain loyal. This in turn can reduce the costs of hiring and training new employees. Improved productivity results when jobs are filled with the most qualified persons. Additionally, when companies hire a diverse local work force, they are more likely to enjoy the goodwill and support of the communities surrounding their facilities. Finally, companies that take steps to eliminate discrimination may receive favorable attention from stakeholder groups such as labor and women's rights groups. This enhances the reputation of the firm overall as well as its brands. Table 10–6 lists steps that Business for Social Responsibility suggests companies take to be proactive on discrimination issues.

## Human Rights

Corporate concern for global human rights emerged in the 1990s as news stories depicting the opportunistic use of child labor, payment of low wages, and abuses in foreign factories helped reshape our attitudes about acceptable behavior for organizations. For example, eight clothing retailers, including Liz Claiborne and Tommy Hilfiger, settled a lawsuit alleging that they were responsible for abuses against foreign workers in textile factories on the Pacific Island of Saipan. As part of the settlement, the factory workers saw improved working conditions, such as relaxed restrictions on bathroom breaks.[19]

| TABLE 10–6 | Steps Companies Can Take to Address Discrimination Issues |
| --- | --- |

1. Establish a company policy on discrimination.

2. Communicate this policy both internally and externally.

3. Determine benchmarks for activities in which discrimination can arise.

4. Identify indicators of possible noncompliance.

5. Establish methods for identifying noncompliance.

6. Develop an action plan.

7. Take action.

Source: "Discrimination," Business for Social Responsibility, www.bsr.org/BSRResources/ WhitePaperDetail.cfm?DocumentID=520 (accessed Mar. 7, 2003).

Companies struggling with human rights issues sometimes make short-term decisions to boost profitability that have negative long-term implications. These issues include concerns about the treatment of minorities and women, as well as the issues of child labor and employee rights. Multinational corporations face even greater challenges in this area because of the nature of their relationships with manufacturers and subcontractors in other cultures. The International Labor Organization estimates that 250 million children between the ages of five and fourteen work in developing countries (61 percent in Asia, 32 percent in Africa, and 7 percent in Latin America). Although only an estimated 5 percent of these child laborers work in export industries, this still represents an ethical issue for multinational corporations.[20]

Although concern about human rights issues is increasing, abuses still occur. Many people believe that multinational companies should view the law as constituting the "floor" of acceptable behavior and strive to improve workers' quality of life in every country. Understanding each country's culture can help MNCs make improvements that will be valued. At an annual Human Rights Survey meeting, the executive director of Human Rights Watch introduced three guidelines that managers should consider to advance human rights. First, companies need to establish an open dialog between workers and management. Second, businesses should be aware of the human rights issues and concerns in each country in which they do business. One source for this information is Amnesty International, an international nonprofit devoted to human rights issues. Finally, companies should adopt the prevailing legal standard but work to improve and embrace a "best practices" approach and standard. Internationally acceptable behavior in any country should be their goal.[21] Several organizations observe and report on corporate behavior:

- *Global Compact:* Developed by the UN Secretary-General, this organization asks businesses to adhere to human rights and labor standards as defined in international treaties.

- *Amnesty International:* The business unit of this London-based human rights group has established Human Rights Guidelines for Companies, a set of principles concerning the link between business and human rights.

- *Fair Labor Association:* A nonprofit whose members include manufacturers, universities, and groups promoting human, consumer, religious, shareholder, and labor rights. Participating firms agree to have their facilities and those of their contractors monitored by both internal and independent external organizations.

- *The Council on Economic Priorities Accreditation Agency:* This organization has established standards for assessing labor conditions in global manufacturing operations.

## Price Discrimination

A major ethical issue in international business is how products sold in other countries are priced. When a firm charges different prices to different groups of customers, it may be accused of **price discrimination.** Differential pricing is legal if it does not substantially reduce competition or if it can be justified on the basis of costs—for example, the costs of taxes and import fees associated with bringing products into another country. However, price discrimination may become an ethical issue, or even be illegal, when (1) the practice violates either country's laws, (2) the market cannot be divided into segments, (3) the cost of segmenting the market exceeds the extra revenue from legal price discrimination, or (4) the practice results in extreme customer dissatisfaction.

When a market is artificially divided into segments and each segment is subject to different prices, inequalities may emerge that cannot be explained by added costs. This creates an ethical concern. Such pricing policies may be judged illegal if courts rule that they substantially decrease competition. In the United States, price discrimination that harms competition is prohibited under the Robinson-Patman Act. In other countries, judgments of illegality result from precedent or fairness rulings. The European Union, for example, has fined numerous companies for price fixing, including European brewers ($201 million fine), the Swiss chemical firm Hoffman-La Roche ($63.5 million euros), and Archer Daniels Midland, a U.S. firm ($40 million euros).[22]

When companies market their products outside their own countries, the costs of transportation, taxes, tariffs, and other expenses can raise their prices. When prices increase beyond the level needed to meet the costs of these additional expenses, an ethical issue emerges. Increasing prices in this way is sometimes referred to as **gouging.** When the EU converted to a single currency—the euro—many Europeans believed that individual shops as well as countries were gouging them.[23] Gouging can also refer to charging exorbitant rates for a limited time to exploit situational shortages—for instance, when lumber suppliers charge premium prices to earthquake victims seeking to rebuild. But gouging can also be endemic. For example, Cemex SA, a cement manufacturer in Mexico, has five thousand cement distributors in poor neighborhoods in Mexico that charge monopoly prices and enjoy monopoly profits. Not surprisingly, cement costs more in Mexico than in any other country, which has a negative effect on poor home builders.[24] Most countries' laws forbid companies from charging exorbitant prices for lifesaving products, which include some pharmaceuticals. However, these laws do not apply to products that are not lifesaving, even if they are in great demand and no substitutes are available.

As mentioned earlier in this chapter, dumping occurs when companies sell products in foreign markets at low prices that do not cover all the costs of exporting the products. Dumping may occur for several reasons. Charging low prices allows a company to enter a market quickly and capture a large market share. Sometimes dumping occurs when the domestic market for a firm's product is too small to support an effi-cient level of production. In other cases, technologically obsolete products that are no longer salable in the country of origin may be dumped overseas. Dumping is unethi-cal if it interferes with competition or hurts firms and workers in other countries. If it substantially reduces competition, it is illegal under many international laws. Dump-ing is difficult to prove, but even the suspicion of dumping can lead to the imposition of import quotas, which can hurt innocent firms. After investigating complaints from U.S. steel producers and labor unions, the U.S. Department of Commerce deter-mined that Russia has been dumping steel in the United States. It recommended as-sessing tariffs as high as 217 percent to reverse the effects of the dumping, which included the loss of ten thousand jobs in the U.S. steel industry. When the Depart-ment of Commerce announced that it would settle the case against Russia and sus-pend the tariffs, the announcement brought protests from attorneys general in four steel-producing states.[25] When the administration of President George W. Bush later attacked European steel imports with new tariffs, the European Union countered with its own tariffs against U.S. exports valued at $2.1 billion.[26]

Price differentials, gouging, and dumping create ethical issues because some groups of consumers have to pay more than a fair price for products. Pricing is cer-tainly a complicated issue in international marketing because of the additional costs imposed by tariffs, taxes, customs fees, and paperwork, as well as the political desire to protect home markets. Nonetheless, businesses should take care to price their products so they recover legitimate expenses and earn a reasonable profit while still competing fairly.

## Bribery

In many cultures, giving bribes—also known as **facilitating payments**—is an acceptable business practice. In Mexico, a bribe is called *la mordida*, while South Africans call it *dash*. In the Middle East, India, and Pakistan, *baksheesh*, a tip or gratuity given by a su-perior, is widely used. The Germans call it *schmiergeld*, grease money, and the Italians call it *bustarella*, a little envelope. Companies that do business internationally should be aware that bribes are an ethical issue and that the practice is more prevalent in some countries than in others. Transparency International has developed a Bribe Payers Index (Table 10–7) to indicate the degree to which international corporations are engaging in paying bribes in specific markets. The index reveals that on a scale of 0 to 10, companies in Russia are highly likely to pay bribes to win or retain business.[27] Bribes or payoff re-quests are frequently associated with large construction projects, turnkey capital proj-ects, and large commodity or equipment contracts, as shown in Table 10–8.

The U.S. **Foreign Corrupt Practices Act (FCPA)** prohibits U.S. companies from offering or providing payments to officials of foreign governments for the purpose of obtaining or retaining business abroad. The FCPA was enacted after a Securities and Exchange Commission investigation in the mid 1970s revealed that four hundred U.S. firms admitted making questionable or illegal payments in excess of $300 million to foreign government officials, politicians, and political parties. Violators of the FCPA face corporate fines of up to $2 million, while company executives face a max-imum of five years in prison or $10,000 in fines, or both. The FCPA does permit small "grease" payments to foreign ministerial or clerical government employees. Such pay-

| TABLE 10–7 | Bribe Payers' Index | |
| --- | --- | --- |

| RANK | COUNTRY | SCORE* |
| --- | --- | --- |
| 1 | Australia | 8.5 |
| 2 | Sweden** | 8.4 |
| 2 | Switzerland | 8.4 |
| 4 | Austria | 8.2 |
| 5 | Canada | 8.1 |
| 6 | Netherlands | 7.8 |
| 6 | Belgium | 7.8 |
| 8 | United Kingdom | 6.9 |
| 8 | Germany | 6.9 |
| 9 | Singapore | 6.3 |
| 11 | Spain | 5.8 |
| 12 | France | 5.5 |
| 13 | United States | 5.3 |
| 13 | Japan | 5.3 |
| 15 | Malaysia | 4.3 |
| 15 | Hong Kong | 4.3 |
| 17 | Italy | 4.1 |
| 18 | South Korea | 3.9 |
| 19 | Taiwan | 3.8 |
| 20 | China | 3.5 |
| | *Domestic companies* | 1.9 |

*A perfect score, indicating zero perceived propensity to pay bribes, is 10.0, and thus the ranking starts with companies from countries that are seen to have a low propensity for foreign bribe paying.

**The same number ranking indicates a tie (for example, Sweden and Switzerland tied for second).

Source: "Transparency International Bribe Payers Index 2002," *Transparency International,* May 14, 2002, www.transparency.org/cpi/2002/bpi2002.en.html. Courtesy of Transparency International. Reprinted with permission.

ments are exempted because of their size and the assumption that they are used to persuade the recipients to perform their normal duties, not to do something critical to the distribution of new goods and services.

Some critics of the FCPA contend that although the law was designed to foster fair and equal treatment for all, it places U.S. firms at a disadvantage in the international business arena. The FCPA applies only to American businesses; other nations have not imposed such restraints on their companies doing business abroad. For example, if three companies—from the United States, France, and Korea—are bidding on a dam-building project in Egypt, the French and Korean firms could bribe Egyptian officials in their efforts to acquire the contract, but it would be illegal for the American firm to do so. Thus, the issue of bribery sets the values of one culture—the U.S. disapproval of bribery—against those of other cultures.

| TABLE 10–8 | Bribery in Business Sectors |
| --- | --- |

How likely is it that senior public officials in this country would demand or accept bribes, e.g., for public tenders, regulations, licensing in the following business sectors?

| BUSINESS SECTOR | SCORE | BUSINESS SECTOR | SCORE |
| --- | --- | --- | --- |
| Public works/construction | 1.3 | Heavy manufacturing | 4.5 |
| Arms and defense | 1.9 | Banking and finance | 4.7 |
| Oil and gas | 2.7 | Civilian aerospace | 4.9 |
| Real estate/property | 3.5 | Forestry | 5.1 |
| Telecoms | 3.7 | Information technology | 5.1 |
| Power generation/transmission | 3.7 | Fishery | 5.9 |
| Mining | 4.0 | Light manufacturing | 5.9 |
| Transportation/storage | 4.3 | Agriculture | 5.9 |
| Pharmaceuticals/medical care | 4.3 | | |

The scores are mean averages from all the responses on a 0 to 10 basis, where 0 represents very high perceived levels of corruption, and 10 represents extremely low perceived levels of corruption.

Source: "Transparency International Bribe Payers Index 2002," *Transparency International,* May 14, 2002, www.transparency.org/cpi/2002/bpi2002.en.html. Reprinted with permission.

In 1988, the **Omnibus Trade and Competitiveness (OTC) Act** reduced FCPA legislation in certain areas and repealed the Eckhardt Amendment. The Eckhardt Amendment had prevented senior managers from using agents or employees as scapegoats when bribes were given. The OTC Act makes prosecution of bribery even more difficult, thus decreasing the power and applicability of the FCPA in global business settings. Subsequent support for the Foreign Corrupt Practices Act has come through a global treaty, the Convention on Combating Bribery of Foreign Public Officials in International Business Transactions, which has been signed by thirty-four nations. The Convention is dominated by some of the largest countries in the world, and the majority in support of the treaty are members of the Organisation of Economic Cooperation and Development (OECD). The treaty requires signatories to make it a criminal offense for any person to "offer, promise or give away undue pecuniary or other advantage . . . to a foreign public official" for the purpose of obtaining "business or other improper advantage in the conduct of international commerce." Punishment is to be swift and effective so as to deter future offenses and is to be determined by the country in which the company operates.[28] However, at the time of the Transparency International Study in, only eighteen of the thirty-four treaty-signing countries had deposited all the necessary ratification documents.[29]

## Harmful Products

Governments in advanced industrialized nations have banned the sale of certain products considered harmful. However, some companies in those nations continue to sell such products in other countries where they remain legal. For example, many recent news stories have focused on the safety of genetically engineered products, which have become very controversial in the United States and Europe. Investors have filed resolutions at American Home Products, Archer Daniels Midland, Dow Chemical, Du Pont, and Monsanto to prevent the marketing of genetically engineered products "until long-term safety testing has shown that they are not harmful to humans, animals, and the environment."[30] Similar proposals made to Coca-Cola and General Mills ask for labeling of genetically engineered ingredients until such ingredients are removed from the companies' products. Many countries, including Japan, Australia, and New Zealand, and those in the European Union, already require labeling of genetically engineered food products.[31]

Another ethical issue involves the export of tobacco products to less-developed countries. Cigarette sales in the United States are declining in the face of stricter tobacco regulations, increasing evidence that smoking causes illness and medical problems, and a decline in the social acceptability of smoking. As U.S. sales decline, tobacco companies have increased their efforts to market cigarettes and other tobacco products in other countries, particularly less-developed ones. U.S. cigarette exports now exceed $200 billion, up from $73.6 billion in 1982.[32] The volume of U.S. tobacco manufacturers' overseas sales now exceeds their domestic sales. The ethical issue becomes whether tobacco marketers should knowingly sell in other countries a product that is considered harmful in their home country.

Many consumers in underdeveloped countries view tobacco as good, both physically and economically. They argue that the tobacco industry provides jobs and stimulates economies and that cigarette consumers enjoy smoking. Many also cite the low longevity rates in these countries as a reason to discount the health hazards of tobacco. In the long run, however, as industrialization raises the standard of living in less-developed countries, in turn increasing longevity rates, those countries may change their views on tobacco. As people live longer and the health hazards of smoking begin to cost both the people and their governments more in time and money, ethical pressure in these countries will increase.

At times, products that are not harmful in some countries become harmful to consumers in others because of illiteracy, unsanitary conditions, or cultural values. For example, products marketed by the Nestlé Corporation in the 1970s included infant formulas, which are used in the supplemental feeding of infants and have been tested as safe when used correctly. When the company introduced its product into African countries as an alternative to breast feeding, local mothers quickly adopted the product. As time passed, however, infant mortality rates rose dramatically. Investigators found that, because of high illiteracy rates, many mothers were not able to follow the instructions for using the formula correctly. In addition, the water they used to mix with the powdered formula was often unsafe, and poor mothers also diluted the formula to save money, which reduced the nutritional value of the feeding. Nestlé was criticized for its aggressive promotion of the infant formula. For example, the company had employed so-called milk nurses to discourage mothers from breast feeding by portraying the practice as primitive and promoted Nestlé's infant formulas as a safer alternative. Under heated pressure from international agencies and boycotts by consumer groups, Nestlé agreed to stop promoting the infant formula. It also revised its product labeling and educational materials to point out the dangers of using the formula incorrectly and to assert that breast feeding was actually preferable.[33] Eventually, however, the company reverted to its previous practices, and the World Health

Organization has maintained its boycott. Thus, even traditionally safe and adequately tested products can create ethical issues when a marketer fails to evaluate foreign markets accurately or respond adequately to the health problems posed by its products in certain markets.

In the twenty-first century, the concern is growing over safe drinking water, genetically modified products, and tainted foodstuffs entering the food chain. For example, ConAgra Foods Inc. had to recall nineteen million pounds of ground beef because sixteen people in the United States became ill with the E. coli bacteria.[34] In some cases, the consequences can be fatal. Among other products, Baxter International Inc. produces kidney-dialysis filters. Unfortunately, when some of the filters proved to be defective at least ten people in Spain died as a result.[35]

Some companies are attempting to address the harmful product issue. For example, PepsiCo, long synonymous with fast food, is attempting to develop healthier snacks even knowing that fat, salt, and sugar are inherently tastier than broccoli, carrots, and tomatoes. The job of marketing healthier snacks with fewer calories and cholesterol is a challenge that PepsiCo is willing to meet to improve public health.[36]

## Pollution and the Natural Environment

Whereas many legal and ethical violations have limited impacts, in the case of environmental issues, the effects of abuses can be far-reaching and long-term. For example, public concern over global warming has increased pressure on companies to dramatically increase energy efficiency. Pressure from environmentalists is also encouraging companies to scrutinize suppliers of wood and paper products to ensure they are not endangered species and are harvesting products using sustainable practices. Many companies are therefore working to create standards for environmental responsibility. For example, Delphi Automotive Systems Corporation is committed to protecting human health, natural resources, and the global environment. Delphi's Design for the Environment process requires teams to evaluate the environmental impacts of product designs, materials, and manufacturing processes before the manufacturing begins. A leading producer of products that reduce emissions and improve fuel efficiency, Delphi is working to gain certification in ISO14001, a global standard that recognizes facilities that proactively adopt systems that manage and reduce environmental impact.[37] Other companies have modified or halted the production and sale of products that have a negative impact on the environment. For example, after tests showed that Scotchguard does not decompose in the environment, 3M announced a voluntary end to production of the forty-year-old product, which had generated $300 million in sales.[38]

Seeking to defend their air and water quality, some countries are taking legal action against polluting firms. In Mexico, for example, firms that fail to cut back emissions or that deny access to inspectors during smog alerts face legal sanctions.[39] In other situations, outside organizations such as Greenpeace issue warnings on countries that engage in environmental abuses. Greenpeace has accused Israel, for example, of defying international convention by dumping toxic waste in the Mediterranean.[40]

In some countries, however, groups have lobbied governments to increase the level of pollution they allow. For instance, Australia's per capita emissions from energy consumption and industrial manufacturing will rise from twenty-one metric tons to twenty-six tons in 2010, making Australia the largest greenhouse-gas emitter in the world. One member of the Australia Institute stated that, "If they had been aware of the facts, other nations would not have agreed to Australia's demand for an increase in emission but would have required us to cut our emissions more than other countries."[41]

For organizations to thrive globally, their governments should form joint agreements, such as the North American Free Trade Agreement between the United States, Canada, and Mexico, that set reasonable standards for emissions for members. Many pollution-control efforts have relatively short payback periods and have a long-term positive effect on profitability. In contrast, violating environmental initiatives has both human and financial costs, with the human cost being the health hazards associated with pollution.

## Telecommunications Issues

With the advent of satellites, e-mail, and the Internet, information can be accessed in a matter of seconds instead of weeks—and as a result businesses can become the victims as well as the perpetrators of unethical actions. The ease of information access poses ethical issues, particularly with regard to privacy, that can differ by country. Some Internet-based firms have responded to privacy issues responsibly whereas others have not. Yahoo!, for example, revised its privacy policy to expand its ability to market its own products to Yahoo users unless they expressly ask it not to. News of the policy change quickly circulated via the Web, and consumers exchanged ideas on how to change their personal preferences on Yahoo to avoid getting spam, junk mail, or telemarketing calls. The animosity was highlighted by a survey that reported that 75 percent of respondents described the new policy as "awful" while only 3 percent said it was good.[42]

Access to Internet users is becoming a huge business. For example, America On-line (AOL) controls 138 million registered users, most with instant messaging, a popular form of Internet chat and a key Web technology. As a result, AOL has become the gatekeeper not only to its own subscribers but also to consumers tapping into the Internet from cell phones and TVs.[43] The relevant ethical issues here relate to access, information mining, and monopolies. Information access gives Internet companies a revenue stream from charging companies to advertise on their server. Many Web sites collect various levels of personal information about their users and sell that information to advertisers. The sale of such information has exploded in the last ten years. One questionable technique that Web sites use is to link or connect one user to others. This tactic involves sending a Web user an e-mail suggesting that if he or she gives them a friend's name, then the company will give him or her discounts on promoted products. The friend then receives the same e-mail, and the result is a cascade of consumer information. Thus, companies are exploiting the human desire to obtain something for nothing.

The Internet seems to foster the something-for-nothing mentality. One of the largest problems associated with the Internet is fraud. The Internet Fraud Complaint Center reported that Americans lost about $18 million to fraud last year, and about half the 16,775 fraud cases the center investigated involved online auctions. Other types of online fraud include failing to deliver promised merchandise, credit-card fraud, and scams like the "Nigerian letter fraud." The latter is a widely distributed unsolicited e-mail purportedly sent by the Nigerian government, which requests that the recipient allow the government to use his or her bank account to hold millions of dollars in funds. The e-mail also requires the victim to pay cash for licenses, taxes, or other fees. The Internet Fraud Center believes the Nigerian scam nets the perpetrators more than $5,000 per victim.[44]

Information overload and Internet slowdowns are becoming more common—and sometimes they are intentionally caused. For example, the number of online attempts to criticize or disrupt corporate operations is increasing. Perpetrators have sent mass e-mail messages, used "distributed denial of service" tools to interrupt company Web site operations, and attempted to deflate stock prices by posting negative comments on online message boards.[45]

The speed of global communications has affected virtually all industries. The fashion industry is a good case in point. Imitations have always been a problem. "Knockoffs" usually entered the market a few months behind the originals by way of a few retailers. The practice has changed dramatically, however. A photograph can be taken at a fashion show in Milan, scanned, and sent electronically to a Hong Kong factory. The next day a sample garment is sent by overnight delivery to a New York showroom for retail buyers. Stores order these lower-priced "interpretations" for their own private-label collections and sometimes even show the costlier designer versions at the same time. Since competition in the malls is fierce and fashion merchandise is highly perishable, the industry has become very competitive. Some designers are countering these imitations by suing and by bringing out affordable knock-off versions of their own before anyone else can.

Another technology-related ethical issue is **day trading,** which involves placing multiple buy and sell orders on select securities and then holding these positions for a very short time—usually minutes or hours, but rarely longer than a day. Day traders, whose activities are made possible by telecommunications technology, seek profits in small increments from fluctuations in stock prices. The Electronic Trading Association estimates that the number of professional traders has grown to forty-five thousand.[46] The ethical issues associated with day trading relate to the huge gains and losses that can occur. For many people, day trading is like gambling because it promises immediate rewards. Some companies exploit day traders by "guaranteeing" huge profits if they buy their publications or take their courses. The Securities and Exchange Commission has guidelines to protect day traders from leveraging themselves into bankruptcy. However, the firms that process trades for brokerage houses and lend money to investors who buy stocks on margin are sometimes lax in enforcing the margin-lending rules that limit how much a customer can borrow. Like compulsive gamblers, some day traders fall into a vicious cycle of borrowing more and more money to make up for past losses, until they may feel that the only option is to do what Mark O. Barton did: go on a shooting spree that ended in his own death.[47]

Questionable financial activities, such as money laundering, have also been made easier by global telecommunications. **Money laundering** means using or transferring illegally received funds in a financial transaction so as to conceal their source or ownership or facilitate an illegal activity. Using telecommunications technology, drug traffickers and smugglers can move funds through wire transfers and checks sent to other countries. Allegations of money laundering have been lodged against officers of Mexican banks. Many Mexicans have lost confidence in their banks due to concerns that banking controls are not enforced despite statements by Mexico's then-president that his country would be a more law-abiding place.[48] Russia has also experienced money-laundering issues at the banking and governmental level. For example, the Bank of New York was accused of helping Russians launder about $7 billion, while Barclays PLC of London was implicated in a $10 billion money-laundering scheme with Russian banks. Whether the money laundering is being done for illegal businesses or just as a tax haven, the global banking community is developing laws and regulations to plug the holes for unethical and illegal activities originating from or going through Russia.[49]

## Intellectual Property Protection

**Intellectual property** refers to the ideas and creative materials people develop to solve problems, carry out applications, educate, and entertain others. It is generally protected through patents, copyrights, and trademarks. A patent is a legal document issued to an inventor that grants him or her the right to exclude any other person from making, using, or selling the invention anywhere for a certain number of years (seventeen years in the United States). The patent document describes the invention in detail, including how to make or use it, and provides protection rights against infringers. India, for example, won a legal battle against Texas-based RiceTec Inc. over the name *basmati*, a particular rice that has been trademarked in India.[50]

Pharmaceuticals raise other patent issues, especially whether multinational corporations have the right to protect their patents on drugs so they can recover their research costs and hinder the introduction of cheaper generic drugs. Future patent issues may relate to whether the human genome that identifies each gene in the human body should be patented. If this is permitted, people will no longer have the rights to their own genes.

A copyright is a protection that covers published and unpublished literary, scientific, and artistic works, in any form of expression, provided that the works are in a tangible or material form. Copyright laws were established to protect the originators of goods such as books and records. However, as use of the Internet and the World Wide Web has proliferated, it has become difficult for copyright owners to protect their works in various countries. The case of the popular song-swapping Web site, Napster, is illustrative. Napster enabled computer users worldwide to send and receive digital music files among themselves for free. The Recording Industry Association of America filed suit against Napster, alleging that its music-sharing service aided large-scale copyright infringement. Napster denied any wrongdoing, arguing that its users were protected by federal law permitting the copying of music for personal use. A federal judge disagreed and ruled that Napster had to halt the downloading of all copyrighted materials, a ruling later upheld on appeal. Napster's efforts to settle the suit were rebuffed by the RIAA,[51] and its attempts to reinvent itself as a fee-based music sharing site have thus far failed. The RIAA continues to battle the proliferation of music-sharing sites.

Many manufacturing firms have been hurt by the fraudulent use of their trademarks, that is, by other parties counterfeiting a major name-brand company's product or ambiguously misrepresenting their own product as a name-brand product. The problems involving name-brand fraud are as varied as the countries in which they occur. In Guatemala City, for example, downtown streets are filled with vendors selling copies of everything from Adidas sneakers to Ferrari jeans. Consumers can buy a fake pair of Lee's $40 rivet jeans for just $9. Business leaders and clothing manufacturers have urged Guatemala's president to veto a new law that would encourage contraband and counterfeiting. The problem with the law, according to an attorney for Lee Apparel Company, Levi Strauss & Co., and Tommy Hilfiger Corp. is that "I can confiscate counterfeit merchandise from a warehouse, but I can't do anything about the people in the street" selling it.[52] Consumer goods companies such as Unilever and Procter & Gamble say they lose millions of dollars annually in India and China to "look-alike" brands that use similar-sounding names and identical packaging. Procter & Gamble estimates its losses in India at more than $370 million annually and in China at about $6.5 million a year. The counterfeiting problem has prompted some companies, including Coca-Cola Ltd. and Colgate-Palmolive Ltd., to form a brand-protection committee. The committee's Web site (http://www.fake-busters.com) was established to help consumers and officials verify packaging and identify the real brands.[53]

### World Trade Organization

The **World Trade Organization (WTO)** was established in 1995 at the Uruguay Round of negotiations of the General Agreement on Tariffs and Trade (GATT). Today, the WTO has 133 member nations and an additional 33 nations that have applied for membership and hold observer status. On behalf of its membership, the WTO administers its own trade agreements, facilitates future trade negotiations, settles trade disputes, and monitors the trade policies of member nations. The WTO addresses economic and social issues involving agriculture, textiles and clothing, banking, telecommunications, government purchases, industrial standards, food sanitation regulations, services, and intellectual property. It also provides legally binding ground rules for international commerce and trade policy. The organization attempts to reduce barriers to trade between and within nations and settle trade disputes.

Although its goals sound lofty, the WTO has been criticized by a number of groups, especially environmental organizations. For example, after the U.S. Marine Mammal Act placed an embargo on tuna caught using methods that can also kill dolphins, Mexico denounced the act and sued the United States. In its Tuna-Dolphin Ruling, the WTO declared the U.S. law illegal under GATT rules, forcing the United States to rescind the law. A similar set of circumstances resulted in the WTO's Shrimp-Turtle Ruling. After the U.S. Environmental Protection Act required that all shrimp fishers use nets with turtle-excluder devices to protect endangered sea turtles, several Asian nations that refused to use the nets were excluded from selling shrimp in the United States. They filed suit, arguing that the United States cannot use import bans to influence fishing practices outside its own borders. The WTO agreed, and the United States eliminated this portion of the law.[54]

## Summary

The global businessperson must not only understand the values, culture, and ethical standards of his or her own country but also be sensitive to those of other countries. In business, the self-reference criterion (SRC) is the idea that "we" differ from "them." Culture comprises everything in our surroundings that is made by people—both tangible items and intangible concepts, including language, law, religion, politics, technology, education, social organizations, and general values and ethical standards. Each nation has a distinctive culture and different beliefs about what business activities are acceptable or unethical. Cultural differences that create ethical issues in international business include differences in language, body language, time perception, and religion. According to cultural relativism, morality varies from one culture to another, and business practices are defined as right or wrong by the particular culture in which they occur.

Numerous attempts have been made to establish a set of global or universal ethical standards. Although many cultures share certain values, differences surface when these values are explained from the perspective of a specific culture.

Multinational corporations (MNCs) operate on a global scale without significant ties to any one nation or region. Because of their size and financial power, MNCs can have a serious impact on the countries where they do business, which may create ethical issues.

Although U.S. laws prohibit American companies from discrimination in employment, discrimination in other countries is often justified on the basis of cultural norms and values. MNCs should strive to understand the human rights issues of each country in which they conduct business.

Price discrimination creates an ethical issue and may be illegal when the practice violates the laws of the countries in which it occurs; when the market cannot be segmented or the cost of segmenting exceeds the extra revenue gained from legal price discrimination; or when price discrimination results in customer dissatisfaction. When the foreign price of a product exceeds the full costs of exporting, the ethical issue of gouging arises. Dumping occurs when companies sell products in their home markets at high prices while selling the same products in foreign markets at low prices that do not cover the full costs of exporting. Price differentials, gouging, and dumping create ethical issues because some groups of consumers have to pay more than a fair price for products.

Bribery is an acceptable practice in many countries, but the U.S. Foreign Corrupt Practices Act (FCPA) prohibits American businesses from offering or providing payments to officials of foreign governments to obtain or retain business. The Omnibus Trade and Competitiveness (OTC) Act reduced the force of the FCPA and has made the prosecution and applicability of the FCPA in global business settings nonthreatening.

Globally, companies have begun working together to minimize the negative effects of pollution and support environmental responsibility. Joint agreements and international cooperatives have successfully policed and prosecuted offenders of reasonable emission standards.

Advances in telecommunications have intensified such ethical issues as privacy protection and fraud as well as patent, copyright, and trademark infringement. They have also made it easier to carry out questionable financial activities, notably, money laundering, which involves transferring illegally received money or using it in financial transactions so as to conceal the source or ownership or to facilitate an illegal activity.

World entities such as the WTO are in the process of redefining themselves in relation to the new global environment. Ethics in the twenty-first century has taken on a new importance and is seen as critical to the economic sustainability of corporations and countries. International entities that do not recognize this new reality face global scrutiny.

| Important Terms for Review | | |
|---|---|---|
| | self-reference criterion (SRC) | Foreign Corrupt Practices Act (FCPA) |
| | dumping | Omnibus Trade and Competitiveness |
| | culture | (OTC) Act |
| | cultural relativism | day trading |
| | multinational corporations (MNCs) | money laundering |
| | price discrimination | intellectual property |
| | gouging | World Trade Organization (WTO) |
| | facilitating payments | |

## A Real-Life Situation*

George Wilson, the operations manager of the CornCo plant in Phoenix, Arizona, has a dilemma. He is in charge of buying corn and producing chips marketed by CornCo in the United States and elsewhere. Several months ago, George's supervisor, CornCo's vice president, Jake Lamont, called to tell him that corn futures were on the rise, which would ultimately increase the overall costs of production. In addition, a new company called Abco Snack Foods had begun marketing corn chips at competitive prices in CornCo's market area. Abco had already shown signs of eroding CornCo's market share. Jake was concerned that George's production costs would not be competitive with Abco's—hence, profitability would decline. Jake had already asked George to find ways to cut costs. If he couldn't, Jake said, then layoffs would begin.

George scoured the Midwest looking for cheap corn and finally found some. But when the railcars started coming in, one of the company's testers reported the presence of aflatoxin—a naturally occurring carcinogen that induces liver cancer in lab animals. Once corn has been ground into corn meal, however, the aflatoxin is virtually impossible

to detect. George knew that by blending the contaminated corn with uncontaminated corn he could reduce the aflatoxin concentrations in the final product, which, he had heard, other managers sometimes did. According to U.S. law, corn contaminated with aflatoxin cannot be used for edible products sold in the United States, and fines are to be imposed for such use. So far, no one has been convicted. No law, however, prohibits shipping the contaminated corn to other countries.

George knows that because of his competitiors' prices, if he doesn't sell the contaminated corn, his production costs will be too high. When he spoke to Jake, Jake's response was, "So how much of the corn coming in is contaminated?" "It's about 10 percent," replied George. "They probably knew that the corn was contaminated. That's why we're getting such good deals on it." Jake thought for a moment and said, "George, call the suspected grain elevators, complain to them, and demand a 50 percent discount. If they agree, buy all they have." "But if we do, the blends will just increase in contamination!" said George. "That's OK. When the blends start getting high, we'll stop shipping into the U.S. market and go foreign," Jake told him. "Remember, there are no fines for contaminated corn in Mexico."

George learned that one other person, Lee Garcia, an operations manager for the breakfast cereals division, had used contaminated wheat once. "Yeah, so what about it? I've got a family to support and house payments. For me there was no alternative. I had to do it or face getting laid off," Lee said.

As George thought about the problem, word spread about his alternatives. The following notes appeared in the plant suggestion box:

Use the corn or we all get laid off!

Process it and ship it off to Mexico!

It's just wrong to use this corn!

When George balked at Jake's solution, Jake said, "George, I understand your situation. I was there once—just like you. But you've got to look at the bigger picture. Hundreds of workers out of a job. Sure, the FDA [Food and Drug Administration] says that aflatoxin is bad, but we're talking rats eating their weight in this stuff. What if it does get detected—so what? The company gets a fine, the FDA tester gets reprimanded for screwing up, and it's back to business as usual."

"Is that all that will happen?" asked George. "Of course, don't worry," replied Jake. But George's sig-

nature, not Jake's, was on the receipts for the contaminated railcars. "So if I do this, at what aflatoxin percentage do I stop, and will you sign off on this?" asked George. "Look," said Jake, "that's up to you. Remember that the more corn chips are produced for the U.S. market, the more profit the company gets and the higher your bonus. As for me signing off on this, I'm shocked that you would even suggest something like that. George, you're the operations manager. You're the one who's responsible for what happens at the plant. It just isn't done that way at CornCo. But whatever you do, you had better do it in the next several hours because, as I see it, the contaminated corn has to be blended with something, and the longer you wait, the higher the percentages will get."

## Questions ■ Exercises

1. Discuss the corporate ethical issue of providing questionable products to other markets.
2. Discuss the suggestions submitted in the suggestion box in light of the decision George must make. Should the suggestions have an influence?
3. Identify the pressures that have caused the ethical and legal issues in this scenario to arise.

\* This case is strictly hypothetical; any resemblance to real persons, companies, or situations is coincidental.

# Cases

# Enron: Questionable Accounting Leads to Collapse[1]

Once upon a time, there was a gleaming headquarters office tower in Houston, with a giant tilted "E" in front, slowly revolving in the Texas sun. Enron's "E" suggested to Chinese *feng shui* practitioner Meihwa Lin a model of instability, which was perhaps an omen of things to come. The Enron Corporation, which once ranked among the top *Fortune* 500 companies, collapsed in 2001 under a mountain of debt that had been concealed through a complex scheme of off-balance-sheet partnerships. Forced to declare bankruptcy, the energy firm laid off four thousand employees; thousands more lost their retirement savings, which had been invested in Enron stock. The company's shareholders lost tens of billions of dollars after the stock price plummeted. The scandal surrounding Enron's demise engendered a global loss of confidence in corporate integrity that continues to plague markets, and eventually it triggered tough new scrutiny of financial reporting practices. To understand what went wrong, we'll examine the history, culture, and major players in the Enron scandal.

The Enron Corporation was created out of the merger of two major gas pipeline companies in 1985. Through its subsidiaries and numerous affiliates, the company provided products and services related to natural gas, electricity, and communications for its wholesale and retail customers. Enron transported natural gas through pipelines to customers all over the United States. It generated, transmitted, and distributed electricity to the northwestern United States, and marketed natural gas, electricity, and other commodities globally. It was also involved in the development, construction, and operation of power plants, pipelines, and other energy-related projects all over the world, including the delivery and management of energy to retail customers in both the industrial and commercial business sectors.

Throughout the 1990s, Chairman Ken Lay, chief executive officer (CEO) Jeffrey Skilling, and chief financial officer (CFO) Andrew Fastow transformed Enron from an old-style electricity and gas company into a $150 billion energy company and Wall Street favorite that traded power contracts in the investment markets. From 1998 to 2000 alone, Enron's revenues grew from about $31 billion to more than $100 billion, making it the seventh-largest company of the *Fortune* 500. Enron's wholesale energy income represented about 93 percent of 2000 revenues, with another 4 percent

[1] This case was prepared by Neil Herndon, University of Missouri - Columbia, under the direction of O. C. Ferrell, for classroom discussion, rather than to illustrate either effective or ineffective handling of an administrative, ethical, or legal decision by management.

## FIGURE C1–1    A BRIEF TIMELINE OF THE ENRON SCANDAL

| | |
|---|---|
| 1985 | Houston Natural Gas merges with Omaha-based InterNorth; the resulting company is eventually named Enron Corp. Ken Lay, who had been CEO of Houston Natural Gas, becomes chairman and chief executive officer the following year. |
| 2000 | Annual revenues reach $100 billion, and the Energy Financial Group ranks Enron as the sixth-largest energy company in the world, based on market capitalization. |
| Feb. 2001 | Jeff Skilling takes over as chief executive officer. Ken Lay remains chairman. |
| Aug. 2001 | Skilling unexpectedly resigns "for personal reasons," and Ken Lay steps back into the CEO job. That same month, a letter from an Enron executive raises serious questions about the company's business and accounting practices. |
| Oct. 2001 | Enron releases third-quarter earnings, showing $1 billion in charges, including $35 million related to investment partnerships headed by Andrew Fastow, Enron's former chief financial officer. Fastow is replaced as CFO. |
| Oct. 22, 2001 | Enron announces that the Securities and Exchange Commission has launched a formal investigation into its "related party transactions." |
| Nov. 8, 2001 | Enron restates earnings for 1997 through 2000 and the first three quarters of 2001. |
| Dec. 2, 2001 | Enron files for protection from creditors in a New York bankruptcy court. |
| Dec. 3, 2001 | Enron announces that it is laying off four thousand employees. |
| Jan. 9, 2002 | The Justice Department announces that it is pursuing a criminal investigation of Enron. |
| Jan. 14, 2002 | U.S. House and Senate lawmakers return campaign contributions from Enron. |
| Jan. 24, 2002 | Ken Lay resigns as chairman and chief executive of Enron. The first of at least eight congressional hearings on Enron begins. |
| Jan. 30, 2002 | Enron names Stephen Cooper, a restructuring specialist, as acting chief executive officer. |
| Feb. 4, 2002 | A report by a special committee of Enron's board investigating the energy trader's collapse portrays a company riddled with improper financial transactions and extensive self-dealing by company officials. |
| May 2, 2002 | Enron announces plans to reorganize as a small company with a new name. |
| Oct. 2, 2002 | Andrew Fastow voluntarily surrenders to federal authorities after prosecutors indicate they will file charges for his role in the company's collapse. |
| Oct. 31, 2002 | Fastow is indicted on seventy-eight counts of masterminding a scheme to artificially inflate the energy company's profits. |
| Feb. 3, 2003 | Creditors of Enron sue Ken Lay and his wife, Linda, to recover more than $70 million in transfers. |
| July 11, 2003 | Enron finally announces a plan to restructure and pay off creditors after five deadline extensions. |

Source: "A Chronology of Enron's Woes: The Accounting Debacle," *Wall Street Journal*, Mar. 20, 2003, http://online.wsj.com; "A Chronology of Enron's Woes: The Investigation," *Wall Street Journal*, Mar. 20, 2003, http://online.wsj.com; and "Enron Timeline," *Houston Chronicle*, Jan. 17, 2002, http://www.chron.com/cs/CDA/story.hts/special/enron/1127125; Kristen Hays, "16 Cents on $1 for Enron Creditors," *Austin American-Statesman*, July 12, 2003, http://statesman.com.

derived from natural gas and electricity. The remaining 3 percent came from broadband services and exploration. However, a bankruptcy examiner later reported that although Enron claimed net income of $979 million in that year, it really earned just $42 million. Moreover, the examiner found that despite Enron's claim of $3 billion in cash flow in 2000, the company actually had a cash flow of negative $154 million.

## Enron's Corporate Culture

When describing the corporate culture of Enron, people like to use the word *arrogant,* perhaps justifiably. A large banner in the lobby at corporate headquarters proclaimed Enron "The World's Leading Company," and Enron executives blithely believed that competitors had no chance against it. Jeffrey Skilling even went so far as to tell utility executives at a conference that he was going to "eat their lunch." There was an overwhelming aura of pride, carrying with it the deep-seated belief that Enron's people could handle increasing risk without danger. The culture also was about a focus on how much money could be made for executives. For example, Enron's compensation plans seemed less concerned with generating profits for shareholders than with enriching officer wealth. Enron's corporate culture reportedly encouraged flouting, if not breaking, the rules.

Skilling appears to be the executive who created a system in which Enron's employees were rated every six months, with those ranked in the bottom 20 percent forced out. This "rank and yank" system helped create a fierce environment in which employees competed against rivals not only outside the company but also at the next desk. Delivering bad news could result in the "death" of the messenger, so problems in the trading operation, for example, were covered up rather than being communicated to management.

Enron Chairman Ken Lay once said that he felt that one of the great successes at Enron was the creation of a corporate culture in which people could reach their full potential. He said that he wanted it to be a highly moral and ethical culture and that he tried to ensure that people did in fact honor the values of respect, integrity, and excellence. On his desk was an Enron paper weight with the slogan "Vision and Values." Some of the people behind Enron, however, believed that nearly anything could be turned into a financial product and, with the aid of complex statistical modeling, traded for profit. Short on assets and heavily reliant on intellectual capital, Enron's corporate culture rewarded innovation and punished employees deemed weak.

## Enron's Accounting Problems

Enron's bankruptcy in December 2001 was the largest in U.S. corporate history at the time. The bankruptcy filing came after a series of revelations that the giant energy trader had been using partnerships, called *special-purpose entities (SPEs),* to conceal losses. In a meeting with Enron's lawyers in August 2001, the company's then chief financial officer, Andrew Fastow, stated that Enron had established the SPEs to move assets and debt off its balance sheet and to increase cash flow by showing that funds were flowing through its books when it sold assets. Although these practices produced a very favorable financial picture, outside observers believed they might constitute fraudulent financial reporting because they did not accurately represent the company's true financial condition. Most of the SPEs were entities in name only, and Enron funded them with its own stock and maintained control over them. When one of these partnerships was unable to meet its obligations, Enron covered the debt with its own stock. This arrangement worked as long as Enron's stock price was high, but when the stock price fell, cash was needed to meet the shortfall.

After Enron restated its financial statements for fiscal 2000 and the first nine months of 2001, its cash flow from operations dropped from a positive $127 million in 2000 to a negative $753 million in 2001. In 2001, with its stock price falling, Enron faced a critical cash shortage. In October 2001, after it was forced to cover some large shortfalls for its partnerships, Enron's stockholder equity fell by $1.2 billion. Already shaken by questions about lack of disclosure in Enron's financial statements and by reports that executives had profited personally from the partnership deals, investor confidence collapsed, taking Enron's stock price with it.

For a time it appeared that Dynegy might save the day by providing $1.5 billion in cash, secured by Enron's premier pipeline Northern Natural Gas, and then purchasing Enron for about $10 billion. But when Standard & Poor downgraded Enron's debt below investment grade on November 28, some $4 billion in off-balance-sheet debt came due, and Enron didn't have the resources to pay. Dynegy terminated the deal. On December 2, 2001, Enron filed for bankruptcy. Enron now faces 22,000 claims totaling about $400 billion.

## The Whistle-Blower

Assigned to work directly with Andrew Fastow in June 2001, Enron vice president Sherron Watkins, an eight-year Enron veteran, was given the task of finding some assets to sell off. With the high-tech bubble bursting and Enron's stock price slipping, Watkins was troubled to find unclear, off-the-books arrangements backed only by Enron's deflating stock. No one seemed to be able to explain to her what was going on. Knowing she faced difficult consequences if she confronted then CEO Jeffrey Skilling, she began looking for another job, planning to confront Skilling just as she left for a new position. Skilling, however, suddenly quit on August 14, saying he wanted to spend more time with his family. Chairman Ken Lay stepped back in as CEO and began inviting employees to express their concerns and put them into a box for later collection. Watkins prepared an anonymous memo and placed it into the box. When CEO Lay held a companywide meeting shortly thereafter and did not mention her memo, however, she arranged a personal meeting with him.

On August 22, Watkins handed Lay a seven-page letter she had prepared outlining her concerns. She told him that Enron would "implode in a wave of accounting scandals" if nothing was done. Lay arranged to have Enron's law firm, Vinson & Elkins, look into the questionable deals, although Watkins advised against having a party investigate that might be compromised by its own involvement in Enron's scam. Near the end of September, Lay sold some $1.5 million of personal stock options, while telling Enron employees that the company had never been stronger. By the middle of October, Enron was reporting a third-quarter loss of $618 million and a $1.2 billion write-off tied to the partnerships that Watkins had warned Lay about.

For her trouble, Watkins had her computer hard drive confiscated and was moved from her plush executive office suite on the top floors of the Houston headquarters tower to a plain office on a lower level with a metal desk. That desk was no longer filled with the high-level projects that had once taken her all over the world on Enron business. Instead, now a vice president in name only, she faced meaningless "make-work" projects. In February 2002, she testified before Congress about Enron's partnerships and resigned from Enron in November.

## The Chief Financial Officer

Chief Financial Officer Andrew Fastow was indicted in October 2002 by the U.S. Justice Department on seventy-eight federal counts for his alleged efforts to inflate Enron's profits. These charges included fraud, money laundering, conspiracy, and one count of obstruction of justice. Fastow faces up to 140 years in jail and millions of dollars in fines if convicted on all counts. Federal officials say they will try to recover all of the money Fastow earned illegally. Having already seized some $37 million of Fastow's gains, they are now seeking their forfeiture.

Federal prosecutors argue that Enron's case is not about exotic accounting practices but fraud and theft. They contend that Fastow was the brain behind the partnerships used to conceal some $1 billion in Enron debt and that this led directly to Enron's bankruptcy. The federal complaints allege that Fastow defrauded Enron and its shareholders through the off-the-balance-sheet partnerships that made Enron appear to be more profitable than it actually was. They also allege that Fastow made about $30 million both by using these partnerships to get kickbacks that were disguised as gifts from family members who invested in them and by taking income himself that should have gone to other entities.

Fastow, who has denied any wrongdoing, says that he was hired to arrange the off-balance-sheet financing and that Enron's board of directors, chairman, and CEO directed and praised his work. He also claims that both lawyers and accountants reviewed his work and approved what was being done and that "at no time did he do anything he believed was a crime." Jeffrey Skilling, chief operating officer (COO) from 1997 to 2000 before becoming CEO, reportedly championed Fastow's rise at Enron and supported his efforts to keep up Enron's stock prices.

The case against Fastow is largely based on information provided by Managing Director Michael Kopper, a key player in the establishment and operation of several of the off-the-balance-sheet partnerships. Kopper, a chief aide to Fastow, pleaded guilty to money laundering and wire fraud. He faces up to fifteen years in prison and has agreed to surrender some $12 million he earned from his dealings with the partnerships. Others charged in the Enron affair include Timothy Belden, Enron's former top energy trader, who pleaded guilty to one count of conspiring to commit wire fraud. He could receive five years in prison, three years' probation, and a $250,000 fine. David Bermingham, Giles Darby, and Gary Mulgrew were indicted in Houston on wire-fraud charges related to a deal at Enron. They were able to use secret investments to take $7.3 million in income that belonged to their employer, according to the Justice Department. The three, employed by the finance group Greenwich NatWest, have not yet been arrested.

Fastow has also been served with a civil lawsuit by the Securities and Exchange Commission (SEC), which claims that Fastow violated securities laws and defrauded investors. The SEC is seeking unspecified penalties and, as mentioned, the return of Fastow's allegedly improperly obtained profits.

## The Chief Executive Officer

Former CEO Jeffrey Skilling, widely seen as Enron's mastermind, will probably be the most difficult case to prosecute. He was so sure he had committed no crime that he waived his right to self-incrimination and testified before Congress that "I was not aware of any inappropriate financial arrangements." However, Jeffrey McMahon, who took over as Enron's president and COO in February 2002, told a congressional subcommittee that he had informed Skilling about the company's off-the-balance-sheet partnerships in March 2000, when he was Enron's treasurer. McMahon said that Skilling had told him "he would remedy the situation."

Calling the Enron collapse a "run on the bank" and a "liquidity crisis," Skilling said that he did not understand how Enron went from where it was to bankruptcy so quickly. He also said that the off-the-balance sheet partnerships were Fastow's creation.

Prosecutors may try to convict Skilling for perjury, but they have reportedly widened their probe to investigate his role in Enron's broadband venture. Skilling is said to have joked that Enron could make "a kazillion dollars" through an exotic new accounting scheme. Skilling is also reported to have sold 39 percent of his Enron holdings before the company disclosed its financial troubles.

## The Chairman

Kenneth Lay became chairman and CEO of the company that was to become Enron in February 1986. A decade later, Lay promoted Jeffrey Skilling to president and chief operating officer and then, as expected, Lay stepped down as CEO in February 2001, to make way for Skilling. Lay remained as chairman of the board. When Skilling resigned in August, Lay resumed the role of CEO.

Lay, who holds a Ph.D. in economics from the University of Houston, contends that he knew little of what was going on even though he had participated in the board meetings that allowed the off-the-balance-sheet partnerships to be created. He said he believed the transactions were legal because they were approved by attorneys and accountants. But by late summer 2001, while he was reassuring employees and investors that all was well at Enron, he had already been informed that there were problems with some of the investments that could eventually cost Enron hundreds of millions of dollars. On February 12, 2002, on the advice of his attorney, Lay told the Senate Commerce Committee that he was invoking his Fifth Amendment rights not to answer questions that could be incriminating.

Ken Lay is expected to be charged with insider trading. Specifically, prosecutors are looking into why Lay began selling about $80 million of his own stock beginning in late 2000, even while he encouraged employees to buy more shares of the company. It appears that Lay drew down his $4 million dollar Enron credit line repeatedly, then repaid the company with Enron shares. These transactions, unlike usual stock sales, do not have to be reported to investors. Lay says that he sold the stock because of margin calls on loans he had secured with Enron stock and that he had no other source of liquidity.

## Vinson & Elkins

Enron was Houston law firm Vinson & Elkins' top client, accounting for about 7 percent of its $450 million revenue. Enron's general counsel and a number of members of Enron's legal department came from Vinson & Elkins. Vinson & Elkins seems to have dismissed Sherron Watkins's allegations of accounting fraud after making some inquiries, but this does not appear to leave it open to civil or criminal liability. Of greater concern are allegations that Vinson & Elkins helped structure some of Enron's special-purpose partnerships. Watkins, in her letter to CEO Ken Lay, indicated that the law firm had written opinion letters supporting the legality of the deals. In fact, Enron could not have done many of the transactions without such opinion letters. Although the law firm denies that it has done anything wrong, legal experts say the key question is whether or not Vinson & Elkins approved deals that it knew were fraudulent.

## Merrill Lynch

The prestigious brokerage and investment banking firm of Merrill Lynch faces scrutiny by federal prosecutors and the SEC for its role in Enron's 1999 sale of Nigerian barges. The sale allowed Enron to improperly record about $12 million in earnings and thereby meet its earnings goals at the end of 1999. Merrill Lynch allegedly bought the barges for $28 million, of which $21 million was financed by Enron through Fastow's oral assurance that Enron would buy Merrill Lynch's investment out in six months with a 15 percent guaranteed rate of return. Merrill Lynch went ahead with the deal despite an internal Merrill Lynch document that suggested that the transaction might be construed as aiding and abetting Enron's fraudulent manipulation of its income statement. Merrill Lynch denies that the transaction was a sham and said that it never knowingly helped Enron to falsify its financial reports.

There are also allegations that Merrill Lynch replaced a research analyst after his coverage of Enron displeased Enron executives. Enron reportedly threatened to exclude Merrill Lynch from a coming $750 million stock offering in retaliation. The replacement analyst is reported to have then upgraded his report on Enron's stock rating. Merrill Lynch maintains that it did nothing improper in its Enron business dealings. However, the firm agreed to pay $80 million to settle SEC charges related to the questionable Nigerian barge deal.

## Arthur Andersen LLP

In its role as Enron's auditor, Arthur Andersen was responsible for ensuring the accuracy of Enron's financial statements and internal bookkeeping. Andersen's reports were used by potential investors to judge Enron's financial soundness and future potential before they decided whether to invest and by current investors to decide if their funds should remain invested there. These investors would expect that Andersen's certifications of accuracy and application of proper accounting procedures were independent and without any conflict of interest. If Andersen's reports were in error, investors could be seriously misled. However, Andersen's independence has been called into question. The accounting firm was a major business partner of Enron, with more than one hundred employees dedicated to its account, and it sold about $50 million a year in consulting services to Enron. Some Andersen executives even accepted jobs with the energy trader.

Andersen was found guilty of obstruction of justice in March 2002 for destroying Enron-related auditing documents during an SEC investigation of Enron. As a result, Anderson has been barred from performing audits.

It is still not clear why Andersen auditors failed to ask Enron to better explain its complex partnerships before certifying Enron's financial statements. Some observers believe that Andersen was unduly influenced by the large consulting fees Enron paid it. However, an Andersen spokesperson said that the firm had looked hard at all available information from Enron at the time. But shortly after she spoke to Enron CEO Ken Lay, Vice President Sherron Watkins had taken her concerns to an Andersen audit partner, who reportedly conveyed her questions to senior Andersen management responsible for the Enron account. It is not clear what action, if any, Andersen took.

## The Fallout

Enron's demise caused tens of billions of dollars of investor losses, triggered a collapse of electricity-trading markets, and ushered in an era of accounting scandals that precipitated a global loss of confidence in corporate integrity. Now companies must defend legitimate but complicated financing arrangements, even legitimate financing tools tainted by association with Enron. On a more personal level, four thousand former Enron employees are struggling to find jobs, while many retirees have been forced to return to work in a bleak job market because their Enron-heavy retirement portfolios were wiped out. One senior Enron executive committed suicide.

In July 2003 Enron announced its intention to restructure and a plan to pay off its creditors. Pending creditor and court approval of the plan, most creditors would receive between 14.4 cents and 18.3 cents for each dollar they were owed—more than most expected. Under the plan, creditors would receive about two-thirds of the amount in cash and the rest in equity in two new companies, neither of which would carry the tainted Enron name. According to the plan, CrossCountry Energy Corp. would retain Enron's interests in three North American natural gas pipelines, while Prisma Energy International Inc. would take over Enron's nineteen international power and pipeline holdings. It remains unclear who owns what, whether assets are available that are free and clear of encumbrances, and what value these assets might have given that Enron now has no auditor, has not issued a financial report for 2001, and is saying that its financial reports after 1997 cannot be relied on.

Enron's auditor, Arthur Andersen, faces some forty shareholder lawsuits claiming damages of more than $32 billion. Enron itself faces many civil actions. A number of current and former Enron executives face federal investigations and possible criminal action, as well as civil lawsuits. The company is also being investigated in California for allegedly colluding with at least two other power sellers in 2000 to obtain excess profits by submitting false information to the manager of California's electricity grid. And, finally, the company is under investigation for tax evasion. As for the giant tilted "E" logo so proudly displayed outside of corporate headquarters, it was auctioned off for $44,000.

*Questions*

1. How did the corporate culture of Enron contribute to its bankruptcy?
2. Did Enron's bankers, auditors, and attorneys contribute to Enron's demise? If so, what was their contribution?
3. What role did the chief financial officer play in creating the problems that led to Enron's financial problems?

---

Sources: These facts are from Alexei Barrionuevo, Jonathan Weil, and John R. Wilke, "Enron's Fastow Charged with Fraud," *Wall Street Journal,* Oct. 3, 2002, pp. A3–A4; Eric Berger, "Report Details Enron's Deception," *Houston Chronicle,* Mar. 6, 2003, pp. 1B, 11B; Christine Y. Chen, "When Good Firms Get Bad Chi," *Fortune,* Nov. 11, 2002, p. 56; Peter Elkind and Bethany McLean, "Feds Move Up Enron Food Chain," *Fortune,* Dec. 30, 2002, pp. 43–44; "Enron Whistle-Blower Resigns," MSNBC News, www.msnbc.com/news/835432.asp (accessed Dec. 2, 2002); Greg Farrell, "Former Enron CFO Charged," *USA Today,* Oct. 3, 2002, p. B1; Greg Farrell, Edward Iwata, and Thor Valdmanis, "Prosecutors Are Far from Finished," *USA Today,* Oct. 3, 2002, pp. 1B–2B; "Fastow Indicted on 78 Counts," MSNBC News, www.msnbc.com/news/828217.asp (accessed Nov. 6, 2002); O. C. Ferrell, "Ethics," *BizEd,* May/June 2002, pp. 43–45; Jeffrey A. Fick, "Report: Merrill Replaced Enron Analyst," *USA Today,* July 30, 2002, p. B1; Daren Fonda, "Enron: Picking over the Carcass," *Fortune,* Dec. 30, 2002 – Jan. 6, 2003, p. 56; "Finger-Pointing Starts As Congress Examines Enron's Fast Collapse," *Investor's Business Daily,* Feb. 8, 2002, p. A1; Mike France, "One Big Client, One Big Hassle," *Business Week,* Jan. 28, 2002, pp. 38–39; Bryan Gruley and Rebecca Smith, "Keys to Success Left Kenneth Lay Open to Disaster," *Wall Street Journal,* Apr. 26, 2002, pp. A1, A5; Tom Hamburger, "Enron CEO Declines to Testify at Hearing," *Wall Street Journal,* Dec. 12, 2001, p. B2; Kristen Hays, "16 Cents on $1 for Enron Creditors," *Austin American-Statesman,* July 12, 2003, http://statesman.com; Edward Iwata, "Merrill Lynch Will Pay $80M to Settle Enron Case," *USA Today,* Feb. 20, 2003, www.usatoday.com; Jeremy Kahn, "The Chief Freaked Out Officer," *Fortune,* Dec. 9, 2002, pp. 197–198, 202; Kathryn Kranhold and Rebecca Smith, "Two Other Firms in Enron Scheme, Documents Say," *Wall Street Journal,* May 9, 2002, pp. C1, C12; Bethany McLean, "Why Enron Went Bust," *Fortune,* Dec. 24, 2001, pp. 58, 60–62, 66, 68; Jodie Morse and Amanda Bower, "The Party Crasher," *Fortune,* Dec. 30, 2002 – Jan. 6, 2003, pp. 53–56; Belverd E. Needles Jr. and Marian Powers, "Accounting for Enron," *Houghton Mifflin's Guide to the Enron Crisis* (Boston: Houghton Mifflin, 2003), pp. 3–6; Mitchell Pacelle, "Enron's Creditors to Get Peanuts," *Wall Street Journal,* July 11, 2003, http://online.wsj.com; "Primer: Accounting Industry and Andersen," *Washington Post,* www.washingtonpost.com (accessed Oct. 2, 2002); Miriam Schulman, "Enron: What Ever Happened to Going Down with the Ship?" Markkula Center for Applied Ethics, www.scu.edu/ethics/publications/ethicalperspectives/schulman0302.html (accessed Sept. 11, 2002); Chris H. Sieroty, "3 Ex-Bankers Charged in Enron Scandal," *Washington Times,* www.washtimes.com (accessed Oct. 2, 2002); William Sigismond, "The Enron Case from a Legal Perspective," *Houghton Mifflin's Guide,* pp. 11–13; Elliot Blair Smith, "Panel Blasts Enron Tax Deals," *USA Today,* Feb. 13, 2003, www.usatoday.com; Rebecca Smith and Kathryn Kranhold, "Enron Knew Portfolio's Value," *Wall Street Journal,* May 6, 2002, pp. C1, C20; Rebecca Smith and Mitchell Pacelle, "Enron Plans Return to Its Roots," *Wall Street Journal,* May 2, 2002, p. A1; Jake Ulick, "Enron: A Year Later," CNN/Money, www.money.cnn.com/2002/11/26/news/companies/enron_anniversary/index.htm (accessed Dec. 2, 2002); Joseph Weber, "Can Andersen Survive?" *Business Week,* Jan. 28, 2002, pp. 39–40; Winthrop Corporation, "Epigraph," *Houghton Mifflin's Guide,* p. 1; Wendy Zellner, "A Hero—and a Smoking-Gun Letter," *Business Week,* Jan. 28, 2002, pp. 34–35.

# Case 2

# Tyco International:
# Leadership Crisis[1]

On September 12, 2002, Tyco International's former chief executive officer, L. Dennis Kozlowski, and former chief financial officer, Mark H. Swartz, were seen in handcuffs on national television after they were arrested and charged with misappropriating more than $170 million from the company. They were also accused of stealing more than $430 million through fraudulent sales of Tyco stock and concealing the information from shareholders. The two executives were charged in a Manhattan federal court with numerous counts of grand larceny, enterprise corruption, and falsifying business records. Another executive, former general counsel Mark A. Belnick, was also charged with concealing $14 million in personal loans. Months after the initial arrests, charges and lawsuits were still being filed in a growing scandal that threatened to eclipse the notoriety of other companies facing accounting fraud charges in the early 2000s.

## Tyco's History

Tyco, Inc., was founded by Arthur J. Rosenberg in 1960, in Waltham, Massachusetts, as an investment and holding company focusing on solid-state science and energy conversion. It developed the first laser with a sustained beam to be used in medical procedures. After shifting its focus to the commercial sector, Tyco became a publicly traded company in 1964. It also began a pattern of acquisitions—sixteen different companies by 1968—that would continue through 1982 as the company sought to fill gaps in its development and distribution network. The rapidly growing and diversifying firm grew from $34 million in consolidated sales in 1973 to $500 million in 1982.

In 1982, Tyco reorganized into three business segments (Fire Protection, Electronics, and Packaging) to strengthen itself from within. By 1986, Tyco had returned to a growth-through-acquisitions mode. In the 1990s Tyco maintained four core segments: Electrical and Electronic Components, Healthcare and Specialty Products, Fire and Security Services, and Flow Control. The company changed its name to Tyco International in 1993 to signal its global presence to the financial community. By

[1] This case was prepared by Linda G. Mullen, Marketing Department, Southern Illinois University at Carbondale, under the direction of O. C. Ferrell, for classroom discussion, rather than to illustrate either effective or ineffective handling of an administrative, ethical, or legal decision by management.

2000, the firm had acquired more than thirty major companies, including well-known firms such as ADT, Raychem, and the CIT Group.

## The Rise of Dennis Kozlowski

Leo Dennis Kozlowski was born in Newark, New Jersey, in 1946. His parents, Leo Kelly and Agnes Kozlowski, were second-generation Polish Americans. His father worked for Public Service Transport (later the New Jersey Transport), and his mother was a school crossing guard in Newark's predominantly Polish neighborhood. Dennis Kozlowski attended public school and graduated from West Side High in 1964. He lived at home while he studied accounting at Seton Hall University in South Orange, New Jersey.

After brief stints at SCM Corp. and Nashua Corporation, Kozlowski went to work for Tyco in 1976. He soon found a friend and mentor in CEO Joseph Gaziano, whose lavish style—including company jets, extravagant vacations, company cars, and country club memberships—impressed Kozlowski. However, the luxurious lifestyle came to an end when Gaziano died of cancer in 1982. Gaziano was replaced by fellow MIT graduate John F. Fort III, who differed sharply in management style. Where Gaziano had been extravagant, Fort was analytical and thrifty, and Wall Street responded approvingly to his new course and direction for Tyco. Fort's goal was to increase the profits for the shareholders of Tyco and cut out the extravagant spending that had characterized Gaziano's tenure.

Kozlowski, who had thrived under Gaziano, had to shift gears to adapt to the abrupt change in leadership. However, Kozlowski's accounting background helped push him through the ranks at Tyco. He was very adept at crunching numbers and helping achieve Fort's vision of taking care of shareholders first. Fort soon noticed Kozlowski's talents.

Kozlowski's first major promotion within Tyco was to president of Grinnell Fire Protection Systems Co., Tyco's largest division. At Grinnell, Kozlowski cut out extras and reduced overhead, eliminated 98 percent of the paperwork, and reworked compensation programs. Although he slashed managers' salaries, he also set up a bonus compensation package that gave them greater control over the money they could earn. He gave public recognition to high achievers at a yearly banquet, but he also recognized the underachievers, giving out an award for the worst producing unit as well as the best. Perhaps most importantly, Kozlowski systematically began to buy out and acquire each of the fire protection division's competitors. As described in a *Business Week* article, he gained a reputation as a "corporate tough guy, respected and feared in roughly equal measure."

Over the next few years, Kozlowski continued his rise up Tyco's corporate ladder, becoming the company's president in 1987, before rising to CFO and eventually CEO in 1992. However, his aggressive approach to acquisitions and mergers during this period became a concern for then-CEO Fort, who wanted to slow the rate of activity in Kozlowski's division. His largest acquisition was Wormald International, a $360 million global fire-protection concern. However, integrating Wormald proved problematic, and Fort was reportedly not happy with so large a purchase. Fort and Kozlowski also disagreed over the rapid changes Kozlowski made in the fire protection division. Kozlowski responded by lobbying to convince Tyco's board of directors that the problems with Wormald were a "bump in the road" and that the firm should continue its strategy of acquiring profitable companies that met its guidelines. The board sided with Kozlowski, and Fort resigned as CEO and later as chairman of the board, although he remained a member of Tyco's board of directors until 2003.

## Kozlowski's Tyco Empire

At the age of forty-six, Dennis Kozlowski found himself at the helm of Tyco International in 1992. He also moved out of his North Hampton home, leaving his wife and two daughters for a waitress, Karen Lee Mayo Locke, whom he eventually married in 2000. His new lifestyle—which included parties that were regular gossip-column fodder and homes in Boca Raton, Nantucket, Beaver Creek, and New York City—appeared to emulate that of Kozlowski's mentor, former CEO Joseph Gaziano. Indeed, Kozlowski's aggressive strategy of mergers and acquisitions made Tyco look more like the company it had been under Gaziano.

Kozlowski had learned Tyco and its businesses from the bottom up, which gave him an advantage in his determination to make Tyco the greatest company of the new century. Among other things, he recognized that one of the conglomerate's major shortcomings was its reliance on cyclical industries. Thus, he decided to diversify into more noncyclical industries. His first major acquisition toward that objective was the Kendall Company, a manufacturer of medical supplies, which had emerged from bankruptcy just two years before. Kozlowski quickly revived the business, which became very profitable and doubled Tyco's earnings. Although Tyco's board of directors had initially balked at the Kendall acquisition, the directors were pleased with the subsidiary's turnaround and contribution to profits. Kozlowski made Kendall the core of his new Tyco Healthcare Group, which quickly grew to become the second-largest producer of medical devices behind Johnson & Johnson. The board rewarded Kozlowski's performance by increasing his salary to $2.1 million and giving him shares of the company's stock.

Kozlowski's next strategic move was the acquisition of ADT Security Services, a British-owned company located in Bermuda, in 1997. By structuring the deal as a "reverse takeover," Tyco acquired a global presence as well as ADT's Bermuda registration, which allowed the firm to create a network of offshore subsidiaries to shelter its foreign earnings from U.S. taxes.

While Kozlowski continued to acquire new companies to build his vision of Tyco, he handpicked a few trusted people and placed them in key positions. One of these individuals was Mark Swartz, who was promoted from director of Mergers and Acquisitions to chief financial officer (CFO). Swartz, who had developed a strong financial background as an auditor for Deloitte & Touche and a reputation for being more approachable than Kozlowski, was aware of Kozlowski's business practices. Kozlowski also recruited Mark Belnick to become Tyco's general counsel.

By this time, Tyco's corporate governance system comprised Kozlowski as CEO and the firm's board of directors, which had eleven members, including Joshua Berman, a vice president of Tyco and former outside counsel; Mark Swartz, CFO; Lord Michael Ashcroft, a British dignitary who came with the ADT merger; James S.

Pasman Jr., also from ADT; W. Peter Slusser, also from ADT; Richard S. Bodman, a venture capitalist; Stephen W. Foss, CEO of a textile concern; Joseph F. Welch, CEO of snack-food maker Bachman Co.; Wendy Lane, a private equity investor; John F. Fort III, former CEO and chairman of Tyco; and Frank E. Walsh Jr., director of the board. Kozlowski particularly liked the prestige of Lord Ashcroft being associated with his company. The majority of the directors had been on the board for ten to twenty years and were very familiar with Tyco's strategies and Kozlowski's management style. As directors, they were responsible for protecting Tyco's shareholders by disclosing any questionable situations or issues that might seem unethical or inappropriate, such as conflicts of interest. However, after the arrests of Kozlowski and Swartz, investigations subsequently uncovered the following troubling relationships among the board's members:

- Mark Swartz participated in loan-forgiveness programs.
- Richard Bodman invested $5 million for Kozlowski in a private stock fund managed by Bodman.
- Frank E. Walsh Jr. received $20 million for helping to arrange the acquisition of CIT Group without the knowledge of the rest of the board of directors.
- Walsh also held controlling interest in two firms that received more than $3.5 million for leasing an aircraft and providing pilot services to Tyco between 1996 and 2002.
- Stephen Foss received $751,101 for supplying a Cessna Citation aircraft and pilot services.
- Lord Michael Ashcroft used $2.5 million in Tyco funds to purchase a home.

With his handpicked board in place, Kozlowski decided to open a Manhattan office overlooking Central Park. However, the firm maintained its humble Exeter, New Hampshire, office, where Kozlowski preferred to be interviewed. According to *Business Week,* he bragged to a guest there, "We don't believe in perks, not even executive parking spots." The unpublicized Manhattan office essentially became the firm's unofficial headquarters, and Kozlowski lavished it with every imaginable perk. He also used Tyco funds to purchase and furnish apartments for key executives and employees in New York's pricey Upper East Side.

Meanwhile, Jeanne Terrile, an analyst for Tyco at Merrill Lynch, was not so impressed with Kozlowski's activities and Tyco's performance. Stock analysts like those at Merrill Lynch make recommendations to investors whether to buy, hold, or sell a particular stock. After Terrile wrote a less than favorable review of Tyco's rapid acquisitions and mergers and refused to upgrade Merrill's position on Tyco's stock, Kozlowski met with David Komansky, the CEO of Merrill Lynch. Although the subject of the meeting was never confirmed, shortly thereafter, Terrile was replaced by Phua Young, who immediately upgraded Merrill's recommendation for Tyco to "buy" from "accumulate." Merrill Lynch continued to be one of Tyco's top underwriters as well as one of its primary advisers for mergers and acquisitions.

Between 1997 and 2001, Tyco's revenues climbed 48.7 percent a year, and its pretax operating margins increased to 22.1 percent. The pace of mergers and acquisitions escalated with the able assistance of Mark Swartz, Tyco's CFO. In February 2002, Tyco announced that it had spent more than $8 billion on more than seven hundred acquisitions in the last three years. Among these were AMP Inc., an electronics maker for $11.3 billion in stock, and CIT Group, a commercial finance company. However, some of the merged companies were less than satisfied with the arrangement. Kozlowski forced acquired companies to scale back sharply and eliminate anything—and anyone—that did not produce revenue. The toll on human capital was enormous. Tyco shareholders and directors, however, were very happy with Kozlowski's performance, as demonstrated by his rapid salary increases from $8 million in 1997, to $67 million in 1998, to $170 million in 1999, which made him the second-highest paid CEO in the United States.

During 1997-2002, Kozlowski's charismatic leadership style together with the firm's decentralized corporate structure meant that few people, including members of the board of directors, had a true picture of the firm's activities and finances. The company was organized into four distinct divisions—fire protection (53 percent); valves, pipes and other "flow control" devices (23 percent); electrical and electronic components (13 percent); and packaging materials (11 percent)—and there was little interaction among them. Each division's president reported directly to Kozlowski, who in turn reported to the board.

Those who saw red flags at Tyco International were shot down, including Jeanne Terrile at Merrill Lynch and David W. Tice, a short seller who questioned whether Tyco's use of large reserves in connection with its acquisitions was obscuring its results. A nonpublic investigation by the Securities and Exchange Commission (SEC) resulted only in Tyco amending its earnings per share for 1999.

## The Fall of Dennis Kozlowski

Everything began to fall apart in January 2002, when the board of directors learned that one of its members, Frank Walsh, had received a $20 million bonus for his part in securing and aiding in the CIT merger. Walsh promptly resigned from the board. Troubled by the idea that Kozlowski had made such a major payment without their knowledge, the remaining board members launched an investigation to determine whether other board members had earned such "commissions." The probe uncovered numerous expense abuses. Finally, after learning that he was about to be indicted for tax evasion, Kozlowski agreed to resign as CEO of Tyco on June 2, 2002.

Months earlier, the New York State Bank Department had observed large sums of money going into and out of Tyco's accounts. This would not have been unusual except that the funds were being transferred into Kozlowski's personal accounts. Eventually, authorities discovered that Kozlowski had allegedly avoided $3.1 million in New York state taxes by appearing to ship rare artwork to New Hampshire when in fact it was sent to New York. On June 3, Kozlowski was arrested for tax evasion, but the scandal was only just beginning.

On September 12, 2002, Dennis Kozlowski and Mark Swartz, who had also resigned from Tyco, were indicted on thirty-eight felony counts for allegedly stealing $170 million from Tyco and fraudulently selling an additional $430 million in stock options. Among other allegations, Kozlowski was accused of taking $242 million from a program intended to help Tyco employees buy company stock in order to buy yachts, fine art, and luxury homes. Together with former legal counsel Mark Belnick, the three face criminal charges, as well as a civil complaint from the SEC. Kozlowski was also accused of granting $106 million to various employees through "loan forgiveness" and relocation programs. Swartz was also charged with falsifying documents in this loan program in the amount of $14 million. Currently awaiting trial, Kozlowski and Swartz face up to twenty-five years in prison if convicted on the charges of enterprise corruption, grand larceny, falsifying documents, and conspiracy. Belnick was charged with larceny and trying to steer a federal investigation, as well as taking more than $26 million from Tyco.

In addition, several board members have been cited for conflict of interest and may yet face charges themselves. Frank Walsh, a former board member who received a $20 million bonus for the CIT merger, pleaded guilty and agreed to repay the $20 million plus an additional $2 million in court costs. Moreover, Jerry Boggess, the president of Tyco Fire and Security Division was fired and accused of creating a number of "bookkeeping issues" that had a negative impact on earnings to shareholders. Richard Scalzo, the PriceWaterhouse auditor who signed off on Tyco's 2002 audit, was removed.

## Rebuilding an Empire

After Kozlowski's resignation, he was replaced as CEO by Edward Breen. The company filed suit against Dennis Kozlowski and Mark Swartz for more than $100 million. The SEC allows companies to sue for profits made by "insiders" who are profiting by buying and selling company stock within a six-month period. A statement by the company stated: "To hold him accountable for his misconduct, we seek not only full payment for the funds he misappropriated but also punitive damages for the serious harm he did to Tyco and its shareholders." Additionally, Tyco is suing for monies paid by Kozlowski to keep some of those closest to him from testifying against him.

Breen launched a review of the company's accounting and corporate governance practices to determine whether any other fraud had occurred. Although the probe uncovered no fraud, the firm announced in late 2002 that it would restate its 2002 financial results by $382.2 million. Tyco's new management declared in a regulatory filing that the firm's previous management had "engaged in a pattern of aggressive accounting which, even when in accordance with Generally Accepted Accounting Principles, was intended to increase reported earnings above what they would have been if more conservative accounting had been employed." Although Tyco's investigations found no further fraud, the company repeatedly restated its financial results or took accounting charges totaling more than $2 billion over the next six months.

Regardless of whether Kozlowski and Swartz are convicted, the scandal has had detrimental consequences, particularly for the company's shareholders. Tyco's stock plunged from $60 per share in January 2002 to $18 per share by December, and investors lost millions of dollars. Many of the firm's 260,000 employees were also shareholders and watched their savings dwindle. Tyco's retirees are worried that their savings and retirement plans, which were tied up in company shares, will plummet with the company's stock price.

To restore investors' faith in the company, Tyco's new management team is working to reorganize the company and recover some of the funds allegedly taken by Kozlowski. At its annual meeting, shareholders elected a completely new board of directors and voted to make future executive severance agreements subject to shareholder approval and to require the board chairman to be an independent person, rather than a Tyco CEO. However, the shareholders elected to keep the company incorporated in Bermuda.

*Questions*

1. What are the ethical and legal issues in this case?
2. What role did Tyco's corporate culture play in the scandal? What roles did the board of directors, CEO, CFO, and legal counsel play?
3. Have Tyco's recent actions been sufficient to restore confidence in the company? What other actions should the company take to demonstrate that it intends to play by the rules?
4. How will the implementation of the Sarbanes-Oxley Act of 2002 prevent future dilemmas in Tyco?

Sources: These facts are from Bud Angst, "The Continuing Tyco Saga: December 2002," *[Valley View, PA] Citizen Standard,* Jan. 1, 2003, via http://budangst.com/news/News763.htm; James Bandler and Jerry Guidera, "Tyco Ex-CEO's Party for Wife Cost $2.1 Million, but Had Elvis," *Wall Street Journal,* Sept. 17, 2002, p. A1; Anthony Bianco, William Symonds, and Nanette Byrnes, "The Rise and Fall of Dennis Kozlowski," *Business Week,* Dec., 23, 2002, pp. 64–77; Laurie P. Cohen, "Tyco Ex-Counsel Claims Auditors Knew of Loans," *Wall Street Journal,* Oct. 22, 2002, http://online.wsj.com/article_print0,, SB103524176089398951,00.html; Laurie P. Cohen and John Hechinger, "Tyco Suits Say Clandestine Pacts Led to Payments," *Wall Street Journal,* June 18, 2002, pp. A3, A10; Laurie P. Cohen and Mark Maremont, "Tyco Ex-Director Faces Possible Criminal Charges," *Wall Street Journal,* Sept. 9, 2002, pp. A3, A11; Laurie P. Cohen and Mark Maremont, "Tyco Relocations to Florida Are Probed," *Wall Street Journal,* June 10, 2002, pp. A3, A6; "Corporate Scandals: Tyco, International," MSNBC, www.msnbc. com/news/corpscandal_front.asp?odm=C2ORB (accessed Apr. 4, 2003); "Former Tyco Execs Face Fraud Charges," Canadian Broadcasting Corporation, Sept. 12, 2002, www.cbc.ca/stories/2002/09/12/ tyco020912; Charles Gaspaino, "Merrill Replaced Its Tyco Analyst After Meeting," *Wall Street Journal,* Sept. 17, 2002, pp. C1, C13; Jerry Guidera, "Veteran Tyco Director Steps Down," *Wall Street Journal,* Nov. 12, 2002, p. A8; "History," Tyco International, www.tyco.com/tyco/history.asp (accessed Apr. 25, 2003); Arianna Huffington, "Pigs at the Trough Sidebars," Arianna Online, www.ariannaonline.com/ books/pigs_updown.html (accessed Apr. 25, 2003); Louis Lavelle, "Rebuilding Trust in Tyco," *Business Week,* Nov. 25, 2002, pp. 94–96; Robin Londner, "Tyco to Consider Reincorporation, Auditor Removed," *[South Florida] Business Journal,* Mar. 10, 2003, http://southflorida.bizjournal.com/southflorida/ stories/2003/03/10/daily2.html; Loann Lublin and Jerry Guidera, "Tyco Board Criticized on Kozlowski," *Wall Street Journal,* June 7, 2002, p. A5; Mark Maremont, "Tyco May Report $1.2 Billion in Fresh Accounting Problems" *Wall Street Journal,* Apr. 30, 2003, http://online.wsj.com/article/ 0,,SB105166908562976400,00.html?mod=home_whats_news_us; Mark Maremont, "Tyco Seeks Hefty Repayments from Former Financial Officer," *Wall Street Journal,* Oct. 7, 2002, p. A6; Mark Maremont and Laurie P. Cohen, "Ex-Tyco CEO Is Likely to Face Charges over Unauthorized Pay," *Wall Street Journal,* Sept. 12, 2002, pp. A1, A8; Mark Maremont and John Hechinger, "Tyco's Ex-CEO Invested in Fund Run by Director," *Wall Street Journal,* Oct. 23, 2002, http://online.wsj.com/article_print 0,,SB1035329530787240111,00.html; Mark Maremont and Jerry Markon, "Former Tyco Chief, Two Others Face New Charges and Lawsuits," *Wall Street Journal,* Sept. 13, 2002, pp. A3, A6; Mark Maremont and Jerry Markon, "Former Tyco Executives Are Charged," *Wall Street Journal,* Sept. 13, 2002, http:// online.wsj.com/article_print0,SB1031836600798528755,00.html; Mark Maremont and Jerry Markon, "Tyco's Kozlowski Is Indicted on Charges of Tax Evasion," *Wall Street Journal,* June 5, 2002, pp. A1, A7; Samuel Maull, "Kozlowski Claims Tyco Owes Him Millions," *Real Cities,* Mar. 14, 2003, www.realcities. com/mld/realcities/business/financial_markets/5395148.htm; Kevin McCoy, "Tyco Acknowledges More Accounting Tricks," *USA Today,* Dec. 31, 2002, p. 3B; Kevin McCoy, "Investigators Scrutinize $20M Tyco Fee," *USA Today,* Sept. 16, 2002, p. 1B; Kevin McCoy, "Directors' Firms on Payroll at Tyco," *USA Today,* Sept. 18, 2002, p. 1B; Gary Panter, "The Big Kozlowski," *Fortune,* Nov. 18, 2002, pp. 123–126;

Stephen Taub, "Tyco on Tyco: Errors Made, But No Fraud," CFO.com, Dec. 31, 2002, www.cfo.com/article/1,5309,8596,00.html?f=related; "Tyco's History Under Kozlowski, *Washington Post,* June 3, 2002, www.washingtonpost.com; "Tyco's Shareholders Defeat Proposal to Leave Bermuda," *USA Today,* Mar. 6, 2003, www.usatoday.com/money/industries/retail/2003-03-06-tyco_x.htm; "Tyco Smells Smoke at Fire Unit," TheStreet.com, Mar. 12, 2003, www.thestreet.com/_yahoo/tech/earnings.10073763.html.

# Case 3

# Global Crossing: Inflated Sales Lead to Bankruptcy[1]

Global Crossing began in 1997 as a grand idea. It was to become the fourth-largest bankruptcy in U.S. history just five years later. The road to that bankruptcy is a story of revenues inflated by what appears to be fraudulent accounting, in which senior executives enriched themselves while Arthur Andersen served as auditor and consultant. Global Crossing employees and shareholders seem to have been left holding the bag, much as in the Enron bankruptcy filed just two months earlier.

## The Global Crossing Business Concept

Global Crossing was Gary Winnick's brainchild. Winnick was a former junk-bond financier who worked with Michael Milken at Drexel Burnham Lambert but escaped untarnished from a 1990s scandal at that firm. Together with a group of financial gurus and chief executive officers, he envisioned a global broadband network that would link continents with undersea fiber-optic cables. This was a risky proposition in 1997 because no such network existed, and no one knew exactly how profitable, or unprofitable, such a network would be. It has always been extremely difficult to forecast the profitability of new services or new technologies, and the Global Crossing proposal was no exception.

Demand for high-speed data services that could span continents exploded in the middle of the 1990s. The fiber-optic networks in the United States were owned by Sprint, AT&T, and MCI, with a few other relatively small players. None of these firms seemed able to keep up with growing business demand for broadband capacity. Level 3, Qwest Communications International, and Williams Communications stepped in to add capacity by building fiber-optic networks that spanned the country, expecting that many businesses would pay extra just to have access to this service. The creators of Global Crossing, as its name implies, envisioned a fiber-optic network that extended globally rather than just domestically.

Global Crossing faced one, not so small obstacle to executing its business plan: It effectively had no assets, and building such a high-tech, undersea network would be

---

[1] This case was prepared by Neil Herndon, University of Missouri - Columbia, under the direction of O. C. Ferrell, for classroom discussion, rather than to illustrate either effective or ineffective handling of an administrative, ethical, or legal decision by management.

tremendously expensive, on the order of $2.7 billion. Fortunately, Wall Street investors valued the Global Crossing concept highly and offered Winnick and his management team about $40 billion in equity financing and $10 billion in debt financing. Investment analysts gave the stock a "strong buy" rating.

If demand for the services Global Crossing offered continued to exceed supply—in other words, creating a "seller's market"—then Global Crossing's plan to create additional fiber-optic broadband capacity had great profit potential because the company could set a high price for its service. However, if supply began to outstrip demand and prices dropped accordingly—a "buyer's market"—then Global Crossing's profits would drop, possibly taking profits into negative territory. In fact, the race to build fiber-optic networks quickly created excess capacity in the industry, which ultimately resulted in customers paying a lower price for broadband service, rather than the premium price executives had hoped for. The bottom line was that Global Crossing's profits could no longer pay the interest on its debt.

At its peak, Global Crossing had a market valuation of more than $50 billion, larger than General Motors on paper, and its fiber-optic telecommunications network connected two hundred cities in twenty-seven countries. However, it amassed about $12.4 billion in debt establishing its global fiber-optic telecommunications network. So when Global Crossing's revenues dropped to $2.4 billion in the first three quarters of 2001, down from about $3.8 billion for the same period in 2000, the writing was on the wall. After finishing 2000 with a loss of some $1.67 billion, Global Crossing was forced to declare bankruptcy on January 28, 2002.

## The Telecommunications Stock Analyst

Jack Grubman, a telecommunications stock analyst for investment house Salomon Smith Barney (owned by Citigroup, Inc.), was consistently "bullish" on Global Crossing after the company went public in August 1998. His support continued until November 2001, when it became clear that demand for broadband capacity was falling short of the demand Grubman and other telecommunications stock analysts had predicted in 1998 and 1999. Although he lowered his price target for Global Crossing stock in May 2001 by $40 per share, from $70 to $30, he also labeled the stock a "core holding" and maintained his "buy" recommendation.

It later emerged that Grubman, though employed by Salomon Smith Barney, helped Global Crossing make key business and management decisions for about two years after the company's initial public offering (IPO). In fact, Global Crossing chairman Gary Winnick and Grubman reportedly communicated almost daily for some time after Global Crossing's debut. Grubman allegedly advised Winnick on his personal stock sales and was reported to be involved in the recommendation to hire Robert Annunziata as Global Crossing's CEO. Grubman also allegedly helped to negotiate mergers with U.S. West, Inc. and Frontier Corporation on Global Crossing's behalf.

Grubman's extensive activities with Global Crossing were unusual given the traditional role of stock analysts, who are generally expected to provide only impartial advice to investors and shareholders. While Grubman's activities do not appear to violate federal securities law, investigators from the New York State Attorney General's Office are looking into the source of Grubman's bonuses. Was he being rewarded for his role as a telecommunications stock analyst or for his role as an advisor to Global Crossing's management?

Jack Grubman was certainly not the only Wall Street analyst enthusiastic about the prospects of the telecommunications industry, but he seems to have had more influence over the telecom sector than any of his peers. One former telecom CEO was quoted as saying that if Grubman didn't endorse a deal, the deal didn't happen. But, in order to get his endorsement, Salomon Smith Barney had to secure a major part of the investment business.

## Concerns about Insider Trading

The laws regulating business in the U.S. emphasize fairness to all involved in commerce, regardless of wealth, fame, position of power, or role, such as consumer, producer, or investor. Some refer to these protections as "maintaining a level playing field," a metaphor that suggests that one team should not have to struggle to move the ball uphill while the other moves the ball easily downhill—aided by gravity. This fairness philosophy, enshrined in many facets of U.S. business law and associated regulations, is especially evident in the laws regarding insider trading.

Insider trading generally occurs when a person has nonpublic information that is material about a security or the company that issues it and then buys or sells that security based on that information. The Securities and Exchange Commission (SEC) requires that an individual who is privy to inside information that might affect a stock's price must not trade in that company's securities unless he or she discloses what is known before buying or selling the stock. The SEC and the courts use three sets of rules to determine whether insider trading has occurred. The traditional rule is that all partners and employees of a firm, including people whose professional activities put them in a relationship of trust or confidence with the firm or its shareholders, must not trade in the securities of the company in which they hold material, nonpublic information. Second, they are not permitted to disclose this information to others if they expect to profit in any way whatsoever from that disclosure. A person who receives a tip from an insider and then trades in that company's securities is generally guilty of insider trading. Finally, the misappropriation rule effectively extends insider liability to people who receive nonpublic, material information from insiders who have a duty to keep that information confidential, including people with whom the insider habitually shares confidential information, such as a spouse. Under tender-offer rules, traditional insiders and any others who obtain material information about the tender offer may not legally trade in that company's securities.

Penalties for insider trading are stiff. Making just over $10,000 in an illegal insider trade would draw a mandatory eight- to fourteen-month jail sentence if convicted. The combined maximum civil and criminal penalties for insider trading are even harsher. Civil penalties assessed to violators may be up to three times the amount of illegal profits gained or losses avoided by the act of insider trading. In addition, the maximum criminal penalties for individuals is twenty years in prison and a $5 million fine. Private parties may also sue the inside trader for damages.

There is evidence that top officials at Global Crossing knew that the company's business future appeared bleak before they sold company stock. These transactions resulted in millions of dollars of income for those involved. Chairman Gary Winnick is reported to have sold stock valued at $123 million on May 23, 2001, but a witness told a congressional committee investigating Global Crossing that he had seen an April forecast projecting a revenue fall of $300 million. A much earlier June 5, 2000, e-mail from then CEO Leo Hindery Jr. encouraged Winnick to offer the assets of Global Crossing for sale to other telecommunications companies. Winnick denies that he sold stock based on his inside information that the company was in financial trouble. Winnick's lawyer, Gary Naftalis, insists the stock sales were proper and had been approved by Global Crossing's counsel. Altogether, it appears that Winnick sold some $734 million in Global Crossing stock before the company filed for bankruptcy.

Other Global Crossing executives also profited from the sale of company stock. Between 1999 and the end of December 2001, they are reported to have sold some $1.3 billion worth. David Walsh, formerly the chief operating officer, sold stock worth $8.7 million on May 31, 2001; Global Crossing co-chairman Lodwrick Cook sold stock worth $9.8 million on May 16, 2001. Cook said that he sold his shares to satisfy a margin call—that is, he had borrowed money to pay for Global Crossing shares and when share prices dropped, needed to sell some of his shares to repay the margin loans.

## The Capacity Swaps

During the "gold rush" fever of the telecommunications boom, start-up fiber-optic telecommunications companies like Global Crossing and Qwest would swap network capacity. In other words, the two companies would simultaneously sell each other the right to use some part of their respective fiber-optic networks, creating in effect a long-term lease that allowed one company to take control of part of the other company's network. The companies would then declare in their quarterly and annual reports the income from selling the rights to use a portion of the network, but would not declare the expense of purchasing the rights. This consequently "boosted" their revenues and overstated their profits, sending their stock price higher. This transaction, called a "capacity swap" or "swap," would have the effect of making the balance sheets of the two companies appear stronger than they actually were. Such deals added about $375 million to Global Crossing's bottom line in the first quarter of 2001.

Signing contracts to gain access to each firm's networks appears to be legal. The issue with such swaps is that one asset is replaced with another, virtually identical asset. It does not appear that any real economic value is created in the transaction, even though the financial statements of the telecommunications firms involved do not reflect this fact. This procedure tended to mislead shareholders and potential investors about the financial health of the company in which they were investing.

Global Crossing senior operations executive Carl Grivner commissioned an internal review of fiber-optic capacity that reported that most of the company's capacity purchases were of limited or no value. Less than 20 percent of the swapped assets could be cost-effectively added to Global Crossing's existing network. In some swaps, the assets were hundreds of miles from a Global Crossing connection point, making interconnection prohibitively expensive. It appears that engineers were sometimes consulted about the swaps and sometimes not, especially when the deals were being made in a quarter's closing minutes. Reportedly, the study was presented to the company's executive vice president of finance, Joseph Perrone, in September 2001.

The SEC looked into Global Crossing's accounting practices after it filed for bankruptcy protection and said that Global Crossing's accounting for these swaps did not comply with generally accepted accounting principles. It ordered Global Crossing to change its financial statements to reflect adherence to these principles, a ruling that would likely apply to other telecommunications companies that had adopted the practice of swapping capacity. Global Crossing indicated that restating its earnings from such capacity swaps to comply with the SEC order for the first nine months of 2001 would cost it about $19 million in revenue. This would lower the $2.44 billion booked in revenue for this period and thereby increase the company's net loss of $4.77 billion by about $13 million. Global Crossing also said that when it accounted for the swaps it had acted in accordance with information provided by Arthur Andersen, its accounting firm. Arthur Andersen reportedly had told Global Crossing that it did not agree with the SEC's interpretation of the accounting rule that Global Crossing used for the swaps.

## The Congressional Investigation

The House of Representatives' Energy and Commerce Committee is looking into possible insider trading by Global Crossing executives. It is also investigating possible efforts by Global Crossing to increase revenues by acquiring other businesses and capacity swaps, which effectively misled investors. The probe was triggered by a former Global Crossing vice president of finance, Roy Olofson, who claimed publicly that the company had improperly increased revenues and underreported costs to improve earnings so it could meet Wall Street expectations and support its stock price. Olofson later lost his job and sued Global Crossing and key executives.

The committee released documents showing that Global Crossing bought 360networks, Inc. in something of a rush during March 2001. Some board members and top company officials objected, but Chairman Gary Winnick reportedly rammed the deal through even though there were limited opportunities for due diligence before the deal was consummated. It appears that the main reason for the rush purchase was to use 360networks' revenue to enhance Global Crossing's financial statements to avoid disappointing Wall Street investors' earnings expectations for Global Crossing.

Some members of Congress expressed concern that capacity swaps were used to inflate Global Crossing's revenue. Its chief financial officer, Dan Cohrs, told the House Financial Services Subcommittee on Oversight and Investigations that his company had not set out to inflate revenue by entering into some twenty-four deals or capacity swaps with other telecommunications companies. Rather, Cohrs said that Global Crossing wanted to expand the capacity and the reach of its global network. But committee members noted that many of these deals dated from 2000 and 2001, a time when there was already overcapacity in the global telecommunications market. These deals added about $375 million to Global Crossing's bottom line in the first quarter of 2001. Qwest Communications International, also involved in deals for network capacity, said it was reversing some $950 million in revenue from capacity swaps and may have to make adjustments of another $531 million in revenue from other sales.

The U.S. Justice Department and the Enforcement Division of the SEC are also probing Global Crossing and Qwest.

The committee is also investigating illegal insider trading. Winnick denied that he sold stock based on inside information that Global Crossing was in financial trouble and said that all of his stock transactions were appropriate. However, witnesses claim that top officials knew that Global Crossing's business outlook was weak before they sold company stock.

The subcommittee expressed concern that Global Crossing relied on nonstandard, pro forma numbers in reports circulated to investors but used generally accepted accounting principles in its public filings with the SEC. These pro forma reports claimed a 50 percent increase, about $531 million, over the statements filed by Global Crossing under generally accepted accounting rules.

There is also evidence that Global Crossing executives deliberately misled investors about the strength of the organization's finances. One report indicates that Winnick learned on February 26, 2001, that Global Crossing would fall some $200 million short of the first quarter financial targets expected by Wall Street investors. However, in April, then CEO Tom Casey told top stock analysts during a conference call that there were "record results in cash revenue" and that Global Crossing's results exceeded the estimates of the stock analysts themselves. This report led analysts to encourage investors to buy Global Crossing stock, sparking a surge in stock prices just before Winnick sold some $123 million of his shares. Winnick's lawyer, Gary Naftalis, said that Global Crossing did not mislead investors, but that it believed it would make its first quarter financial targets legitimately.

Jack Grubman, the telecommunications stock analyst for investment house Salomon Smith Barney, is also of interest to the committee. They would like to know more about the ties between Global Crossing and Salomon Smith Barney and also about the positive research reports Grubman was writing about telecommunications firms that later crashed.

## After the Fall

Global Crossing hopes to emerge from bankruptcy protection in 2003. Its restatements of financial results related to its capacity swaps will have very limited impact on its continuing operations because it will use so-called "fresh-start" accounting procedures, which do not include any previous financial results. The company has also indicated that its use of nonstandard, pro forma numbers in reports to investors should be disregarded.

Global Crossing will have its debt load cut from about $6.6 billion to about $200 million and its work force reduced from some fifteen thousand people to about five thousand. Some observers believe it will no longer be a market leader but rather exist as more of a niche player, with a network connecting about two hundred cities. At least four other competitors are also emerging from bankruptcy proceedings at about the same time: Williams Communications, Flag Telecom, 360networks, and World-Com. With excess network capacity available, it's a buyer's market now. Price wars, in which competitors compete away profits until, potentially, only those with the deepest pockets remain, could easily become a facet of telecom competitive life. And

Global Crossing CEO John Legere has already said that his company could indeed cut prices after it emerges from Chapter 11 protection.

The bankruptcy process may be hastened by a bidding war for controlling interest in Global Crossing. Hutchison Whampoa of Hong Kong and Singapore Technologies Telemedia proposed a $250 million offer for Global Crossing, which was approved by the judge presiding over Global Crossing's bankruptcy case. However, a rival bid of $255 million from IDT Corporation may ultimately be successful because of the U.S. government's concern over potential national security issues resulting from Asian ownership of Global Crossing's fiber-optic network in the United States.

Global Crossing's creditors are owed about $12.4 billion; Global Crossing investors lost a total of about $54 billion. Some fourteen thousand current and former employees lost 401(k) funds and pension funds, as well as health and severance benefits. The employees' 401(k) funds alone appear to have declined in value about $191 million, from about $200 million to $8.9 million as of December 2001. Leo Hindery, Global Crossing's CEO from March to October 2000, is asking U.S. Bankruptcy Judge Robert Gerber to order Global Crossing to treat him as an administrative creditor. This would give his claims precedent over other creditors in the bankruptcy proceeding. Hindrey claims $817,714 dollars in unpaid severance benefits, which include $22,378 a month rent on his apartment in the Waldorf-Astoria Towers on Manhattan's Park Avenue. His claims are partly based on agreements that he stay on as the chairman and CEO of Global Center, Global Crossing's Web-hosting unit, for about a million dollars a year. Global Center was sold in January 2001 to Exodus Communications for $1.91 billion in stock.

Telecommunications stock analyst Jack Grubman would be banned for life from the securities industry and pay a $15 million fine for his role in the Global Crossing debacle under a tentative agreement with the New York State Attorney General's Office. Under this deal Grubman neither admitted nor denied guilt, and he would remain subject to further investigations.

Global Crossing founder and chairman Gary Winnick resigned from the board on December 31, 2002, under pressure from investor groups. All together, it appears that Winnick profited by about $734 million from his sales of Global Crossing stock before the company filed bankruptcy. However, he and more than twenty Global Crossing executives and directors face a lawsuit filed in the Federal District Court in Manhattan that consolidates several class-action complaints on behalf of investors who lost billions of dollars on Global Crossing stocks and bonds.

The investigations of the events surrounding Global Crossing's bankruptcy continue. The Congress, SEC, U.S. Department of Justice, Federal Bureau of Investigation, and New York State Attorney General's Office could still bring civil or criminal proceedings against Global Crossing executives and other involved parties at any time. The scandal took a new twist when Richard N. Perle, who the firm retained to help overcome Defense Department concerns about the proposed sale to two Asian firms, was forced to resign as chairman of the Defense Policy Board after the press suggested that the two roles created a conflict of interest, perhaps violating ethics rules. Although Perle remained a member of the Defense Policy Board, which advises the Pentagon and Secretary of Defense on war matters including the recent conflict in Iraq, he withdrew from his role as advisor to Global Crossing.

Interestingly, Global Crossing shareholders were not the greatest beneficiaries of their risk-taking; they will lose almost all of their investment. The real beneficiaries are the customers of the telecommunications services market. They will have more fiber-optic broadband capacity connected to more locations at a lower price than would have been possible if Global Crossing and other telecommunications companies had not invested in the creation of these networks.

*Questions*

1. How did the pressure to meet earnings forecasts for Wall Street investors contribute to unethical conduct at Global Crossing?
2. Was there some unacceptable level of greed at Global Crossing that contributed to its bankruptcy? Support your position with facts from the case.
3. Are there similarities between the bankruptcy at Global Crossing and the bankruptcy at Enron (Case 1)? If so, what are they?

Sources: These facts are from Andrew Backover, "Global Crossing Plans Bold End to Chapter 11," *USA Today,* Oct. 16, 2002, www.usatoday.com/money/industries/telecom/2002-10-16-global_x.htm; Andrew Backover, "Spring CEO Says Strong Will Survive," *USA Today,* Oct. 21, 2002, www.usatoday.com/money/industries/telecom/2002-10-21-sprint_x.htm; Andrew Backover, "Telecom Executives Deny Wrongdoing," *USA Today,* Oct. 2, 2002, p. B1; Dennis K. Berman, "Global Crossing's Accounting for 'Swap' Trades to Be Amended," *Wall Street Journal,* Oct. 22, 2002, p. A10; Dennis K. Berman, "Global Crossing Faces More Accusations," *Wall Street Journal,* Feb. 6, 2002, p. B6; Dennis K. Berman, "Hindery Wants Global Crossing to Give Him Pay," *Wall Street Journal,* Oct. 14, 2002, p. B6; Dennis K. Berman, "Study Questioned Global Crossing Deals," *Wall Street Journal,* Feb. 19, 2002, p. B6; Dennis K. Berman and Laurie P. Cohen, "SEC to Investigate Insiders' Trades at Global Crossing," *Wall Street Journal,* June 3, 2002, pp. A1, A8; Laurie P. Cohen and Dennis K. Berman, "How Analyst Grubman Helped Call Shots at Global Crossing," *Wall Street Journal,* May 31, 2002, pp. A1, A6; Julie Creswell, "The Emperor of Greed," *Fortune,* June 24, 2002, pp. 106–116; "Ex-Global Crossing CEO Seeks $821,714 in Severance Benefits," *Boston Globe,* Oct. 15, 2002, p. D4; Harold Furchtgott-Roth, "Manager's Journal: Global Crossing's Bankruptcy Is a Success Story," *Wall Street Journal,* Feb. 5, 2002, p. A18; "Global Crossing Exec Denies Insider Trading," *USA Today,* Oct. 1, 2002, www.usatoday.com/money/industries/telecom/2002-10-01-global-crossing-hearing_x.htm; "Global Crossing Probe Eyes 2001 Accounts," *InfoWorld Media Group, Inc.,* Oct. 14, 2002, http://staging.infoworld.com/articles; Tom Hamburger and Dennis K. Berman, "U.S. Adviser Perle Resigns As Head of Defense Board," *Wall Street Journal,* Mar. 28, 2003, http://online.wsj.com; Jim Hopkins, "Winnick Quits Board at Global Crossing," *USA Today,* December 31, 2002, p. B03; Susan Ivancevich, Lucian C. Jones, and Thomas Keaveney, "Don't Run the Risk," *Journal of Accountancy,* 194 (Dec. 2002): 47–51; Siobhan Kennedy, "Global Crossing Restates Earnings," *Reuters,* Oct. 21, 2002, http://reuters.com; Jonathan Krim, "Panel Widens Probe of Global Crossing," *Washington Post,* Aug. 30, 2002, p. E01, www.washingtonpost.com; Stephen Labaton, "Pentagon Adviser Is Also Advising Global Crossing," *New York Times,* Mar. 21, 2003, www.nytimes.com/2003/03/21/business/21GLOB.html; Stephanie N. Mehta, "Birds of a Feather," *Fortune,* Oct. 14, 2002, pp. 197–202; "A Guide to Corporate Scandals," *The Economist Newspaper,* July 10, 2002, p. 1; Jeremy Pelofsky, "Ex-Global Crossing CEO Demands Rent Paid," *Reuters,* Oct. 14, 2002, www.reuters.com; Simon Romero, "Adding to Claims Against Global Crossing," *New York Times,* Jan. 30, 2003, p. C4; Simon Romero, "Technology; IDT Offers $255 Million to Control Global Crossing," *New York Times,* Feb. 25, 2003, www.nytimes.com; Christopher Stern, "At Global Crossing, 'No Enron'," *Washington Post,* Mar. 22, 2002, p. E04; James Toedtman, "Telecom Head Pledges $25M," *Newsday,* Oct. 2, 2002, www.newsday.com; "Under Fire: These Execs, Too, Are Embroiled in a Range of Investigations," *Business Week,* Jan. 13, 2003, pp. 87, 89; Michael Weisskopf, "Global Crossing: What Did Winnick Know?" *Time,* Oct. 7, 2002, p. 28; "Winnick Was Told of Telecom Risks," *Washington Post,* Oct. 1, 2002, p. E03.

# Case 4

# WorldCom: Actions Lead to Corporate Reform[1]

The story of WorldCom began in 1983 when businessmen Murray Waldron and William Rector sketched out a plan to create a long-distance telephone service provider on a napkin in a coffee shop in Hattiesburg, Mississippi. Their new company, Long Distance Discount Service (LDDS), began operating as a long distance reseller in 1984. Early investor Bernard Ebbers was named CEO the following year. Through acquisitions and mergers, LDDS grew quickly over the next fifteen years. It changed its name to WorldCom, achieved a worldwide presence, acquired telecommunications giant MCI, and eventually expanded beyond long-distance service to offer the whole range of telecommunications services. It seemed poised to become one of the largest telecommunications corporations in the world. Instead, it became the largest bankruptcy filing in U.S. history to date and another name on a long list of those disgraced by the accounting scandals of the early twenty-first century.

## Financial Implications of Accounting Fraud

Unfortunately, for thousands of employees and shareholders, WorldCom used questionable accounting practices and improperly recorded $3.8 billion in capital expenditures, which boosted cash flows and profit over all four quarters in 2001 as well as the first quarter of 2002. This disguised the firm's actual net losses for the five quarters because capital expenditures can be deducted over a longer period of time, whereas expenses must be immediately subtracted from revenue. Investors, unaware of the alleged fraud, continued to buy the company's stock, which accelerated the stock's price. Internal investigations uncovered questionable accounting practices stretching as far back as 1999.

Even before the improper accounting practices were disclosed, however, by 2001 WorldCom was already in financial turmoil. Declining rates and revenues and an ambitious buying spree had pushed the company deeper into debt. In addition, chief executive Bernard Ebbers received a controversial $408 million loan to cover margin calls on loans that were secured by company stock. In July 2001, WorldCom signed a

---

[1] This case was prepared by Linda Ferrell and Nichole Scheele, University of Wyoming, and Reneé Galvin, Colorado State University, for classroom discussion, rather than to illustrate either effective or ineffective handling of an administrative, ethical, or legal decision by management.

credit agreement with multiple banks to borrow up to $2.65 billion and repay it within a year. According to the banks, WorldCom tapped the entire amount six weeks before the accounting irregularities were disclosed. The banks contend that if they had known WorldCom's true financial picture, they would not have extended the financing without demanding additional collateral.

On June 28, 2002, the Securities and Exchange Commission (SEC) directed WorldCom to detail the facts underlying the events the company had described in a June 25, 2002, press release. That press release had stated that WorldCom intended to restate its 2001 and first quarter 2002 financial statements and that Scott Sullivan—who reported to Bernard Ebbers until he resigned in April 2002—had prepared the financial statements for 2001 and the first quarter of 2002. On February 6, 2002, a meeting had been held between the board's audit committee and Arthur Andersen, the firm's outside auditor, to discuss the audit for fiscal year 2001. Andersen assessed WorldCom's accounting practices to determine whether it had adequate controls to prevent material errors in its financial statements and attested that WorldCom's processes were, in fact, effective. When the committee asked Andersen whether its auditors had had any disagreements with WorldCom's management, Andersen replied that they had not; they were comfortable with the accounting positions WorldCom had taken.

WorldCom did not have the cash needed to pay $7.7 billion in debt, and therefore, filed for Chapter 11 bankruptcy protection on July 21, 2002. In its bankruptcy filing, the firm listed $107 billion in assets and $41 billion in debt. WorldCom's bankruptcy filing allowed it to pay current employees, continue service to customers, retain possession of assets, and gain a little breathing room to reorganize. However, the telecom giant lost credibility along with the business of many large corporate and government clients, organizations that typically do not do business with companies in Chapter 11 proceedings.

## Who Is to Blame?

Naturally, no one has stepped forward to shoulder the blame for WorldCom's accounting scandal, not its auditors, executives, board of directors, or its analysts. As the primary outside auditor, Arthur Andersen—also under fire for alleged mismanagement of many other large scandal-plagued audits—has been faulted for failing to uncover the accounting irregularities. In its defense, Andersen claimed that it could not have known about the improper accounting because former CFO Scott Sullivan never informed Andersen's auditors about the firm's questionable accounting practices. But, in WorldCom's statement to the SEC, the company claimed that Andersen did know about these accounting practices, had no disagreement with WorldCom's management, and was not uncomfortable with any accounting positions taken by WorldCom.

Several former WorldCom finance and accounting executives, including David Myers, Buford Yates, Betty Vinson, and Troy Normand, pleaded guilty to securities-fraud charges. They claimed that they were directed by top managers to cover up WorldCom's worsening financial situation. Although they protested that these directions were improper, they say they agreed to follow orders after their superiors told them it was the only way to save the company. However, Scott Sullivan, who worked above

## FIGURE C4–1 BANKRUPTCY TIMELINE

| | |
|---|---|
| Early 2001 | WorldCom shows signs of financial troubles: rates and revenues decline and debt rises. |
| July 2001 | WorldCom receives $2.65 billion in loans from twenty-six banks—to be repaid by the end of 2001. |
| Feb. 6, 2002 | Arthur Andersen, LLP, and WorldCom's audit team meet to discuss the 2001 audit. Everything is deemed correct, and Andersen gives its approval. |
| Mar. 11, 2002 | The U.S. Securities and Exchange Commission (SEC) requests more information concerning accounting procedures and loans to officers. |
| Apr. 30, 2002 | Bernard Ebbers resigns as CEO of WorldCom and is replaced by vice chairman John Sidgmore. |
| June 25, 2002 | CFO Scott Sullivan is fired after improper accounting of $3.8 billion in expenses is discovered, which covered up a net loss for 2001 and the first quarter of 2002. |
| June 28, 2002 | WorldCom fires seventeen thousand employees to cut costs. |
| July 8, 2002 | John Sidgmore testifies before a congressional committee to explain how internal investigations uncovered the accounting problems. |
| July 21, 2002 | WorldCom files for reorganization under Chapter 11 bankruptcy, an action that affects only the firm's U.S. operations, not its overseas subsidiaries. |
| Aug. 9, 2002 | Continued internal investigations uncover an additional $3.8 billion in improperly reported earnings for 1999, 2000, 2001, and the first quarter of 2002, bringing the total amount of accounting errors to more than $7.6 billion. |
| Aug. 13, 2002 | WorldCom names Greg Rayburn as chief restructuring officer and John Dubel as chief financial officer to lead the company through the reorganization process. |
| Sept. 10, 2002 | WorldCom formally announces it is seeking a permanent chief executive officer. |
| Oct. 1, 2002 | The U.S. Bankruptcy Court approves WorldCom's request to pay full severance and benefits to former employees, which had been limited under the company's Chapter 11 filing. |
| Oct. 15, 2002 | The U.S. Bankruptcy Court approves up to $1.1 billion in debtor-in-possession (DIP) financing for WorldCom while it undergoes reorganization. |
| Nov. 8, 2002 | WorldCom files additional bankruptcy petitions for forty-three of its subsidiaries. |
| Nov. 15, 2002 | Michael D. Capellas, former president of Hewlett-Packard Company, is named chairman and CEO. |
| July 8, 2003 | WorldCom, now operating under the name MCI, agrees to pay $750 million to settle the SEC's civil fraud charges. |

many of these employees, pleaded not guilty. Chief executive Bernard Ebbers stated that he did nothing fraudulent and has nothing to hide. WorldCom's lawyers have said that Ebbers did not know of the money shifted into the capital expenditure accounts. However, the *Wall Street Journal* reported that an internal WorldCom report identified an e-mail and a voice mail that suggested otherwise. Former CEO Ebbers has not been charged with any crime as of this writing.

John Sidgmore, who briefly replaced Bernard Ebbers as CEO, blames WorldCom's former management for the company's woes. Richard Thornburgh, the independent investigator appointed by WorldCom's bankruptcy court, asserted that there was a "cause for substantial concern" regarding WorldCom's board of directors and independent auditors. The board has been accused of lax oversight, and the board's compensation committee has been attacked for approving Bernard Ebber's generous compensation package. Moreover, Thornburgh's report claimed that Ebbers and Sullivan ran WorldCom "with virtually no checks or restraints placed on their actions by the board of directors or other management." Another report, prepared for the firm's new board of directors, also criticized Ebbers for bucking efforts to develop a code of conduct, which Ebbers was said to have called a "colossal waste of time."

Additionally, Jack Grubman, a Wall Street analyst specializing in the telecommunications industry, who rated WorldCom's stock highly, has admitted he did so for too long. However, he insists he was unaware of the company's true financial shape. Grubman was later fired by Salomon Smith Barney because of accusations that he hyped telecommunications stocks, including Global Crossing and WorldCom, even after it became public that the stocks were poor investments.

Many people have blamed the rising number of telecommunication company failures and scandals on neophytes who had no experience in the telecommunication industry. Among these telecom outsiders are a junk bond financier (Gary Winnick of Global Crossing), a railroad baron (Phil Anschutz, who founded Qwest), and Bernard Ebbers, who operated a motel before he took the helm of WorldCom. They tried to transform their startups into gigantic full-service providers like AT&T, but in an increasingly competitive industry it was unlikely that so many large companies could survive.

## Effect on Investors

A Chapter 11 reorganization bankruptcy filing means different things to different investor groups, but the reality is that in the end, few investors will get back what they put into WorldCom. In a bankruptcy proceeding, shareholders have a legal right to some money, but because they essentially sit at the bottom of the list of creditors, they will not likely see anything at all.

In 2001 WorldCom created a separate "tracking" stock for its declining MCI consumer long-distance business in the hopes of isolating MCI from WorldCom's Internet and international operations, which were seemingly stronger. WorldCom announced the elimination of the MCI tracking stock and suspended its dividend in May 2002 in the hopes of saving $284 million a year. The actual savings was just $71 million. The S&P 500 cut WorldCom's long-term and short-term corporate credit rating to "junk" status on May 10, 2002, and the NASDAQ de-listed WorldCom's stock on June 28, 2002, when the price dropped to $0.09.

Likewise, holders of WorldCom's bonds, which include banks' investment departments, insurance companies, and pension funds, are not expected to receive interest and principal payments on those bonds. Although they may receive new stock, new bonds, or a combination of stocks and bonds in exchange for the bonds they hold, any new stock is unlikely to be worth nearly as much as investors lost. Various state funds alone lost $277 million when WorldCom's stock tanked.

After WorldCom emerges from bankruptcy, shareholders may be able to exchange current stock for new stock in the reorganized company, but, as with bonds, any new shares may be fewer and worth less. Of course, if WorldCom's attempt to reorganize proves futile and is declared insolvent, then both bond and shareholders will be left with nothing at all.

## Effect on Consumers

The greatest effect on consumers could be any change in service by MCI, the long-distance giant acquired by WorldCom years ago. MCI, touted as the second-largest long-distance carrier, is continuing service during WorldCom's Chapter 11 bankruptcy reorganization. If WorldCom's reorganization ultimately proves unsuccessful, its assets would be liquidated, thus ending MCI long-distance service. In that event, the FCC would have to receive a thirty-day warning from MCI before any service is cut, which hopefully would give consumers sufficient time to find another long-distance carrier.

The potential termination of MCI's long-distance services brings up a historical debate about the relative merits of having a single network provider versus having two or more carriers. Many WorldCom customers, along with Qwest and Global Crossing customers, may wish they had implemented a backup provider. Ted Chamberlin, a networking analyst for the research firm Gartner, believes that "For any customer of a network service provider, the potential is there for gloomy times. So we tell our customers that having a dual-carrier strategy is essential." Gartner has also advised all information technology (IT) decision makers to delay signing up for new services with WorldCom, to extend expiring contracts for only six months, to consider a second Internet service provider for Internet access, to research alternative Web-hosting sites, and to document all their WorldCom services and networking needs.

## Where Now? Reorganization

In March 2003, WorldCom announced that it would write down close to $80 billion in good will, write off $45 billion of goodwill as impaired, and adjust $39.2 billion of property- and-equipment accounts and $5.6 billion of other intangible assets down to a value of about $10 billion. These figures join a growing list of similar write-offs and write-downs by companies in the telecom, Internet, and high-tech industries which have admitted that they overpaid for acquisitions during the booming 1990s. Such charges also reflect downturns in various sectors. Deutsche Telekom recently took $21 billion in charges; France Telecom, $20 billion; AOL Time Warner, $45.5 billion; Qwest Communications, $41 billion; and JDS Uniphase took $50 billion. A few months later, WorldCom filed its plan for restructuring its debt in order to emerge from bankruptcy proceedings. Among other provisions, the plan included changing the firm's name to MCI. In July, the company agreed to settle the SEC's civil fraud charges and to pay $750 million in cash and stock to investors who lost money as a result of the fraud.

Will WorldCom survive restructuring in bankruptcy court? Many signs point to yes, but there are skeptics who don't think the telecom giant can be pulled out of the hole it has found itself in. WorldCom's greatest problem is accountability. It has taken many steps toward a successful reorganization, including securing $1.1 billion in loans and appointing Michael Capellas as chairman and CEO. WorldCom has also taken many actions to restore confidence in the company, including replacing the board members who failed to prevent the accounting scandal, firing many managers, reorganizing its finance and accounting functions, and making other changes designed to help correct past problems and prevent them from recurring. The hiring of four line controllers to oversee revenue accounting, operational accounting, financial accounting, and financial controls and procedures is also in process. Additionally, the audit department staff is being increased and will now report directly to the audit committee of the company's new board. "We are working to create a new WorldCom," John Sidgmore said. "We have developed and implemented new systems, policies, and procedures."

*Questions*

1. What are some things that WorldCom executives could have done to prevent the accounting scandal?
2. How could corporate ethics have played a part in this failure? How could they help to bring about a new and successful WorldCom?
3. Give a thorough update on WorldCom's struggle to reorganize. What penalties have WorldCom executives paid for their part in the fiasco? Do you think these penalties are sufficient?

Sources: "02 CV 8083 (JSR) Complaint (Securities Fraud)," Securities and Exchange Commission, Oct. 31, 2002, www.sec.gov/litigation/complaints/comp17783.htm; "Accounting Fraud," WorldCom News, http://Worldcomnews.com/accountingfraud.html (accessed Apr. 3, 2003); Andrew Backover, "Overseer Confident WorldCom Will Come Back," *USA Today*, Dec. 31, 2002, p. 8A; "Bankruptcy," Worldcom News, http://Worldcomnews.com/bankruptcy.html (accessed Apr. 3, 2003); Andrew Barakat, "Reports Detail How Ebbers, Officers Ran Wild at WorldCom," *Austin American-Statesman*, June 10, 2003, http://statesman.com; Rebecca Blumenstein and Ken Brown, "Scrapped Worldcom Merger Sparked Sprint Tax Shelter," Yahoo! News, Feb. 27, 2003, http://story.news.yahoo.com/news?tmpl=story&u=/dowjones/20030207/bs_dowjones/200302070218000057; "Capellas Close to Leading WorldCom," *CNN/Money*, Nov. 13, 2002, http://cnnmoney.printthis.clickability.com/pt/cpt?action=cpt&expire=&urlID=4597701&fb; "Corporate Scandals: WorldCom," MSNBC, www.msnbc.com/news/corpscandal_front.asp?odm=C2ORB (accessed Apr. 4, 2003); Nora Devine, "WorldCom to Write Off $45B Goodwill, Adjust Intangibles," Dow Jones Newswires, Mar. 13, 2003, http://story.news.yahoo.com/news?tmpl=story&u=/dowjones/20030313/bs_dowjones/200303131736001097; "Ebbers Reportedly Knew of Fraud," *MSNBC*, Mar. 12, 2003, www.msnbc.com/news/884175.asp; "Effect on Consumer," WorldCom News, http://Worldcomnews.com/effectonconsumer.html (accessed Apr. 3, 2003); "Effect on Investors," WorldCom News, http://Worldcomnews.com/effectoninvestors.html (accessed Apr. 3, 2003); Janet Elliott, "AG Would Have More Investigative Power — Bill Focuses on Integrity in Business," *Houston Chronicle*, Mar. 11, 2003, www.chron.com/cs/CDA/story.hts/metropolitan/1812842; "Enron &

WorldCom Scandals Inspire Movie and National Ethics Scholarship for Students," Yahoo! News, Mar. 12, 2003, http://biz.yahoo.com/prnews/030312/daw022_1.html; "Former WorldCom CEO, CFO Take the Fifth," *eWeek*, July 8, 2002, www.eweek.com/article2/0,3959,362703,00.asp; Charles Gasparino, "Grubman Informed Weill of AT&T Meetings," *Wall Street Journal*, Nov. 15, 2002, pp. C1, C13; "Investment and Litigation," WorldCom News, http://Worldcomnews.com/investmentandlitigation.html (accessed Apr. 3, 2003); Carrie Johnson, "More Guilty Pleas from WorldCom Managers," *Washington Post*, Oct. 11, 2002, http://nl12.newsbank.com/nl-search/we/Archives?p_action=list&p_topdoc=126; "Judge Outlines Budget Plan for WorldCom," Yahoo! News, Mar. 6, 2003, http://story.news.yahoo.com/news?tmpl=story2&cid=509&ncid=509&e=41&u=/ap/20030306/ap_on_bi_ge/worldcom_budget_1; Gina Keating, "U. of Calif. Files $353 Million WorldCom Lawsuit," Yahoo! News, Feb. 13, 2003, http://story.news.yahoo.com/news?tmpl=story&u=/nm/20030213/tc_nm/telecoms_worldcom_lawsuit_dc_1; Peter Kennedy, "WorldCom Puts Ebbers' B.C. Ranch Up for Sale," *Globe and Mail*, Jan. 28, 2003, p. B5, http://www.globeandmail.com/servlet/ArticleNews/PEstory/TGAM/20030128/RANCH/Headlines/headdex/headdexBusiness_temp/52/52/58/; Stephanie Kirchgaessner, "WorldCom Mulls Further $16Bn Write-off," Yahoo! News, Jan. 30, 2003, http://story.news.yahoo.com/news?tmpl=story2&cid=1106&ncid=1106&e=5&u=/ft/20030130/bs_ft/1042491347715; Matt Krantz, "Capitalizing on the Oldest Trick in Book: How WorldCom, and Others, Fudged Results," *USA Today*, June 27, 2002, www.usatoday.com/tech/techinvestor/2002/06/27/worldcom-whatdo.htm; Adam Lahinsky, "WorldCom: Picking Up the Pieces," *Business 2.0*, May 2, 2002, www.business2.com/articles/web/print/0,1650,40140,FF.html; Joseph McCafferty, "Scott Sullivan," *CFO Magazine*, Sept. 1998, www.findarticles.com/cf_0/m3870/n9_v14/21119225/print.jhtml; Jack McCarthy, "WorldCom Woes," *InfoWorld*, Aug. 2, 2002, www.infoworld.com/article/02/08/02/020805cttelco_1.html; Stephanie Mehata, "Birds of a Feather," *Fortune*, Oct. 2002, www.business2.com/articles/mag/print/0,1643,43957,00.html; Adrian Michaels, "SEC Extends Charges Against WorldCom," *Financial Times*, Nov. 6, 2002, http://news.ft.com/servlet/ContentServer?pagename=Synd/StoryFT/FTFull&artid=10358730; Susan Pulliam, "Ordered to Commit Fraud, A Staffer Balked, Then Caved," *Wall Street Journal*, June 23, 2003, http://online.wsj.com; Amanda Ripley, "The Night Detective," *Time*, Dec. 22, 2002, www.time.com/time/personoftheyear/2002/poycooper.html; Simon Romero, "WorldCom to Write Down $79.8 Billion of Good Will," *New York Times*, Mar. 14, 2003, www.nytimes.com/2003/03/14/technology/14TELE.html; Mathew Secker, "WorldCom. (Company Operations)," *Telecommunications*, Mar. 2001, www.mobilepaymentforum.org/pdfs/TelecommunicationsIntlEd.pdf; Ben Silverman, "WorldCom Waits for Blame Game," *New York Post*, Mar. 10, 2003, www.nypost.com/business/70283.htm; Christopher Stern, "6 Resign from WorldCom Board," *Washington Post*, Dec. 18, 2002, p. E04, http://www.washingtonpost.com/ac2/wp-dyn?pagename=article&node=&contentId=A3966-2002Dec17&notFound=true; Christopher Stern, "Cost-Cutting World Com Considers More Layoffs," *Washington Post*, Feb. 2, 2003, p. A02, www.washingtonpost.com/ac2/wp-dyn?pagename=article&node=&contentId=A16324-2003Feb2&notFound=true; David Teather, "Former WorldCom Controller Admits Fraudulent Entries," *The Guardian*, Sept. 27, 2002; David Teather, "To Ebber's Wedding, on Expenses," *The Guardian*, Aug. 30, 2002; Steven Titch, "Deconstructing WorldCom: A Revealing Autopsy of the 1998 Mega-Merger," *America's Network*, May 1, 2001, www.findarticles.com/cf_0/m0DUJ/6_105/74651470/print.jhtml; John Van and Michael Oneal, "$750 Million WorldCom Settlement Is Approved," *Austin American-Statesman*, July 8, 2003, http://statesman.com; Lingling Wei, "More WorldCom Restatements?" *Wall Street Journal*, Nov. 4, 2002, http://www.msnbc.com/news/83048.asp; "Who Is to Blame?" WorldCom News, http://Worldcomnews.com/whoistoblame.html (accessed Apr. 3, 2003); "WorldCom Announces Its Post-Restructuring Management Plan," WorldCom, press release, Sept. 10, 2002, www1.worldcom.com/infodesk/news/news2.xml?newsid= 4392&mode=long&lang=e; "WorldCom Finances," WorldCom News, http://Worldcomnews.com/worldcomfinances.html (accessed Apr. 3, 2003); "WorldCom Issues July and August 2002 Operating Results," WorldCom, press release, Oct. 22, 2002, www.worldcom.com/global/about/news/news2.xml? newsid=4870&mode=long&lang=en&width=530&root=global/about/; "WorldCom's Latest Development," *CNN/Money*, Nov. 11, 2002, www.cnnmoney.printthis.clickability.com/pt/cpt?action=cpt&expire=urlID=4580252&fb; "WorldCom Milestones," *Washington Post*, Aug. 9, 2002, www.washingtonpost.com/ac2/wp-dyn/A49156-2002Jun26?language=printer; "WorldCom Report Suggests Ebbers Knew of Accounting Fraud," Quicken Brokerage, Mar. 12, 2003, www.quicken.com/investments/news_center/story/?story=NewsStory/dowJones/20030312/ON2003031204 06000594.var&column=P0DFP; "World Com Report Suggests Ebbers Knew of Fraud," *Forbes*, Mar. 12, 2003, www.forbes.com/technology/newswire/2003/03/12/rtr904375.html; "WorldCom Revised Statement Pursuant to Section 21 (a)(1) of the Securities Exchange Act of 1934," Securities and Exchange Commission, July 8, 2002, www.sec. gov/news/extra/wcresponserv.htm; "WorldCom, SEC to Settle Charges," *CNN*, Nov. 5, 2002, www.cnn.com/2002/BUSINESS/11/05/worldcom.reut/index.html; "WorldCom to Cut 2,000 Jobs," *CNN*, Sep. 16, 2002, www.cnn.com/2002/BUSINESS/09/16/worldcom/index.html.

# Case 5

# Arthur Andersen: Questionable Accounting Practices[1]

Arthur Andersen LLP was founded in Chicago in 1913 by Arthur Andersen and partner Clarence DeLany. Over a span of nearly ninety years, the Chicago accounting firm would become known as one of the "Big Five" largest accounting firms in the United States, together with Deloitte & Touche, PricewaterhouseCoopers, Ernst & Young, and KPMG. For most of those years, the firm's name was nearly synonymous with trust, integrity, and ethics. Such values are crucial for a firm charged with independently auditing and confirming the financial statements of public corporations, whose accuracy investors depend on for investment decisions.

In its earlier days, Andersen set standards for the accounting profession and advanced new initiatives on the strength of its then undeniable integrity. One example of Andersen's leadership in the profession occurred in the late 1970s when companies began acquiring IBM's new 360 mainframe computer system, the most expensive new computer technology available at the time. Many companies had been depreciating computer hardware on the basis of an assumed ten-year useful life. Andersen, under the leadership of Leonard Spacek, determined that a more realistic life span for the machines was five years. Andersen therefore advised its accounting clients to use the shorter time period for depreciation purposes, although this resulted in higher expenses charged against income and a smaller bottom line. Public corporations that failed to adopt the more conservative measure would receive an "adverse" opinion from Andersen's auditors, something they could ill afford.

Arthur Andersen once exemplified the rock-solid character and integrity that was synonymous with the accounting profession. But high-profile bankruptcies of clients such as Enron and WorldCom capped a string of accounting scandals that eventually cost investors nearly $300 billion and hundreds of thousands of people their jobs. As a result, the Chicago-based accounting firm was forced to close its doors after ninety years of business.

---

[1] This case was prepared by Heather Stein, Colorado State University, for classroom discussion, rather than to illustrate either effective or ineffective handling of an administrative, ethical, or legal decision by management.

## The Advent of Consulting

Leonard Spacek joined the company in 1947 following the death of founder Arthur Andersen. He was perhaps best known for his uncompromising insistence on auditor independence, which was in stark contrast to the philosophy of combining auditing and consulting services that many firms, including Andersen itself, later adopted. Andersen began providing consulting services to large clients such as General Electric and Schlitz Brewing in the 1950s. Over the next thirty years, Andersen's consulting business became more profitable per partner than its core accounting and tax services businesses.

According to the American Institute of Certified Public Accountants (AICPA), the objective of an independent audit of a client's financial statements is "the expression of an opinion on the fairness with which [the financial statements] present, in all material respects, financial position, results of operations, and its cash flows in conformity with generally accepted accounting principles." The primary responsibility of an auditor is to express an opinion on a client firm's financial statements after conducting an audit to obtain reasonable assurance that the client's financial statements are free of material misstatement. It is important to note that financial statements are the responsibility of a company's management and not the outside auditor.

At Andersen, growth became the priority, and its emphasis on recruiting and retaining big clients perhaps came at the expense of quality and independent audits. The company linked its consulting business in a joint cooperative relationship with its audit arm, which compromised its auditors' independence, a quality crucial to the execution of a credible audit. The firm's focus on growth also generated a fundamental change in its corporate culture, one in which obtaining high-profit consulting business seems to have been regarded more highly than providing objective auditing services. Those individuals who could deliver the big accounts were often promoted ahead of the practitioners of quality audits.

Andersen's consulting business became recognized as one of the fastest-growing and most profitable consulting networks in the world. Revenues from consulting began catching up with the auditing unit in the early 1980s, and surpassed them for the first time in 1984. Although Andersen's consulting business was growing at a rapid pace, its audit practice remained the company's bread and butter. Ten years later, Arthur Andersen merged its operational and business systems consulting units and set up a separate business consulting practice in order to offer clients a broader range of integrated services. Throughout the 1990s, Andersen reaped huge profits by selling consulting services to many clients whose financial statements it also audited. This lucrative full-service strategy would later pose an ethical dilemma for some Andersen partners, who had to decide how to treat questionable accounting practices discovered at some of Andersen's largest clients.

Thanks to the growth of Andersen's consulting services, many viewed it as a successful model that other large accounting firms should emulate. However, this same model eventually raised alarm bells at the Securities and Exchange Commission (SEC), concerned over its potential for compromising the independence of audits. In 1998, then SEC chairman Arthur Levitt publicly voiced these concerns and recommended new rules that would restrict the nonaudit services that accounting firms could provide to their audit clients—a suggestion that Andersen vehemently opposed.

Nonetheless, in 1999 Andersen chose to split its accounting and consulting function into two separate—and often competing—units. Reportedly, under this arrangement, competition between the two units for accounts tended to discourage a team spirit and instead fostered secrecy and selfishness. Communication suffered, hampering the firm's ability to respond quickly and effectively to crises. As revenues grew, the consulting unit demanded greater compensation and recognition. Infighting between the consulting and auditing units grew until the company was essentially split into two opposing factions.

In August 2000, following an arbitration hearing, a judge ruled that Andersen's consulting arm could effectively divorce the accounting firm and operate independently. By that time, Andersen's consulting business consisted of about eleven thousand consultants and brought in global revenues of nearly $2 billion. Arthur Andersen as a whole employed more than eighty-five thousand people worldwide. The new consulting company promptly changed its name to Accenture the following January. The court later ordered Arthur Andersen to change its name to Andersen Worldwide in order to better represent its new global brand of accounting services.

Meanwhile, in January 2001 Andersen named Joseph Berardino as the new CEO of the U.S. audit practice. His first task was to navigate the smaller company through a number of lawsuits that had developed in prior years. The company paid $110 million in May 2001 to settle claims brought by Sunbeam shareholders for accounting irregularities and $100 million to settle with Waste Management shareholders over similar charges a month later. In the meantime, news that Enron had overstated earnings became public, sending shock waves through the financial markets. Over the following year, many companies, a number of them Andersen clients, were forced to restate earnings. The following sections describe a few of the cases that helped lead to Andersen's collapse.

## Baptist Foundation of Arizona

In what would become the largest bankruptcy of a nonprofit charity in U.S history, the Baptist Foundation of Arizona (BFA), which Andersen served as auditor, bilked investors out of about $570 million. BFA, an agency of the Arizona Southern Baptist Convention, was founded in 1948 to raise and manage endowments for church work in Arizona. It operated like a bank, paying interest on deposits that were used mostly to invest in Arizona real estate. The foundation also offered estate and financial planning services to the state's more than four hundred Southern Baptist churches, and was one of the few foundations to offer investments to individuals.

BFA invested heavily in real estate, a more speculative investment strategy than other Baptist foundations in the state traditionally used. Profits from investments were supposed to be used to fund the churches' ministries and numerous charitable causes. Problems began when the real estate market in Arizona suffered a downturn, and BFA's management came under pressure to show a profit. To do so, foundation officials allegedly concealed losses from investors beginning in 1986 by selling some properties at inflated prices to entities that had borrowed money from the foundation and were unlikely to pay for the properties unless the real estate market turned around. In what court documents would later label a "Ponzi scheme" after a famous swindling case, foundation officials allegedly took money from new investors to pay off existing investors in order to keep cash flowing. In the meantime, the foundation's top officers received six-figure salaries. With obligations to investors mounting, the scheme eventually unraveled, leading to criminal investigations and investor lawsuits against BFA and Andersen; more than half of the foundation's 133 employees were laid off. Finally, the foundation petitioned for Chapter 11 bankruptcy protection in 1999, listing debts of about $640 million against assets of about $240 million.

The investor lawsuit against Andersen accused the auditing firm of issuing false and misleading approvals of BFA's financial statements, which allowed the foundation to perpetuate the fraud. Andersen, in a February 2000 statement, responded that it sympathized with BFA investors but stood by the accuracy of its audit opinions. The firm blamed BFA management for the collapse, arguing that it was given misleading information on which to conduct the audits. However, during nearly two years of investigation, reports surfaced that Andersen had been warned of possible fraudulent activity by some BFA employees, and the firm eventually agreed to pay $217 million to settle the shareholder lawsuit in May 2002.

## Sunbeam

Andersen's troubles over Sunbeam Corp. began when its audits failed to address serious accounting errors that eventually led to a class-action lawsuit by Sunbeam investors and the ouster of CEO Albert Dunlap in 1998. Boca Raton-based Sunbeam is the maker of such notable home appliance brands as Mr. Coffee, Mixmaster, Oster, Powermate, and others. Both the lawsuit and a civil injunction filed by the SEC accused Sunbeam of inflating earnings through fraudulent accounting strategies such as "cookie jar" revenues, recording revenue on contingent sales, and accelerating sales from later periods into the present quarter. The company was also accused of using improper "bill and hold" transactions, which involves booking sales months ahead of actual shipment or billing, temporarily inflating revenue through accounts receivable, and artificially boosting quarterly net income. As a result, Sunbeam was forced to restate six quarters of financial statements. The SEC's injunction also accused Phillip Harlow, then a partner at Arthur Andersen, of authorizing clean or "unqualified" opinions on Sunbeam's 1996 and 1997 financial statements despite his awareness of many of Sunbeam's accounting and disclosure improprieties.

In August 2002, a federal judge approved a $141 million settlement in the case. In it, Andersen agreed to pay $110 million to resolve the claims without admitting fault or liability. As of this writing, losses to Sunbeam shareholders have amounted to about $4.4 billion and job losses have totaled about 1,700.

## Waste Management

Andersen also found itself in court over questionable accounting practices with regard to $1.4 billion of overstated earnings at Waste Management. A complaint filed by the SEC charged Waste Management with perpetrating a "massive" financial fraud over a period of more than five years. According to the complaint, the company's senior management itself violated and aided and abetted others' violations of antifraud, reporting, and recordkeeping provisions of federal securities laws, resulting in a loss to investors of more than $6 billion. Andersen was named in the case as having aided the fraud by repeatedly issuing unqualified audit opinions on Waste Management's materially misleading financial statements.

According to SEC documents, Waste Management capped the amount of fees it would pay for Andersen's auditing services, but it advised Andersen that it could earn additional fees through "special work." At first, Andersen identified improper accounting practices and presented them to Waste Management officials in a report called "Proposed Adjusting Journal Entries," which outlined entries that needed to be corrected to avoid understating Waste Management's expenses and overstating its earnings. However, Waste officials refused to make the corrections, and instead allegedly entered into a closed-door agreement with Andersen to write off the accumulated errors over a ten-year period and change its underlying accounting practices, but only in future periods. The SEC viewed this agreement as an attempt to cover up past frauds and to commit future frauds.

The result of these cases was that Andersen paid some $220 million to Waste Management shareholders and $7 million to the SEC. Four Andersen partners were sanctioned, and an injunction was obtained against the firm. Andersen, as part of its consent decree, was forced to promise not to sign off on spurious financial statements in the future or it would face disbarment from practicing before the SEC—a promise that it would later break with Enron. After the dust settled, Waste Management shareholders lost about $20.5 billion and about eleven thousand employees were laid off.

## Enron

In October 2001, the Securities and Exchange Commission announced that it was launching an investigation into the accounting of Enron, one of Andersen's biggest clients. Indeed, Andersen's new CEO, Joseph Berardino, had perhaps viewed the $1 million a week in audit fees Enron paid to Andersen, along with the consulting fees it paid to Andersen's spin-off firm, Accenture, as a significant opportunity to expand revenues at Andersen. And, with Enron as a client, Andersen had been able to make 80 percent of the companies in the oil and gas industry its clients. However, on November 8, 2001, Enron was forced to restate five years worth of financial statements that Andersen had signed off on, accounting for $586 million in losses. Within a month, Enron filed for bankruptcy. The U.S. Justice Department began a criminal investigation into Andersen in January 2002, prompting both Andersen's clients and its employees to jump ship. The auditing firm eventually admitted to destroying a number of documents concerning its auditing of Enron, which led to an indictment for obstruction of justice on March 14, 2002. CEO Bernardino stepped down by the end of the month.

As Andersen's obstruction-of-justice trial progressed, Nancy Temple, Andersen's Chicago-based lawyer, demanded Fifth Amendment protection and thus did not have to testify. Many others named her as the "corrupt persuader" who led others astray. She allegedly instructed David Duncan, Andersen's supervisor of the Enron account, to remove her name from memos that could have incriminated her. On June 15, 2002, the jury found Andersen guilty of obstruction of justice, the first accounting firm ever to be convicted of a felony. The company agreed to stop auditing public companies by August 31, 2002, essentially shutting down the business.

## Trouble with Telecoms

Unfortunately for Andersen, the accusations of accounting fraud did not end with Enron. News soon surfaced that WorldCom, Andersen's largest client, had improperly accounted for nearly $3.9 billion of expenses and had overstated earnings in 2001 and the first part of 2002. After WorldCom restated its earnings, its stock price plummeted, and investors launched a barrage of lawsuits that sent the telecom into bankruptcy court. WorldCom's bankruptcy filing eclipsed Enron's as the largest in U.S. history. Andersen blamed WorldCom for the scandal, insisting that the expense irregularities had not been disclosed to its auditors and that it had complied with SEC standards in its auditing of WorldCom. WorldCom, however, pointed the finger of blame not only at its former managers but also at Andersen for failing to find the accounting irregularities. The SEC filed fraud charges against WorldCom, which fired its CFO.

While the Enron and WorldCom scandals continued, more telecommunications firms, including Global Crossing and Qwest Communications, came under investigation for alleged accounting improprieties. Both firms had been issued unqualified or clean opinions on audits by Andersen. At the heart of both cases is the issue of fake asset swaps, in which the accused telecom companies allegedly exchanged fiber-optic broadband capacity at inflated prices in order to show huge gains. An investor lawsuit was filed against Global Crossing and Andersen alleging that Global Crossing had artificially inflated earnings and that Andersen had violated federal securities laws by issuing unqualified (positive) audit opinions on Global Crossing's financial statements, though it knew or failed to discover they contained material misstatements. Global Crossing filed for Chapter 11 bankruptcy protection and fired Andersen as its auditor. Qwest, which thus far has avoided bankruptcy court, admitted to using improper accounting methods and will likely be forced to restate profits for 1999, 2000, and 2001, including $950 million in relation to the swaps and up to $531 million in cash sales of optical capacity.

## Corporate Culture and Ethical Ramifications

As the details of these investigations into accounting irregularities and fraud came to light, it became apparent that Andersen was more concerned about its own revenue growth than where the revenue came from or whether its independence as an auditor had been compromised. One of the reasons for this confusion in its corporate culture may have been that numerous inexperienced business consultants and untrained auditors were sent to client sites who were largely ignorant of company policies. Another factor may have been its partners' limited involvement in the process of issuing opinions. As the company grew, the number of partners stagnated. There is also evidence that Andersen had limited oversight over its audit teams and that such visibility was impaired by a relative lack of checks and balances that could have identified when audit teams had strayed from accepted policies. Audit teams had great discretion in terms of issuing financials and restatements.

In February 2002, Andersen hired former Federal Reserve Board chairman Paul Volcker to institute reform and help restore its reputation. Soon after Volcker came on board, however, Andersen was indicted for obstruction of justice in connection with the shredding of Enron documents. During the investigations, Andersen had been trying to negotiate merger deals for its international partnerships and salvage what was left of its U.S operations. But amid a mass exodus of clients and partners and the resignation of Berardino, the company was forced to begin selling off various business units, and ultimately laid off more than seven thousand employees in the United States.

During this time, Alaska Air Group, an Andersen client, restated its 2001 results, which resulted in an *increase* in shareholder equity of $31 million. Alaska Air made the restatement on the recommendation of its new auditor, Deloitte and Touche, which had replaced Andersen in May 2002.

After Andersen was convicted of obstruction of justice, it was fined $500,000, among other penalties. Andersen agreed to cease auditing public corporations by the end of August, essentially marking the end of the ninety-year-old accounting institution. Accenture, its spin-off consulting unit, is free and clear of all charges, although the consulting firm seems reluctant to mention its origins and association with Andersen: nowhere on Accenture's Web site is the word *Andersen* to be found.

## Implications for Regulation and Accounting Ethics

The accounting scandals of the early twenty-first century sent many Andersen clients into bankruptcy court and subjected even more to greater scrutiny. They also helped spur a new focus on business ethics, driven largely by public demands for greater corporate transparency and accountability. In response, Congress passed the Sarbanes-Oxley Act of 2002, which established new guidelines and direction for corporate and accounting responsibility. The act was enacted to combat securities and accounting fraud and includes, among other things, provisions for a new accounting oversight board, stiffer penalties for violators, and higher standards of corporate governance. Table C5–1 discusses some of the components of the act and how it could prevent these types of situations from occurring again.

For the accounting profession, Sarbanes-Oxley emphasizes auditor independence and quality, restricts accounting firms' ability to provide both audit and nonaudit services for the same clients, and requires periodic reviews of audit firms. All are provisions that the Arthur Andersen of the past would likely have supported wholeheartedly. Some are concerned, however, that such sweeping legislative and regulatory reform may be occurring too quickly in response to intense public and political pressure. The worry is that these reforms may not have been given enough forethought and cost-benefit consideration for those public corporations that operate within the law, which comprise the vast majority of corporate America.

| TABLE C5-1 | Sarbanes-Oxley Act Intended to Prevent Accounting Misconduct |
|---|---|

| SARBANES-OXLEY ACT | WHAT IT WILL DO | WHAT IT COULD PREVENT |
|---|---|---|
| **Section 104:** Inspection of Registered Public Accounting Firms | Verify that financial statements are accurate | Use of questionable/illegal accounting practices |
| **Section 201:** Services Outside the Scope of Auditors; Prohibited Activities | Restrict auditors to audit activities only | Improper relationships, reduce likelihood of compromising good audit for more revenue |
| **Section 203:** Audit Partner Rotation | Rotate partners assigned to client, so fresh eyes see work papers | "Partner in Crime" relationship |
| **Section 204:** Auditor Reports to Audit Committees | Auditors must report to committee,who work for the board, not the company | Powerlessness of auditors by giving board power to investigate and rectify |
| **Section 302:** Corporate Responsibility for Financial Reports | Making executive personally liable for ensuring that statements are reported accurately | Companies from publishing misleading statements |
| **Section 303:** Improper Influence on Conduct of Audits | Removes power from company personnel | Withholding of information from auditors by making this illegal |
| **Section 404:** Management Assessment of Internal Controls | Gives auditor a voice outside of the audit to attest to policies demonstrated by the company | Information slipping by the SEC and stakeholders by giving more visibility to the firm |
| **Title VIII:** Corporate and Criminal Fraud Accountability Act of 2002 | Makes it a felony to impede federal investigation, provides whistle-blower protection | Destruction of documents, will allow investigators to review work of auditors |
| **Section 1102:** Tampering with a Record or Otherwise Impeding an Official Proceeding | Persons acting to corrupt or destroy evidence liable for extended prison term | Others from attempting to interfere in an official investigation |

Source: Table adapted from Mandy Storeim, *Andersen LLP: An Assessment of the Company's Dilemmas in Corporate Crisis*, BG660 Final Project, Colorado State University, Nov. 13, 2002.

*Questions*

1. Describe the legal and ethical issues surrounding Andersen's auditing of companies accused of accounting improprieties.
2. What evidence is there that Andersen's corporate culture contributed to its downfall?
3. How can the provisions of the Sarbanes-Oxley Act help minimize the likelihood of auditors failing to identify accounting irregularities?

Sources: These facts are from "$141M Sunbeam Fraud Case Settled; Andersen to Pay Bulk," New York State Society of Certified Public Accountants, Aug. 9, 2002, http://nysscpa.org/home/2002/802/ 1week/article58.htm; "Alaska Air Restatement Adds Shareholder Value," *Seattle Times*, Jan. 11, 2003, p. C1; "Andersen's Fall from Grace," BBC News, June 17, 2002, www.news.bbc.co.uk/1/hi/business/ 2049237.stm; John A. Byrne, "Fall from Grace," *Business Week*, Aug. 12, 2002, pp. 50–56; Nanette

Byrnes, Mike McNamee, Diane Brady, Louis Lavelle, Christopher Palmeri, et al., "Accounting in Crisis," *Business Week,* Jan. 28, 2002, pp. 44–48; Dave Carpenter, "Andersen's WorldCom Story Familiar to Enron Excuse," *Houston Chronicle,* June 27, 2002, www.chron.com/cs/CDA/printstory.hts/special/andersen/1474232; "The Fall of Andersen," *Chicago Tribune,* Sept. 1, 2002, www.chicagotribune.com/business/showcase/chi-0209010315sep01.story; Greg Farrell, "Jury Will Hear of Andersen's Past Scandals," *USA Today,* May 8, 2003, www.usatoday.com/money/energy/enron/2002-05-07-andersen-trial.htm; "First Trial of Arizona Baptist Foundation Case Starts This Week," *Baptist Standard,* Mar. 4, 2002, http://baptiststandard.com/2002/3_4/print/arizona.html; Jonathan D. Glater, "Auditor to Pay $217 Million to Settle Suits," *Yahoo News,* Mar. 2, 2002, http://premium.news.yahoo.com/news?tmpl=story&u=/nytp/20020302/880914; "Global Crossing Drops Andersen; Being Investigated by FBI, SEC," New York State Society of Certified Public Accountants, Feb. 2, 2002, www.nysscpa.org/home/2002/202/1week/ article45.htm; Floyd Norris, "$217 Million New Settlement by Andersen in Baptist Case," Yahoo News, May 7, 2002, http://premium.news.yahoo.com/news?tmpl=story&u=/nytp/20020507/918059; Bruce Nussbaum, "Can You Trust Anybody Anymore?" *Business Week,* January 28, 2002, pp. 31–32; Barbara Powell, "Bankrupt WorldCom Says Financial Woes Persisting," *Yahoo News,* Oct. 22, 2002, http://story.news.yahoo.com/news?tmpl=story&u=/ap/20021022/ap_wo_en_po/us_worldcom_110/27/02; "Q&A: What Now for Andersen?" *BBC News,* June 16, 2002, http://news.bbc.co.uk/1/hi/business/2048325.stm; "Qwest Admits Improper Accounts," *BBC News,* July 29, 2002, http://news.bbc.co.uk/2/hi/business/2158135.stm; David Schepp, "Analysis: Verdict Signals Andersen's End," *BBC News,* June 15, 2002, http://news.bbc.co.uk/1/hi/business/2047381.stm; "SEC Sues Former CEO, CFO, Other Top Officers of Sunbeam Corporation in Massive Financial Fraud," U.S. Securities and Exchange Commission, May 15, 2001, www.sec.gov/news/headlines/sunbeamfraud.htm; Stephen Taub, "Andersen Pays $110 Million in Sunbeam Settlement," *CFO.com,* May 2, 2001, www.cfo.com/printarticle/0,53172947,/A,00.html; "Telecoms Bosses Deny 'Fake' Swap Deals," *BBC News,* Oct. 1, 2002, http://news.bbc.co.uk/2/hi/business/2290679.stm; Kathy Booth Thomas, "Called to Account," *Time,* June 18, 2002, pp. 43–45; "Waste Management Founder, Five Other Former Top Officers Sued for Massive Fraud," U.S. Securities and Exchange Commission, Mar. 26, 2002, www.sec.gov/news/headlines/wastemgmt6.htm; "WorldCom, Andersen Play Blame Game," *USA Today,* July 8, 2002, www.usatoday.com/money/telecom/2002-07-08-worldcom-hearings-ap.htm; "WorldCom Revelations Another Mark Against Andersen," *Atlanta Journal-Constitution,* June 27, 2002, www.accessatlanta.com/ajc/business/0602/worldcom/27andersen.html; Wendy Zellner, Stephanie Forest Anderson, and Laura Cohn, "A Hero—And a Smoking-Gun Letter," *Business Week,* Jan. 28, 2002, pp. 34–35.

# Case 6

# Sunbeam Corporation: "Chainsaw Al" and Greed[1]

W hen John Stewart and Thomas Clark founded the Chicago Flexible Shaft Company in Dundee, Illinois, in 1897 they probably never expected that their fledgling company would grow into a huge conglomerate and face ethical and financial dilemmas more than a hundred years later. Like many corporations, the firm has changed and faced many crises. It has changed its name several times, acquired rival companies, added totally new product lines, gone through bankruptcy, rebounded, restructured, relocated, and hired and fired many CEOs, including "Chainsaw Al" Dunlap. Today, Sunbeam has grown into a well-known designer, manufacturer, and marketer of consumer products used for cooking, health care, and personal care. A few of the most recognized brand names owned by Sunbeam include Coleman, First Alert, Grillmaster, Health-O-Meter, Mixmaster, Mr. Coffee, Oster, Osterizer, Powermate, and Campingaz.

## More Than One Hundred Years of Change

The first products that Sunbeam manufactured and sold were agricultural tools. In 1910 the company began manufacturing electrical appliances, one of the first being a clothes iron. At that time, Stewart and Clark began using the name Sunbeam in advertising campaigns, although the company would not officially change its name to the Sunbeam Corporation until 1946. Sunbeam's electric products sold well even during the Great Depression of the 1930s when housewives throughout the country quickly accepted the Sunbeam Mixmaster, automatic coffee maker, and pop-up toaster. The years following the Great Depression were times of growth and innovation for Sunbeam. The next major development came in 1960 when Sunbeam acquired rival appliance maker John Oster Manufacturing Company, which helped make Sunbeam the leading manufacturer of electric appliances.

During the 1980s, a period of relatively high inflation and interest rates, corporations were going through acquisitions, mergers, restructurings, and closings—doing whatever they could to continue operating profitably. In 1981 Sunbeam was acquired by Allegheny International, an industrial conglomerate. Allegheny retained the Sun-

[1] This case was prepared by Carol A. Rustad and Linda E. Rustad for classroom discussion, rather than to illustrate either effective or ineffective handling of an administrative, ethical, or legal decision by management. It is reprinted with the author's permission.

beam name and added John Zink (air-pollution control devices) and Hanson Scale (bathroom scales) to the Sunbeam product line. After sales of other divisions of Allegheny International declined, the company was forced into bankruptcy in 1988.

In 1990 investors Michael Price, Michael Steinhardt, and Paul Kazarian bought the Sunbeam division from Allegheny International's creditors. They renamed the division the Sunbeam-Oster Company and took it public two years later. The following year, Kazarian was forced out of his chairman position and out of the company. Sunbeam-Oster also relocated to Florida and purchased the consumer products unit of DeVilbiss Health Care. In 1994 Sunbeam-Oster acquired Rubbermaid's outdoor furniture business. The company changed its name back to Sunbeam Corporation in 1995.

By the time Albert Dunlap took over the company in 1996, Sunbeam had more than twelve thousand stock-keeping units (SKUs or individual variations of its product lines). The company also had twelve thousand employees, as well as twenty-six factories worldwide, sixty-one warehouses, and six headquarters. Its earnings had been declining since December 1994, and by 1996 the stock was down 52 percent and its earnings had declined by 83 percent. The company needed help.

## Albert Dunlap, A.K.A. "Chainsaw Al"

Before taking the reins at Sunbeam, Dunlap had acquired a reputation as one of the country's toughest executives—as well as nicknames like "Chainsaw Al," "Rambo in Pinstripes," and "The Shredder"—because he eliminated thousands of jobs while restructuring and turning around financially troubled companies. His reputation and business philosophy were recognized throughout the world. His operating philosophy was to make extreme cuts in all areas of operations, including extensive layoffs, so as to streamline a business and return it to profitability. He even authored a book, entitled *Mean Business,* in which he stressed that the most important goal of any business is making money for shareholders. To achieve this goal, Dunlap developed four simple rules of business: (1) get the right management team, (2) cut back to the lowest costs, (3) focus on the core business, and (4) get a real strategy. By following those four rules, Dunlap helped turn around companies in seventeen states and across three continents, including—according to Dunlap—Sterling Pulp & Paper, American Can, Lily-Tulip, Diamond International, Canenham Forest Industries (formerly Crown-Zellerback), Australian National Industries, Consolidated Press Holdings, and Scott Paper Company.

Michael Price and Michael Steinhardt hired Dunlap as the CEO and chairman of the board for Sunbeam Corporation in July 1996. Price and Steinhardt, two of the original investors who had bought Sunbeam from bankrupt Allegheny International and together owned 42 percent of the stock, had originally tried to sell Sunbeam. Unsuccessful in that effort, they decided to see if "Chainsaw Al" could save their company, although they well knew Dunlap's reputation for extensive layoffs and huge operating cuts. They believed, however, that such drastic efforts were necessary to turn Sunbeam around and increase stock prices and profits.

In fact, Sunbeam's stock price did increase, almost instantly, vaulting 49 percent on July 19, 1996, the day Dunlap was named chairman and CEO. The rise from $12 1/2 to $18 5/8 added $500 million to Sunbeam's market value. The stock continued to increase, reaching a record high of $52 per share in March 1998. Although Dunlap's acceptance of the helm at Sunbeam helped boost the company's stock, he realized that his reputation alone would not hold the stock price up and that he needed to start the process of turning Sunbeam around.

## Al's First Step at Sunbeam

In accordance with his management rules, Dunlap's first move at Sunbeam was to get the right management team. His very first hire was Russ Kersh, a former employee of Dunlap, as executive vice president of finance and administration. The new management team also included twenty-five people who had previously worked for Dunlap at various companies. Dunlap saw logic in hiring these people because they had all worked with him and had been successful in past turnarounds. He retained only one senior executive from Sunbeam's old management team. Once this first step had been accomplished, Dunlap and his "Dream Team for Sunbeam" quickly went into action implementing his second rule: cutting back to the lowest costs.

## Second Step: Cut Back

In his book *Mean Business,* Dunlap had written, "Sunbeam's employees wanted a leader and knew things had to change. Employees want stability. Restructuring actually brings stability, because the future is more clear." Sunbeam's employees certainly knew of Dunlap's reputation for slashing jobs. Some would argue, however, that what people want and need is job security, and knowing Dunlap's reputation did not make Sunbeam's employees feel secure. The need for security relates to psychologist Abraham Maslow's hierarchy of needs, which can be applied to employee motivation. According to Maslow, people strive to satisfy five basic needs—physiological, security, social, esteem, and self-actualization—in a hierarchical order. Security needs—second in the hierarchy of needs—relate to protecting oneself from physical and economic harm. At Sunbeam, Dunlap's reputation for layoffs left many employees feeling threatened and insecure.

As expected, after less than four months as the chairman and CEO of Sunbeam, Dunlap announced plans to eliminate half of Sunbeam's twelve thousand employees worldwide. The layoffs affected all levels at Sunbeam. Management and clerical staff positions were cut from 1,529 to 697, and headquarters staff was cut by 60 percent, from 308 to 123 employees. On hearing of Dunlap's layoff plans, U.S. Labor Secretary Robert Reich reportedly remarked, "There is no excuse for treating employees as if they are disposable pieces of equipment." Around the same time the company's share prices rose to the mid-20s, and one of the original investors, Michael Steinhardt, sold his shares and divested himself of his Sunbeam connection altogether.

Another method used by Dunlap to cut back to the lowest costs was to reduce the number of SKUs from twelve thousand to fifteen hundred. When Dunlap took over, Sunbeam had thirty-six variations of styles and colors for one clothes iron. Such variation allows for product differentiation, a common business strategy, but some argued that thirty-six variations of a consumer product such as an iron was unnecessary and costly to maintain. Instead of many product variations, Dunlap pursued service as the area to differentiate Sunbeam from competitors in the appliance business.

Eliminating 10,500 SKUs also enabled Dunlap to close a number of factories and warehouses—another cost-saving method. He disposed of eighteen factories world-wide, reducing their number from twenty-six to eight, and reduced the number of warehouses from sixty-one to eighteen. The layoff of thousands of employees, coupled with the reduction of SKUs, factories, and warehouses meant that fewer headquarter locations would be needed. Thus, Dunlap consolidated Sunbeam's six headquarters into one facility in Delray Beach, Florida—Dunlap's primary residence.

## Steps Three and Four

Once the cost-cutting strategies had been implemented, Dunlap began to practice his third rule: that is, to focus on Sunbeam's core business, which first needed to be defined. Dunlap and his Dream Team defined Sunbeam's core business as electric appliances and appliance-related businesses. They identified five categories surrounding the core business as vital to Sunbeam's success: kitchen appliances, health and home, outdoor cooking, personal care and comfort, and professional products. Any product that did not fit into one of the five categories was sold. Dunlap applied a simple criterion to decide whether to keep or divest a product line. Because he believed firmly that consumers recalled the Sunbeam brand name fondly, he retained any product that related to the Sunbeam brand name. Identifying Sunbeam's core business and paring down to it was the goal in implementing the third rule.

The final of Dunlap's four rules of business called for developing and implementing a real strategy. Dunlap and his team defined Sunbeam's strategy as driving the growth of the company through core business expansions by further differentiating Sunbeam's products from competitors', moving into new geographic areas around the globe, and introducing new products that were linked directly to emerging customer trends as lifestyles evolved around the world. As the first step in implementing this strategy, the company re-engineered electrical appliances to 220 volts so they could be marketed and used internationally. Another step was reclaiming the differentiation between the Oster and Sunbeam lines. Each was designed, packaged, and advertised to target different markets. Oster products were positioned as upscale, higher-end brands and sold at completely different retailers than the Sunbeam lines. The Sunbeam line of products was positioned as an affordable, middle-class brand. Early in 1997 Sunbeam opened ten factory outlet stores to increase brand awareness, sales, and ultimately shareholder wealth. Dunlap made all these changes within seven months of taking up the challenge to turn around Sunbeam. The stock rose to more than $48 per share, a 284 percent increase since July 1996.

## The Turnaround of Sunbeam

Just fifteen months after accepting the position as chairman and CEO, Dunlap issued a press release in October 1997 announcing that the turnaround of Sunbeam was complete and that Morgan Stanley of Stanley Dean Witter & Co. had been hired to find a buyer for Sunbeam. However, according to John A. Byrne in his book *Chainsaw,* "no one was the least bit interested." Byrne also reported that Dunlap misled a journalist into reporting that Philips, a Dutch electronics giant, was interested in purchasing Sunbeam for $50+ per share but that Dunlap wanted $70.

On March 2, 1998, Dunlap announced plans to buy three consumer products companies. Sunbeam acquired 82 percent of Coleman (camping gear) from Ronald Perelman for $2.2 billion. Perelman received a combination of cash and stock, which gave him 14 percent ownership of Sunbeam. Sunbeam also acquired 98.5 percent of Signature Brands (Mr. Coffee) and 95.7 percent of First Alert (smoke and gas alarms) from Thomas Lee for $425 million in cash. Two days after announcing the purchase of the three companies, Sunbeam's stock closed at a record high of $52 a share. With the stock price at an all-time high and 1997 net income reported at $109.4 million, Sunbeam truly seemed to have been turned around—at least on paper.

Dunlap publicly praised himself and his "Dream Team for Sunbeam" for turning around the failing corporation within seven months of taking over. He was so confident in the success of their mission at Sunbeam that he added a complete chapter to his book *Mean Business* titled, "Now There's a Bright Idea. Lesson: Everything You've Read So Far About Restructuring Works. This Chapter Proves It—Again." Dunlap stated that Kersh and a dozen other people tried to dissuade him from taking the Sunbeam job because they were convinced that even he could not save the troubled company. Dunlap had disagreed with them, pointing out that he saw opportunity where others saw the impossible. He mentioned that he did not need to take the position at Sunbeam or with any other company because of his wealth. Dunlap also wrote that the tremendous media attention given to the first edition of his book made it an unofficial handbook for Sunbeam employees and also provided free publicity for the company. A whole section of the chapter recalled how the media arrived in full force to cover the promotional tour and signing of his book. Dunlap also mentioned how strangers, including a Greek Orthodox cleric, praised him and his book, and pointed out that he was at the top of the most admired CEOs list in a survey of business students at U.S. colleges and universities. In the concluding paragraph of the chapter, Dunlap suggested that all CEOs and boards of directors should read his book and use him as a role model in running their companies.

At the time, Dunlap's management philosophy seemed to underlie his success at Sunbeam. He streamlined the company and attained what he considered the most important goal of any business: to make money for shareholders. In February 1998 Sunbeam's board of directors expressed satisfaction with Dunlap's leadership and signed a three-year employment contract with him that included 3.75 million shares of stock.

## Sunbeam's Accounting Practices Raise Questions

Although Dunlap accomplished what he had set out to do at Sunbeam, the shareholder wealth did not last. Nor did the board's satisfaction. Sunbeam again faced tough times—and not because of excessive costs or lack of a strategy. The three purchases that more than doubled Sunbeam's size and helped push the company's stock price to $52 also helped cause a second upheaval and restructuring of Sunbeam. Rumors began surfacing that these purchases had been made to disguise losses through write-offs.

Paine Webber, Inc. analyst Andrew Shore had been following Sunbeam since the day Dunlap was hired. As an analyst, Shore's job was to make educated guesses about investing clients' money in stocks. Thus, he had been scrutinizing Sunbeam's financial statements every quarter and considered Sunbeam's reported levels of inventory for certain items to be unusual for the time of year. For example, he noted massive increases in the sales of electric blankets in the third quarter, although they usually sell well in the fourth quarter. He also observed that sales of grills were high in the fourth quarter, which is an unusual time of year for grills to be sold, and noted that accounts receivable were high. On April 3, 1998, just hours before Sunbeam announced a first-quarter loss of $44.6 million, Shore downgraded his assessment of the stock. By the end of the day Sunbeam's stock prices had fallen 25 percent.

Shore's observations were indeed cause for concern. In fact, Dunlap had been using a "bill-and-hold" strategy with retailers, which boosted Sunbeam's revenue, at least on the balance sheet. A bill-and-hold strategy entails selling products at large discounts to retailers and holding them in third-party warehouses to be delivered at a later date. By booking sales months ahead of the actual shipment or billing, Sunbeam was able to report higher revenues in the form of accounts receivable, which inflated its quarterly earnings. The strategy essentially shifted sales from future quarters to the current one, and in 1997 the strategy helped Dunlap boost Sunbeam's revenues by 18 percent.

The "bill-and-hold" strategy is not illegal and follows the Generally Accepted Accounting Principles (GAAP) of financial reporting. Nevertheless, Sunbeam's shareholders filed lawsuits, alleging that the company had made misleading statements about its finances and deceived them so they would buy Sunbeam's artificially inflated stock. A class-action lawsuit was filed on April 23, 1998, naming both Sunbeam Corporation and CEO Albert Dunlap as defendants. The lawsuit alleged that Sunbeam and Dunlap had violated the Securities and Exchange Act of 1934 by misrepresenting and/or omitting material information concerning the business operations, sales, and sales trends of the company. The lawsuit also alleged that the motivation for artificially inflating the price of the common stock was to enable Sunbeam to complete millions of dollars of debt financing in order to acquire Coleman, First Alert, and Signature Brands. Sunbeam's subsequent reporting of earnings significantly below the original estimate caused a huge drop in its stock.

Dunlap continued to run Sunbeam and the newly purchased companies as if nothing had happened. On May 11, 1998, he tried to reassure two hundred major investors and Wall Street analysts that the first-quarter loss would not be repeated and that Sunbeam would post increased earnings in the second quarter. That same day he announced another 5,100 layoffs at Sunbeam and the acquired companies, possibly to gain back investor confidence and divert attention away from the losses and lawsuits. The tactic failed. The press continued to report on Sunbeam's bill-and-hold strategy and the accounting practices that Dunlap had allegedly used to artificially inflate revenues and profits.

## Chainsaw Al's Reputation Backfires

Dunlap called an impromptu board meeting on June 9, 1998, to address and rebut the reported charges. A partner from Sunbeam's outside auditors, Arthur Andersen

LLP, assured the board that the company's 1997 numbers were in compliance with accounting standards and firmly stood by Arthur Andersen's audit of Sunbeam's financial statements. Robert J. Gluck, the controller at Sunbeam, who was also present at the board meeting, did not counter the auditor's statement. The meeting seemed to be going well until Dunlap was asked if the company would make its projected second-quarter earnings. His response that sales were soft was not what the board expected to hear. Nor was his statement that he had a document in his briefcase outlining a settlement of his contract for his departure from Sunbeam. The document was never reviewed. However, Dunlap's behavior made board members suspicious, which led to an in-depth review of Dunlap's practices.

The review took place during the next four days in the form of personal phone calls and interviews between board members and select employees—without Dunlap's knowledge. A personal conversation with Sunbeam's executive vice president, David Fannin, reportedly revealed that the 1998 second-quarter sales were considerably below Dunlap's forecast and that the company was in crisis. Dunlap had forecast a small increase, but the numbers provided by Fannin indicated that Sunbeam could lose as much as $60 million that quarter. Outside the boardroom and away from Dunlap, controller Robert J. Gluck revealed that the company had tried to do things in accordance with GAAP, but allegedly everything had been pushed to the limit.

These revelations led the board of directors to call an emergency meeting. On Saturday, June 13, 1998, the board of directors, along with Fannin, and a pair of lawyers, discussed the informal findings. They agreed that they had lost confidence in Dunlap and his ability to turn Sunbeam around. The board of directors unanimously agreed that Dunlap had to go and drafted a letter calling for his immediate departure. "Chainsaw Al" was told that same day, in a one-minute conference call, that he was the next person to be cut at Sunbeam.

## Sunbeam Looks Forward

Once again, Sunbeam faced the need to revitalize itself. It was again looking for a new CEO; its stock price had dropped to as low as $10 per share; shareholder lawsuits had been filed; legal action regarding Dunlap's firing was under way; the Securities and Exchange Commission (SEC) was scrutinizing Sunbeam's accounting practices; the audit committee of the board of directors was requiring Sunbeam to restate its audited financial statements of 1997, possibly for 1996, as well as for the first quarter of 1998; and creditors were demanding payment in full. Additionally, on August 24, 1998, Sunbeam announced that it would discontinue a quarterly dividend of $0.01 per share. Shareholder confidence was at an all-time low.

Less than two years after Dunlap was hired, Sunbeam again reorganized and brought in a new senior management team. Jerry W. Levin accepted the position of president and CEO. He outlined a new strategy for Sunbeam focusing on growth through increased product quality and customer service. The plan was to decentralize operations while maintaining centralized support and organizing into three operating groups. Four of the eight plants that were scheduled to be closed under Dunlap's management remained open to ensure consistency of supply. In a press release, Levin outlined his strategy for revitalizing Sunbeam: "Our goal is to increase accountability at the business unit level, and to give our employees the tools they need to build their businesses. We are shifting Sunbeam's focus to increasing quality in products and customer service."

On October 21, 1998, Sunbeam announced that it had signed a memorandum of understanding to settle, subject to court approval, the class-action lawsuit brought by public shareholders of Coleman Co., Inc. The court approved, and on January 6, 2000, Sunbeam completed the acquisition of the publicly held shares of Coleman. The terms of the merger allowed all public stockholders of Coleman to receive $6.44 in cash, 0.5677 of a share of Sunbeam common stock, and 0.381 of a warrant to purchase one share of Sunbeam common stock for each of their shares of Coleman stock.

There were legal ramifications from Dunlap's firing. In an interview on July 9, 1998, Dunlap stated that he intended to challenge Sunbeam's efforts to deny him severance under his contract, although both Dunlap and Sunbeam agreed not to take legal action against each other for a period of six months. Dunlap claimed that his mission was aborted prematurely and that three days after receiving the board of director's support, he was fired without being given a reason. On March 15, 1999, Dunlap filed an arbitration claim against Sunbeam to recover $5.5 million in unpaid salary, $58,000 worth of accrued vacation, and $150,000 in benefits as well as to have his stock options repriced at $7 a share. Additionally, he sued the company for dragging its feet in reimbursing him for more than $1.4 million in legal and accounting fees he had racked up defending himself in lawsuits that alleged securities fraud. Although the board made it clear that they had no intention of paying Dunlap any more money, a judge ruled in his favor in June 1999.

In a letter to the shareholders at the beginning of 1999, Levin stated that Sunbeam had gone back to basics and intensified its focus on its powerful family of brands. He also wrote that the lending banks had extended covenant relief and waivers of past defaults until April 10, 2000. The $1.7 billion credit agreement was extended until April 14, 2000, at which time Sunbeam hoped to have a definitive agreement extending the covenant relief and waivers for an additional year. Sunbeam was required to restate its audited accounting reports. It took auditors four months to unravel the accounting statements from Dunlap's tenure, which were confirmed to be legal—just inaccurate. The 1997 net income was restated from $109.4 million to $38.3 million.

In the meantime, Sunbeam moved forward, creating a new company—Thalia Products, Inc. (Thinking and Linking Intelligent Appliances)—to produce smart appliances and services and to license HLT (home linking technology) to other manufacturers. At the International Housewares show in January 2000, Sunbeam and Thalia introduced nine new products, which automatically network when plugged in and "talk" to each other to coordinate tasks. Such tasks include an alarm clock turning on the coffee pot ten minutes before the alarm goes off—no matter what time it is set for—and an alarm that will ring if water has not been added to the coffee pot. Sunbeam announced on March 23, 2000, that its Thalia Products division had an agreement with Microsoft Corp. to join the Universal Plug and Play (UPnP) Forum, which would further the companies' shared objective of establishing industry-leading standards for home appliance networking.

At this point, CEO Levin still had confidence in Sunbeam's ability to recover. A press release on May 10, 2000, stated that the first-quarter results showed that net sales had increased 3 percent to $539 million and that operating results had narrowed to a loss of $3 million. Levin stated:

> These results, though improved, are not indicative of the value we have created, and will continue to create for Sunbeam's shareholders. Looking forward, we expect operating results to further improve as we execute our long-range strategy that focuses on consumer-oriented new products.

However, on January 25, 2001, Sunbeam announced that it had been notified by the New York Stock Exchange (NYSE) that the company was not in compliance with minimum listing criteria. As a result, the NYSE "de-listed" the company's common stock. This meant that the stock ceased to be traded. The bad news continued when Sunbeam announced on February 6, 2001, that it planned to reorganize under Chapter 11 of the U.S. Bankruptcy Code due to its $3.2 billion in debt, some of which accrued from Dunlap's acquisitions. The company expected no interruption in production or distribution. Senior management committed themselves to remaining in place and leading Sunbeam throughout the bankruptcy process and beyond.

In September 2002, Dunlap agreed to pay $500,000 to settle the SEC's charges that he defrauded investors by inflating sales at Sunbeam so as to make the company more attractive to a prospective buyer. According to the SEC, Sunbeam's accounting practices inflated the company's income by $60 million in 1997, "contributing to the false picture of a rapid turnaround in Sunbeam's financial performance." In settling the charges, Dunlap did not admit or deny any wrongdoing, and agreed never to work as an executive or director of a public corporation again. Dunlap's chief financial officer, Russell Kersh, agreed to the same ban and paid $200,000 to settle the SEC's suit. The month before, Dunlap paid $15 million to settle a class-action lawsuit brought by shareholders with similar allegations. Sunbeam emerged from Chapter 11 bankruptcy proceedings in December 2002 and changed its name to American Household Inc.

*Questions*

1. How did pressures for financial performance contribute to Sunbeam's culture where quarterly sales were manipulated to influence investors?
2. What were Al Dunlap's contributions to the financial and public relations embarrassments at Sunbeam that caused investors and the public to question Sunbeam's integrity?
3. Identify ethical issues that Al Dunlap's management team may have created by adopting a short-run focus on financial performance. What lessons could be learned from the outcome?

---

Sources: These facts are from the Alexander Law Firm, http://defrauded.com/sunbeam.shtml (accessed Sept. 13, 1998); "American Household, Inc.," Hoover's Online, www.hoovers.com/co/capsule/4/ 0,2163,11414,00.html (accessed Apr. 16, 2003); Douglas Bell, "Take Me to Your Leader," *ROB Magazine,* June 10, 2000, www.robmagazine.com/archive/2000ROBfebruary/html/idea_log.html; Martha Brannigan and Ellen Joan Pollock, "Dunlap Offers Tears and a Defense," *Wall Street Journal,* July 9, 1998, p. B1; John A. Byrne, "Chainsaw Al Dunlap Cuts His Last Deal," *Business Week Online,* Sept. 5, 2002, www.businessweek.com/bwdaily/dnflash/sep2002/nf2002095_2847.htm; John A. Byrne, "How Al Dunlap Self-Destructed," *Business Week,* July 6, 1998, pp. 58–65; John A. Byrne, "The Notorious Career of Al

Dunlap in the Era of Profit-at-Any-Price," *Chainsaw* (New York: HarperCollins Publishers, 1999); Albert J. Dunlap and Bob Aldeman, "How I Save Bad Companies and Make Good Companies Great," *Mean Business,* rev. ed. (New York: Simon and Schuster, 1997); "Dunlap and Kersh Resign from Sunbeam Board of Directors," *Company News On-Call,* www.prnewswire.com (accessed Sept. 13, 1998); Daniel Kadlec, "Chainsaw Al Gets the Chop," *Time,* June 29, 1998, http://cgi.pathfinder.com/time/ham...29/business.chainsaw-al-get15.html; "Letter from CEO Jerry W. Levin," Sunbeam, June 10, 2000, www.sunbeam.com; Steve Matthews, "Sunbeam's Ex-CEO Seeks $5.25 Million in Arbitration Claim," *Bloomberg News,* Mar. 15, 1999; Andy Ostmeyer, "'Chainsaw Al' Agrees to Settle Suit," *Joplin Globe,* Jan. 16, 2002, www.joplinglobe.com/archives/2002/020116/regional/story5.html; Andy Ostmeyer, "Sunbeam's Bankruptcy Protection Plan OK'd," *Joplin Globe,* Nov. 27, 2002, www.joplinglobe.com/archives/2002/021127/regional/story2.html; Neil Roland and Judy Mathewson, with Robert Schmidt, "Sunbeam Ex-CEO 'Chainsaw Al' Dunlap Settles SEC Case," *Bloomberg News,* Sept. 4, 2002; Matthew Schifrin, "Chainsaw Al to the Rescue," *Forbes,* Aug. 26, 1996, www.forbes.com/forbes/082696/5805042a.htm; Matthew Schifrin, "The Sunbeam Soap Opera: Chapter 6," *Forbes,* July 6, 1998, pp. 44–45; Matthew Schifrin, "The Unkindest Cuts," *Forbes,* May 4, 1998, www.forbes.com/forbes/98/0504/6109044a. htm; Patricia Sellers, "First: Sunbeam's Investors Draw Their Knives—Exit for Chainsaw?" *Fortune,* June 8, 1998, pp. 30–31; "Sunbeam Announces Eastpak Sale Complete," *PR Newswire,* May 30, 2000, www. prnewswire.com; "Sunbeam Balks at Dunlap's Demand for $5.5 Million," *Naples Daily News,* Mar. 17, 1999; "Sunbeam Completes Acquisition of Coleman Publicly Held Shares," Sunbeam, press release, Jan. 6, 2000, www.sunbeam.com; "Sunbeam Corporation," *Hoover's Online,* www.hoovers.com/premium/profiles/11414.html (accessed Sept. 19, 1998); "Sunbeam Corporation Announces Plan to Reorganize under Chapter 11," Sunbeam, press release, Feb. 6, 2001, www.sunbeam.com/media_room/soc_reorg.htm; "Sunbeam Credit Waivers Extended to April 14, 2000," Apr. 11, 2000, www. prnewswire.com; "Sunbeam Joins Microsoft in the Universal Plug and Play Forum to Establish a 'Universal' Smart Appliance Technology Standard," Sunbeam, press release, Mar. 23, 2000, www.sunbeam.com; "Sunbeam Outlines New Strategy, Organizational Structure, Senior Management Team," *Company News On-Call,* www.prnewswire.com (accessed Sept. 13, 1998); "Sunbeam Reports First Quarter 2000 Results," Sunbeam, press release, May 10, 2000, www.sunbeam.com; "Sunbeam Signs Memorandum of Understanding to Settle Coleman Shareholder Litigation," *PR Newswire,* Oct. 21, 1998, www. prnewswire.com; "Sunbeam to Restate Financial Results," *Company News On-Call,* www.prnewswire.com (accessed Sept. 13, 1998); "Time for Smart Talk Is Over," Sunbeam, press release, Jan. 14, 2000, www.sunbeam.com; "VF To Acquire Eastpak Brand," Sunbeam, press release, Mar. 20, 2000, www. sunbeam.com.

# Case 7

# Martha Stewart: Insider-Trading Scandal[1]

artha Stewart is one of the latest chief executive officers to become embroiled in a widening series of corporate scandals across the United States. She founded Martha Stewart Living Omnimedia Inc., a company with interests in publishing, television, merchandising, electronic commerce, and related international partnerships. Along the way, she became America's most famous homemaker and one of its richest women executives. In late 2001, however, she became the center of headlines, speculations, and eventually a federal investigation and indictment on charges related to her sale of four thousand shares of ImClone stock one day before that firm's stock price plummeted. Although Stewart's case had not come to trial at the time of this writing, the scandal harmed the empire she created in her name.

## Evolution of a Media Empire

Born in 1941, Martha Kostyra grew up in Nutley, New Jersey, in a Polish-American family with six children. During her childhood years, she developed a passion for cooking, gardening, and home keeping. She learned the basics of cooking, baking, canning, and sewing from her mother; her father introduced her to gardening at a very early age. While earning a bachelor's degree in history and architectural history at Barnard College, she worked as a model to pay her tuition. She became Martha Stewart when she married in her sophomore year. Although she became a successful stockbroker on Wall Street, she left to open a gourmet-food shop that later became a catering business in Westport, Connecticut. She used the distinct visual presentations and stylish recipes she developed for her catering business as a source for her first book, the best-selling *Entertaining*, which was first published in 1982.

Stewart's natural business instincts and leadership skills helped her make smart choices as she transformed her small business into a media empire and her name into a well-recognized brand. She joined Kmart as an image and product consultant in 1987, and persuaded the retailer to sell her growing line of products. She eventually became partners with the firm. This partnership helped her gain the capital necessary

[1] This case was prepared by Leyla Baykal and Debbie Thorne McAlister for classroom discussion, rather than to illustrate either effective or ineffective handling of an administrative, ethical, or legal decision by an individual or management. Reprinted with the permission of Debbie Thorne McAlister.

to break free of Time Warner, publisher of her highly successful *Martha Stewart Living* magazine. When Stewart and Time Warner disagreed over her plan to cross-sell and market her publishing, television, merchandising, and Web interests, she used everything she owned to buy back the brand rights of her products and publishing for an estimated $75 million. In 1999, she took her rapidly growing business public. Martha Stewart Living Omnimedia, the company she created, now owns three magazines, a TV and cable program, thirty-four books, a newspaper column, a radio program, a Web site, and a merchandising line, as well as the Martha by Mail catalog business. The company earns 65 percent of its revenues from publishing, and its media properties reach 88 million people a month around the world, which allows Martha Stewart Living Omnimedia to command top advertising rates.

Martha Stewart's successes have been widely recognized. Her television show has won an Emmy, and *Adweek* named her "Publishing Executive of the Year" in 1996. She has been named one of "New York's 100 Most Influential Women in Business" by *Forbes* 400, one of the "50 Most Powerful Women" by *Fortune,* and one of "America's 25 Most Influential People" by *Time.* In 1998, she was the recipient of an Edison Achievement Award from the American Marketing Association, among many other national awards and honors.

Martha Stewart Living Omnimedia is clearly a classic success story: the small catering business transformed into a well-known brand, in the process making its founder synonymous with stylish living and good taste. Even those who have ridiculed Stewart's cheery perfect-housewife image acknowledge her confidence and business acumen. One author commented, "To the degree that her business partners were prepared to help advance the success of Martha Stewart, she was prepared to work with them. To the degree that they got in her way, she was willing to roll right over them." Another admired her hard-working nature by saying, "Anyone who spends more than a few minutes with America's most famous homemaker learns that she is one heck of a juggler."

## The Insider-Trading Scandal

Despite her reputation and business successes, Stewart was indicted in 2003 on criminal charges and faced several civil lawsuits related to her sale of the ImClone stock. Stewart sold the stock on December 27, 2001, one day before the Food and Drug Administration refused to review ImClone System's cancer drug Erbitux; the company's stock tumbled following the FDA's announcement. The scandal also touches a number of other ImClone insiders, including the company's counsel, John Landes, who dumped $2.5 million worth of the company's stock on December 6; Ronald Martell, ImClone's vice president of marketing, who sold $2.1 million worth of company stock on December 11; and four other company executives who cashed in shares between December 12 and December 21.

*Developments in the Scandal.* After learning that FDA would refuse to review Erbitux, Sam Waksal, the CEO of ImClone and a close friend of Stewart's, instructed his broker Peter Bacanovic, who is also Stewart's broker, to transfer $4.9 million in ImClone stock to the account of his daughter Aliza Waksal. His daughter also requested that Bacanovic sell $2.5 million of her own ImClone stock. Sam Waksal then tried to sell the shares he had transferred to his daughter, but was blocked by brokerage firm Merrill Lynch. Phone records indicate that Bacanovic called Martha Stewart's office on December 27 shortly after Waksal's daughter dumped her shares. Stewart's stock was sold ten minutes later.

Sam Waksal was arrested on June 12, 2002, on charges of insider trading, obstruction of justice, and bank fraud in addition to previously filed securities fraud and perjury charges. Although he pleaded innocent for nine months, Sam Waksal eventually pleaded guilty to insider trading and another six out of thirteen charges. In his plea, Waksal said that, "I am aware that my conduct, while I was in possession of material non-public information, was wrong. I've made some terrible mistakes and I deeply regret what has happened." He was later sentenced to more than seven years in prison—the maximum allowed by federal sentencing guidelines—and ordered to pay a $3 million fine. Prosecutors continue to investigate whether he tipped off others, including family members and an individual who sold $30 million of the biotechnology company's shares. Sam Waksal's father and daughter also face a criminal investigation and the possible forfeiture of nearly $10 million that the government contends were obtained from illegal insider trading.

Martha Stewart denied that she engaged in any improper trading when she sold her shares of ImClone stock. On December 27, Stewart says she was flying in her private jet to Mexico for a vacation with two friends. En route, she called her office to check her messages, which included one from her broker Peter Bacanovic, with news that her ImClone stock had dropped below $60 per share. Stewart claims she had previously issued a "stop-loss" order to sell the stock if it fell below $60 per share. Stewart called Bacanovic and asked him to sell her 3,928 shares; she also called her friend Sam Waksal, but could not reach him. Stewart's assistant left a message for Sam Waksal saying, "Something's going on with ImClone, and she wants to know what it is. She's staying at Los Ventanos." Waksal did not call her back. Investigators are also looking into the sale of another ten thousand shares of ImClone stock by Dr. Bart Pasternak, a close friend of Stewart. At about the time Stewart made her sale, she was on her way to Mexico with Pasternak's estranged wife, Mariana.

However, Stewart's explanation that she unloaded her stock because of a pre-arranged sell order collapsed when Douglas Faneuil, the broker's assistant who handled the sale of the ImClone stock for Stewart, told Merrill Lynch lawyers that his boss, Peter Bacanovic, had pressured him to lie about a stop-loss order. Although Faneuil initially backed Stewart's story, he later told prosecutors that Bacanovic prompted him to advise Stewart that Waksal family members were dumping their stock and that she should consider doing the same. During interviews with law enforcement officials, Faneuil said, "I did not truthfully reveal everything I knew about the actions of my immediate supervisor and the true reason for the sales." He reportedly received money or other valuables for hiding his knowledge from investigators. Faneuil pleaded guilty to a misdemeanor charge on October 2 and is expected to testify against Stewart, who resigned from her board membership of the New York Stock Exchange a day after Faneuil pleaded guilty. Merrill Lynch fired Faneuil after he pleaded guilty; Bacanovic was also fired for declining to cooperate with investigators looking into trading activity of ImClone's shares.

*The Probe.* In August 2002, investigators requested Stewart's phone and e-mail records on the ImClone stock trade and her Merrill Lynch account as well as those of her business manager. Stewart and Bacanovic have yet to provide investigators with proof that a stop-loss order existed. Congressional investigators for the U.S. House of Representatives' Energy and Commerce Committee could not find any credible record of such an order between Stewart and her broker. However, portions of the documents presented to the committee were unreadable because they were blacked out. Stewart's lawyers later agreed to return to Capitol Hill with unedited documents. The committee did not call Martha Stewart to testify as her lawyers had made it clear that she would invoke her Fifth Amendment right to remain silent. Investigators, who had been negotiating unsuccessfully with Stewart's lawyers to arrange for her voluntary testimony, came to believe that Stewart was "stonewalling" and would not cooperate. Many wondered, "If Ms. Stewart has been straight about her story, then why wouldn't she tell it under oath?" After the scandal broke, however, Stewart and her spokespeople declined to comment or could not be reached. The House Energy and Commerce Committee ultimately handed the Martha Stewart/ImClone investigation over to the U.S. Justice Department, with a strong suggestion that it investigate whether Stewart had lied to the committee.

Additionally, the SEC indicated that it was ready to file civil securities fraud charges against Stewart for her alleged role in the insider-trading scandal and her public statement about the stop-loss arrangement with her broker. Federal prosecutors soon widened their investigation to include determining whether Stewart had tampered with a computerized phone log to delete a message from her broker as well as whether she had made her public statements about why she sold ImClone shares in order to maintain the price of her own company's stock. Federal law bars officers of public corporations from knowingly making false statements that are material in effect—meaning they have the potential to shape a reasonable investor's decision to buy or sell stock in a particular company. If prosecutors could prove that Stewart made a deceptive statement to repair her credibility and keep her firm's stock price from falling, it could charge her with securities fraud. Already, one shareholder has filed suit against Stewart.

*The Charges.* Finally, on June 4, 2003, a federal grand jury indicted Stewart on charges of securities fraud, conspiracy (together with Peter Bacanovic), making false statements, and obstruction of justice. Although the forty-one page indictment did not specifically charge Stewart with insider trading, it alleged that she lied to federal investigators about the stock sale, attempted to cover up her activities, and defrauded Martha Stewart Living Omnimedia shareholders by misleading them about the gravity of the situation and thereby keeping the stock price from falling. The indictment further accused Stewart of deleting a computer log of the telephone message from Bacanovic informing her that he thought ImClone's stock "was going to start trading downward." Peter Bacanovic was also indicted on charges of making false statements, making and using false documents, perjury, and obstruction of justice. The indictment alleged that Bacanovic had altered his personal notes to create the impression of a prior agreement to sell Stewart's ImClone shares if the price fell below $60/share. Both Stewart and Bacanovic pleaded "not guilty" to all charges. If convicted, Martha Stewart could be sentenced to up to thirty years in prison and fined up to $2 million.

Additionally, the SEC filed a civil lawsuit accusing both Stewart and Bacanovic of insider trading, demanding more than $45,000 in re-compensation, and seeking to bar Stewart from being an officer or director of a public company. Although Stewart denied the charges, she resigned her positions as chief executive officer and chairman of the board of Martha Stewart Living Omnimedia just hours after the indictment, avowing, "I love this company, its people and everything it stands for, and I am stepping aside as chairman and CEO because it is the right thing to do." She retains a seat on the firm's board of directors and remains its chief shareholder. Sharon Patrick, the company's president and chief operating officer, replaced Stewart as CEO, while Jeffrey Ubben, the founder of an investment group that owns Omnimedia stock, was named chairman.

Ironically, Martha Stewart could have sold her ImClone stock on December 31 instead of December 27 and collected $180,000 in profit without raising any concerns. That's just $48,000 less than what she gained through the earlier sale. That $48,000 gain has already cost Stewart $261,371,672 plus legal fees, an amount that grows daily due to the damage the scandal may create for her image and brand. Despite Stewart's denials of any wrongdoing, the scandal has sliced more than 70 percent off the stock price of Omnimedia and according to one estimate, washed away more than a quarter of her net worth. Before the scandal Stewart had an estimated net worth of $650 million.

After the indictment and Stewart's resignation, she took out a full-page newspaper ad in which she reiterated her innocence and appealed to her customers to remain loyal. Stewart insisted in the ad that, "I simply returned a call from my stockbroker. . . . Based in large part on prior discussions with my broker about price, I authorized a sale of my remaining shares in a biotech company called ImClone. I later denied any wrongdoing in public statements and voluntary interviews with prosecutors. The government's attempt to criminalize these actions makes no sense to me." Stewart also retained a public-relations firm to help her firm weather the crisis and set up a Web site, www.marthatalks.com, to update her customers and fans about the case.

## Implications of the Scandal

After the scandal became public, Martha Stewart began a campaign to detach herself from the events. However, she couldn't escape questions about the insider-trading scandal. Even in her regular weekly cooking segment on CBS's *The Early Show*, host Jane Clayson attempted to ask about the scandal, but Stewart responded: "I want to focus on my salad . . ." Her appearances on the morning program have since been put on hold.

If convicted on all charges, Stewart could face a prison sentence and be forced to give up her seat on the board of directors. Separating Martha Stewart from Omnimedia, the company she personifies, would be no simple task. Her most important role in the company is as its highly recognizable spokesperson, brand, and television personality. Finding someone to replace her in that role would be far more difficult than finding a replacement chairwoman and CEO.

## The Future of Stewart's Image and Business

There are few companies so closely identified with their founders as Martha Stewart Living Omnimedia Inc. Although many companies have survived scandals and the exit of their founders, Martha Stewart has a one-of-a-kind relationship with her company, its brands, and products. Regardless of whether she is convicted, the insider-trading scandal has affected Stewart's company: the stock price has fallen by 50 percent, and magazine revenues and subscription renewals have declined. Many wonder whether the firm can truly recover without Stewart's presence. Organizational psychologist Ken Siegel, commenting for *CBS News*, suggested that, "Even if she is legally exonerated, her image as the mistress of homeyness is significantly tarnished. She's playing this a little too close to the vest. It's a contradiction of the marketplace image of open, warm, and domestic." On *CBS News*, Steven Fink, president of Lexicon Communications, likewise questioned Stewart's choice of avoiding the questions: "Someone as culturally prominent as Stewart would be expected to address the public, and she has not really done that, resulting, rightly or wrongly, in the perception that she has something to hide. She branded herself as the ultimate last word on perfect living but now her image is looking like a complete act, and the dishonored reputation of its creator is sure to have severe costs for Omnimedia."

The scandal occurred at an unfortunate time for Martha Stewart Living Omnimedia. The company's publishing arm was in its mature stage, its television show was suffering declining ratings, and the Internet operation was taking heavy losses. Moreover, some market analysts have expressed concern that the company depends too heavily on the name and image of its celebrated founder. One shareholder voiced the concern felt by many: "Without Martha, the company is only a shell. She's it." Stewart personifies the brand that is associated with her credibility and honesty—traits the public and investigators now question. In this case, the strength of the brand also becomes its weakness, as it is hard to tell where the person ends and the brand begins. Market analysts agree that Stewart needs to take steps to ensure that the brand can go beyond the person. With the tremendous growth of her company, Stewart has surrounded herself with a group of trustworthy professionals to deal with the fine points who are as detail oriented as she is. She believes that her business can live on without her because it is now a combination of her artistic philosophy and spirit and the creativity of others. Although Stewart has taken strides to make the brand more independent, there are lingering doubts about the long-term effects of the scandal.

Others, however, believe that Martha Stewart's drive and spirit will help her overcome this setback. Jerry Della Femina, an advertising executive, said, "The brand will survive because Martha has gone beyond being a person who represents a brand." She built an empire and became famous by making the most discouraging circumstances seem neat and elegant. The question now is whether the billionaire "diva of domesticity" can survive an insider-trading scandal that has already resulted in the convictions of two people. Before the scandal broke, Stewart was asked about her close ties with her brand. She replied, "I think that my role is Walt Disney. There are very few brands that were really started by a person, with a person's name, that have survived as nicely as that. Estee Lauder has certainly survived beautifully, despite Mrs. Lauder's absence from the business in the last, maybe, 15 years. I would like to engender that same kind of spirit and same kind of high quality."

*Questions*

1. Martha Stewart has repeatedly denied any wrongdoing, despite the indictment. Why is her company being damaged by the scandal?
2. What role has Stewart's image played in the insider-trading scandal?
3. Will Martha Stewart Living Omnimedia survive if Stewart is convicted? In order to survive, what changes will need to be made at the company?

---

Sources: These facts are from Christopher M. Byron, *Martha Inc.: The Incredible Story of Martha Stewart Living Omnimedia* (New York: John Wiley & Sons, Inc., 2002); Diane Brady, "Martha Inc. Inside the Growing Empire of America's Lifestyle Queen," *Business Week,* Jan. 17, 2000; Julie Creswell, "Will Martha Walk?" *Fortune,* Nov. 25, 2002, pp. 121–124; Mike Duff, "Martha Scandal Raises Questions, What's in Store for Kmart?" *DSN Retailing Today,* July 8, 2002, pp. 1, 45; Anne D'Innocenzio, "Charges Imperil Stewart Company," *[Fort Collins] Coloradoan,* June 5, 2003, pp. D1, D7; Shelley Emling, "Martha Stewart Indicted on Fraud," *Austin American-Statesman,* June 5, 2003, www.statesman.com; Shelley Emling, "Stewart Defends Her Name with Ad," *Austin American-Statesman,* June 6, 2003, www.statesman.com; "Feds Tighten Noose on Martha," CNN/Money, Feb. 6, 2003, http://money.cnn.com/2003/02/06/ news/companies/martha/index.htm; Charles Gasparino and Kara Scannell, "Probe of Martha Stewart's Sale of Stock Enters Its Final Phase," *Wall Street Journal,* Jan. 24, 2003, p. C7; Constance L. Hays, "Stiff Sentence for ImClone Founder," *Austin American-Statesman,* June 11, 2003, http://www.statesman.com; "ImClone Founder Pleads Guilty," CBS News, Oct. 15, 2002, www.cbsnews.com/stories/2002/08/12/ national/main518354.shtml; "ImClone Probe Costly for Martha Stewart," MSNBC, Jan. 27, 2003, http://stacks.msnbc.com/news/864675.asp; Charles M. Madigan, "Woman Behaving Badly," *Across the Board,* July/Aug. 2002, p. 75; Jerry Markon, "Martha Stewart Could Be Charged As 'Tippee,'" *Wall Street Journal,* Oct. 3, 2002, pp. C1, C9; "Martha Stewart Enters Not Guilty Plea to Charges," *Wall Street Journal,* June 4, 2003, http://online.wsj.com; "Martha's Mouthpiece: We'll Deliver," CBS News, Aug. 20, 2002, www.cbsnews.com/stories/2002/08/20/national/main519320.shtml; "Martha Stewart Living Slides into Red, Expects More Losses," *Wall Street Journal,* Mar. 4, 2003, http://online.wsj.com/article/0,,SB1046721988332486840,00.html; Erin McClam, "Martha Stewart Indicted in Stock Scandal," *Coloradoan,* June 5, 2003, p. A1; Amy Merrick, "Can Martha Deliver Merry?" *Wall Street Journal,* Oct. 8, 2002, pp. B1, B3; Keith Naughton, "Martha's Tabloid Dish," *Newsweek,* June 24, 2002, p. 36; Keith Naughton and Mark Hosenball, "Setting the Table," *Newsweek,* Sept. 23, 2002, p. 7; "New Witness in Martha Probe," CBSNews, Aug. 9, 2002, www.cbsnews.com/stories/2002/08/12/national/main518448. shtml; Marc Peyser, "The Insiders," *Newsweek,* July 1, 2002, pp. 38–53; Thomas A. Stewart, "Martha Stewart's Recipe for Disaster," *Business2.com,* July 3, 2002; Jeffrey Toobin, "Lunch at Martha's," *New Yorker,* Feb. 3, 2003, pp. 38–44; Thor Valdmanis, "Martha Stewart Leaves NYSE Post," *USA Today,* Oct. 4, 2002, p. 3B.

# Astra USA: A Sexual Discrimination Scandal[1]

A stra USA was a wholly owned subsidiary of the international pharmaceutical company Astra AB of Sweden. To understand Astra USA and its former president CEO, Lars Bildman, one needs to understand the parent company. Established in the early 1900s, Astra began manufacturing its first pharmaceutical drug, called Digitotal, a heart medicine, after the abolishment of the drug monopolies in Sweden and other countries. Over the next twenty years, Astra continued to be aggressive in marketing and research and development, forming subsidiaries in Finland and Latvia. By the 1950s Astra had subsidiaries in Italy, Canada, West Germany, Colombia, Mexico, Australia, and the United States. The drug that propelled Astra into an elite group of competitors was Xylocaine, a local anesthetic. In the 1960s and 1970s Astra diversified heavily into a wide variety of medical drugs and products. It developed a four-pronged strategy in the following areas: cardiovascular preparations, local anesthetics, anti-asthma agents, and antibiotics. In 1982 Astra signed a long-term agreement in the U.S. market with the conglomerate Merck & Co. During the 1980s Astra shares were introduced onto the London stock exchange. It introduced profit sharing and established research centers in India and England.

## Håkan Mögren

In 1987 Håkan Mögren was appointed president of the company. Before Mögren came to Astra it had been a slow-moving, sedate company. When the wealthy Wallenberg family of Sweden who owned Astra chose Mögren, many in the industry thought it was a mistake. After all, Håkan Mögren knew nothing of molecular research or the drug business. He had been the chief executive of a local chocolate and foodstuff company. Soon after being hired, Mögren shook up the sleepy company. He took an unknown anti-ulcer drug, Losec, and marketed it globally. He tripled the international sales staff, built subsidiaries overseas, and bought back licenses in strategically located markets.

Under Mögren, Astra's international marketing intensified. It signed several licensing

[1] This case was prepared by John Fraedrich and Barbara Gilmer for classroom discussion rather than to illustrate either effective or ineffective handling of an administrative, ethical, or legal decision by management.

agreements, which gave it significant marketing control in Italy, Spain, Japan, and the United States. Astra shares were finally listed on the New York Stock Exchange in 1996, and in 1998 Astra's market capitalization surpassed $30 billion. The highest sales increase was in the North American market, where sales rose more than 50 percent, to nearly $1 billion. Astra spent more than 21 percent of its revenues on research and development in 1998. The restructuring relationship between Astra USA with Merck & Co. in early 1998 gave it strategic marketing freedom within the United States, as well as the right to buy out Merck's interest in 2008.

Mögren's appetite for growth seemed to know no bounds. In late 1998, Mögren, who said that he was not interested in rapid growth, decided first to sever and then to buy out the joint venture it had with Merck. It cost Astra approximately $10 billion to acquire control of the Merck joint venture. The move paved the way for Astra, one of Europe's strongest pharmaceutical companies, to pursue a multibillion-dollar merger in the consolidating global drugs industry. On April 6, 1999, Astra AB of Sweden and Zeneca Group PLC of the United Kingdom officially merged to form AstraZeneca PLC. Based in London, the combined company has become a giant in the industry with fifty-eight thousand employees worldwide and sales in 2002 of nearly $18 billion. Sir Tom McKillip is the chief executive, and Håkan Mögren serves as deputy chairman.

Håkan Mögren's style certainly was not traditionally Swedish, that is, conservative and group oriented. Some former employees spoke of his extravagant personal indulgences. Allegedly, suppliers and subordinates gave tax-free "gifts" of expensive wines and other items to Mögren because of his known love of such things. Mögren also loved the opera and would fly his family to other countries to attend performances. His lifestyle helps to shed light both on the type of culture he established at Astra and what subsequently befell the company.

## Lars Bildman and the Astra Way

Whether Mögren influenced Lars Bildman's business approach and lifestyle or whether Bildman's business approach and lifestyle were already set before he came to Astra USA is still in question. Bildman started out with the company as a young chemical engineer. He was vice president of the company's German subsidiary and from there went to Astra USA as CEO. A lanky man with piercing eyes, he was a charismatic, if somewhat quirky, employer. For example, Bildman favored suits in colors like purple, coral, or traffic-cone orange. Insiders report that he was also a connoisseur of fine wines, caviar, and Dom Perignon champagne. Many believed these eccentricities were acceptable, especially for a man who had taken a company from annual revenues of $30 million to $360 million. People around Bildman described him as a very disciplined, goal-oriented man, who ruled firmly over his fifteen hundred plus "troops" in Westborough, Massachusetts, a Boston suburb.

Bildman's management style was described as autocratic. He established a rigid, militaristic atmosphere at Astra headquarters. For example, most staffers were required to go to lunch at precisely the same time every day and had to get permission to hang anything personal on their cubicle walls. All but the highest-ranking executives had to share one centralized fax number, and Bildman received copies of all messages. Others told about the way he exercised power. For example, at one meeting he disliked the suit one of his executives was wearing and told him to change it; the executive did so quickly. Bildman also insisted that everyone wear the Astra pin. Employees who forgot their pin were severely reprimanded. One employee said, "The fear got so out of hand that I recall at least six times that I gave somebody an extra pin and they were literally shaken by the fact that they had lost theirs."

To fuel the growth that was taking place at Astra USA, Bildman began to hire hundreds of young salespeople. For female recruits, appearance seemed to be especially important. One employee's comment illustrates the prevailing attitude: "They told me in no uncertain terms why they wanted her hired—because she was extremely attractive." An Astra executive said about someone else: "We're not hiring her. I can't see me sitting at a bar having a drink with her."

Selling pharmaceuticals is a high-paying, much-sought-after profession. Starting salaries are high and include a car and hefty bonuses—and compensation at Astra was even better. However, the new hires that Astra recruited rarely had prior pharmaceutical experience. All had to attend a rigorous nine-week training course, which included in-depth sales instruction as well as such topics as anatomy and physiology. Tests, studying, and physical activities were the standard for the nine-week period. The training program also immersed the new hires in the Astra culture, known as the "Astra Way." Each class of up to a hundred was lodged for the entire nine weeks at the Westborough Marriott near Astra headquarters. The company paid for just one plane ticket home and discouraged trainees from having any visitors or leaving before the nine weeks were completed. The Astra Way consisted of a set of rigid rules covering everything from sales techniques—presentations had to be memorized and delivered to doctors virtually by rote—to acceptable casual dress (no jeans, no shorts; socks required). Trainees were also taught and expected to use European etiquette. New recruits were marched around buildings in sweats for a day, as managers, dressed in fatigues, barked questions. Those who could not answer quickly enough were made to do pushups. The atmosphere was one of domination.

Socializing also appeared to play a key role in the Astra Way. Recruits were told that to succeed they had to play hard as well as work hard. "Work eight hours, play eight hours, sleep eight hours" was a phrase Bildman and other top managers frequently used. Because entertaining was the Astra Way, open-bar nights were frequent. Managers would take new hires to drinking parties, which usually went on until the early-morning hours, three or four nights a week. At these open-bar nights, the attractive women drew most of the attention. "Upper management was barely paying attention to the male students, but they were all over the female students," said a 1993 trainee who left Astra a year later. The pressure to go to these events was high, especially when Bildman and other executives were in attendance. With a 15 percent washout rate, trainees realized that making the right impression could mean the difference between being assigned to San Francisco or to Fargo, North Dakota. "You had to go to the bar," said one female rep. Another former employee had this comment: "They would use their power and authority to make you think you didn't have a job if you didn't go along."

It has been claimed that Bildman and other managers would also invite new hires out on the town. For example, on one occasion Bildman supposedly organized a night out with six trainees—four women and two men. After dinner, the group retired to a darkly lit piano bar, where Bildman ordered people to dance. One trainee remembered it as a "come-on" bar, "the type of place where you'd meet somebody, have a steamy dance, and go home." As the party moved to another nightclub, it is alleged sexual improprieties began occurring. "I didn't feel I could say no," recalled one trainee, whom Bildman allegedly steered to a bed at one of the private parties. "I kept thinking: He's the president of the company. Is there any way to get out of this discreetly?"

This seemed to be a pattern during Bildman's tenure at Astra USA. In addition, it was also alleged that Bildman and his colleagues chartered yachts with high-priced prostitutes, and took relatives and family on vacations using company funds. Bildman also allegedly renovated his house and his Vermont ski lodge with more than $2 million in Astra money. According to prosecutors, Bildman's Boston suburban home was furnished with a sauna, pool, wine cellar, and a martial arts facility for his children—all on company funds.

What is not in question is that Lars Bildman was terminated as president and CEO on June 26, 1996, after an internal investigation prompted by an exposé in *Business Week* magazine raised numerous sexual harassment allegations. Astra refused at the time to comment on specific sexual-harassment allegations, but Carl-Gustav Johansson, an executive vice president, said the investigation had found that Bildman had "exhibited inappropriate behavior at company functions" and had "abused his power." The company also accused Bildman of misappropriating $2 million in company funds to renovate three homes and pay for lavish vacations and other personal expenses. Bildman vehemently denied both sets of charges. The company also fired another executive, George Roadman; two others, Edward Aarons and Anders Lonner, resigned.

In January 1998, U.S. authorities' case against Bildman was concluded with a plea bargain in which Bildman pleaded guilty to three counts of filing false federal income tax returns. In exchange for the plea, prosecutors dropped fraud and conspiracy charges. Bildman was sentenced to twenty-one months in prison, to be followed by three years' probation, and was forced to pay $281,190 in back taxes and a $30,000 fine. Bildman was released from the Oakdale (Louisiana) Federal Correctional Institution in December 1999.

After a yearlong investigation, the U.S. Equal Employment Opportunity Commission (EEOC) found that Bildman was guilty of extensive sexual harassment. In a settlement with the EEOC, Astra agreed to establish a claim fund of $9.85 million to be apportioned among eligible claimants. Of the 181 claims made, 124 have been substantiated. To date, litigants have received compensation as follows:

| NUMBER OF LITIGANTS | COMPENSATION RECEIVED |
| --- | --- |
| 20 | $12,000 |
| 16 | 25,000 |
| 20 | 30,000 |
| 13 | 40,000 |
| 10 | 50,000 |
| 3 | 75,000 |

| 15 | 100,000 |
|----|---------|
| 10 | 150,000 |
| 1 | 200,000 |
| 10 | 250,000 |
| 6 | 300,000 |

Astra filed suit against Bildman, demanding damages of $15 million.

## The Response from Mögren and Sweden

In contrast to many other scandal-plagued companies in recent years, Astra addressed the problems in a very open way. The following is part of a speech given by Mögren:

> . . . As a result of a preliminary investigation . . . we were able to confirm that a violation had been made of the fundamental principles for working at Astra and of the culture that we have developed. . . .
>
> . . . Concerning the sexual harassment now in question, it should be said that what has occurred is at best a violation of good style and form. At worst, a number of our employees have also been caused inconveniences or suffering. To the extent this may have occurred, we are deeply regretful. We will do everything we can to prevent it from ever happening again. . . .
>
> . . . We have decided to review the adherence to all applicable rules. At first glance our view is that it is not the rules that are at fault. What has happened is that some people have tried to put themselves above the rules, at the same time that they have made great efforts to cover up what has happened. . . .
>
> . . . We have adopted measures aimed at strengthening the staff's position. We have established a telephone hotline in the U.S. with an impartial party, where persons who feel they are exposed to any form of harassment can call under protection of anonymity. . . .
>
> . . . We have also conducted a great deal of self-reflection . . . and asked ourselves what we can improve upon. . . .
>
> . . . I would like to [note] that sexual harassment is not viewed in the same way in all cultures. . . . Since views differ, it is all the more important for a company that is active around the world to work according to a carefully thought-out policy. But there is no doubt about the principal objective: no employee . . . should have to tolerate harassment of any kind. All misuse of power must be condemned.[2]

AstraZeneca, recognizing that diversity and creative potential are valuable assets, stated that one of its priorities since the merger "has been to develop and widely communicate the new company values and principles, and to build a culture which unites employees in a common purpose." AstraZeneca's code of conduct was published in June 2000, and all employees are required to comply with the letter and spirit of the code.

[2] *Håkan Mögren, "Address to Astra's Annual Meeting, May 13, 1996," Astra AB of Sweden.

*Questions*

1. Discuss the interaction between Bildman and Mögren as well as Astra's corporate culture. Who or what was ultimately responsible, and why?
2. Evaluate Astra's corporate culture during Bildman's tenure and discuss whether or not it has changed.
3. Was Bildman a rogue executive who was not following Astra's corporate culture, or was he its epitome? Discuss both sides of the argument.

---

Sources: These facts are from "Board and Management," AstraZeneca International, www.astrazeneca. com/mainnav1/about/s_board/c_board_i/index.html (accessed Apr. 11, 2003): "Clarification from Astra Concerning Information in the Swedish Newspaper *Dagens Industri*," March 4, 1998, Astra, news release, www.astrazeneca.com/NewSection/newsreleases/2_1_65e.htm; "EEOC v. ASTRA USA, INC.," Emory University School of Law, Oct. 11, 1996, www.law.emory.edu/1circuit/sept96/96-1751.01a. html; "Key Facts," AstraZeneca, www.astrazeneca.com/mainnav1/about/keyfacts/c_keyfacts/index. html (accessed Apr. 11, 2003); Bob Kievra, "Astra Sex-Harassment Payments OK'd. $9.1M Ready to Go to 120 Claimants," *Worcester Telegram & Gazette*, May 27, 1999, p. E1; Bob Kievra, "Former Astra CEO Bildman Released from Federal Prison," *Worcester Telegram & Gazette*, Nov. 9, 1999; Mark Maremont, "Aftershocks Are Rumbling through Astra," *Business Week*, May 20, 1996, www.businessweek.com/1996/ 21/b347654.htm; Mark Maremont, "Day of Reckoning at Astra," *Business Week*, July 8, 1996, www. businessweek.com/1996/28/b348355.htm; Mark Maremont, with Jane A. Sasseen, "Abuse of Power," *Business Week*, May 13, 1996, www.businessweek.com/1996/20/b34751.htm and www.businessweek.com/ 1996/20/b34752.htm; Leslie Miller, "Astra USA Agrees to Largest Sex Harassment Settlement Ever," *South Coast Today*, Feb. 6, 1998, www.s-t.com/daily/02-98/02-06-98/a06bu038.htm; "People, Culture & Values," AstraZeneca, www.astrazeneca.com/mainnav1/about/s_pcv/c_pcv/index.html (accessed Apr. 11, 2003); www.astra.com/astra/news/2_4_5.HTM; www.astra.com/Astra/ news/enewsrel/ 2_1_59e.htm; www.astra.com/Astra/news/ENEWSREL/2_1_65e.htm; www.astra.se/om_astra/pressm eddelanden/pm/pm59.htm; http://lawlibrary.ucdavis.edu/LAWLIB/March98/0139.html; www.wcinet. com/th/News/020698/National/94318.htm; www.consult-dtc.com/news.html; www.civiljustice.com/ astra515.htm; www.communityadvocate.com/; www.uiowa.edu/; www.civiljustice.com/astra72.htm; and www.newsday.com/mainnews/rnmi012a.htm.

# Case 9

# Firestone: A Reputation Blowout[1]

Harvey Firestone founded the Firestone Tire & Rubber Company in 1900 in Akron, Ohio. The company was acquired by Bridgestone USA, Inc., a subsidiary of Tokyo-based Bridgestone Corporation, in 1990 for $2.6 billion. Firestone's long relationship with Ford Motor Company began in 1906, when Henry Ford bought two thousand sets of tires from Harvey Firestone. Since that initial transaction, both companies have grown and become major players in their industries. Ford, which boasts a global portfolio of more than five thousand patents, now owns many well-known automotive brands, including Ford, Volvo, Mazda, Lincoln, Mercury, Jaguar, Land Rover, and Aston Martin. Firestone markets eight thousand different types and sizes of tires and a host of other products.

Despite its growth over the past hundred years, Firestone has faced more turbulence than Ford. In 1978, Firestone recalled 14.5 million tires—the largest tire recall in history. Excess application of the adhesive that binds the rubber and steel had caused five hundred tread separations and blowouts. Firestone paid a $500,000 fine for concealing safety problems. This recall weakened the financial position of the company and resulted in its merger with Bridgestone. The parent company, founded in 1931 by Shojiro Ishibashi, developed its name from the English translation of the founder's family name, "stone bridge." Bridgestone successfully restored the struggling company back to profitability. Firestone now accounts for 40 percent of the parent company's sales.

Tire recalls have plagued other manufacturers as well. On March 12, 1980, Uniroyal recalled almost 2 million tires because of tread separation. B.F. Goodrich recalled a million tires on August 13, 1974, because of improper inflation and installation. Kelly-Springfield faced a recall on January 28, 1976, when 300,000 tires were recalled because of tread separation. General Tire recalled 187,000 tires on January 24, 1979, because of exposed belt wire. Cooper Tire & Rubber recalled more than 156,000 tires on August 11, 1988, because of bead flaw. More recently, on April 14, 1998, Kelly-Springfield recalled more than 500,000 tires because of sidewall cracking. The high number of recalls indicates that tire failure have been an industrywide problem for more than twenty-five years.

---

[1] This case was prepared by Dana Schubert and O. C. Ferrell for classroom discussion rather than to illustrate either the effective or ineffective handling of an administrative, ethical, or legal decision by management.

## The Timeline for the Firestone Recall

In July 1998, Sam Boyden, an associate research administrator for State Farm Insurance, received a phone call from a claims handler asking him to determine if there were other cases of Firestone tire tread failure besides the one he was handling. He discovered twenty such cases dating back to 1992. A car fanatic, Boyden recognized that this was more than a coincidence. He sent an e-mail advising the National Highway Traffic Safety Administration (NHTSA) of his findings. He was politely thanked, but no action occurred until early 2000.

In January 2000, Anna Werner, a reporter for KHOU-TV in Houston, and two colleagues researched accidents caused by tire tread separation in Texas after an attorney mentioned the issue. Based on the results of their investigation, the television station aired a nine-minute segment. Werner also reported her findings to Joan Claybrook, a former chief of the NHTSA. In the weeks that followed the airing of the story, KHOU was flooded with calls from citizens who wanted to relate their own stories of Firestone tire failures, most of them on Ford Explorer sport-utility vehicles (SUVs). KHOU eventually began directing the calls to the NHTSA.

Despite the flow of information from Sam Boyden and KHOU, NHTSA was slow to take action. In early March, investigators Steve Beretzky and Rob Wahl found twenty-two complaints of tread separation that they marked for "initial evaluation." Between March and May, the number of complaints skyrocketed. On May 2, three senior NHTSA officials increased the status of the inquiry to "preliminary investigation." Within six days, the NHTSA requested that Firestone supply production data and complaint files, which the company provided on July 27, with a copy going to Ford Motor the following day.

Sean Kane, a former employee of the Center for Auto Safety, had also tried to alert the NHTSA about the problems. Kane, who founded Strategic Safety, a research group interested in product-liability issues, received an e-mail in late July 2000 from a Venezuelan source who disclosed Ford's tire-replacement program there. Ford had recalled the tires, without Firestone's backing, because of problems with tread separation and mislabeled products dating back to 1998. Ford had discovered that the defect rates from the Valencia, Venezuela, plant were a thousand times higher than from the Decatur, Illinois, plant. On August 1, Strategic Safety, along with the political action group Public Citizen, issued a press release asking Ford for a vehicle recall.

After Ford received Firestone's report, it immediately began analyzing the data using Cray supercomputers. Of the 2,498 complaints logged on tire failure, 81 percent involved the fifteen-inch P235/75R15 models. When the complaints were screened for tread separation, 84 percent of some 1,699 complaints involved Ford's Explorer, Bronco, Ranger, or F-150 SUVs and trucks. Ford relayed the results to Firestone, and representatives from the two companies met in Dearborn, Michigan, to discuss the issue on August 5. By this time, the NHTSA was investigating twenty-one deaths that were possibly related to tread separation on Firestone tires. One of the deaths was civil-rights leader Earl Shinhoster, who was killed while riding in a Ford Explorer that crashed on June 11, 2000, while part of a motorcade accompanying the first lady of Nigeria, Jewel Howard-Taylor. Within days, the investigation had grown to include forty-six possible deaths, and Ford and Bridgestone/Firestone met with NHTSA officials to discuss a plan of action. The following day, August 9, they issued a recall of 6.5 million tires.

## The Recall

The recall included 3.8 million P235/75R15 radial ATX and ATXII and 2.7 million Wilderness AT tires, all manufactured in Firestone's Decatur, Illinois, plant. Firestone organized the official recall by state, giving priority to Arizona, California, Florida, and Texas, where the greatest percentage of casualties had occurred. Based on NHTSA data, Florida and Texas each accounted for 22 percent of the complaints, followed by California with 20 percent and Arizona with 5 percent. This first phase of the recall was expected to be complete by October 2000. The second phase, involving Alabama, Georgia, Louisiana, Mississippi, Nevada, Oklahoma, and Tennessee, was expected to be concluded by the end of 2000. Firestone announced that the recall in all remaining states would be complete by the end of 2001. It was 90 percent complete in late December 2000.

Firestone issued letters to all affected customers detailing the procedure for replacement. Customers affected by the recall could take their tires to Firestone retailers, Ford dealerships, or other tire retail outlets and receive a similar Firestone tire or equivalent competitor's model. In addition to the tire cost, the replacement included mounting and balancing fees. If replacements had been purchased before the official recall, customers who provided a receipt would be issued a reimbursement of up to $100 per tire. Ford also began testing other brands on the Explorer and identified thirty-four acceptable replacements.

Both companies ran advertisements and public information announcements to inform consumers how to determine whether their tires were included in the recall. Consumers could call a toll-free number if they had questions about tire models or eligibility. Despite Firestone's gradual plan, Ford encouraged all concerned motorists included in the recall, regardless of their location, to replace questionable tires immediately and, if necessary, to save the receipts for later reimbursement. Consumers not directly included in the recall could purchase new Firestone tires based on a credit system determined by the age and wear of their current tires.

After continued investigations, the NHTSA encouraged Firestone to expand the recall to other sizes and models of tires, but Firestone declined. On September 1, the NHTSA issued a consumer advisory to warn of potential problems with other Firestone tires, including ATXP205/75R15 tires on Chevy Blazers, ATX 31X10. 50R15LT tires on 1991 through 1994 Nissan pickups, and other sizes of ATX, Firehawk ATX, ATX23 Degree, Widetrack Radial Baja, and Wilderness AT tires—mostly those originating from the Decatur factory. Because these tires were not included in the official recall, replacements were not free. The NHTSA suggested that consumers save receipts in the event that Firestone increased the depth of the recall. Included in this advisory was a list of precautionary measures consumers could take to avoid tire failure.

## Firestone's Response to the Crisis

- Firestone successfully negotiated with union officials to avoid a potentially disruptive strike by the United Steelworkers of America that would have affected production at nine of eleven U.S. plants.

- Firestone began receiving replacement tires from its parent company's plant in Japan on August 23 and expected between 325,000 and 350,000 to arrive by September 1. Bridgestone/Firestone planned to send at least one shipment per day until the recall was complete.

- Firestone's U.S. factories doubled the number of tire molds in use and increased production by seven thousand tires per day.

- During Senate hearings into the growing number of complaints and accidents, evidence surfaced that the company had known about potential tread separation problems as far back as 1994. The company admitted that it had increased production during this time to dilute the failure rate. Additionally, internal memos warned of bubbles on the tire shoulder. Company officials stated that they did not investigate further because failure rates as determined by warranty claims had not demonstrated significant patterns. Bridgestone/Firestone officials accepted full responsibility and admitted the company had made "bad tires."

- Masatoshi Ono stepped down as CEO, and was replaced by former Executive Vice President John Lampe.

## Ford's Response to the Crisis

- Ford increased the staff monitoring its help line from three hundred to eight hundred employees and kept it open twenty-four hours a day.

- Ford closed new car production plants for three weeks so all its available tires could be used to replace the recalled tires rather than being used on new vehicles. The company continued to pay the six thousand workers from the three closed plants, who spent much of that time helping to distribute replacement tires to dispersal outlets.

- Ford created a five hundred-person crisis-management team to devise creative tactics to speed the recall procedure.

- Ford purchased tire molds from Firestone competitors to enable the entire industry to produce a greater quantity of replacement tires.

- Ford approached other tire manufacturers to request that they increase production of suitable replacement tires.

## "The Blame Game," or Whose Fault Was It?

The matter of fault in this recall has been much debated. When Ford analyzed Firestone's data, the auto maker noticed ten times more complaints stemming from tires originating in Firestone's Decatur factory than from other plants and specifically for tires made in 1994 and 1995. In particular, questions have arisen about the skill of replacement workers who filled in at the Decatur factory during a two-year strike known as "The War of '94–'95." Some have suggested that quality inspections were compromised as tires piled up on the factory floor and that old, dried rubber was used in production when employees returned from the strike.

Another factor under consideration is the quality of the Decatur facility itself. Constructed in 1942, the building was used to store telecommunications for the United States Armed Forces for nineteen years before being purchased by Firestone in 1962. The Decatur plant was insufficiently air conditioned and therefore may have had a high humidity level, which decreases the adhesive properties required to bind rubber to steel. This effect became apparent when it was shown that tires produced in the winter when humidity is low were of higher quality than those produced during the more humid summer months. Another contributing factor may have been the age and condition of the equipment used to mix raw materials and press steel together. In addition, the plant's vulcanization process, which uses heat and pressure to unite the rubber fragments into one product, is suspected of having had temperature-control problems. Poor quality can result when temperatures are too hot or not hot enough.

Although many people were quick to point a blaming finger at Firestone, others believe that Ford should share in the blame. The Ford Explorer's design as well as Ford's tire-pressure recommendations have been cited as possible factors contributing to the rate of tire separations and rollover accidents. Ford initially recommended a low tire pressure of 26 psi for two reasons. First, lower tire pressure compensates for the stiff suspension and thus produces a softer ride. Underinflated tires are problematic, however, because they have greater surface area in contact with the road, which creates more wear and more flexible sidewalls, which ultimately leads to overheated tires. Second, the Explorer SUV was designed with a high center of gravity and short wheelbase—traits associated with high rollover frequency. Moreover, low tire pressure results in diminished steering and responsiveness, which could increase the likelihood that an Explorer driver could roll over while overcorrecting or making sudden maneuvers. Because Ford Explorers are often overloaded with passengers, luggage, and other items, investigators are also looking into whether excess weight, which can lead to high friction and high heat, could be a contributing factor.

After the tire tread separation issue came to light, Ford requested that Firestone complete tests to determine whether there was a problem in the specific combination of Ford Explorers and Firestone tires. These tests, completed in Arizona in late February and early March, involved 243 heavily worn tires from sixty-three Explorers. No problems were discovered at that time, and both companies dropped the issue.

## Legal and Financial Implications for Ford and Firestone

For Bridgestone/Firestone, the financial implications of the recall have been devastating. Although the company attempted to isolate the public perception of the problem as involving only certain tires made in one Illinois plant, maintaining an image of overall quality for its products proved difficult. A Harris poll that asked "How likely is it that this tire recall would influence your decision to purchase a Firestone product?" found that 67 percent of 814 people responded "extremely to very likely." An additional 18 percent responded "somewhat likely." After the recall announcement, the company's stock price dropped 47 percent in just one month, and it reported a $750 million loss in 2000. It is yet to be determined whether Firestone will recover from this substantial blow.

Although Ford suffered less than Firestone, its image and stock price were harmed. Ford is not directly liable under current law for the recall costs, but it is subject to private lawsuits and criminal charges for the thousands of complaints, 700 injuries, and 271 deaths in the United States. In addition, the Venezuelan government and its consumer protection agency are pursuing Ford concerning forty-six deaths in Venezuela that involved Explorers. In the same poll mentioned above, 25 percent of respondents said the tire recall was "extremely or very likely" to influence their decision to purchase a Ford product, while 22 percent said the recall was "somewhat likely" to influence their decision. Ford attempted to focus the problem on Firestone by insisting that it was a "tire issue" not a "vehicle issue." Nonetheless, Ford's stock price dropped 18 percent in the month after the recall announcement, partially because of decreased consumer confidence.

Both companies faced an estimated three hundred lawsuits stemming from the deaths and injuries caused by the tread-separation incidents, including one related to the death of civil-rights leader Shinhoster. Firestone settled the first of these suits, which went to trial in Texas in August 2001, out of court for $7.85 million. Ford, which also was named in that suit, settled for $6 million before the trial began. Most of the other suits were also settled out of court with confidential agreements. On November 8, 2001, Bridgestone/Firestone settled lawsuits brought by fifty-three U.S. states and territories by agreeing to pay $500,000 to each plus $10 million in attorneys' fees and $5 million to fund a consumer education campaign. As part of the settlement, the company also agreed to review claims that it had previously denied seeking reimbursement for replacement tires from competitors. Although the company said it strongly disagreed with many of the states' claims and did not admit to any wrongdoing, CEO John Lampe said, "we believe that significant portions of the settlement, such as those related to consumer education, are very much in line with the company's own initiatives."

## The Impact on Other Companies

Many other firms were affected by the recall, including tire distributors nationwide. Many large retailers took a proactive stance and removed Firestone brands from their sales floors. Sears made the decision to remove Firestone tires even before the recall was officially announced. Sears, National Tire and Battery, and other retailers fully refunded customers who had purchased recalled tires and absorbed the mounting and balancing costs if customers purchased replacements. Many small retail operations that focused exclusively on Firestone tires changed their names and expanded or altered their product lines to avoid going bankrupt.

The recall affected competing tire manufacturers as well. Goodyear, Michelin, and other firms helped ease the recall effort by increasing their own production to reduce the tire shortage caused when so many consumers sought replacements. However, many consumers speculated that competitors may have benefited from the crisis.

Goodyear spent an extra $1 million on television and radio promotions, full-page newspaper ads, and banner ads on Yahoo! and AOL, admitting that its intensified promotion efforts were "in specific response to the recall, but done with good taste." Michelin continued its normal advertising plans, which happened to coincide with the recall news. Before the crisis, each tire company had a brand image it hoped to promote: Goodyear produced reliable tires; Michelin produced safe tires; and Firestone made high-performance tires. Now the companies are calling on those images to help customers associate desired benefits with the companies that provide them.

## The Future

In addition to the financial and legal implications for Ford and Firestone, the tire problems and subsequent recall will also affect the government, regulatory agencies, and other businesses. Many suggestions for improvement have been raised at the organizational, industry, and national levels. These include implementing a nylon layer, or cap, to brace the tire and reduce the risks of separation and creating stricter quality-inspection procedures and requirements within the individual companies. On an industry level, it has been suggested that tires pass more rigorous testing by nonbiased parties. Currently, consumers can research all aspects of car quality except tires. Creating consumer reports on tire durability, traction, strength, and other important traits has been suggested.

On September 7, 2000, the Senate introduced a bill that would hold executives criminally liable for withholding information on foreign recalls or defective products that result in death. The charge would be second-degree murder with a punishment of up to fifteen years in prison for selling unsafe merchandise. The bill passed on October 11, 2000. Additionally, on September 14, 2000, the Tread Act was proposed to improve consumer protection and increase communication between the government, tire manufacturers, and motor vehicle companies.

## Questions

1. To what extent do companies need to make a proactive effort to collect and analyze data concerning possible safety issues?
2. What mistakes did Ford, Firestone, and the NHTSA each make in their early attempts to handle the crisis?
3. What are the possible ethical implications of accepting responsibility versus blaming others?
4. Suggest measures that Firestone could take to improve tire quality in the future.

Sources: These facts are from Timothy Aeppel, "Firestone Milestone Brings on Dilemma," *Wall Street Journal,* Aug. 18, 2000, p. B8; Bridgestone/Firestone, www.firestone.com (accessed Aug. 30, 2001, and Apr. 16, 2003); "Bridgestone-Firestone and Ford on Trial," CBS News, Jan. 6, 2003, www.cbsnews.com/stories/2003/01/07/national/main535494.shtml; Lauren Comander, "Firestone Tires Shipped from Japan to Boost Supply," *Chicago Tribune,* Aug. 23, 2000, pp. 1, 2; "Consumer Advisory: Potentially Dangerous Tires," *Fox Market Wire,* Sept. 1, 2000, www.foxmarketwire.com/090100/tiredeaths_list.sml; Claudia H. Deutsch, "Where Rubber Meets the Road; Recall of Firestone Tires Is Aimed at Damage Control," *New York Times,* Aug. 10, 2000, http://archives.nytimes.com; "Firestone Reaches Agreement with State Attorneys General," Bridgestone/Firestone, press release, Nov. 8, 2001, www.bridgestone-firestone.com/news/mediacenter/news/011108a.html; "Ford, Firestone Settle Rollover Suit," CBS News, July 16, 2002, www.cbsnews.com/stories/2002/07/16/national/main515326.shtml; Melita Marie Garza, Lauren Comander, and Patrick Cole, "Problems at Tire Plant Alleged," *Chicago Tribune,* Aug. 20, 2000, pp. 1, 10; Milo Geyelin and Timothy Aeppel, "For Firestone, Tire Trial Is Mixed Victory," *Wall Street Journal,* Aug. 27, 2001, pp. A3, A4; Lori Grant, "More Retailers Pull 3 Firestone Tires from Stock," *USA Today,* Aug. 7, 2000, p. 1B; James R. Healey, "What You Don't Know About Your Tires," *USA Today,* Aug. 11, 2000, p. B1; David Kiley, "Bridgestone Exec Will Speak to Congress," *[Fort Collins] Coloradoan,* Aug. 30, 2000, p. D7; Kathryn Kranhold and Erin White, "The Perils and Potential Rewards of Crisis Management for Firestone," *Wall Street Journal,* Sept. 8, 2000, pp. B1, B4; Robert Guy Matthews, "How the Rubber Meets the Road," *Wall Street Journal,* Sept. 8, 2000, pp. B1, B4; Stephen Power, "Update Needed for Tire Rules, Activists Argue," *Wall Street Journal,* Sept. 8, 2000, pp. B1, B4; Stephen Power and Clare Ansberry, "Bridgestone/Firestone Says It Made 'Bad Tires'," *Wall Street Journal,* Sept. 13, 2000, pp. A3, A6; Robert L. Simison, "For Ford CEO Nasser, Damage Control Is the New 'Job One'," *Wall Street Journal,* Sept. 11, 2000, pp. A1, A8; Calvin Sims, "A Takeover with Problems for Japanese Tire Maker," *New York Times,* Aug. 10, 2000, http://archives.nytimes.com; Devon Spurgeon, "State Farm Researcher's Sleuthing Helped Prompt Firestone Recall," *Wall Street Journal,* Sept. 1, 2000, pp. B1, B6; Jason Szip, "Firestone's Japanese Parent Hit Again," *Fox Market Wire,* Sept. 1, 2000, http://foxmarketwire.com/090100/tirestrike_side2.sml; Lawrence Viele, "Ford, Bridgestone Testimony Sought," *Beacon Journal,* Feb. 27, 2003, www.ohio.com/mld/ohio/5274001.htm; Bill Vlasic, "Anatomy of a Crisis," *The Coloradoan,* Sept. 4, 2000, pp. C1, C2.

# Case 10

# *Exxon Valdez:* Revisited[1]

I n 1989, Exxon Corporation and Alyeska Pipeline Service Co., an eight-company consortium that operates the Trans-Alaska pipeline and the shipping terminal in Valdez, Alaska, were severely criticized for their handling of a major oil spill from an Exxon tanker. The *Exxon Valdez* ran aground near Valdez, Alaska, on March 24, 1989, and spilled two hundred forty thousand barrels—eleven million gallons—of crude oil, which eventually covered twenty-six hundred square miles of Prince William Sound and the Gulf of Alaska. Although the Exxon spill was not the largest ever, it was the worst in terms of environmental damage and disruption of industry, and it jeopardized the future of oil production in environmentally sensitive areas of Alaska. The effects of the spill could still be seen more than ten years after the wreck.

## The Wreck

At 12:04 A.M. on March 24, 1989, the *Exxon Valdez* was under the command of Third Mate Gregory Cousins, who was not licensed to pilot the vessel through the waters of Prince William Sound. The ship's captain, Joseph Hazelwood, apparently was asleep below deck. In an effort to dodge floating ice in the sound, Cousins performed what officials later described as an unusual series of right turns. The ship ran aground on Bligh Reef, spilling much of its cargo through the ruptured hull. The spill spread rapidly during the next few days, killing thousands of sea birds, sea otters, and other wildlife; covering the coastline with oil; and eliminating the fishing season in the sound for several years.

The Prince William Sound area was home to abundant wildlife. More than two hundred species of birds had been reported there, including one-fifth of the world's trumpeter swans. The fishing industry derived annual sales of $100 million from the sound's herring, salmon, Pacific cod, Alaska pollock, rockfish, halibut, flounder, and sharks, as well as crabs and shrimp. The world's largest concentration of killer whales and about one-fourth of the total U.S. sea otter population had inhabited the sound at the time of the wreck.

[1] This case was prepared by O. C. Ferrell, John Fraedrich, and Gwyneth Vaughn Walters for classroom discussion rather than to illustrate either effective or ineffective handling of an administrative, ethical, or legal decision by management.

## *Response to the Disaster*

The events following the March 24 spill reveal what some observers say was a pattern of unpreparedness, mismanagement, and negligence. According to the transcripts of radio conversations between Captain Hazelwood and the Coast Guard immediately after the accident, the captain tried for an hour to rock the tanker free from the reef, an action that Coast Guard officials claim might have sunk the ship and spilled more oil. They say that Hazelwood ignored their warnings that rocking the ship might make the oil spill almost five times as bad.

When Coast Guard officers boarded the tanker at 3:30 A.M., they reported that 138,000 barrels of crude oil had already been spilled. According to a contingency plan filed when the Valdez terminal first began operations, Alyeska crews should have arrived at the ship with containment equipment within a very short period of time; they did not. A frantic Coast Guard officer radioed, "We've got a serious problem. . . . She's leaking and groaning. There's nobody here. . . . Where's Alyeska?"

After being notified of the accident, Alyeska Pipeline Service initiated the first line of defense against oil spills: sending an observation tug to the scene and beginning to assemble its oil-spill containment equipment, much of which was in disarray. It loaded containment boom and lightering equipment (emergency pumps to suction oil from the *Exxon Valdez* onto other vessels) onto a damaged barge. The Coast Guard decided, however, that the barge was too slow and the need for the lightering equipment more urgent, so Alyeska crews had to reload the lightering equipment onto a tugboat, losing still more time.

The first Alyeska containment equipment did not arrive at the scene until 2:30 in the afternoon; the rest of the equipment came the next morning. Neither Alyeska nor Exxon had enough containment booms and chemical dispersants to fight the spill. They were not ready to test the effectiveness of the dispersants until eighteen hours after the spill, and then they conducted the test by tossing buckets of chemicals out the door of a helicopter. The helicopter's rotor dispersed the chemicals, and they missed their target. Moreover, the skimmer boats used to scoop oil out of the sea were old and kept breaking down. The skimmers filled up rapidly and had to be emptied into nearby barges, taking them out of action for long periods of time. Some of the makeshift work crews were assigned to boats without any apparent mission. Cleanup efforts were further hampered by communication breakdowns between coordinators on shore and crews at the scene caused by technical problems and devices' limited range. Instead, messages had to be relayed through local fishermen. In addition, although a fleet of private fishing boats was standing by ready to assist with the containment and cleanup, Exxon and Alyeska failed to mobilize their help. Exxon has admitted that the early efforts were chaotic but says that they were no more so than the usual response to any major disaster.

The *Exxon Valdez* was not fully encircled by containment booms until Saturday afternoon, thirty-six hours after the accident. By then the oil spill covered an area of twelve square miles. Exxon conducted more tests with chemical dispersants Saturday night, but the tests were inconclusive because conditions were too calm. (The chemical dispersants require wave action to be effective.) On Sunday afternoon the Coast Guard gave Exxon permission to use the dispersants on the spill. But that night a storm with winds as high as seventy-three miles an hour drove the oil slick thirty-seven miles into the southwestern section of the sound. All cleanup efforts were halted until the next afternoon because of the weather. Exxon eventually applied 5,500 gallons of chemical dispersants. However, by then, because of the delay caused by the storm, the oil had become too emulsified for dispersants to work properly. By the end of the week, the oil slick had spread to cover twenty-six hundred miles of coastline and sea.

Coast Guard officers tested Captain Hazelwood for alcohol nine hours after the wreck. They apparently did not realize that the ship was equipped with a testing kit. The test showed that Hazelwood had a blood-alcohol content of 0.061. It is a violation of Coast Guard regulations for a person operating a ship to have a blood-alcohol level in excess of 0.04. Four other crewmen, including the third mate, tested negative for alcohol. Exxon officials later admitted that they knew the captain had gone through an alcohol detoxification program, yet they still gave him command of the *Exxon Valdez,* Exxon's largest tanker.

## Alyeska's Containment Plan

Since the early 1970s, Alaskan officials and fishermen had expressed concern that a major oil spill was inevitable. In response, Alyeska Pipeline Service, its eight oil-company owners, and federal officials promised in 1972 that the tanker fleet operating out of Valdez would incorporate safety features such as double hulls and protective ballast tanks to minimize the possibility of spills. By 1977, however, Alyeska had convinced the Coast Guard that the safety features were not necessary, and only a few ships in the Valdez fleet incorporated them. The *Exxon Valdez* did not.

Alyeska Pipeline Service had filed a comprehensive contingency plan detailing how it would handle spills from the pipeline or from the Valdez terminal. In the event of an oil spill from a tanker, emergency crews were to encircle the spill with containment booms within five hours—yet it took them a day and a half to encircle the *Exxon Valdez.* Alyeska's contingency plan further specified that an emergency crew of at least fifteen people would be on hand at all times. However, in 1981 much of the team had been disbanded to cut costs. In 1989 Alyeska maintained a crew of eleven to monitor terminal operations, but because the *Exxon Valdez* spill occurred at the beginning of the Easter holiday weekend, the company had trouble rounding up the team. Furthermore, Exxon's staff of oil-spill experts had been reduced since 1985. At least nine oil-spill managers, including Exxon's chief environmental officer, had left or retired. An Exxon spokesman said that he was not aware that the cutbacks affected Alyeska's initial readiness to combat a spill.

A state audit of Alyeska's equipment demonstrated that the company was unprepared for the spill. It was supposed to have three tugboats and thirteen oil skimmers available but had only two and seven, respectively. Furthermore, the company had only fourteen thousand feet of boom for containing spills rather than the twenty-one thousand feet specified in the contingency plan. Moreover, the barge that carried the booms and stored skimmed oil was out of service because it had been damaged in an earlier storm. However, even if it had been available, the required equipment would not have been enough because a tanker like the *Exxon Valdez* is almost one thousand feet long and holds 1.2 million barrels of oil. The booms available could barely encircle the giant ship, much less a sizable slick.

Alyeska violated its own contingency plans when it failed to notify state officials that the barge was out of service. A key piece of equipment in the contingency plan, the barge should have been loaded with seven thousand feet of boom. But the boom had been removed during the repair. A replacement barge had been ordered and was on its way from Texas. On March 24, it was in Seattle.

Although Alyeska conducted regular "spill drills," state monitors said that drills in the previous few years had been bungled and were considered unsuccessful. Among other things, the drills showed that crew members often did not know how to operate their assigned equipment. It was also noted that Alyeska's equipment and the crew's responses were inadequate for a real spill. Reporters Ken Wells and Charles McCoy wrote in the *Wall Street Journal:* "The oil companies' lack of preparedness makes a mockery of a 250-page containment plan, approved by the state, for fighting spills in Prince William Sound." Arlon R. Tussing, a Seattle oil consultant, commented, "The system that was set up early on has disintegrated."

## Cleaning Up

Exxon's chairman, Lawrence Rawl, apologized to the public for the spill in full-page advertisements in many newspapers and in a letter to Exxon shareholders. The company accepted liability for the spill and responsibility for its cleanup. By summer, Exxon had ten thousand people, one thousand vessels, thirty-eight oil skimmers, and seventy-two aircraft working to clean up beaches and wildlife.

Exxon hoped to have completed its cleanup before September 15, 1989, but a 1990 survey showed that much work remained to be done. Shoreline surveys and limited cleanup efforts were made in 1991, 1992, 1993, and 1994. In 1992 crews from Exxon and the state and federal governments reported that an estimated 7 miles of the 21.4 miles of shoreline surveyed still showed some surface oiling. The surveys also indicated that subsurface oil remained at many of the sites that were heavily oiled in 1989. The surveys determined that the potential environmental impact of further cleanup, as well as the cost, was greater than the problems caused by leaving the oil in place. The 1992 cleanup and the 1993 shoreline assessment were concentrated in those areas where oil remained to a greater degree: Prince William Sound and the Kenai Peninsula. In 1994 restoration workers cleaned a dozen important subsistence and recreation beaches in western Prince William Sound.

Exxon claims that it saved $22 million by not building the *Exxon Valdez* with a second hull. During the period of the oil spill, Exxon spent more than $2.2 billion for cleanup and for reimbursements to the federal, state, and local governments for their expenses in response to the oil spill. In addition, thirty-one lawsuits and thirteen hundred claims had been filed against Exxon within a month of the spill. On August 15, 1989, the state of Alaska also filed a suit against Exxon for mismanaging the response to the oil spill. The suit demanded both compensatory and punitive damages that would exceed $1 billion. Captain Hazelwood, who was fired by Exxon soon after the accident, was found guilty in March 1990 of negligent discharge of oil, a misdemeanor. He was acquitted on three other more serious charges, including drunk driving.

Exxon also faced heated criticism from the public and from state and federal officials, who believed the cleanup efforts were inadequate. A Coast Guard spokesman in Valdez said, "We're running into a problem with the definition of the word 'clean.' The concept of being clean makes you think no oil is there. The oil is still there, but it may be three feet or two feet beneath the surface." Lee Raymond, Exxon's president, said, "Assuming that we can have people working till mid-September, we have a good shot at having all the beaches treated. But not clean like Mr. Clean who shows up in your kitchen. Our objective is to make sure the ecosystems are back in shape." Many Alaskans and environmentalists did not believe Exxon's idea of "clean" was clean enough. In addition, there were disputes as to how much oil had actually been cleaned up. By 1989 six hundred miles of shoreline had been "treated," but another two hundred miles still required treatment. Moreover, incoming tides often brought new oil slicks to cover just-treated beaches, slowing cleanup efforts considerably.

In addition, Exxon came under fire for the way it had managed the crisis. Chairman Lawrence Rawl did not comment on the spill for nearly six days, and then he did so from New York. Although Rawl personally apologized for the spill, crisis-management experts say that it is important for the chief executive to be present at the site of an emergency. Harry Nicolay, a Boston crisis-management consultant, said, "When the most senior person in the company comes forward, it's telling the whole world that we take this as a most serious concern." The crisis-management experts believe that Rawl's delayed response and failure to appear on the scene angered the public even despite Exxon's efforts to clean up the spill.

Some of Exxon's statements to the public have also been criticized as bad public relations moves. For example, one Exxon executive told reporters that consumers would pay for the costs of the cleanup in the form of higher gas prices. Although that statement may have been truthful, it did nothing to placate already angry consumers. The public also reacted skeptically to Exxon officials' attempts to blame cleanup delays on the Coast Guard and Alaskan officials. Gerald C. Meyers, a specialist in corporate crisis management, said that Exxon's newspaper apology was "absolutely insincere. They were ill advised to say they sent 'several hundred people' to the scene. This is a company with more than 100,000 employees." Furthermore, Exxon insisted that it would stop all cleanup operations on September 15, 1989, regardless of how much shoreline remained to be cleaned. In a memorandum released in July 1989, that September deadline was said to be "not negotiable." After much public and government protest, however, the company's president promised that Exxon would return in the spring of 1990 if the Coast Guard determined that further cleanup was warranted. "It's our best guess that there will be a lot less oil than people think," he said. "But if the conclusion is reached by the Coast Guard that something needs to be made right and it can be made right, we'll be there. We're not trying to run off." Exxon did return that spring and the next four years for further cleanup efforts.

Exxon's response to the crisis certainly hurt its reputation and credibility with the public. National consumer groups urged the public to boycott all Exxon products, and nearly twenty thousand Exxon credit card holders cut up their cards and returned them to the company to express their dissatisfaction with its cleanup efforts. Indeed, anger and resentment toward Exxon linger more than a decade after the disaster, and some consumers still refuse to patronize the company because of its handling of the spill.

## The Effects of the Exxon Valdez Disaster in the Twenty-First Century

Many changes have occurred since the *Exxon Valdez* incident. Because Captain Hazelwood was found to have had a high blood-alcohol content after the spill, three of Alyeska's largest owners (including Exxon) began mandatory random drug and alcohol searches of all ships using the Valdez port. In 1999, Captain Hazelwood began serving a sentence of one thousand hours of community service after he failed in a nine-year appeal of his 1990 conviction for negligent discharge of oil. Alaska's Governor Steve Cowper ordered Alyeska Pipeline to restock the Valdez terminal with all the booms, skimmers, and other equipment that were required by the original contingency plan. Alyeska was also ordered to form an emergency crew to respond immediately to spills. Governor Cowper demanded that Alyeska stock enough additional equipment to allow it to respond within two hours to a ten-million-gallon spill in Prince William Sound. Alyeska is now required to encircle all tankers with containment booms as they are loading and unloading, and it also had to change other procedures. The state of Alaska also eliminated many of the tax exemptions granted to oil companies producing in many Alaskan oil fields. The elimination of the tax breaks was expected to cost the affected oil companies about $2 billion over the next twenty years. The *Exxon Valdez* was renamed the *SeaRiver Mediterranean,* but the new name failed to prevent environmentalists from regularly protesting the ship in ports along its new Middle East–Europe route. Prevented by law from entering Alaskan waters and too large and expensive for the Middle Eastern route, the ship was retired from service in the early 2000s.

In a civil settlement with the state of Alaska and the federal government, Exxon agreed to make ten annual payments—ending in the twenty-first century—totaling $900 million, for injuries to natural resources and services and for the restoration and replacement of natural resources. In addition, $5 billion was awarded in punitive damages, which must be divided evenly among the fourteen thousand commercial fishermen, natives, business owners, landowners, and native corporations that were part of the class-action suit. Exxon appealed this judgment, but in late 2000, the Supreme Court refused to free the company from having to pay the $5 billion in damages; a U.S. District Judge later reduced the punitive damages to $4 billion.

In a criminal plea agreement, Exxon was fined $150 million, of which $125 million was remitted in recognition of its cooperation in cleaning up the spill and paying private claims. Of the remaining $25 million, $12 million went to the North American Wetlands Conservation Fund and $13 million to the Victims of Crime Fund. In addition, Exxon agreed to pay restitution of $50 million to the United States and $50 million to the state of Alaska.

But the court debate has not ended. Exxon is involved in a highly contested lawsuit with its numerous insurance providers over their refusal to pay Exxon for its spill-cleanup efforts. The insurance companies, led by Lloyd's of London, refused to pay Exxon because (1) the cleanup efforts engaged in were not required by law; (2) the efforts were conducted in substandard fashion; (3) Exxon's level of liability coverage was well below the expenses sought; and (4) the spill itself was a result of "intentional misconduct," thus disqualifying insurance coverage of the accident. In short, the insurance companies contend that Exxon's cleanup activities were little more than "an expensive public relations exercise," designed to make the public think of Exxon as an ethical and socially responsible corporation. Claiming that it had incurred between $3.5 billion and $4 billion in expenses for the cleanup, Exxon in turn filed suit against the 250 insurance companies, originally seeking around $3 billion in compensation, though it was covered for only $850 million. Most of the original amount Exxon sought from the insurers, $2.15 billion, was for their "bad-faith" conduct in initially refusing to pay as well as interest charges and attorneys' fees. The original figure of $3 billion was later reduced to about $1 billion, and insurers agreed to pay Exxon $300 million as a partial settlement of claims related to cleanup activities.

The one positive consequence of the *Exxon Valdez* oil spill has been better industry response to spills. According to one analyst, "We're still seeing the same number of spills. What has improved is the response to those spills." However, this hardly compensates for the harm inflicted by Exxon's negligent spillage of eleven million gallons of crude oil into the Prince William Sound area. Exxon, now called ExxonMobil, insists the area has completely recovered. However, a study by the National Marine Fisheries Service found that toxins leaching from *Valdez* oil that remains on the beaches continued to harm sea life more than twelve years after the disaster.

*Questions*

1. In the context of this incident and the circumstances that led up to it, discuss the role of individual moral development, organizational factors, and significant others in the decisions made after the spill.

2. If Exxon had had an ethics program, would this have prevented the wreck of the *Exxon Valdez*?

3. Should Exxon and Alyeska be held responsible for cleaning up the spill, or should taxpayers and consumers pay for it (in the form of higher gasoline prices and taxes)? Why?

4. In future oil-production efforts, which should take precedence: the environment or consumers' desires for low-priced gasoline and heating oil? Why?

Sources: These facts are from Scott Allen, "Oil Spills: A Fossil-Fuel Fact of Life," *Boston Globe*, Jan. 27, 1996, p. 13; Ronald Alsop, "Corporate Reputations Are Earned with Trust, Reliability, Study Shows," *Wall Street Journal*, Sept. 23, 1999, http://interactive.wsj.com; American Petroleum Institute, "Oil Spill Prevention and Response: It's in Everyone's Best Interest," www.api.org/resources/ valdez/ (accessed June 14, 1999); Reed Abelson, "Tax Reformers, Take Your Mark," *New York Times*, Feb. 11, 1996, sec. 3, p. 1; Scott Allen, "Oil Spills. A Fossil-Fuel Fact of Life," *Boston Globe*, Jan. 27, 1996, p. 13; Wayne Beissert, "In *Valdez*'s Wake, Uncertainty," *USA Today*, July 28, 1989, p. 3A; Amanda Bennett, Julie Solomon, and Allanna Sullivan, "Firms Debate Hard Line on Alcoholics," *Wall Street Journal*, Apr. 13, 1989, p. 131; CNN, Mar. 22, 1990; Carrie Dolan, "Exxon to Bolster Oil-Cleanup Effort After Criticism," *Wall Street Journal*, May 11, 1989, p. A10; Carrie Dolan and Charles McCoy, "Military Transports Begin Delivering Equipment to Battle Alaskan Oil Spill," *Wall Street Journal*, Apr. 10, 1989, p. A8; Stuart Elliot, "Public Angry at Slow Action on Oil Spill," *USA Today*, Apr. 21, 1989, pp. B1, 132; "Exxon Mobil Must Pay *Valdez* Fine," *USA Today*, Oct. 2, 2000, www.usatoday.com/news/court/nsco1379.htm; "Exxon Valdez Disaster Haunts Alaska 14 Years On," *Sydney Morning Herald*, Jan. 16, 2003, www.smh.com.au/articles/2003/01/15/1042520672374.html; "Exxon Will Pay $3.5 Million to Settle Claims in Phase Four of *Valdez* Case," *BNA State Environment Daily*, Jan. 19, 1996; Aliza Fan, "Exxon May Still Get More Than $3 Billion in Dispute with Lloyd's," *Oil Daily*, Jan. 22, 1996, p. 3; Tony Freemantle, "Billion-Dollar Battle Looms over Spill Costs: Exxon Corp. Trying to Collect from Its Insurance Companies," *Anchorage Daily News*, Sept. 5, 1995, p. IA; William Glasgall and Vicky Cahan, "Questions That Keep Surfacing After the Spill," *Business Week,* Apr. 17, 1989, p. 18; Kathy Barks Hoffman, "Oil Spill's Cleanup Costs Exceed $1.3B," *USA Today,* July 25, 1989, p. B1; *Institute for Crisis Management Newsletter,* 4 (March 1995): 3; "Judge Cuts Exxon Valdez Punitive Damage Award," *Alaska Journal,* Dec. 16, 2002, www.alaskajournal. com/stories/121602/loc_20021216003.shtml; Dave Lenckus, "Exxon Seeks More Spill Cover: Oil Giant Reaches Partial Agreement with Insurers," *Business Insurance,* Jan. 22, 1996, p. 1; Charles McCoy, "Alaska Drops Criminal Probe of Oil Disaster," *Wall Street Journal,* July 28, 1989, p. A3; Charles McCoy, "Alaskans End Big Tax Breaks for Oil Firms," *Wall Street Journal,* May 10, 1989, p. A6; Charles McCoy, "Heartbreaking Fight Unfolds in Hospital for Valdez Otters," *Wall Street Journal,* Apr. 20, 1989, pp. A1, A4; Charles McCoy and Ken Wells, "Alaska, U.S. Knew of Flaws in Oil-Spill Response Plans," *Wall Street Journal,* Apr. 7, 1989, p. A3; Peter Nulty, "The Future of Big Oil," *Fortune,* May 8, 1989, pp. 46–49; Wayne Owens, "Turn the Valdez Cleanup Over to Mother Nature," editorial, *Wall Street Journal,* July 27, 1989, p. A8; Natalie Phillips, "$3.5 Million Settles Exxon Spill Suit," *Anchorage Daily News,* Jan. 18, 1996, p. 113; "In Ten Years You'll See 'Nothing'" (interview with Exxon chairman, Lawrence Rawl), *Fortune,* May 8, 1989, pp. 50–54; Lawrence G. Rawl, letter to Exxon shareholders, Apr. 14, 1989; "Recordings Reveal Exxon Captain Rocked Tanker to Free It from Reef," [Texas A&M University] *Battalion,* Apr. 26, 1989, p. 1; Michael Satchell, with Steve Lindbeck, "Tug of War Over Oil Drilling," *U.S. News & World Report,* Apr. 10, 1989, pp. 47–48; Richard B. Schmitt, "Exxon, Alyeska May Be Exposed on Damages," *Wall Street Journal,* Apr. 10, 1989, p. A8; Stratford P. Sherman, "Smart Way to Handle the Press," *Fortune,* June 19, 1989, pp. 69–75; Caleb Solomon and Allanna Sullivan, "For the Petroleum Industry, Pouring Oil Is in Fact the Cause of Troubled Waters," *Wall Street Journal,* Mar. 31, 1989, p. A4; Allanna Sullivan, "Agencies Clear Exxon Oil-Cleanup Plan Despite Coast Guard Doubts on Deadline," *Wall Street Journal,* Apr. 19, 1989, p. A2; Allanna Sullivan, "Alaska Sues Exxon Corp., 6 Other Firms," *Wall Street Journal,* Aug. 16, 1989, pp. A3, A4; Allanna Sullivan and Amanda Bennett, "Critics Fault Chief Executive of Exxon on Handling of Recent Alaskan Oil Spill," *Wall Street Journal,* Mar. 31, 1989, p. B1; Kim Todd, "Last Voyage of the Valdez?" *Sierra,* Jan./Feb. 2003, www.sierraclub.org/sierra/200301/lol6_printable. asp; "*Valdez* Captain Serves Sentence," Associated Press, June 22, 1999; Ken Wells, "Alaska Begins Criminal Inquiry of Valdez Spill," *Wall Street Journal,* Mar. 30, 1989, p. A4; Ken Wells, "Blood-Alcohol Level of Captain of Exxon Tanker Exceeded Limits," *Wall Street Journal,* Mar. 31, 1989, p. A4; Ken Wells, "For Exxon, Cleanup Costs May Be Just the Beginning," *Wall Street Journal,* Apr. 14, 1989, pp. B1, B2; Ken Wells and Marilyn Chase, "Paradise Lost: Heartbreaking Scenes of Beauty Disfigured Follow Alaska Oil Spill," *Wall Street Journal,* Mar. 31, 1989, pp. A1, A4; Ken Wells and Charles McCoy, "How Unpreparedness Turned the Alaska Spill into Ecological Debacle," *Wall Street Journal,* Apr. 3, 1989, pp. A1, A4; Ken Wells and Allanna Sullivan, "Stuck in Alaska: Exxon's Army Scrubs the Beaches, but They Don't Stay Cleaned," *Wall Street Journal,* July 27, 1989, pp. A1, A5.

# Case 11

# Tobacco Under Fire: Advertising a Harmful Product[1]

The detrimental effects of tobacco use have been well documented. It is one of the primary factors in illnesses such as cancer, heart and circulatory disease, and respiratory disease. Smoking causes nearly 90 percent of all lung cancers, and secondhand smoke has been shown to contribute to the development of lung cancer in nonsmokers. Experts estimate that there are approximately 4.2 million tobacco-related deaths per year worldwide; given current trends, this statistic is projected to rise to 10 million by 2030.

## History of Cigarette Advertising

The advertising of cigarettes began as early as 1929. One of the first ads, by Lucky Strike, touted the fact that more than twenty thousand physicians had said Lucky Strike was less irritating than other cigarettes and that prominent athletes smoked its products with no harmful effects. In 1939 Philip Morris promoted its cigarettes as having advantages for the nose and throat. A decade later Camel was also extolling the health benefits of its product. Nevertheless, by the early 1950s consumers had begun to suspect that smoking might be harmful. To counter this perception, Kent ran an ad arguing that if you were one of those "sensitive smokers" who worried about the harmful effects of smoking, Kent provided you with health protection and gave "taste satisfaction."

As a result of growing public concern, however, investigations into the health hazards of cigarette smoking began in the early 1950s. In 1953 a report from the Memorial Sloan-Kettering Cancer Center linked smoking to cancer in rats. The first attempt to regulate the cigarette industry came in 1955, when the Federal Trade Commission (FTC) prohibited companies from claiming the presence or absence of any positive physical effects from smoking in their cigarette advertising or labeling.

In the 1960s and 1970s, consumers and the U.S. government began to understand the harmful effects of smoking. In 1964, U.S. Surgeon General Luther Terry declared cigarettes to be a cause of cancer. The following year trade regulation rules were formulated that mandated a health warning on all cigarette packaging and prohibited

[1] This case was prepared by John Fraedrich and Barbara Gilmer for classroom discussion rather than to illustrate either effective or ineffective handling of an administrative, ethical, or legal decision by management.

advertising cigarettes to people under twenty-five. In addition, several countries began banning television advertisements for cigarettes. Nevertheless, consumption continued to increase.

Smoking did not begin to decline until soon after the "fairness doctrine" was implemented in 1967. Although developed for political advertising, the fairness doctrine as applied to tobacco advertising, requires radio and television broadcasters to give equal time to antismoking advertisements. In 1971, the Cigarette Advertising and Labeling Act banned cigarette advertisements from U.S. television and radio altogether. A 1984 amendment required cigarette manufacturers or importers to display on all cigarette packaging and advertising one of four different health warnings, which were rotated every quarter.

In the 1980s, however, the tobacco industry discovered a new promotional vehicle, which soon became an industry standard—movie endorsements. Film star Sylvester Stallone, for example, agreed to smoke Brown & Williamson (B&W) cigarettes in four movies—*Rhinestone Cowboy, Rambo, 50/50,* and *Rocky IV,* for $500,000. The tobacco industry had vehemently opposed all legislation restricting cigarette advertising. In contrast, the medical profession and various consumer groups demanded even more stringent regulation of the industry. Many advocated a complete ban on cigarette advertising.

## The Multistate Master Settlement Agreement

Consumers and the medical community were rewarded in 1998 when the five largest tobacco manufacturers in the United States reached a landmark $246 billion settlement with the attorneys general of forty-six states. The master settlement agreement (MSA) required the companies to give billions of dollars to those state governments every year to help relieve the financial burden that smoking-related illnesses placed on state health care systems as well as to fund campaigns to discourage smoking, especially among children. The settlement requires the companies to stop using cartoon characters, like R.J. Reynold's Joe Camel, and bars them from a number of traditional promotion strategies, such as using billboards, direct mail advertising, or samples passed out at shopping malls. To help pay for the costs of the settlement, the companies were forced to raise prices by 44 percent over the next two years.

To comply with the terms of the settlement, the cigarette marketers were forced to make significant changes to their marketing strategies. All of the firms contributed to the funding of the Washington-based antismoking group, American Legacy Foundation, and shifted some of their promotion budgets to image campaigns. Philip Morris, for example, ran commercials explaining the provisions of the MSA, while R.J. Reynolds Tobacco launched the "Right Decisions, Right Now" program, which created and distributed antismoking materials to teachers. Brown & Williamson and other companies contributed funds to support the "We Card" program for retailers.

Despite agreeing in the settlement not to target youths in advertisements, studies by the Massachusetts Department of Public Health and the American Legacy Foundation found that in the year after the settlement advertising in magazines with large teen readerships actually increased. Cigarette makers spent $119.9 million on advertising in magazines popular among youths, a 30 percent increase over the amount spent in the period before the settlement. Faced with investigations into whether its advertising violated the 1998 settlements, Philip Morris, the nation's largest tobacco company, announced that it would stop placing ads in forty-two magazines that had more than 15 percent teen readers. However, a spokesman for *Sports Illustrated* said the readership figures used by Philip Morris were inaccurate, and *Entertainment Weekly's* publisher said that the move by Philip Morris was "a suspension and not a forever cancellation."

## High Stakes

Cigarettes are big business. With approximately six trillion cigarettes purchased annually at a cost of $50 billion, the economic stakes are enormous. Twenty-two states grow tobacco, making it the sixth-largest cash crop in the United States. The vast and complex tobacco-supply network extends the chain of economic dependence on tobacco to include manufacturers of farm equipment, advertising agencies, advertising media, and other businesses around the world. Additionally, state and federal governments generate significant revenues from excise and other taxes on tobacco products. Arguably, banning cigarettes and their advertising could have serious repercussions for the economy. Moreover, even many nonsmokers believe that cigarette advertising is commercial speech protected under the First Amendment. There are also those who fear that a ban on cigarette advertising would set a dangerous precedent for more government interference in commercial activities.

Opponents of the free-speech argument counter that if commercial speech is to be free, it should not be deceptive and misleading. For example, in 1985 R. J. Reynolds ran an advertisement in the *New York Times* and other newspapers around the United States entitled "Of Cigarettes and Science." The FTC filed a formal complaint against the company, charging that the advertisement distorted an important study demonstrating the relationship between a number of risk factors and heart disease. R. J. Reynolds countered by arguing that "Of Cigarettes and Science" was an expression of opinion on an issue of social and political importance and was therefore protected by the First Amendment. A commercial law judge dismissed the complaint, concluding that "Of Cigarettes and Science" was not commercial speech and therefore not subject to FTC regulation. The court did not consider whether the advertisement was deceptive, false, or misleading.

## The Future

Class-action lawsuits, the multistate agreement, and increasing pressure from antismoking activists have sent a message to the tobacco industry that its product is increasingly unwelcome—but not the taxes it brings in. This new era may have begun with Jeffrey Wigand, a former research executive of Brown & Williamson, who came forward to testify against the tobacco giants. Wigand's decision to blow the whistle on "big Tobacco" was later dramatized in the award-winning movie *The Insider.* He now travels the country giving guest lectures to children in grades K–6 about the dangers of smoking. Government statistics indicate that 80 percent of the fifty to sixty million Americans habituated to cigarettes began smoking as children. National news shows such as *60 Minutes* widened the debate as to whether tobacco companies should be legally liable for damages caused by smoking.

If there are no dramatic changes in cessation rates and no new interventions and if children start smoking at expected rates, then the current number of smokers in the world, 1.1 billion, is predicted to rise to 1.64 billion by 2025. In developing countries, women will be a particular focus of tobacco companies as smoking rates are now much lower among women than men. The prevalence of smoking among women in developing countries is currently 12 percent, but that figure is likely to triple by 2025. It is in the developing countries that the tobacco companies see their future, as the following statements suggest:

> They have to find a way to feed the monsters they've built. Just about the only way will be to increase sales to the developing world.[2]
>
> Tobacco use in the developed nations will trend down slightly through the end of the century, while in the developing countries use could rise by about three percent annually. A bright picture indeed! Not a smoke-free society, but continued growth for the tobacco industry.[3] We should not be depressed simply because the total free world market appears to be declining. Within the total market, there are areas of strong growth, particularly in Asia and Africa; there are new markets opening up for our exports, such as Indo-China and the Comecon countries; and there are great opportunities to increase our market share in areas like Europe. . . . This industry is consistently profitable. And there are opportunities to increase that profitability still further.[4]
>
> You know what we want . . . we want Asia.[5]

In the post-MSA twenty-first century, tobacco companies in the United States and Europe appear to be rethinking their strategies for developed countries. In the United States, tobacco firms are concentrating their marketing efforts on areas where adult smokers are readily found. Representatives of Brown & Williamson, for example, seek out smokers on the streets (because smoking is prohibited inside most public buildings in most U.S. municipalities) and offer them coffee and free samples. Marketing representatives are also passing out free samples to bar patrons, but only after observing them smoking and checking their IDs. Point-of-sale promotions in convenience stores have become crucial because these retailers represent the last large public spaces available to larger cigarette ads. However, Mike Pfeil, vice president of communications and public affairs at Philip Morris, insists that his company has not shifted billboard spending to retail point-of-sale. Rather, he says, Philip Morris' strategy is to "lower the profile of cigarette ads in stores because that's what the public expects of a tobacco company."

Additionally, several companies are working to create a "safer" cigarette. Star Scientific, Inc., for example, has test-marketed a new cigarette that combines a charcoal filter and cured tobacco to reduce nitrosamine, a carcinogen. R. J. Reynolds' *Eclipse* brand is the result of a technology explored in the 1980s that relies on heating tobacco rather than burning it, thus producing fewer toxic substances. The hope is that

---

[2] R. Morelli, "Packing It In," *Marketing Week,* Jun. 28, 1991, pp. 30–34.
[3] "Growth Through 2000," *Tobacco Reporter,* Feb. 1989.
[4] L. Heise, "Unhealthy Alliance," *World Watch,* Oct. 1988, p. 20 [c. 7].
[5] L. Heise, "Unhealthy Alliance," *World Watch,* Oct. 1988, p. 20 [c. 7].

the risk of cancer, chronic bronchitis, and possibly emphysema will be reduced. However, *Eclipse*'s filter can release glass fibers into the lungs.

Although the use of tobacco products is not expected to be banned in the United States, antismoking campaigns and increased public awareness have helped reduce the number of cigarettes smoked within the last two decades by 42 percent in the United States. Additionally, a number of municipalities, including New York City, have enacted ordinances that sharply limit smoking in public places. Also contributing to this reduction is the fact that the price of cigarettes rose 80 percent over the last four years. The average state tax on a pack of cigarettes is 34 cents.

While tobacco consumption will continue to decrease overall in developed countries, a more aggressive marketing strategy is being pursued in developing countries. There tobacco companies are sponsoring sporting and other events and aiming their advertising toward younger people. The World Health Organization (WHO) anticipates that 70 percent of tobacco-related deaths will be in developing countries by 2030. In March 2003, all but 2 of the 171 nations at the World Health Organization conference in Geneva, Switzerland, agreed on a treaty that would ban tobacco advertising. Most of the opposition to the treaty came from the United States. WHO and the World Bank are also trying to convince developing countries to follow the U.S. example of raising cigarette taxes in order to prevent the tobacco companies from gaining new and larger markets in these countries. It is likely that the lessons learned by the tobacco companies in the U.S. court system will be applied to emerging markets so future litigation can be kept to a minimum.

*Questions*

1. What are the arguments for and against the issue of tobacco use, tobacco advertising, and free speech?
2. Does selling a potentially harmful or addictive product that is nevertheless legal represent an ethical problem for businesspeople? How should a society regulate such products and protect its citizens from them?
3. If the cost of cigarettes becomes prohibitive in the United States, what, if any, are the ethical ramifications of selling cigarettes in other countries?

Sources: These facts are from "America Smokes, Exports Fewer Cigarettes," *Detroit News,* May 22, 2000, p. 8; *American Voices: Prize Winning Essays on Freedom of Speech, Censorship, and Advertising Bans* (New York: Philip Morris USA, 1987); "Africa: Ashtray of the World," *[London] Sunday Times,* May 13, 1990; "Are Tobacco Companies More Responsible?" in Debbie Thorne McAlister, O. C. Ferrell, and Linda Ferrell, *Business and Society: A Strategic Approach to Corporate Citizenship* (Boston: Houghton Mifflin, 2003), pp. 210–211; Rekha Balu and Ernest Beck, "Heeding Critics, Sara Lee Corp. Kicks Tobacco," *Wall Street Journal,* Apr. 8, 1998, pp. B1, B4; Sally Beatty, "Tobacco Pact Pays to Combat Teen Smoking," *Wall Street Journal,* Apr. 13, 1998, pp. B1, B12; L. Bird, "Joe Smooth for President," *Adweek's Marketing Week,* May 20, 1991; Alan Blum, *New England Journal of Medicine,* Mar. 28, 1991, pp. 913–916; "Cigarette Sales on Web Will Resolve Tax Issues," *Portland Press Herald,* Aug. 30, 2000, p. 10A; Ann Davis, "Top Ad Agency Defends Tossing Joe Camel Files," *Wall Street Journal,* Apr. 30, 1998, pp. B1, B5; Ann Davis and Ernest Beck, "U.S. Tactics Stoke Britain's War on Tobacco," *Wall Street Journal,* Apr. 9, 1998, pp. B1, B9; "Deaths from Tobacco Will Soar," *Chicago Sun-Times,* Aug. 8, 2000, p. 12; Kathleen Deveny, "Joe Camel Is Also Pied Piper, Research Finds," *Wall Street Journal,* Dec. 11, 1992, pp. B1, B4; "Dying to Quit," *Advocate,* Aug. 3, 2000, p. 2A; William Ecenbarger, "America's New Merchants of Death," *Reader's Digest,* Apr. 1993; "Expecting a World Which Is Free from Tobacco," *Jakarta Post,* May 31, 2000, p. 3; Paul M. Fischer, Meyer P. Schwartz, John W. Richards Jr., Adam O. Goldstein, and Tina H. Rojas, "Brand Logo Recognition by Children Aged Three to Six Years," *Journal of the American Medical Association (JAMA),* Dec. 11, 1991, pp. 3145–3148; Joseph R. DiFranza, John W. Richards, Paul M. Paulman, Nancy Wolf-Gillespie, Christopher Fletcher, Robert D. Jaffe, and David Murray, "RJR Nabisco's Cartoon Camel Promotes Camel Cigarettes to Children," *JAMA,* Dec. 11, 1991, pp. 3149–3153; Milo Geyelin, "Airline Staff Objects to Deal in Smoke Case," *Wall Street Journal,* Jan. 7, 1998, p. B5; Milo Geyelin, "An Ex-Official of Philip Morris Invokes Fifth Amendment Rights," *Wall Street Journal,* Feb. 18, 1998, p. B2; Gordon Fairclough, "Magazines Brace for Cigarette Ad Pullout," *Wall Street Journal,* June 7, 2000, p. B5; Milo Geyelin, "Gallup Big Tobacco of Misusing Poll in Court," *Wall Street Journal,* June 26, 1998, pp. B1, B7; Milo Geyelin, "Lonely Lawyers for Liggett Feel Minnesota Chill," *Wall Street Journal,* Feb. 6, 1998, pp. B1, B18; Milo Geyelin, "Texas, Tobacco Industry Are Close to 14.5 Billion Settlement of Suit," *Wall Street Journal,* Jan. 12, 1998, p. B8; Milo Geyelin and Ann Davis, "Tobacco's Foes Target Role of Lawyers," *Wall Street Journal,* Apr. 23, 1998, pp. B1, B2; Kevin Goldman, "Philip Morris Dresses Up Virginia Slims," *Wall Street Journal,* Feb. 26, 1993; A. O. Goldstein, P. M. Fischer, J. W. Richards, and D. Creten, "The Influence of Cigarette Advertising on Adolescent Smoking," Action on Smoking and Health, white paper, June 25, 1998, www.ash.org.uk/papers/tobexpld7.html; L. Heise, "Unhealthy Alliance," *World Watch,* Oct. 1988, p. 20 [c. 7]; Suein L. Hwang, "Tobacco Memos Detail Passive-Smoke Attack," *Wall Street Journal,* Apr. 28, 1998, pp. B1, B4; Suein L. Hwang, "Tobacco Takes New Stab at a Settlement," *Wall Street Journal,* July 10, 1998, pp. B1, B5; Suein L. Hwang, "A Vast Trove of Tobacco Documents Opens Up," *Wall Street Journal,* Apr. 23, 1998, pp. B1, B12; Suein L. Hwang and John Lippman, "Hollywood to Antismoking Activist: Butt Out," *Wall Street Journal,* Mar. 17, 1998, pp. B1, B8; John Harwood and Jeffrey Taylor, "Voter Backlash Could Be Proud for New Tobacco Bill," *Wall Street Journal,* June 19, 1998, pp. B1, B5; "Increased Cigarette Company Marketing Since the Multistate Settlement Agreement Went into Effect," Campaign for Tobacco-Free Kids, http://tobaccofreekids.org/research/factsheets/pdf/0128.pdf (accessed Apr. 23, 2003); "Judge Limits Tobacco Cases: Health Laws Can't Be Used to Recover Costs of Sick Smokers," *Detroit News,* Sept. 29, 2000, p. 3; Walecia Konrad, "I'd Toddle a Mile for Camel," *Business Week,* Dec. 23, 1991, p. 34; Gary Levin, "Poll: Camel Ads Effective with Kids: Brand Recognition Highest Among Preteens," *Advertising Age,* Apr. 27, 1992; Karen Lewis, "Addicting the Young: Tobacco Pushers and Kids," *Multinational Monitor,* Jan.-Feb. 1992; Joanne Lipman, "Why Activists Fume at Anti-Smoking Ads," *Wall Street Journal,* Feb. 20, 1992, p. B3; Barbara Lippert, "Camel's Old Joe Poses the Question: What Is Sexy?" *AdWeek's Marketing Week,* Oct. 3, 1988, p. 55; Judith Mackay and Michael Eriksen, *The Tobacco Atlas* (Geneva, Switzerland: World Health Organization, 2002), available at http://tobacco.who.int/page.cfm?sid=84; "Memo on Tobacco Trends in 21st Century: Domestic and Global Outlook," *U.S. Newswire,* Dec. 16, 1999, pp. 1–2; National Institute on Drug Abuse, "Monitoring the Future Survey," 1989 National High School Senior Drug Abuse Survey, press release, Feb. 13, 1990; "NYC Smoking Ban Debuts," CBSNews, Mar. 30, 2003, www.cbsnews.com/stories/2003/03/29/national/main546751.shtml; "R. J. Reynolds Takes on the AMA, Defending Joe Camel Cartoon Ad," *Wall Street Journal,* Feb. 5, 1992, p. B8; A. J. S. Rayl, "Tobacco Targets Kids, Threatens Health," *USA Today,* Mar. 31, 2000, www.usatoday.com/life/health/doctor/lhdoc122.htm; Camille P. Schuster and Christine Pacelli Powell, "Comparison of Cigarette and Alcohol Advertising Controversies," *Journal of Advertising,* 16 (2, 1987): 26–33; Daniel Seligman, "Camel Rights," *Fortune,* May 18, 1992, p. 120; Nancy Shute, "Building a Better Butt," *U.S. News & World Report,* Sept. 18, 2000, p. 66; Suzanne Smalley, *Newsweek,* Mar. 10, 2003, p. 10; Stop Teen Addiction to Tobacco (STAT), "Cigarette Advertising Increases Smoking," *Tobacco Free Youth Reporter,* Fall 1992; Stop Teenage Addiction to Tobacco (STAT), "RJRNabisco: Targeting Teens for Addiction," *Tobacco Free Youth Reporter,* Fall 1992; and Jeffrey Taylor, "Lawyers, Once Chary of Big Tobacco, Rush to Line Up Plaintiffs," *Wall Street Journal,* Apr. 1, 1998, pp. A1, A7; "Tobacco Explained: 7. Emerging Markets," Action on Smoking and Health, white paper, June 25, 1998, www.ash.org.uk/html/conduct/html/tobexpld7.html; "Tobacco Trials Research," The Wilmington Institute, 1998, www.tobacco-litigation.com/index.html-ssi (accessed June 16, 1999); Joe B. Tye, "Lusting After Children: The Tobacco Industry's Investment in a Profitable Future," *Social Science Record,* Fall 1988; U.S. Department of Health and Human Services, National Center for Chronic Disease Prevention and Health Promotion Study, cited in *Wall Street Journal,* Apr. 2, 1993, p. A1; "U.S. House Approval of Foreign Sales Corporation Bill Providing $100 Million in Tax Breaks for U.S. Tobacco Companies," *U.S. Newswire,* Sept. 13, 2000, p. 1; Fara Warner, "Novello Throws Down the Gauntlet: The Surgeon General's Crusade to Kill Off Joe Cool," *AdWeek's Marketing Week,* Mar. 16, 1992, pp. 4–5; Larry C. White, *Merchants of Death* (New York: Beech Tree Books, 1988); "World No-Tobacco Day: Health Versus Smoking," World Health Organization, press release, May 27, 1993; "You're Going Too Far, Baby," *The Village Voice,* Aug. 15, 2000, pp. 62–63.

# Microsoft: Antitrust Battles[1]

M icrosoft Corporation was founded in 1975 by William H. (Bill) Gates III and Paul G. Allen. Since that time the company's innovative products and marketing prowess have made it the world's leading marketer of computer software. Among its many product lines are operating systems for personal computers (PCs), network servers, and other devices; office productivity software; software development tools; Internet products such as Internet Explorer and the MSN online network; and gaming devices like the Xbox. The company has grown to nearly fifty-one thousand employees worldwide with annual revenues of $28.37 billion in fiscal year 2002. Microsoft's stated mission is "to enable people and businesses throughout the world to realize their full potential" through its products.

Along with its innovative products and marketing, Microsoft contributes substantially to charities. In 2002, the company and its employees donated $246.9 million, as well as thousands of volunteer hours. For example, when Microsoft employees donate to the annual giving campaign, the company matches their contributions, up to $12,000. Organizations that have benefited from these contributions include low-income housing developments, the YMCA, Easter Seals, Boys and Girls Club of America, museums, and schools. Another important program is Libraries Online, through which Microsoft provides computers, cash, and software to help link libraries to the Internet. The goal is to enable people who may not have access to computers to learn about PCs, explore the latest software, and experience the Internet. The company focuses its philanthropic contributions on four areas: helping to provide technology access to underserved communities around the world, strengthening nonprofit organizations, supporting technology training and education for underserved people around the world, and building communities.

## Legal Issues Demeaning Microsoft's Reputation

Regardless of Microsoft's reputation for innovation and charity, the company has faced significant ethical and legal issues stemming from its dominance of particular software markets. In 1990, for example, the Federal Trade Commission (FTC) began

[1] This case was prepared by Robyn Smith and John Fraedrich for classroom discussion, rather than to illustrate either effective or ineffective handling of an administrative, ethical, or legal decision by management.

investigating Microsoft for possible violations of the Sherman and Clayton Antitrust Acts. By August 1993, the FTC was deadlocked on a decision regarding possible Microsoft violations and handed the case over to the U.S. Department of Justice (DOJ). Microsoft eventually agreed to settle those charges without admitting any wrongdoing. Part of the settlement provided the Justice Department with complete access to Microsoft's documents for use in subsequent investigations.

Another important part of that settlement was a provision to end Microsoft's practice of selling its MS-DOS operating system to original equipment manufacturers (OEMs) at a 60 percent discount. Those manufacturers received the discount if they agreed to pay Microsoft for every computer they sold (a "per processor" agreement) as opposed to paying Microsoft for every computer they sold that had MS-DOS preinstalled (a "per copy" agreement). If an original equipment manufacturer wished to install a different operating system in some of its computers, the manufacturer would, in effect, be paying for both the Microsoft and the other operating system—that is, paying "double royalties." Critics argued that this practice was unfair to both consumers—who effectively paid Microsoft even when they bought a rival operating system—and manufacturers, because it made it uneconomical to give up the 60 percent Microsoft discount in order to install a less popular operating system on some of its computers. Competitors claimed the practice was monopolistic.

The Supreme Court has defined monopoly power as the "power to control prices or exclude competition." In other words, a monopolist is a company that can significantly raise the barriers to entry within the relevant market. A monopolist may engage in practices that any company, regardless of size, could legally employ. However, it cannot use its market power in such a way so as to prevent competition. In essence, a company is allowed to be a monopoly, but when a monopolist acts in a way that only a monopolist can, it has broken the law.

Despite the settlement, Microsoft's legal woes were far from over. The next battle was against Apple Computer. Apple alleged that Microsoft's chief executive officer, Bill Gates, threatened to stop making Macintosh-compatible products if Apple did not stop developing a program that was to compete with a similar Microsoft program. Because Microsoft is the largest producer of Macintosh-compatible programs, Apple argued that it was being forced to choose between a bad deal or extinction. Apple also alleged that Microsoft would not send it a copy of Windows 95 until Apple dropped Microsoft's name from a lawsuit. Over the years, the two companies worked out their differences. And, in late 1998, Microsoft bought $150 million of nonvoting stock in Apple, as well as paying $100 million for access to Apple's patents.

The next legal battle was Sun Microsystems' trademark and breach-of-contract case against Microsoft. The case accused Microsoft of deliberately trying to sabotage Sun's Java "write once, run anywhere" promise by making Windows implementations incompatible with those that run on other platforms. Specifically, the suit alleged that Microsoft's Java-compatible products omitted a so-called Java native interface (JNI), as well as a remote method invocation (RMI)—features that help developers write Java code. Sun claimed Microsoft replaced certain parts of the Java code with Windows-specific code in a way that confused programmers into thinking they were using pure Java. Sun acknowledged that Microsoft fixed some of the earlier problems, but added two new alleged incompatibilities to its list. One allegation concerned the addition of new keywords that are available to programmers, and the other revolved around new directives in Microsoft's Java compiler that make it dependent on Windows implementations.

In 1998 Sun added new allegations of exclusionary conduct on Microsoft's part and requested an injunction that would require Microsoft either to make the Java features in its new Windows 98 operating system compatible with its tests or to include Sun's version of Java with every copy of Windows sold. In 2000, the Ninth District Court of Appeals ruled that it was software developers and consumers, not Sun, who would decide the value of Microsoft's language extensions. Therefore, Microsoft was allowed to support its development tools with its own Java enhancements. Furthermore, Sun's motion to reinstate the injunction on the basis of copyright infringement was denied. The court ruled that the compatibility test was a contractual issue, not a copyright issue.

After various companies, particularly Netscape Communications, continued to complain about Microsoft's competitive practices, the federal government took an aggressive stand. It charged Microsoft with creating a monopolistic environment that substantially reduced competition in the industry. The company settled the charges in 1995 and consented to a decree that prohibited it from imposing anticompetitive licensing terms on PC manufacturers.

In October 1997, however, the Justice Department asked a federal court to hold Microsoft in civil contempt for violating the terms of that consent decree and to impose a $1 million-per-day fine. This time the issue was over Microsoft's "bundling" of its Internet Explorer Web browser into the Windows 95 operating system. Microsoft argued that Internet Explorer was an integral, inseparable part of Windows 95 and that it had not integrated the browser technology solely to disadvantage rivals such as Netscape. A U.S. District Court judge disagreed and issued an injunction prohibiting the company from requiring Windows 95 licensees to bundle Internet Explorer with the operating system. Microsoft filed an appeal and asked for the petition to be heard on an expedited basis, while it supplied PC makers with an older version of Windows 95 without the Internet Explorer files or with a current version of Windows 95 stripped of all Internet Explorer files. The modified product would not boot up, however, a problem that Microsoft later admitted it knew about beforehand. Consequently, the Justice Department asked the district court to hold Microsoft in contempt. Microsoft's stock price began to drop. Possibly fearing larger stock devaluation, Microsoft agreed to provide computer vendors with the most up-to-date version of Windows 95 without the Internet Explorer desktop icon.

## Microsoft's Rebuttal to the Allegations

In response to its detractors, twenty state attorneys general, and the Justice Department, Microsoft denied all of the essential allegations, arguing that it had planned to integrate Internet Explorer into the Windows operating system long before rival Netscape even existed. Microsoft also refuted the government's central accusation that it incorporated its browser technologies into Windows only to disadvantage Netscape. Microsoft argued that its Internet Explorer was gaining popularity with consumers for the simple reason that it offered superior technology. In addition, Microsoft rejected government allegations that it tried to "illegally divide the browser market" with rival Netscape and that it had entered into exclusionary contracts with Internet service providers or Internet content providers. Finally, Microsoft argued that it did not illegally restrict computer manufacturers from altering the Windows desktop screen that users see when they turn on their computers for the first time.

Like other software products, the various versions of Microsoft's Windows operating system products are protected by the Federal Copyright Act of 1976. This act states that copyright owners have the right to license their products to third parties in an unaltered form. Thus, Microsoft asserted a counterclaim against the state attorneys general because it believed the state attorneys general were inappropriately trying to use state antitrust laws to infringe on Microsoft's federal rights.

## Microsoft on Trial

After two years of negotiations, the federal government, along with twenty states, charged Microsoft with abusing its monopoly in the computer software business. The three primary issues raised in the lawsuit were (1) bundling the Internet Explorer Web browser with the Windows 98 operating system to damage competition, particularly Netscape Communications Inc.; (2) using cross-promotional deals with Internet providers to extend its monopoly; and (3) illegally preventing PC makers from customizing the opening screen showing Microsoft.

*The Depositions.* In August 1998, the deposition of Microsoft management began in Redmond, Washington. Bill Gates was placed under oath and before a camera for a total of thirty hours. During the deposition, Gates refused to answer most questions on his own. He also quibbled over the exact meaning of words such as *complete* and *ask* when they were used in questions throughout the deposition. When questioned about controversial e-mails sent throughout the company regarding treatment of competition, he did not provide an effective argument as to their exact meaning. It seemed at this point that Gates was not concerned about the forthcoming trial.

*The Trial.* The trial began on October 19, 1998, when the government specifically accused Gates of illegal bullying, coercion, and predatory pricing to undermine Netscape because that company's products were becoming more popular than Microsoft's. Gates denied being concerned about Netscape's increasing browser market, but memorandums and e-mail messages presented in court suggested otherwise. Moreover, Netscape's CEO, James Barksdale, told the court that Microsoft and Netscape executives had met in June 1995 to discuss "ways to work together." Barksdale testified that Microsoft's proposal at the time involved illegally dividing the market. When Netscape rejected the proposal, Microsoft supposedly used predatory pricing, along with other tactics, to "crush" the company.

By the time Microsoft began its defense in January 1999, its credibility had been severely damaged. During this time, several company witnesses testified regarding the e-mails in question. However, the prosecutor was usually able to rebut their versions of the story. The most damaging testimony came from Jim Allchin, who was often referred to as "Microsoft's lord of Windows." Allchin's testimony was supposed to demonstrate that Internet Explorer could not be separated from Windows without detrimental effects. His demonstration lost its credibility, however, when a reappearing Explorer icon made it apparent that the videotape had been doctored.

This led Microsoft to attempt to settle the case, but the two sides could not agree to the terms of a settlement. By the end of February 1999, Microsoft had three proposals ready for the Justice Department. The government wanted to assign government-appointed people as active members of Microsoft's board of directors, which Microsoft viewed as an attempt by the government to take control of the company. In November 1999, Judge Thomas Penfield Jackson released his findings of facts, a document consisting of 412 paragraphs, only 4 of which were favorable toward Microsoft. Jackson also named Jim Allchin, a computer expert and long-time Microsoft employee, as the mastermind behind the bundling of Internet Explorer and the operating system so as to destroy Netscape.

Judge Jackson appointed Judge Richard Posner, a well-respected member of the Seventh Circuit Court, to try one more time to make a deal, but the gap between the two sides remained insurmountable. The last meeting took place on June 2, 2000. All that was left was the judge's decision.

*The Ruling.* On June 7, 2000, Judge Jackson ordered Microsoft to split into two independent companies—one company to sell Windows and the other to sell everything else. Jackson offered several grounds for his dramatic decision, the first being simply that Microsoft would not admit to any wrongdoing. He also stated that one intent of his decision was to prevent Microsoft from insulting the government by refusing to comply with antitrust laws. Jackson said he found Microsoft to be "untrustworthy" because of its past behavior, including sending defective Windows software after it had been ordered to unbundle the Internet browser from the operating system. Jackson further indicated that he was trying to prevent Microsoft from bullying its competitors. By splitting Microsoft into two independent companies, Jackson expressed the hope of achieving several objectives. First, the split was intended to reignite competition in the industry. Second, it could potentially spur some innovation that had been stifled by the software giant's size and force. Third, the split might rejuvenate some of the "dead zones" in the industry, such as word processing, spreadsheets, databases, and e-mail. Fourth, and perhaps most importantly, lessening Microsoft's power in the industry would hopefully renew creativity among software engineers.

Of course, Microsoft didn't see it that way. Instead, Gates and other executives viewed the idea of splitting the company into two as the equivalent of a "corporate death sentence." They countered that rather than spur innovation, it would stifle it. The split would make software development more complex and effectively integrating two or more programs across two businesses much more difficult. They further argued that the separate marketing of Windows and Microsoft's non-Windows software would drive up prices for consumers. Finally, Microsoft saw the split as leading to delays in completing and introducing new products.

Microsoft has long viewed itself as the symbol of the American Dream for its customers, and a public opinion poll conducted by Harris Interactive supported that notion. A few more than half of 3,830 people surveyed agreed that Bill Gates was a positive role model. The respondents were randomly selected to participate in the survey examining the possible splitting of Microsoft. Of the respondents, nearly half said they disagreed with the government's proposal to split Microsoft into two companies.

However, there were negative responses as well. Of those surveyed, 42 percent believed that Microsoft was a monopolist, and only 23 percent felt that Microsoft treated its competitors in an appropriate manner. Another survey showed that 55 percent of 137 respondents felt that Microsoft was guilty of deliberately trying to crush its competitors.

*The Appeal.* Clearly unhappy with Judge Jackson's decision, Microsoft appealed it, thereby suspending the implementation of the ruling. Although the Justice Department wanted the Supreme Court to review the case, bypassing the D.C. (District of Columbia) Circuit Court of Appeals, the Supreme Court declined the case. In June 2001, a federal appeals panel agreed with Jackson's ruling that Microsoft had violated antitrust laws, but reversed his breakup order and returned the case to the lower court for a new remedy. While attempting to have the Supreme Court vacate that ruling, the various parties continued to negotiate to settle the suit. In November 2001, the U.S. government and nine states reached agreement with Microsoft on a tentative settlement, although California and eight other states continued to hold out for stricter remedies and stronger enforcement.

Finally, on November 1, 2002, U.S. District Judge Colleen Kollar-Kotelly approved most of the provisions of the settlement, which bars Microsoft from retaliating against computer manufacturers, permits customers to delete desktop icons for some Microsoft features, and requires the company to disclose specific technical data to software developers. To satisfy the hold-out states, Kollar-Kotelly included a provision in the settlement that made independent Microsoft board members responsible for the company's compliance efforts instead of the technical committee that Microsoft had wanted to oversee compliance. CEO Gates declared, "It represents a fair resolution of this case. I am personally committed to full compliance." Although the company's stock rose on the news of the final settlement, some critics expressed concern that the decision failed to eliminate Microsoft's virtual monopoly over some aspects of the computer industry. Sun Microsystems' special counsel, Mike Morris, said, "The weak steps that Microsoft has taken to comply with the requirements already show that the settlement will be ineffective in curbing Microsoft's monopolistic and anti-competitive practices and how difficult it will be to enforce."

## Where Does Microsoft Go from Here?

Bill Gates stepped down as CEO in January 2000 and was replaced by Steve Ballmer. However, Gates remains chairman of Microsoft's board and the company's self-appointed "chief software architect." With most of its major legal battles resolved, Microsoft can now turn its full attention to fulfilling its mission and developing new products.

*Questions*

1. Why has there been so much debate about the software industry and Bill Gates?
2. What legal and ethical issues in the Microsoft case relate to U.S. culture, and do these same issues extend to other countries that use Microsoft products?

3. Discuss Microsoft's corporate culture with respect to the ethical and legal issues involved.
4. Identify the types of power associated with each player in this case and discuss how and why each player is using these types of power. What are the potential ramifications of their actions?

Sources: These facts are from "About Microsoft," Microsoft, www.microsoft.com/presspass/inside_ms. asp (accessed Apr. 23, 2003); Christopher Barr, "The Justice Department's Lawsuit Against Microsoft," Cnet, www.cnet.com/content/voices/Barr/012698/ss01.html (accessed July 13, 1998); Rebecca Buckman, "Go Figure: In Valuing a Split Microsoft, Analysts Offer a Wide Range of Numbers," *Wall Street Journal,* May 2, 2000, pp. C1, C3; Rebecca Buckman, "Looking Through Microsoft's Window: On the Firm's Sprawling Campus, It's Almost Business As Usual As Talk of Breakup Brews," *Wall Street Journal,* May 1, 2000, pp. B1, B10; Dan Check, "The Case Against Microsoft," http://ourworld.compuserve.com/homepages/spazz/mspaper.htm (accessed Spring 1996); Don Clark and Ted Bridis, "Creating Two Behemoths? Company Bets Appeals Court Will Overturn Jackson, Making Any Remedy Moot," *Wall Street Journal,* Apr. 28, 2000, pp. B1, B4; Tim Clark, "Go Away," Cnet News, http://ne2.news.com/News/Item/0,4,2076,00.html (accessed Aug. 7, 1996); Paul Davidson, "Expert's View May Influence Ruling," *USA Today,* Feb. 2, 2000, p. B1; Paul Davidson, "Microsoft Awaits a New Hand: Executives Expect Appeals Judges to Be More Amenable," *USA Today,* June 8, 2000, pp. B1, B2; Paul Davidson, "Microsoft Responds to Judge's Findings," *USA Today,* Jan. 19, 2000, p. B1; Paul Davidson, "Microsoft Split Ordered: Appeal Could Go Directly to Supreme Court," *USA Today,* June 8, 2000, p. A1; "Feud Heats Up," Cnet News, http://ne2.news.com/SpecialFeature...d/0,6,2216_2,00.html'st.ne.ni.prev (accessed July 13, 1998); Dana Gardner, "Java Is an Unleashed Force of Nature, Says JavaOne Panel," *InfoWorld Electric,* Mar. 26, 1998; Bill Gates and Steve Ballmer, "To Our Customers, Partners and Shareholders," *USA Today,* Apr. 5, 2000, p. B7; Lee Gomes and Rebecca Buckman, "Creating Two Behemoths? Microsoft Split Might Not Be Much Help for Competitors and Could Harm Consumer," *Wall Street Journal,* Apr. 28, 2000, p. B1; Dan Goodin, "New Microsoft Java Flaws Alleged," www.news.com/News/Item/Textonly/0,25,24007,00.html'st.ne.ni.pfv (accessed Aug. 3, 1998); Dan Goodin, "New Microsoft Java Flaws Alleged," www.microsoft.com/ BillGates/billgates_1/speeches/6-25win98launch. htm#bill (accessed July 9, 1998); John Harwood and David Bank, "CyberSpectacle: Senate Meets Electronic Elite," *Wall Street Journal,* Mar. 4, 1998, pp. B1, B13; "International Design for Office 2000," Microsoft, www.microsoft.com/Office/ORK/2000Journ/LangPack.htm (accessed Sept. 8, 2000); Edward Iwata and John Swartz, "Bill Gates Won't Be Dethroned So Easily: Software King—and His Myth—to Survive on Iron Will, Talent," *USA Today,* June 8, 2000, p. B3; Margaret A. Jacobs, "Injunction Looms As Showdown for Microsoft," *Wall Street Journal,* May 20, 1998, pp. B1, B6; "Java Contract Lawsuit Update," Microsoft's Visual Studio.net, http://msdn.microsoft.com/visualj/lawsuitruling.asp (accessed Sept. 8, 2000); Eun-Kyung Kim, "Microsoft Court Gets Lesson on Monopolies," *[Fort Collins] Coloradoan,* Nov. 20, 1998, p. B2; Malcolm Maclachlan, "New Lawsuit Is Over Java, Sun Says," *TechWeb News,* May 12, 1998, www.techweb.com/wire/story/TWB19980512S0012; Malcolm Maclachlan, "Sun Attacks an Embattled Microsoft," *TechWeb News,* May 14, 1998, www.techweb.com/wire/story/msftdoj/TWB19980514S0002; Malcolm Maclachlan, "Sun Targets Microsoft: Software Maker Says Windows 98 Must Be Java Compatible," *Tech Web News,* www.techweb.com/news/story/TWB19980512S0012 (accessed May 12, 1998); Kevin Maney, "Microsoft's Uncertain Future Rattles Investors: Justice Must Make Recommendation: Breakup Possible," *USA Today,* Apr. 25, 2000, p. B1; Michael J. Martinez, "Microsoft Buys Time to Retool," *[Fort Collins] Coloradoan,* Sept. 27, 2000, pp. A1, A2; Richard B. McKenzie, *Trust on Trial: How the Microsoft Case Is Reframing the Rules of Competition* (Cambridge, Mass: Perseus Publishing, 2000); Patrick McMahon, "Stoic Staffers Shake Heads, Return to Work," *USA Today,* June 8, 2000, p. B3; Joseph Menn and Jube Shiver, "The Microsoft Decision," *Los Angeles Times,* Nov. 2, 2002, sec. 1, p. 1; "Microsoft Antitrust Ruling," CourtTV, www.courttv.com/legaldocs/cyberlaw/mseruling.html (accessed Jul. 13, 1998); "Microsoft Asks Court to Limit Gates Deposition," Yahoo News, http://dailynews.yahoo.com/headlines/politics/story.html/s=z/reuters/980805/politics/stories/microsoft_1. html; "Microsoft Corporate Information: What We Do," Microsoft, www.microsoft.com/mscorp/ (accessed Aug. 3, 1998); Michael Moeller, "Amended Complaint: Microsoft Wants Access to 'Highly Confidential' Documents," *PC Week Online,* Aug. 4, 1998; "Notice Regarding Java Lawsuit Ruling: Notice to Customers," Microsoft's Visual Studio.net, http://msdn.microsoft.com/visualj/ statement.asp (accessed

Sep. 8, 2000); Robert O'Brien, "Kodak, Lexmark Lead Decline as Profit Warnings Hurt Stocks," *Wall Street Journal,* Sept. 27, 2000, p. C2; Lisa Picarille, "Microsoft, Sun Postpone Java Hearing," *Computer Reseller News,* http://headlines.yahoo.com/Full_Coverage/Tech/Sun_Microsoft_ Lawsuit/ (accessed July 7, 1998); Jared Sandberg, "Bring on the Chopping Block," *Newsweek,* May 8, 2000, pp. 34–35; Jared Sandberg, "Microsoft's Six Fatal Errors," *Newsweek,* June 19, 2000, pp. 23–27; "Survey Results: May 2000 Final Survey Results," E-businessethics.com, http://e-businessethics.com/view_results.htm (accessed Apr. 23, 2003); Julie Schmit, "Tech Industry's Direction Hangs in Balance," *USA Today,* Oct. 16, 1998, p. 3B; Jon Swartz, "Microsoft Split Ordered: Will Breakup Help or Hurt Consumers?" *USA Today,* June 8, 2000, pp. A1, A2; Bob Trott and David Pendery, "Allchin E-Mail Adds to Microsoft's Legal Woes"; Ted Bridis, "More Accusations Hit Microsoft," *Denver Post,* Oct. 23, 1998, sec. B; Geri Coleman Tucker and Will Rodger, "Facing Breakup, Gates to Take Case to People; Microsoft Says Don't Punish Success," *USA Today,* May 1, 2000, pp. B1; B2; U.S. Justice Department and State Attorneys General, "Statement by Microsoft Corporation," Microsoft, www.microsoft.com/presspass.doj.7-28formalresponse.htm (accessed Aug. 3, 1998); "U.S. Vs. Microsoft," *New York Times,* Nov. 2, 2002, p. C4; John R. Wilke and David Bank, "Microsoft's Chief Concedes Hardball Tactics," *Wall Street Journal,* Mar. 4, 1998, pp. B1, B13; Nick Wingfield, "Net Assault," Cnet News, http://ne2.news.com/News/Item/0,4,1940,00.html (accessed July 25, 1996); Nick Wingfield and Tim Clark, "Dirty," Cnet News, http://ne2.news.com/News/Item/0,4,2072,00.html (accessed Aug. 7, 1996); Aaron Zitner, "Feds Assail Gates," *Denver Post,* Oct. 30, 1998, sec. C.

# Case 13

# HCA, Inc.: Learning from Past Mistakes[1]

I n 1968, Dr. Thomas Frist Sr., Jack C. Massey, and Dr. Thomas Frist Jr. founded the Hospital Corporation of America (HCA) to manage Park View Hospital in Nashville, Tennessee. The firm grew rapidly over the next two decades by acquiring and building new hospitals and contracting to manage additional facilities for their owners. The firm merged with Columbia Hospital Corporation to become Columbia/HCA Healthcare Corporation in 1994, and Columbia founder Richard Scott became chairman and CEO of the combined companies. By 1997, Columbia/HCA Healthcare Corporation had grown to become one of the largest health care services companies in the United States, operating 343 hospitals, 136 outpatient surgery centers, and approximately 550 home-health locations. It also provided extensive outpatient and ancillary services in thirty-seven states, as well as in the United Kingdom and Switzerland. The firm's comprehensive network included more than 285,000 employees and used economies of scale to increase profits.

Columbia/HCA's stated mission was "to work with our employees, affiliated physicians and volunteers to provide a continuum of quality healthcare, cost-effectively for the people in the communities we serve." Its vision was "to work with employees and physicians, to build a company that is focused on the well-being of people, that is patient-oriented, that offers the most advanced technology and information systems, that is financially sound, and that is synonymous with quality, cost-effective healthcare." Columbia/HCA's goals included measuring and improving clinical outcome and patient satisfaction as well as reducing costs and providing services with compassion. With these goals, the company built the nation's largest chain of hospitals based on cost-effectiveness and financial performance. It competed by capitalizing on its size and creating economies of scale in the internal control of its costs and sales activities. The focus was bottom-line performance and new business acquisitions.

However, a number of critics charged that health care services and staffing at Columbia/HCA often took a back seat to the focus on profits. For example, the company employed shorter training periods than competing hospitals provided. One former administrator reported that training that typically should take six months was sometimes accomplished in as little as two weeks at a Columbia/HCA hospital. In

---

[1] This case was prepared by John Fraedrich and O.C. Ferrell for classroom discussion, rather than to illustrate either effective or ineffective handling of an administrative, ethical, or legal decision by management.

addition, the company was accused of "patient dumping"—discharging emergency-room patients or transferring them to other hospitals when they are not yet in stable condition. In 1997 officials at the Department of Health and Human Services Inspector General's Office indicated that they were considering imposing fines on Columbia/HCA for an unspecified number of patient-dumping cases. Additionally, the corporate watchdog INFACT publicly challenged the company's practices, inducting Columbia/HCA into its "Hall of Shame" for corporations that manipulate public policy to the detriment of public health.

## Ethical and Legal Problems Begin

In late July 1997, Fawcett Memorial Hospital in Port Charlotte, Florida, a Columbia/HCA hospital, became the focal point of the biggest case of health care fraud in the industry. A government investigation resulted in the indictment of three mid-level Columbia/HCA Healthcare Corporation executives for filing false cost reports for Fawcett, which resulted in losses of more than $4.4 million from government programs. The government alleged that Columbia/HCA had gained at least part of its profit by overcharging for Medicare and other federal health programs; that is, executives had billed the government for nonreimbursable interest expenses. Other concerns were alleged illegal incentives to physicians and the possible overuse of home-health services. Federal investigators accused Columbia/HCA of engaging in a "systematic effort to defraud government health care programs." In a seventy-four-page document, federal investigators quoted confidential witnesses who stated that Columbia/HCA's former CEO, Richard Scott, and former president, David Vandewater, were briefed routinely on issues relating to Medicare reimbursement claims that the government charged were fraudulent. Samuel Greco, Columbia/HCA's former chief of operations, was also implicated in the scandal.

One of the issues was whether Columbia/HCA had fraudulently overstated home health care laboratory test expenses and knowingly miscategorized other expenditures so as to inflate the amounts for which it sought reimbursement. For example, Columbia/HCA's Southwest Florida Regional Medical Center in Fort Myers reportedly claimed $68,000 more in property taxes than it paid. Moreover, documents showed that the hospital had set aside money to return to the government in case auditors caught the inflated figure. Technically, expenses claimed on cost reports must be related to patient care and fall within the realm of allowable Medicare reimbursements. However, medical billing can be confusing, chaotic, imprecise, and subject to interpretation. Hence, it is not unusual for hospitals to keep two sets of accounting books. One set is provided to Medicare, and the other set, which includes records for set-aside money, is held in case auditors interpret the Medicare cost report differently than the hospital does. Some believe it is appropriate for a hospital to set aside money to return to the government if the hospital in good faith believes the Medicare cost claims are legitimate. However, if administrators believe strongly or know that certain claims are not allowable yet still file the claims and note them in the second set of books, charges of fraud may result.

Confidential witnesses said that Columbia/HCA had made an effort to hide from federal regulators internal documents that could have disclosed the alleged fraud. In addition, Columbia/HCA's top executive in charge of internal audits had instructed employees to soften the language used in internal financial audits that were critical of Columbia/HCA's practices. According to FBI agent Joseph Ford, "investigation by the [Federal Bureau of Investigation] and the [Defense Criminal Investigative Service] has uncovered a systematic corporate scheme perpetrated by corporate officers and managers of Columbia/HCA's hospitals, home health agencies, and other facilities in the states of Tennessee, Florida, Georgia, Texas, and elsewhere to defraud Medicare, Medicaid, and the [Civilian Health and Medical Program of the Uniformed Services]." Indicted Columbia/HCA officials pleaded not guilty, and defense lawyers for Columbia/HCA tried to diminish the importance of the allegations contained in the government's affidavits.

## Developing a New Ethical Climate at Columbia/HCA

Soon after the investigation was launched, Dr. Thomas Frist Jr. was hired as chairman and chief executive of Columbia/HCA. Frist, who had been president of Hospital Corporation of America (HCA) before it merged with Columbia, vowed to cooperate fully with the government and to develop a one-hundred-day plan to change the troubled firm's corporate culture. Under the Federal Sentencing Guidelines for Organizations (FSGO), companies that have effective due diligence compliance programs can reduce their fines if they are convicted of fraud. For penalties to be reduced, however, an effective compliance program must be in place before misconduct occurs. Although the FSGO requires that a senior executive be in charge of the due diligence compliance program, Columbia/HCA's general counsel had been designated to take charge of the program.

After a hundred days as chairman and chief executive of Columbia/HCA, Frist outlined changes that would reshape the company. His reforms included a new mission statement as well as plans to create a new senior executive position to oversee ethical compliance and quality issues. Columbia/ HCA's new mission statement emphasized a commitment to quality medical care and honesty in business practices. It did not, however, mention financial performance. "We have to take the company in a new direction," Frist said. "The days when Columbia/HCA was seen as an adversarial or in your face, a behind-closed-doors kind of place, is a thing of the past." (It has been claimed that some managers viewed Columbia/HCA's corporate culture as so unethical that they resigned before the fraud investigation had even started.)

Columbia/HCA hired Alan Yuspeh as the senior executive to oversee ethical compliance and quality issues. Yuspeh, senior vice president of ethics, compliance, and corporate responsibility, was given a staff of twelve at the corporate headquarters and assigned to work with group, division, and facility presidents to create a "corporate culture where Columbia workers feel compelled to do what is right." Yuspeh's first initiatives were to refine monitoring techniques, boost workers' ethics and compliance training, develop a code of conduct for employees, and create an internal mechanism for workers to report any wrongdoing.

Because of the investigation, consumers, doctors, and the general public lost confidence in Columbia/HCA, and its stock price dropped more than 50 percent from its all-time high. The new management seemed more concerned about developing the corporation's ethical compliance program than about its growth and profits. For instance, at a conference in Phoenix, Arizona, twenty Columbia managers were asked to indicate by a show of hands how many of them had escaped taunts from friends that they were crooks. Not a single hand went up. The discussion that followed that question did not focus on surgery profit margins. It focused on resolving the investigation and on the importance of the corporation's intangible image and values.

## Columbia/HCA Launches an Ethics, Compliance, and Corporate Responsibility Program

Columbia/HCA released a press statement indicating that it was taking a critical step in developing a companywide ethics, compliance, and corporate responsibility program. To initiate the program, the company designated more than five hundred employees as facility ethics and compliance officers (ECOs). The new ECOs began their roles with a two-day training session in Nashville, Tennessee. The local leadership provided by these facility ECOs was thought to be the key link in ensuring that the company continued to develop a culture of ethical conduct and corporate responsibility.

As part of the program, Yuspeh made a fifteen-minute videotape that was sent to managers throughout the Columbia/HCA system. The tape announced the launching of the compliance training program and the unveiling of a code of ethics that was designed to effectively communicate Columbia/HCA's new emphasis on compliance, integrity, and social responsibility. Frist stated that "we are making a substantial investment in our ethics and compliance program in order to ensure its success" and that "instituting a values-based culture throughout this company is something our employees have told us is critical to forming our future. The ethics and compliance initiative is a key part of that effort."

Training seminars for all employees, conducted by each facility's ECO, included introductions to the training program, the Columbia/HCA code of conduct, and the company's overall ethics and compliance program. The training seminars also included presentations by members of senior management and small-group discussions in which participants discussed how to apply the new Columbia/HCA code of conduct in ethics-related scenarios.

Although the company wanted individuals to bring their highest sense of personal values to work each day, the purpose of the program was to help employees understand the company's strict definition of ethical behavior rather than to change their personal values. Columbia/HCA's ethical guidelines tackled basic issues, such as whether nurses can accept $100 tips—they cannot—as well as complicated topics, such as what constitutes Medicare fraud. In addition, the company developed certification tests for the employees who determine billing codes. In 1998 a forty-minute training video was shown to all the firm's employees; it featured three ethical scenarios for employees to examine. Columbia/HCA apparently recognized the importance of ethical conduct and quality service to all of its constituents.

## Resolving the Charges

In 1997–1998 Columbia/HCA Healthcare settled with the Internal Revenue Service (IRS) for $71 million over allegations that it had made excessive compensation and golden parachute payments to some one hundred executives. As a result of the settlement, the IRS, which had sought $276 million in taxes and interest, agreed to drop its charges that Columbia/HCA had awarded excessive compensation by allowing the executives to exercise stock options after a new public offering of Columbia/HCA stock. Frist had reportedly earned about $125 million by exercising stock options after that public offering, and seventeen other top executives each made millions on the deals.

In August 2000, Columbia/HCA became the first corporation ever to be removed from INFACT's Hall of Shame. The executive director of INFACT announced that Columbia/HCA had drastically reduced its political activity and influence. For example, the corporation has no active federal lobbyists and has a registered lobbying presence in only twelve states. According to INFACT's executive director, "This response to grassroots pressure constitutes a landmark development in business ethics overall and challenges prevailing practices among for-profit health care corporations."

In December 2000, Columbia/HCA announced that it would pay the federal government more than $840 million in criminal fines and civil penalties. The company agreed in June 2003 to pay $631 million to settle the last of the government's charges that it had filed false Medicare claims, paid kickbacks to doctors, and overcharged at wound-care centers. No senior executives of the company have ever been charged with a crime. However, the company has paid out a total of $1.7 billion in fines, refunds, and lawsuit settlements after admitting that it had, through two subsidiaries, offered financial incentives to doctors in violation of anti-kickback laws, falsified records to generate higher payments for minor treatments or treatments that never occurred, charged for lab tests that were never ordered, charged for home health care for patients who did not qualify for it, and falsely labeled ads as "community education." KPMG, the firm's auditor, denied any wrongdoing on its part but agreed to pay $9 million to settle a whistle-blower lawsuit related to the charges. Columbia/HCA also signed a "Corporate Integrity Agreement" in 2000 that subjects the firm to intense scrutiny until 2009. In the same year, the company was officially renamed HCA—The Healthcare Company.

In January 2001, Frist relinquished the title of CEO to focus on other interests but remained involved in corporate strategy as chairman of HCA's board of directors. Jack Bovender Jr. (formerly chief operating officer) replaced him. Of the fraud investigation, Bovender said, "We think the major issues have been settled," although the company still has some "physician relations issues and cost report issues" to resolve in civil actions involving individual hospitals. Since 1997, the company has closed or consolidated more than one hundred hospitals. It is currently composed of locally managed facilities that include 175 hospitals and 80 outpatient surgery centers in twenty-four states, England, and Switzerland.

## HCA's Compliance Program at Work

Today, HCA spends $4 million a year on its ethics program, which includes an ethics and compliance committee of independent board directors, two separate corporate committees that draft ethics policy and monitor its use, and a twenty-member department that implements the program. In all, twenty-six executives oversee ethics and compliance for a variety of issues, ranging from taxes to pollution to the Americans with Disabilities Act.

The ethics compliance program set up by Alan Yuspeh includes seven components: (1) articulating ethics through a code of conduct and a series of company policies and procedures; (2) creating awareness of these standards of compliance and promoting ethical conduct among everyone in the company through ethics training, compliance training, and other ongoing communication efforts; (3) providing a twenty-four-hour, toll-free telephone hotline to report possible misconduct; (4) monitoring and auditing employees' performance in areas of compliance risk to ensure that established policies and procedures are being followed and are effective; (5) establishing organizational supports for the ethics compliance effort; (6) overseeing the company's implementation of and adherence to the Corporate Integrity Agreement; and (7) undertaking other efforts such as clinical ethics and pastoral services.

Training continues to play a major role in helping employees understand HCA's new focus on ethics and legal compliance. Every new employee is required to undergo two hours of "orientation" on the firm's code of conduct within thirty days of employment. At that time, new employees receive a copy of the code of conduct, participate in training using videotapes and games, and sign an acknowledgment card. All employees complete one hour of annual refresher training on the firm's code of conduct every year.

HCA's new ethics hotline helps the firm identify misconduct and take corrective action where necessary. For example, in the spring of 2002 an anonymous caller to the toll-free line accused a hospital supply clerk of stealing medical gear and reselling it online through eBay. After investigators verified the complaint, the clerk was fired. Since its inception, the ethics program has fielded hundreds of such ethics-related complaints.

The effort to change HCA's corporate culture quickly and become the model corporate citizen in the health care industry was a real challenge. This health care provider learned the hard way that maintaining an organizational ethical climate is the responsibility of top management. As Jack Bovender says, "Internal controls can always be corrupted. We've tried to come up with a system that would require a lot of people to conspire. It would be very hard for Tyco-type things to happen here."

### Questions

1. What were the organizational ethical leadership problems that resulted in Columbia/HCA's misconduct?
2. Discuss the strengths and weaknesses of HCA's current ethics program. Does this program appear to satisfy the provisions of the Federal Sentencing Guidelines for Organizations and the Sarbanes-Oxley Act?
3. What other suggestions could Columbia/ HCA have implemented to sensitize its employees to ethical issues?

Sources: These facts are from Columbia/HCA Healthcare Corporation, *1996 Annual Report to Stockholders;* "Columbia/HCA Launches Ethics and Compliance Training Program," *AOL News,* Feb. 12, 1998, http://cbs.aol.com; "Columbia/HCA to Sell Part of Business," *Commercial Appeal,* June 3, 1998, p. B8; "Corporate Influence Curtailed," *PR Newswire,* Aug. 2, 2000; Kurt Eichenwald, "Reshaping the Culture at Columbia/HCA," *New York Times,* Nov. 4, 1997, p. C2; Kurt Eichenwald and N. R. Kleinfield, "At Columbia/HCA, Scandal Hurts," *Commercial Appeal,* Dec. 21, 1997, pp. C1, C3; "Ethics, Compliance, and Corporate Responsibility: Introduction," HCA, http://ec.hcahealthcare.com/ (accessed Apr. 24, 2003); "HCA Tentatively Agrees to Multimillion Fraud Settlement," American Medical News, Jan. 27, 2003, www.ama-assn.org/sci-pubs/amnews/pick_03/gvbf0127.htm; "History," HCA, http://hca.hcahealthcare.com/CustomPage.asp?guidCustomContentID=C2E6928A-D8B1-42AF-BA44-6C2B591282D5 (accessed Apr. 24, 2003); "INFACT Urges Columbia/HCA to Remove Itself from the Hall of Shame," *PR Newswire,* www.prnewswire.com (accessed May 27, 1999); Lucette Lagnado, "Columbia Taps Lawyer for Ethics Post: Yuspeh Led Defense Initiative of 1980s," *Wall Street Journal,* Oct. 14, 1997, p. B6; Tom Lowry, "Columbia/HCA Hires Ethics Expert," *USA Today,* Oct. 14, 1997, p. 4B; Tom Lowry, "Loss Warning Hits Columbia/HCA Stock," *USA Today,* Feb. 9, 1998, p. 2B; Duncan Mansfield, "HCA Names Bovender Chief Executive," Jan. 8, 2001, Yahoo News, http://biz.yahoo.com/apf/ 010108/hca_change_2.html (accessed Jan. 16, 2001); Charles Ornstein, "Columbia/HCA Prescribes Employee Ethics Program," *Tampa Tribune,* Feb. 20, 1998, p. 4; Eva M. Rodriguez, "Columbia/HCA Probe Turns to Marketing Billing," *Wall Street Journal,* Aug. 21, 1997, p. A2; Neil Weinberg, "Healing Thyself," *Forbes,* Mar. 17, 2003, www.forbes.com/forbes/2003/0317/064.html; and Chris Woodyard, "FBI Alleges Systemic Fraud at Columbia," *USA Today,* Oct. 7, 1997, p. 1B.

# Ethics Officer Association: Sharing Best Practices[1]

The Ethics Officer Association (EOA) is a professional organization of managers of ethics, compliance, and business conduct programs. Founded in 1992 by twelve ethics officers, the Massachusetts-based association has grown to more than 890 members representing multiple and diverse industries and nonprofit organizations. EOA members include companies such as General Motors, Bell Atlantic, Boeing, AmeriSteel, Comdisco, KeySpan Energy, Pall Corporation, Raytheon, United Airlines, as well as such nonprofit and other organizations as the American Cancer Society, the City of Philadelphia, and the New York Stock Exchange. The organization's reach is not limited to North America, with members from Canada, Great Britain, India, Japan, the Netherlands, and Switzerland. Thus, the EOA has established a focus on business ethics that spans industries, geographic regions, and organizations of all types and sizes.

The EOA's mission is "dedicated to promoting ethical business practices and serving as a global forum for the exchange of information and strategies among organizations and individuals responsible for ethics, compliance and business conduct programs." It is committed to educating and supporting those individuals who have the responsibility to ensure that their organizations are fulfilling their legal and ethical responsibilities.

## The Need for an Association of Ethics Officers

The ethics officer position is relatively new. As recently as fifteen years ago, few organizations had ethics officers. Now, as a result of initiatives such as the Sarbanes-Oxley Act, the Federal Sentencing Guidelines for Organizations (FSGO), the Foreign Corrupt Practices Act, and the Defense Industry Initiative, these positions are emerging in companies throughout the world. Today, companies want to develop a reputation for credibility, honesty, and responsibility, and establishing an ethics officer is one component of that strategy.

[1] This case was prepared by Debbie Thorne McAlister and Kevin Sample for classroom discussion, rather than to illustrate either effective or ineffective handling of an administrative, ethical or legal decision by individuals or management. The research assistance of Jason De Los Santos is gratefully acknowledged. Reprinted with permission of Debbie Thorne McAlister.

Throughout the 1980s, white-collar crime and other legal issues sparked public and government concern about corporate control and power. This decade prompted a formal focus on business ethics, and increased media attention on and public scrutiny of companies led to more ethics officers. Other ethical and legal scandals in the 1990s and early 2000s further eroded public confidence in corporate ethics and elevated the importance of the ethics officer's role in creating and overseeing strong ethics and legal compliance programs designed to deter misconduct. Many companies, however, have created ethics officer positions out of a sincere emphasis on business ethics and social responsibility rather than in response to any unethical activities. These firms have invested time, money, and other resources to develop a formal ethics office so they can demonstrate their commitment to strong business ethics and their implementation of companywide ethics programs.

Companies usually create ethics offices because they want to fulfill their legal and ethical obligations effectively. In committing to this new management role, firms must consider a range of stakeholder issues, including the industry in which they compete and how the public feels about their activities. By understanding the concerns of internal and external stakeholders, a company can evaluate its ethics position and develop the proper guidance, communication tools, and resources for employees and business partners to use when dealing with difficult ethical situations.

In the workplace, an ethics officer performs a number of tasks related to ethics and compliance. To ensure that corporate priorities on ethics and compliance are integrated throughout the organization, ethics officers interact with the different levels of management, with employees, and even with outside stakeholders to monitor any new developments in their organization and industry that may have ethical consequences. Ethics officers coordinate with top management over the best way to create and instill a code of ethics and an ethical corporate culture. Once a program is established, an ethics officer will develop control systems to ensure that employees and organizational agents do not deviate from the ethics code. Officers work to continually refine the code to make it more effective. They also respond to employee questions and concerns, often through a toll-free hot line. An effective ethics officer also devotes time to training, communications, and continuously improving the program. Part of this continuous improvement may occur through EOA educational programs and networking opportunities. These factors created the initial need and the expectations they raise have continued to fuel the demand for an association of ethics officers.

## EOA Membership

Membership in the Ethics Officer Association is limited to organizations that have business ethics and compliance programs as well as to the managers of these initiatives. Although these individuals are generally known as "ethics officers," their actual titles vary from "director of corporate ethics," "vice president of ethics and compliance," or "vice president of ethics and integrity" to "vice president of business practices," "director of business conduct," and "chief compliance officer," among others. For these individuals and their organizations, a key advantage of EOA membership is the educational focus of the EOA's activities. Members have an opportunity to be both teacher and student as they learn from each other about different practices and solutions to

| TABLE C14–1 | Ethics Officer Responsibilities |

| TASK | ETHICS OFFICERS REPORTING RESPONSIBILITY FOR |
|---|---|
| Oversight of hot line/guideline/internal reporting | 89% |
| Preparing and delivering internal presentations | 89% |
| Organizationwide communications | 88% |
| Senior management and/or board briefings/communications | 85% |
| Training design | 84% |
| Assessing/reviewing vulnerabilities | 83% |
| Assessing/reviewing success or failure of initiatives | 83% |
| Overseeing investigations of wrongdoing | 79% |
| Managing program documentation | 79% |
| Direct handling of hot line/guideline/internal reporting | 77% |
| Preparing and delivering external presentations | 72% |
| Establishing company policy and procedures | 68% |
| Developing international programs | 64% |
| Training delivery | 61% |
| Implementing international programs | 56% |
| Conducting investigations of wrongdoing | 52% |

*Source:* "EOA Member Survey 2000, Public Version," Ethics Officer Association, Feb. 2001, p. 12, www.eoa.org/EOA_Resources/Reports/MS2000_wo$.pdf.

ethical dilemmas and concerns. Through the EOA, members can discuss issues in a comfortable and professional environment and review policies, dilemmas, and strategies of shared concern. They also have the opportunity to network with other ethics professionals, attend annual conferences and workshops, and access the EOA's resources, such as its extensive ethics-related library and online discussion forum. Thus, the EOA provides one of the few forums in which companies can share their ethics concerns and successes. The U.S. government has indicated that such cooperation is lawful, as long as it does not set a low standard of conduct or evolve into collusion.

As with many organizations, EOA members receive different benefits according to which of the two types of membership they hold: sponsoring partners or basic members. Sponsoring partners join on an organizational level, which demonstrates the company's strong interest in helping the EOA promote ethical practices in the workplace. The EOA's basic membership is a limited membership designed primarily for small businesses and nonprofit organizations. The EOA provides a range of programs and benefits targeted to the needs of these two types of members.

Sponsoring partners take active roles as stakeholders, leaders, and guides in developing EOA's future structure and activities. These members work jointly with the EOA's board of directors, providing funds to EOA as well as experience, knowledge of specific ethics areas or issues, and networking channels. The fee for Sponsoring

Partners is $3,000 a year; any additional individuals from the sponsor's organization can join as Sponsoring Partner Associates for $150 annually. Sponsors can appoint any person within their organization to act as their representative in determining EOA's future direction.

The basic membership is also held in the organization's name, and the membership fee is $750 per person. Additional employees can also be added at $750 each.

## EOA Services and Programs

The EOA draws on its understanding of its member characteristics and general trends in business ethics to develop services and programs to fulfill its mission and members' needs. Among these services are the Sponsoring Partner Forum, ethics administration software, a corporate ethics and compliance library, the "Managing Ethics in Organizations" program, an annual conference and skill enhancement courses, online resources, and research conducted by the EOA for the benefit of its members. The availability of some of these offerings is dependent on member status, and are offered only to sponsoring partners.

For example, the Sponsoring Partner Forum is an annual conference for senior-level ethics officers that provides an open and trusting environment in which successes can be shared, problem areas reviewed, and company ethics initiatives generally improved. Company representatives participate in workshops and provide direction to the EOA by reviewing the status of its activities. In the forum, ethics and compliance professionals can openly discuss ethical and compliance-related issues that affect their organizations. These exclusive forums enable members to have strong interaction and learning experiences, thus improving the effectiveness of the ethics officers and their ethics programs.

One of the most significant benefits of being an EOA member is the option to use its Ethics Administration Software (EAS). EAS was created by Hughes Aircraft to assist its ethics officers in collecting, reporting, managing, and graphing data related to ethics allegations, human resources, and ethics inquiries. Using the program enables members to avoid the significant time and resources required to develop such software themselves.

Another important benefit of being an EOA member is the right to use its extensive library on business ethics, compliance, and "best practices" in business ethics. The library includes codes of conduct from member companies, videos, and other communication tools that ethics officers can use to relay ethics messages to employees.

The "Managing Ethics in Organizations" program is a professional weeklong development course offered in conjunction with the Center for Business Ethics at Bentley College. The course is intended for newly appointed ethics officers and others who are responsible for their organizations' ethics, compliance, or business conduct programs. The course offers new officers the knowledge, fundamental theories, and general skills needed to execute their positions. Topics covered in past sessions have included setting up an ethics office, crisis management skills, ethics and the law, globalizing an ethics program, and diversity, among many others. The faculty for these sessions include experienced EOA ethics officers, consultants, and academics who are widely recognized leaders in their fields. The fee for nonmembers of the EOA is roughly $3,500; members pay a reduced fee.

The EOA also hosts an annual conference that is designed to explore business ethics and related subjects in more detail. These conferences draw together ethics officers and other industry personnel for several days of learning and sharing on timely topics and issues. In addition, the association sponsors skill-enhancement courses taught by ethics officers and subject matter experts who provide hands-on experience on such topics as ethics and the law, ethical reasoning, and assessing the ethical environment, among others.

Like most organizations today, the EOA has a Web site for communicating with members and other stakeholders. The site contains most of the information that members need, including descriptions of the organization's activities, upcoming events, the online library, current newsletters, links to other members' Web sites, and general information about the organization. The Web site is updated regularly, and allows members and guests of the site to leave feedback and suggestions. JobLink is a job-search service on the EOA Web site that helps individuals find ethics-related job opportunities and companies advertise and fill these positions.

As part of its mission, the EOA conducts research on topics of interest to its members. For example, two recent national studies—on workplace pressure and ethics and new technologies and ethics—were conducted by the EOA together with the American Society of Chartered Life Underwriters (CLU) & Chartered Financial Consultants (ChFC), now called the Society of Financial Service Professionals. The association also conducts research on member-specific issues, such as cutting-edge corporate training initiatives, reporting relationships to the ethics officer, and compensation for ethics officers. These studies are often released to the general public and enable the EOA to communicate with many stakeholders. For example, results of EOA research have been published in *USA Today, The Wall Street Journal, Success, HRMagazine,* and other media outlets.

One example of EOA research is the "Workplace Pressure and Ethics" survey, which was conducted to determine whether workplace pressures increase the risk of unethical and illegal business practices, to uncover the sources that contribute to these pressures, and to find ways for management to address concerns in this area. This survey generated widespread media attention and speculation about its findings. According to the study, 48 percent of employees surveyed —almost half of all workers—have engaged in unethical or illegal activities because of job pressure. The study also reported that 58 percent of surveyed employees have at least considered acting unethically or illegally on the job. The most common types of unethical behavior reported were cutting corners on quality control (16 percent), covering up incidents (14 percent), abusing or lying about sick leave (11 percent), and lying to or deceiving customers (9 percent).

Stuart G. Tugman Jr., president of the American Society of Chartered Life Underwriters & Chartered Financial Consultants, says that "The survey sends a serious message to the American business leaders, we are putting too much pressure on our economy's most valuable resource—our employees—and they are looking to us, the leadership of corporate America, to solve the problem." According to the study, the status of business ethics is not as bad as it seems, since 60 percent of the respondents believe that ethical quandaries can be avoided. "For years the term *business ethics* was considered an oxymoron, a contradiction in terms," says William T. Redgate, emeritus member of the Ethics Officer Association. "The fact that American workers no longer see ethical dilemmas as unavoidable consequences of doing business means that there is a new era in business, an era in which a majority of workers believe that business and ethics can mix and that ethical dilemmas can be reduced."

The survey also asked respondents how to reduce the pressure that leads to unethical behavior. Seventy-three percent of respondents suggested improved communications, while 71 percent said a greater commitment by senior management was needed to reduce pressure. Of all the industries surveyed, the computer/software industry had the highest degree of unethical behavior, but employees in the manufacturing and health care industries seem to face more pressure.

Another EOA research project, the "New Technologies and Ethics" study, focused on how the use of the Internet, e-mail, pagers, computers, voice mail, cell phones, and other workplace technologies have changed the way people interact with one another as well as whether they contribute to pressure that can lead to unethical or illegal business practices. With this survey, the EOA found itself on the cutting edge of issues affecting not only its members but most organizations today. Among the results of the survey were the following:

- 14 percent of respondents had wrongly blamed an error they made at work on a technological glitch
- 6 percent accessed private computer files without permission and intruded on coworkers' privacy
- 13 percent copied the company's software for home use; this same percentage used office equipment to shop on the Internet for personal reasons; and 11 percent used office equipment to search for another job
- 5 percent listened to a private cellular phone conversation; this same percentage visited pornographic sites using office equipment
- 19 percent admitted having created a potentially dangerous situation by using new technology while driving.

Through the survey process, some company respondents offered suggestions for remedying these ethical dilemmas. For example, organizations should create guidelines that dictate personal use of resources, develop policies on personal use of technology, and encourage employees to police themselves. In addition, researchers suggested that companies should install Internet blocking software and start a corporate training program on ethics and technology.

## The Business Conduct Management System Standard

The EOA has developed into a strong association with a growing and diverse membership. At the same time, business ethics has grown in prominence within organizations and moved to the forefront of media and public consideration. The EOA has also taken a leadership role in standardizing expectations about business conduct principles and practices around the world. Association members believe that in order for an ethics program to be judged effective, there should be a recognized standard for what constitutes effectiveness. Thus, ethics officers need a standard for not only assessing their programs but for comparing them to generally accepted best practices and systems. Such a standard could also be used by companies establishing or updating ethics programs. As a result, the EOA proposed the development of an internationally recognized business conduct management system (BCMS) to the American National Standards Institute (ANSI), which is the U.S. representative to the International Organization for Standardization (ISO). The proposal was accepted in May 2002.

The EOA's business conduct management system creates a set of standards for business conduct much like the ISO 9000 standard for quality management and ISO 14000 standard for environmental management. All ISO standards include these elements: (1) policy, (2) planning, (3) implementation and operation, (4) performance assessment, (5) improvement, and (6) management review. These elements are also quite similar to the compliance program recommendations of the Federal Sentencing Guidelines for Organizations. According to project director C. Lee Essrig, the BCMS "would define business conduct and would include the means to measure and credibly demonstrate compliance with the standard. The management system standard could be a tool for any organization to use, among other things, as a benchmark in measuring and demonstrating the effectiveness of its business conduct program and/ or as a standard for business partners to meet."

EOA members believe that an effective business conduct management system standard can help organizations protect and enhance their reputations, minimize their liability, and maintain their long-term viability. Implementing a management system can help a firm (1) assure interested stakeholders that management is committed to the system's policy, objectives, and targets; (2) demonstrate an emphasis on prevention rather than corrective action; (3) demonstrate reasonable care and regulatory compliance; and (4) facilitate the process of continual evaluation and improvement.

In addition to the BCMS project, the EOA is engaged in other initiatives to strengthen and improve standards for compliance and business ethics. For example, the association recently responded to a U.S. Sentencing Commission (USSC) request for comment on possible enhancements to the FSGO. The EOA Board of Directors drafted a statement of commitment to the guidelines and then made a number of suggestions for improving them. The USSC is listed as a partner on the EOA Web site.

## The Future of EOA

The Ethics Officer Association provides many valuable services to the organizations it works with as well as indirectly to other stakeholders who have an interest in business ethics and related topics. Although the EOA was primarily established to assist ethics officers, it is also proactive in examining the status of ethics in the workplace and advocating an increased focus on ethics. Since the accounting scandals of the early 2000s, the EOA has significantly increased its membership and conference attendance rates. For example, it added one hundred new members between August and November 2002 alone. More and more companies are recognizing the value of the EOA and adopting a formal focus on business ethics.

*Questions*

1. What are the benefits and drawbacks to organizations of sharing their experiences on ethics and compliance with other members of the EOA?
2. Compare the role and responsibilities of ethics officers to other employees, including managers of the marketing, accounting, legal, and human resources functions. Where does ethics officers' work overlap with each of these managers' traditional responsibilities? How can these four functional areas help an ethics officer develop and implement an effective ethics program?
3. How will the BCMS project affect the general nature of business ethics and social responsibility today?

Sources: These facts are from Stephen A. Banning, "The Professionalization of Journalism," *Journalism History,* 24 (Winter 1998/1999): 157-164; Dawn-Marie Driscoll, W. Michael Hoffman, and Edward S. Petry, *The Ethical Edge: Tales of Organizations That Have Faced Moral Crises* (New York: MasterMedia, 1995); C. Lee Essrig, "An International Management System Standard for Business Conduct," *ethikos,* Nov./Dec. 2001, via www.singerpubs.com/ethikos/Essrig.htm; "Ethics: A New Profession in American Business," *HR Focus,* 70 (May 1993): 22; The Ethics Center, www.taknosys.com/ethics/ (accessed July 3, 2000); Ethics Officer Association, www.eoa.org/ (accessed Apr. 18, 2003); Leslie S. Laffie, "Tax Technology," *Tax Adviser,* 29 (July 1998): 441; Debbie Thorne LeClair, O. C. Ferrell, and John P. Fraedrich, *Integrity Management: A Guide to Managing Legal and Ethical Issues in the Workplace* (Tampa, FL: University of Tampa Press, 1998); Elaine McShulskis, "Job Stress Can Prompt Unethical Behavior," *Society for Human Resource Management Magazine,* 7 (July 1997): 22; Edward Petry, "Appointing an Ethics Officer," *Healthcare Executive,* 13 (Nov./Dec. 1998): 35; Edward S. Petry Jr., and Fred Tietz, "Can Ethics Officers Improve Office Ethics?" *Business and Society Review,* 82 (Summer 1992): 21–25; Cheryl J. Polson, "Fostering Graduate Socialization into Adult Education," *Adult Learning,* 10 (Winter 1998/1999): 23–27; Alynda Wheat, "Keeping an Eye on Corporate America," *Fortune,* Nov. 11, 2002, www.fortune.com/fortune/articles/0,15114,390033,00.html.

# Ben & Jerry's Homemade: Managing Social Responsibility and Growth[1]

en Cohen and Jerry Greenfield opened their first ice cream shop on May 5, 1978, in a converted gas station in Burlington, Vermont, with $12,000 worth of secondhand equipment. Their business credentials consisted of much enthusiasm and a $5 correspondence course in ice-cream making from Pennsylvania State University. Driven by Cohen and Greenfield's 1960s ideals, Ben & Jerry's Homemade, Inc., has grown very successful, achieving an enviable level of brand-name recognition for the firm's internationally distributed frozen dessert products, including ice cream, frozen yogurt, and sorbets. In addition, there are 337 franchise or company-owned "scoop shops" in the United States, United Kingdom, Holland, France, Israel, Spain, and Lebanon.

From the beginning, Cohen and Greenfield incorporated into their business a strong sense of social responsibility—to their employees, the community, and the world at large. Unlike most companies, Ben & Jerry's Homemade has a three-part mission statement—product, economic, and social. According to the company, it "is the belief that all three parts must thrive equally in a manner that commands deep respect for individuals in and outside the company and supports the communities of which they are a part." Although Ben & Jerry's has experienced some trying times, it remains firmly grounded in its original, socially responsible corporate vision.

## The Ben & Jerry Story

Cohen and Greenfield's converted gas station served rich, all-natural ice cream, which quickly became popular with local residents. During the winter months, however, the customers turned to warmer treats, so Cohen and Greenfield had to come up with new ideas to survive their first year. Soon they were packaging their ice cream and hauling it around to local restaurants. Gradually, they began to include grocery stores among their customers and soon gained shelf space in 150 stores across the state. The

[1] This case was prepared by O.C. Ferrell, John Fraedrich, and Terry Gable for classroom discussion, rather than to illustrate either effective or ineffective handling of an administrative, ethical, or legal decision by management.

first franchise store opened in 1981, and by 1985 Ben & Jerry's was selling pints in stores outside of New England.

Ben & Jerry's has always been a bit unorthodox in its business practices, which range from Greenfield's formal executive title of "Big Cheese" to its products. For example, a popular Ben & Jerry's ice cream flavor is Cherry Garcia, named after (now deceased) guitarist Jerry Garcia of the Grateful Dead. Another flavor, Wavy Gravy, was named after the master of ceremonies at Woodstock and, naturally, was packaged in a tie-dyed container. Another perennial favorite is Phish, named in honor of a popular band from Vermont. The company has also employed some unconventional promotional tactics, like the "Cowmobile," a modified mobile home that Cohen and Greenfield drove cross country to distribute free ice cream scoops.

When the company went public in 1984 as Ben & Jerry's Homemade, Inc., Cohen initially limited the sale of the company's stock to Vermont residents. His idea was that if local residents were part owners of the firm, the community would share in the success of the business. In Cohen's words, "What a strange thing we're discovering: As our business supports the community, the community supports us back." A national stock offering did follow two years later, but the company has continued its philosophy of supporting the local community.

## Caring Capitalism

When Cohen and Greenfield first went into business together, they wrote their own rules. Their corporate mission statement listed not only the goals of making and selling the finest-quality natural ice cream and operating in such a way as to achieve success for both shareholders and employees, but also the requirement that they initiate "innovative ways to improve the quality of life of a broad community—local, national, and international."

In the early 1990s, Ben & Jerry's was selling more than $100 million worth of ice cream products annually, and Cohen and Greenfield felt they were losing control of their company—its growth, creativity, organization, and values. Greenfield even dropped out of the business for a while. Cohen considered selling the company until a friend pointed out to him that he could make it into whatever he wanted. He then developed the concept of "caring capitalism," which he applies by donating part of the company's profits to worthy causes as well as by finding creative ways to improve the quality of life of the firm's employees and of the local community. Greenfield rejoined the company soon after.

Shortly after Greenfield rejoined, Cohen set up the Ben & Jerry's Foundation, which is dedicated to encouraging social change through the donation of 7.5 percent of the company's yearly pretax profits. Ben & Jerry's social concern can also be seen in some of its products. One of the firm's ventures was the Peace Pop, an ice cream bar on a stick, from which 1 percent of profits were used to build awareness and raise funds for peace. The company purchases rain-forest nuts for its Rainforest Crunch ice cream, thus providing a market for goods from the rain forests that do not require their destruction. Additionally, sales of Rainforest Crunch are funneled back into rain-forest preservation efforts. Ben & Jerry's environmental concern was apparent when it switched to the "Eco-Pint," a more environmentally friendly unbleached paperboard container. Standard papermaking uses chlorine compounds for bleaching, a process that discharges millions of gallons of organochlorine-laced water daily. Chemicals found in this water are considered hazardous to human health. The company also joined in sponsoring the Rosebud Sioux Tribe Wind Turbine Project in South Dakota, the first large-scale American-Indian-owned wind farm. By purchasing credits in the project, the company can neutralize some of the effects of the carbon monoxide generated by the energy used in its facilities.

Cohen and Greenfield extend their social awareness to their own employees. A salary ratio at the firm keeps the salaries of top executives in line with nonmanagerial employees. This helps give all employees a sense that they're working together as a team. And when it seemed that Ben & Jerry's was expanding too quickly (the company went from a hundred and fifty employees to three hundred almost overnight), company executives made a conscious decision to slow growth to ensure that the company's family atmosphere and core values would not be lost. Among the additional benefits employees receive are three pints of ice cream a week, free health-club memberships, and use of a partially subsidized company child care center.

Another of Ben & Jerry's efforts to utilize the "caring capitalism" concept was in advertising techniques. Rather than buy television, radio, or newspaper advertising, Ben & Jerry's promotes things and events of value to the community. It sponsors peace, music, and art festivals around the country—including the Newport Folk Festival, FarmAid, and its own One World, One Heart festivals—and tries to draw attention to the many social causes it undertakes. One such cause is the founders' opposition to the bovine growth hormone (a substance injected into cows to increase milk production), which they fear will drive small dairy farmers out of business. A venture targeted directly to Burlington residents is the Giraffe Project, which recognizes people who have been willing to stick their own necks out and stand tall for what they believe. Local residents and customers of Ben & Jerry's scoop shops nominate the recipients of these Giraffe Commendations.

## Auditing Social Performance

As a public corporation operating on a much-publicized socially responsible platform, Ben & Jerry's must answer to many stakeholders not only for its financial performance but also its conduct. Although a relatively small firm with fewer than one thousand employees, Ben & Jerry's was one of the first corporations to formally report on its performance with respect to its social responsibility vision and goals. The company began reporting its auditing results in 1999.

Ben & Jerry's most recent social audit examined the firm's performance in a number of significant areas, including employee, supplier, and consumer relations; workplace safety; franchise and international operations; the natural environment; and philanthropy. For example, in the area of "workplace and employees," Ben & Jerry's audit examined the firm's benefit programs for employees, including its "livable wage" policy, compensation ratios, relations with unions, and gender and racial equity. Another section of the report identified the firm's continuing efforts to improve workplace safety using measures such as lost-time days and accident rates. Ben & Jerry's has long taken a proactive position on environmental issues, so the social audit devoted considerable space to measures of environmental performance, such as use of water, discharge of wastewater, and overall energy conservation.

Ben & Jerry's social audit also reported on its philanthropic efforts, especially with regard to the Ben & Jerry's Foundation. The company donated $1.2 million to its foundation to support various social causes related to children and families, environmental restoration, sustainable agriculture, and peace. The report also identified numerous organizations and programs supported by the foundation's donations, such as the Vermont Dairy Farm Sustainability Project and Grounds for Health, Inc. in the United States and The Children's Society, ChildLine, and the National Missing Person's Helpline in the United Kingdom.

## Long-Term Goals Versus Cost Efficiency

David Korten, a former Harvard Business School professor with years of experience in international development and citizen action, has argued that long-term-oriented, socially responsible companies often face challenges in today's fast-paced, often short-sighted, and profit-minded economic system. According to his perspective, the economic system focuses on the current value of a company's stock, rewarding cost efficiency and punishing inefficiency. Thus, firms that can outsource or otherwise shift their costs to other parties are rewarded, whereas socially responsible organizations are often considered inefficient and wasteful. Consequently, the stock price of such firms suffers, and they may be labeled as "in trouble." According to Korten,

> With financial markets demanding maximum short-term gains and corporate raiders standing by to trash any company that isn't externalizing every possible cost, efforts to fix the problem by raising the social consciousness of managers misdefine the problem. There are plenty of socially conscious managers. The problem is a predatory system that makes it difficult for them to survive. . . . They must either compromise their vision or run a great risk of being expelled by the system. . . . Corporate managers live and work in a system that is virtually feeding on the socially responsible.[2]

Ben & Jerry's has certainly faced its share of difficulties while striving to live up to the ideals established by its founders. One of the firm's biggest challenges occurred when the company was acquired by Unilever, an Anglo-Dutch conglomerate, in April 2000 for $326 million. Under the terms of the sale, Ben & Jerry's retained its independent board of directors so it could provide leadership for the company's social mission and brand integrity. The transaction also rewarded shareholders for their investments; protected Ben & Jerry's employees; maintained agreements to purchase from local, socially minded suppliers; and continued to encourage and fund the firm's social mission. The agreement also provided an opportunity for Ben & Jerry's to contribute to Unilever's social practices worldwide. Both co-founders of the company were to continue to be involved.

In November 2000, Yves Couette was named the new CEO of Ben & Jerry's. One of Unilever's leading ice cream professionals, Couette had worked in the United

---

[2] David C. Korten, *When Corporations Rule the World* (West Hartford, Conn.: Kumarian Press, 1995), pp. 212–214.

States, Mexico, Indonesia, and the United Kingdom. Vowing to build on Ben & Jerry's achievements, he said, "I am determined to deliver on Ben & Jerry's social mission commitment." However, Ben Cohen expressed dissatisfaction not only with Unilever's choice of Couette but also that a co-CEO had not been named. Threatening to leave the company he cofounded, Cohen declared, "The only way the social mission of Ben & Jerry's and the heart and soul of the company will be maintained is to have a CEO running the company who has a deep understanding of our values-led social business philosophy, who had experience with the company and with how that worked in practice." Cohen also expressed concern that a promised "social audit" of Unilever's operations had not been completed. He was also upset that Unilever would not allow the creation of a $5 million fund bearing Ben & Jerry's name to help new businesses with a social agenda get on their feet.

Unilever countered Cohen's claims by pointing out that Couette had the needed experience. While he was working in Mexico, Unilever had established an ice cream shop, run by a nonprofit organization, to support disabled children. Couette said, "Working in countries like Mexico and Indonesia, I have seen first hand the glaring social problems people face everyday. This has strengthened my belief that business has an important role to play in achieving social progress." Unilever also offered a list of the company's social objectives for 2001, which included helping to build playgrounds and launching a new flavor tied to that effort; lobbying to extend the life of the Northeast Interstate Dairy Compact, which provides more income for farmers; and developing more environmentally friendly packaging. As for Cohen's concern about the $5 million fund not carrying the Ben & Jerry name, a Unilever spokesman replied that Unilever wants to protect the Ben & Jerry's brand name and so the fund could be called "Ben's Venture Capital Fund" but not "Ben & Jerry's Venture Capital Fund." The spokesman said, "We understand that Ben's very concerned. He's a founder of the company. He has a huge emotional stake in the company. Our view is, judge us by our actions."

James Heard, who audited Ben & Jerry's social report, also sounded a note of cautious optimism: "There is definitely an irony to a counterculture company such as Ben & Jerry's being acquired by a global behemoth such as Unilever, and many members of the Ben & Jerry's family are acutely aware of the irony. But fears that Ben & Jerry's would abandon its commitment to caring capitalism have so far proved unfounded."

## *Questions*

1. Discuss how the corporate culture at Ben & Jerry's, as described in this case, influences the daily implementation of ethical decisions at the firm.
2. Visit Ben & Jerry's Web site (www.benjerry.com) and find its most recent social audit. Compare the areas covered in this audit to the audit process described in Chapter 9 of your text. In what other ways could Ben & Jerry's demonstrate to stakeholders its commitment to ethical and socially responsible conduct?
3. Like Ben & Jerry's, many small businesses were founded and grew successful on a platform of ethics and social responsibility. However, more than a few of these companies became so successful that they were acquired by larger firms that may or may not respect the principles and values on which they were founded. How

can such companies protect their core values as they grow from small firms into large ones and/or are acquired by multinational conglomerates?

Sources: These facts are from Mark Albright, "At Ben & Jerry's, Social Agenda Churns with Ice Cream," *St. Petersburg Times,* Nov. 11, 1995, p. 1E; "Ben & Jerry's 2001 Social Audit," Ben & Jerry's Homemade, May 2002, www.benjerry.com/our_company/about_us/social_mission/social_audits/2001/letter01.cfm; "Ben & Jerry's & Unilever to Join Forces," Ben & Jerry's Homemade, April 12, 2000, http://lib.benjerry. com/pressrel/join-forces.html; "Ben & Jerry's Announces Environmentally-Friendly Packaging Innovation," Ben & Jerry's Homemade, Feb. 22, 1999, http://lib.benjerry.com/pressrel/unbleached.html; "Ben & Jerry's Appoints Yves Couette as Chief Executive Officer," Ben & Jerry's Homemade, Nov. 20, 2000, http://lib.benjerry.com/pressrel/press1120.html; "Clif Bar Forms Wind-Farm Partnership to Offset $CO_2$ Footprint," GreenBiz.com, Mar. 26, 2003, www.greenbiz.com/news/news_third. cfm?NewsID =24244; Simon Goodley, "Ben & Jerry Frosty over Unilever Choice for Key Job," *Electronic Telegraph,* Dec. 4, 2000, www.telegraph.co.uk/; David Gram, "Ben Worried Ben & Jerry's Good Work Is Melting Away After Merger," *Register Citizen,* Dec. 1, 2000, www.zwire.com; David C. Korten, *When Corporations Rule the World* (West Hartford, Conn.: Kumarian Press, 1995), pp. 212–214; Erik Larson, "Forever Young," *Inc.,* July 1988: pp. 50–62; Maxine Lipner, "Ben & Jerry's: Sweet Ethics Evince Social Awareness," *Compass Readings* July 1991, pp. 22–30; Peter Newcomb, "Is Ben & Jerry's BST-free?" *Forbes,* Sept. 25, 1995, p. 98; Hanna Rosin, "The Evil Empire: The Scoop on Ben & Jerry's Crunchy Capitalism," *New Republic,* Sept. 11, 1995, p. 22; Andrew E. Serwer, "Ben & Jerry's Corporate Ogre," *Fortune,* July 10, 1995, p. 30; "TimeLine," Ben & Jerry's Homemade, www.benjerry.com/our_company/about_us/ our_history/timeline/index.cfm (accessed Apr. 18, 2003); Blair S. Walker, "Good-Humored Activist Back to the Fray," *USA Today,* Dec. 8, 1992, pp. 1B, 213; and Eric J. Wieffering, "Trouble in Camelot," *Business Ethics* 5 (Jan.-Feb. 1991): 16–19.

# Case 16

# New Belgium Brewing: Environmental and Social Responsibilities[1]

Although most of the companies frequently cited as examples of ethical and socially responsible firms are large corporations, it is the social responsibility initiatives of small businesses that often have the greatest impact on local communities and neighborhoods. These businesses create jobs and provide goods and services for customers in smaller markets that larger corporations often are not interested in serving. Moreover, they also contribute money, resources, and volunteer time to local causes. Their owners often serve as community and neighborhood leaders, and many choose to apply their skills and some of the fruits of their success to tackling local problems and issues that benefit everyone in the community. One such small business is the New Belgium Brewing Company, Inc., based in Fort Collins, Colorado.

## History of the New Belgium Brewing Company

The idea for the New Belgium Brewing Company began with a bicycling trip through Belgium. Belgium is arguably the home of some of the world's finest ales, some of which have been brewed for centuries in that country's monasteries. As Jeff Lebesch, an American electrical engineer, cruised around that country on his fat-tired mountain bike, he wondered if he could produce such high-quality beers back home in Colorado. After acquiring the special strain of yeast used to brew Belgian-style ales, Lebesch returned home and began to experiment in his Colorado basement. When his beers earned thumbs up from friends, Lebesch decided to market them.

The New Belgium Brewing Company (NBB) opened for business in 1991 as a tiny basement operation in Lebesch's home in Fort Collins. Lebesch's wife, Kim Jordan, became the firm's marketing director. They named their first brew Fat Tire Amber Ale in honor of Lebesch's bike ride through Belgium. New Belgium beers quickly developed a small but devoted customer base, first in Fort Collins and then throughout Colorado. The brewery soon outgrew the couple's basement and moved into an old

[1] This case was prepared by Nikole Haiar under the direction of O. C. Ferrell for classroom discussion, rather than to illustrate either effective or ineffective handling of an administrative, ethical, or legal decision by individuals or management.

railroad depot before settling into its present custom-built facility in 1995. The brewery includes an automated brewhouse, two quality assurance labs, and numerous technological innovations for which New Belgium has become nationally recognized as a "paradigm of environmental efficiencies."

Today, New Belgium Brewing Company offers a variety of permanent and seasonal ales and pilsners. The company's standard line includes Sunshine Wheat, Blue Paddle Pilsner, Abbey Ale, Trippel Ale, 1554 Black Ale, and the original Fat Tire Amber Ale, still the firm's best-seller. Some customers even refer to the company as the Fat Tire Brewery. The brewery also markets two types of specialty beers on a seasonal basis. Seasonal ales include Frambozen and Abbey Grand Cru, which are released at Thanksgiving, and Christmas and Farmhouse Ale, which are sold during the early fall months. The firm occasionally offers one-time-only brews, such as LaFolie, a wood-aged beer, which are sold only until the batch runs out.

Since its founding, NBB's most effective form of advertising has been its customers' word of mouth. Indeed, before New Belgium beers were widely distributed throughout Colorado, one liquor store owner in Telluride is purported to have offered people gas money if they would stop by and pick up New Belgium beer on their way through Ft. Collins. Although New Belgium beers are distributed in just one-third of the United States, the brewery receives numerous e-mails and phone calls every day inquiring when its beers will be available elsewhere.

## New Belgium's Purpose and Core Beliefs

New Belgium's dedication to quality, the environment, and its employees and customers is expressed in its mission statement: "To operate a profitable brewery which makes our love and talent manifest." The company's stated core values and beliefs about its role as an environmentally concerned and socially responsible brewer include:

- Producing world-class beers
- Promoting beer culture and the responsible enjoyment of beer
- Continuous, innovative quality and efficiency improvements
- Transcending customers' expectations
- Environmental stewardship: minimizing resource consumption, maximizing energy efficiency, and recycling
- Kindling social, environmental, and cultural change as a business role model
- Cultivating potential: through learning, participative management, and the pursuit of opportunities
- Balancing the myriad needs of the company, staff, and their families
- Committing ourselves to authentic relationships, communications, and promises
- Having Fun.

David Kemp, a longtime brewery employee, believes that these statements help communicate to customers and other stakeholders what New Belgium, as a company, is about.

## Employee Concerns

Recognizing employees' role in the company's success, New Belgium provides many generous benefits. In addition to the usual paid health and dental insurance and retirement plans, employees get a free lunch every other week as well as a free massage once a year, and they can bring their children and dogs to work. Employees who stay with the company for five years earn an all-expenses paid trip to Belgium to "study beer culture." Perhaps most importantly, employees can also earn stock in the privately held corporation, which grants them a vote in company decisions. New Belgium's employees now own one-third of the growing brewery.

## Environmental Concerns

New Belgium's marketing strategy involves linking the quality of its products, as well as their name and look, with the company's philosophy toward affecting the planet. From leading-edge environmental gadgets and high-tech industry advancements to employee-ownership programs and a strong belief in giving back to the community, New Belgium demonstrates its desire to create a living, learning community.

NBB strives for cost-efficient energy-saving alternatives to conducting its business and reducing its impact on the environment. In staying true to the company's core values and beliefs, the brewery's employee-owners unanimously agreed to invest in a wind turbine, making New Belgium the first fully wind-powered brewery in the United States. Since the switch from coal power, New Belgium has been able to reduce its $CO_2$ emissions by 1,800 metric tons per year. The company further reduces its energy use by employing a steam condenser that captures and reuses the hot water that boils the barley and hops in the production process to start the next brew. The steam is redirected to heat the floor tiles and de-ice the loading docks in cold weather. Another way that NBB conserves energy is by using "sun tubes," which provide natural daytime lighting throughout the brew house all year long.

New Belgium also takes pride in reducing waste through recycling and creative reuse strategies. The company strives to recycle as many supplies as possible, including cardboard boxes, keg caps, office materials, and the amber glass used in bottling. The brewery also stores spent barley and hop grains in an on-premise silo and invites local farmers to pick up the grains, free of charge, to feed their pigs. NBB even encourages its employees to reduce air pollution by using alternative transportation. As an incentive, NBB gives its employees "cruiser bikes"— like the one pictured on its Fat Tire Amber Ale label—after one year of employment and encourages them to ride to work.

## Social Concerns

Beyond its use of environment-friendly technologies and innovations, New Belgium Brewing Company strives to improve communities and enhance people's lives through corporate giving, event sponsorship, and philanthropic involvement.

One way that New Belgium demonstrates its corporate citizenship is by donating $1 per barrel of beer sold to various cultural, social, environmental, and drug- and alcohol-awareness programs across the thirteen western states in which it distributes beer. Typical grants range from $2,500 to $5,000. Involvement is spread equally among the thirteen states, unless there is a special need that requires more participation or funding.

NBB also maintains a community bulletin board in its facility where it posts an array of community involvement activities and proposals. This community board allows tourists and employees to see the different ways they can help out the community, and it gives nonprofit organizations a chance to make their needs known. Organizations can even apply for grants through the New Belgium Brewing Company Web site, which has a link designated for this purpose.

NBB also sponsors a number of events, with a special focus on those that involve "human-powered" sports that cause minimal damage to the natural environment. Through event sponsorships, such as the Tour de Fat, NBB has raised more than $15,000 for various environmental, social, and cycling nonprofit organizations. In 2000, New Belgium also sponsored the MS 150 "Best Damn Bike Tour," a two-day, fully catered bike tour, from which all proceeds went to benefit more than five thousand local people with multiple sclerosis. In the same year, NBB also sponsored the Ride the Rockies bike tour, which donated the proceeds from beer sales to local nonprofit groups. The money raised from this annual event funds local projects, such as improving parks and bike trails. In the course of one year, New Belgium can be found at anywhere from 150 to 200 festivals and events, across all thirteen western states.

## Organizational Success

New Belgium Brewing Company's efforts to live up to its own high standards have paid off with numerous awards and a very loyal following. It was one of three winners of *Business Ethics* magazine's 2002 Business Ethics Awards for its "dedication to environmental excellence in every part of its innovative brewing process." It also won an honorable mention in the Better Business Bureau's 2002 Torch Award for Outstanding Marketplace Ethics competition. Kim Jordan and Jeff Lebesch were named the 1999 recipients of the Rocky Mountain Region Entrepreneur of the Year Award for manufacturing. The company also captured the award for best mid-sized brewing company of the year and best mid-sized brewmaster at the Great American Beer Festival. In addition, New Belgium took home medals for three different brews, Abbey Belgian Style Ale, Blue Paddle Pilsner, and LaFolie specialty ale. One member of the staff of the Association of Brewers commented that Fat Tire is one of the only brews he'd pay for in a bar.

According to David Edgar, director of the Institute for Brewing Studies, "They've created a very positive image for their company in the beer-consuming public with smart decision-making." Although some members of society do not believe that a company whose major product is alcohol can be socially responsible, New Belgium has set out to prove that for those who make a choice to drink responsibly, the company can do everything possible to contribute to society. Its efforts to promote beer culture and the connoisseurship of beer has even led it to design a special "Worthy Glass," the shape of which is intended to retain foam, show off color, enhance the visual presentation, and release aroma. New Belgium Brewing Company also promotes the responsible appreciation of beer through its participation in and support of the culinary arts. For instance, it frequently hosts New Belgium Beer Dinners, in which every course of the meal is served with a complementary culinary treat.

Every six-pack of New Belgium Beer displays the phrase, "In this box is our labor of love, we feel incredibly lucky to be creating something fine that enhances people's lives." Although Jeff Lebesch has "semi-retired" from the company to focus on other interests, the founders of New Belgium hope this statement captures the spirit of the company. According to employee Dave Kemp, NBB's environmental concern and social responsibility give it a competitive advantage because consumers want to believe in and feel good about the products they purchase. NBB's most important asset is its image—a corporate brand that stands for quality, responsibility, and concern for society. Defining itself as more than just a beer company, the brewer also sees itself as a caring organization that is concerned with all stakeholders, including the community, the environment, and employees.

*Questions*

1. What environmental issues does the New Belgium Brewing Company work to address? How has NBB taken a strategic approach to addressing these issues? Why do you think the company has chosen to focus on environmental issues?
2. Are New Belgium's social initiatives indicative of strategic philanthropy? Why or why not?
3. Some segments of society vigorously contend that companies that sell alcoholic beverages and tobacco products cannot be socially responsible organizations because of the nature of their primary products. Do you believe that New Belgium Brewing Company's actions and initiatives are indicative of an ethical and socially responsible corporation? Why or why not?
4. What else could New Belgium do to foster ethical and responsible conduct?

Sources: These facts are from Peter Asmus, "Goodbye Coal, Hello Wind," *Business Ethics,* 13 (July/Aug. 1999): 10–11; Robert Baun, "What's in a Name? Ask the Makers of Fat Tire," *[Fort Collins] Coloradoan,* Oct. 8, 2000, pp. E1, E3; Rachel Brand, "Colorado Breweries Bring Home 12 Medals in Festival," *Rocky Mountain News,* www.insidedenver.com/news/1008beer6.shtml, (accessed Nov. 6, 2000); Stevi Deter, "Fat Tire Amber Ale," The Net Net, www.thenetnet.com/reviews/fat.html (accessed Apr. 29, 2003); DirtWorld.com, www.dirtworld.com/races/Colorado_race745.htm (accessed Nov. 6, 2000); Robert F. Dwyer and John F. Tanner Jr., *Business Marketing* (Irwin McGraw-Hill, 1999), p. 104; "Fat Tire Amber Ale," Achwiegut (The Guide to Austrian Beer), www.austrianbeer.com/beer/b000688.shtml, (accessed Jan. 19, 2001); "Four Businesses Honored with Prestigious International Award for Outstanding Marketplace Ethics," Better Business Bureau, press release, Sept. 23, 2002, www.bbb.org/alerts/2002torchwinners. asp; Del I. Hawkins, Roger J. Best, and Kenneth A. Coney, *Consumer Behavior: Building Marketing Strategy,* 8th ed. (Irwin McGraw-Hill, 2001); David Kemp, Tour Connoisseur, New Belgium Brewing Company, personal interview by Nikole Haiar, Nov. 21, 2000, 1:00 PM; Julie Gordon, "Lebesch Balances Interests in Business, Community," *Coloradoan,* Feb. 26, 2003; New Belgium Brewing Company, Ft. Collins, CO, www.newbelgium.com (accessed Apr. 29, 2003); New Belgium Brewing Company Tour by Nikole Haiar, Nov. 20, 2000, 2:00 PM; "New Belgium Brewing Wins Ethics Award," *Denver Business Journal,* Jan. 2, 2003, http://denver.bizjournals.com/denver/stories/2002/12/30/daily21.html; and Dan Rabin, "New Belgium Pours It on for Bike Riders," *Celebrator Beer News,* Aug./Sept. 1998, www. celebrator.com/9808/rabin.html.

# Case 17

# Mattel: Ethics Is No Game[1]

Mattel, Inc.—with nearly $5 billion in annual revenues—is a world leader in the design, manufacture, and marketing of family products. The company's well-known toy brands include Barbie (which encompasses more than 120 different Barbie doll models), Fisher-Price, Disney entertainment lines, Hot Wheels and Matchbox cars, Tyco Toys, Cabbage Patch Kids, and board games such as Scrabble. In addition, Mattel promotes international sales by tailoring toys for specific international markets rather than simply modifying favorites in the United States. The company has its headquarters in El Segundo, California, and offices in thirty-six countries. It markets its products in more than 150 nations throughout the world.

The toy manufacturer was under the managerial control of CEO Jill Barad from January 1997 to February 2000. The chief executive's management style has been characterized both as strict and business- and people-oriented. When Barad was named chief executive in January 1997, Mattel's stock was trading for less than $30 a share. By March 1997, however, it had risen to more than $46. Before being made CEO, Barad had also helped build the sales of Barbie from $200 million in 1982 to $1.9 billion in 1997. Her tenure at Mattel's helm would prove challenging, however. Mattel announced in October 1998 that earnings growth for the year would be between 9 and 12 percent, rather than the 18 percent that Wall Street had anticipated. This was due to the declining sales to Toys "R" Us, the retail chain that accounted for 18 percent of Mattel's revenue in 1997. Barad stated in an interview that if performance continued to deteriorate sharply, the generous rewards given to employees would have to be cut back. Problems continued during Barad's three-year tenure. Mattel bought software maker The Learning Co., which immediately began draining $1 million a day in cash from Mattel. Also during this time, sales of Barbie fell 20 percent, earnings per share dropped to 43 cents, and Mattel's stock price plummeted. Barad resigned in 2000.

New CEO Robert Eckert sold the money-losing Learning Co. unit, cut 350 jobs, and eliminated marginally profitable toy lines. Also in 2000, Mattel was granted the highly sought-after licensing agreement for products related to the literary phenomenon *Harry Potter*. In addition, Nickelodeon and Mattel signed a new, multiyear,

[1] This case was prepared by Marisol Paradoa and Debbie Thorne McAlister for classroom discussion rather than to illustrate either effective or ineffective handling of an administrative, ethical, or legal decision by management. Reprinted with permission.

worldwide licensing agreement that gives Mattel the master toy license for all Nickelodeon's entertainment properties.

## Mattel's Core Products

*Barbie and American Girl.* The Barbie doll is one of Mattel's most important product lines, and the number one girls' brand in the world. Approximately one billion Barbie dolls have been sold since its introduction in 1959. The average American girl aged three to eleven owns ten Barbie dolls, and the doll is currently sold in more than 150 countries. Although Mattel tailors Barbie's appearance for each country, company research found that girls in Asia like the original blonde-haired, blue-eyed Barbie just as much as American girls do. As a result, Mattel is increasingly marketing the same dolls the world over, including the recently launched Rapunzel Barbie, who shares the fairy-tale heroine's long locks. Nearly 50 percent of that doll's first six month's sales came from outside the United States from its launch in the fall of 2002 to the spring of 2003. The Barbie line today includes not only dolls and accessories but also Barbie software and a broad assortment of licensed products such as books, apparel, food, home furnishings, home electronics, and even a movie, *Barbie As Rapunzel.*

To augment Barbie, Mattel announced in 1998 that it would pay $700 million to Pleasant Co., for its American Girl collection, a well-known line of historical dolls, books, and accessories. Sold exclusively through catalogs, the American Girl dolls, which are made to look like nine-year-olds, have a wholesome and educational image. The American Girl brand is the number-two girls' brand in the world, and Mattel's purchase reflected its long-term strategy to reduce its reliance on its traditional products.

*Hot Wheels.* Hot Wheels roared into the toy world in 1968. More than thirty years later, the brand is hotter than ever and includes high-end collectibles, models for adults such as NASCAR (National Association for Stock Car Auto Racing) and Formula One, and high-performance cars, track sets, and play sets for children of all ages. The brand is involved in almost every racing circuit in the world, including NASCAR, Formula One, NHRA (National Hot Rod Association), CART (Championship Auto Racing Teams), and AMA (American Motorcyclist Association). More than 15 million boys aged five to fifteen are avid collectors, with the average collector owning more than forty-one Hot Wheels cars. Somewhere in the world, two Hot Wheels cars are sold every second of every day. The brand that started with cars on a track has evolved into a "lifestyle" brand that encompasses licensed Hot Wheels shirts, caps, lunch boxes, backpacks, and more. Together, Hot Wheels and Barbie generate 45 percent of Mattel's revenue and 65 percent of its profits.

*Cabbage Patch Kids.* Since the introduction of Cabbage Patch Kids in 1983, more than 90 million of the dolls have been purchased around the world. The dolls are unique in many respects, including their representation of many races and ethnicities through individualized facial and body features. When Mattel introduced the Cabbage Patch Kids Snacktime Kids line in the fall of 1996, it expected the dolls to continue the success of the original product line. The Snacktime Kids had moving mouths that enabled children to "feed" the doll. However, this unique feature proved dangerous to some children. Reports of children getting their fingers or hair caught in the dolls' mouths surfaced soon after the 1996 holiday season, and Mattel voluntarily pulled all the dolls from store shelves by the following January. The company also offered consumers a cash refund of $40 when returning the dolls. The U.S. Consumer Product Safety Commission applauded Mattel's handling of the Snacktime Kids situation. Current "hot" products in the Cabbage Patch Kids line include Preemie Surprise and Butterfly Fairies.

## Mattel's Commitment to Ethics and Social Responsibility

Mattel's core products and business environment can present it with unique ethical issues. For example, because the company's products are designed primarily for children, it must be sensitive to social concerns about children's rights. In addition, the international environment often complicates business transactions. Different legal systems and cultural expectations about business can create ethical conflict. Finally, the use of technology may present ethical dilemmas, especially regarding protecting consumer privacy. Mattel has recognized these potential issues and taken steps to strengthen its commitment to business ethics and social responsibility.

*Privacy and Marketing Technology.* Advances in technology have created special issues for Mattel's marketing efforts. Mattel has recognized that, because it markets to children, it has the responsibility to communicate with parents about its marketing strategy. The company has taken special steps to inform both children and adults about its philosophy on Internet-based marketing tools, such as the Hot Wheels Web site. For example, the Web site for Hot Wheels contains a lengthy online privacy policy, which includes the following:

> Mattel is committed to protecting your on-line privacy when visiting a web site operated by us or our family of companies. We do not collect and keep any personal information online from you unless you volunteer it and you are 13 or older. We also do not collect and keep personal information online from children under the age of 13 without their parents' consent except in limited circumstances authorized by law and described in this policy. . . .
>
> A SPECIAL NOTE FOR PARENTS: Mattel adheres to the Children's Online Privacy Protection Act of 1998 and the guidelines of the Children's Advertising Review Unit (CARU) of the Council of Better Business Bureaus, Inc. in each of our web sites for children. Parents, you can help by spending time online with your children and monitoring your children's online use. Please help us protect your child's privacy by instructing them never to provide personal information on this site or any other without your permission.
>
> IF YOU ARE UNDER 18, PLEASE BE SURE TO READ THIS POLICY WITH YOUR PARENTS AND ASK QUESTIONS ABOUT THINGS YOU DO NOT UNDERSTAND. CHILDREN UNDER 13 SHOULD GET YOUR PARENTS'

PERMISSION BEFORE GIVING OUT YOUR E-MAIL ADDRESS OR ANY PER-
SONAL INFORMATION TO MATTEL - OR TO ANYONE ELSE ON THE IN-
TERNET.[2]

*Expectations of Mattel's Business Partners.* Beyond concerns about marketing to
children, Mattel, Inc. is making a serious commitment to business ethics. In late 1997
the company completed its first full ethics audit of each of its manufacturing sites as
well as the facilities of its primary contractors. The audit found that Mattel was not using any child or forced labor, a problem that has plagued other overseas consumer
products' manufacturers. However, several contractors were found to be in violation
of Mattel's standards and were asked to change their operations or risk losing Mattel's
business. The company now has an independent monitoring council audit its manufacturing facilities every three years.

In an effort to continue its strong record on human rights and related ethical standards, Mattel instituted a code of conduct called "Global Manufacturing Principles."
One of these principles requires all Mattel-owned and contracted manufacturing facilities to favor business partners who are committed to ethical standards that are
comparable to Mattel's. Other principles relate to safety, wages, and adherence to local laws.

Mattel's audits and the code of conduct that emerged from them were not designed as punitive measures against its employees or other organizations. Rather, the
international company is dedicated to creating and encouraging responsible business
practices. As one company consultant has noted, "Mattel is committed to improving
the skill level of workers . . . [so that they] will experience increased opportunities and
productivity." This statement reflects Mattel's concern for building relationships with
employees and business partners that extend beyond pure profit considerations. Although the company will benefit from the code's principles, Mattel has formally acknowledged its willingness to consider incorporating multiple stakeholders' interests
and benefits in its business philosophy. The company's code is a signal to potential
partners, customers, and other stakeholders that Mattel is making a serious commitment to ethical values and is willing to base business decisions on them.

*International Manufacturing Principles.* As a U.S.-based multinational company
that owns and operates facilities and has contractor relationships around the world,
Mattel's Global Manufacturing Principles reflect not only its need to conduct all its
manufacturing responsibly, but also to respect the cultural, ethical, and philosophical
differences of the many countries in which it operates. In addition, these principles set
standards for every facility that manufactures Mattel products wherever they are
made. The principles not only benefit the men and women who manufacture Mattel's
products, but also ensure that Mattel's customers can continue to buy its products
with the confidence that they have been made in an environment that emphasizes
both safety and respect for individual rights.

Mattel's Global Manufacturing Principles cover such issues as wages and work
hours at Mattel, child labor, forced labor, discrimination, freedom of association, and
working conditions. All Mattel factories and vendors set working hours, wages, and

[2] Mattel, Inc., Online Privacy Policy, http://www.hotwheels.com/policy.asp (accessed Apr. 30, 2003).

overtime pay so they comply with the governing laws. Workers must be paid at least minimum wage or a wage that meets local industry standards, whichever is greater, and no one under sixteen or the local age limit (whichever is higher) may be allowed to work in a facility that produces products for Mattel. Furthermore, under no circumstances will Mattel use forced or prison labor of any kind, nor will it work with any manufacturer or supplier that does. As for discrimination, it is absolutely not tolerated by the company. Mattel firmly believes that individuals should be employed on the basis of their ability to do a job—not on the basis of individual characteristics or beliefs. Its concept of freedom of association is linked to its adherence to all the laws and regulations of every country in which it operates. The company recognizes all employees' rights to choose to affiliate—or not to affiliate—with legally sanctioned organizations or associations without unlawful interference.

In regard to working conditions, all Mattel facilities and those of its business partners must provide a safe working environment for their employees. The requirements include the following:

- Complying with all applicable local laws regarding sanitation and risk protection as well as meeting Mattel's own stringent standards
- Maintaining proper lighting and keeping aisles and exits accessible at all times
- Properly maintaining and servicing all machinery
- Sensibly storing and responsibly disposing of hazardous material
- Having an appropriate emergency medical and evacuation response plan for employees
- Never using corporal punishment or any other form of physical or psychological coercion on any employee.

*Legal and Ethical Business Practices.* Mattel favors business partners who are committed to ethical standards that are compatible with its own. At a minimum, all the company's business partners must comply with the local and national laws of the countries in which they operate. In addition, all Mattel partners must respect the significance of all patents, trademarks, and copyrights of Mattel's and other products and support Mattel in protecting these valuable assets. They also have responsibilities in the five areas that fall under legal and ethical practices: product safety and quality, the environment, customs, evaluation and monitoring, and compliance.

First, all of Mattel's business partners must share a commitment to product safety and quality and adhere to workplace practices that are necessary to meet Mattel's stringent safety and quality standards. Second, Mattel will work only with those manufacturers or suppliers that comply with all applicable laws and regulations and that share its commitment to the environment. Third, because of the global nature of Mattel's business and its history of leadership in this area, the company insists that all its business partners strictly adhere to all local and international customs laws. These partners must also comply with all import and export regulations. When it comes to evaluation and monitoring, Mattel audits manufacturing facilities to ensure that they comply with the Global Manufacturing Principles. Mattel also insists that all manufacturing facilities provide it with the following:

- Full access for on-site inspections by Mattel or parties designated by Mattel

- Full access to those records that will enable Mattel to determine whether facilities are complying with its principles

- An annual statement from facilities that they are complying with Mattel's Global Manufacturing Principles, signed by an officer of the manufacturer or manufacturing facility.

Acceptance of and compliance with the Mattel Global Manufacturing Principles are part of every contract agreement signed with all Mattel's manufacturing business partners.

Supporting Mattel's Global Manufacturing Principles is an independent monitoring system created to provide objective checks and balances to ensure that its standards are consistently met. With the creation of the Mattel Independent Monitoring Council (MIMCO), Mattel became the first global consumer products company to apply such a system to facilities and core contractors on a worldwide basis.

*Mattel Children's Foundation.* The Mattel Children's Foundation promotes the spirit of philanthropy and community involvement among its employees and makes charitable investments to further Mattel's goal of bettering the lives of children in need. Foundation staff carefully examine and evaluate its initiatives and grants to ensure that its financial resources are invested in ways that maximize impact. Current funding priorities include building the Mattel Children's Hospital at the University of California, Los Angeles (UCLA); sustaining the Mattel Family Learning Program; and continuing to promote the spirit of giving among Mattel employees.

In November 1998, Mattel announced a multiyear, $25 million gift to UCLA Children's Hospital to support that hospital and provide for a new state-of-the-art facility, which is currently being built. In honor of Mattel's donation, the hospital, expected to be completed by 2004, was renamed the Mattel Children's Hospital at UCLA.

The Mattel Family Learning Program establishes computer learning labs as part of the company's commitment to advancing the basic skills of children worldwide. Now numbering more than eighty throughout the United States, Hong Kong, Canada, and Mexico, the labs offer literacy software and adaptive technology that is specifically designed to help children who have special needs or limited English proficiency.

Mattel employees at its California headquarters as well as other locations are encouraged to participate in a wide range of activities as part of a volunteer program called "Mattel Volunteers: Happy to Help." Employees who serve on the boards of local nonprofit organizations or who help with ongoing programs at such organizations are eligible to apply for Volunteer Grants to support those organizations. Mattel employees who contribute to higher education or to nonprofit organizations that serve children in need are eligible to have their personal donations matched dollar for dollar, up to $5,000 per employee per year. And recognizing that many employees require financial assistance in order to send their children to college, Mattel has established a scholarship fund for them.

## Mattel's Future Challenges

Mattel's principles are intended to create and encourage responsible manufacturing business practices around the world rather than to serve as a guideline for punishment.

Moreover, Mattel expects its business partners to abide by these principles on an ongoing basis. But if certain aspects of the principles are not being met, Mattel's partners can expect the company to work with them to effect change. Potential business partners will not be engaged unless they meet all of Mattel's manufacturing principles. If the company determines that any one of its manufacturing facilities or any vendor has violated these principles, it can either terminate its business relationship or require the facility to implement a corrective action plan. If corrective action is advised but not taken, Mattel will immediately terminate current production and suspend placement of future orders. Thus, a key challenge for Mattel is the certification of its business partners and potential partners for compliance with Mattel's manufacturing principles.

Because Mattel is actively engaged in business around the world, it must be sensitive to economic downturns in other parts of the world. Shifts in the economic viability of markets can put pressure on sales targets, business relationships, and plans for new business ventures. As economic pressures increase, employees or organizations may change their normal business procedures, resulting in unethical and sometimes illegal practices. To cut corners and meet financial goals, managers and employees may purposely or inadvertently ignore the high ground established by regulations and agreements on ethical standards. Mattel, however, relies on overseas manufacturers to uphold key ethical principles, regardless of economic stability.

Overall, Mattel is very committed to both business success and ethical standards, but it recognizes that this commitment is part of a continuous improvement process. The company's position is made very clear in this statement: "[At Mattel, Inc.,] management is concerned not only with the safety and quality of the products manufactured, but with the safety and fair treatment of the men and women who manufacture these products as well."

*Questions*

1. What role does the chief executive officer have in creating an organizational culture that values ethics and compliance?
2. Do manufacturers of products for children have special obligations to consumers and society? If so, what are these responsibilities? If not, why not?
3. How effective has Mattel been at encouraging ethical and legal conduct by its manufacturers? What changes and additions would you make to the company's Global Manufacturing Principles? What are other companies doing in this area?

Sources: These facts are from "About Mattel-Company History," "Responsibility-Executive Summary," "Cabbage Patch Kids Overview," "Barbie Overview," "Hot Wheels Overview," "Mattel Press Releases: 9/29/00," "Responsibility-Independent Monitoring," and "Mattel Children's Foundation" Mattel, www.mattel.com (all accessed Jan. 17, 2001); Lisa Bannon and Carla Vitzhum, "One-Toy-Fits-All: How Industry Learned to Love the Global Kid," *Wall Street Journal,* Apr. 30, 2003, http://online.wsj.com; Adam Bryant, "Mattel CEO Jill Barad and a Toyshop That Doesn't Forget to Play," *New York Times,* Oct. 11, 1998; Bill Duryea, "Barbie-holics: They're Devoted to the Doll," *St. Petersburg Times,* Aug. 7, 1998; Rachel Engers, "Mattel Board Members Buy $30 Million in Stock: Insider Focus," *Bloomberg.com,* Dec. 22, 2000; "Global Manufacturing Principles," Mattel, 1998, p. 1; James Heckman, "Legislation," *Marketing News,* Dec. 7, 1998, pp. 1, 16; Mattel, Inc., Hot Wheels Web site, www.hotwheels.com/; "Independent Monitoring Council Completes Audits of Mattel Manufacturing Facilities in Indonesia, Malaysia and Thailand," Mattel, press release, Nov. 15, 2002, www.shareholder.com/mattel/news/20021115-95295.cfm; "Investors and Media," "Mattel Children's Foundation," and "Mattel Independent

Monitoring Council," Mattel, www.mattel.com/about_us/ (all accessed Apr. 30, 2003); "Mattel and U.S. Consumer Product Safety Commission Announce Voluntary Refund Program for Cabbage Patch Kids Snacktime Kids Dolls," U.S. Consumer Product Safety Commission, Office of Information and Public Affairs, Release No. 97-055, Jan. 6, 1997; "Mattel, Inc., Launches Global Code of Conduct Intended to Improve Workplace, Workers' Standard of Living," *Canada NewsWire,* Nov. 21, 1997 (for more information on Mattel's code, the company can be contacted at 310 252-3524); "Mattel, Inc., Online Privacy Policy," Mattel www.hotwheels.com/policy.asp (accessed Apr. 30, 2003); Marla Matzer, "Deals on Hot Wheels," *Los Angeles Times,* July 22, 1998; Patricia Sellers, "The 50 Most Powerful Women in American Business," *Fortune,* Oct. 12, 1998; "Toymaker Mattel Bans Child Labor," *Denver Post,* Nov. 21, 1998; Michael White, "Barbie Will Lose Some Curves When Mattel Modernizes Icon," *Detroit News,* Nov. 18, 1997.

# Case 18

# Conoco's Decision: The First Annual President's Award for Business Ethics[1]

On a December Friday in 1999, Steve L. Scheck, General Auditor for Conoco Inc., directed the other members of the award selection team toward lunch in the corporate dining room. They had spent the morning reviewing all the nominees for Conoco's first annual President's Award in Business Ethics. The heavy lifting would take place that afternoon. The team was charged with deciding who should receive the award and how the process should be improved for the following year.

As they walked through the corridors of the headquarters campus in Houston, Steve reflected on the events that had brought this group together. He recalled the meeting with Archie Dunham, Conoco's president, chairman, and CEO, when the idea first surfaced. In their discussion, Dunham had indicated that he wanted to initiate a "President's Award for Business Ethics." "We have a President's award for the other core values of safety and health, environmental stewardship, and valuing all people," he stated. "Why don't we have an award for business ethics?" Steve had agreed to get started on the project right away. Now a year later and after a great deal of planning, the process was coming to fruition. The award recipient or recipients would be presented with a trophy at the company's honors banquet and featured in an awards video circulated internally and externally. All the nominees would receive a note of congratulations from the president, chairman, and CEO, which certainly would provide some carryover in their annual performance evaluations. After the discussion of the candidates that morning, Steve had his own preliminary judgments on who should be selected, but he was curious to see what the other members of the selection team thought.

## Background and History of the Company

In 1999 Conoco was a large integrated oil company. The firm traced its origins back to the Continental Oil and Transportation Company first incorporated in Utah in 1875. At the time of the case it was a global firm operating in more than forty countries in the oil exploration, transportation, refining, and marketing sectors of the industry. The company had approximately 16,700 employees plus contractors and joint venture partners.

The firm's history has not been without difficulties. During the oil shocks of the early 1980s, the company lost its independence. In 1981, DuPont acquired Conoco in order to ensure adequate feed stocks for DuPont's chemical business. In 1992, the international oil analyst Schroder and Co. rated Conoco last in overall exploration results among the fourteen firms it surveyed.

As the oil crisis abated, the need to secure feed stocks seemed less important to DuPont. Wall Street was pressuring the company to improve its performance. DuPont's response was to streamline its operations. In the early 1990s, Conoco's new president, Archie Dunham, began a program of rationalizing Conoco's assets and developing new sources of supply. The company was successfully spun off from DuPont in a complex public offering and stock swap in 1999. In 1999 the Schroder survey ranked the firm number one in exploration efficiency among the major oil companies.

The newly independent company had the task of reintroducing itself to the stock market and establishing its own identity. While retaining its decades-old retailing identity as "The Hottest Brand Going!" Conoco's new corporate identity campaign centered on Domino, the fast cat, emphasizing that in the new global energy environment speed and agility matter more than size. Internally, the company emphasized a culture based on Conoco's core values of safety, environmental stewardship, valuing all people, and business ethics. The company developed compensation plans that closely align employees' interests with those of their shareholders. Under these plans, a portion of an employee's pay was tied to the total shareholder return, as well as other performance objectives, including upholding Conoco's core values. Conoco maintained that upholding these core values provided a powerful advantage for a company intent on global growth and that they were one of the reasons Conoco was welcomed around the world by customers, partners, governments, and communities.

The management believed that this values focus was particularly important for a global oil producer. The nature of the product, business, and technology required that the company have a big footprint. The firm must go where the oil is, move it, refine it, and sell it where it is needed. Conoco employees are natives of many countries and expatriates in many countries. They deal with governments, suppliers, joint venture partners, contractors, workers, and civilian populations in many places in the world. All of this means dealing with the environmental and moral hazards of the world community. The oil industry has a bad press, some of it, possibly, well deserved.

However, the world economy depends on the flow of oil, and the industry is not going away any time soon.

Conoco was proud to have avoided major disasters, such as the Exxon Valdez oil spill. In 1998, it was the first of the major oil companies to have converted completely to double-hulled tankers, a full seventeen years before the U.S. government's deadline in 2015. It promoted this and other safety and environmental accomplishments prominently in its annual report. One of the ways it did this is by having awards and contests in these areas. The winners received a letter from the president, and their accomplishments and pictures were published in the annual report.

## Development of the Award

Conoco had formal programs throughout the company to ensure that employees understood and put into practice the company's core values of safety and occupational health, care for the environment, valuing all people, and business ethics (see 1999 Annual Report, 22-24, Exhibit 1). The ethics program included a formal ethics policy, procedures for ensuring integrity and compliance with laws and ethics, and a twenty-four-hour ethics action line for employees to seek guidance and report possible violations. In developing the Business Ethics Award to complement this program, Steve had decided to work with a team of managers who were interested in the ethics process and who represented areas in which ethics questions would be a part of daily business. Debbie Tellez, Assistant General Counsel, Business Development; L. Cathy Wining, General Manager, Materials and Services; and Barbara Govan, Human Resources Generalist, formed the core team that was completed by several key persons around the world to ensure that global perspectives were included. The team met over several months, and circulated and revised a number of drafts so as to design a process for soliciting and judging nominees for the award (see Award Guidelines, Exhibit 2).

## Award Guidelines

The purpose of the award was to "support and recognize ethics as one of Conoco's four core values," to recognize "extraordinary examples" of "leadership" that demonstrate "excellence" in "conduct," and to provide "role models whose behavior embodies what Conoco stands for" (Exhibit 2). Rather than simply stating that the award was to be given for ethical conduct, the guidelines made a number of distinctions. The award was to reward individuals or groups for good conduct and to inspire it in the actions, attitudes, and opinions of others. It sought to reward both individuals and groups, to recognize both significant and sustainable activities, to include both business and personal conduct, to be concerned with both ethics and law, and to represent Conoco's values both internally and externally. Conoco's business conduct guide, *Doing the Right Thing,* set the standards with which every employee was expected to comply. The Ethics Award was to recognize individuals who had gone beyond compliance.

Instead of simply assuming that good conduct is worthwhile, the award guidelines spelled out why this and the other core values were important to Conoco:

**EXHIBIT 1**
**THINK BIG, MOVE FAST: DELIVERING ON OUR PROMISES**

(Conoco 1999 Annual Report, p. 22–24)

Our vision is to be recognized around the world as a truly great, integrated, international energy company that gets to the future first. Conoco operates in more than 40 countries worldwide and at year-end 1999 had approximately 16,700 employees. Conoco is active in both the upstream and downstream segments of the global petroleum industry.

*Distinctive Corporate Culture Defines Conoco—Past, Present and Future*
*Core Values—An Unwavering Commitment*

Safety and Health: Conoco is dedicated to protecting the safety and health of our employees, who maintained an outstanding safety performance in 1999. The total recordable injury rate of 0.36 per 100 full-time employees was just slightly above the previous year's record low. During the past five years, employee safety performance has improved more than 60 percent. Conoco has achieved these outstanding results through the company's efforts to continuously improve safety systems and processes, and because employees take personal responsibility for their safety and the safety of their co-workers. This sense of shared concern was reflected in the safety performance of the thousands of contractors who work at Conoco facilities. Contractor safety performance improved 17 percent in 1999, and 64 percent during the last five years. . . . .

Environmental Stewardship: Conoco is working to minimize the impact of the company's activities on the environment. The number of significant environmental incidents was reduced to zero in 1998, with one occurring in 1999. "Significant" incidents are major releases or spills with the potential to affect our neighbors. Over the past five years, emissions of volatile organic compounds (which contribute to smog) have been reduced by an estimated one-third, while Conoco's global refining operations have continued to reduce flaring and sulfur emissions. Ernst & Young, a global accounting and auditing firm, is conducting an independent evaluation of Conoco's worldwide reporting processes for future data on safety, health and environmental performance. This audit will help us better measure the company's progress in these areas. In the communities where Conoco operates major facilities, we maintain a flow of information to local residents through Citizens Advisory Councils, which bring together community representatives and Conoco managers. . . . .

Valuing All People: Conoco operates in more than 40 countries and has a diverse global workforce. We draw on the different perspectives and cultures of our employees, along with their combined experience, knowledge and creativity, to gain a powerful business advantage around the world. Throughout the company, we strive to create an inclusive work environment that treats all people with dignity and respect. In such an environment, employees are recognized and valued for their experience, intellect and leadership.

Business Ethics: Conducting business with the highest ethical standards is critical to Conoco's continuing success. As Conoco becomes more global, the company is subject to an ever-widening variety of laws, customs and regulations. This requires us to be flexible and innovative in our business dealings, while at the same time resolute about doing what's right, both legally and ethically.

> Adherence to the highest ethical standards is a condition of employment at Conoco. The company has a formal ethics policy and procedures for conducting business with integrity and in compliance with all applicable laws. Employees are required to review the policies and procedures regularly and complete an annual certificate of compliance. A 24-hour telephone hot line also provides employees a way to seek guidance or report possible conflicts.

> Living up to Conoco's core values in everything we do, individually and as a company, is fundamental to Conoco's continuing success. Conoco must conduct its business with the highest ethical standards. As our activities grow and extend into new areas of the world, we are subject to an ever-widening variety of laws, customs and regulations. We need to be flexible and innovative, and at the same time absolutely unwavering in doing what is right, ethically and legally, so that we may enhance our corporate image, and still gain competitive advantage and increase shareholder value (Exhibit 2).

According to the Guidelines, the specific criteria for judging the Award candidates were:

1. significance of the achievement
2. degree of innovation/creativity
3. degree of employee involvement
4. leadership qualities exhibited
5. impact on Conoco's image/value

The form on which all employees were invited to submit nominations asked for a description of:

1. the reason for the nomination, in terms of the results that were accomplished;
2. strategy and tactics, describing how the results were achieved, including obstacles and innovations; and
3. people involved and why they made a difference, including aspects of leadership and teamwork.

Those eligible for the award included individual employees (regular or temporary), a team, an entire work unit, or retiree of Conoco, for leadership or conduct while in Conoco service in the year of the nomination. Contractors could be included in work units, and multiple recipients were possible. The award winner(s) were to be decided by a selection team representing diverse constituencies, and confirmed by Archie Dunham, the president, CEO, and chairman. Persons outside the company (global external resources) were asked to participate in order to provide additional perspectives. For new perspective and continuity, one-third of the team was expected to change each year, and about one-third was to be comprised of former recipients of the award (Exhibit 2).

# EXHIBIT 2
# GUIDELINES: PRESIDENT'S AWARD FOR BUSINESS ETHICS

(Conoco Inc., 1999)

## Purpose

The **President's Award for Business Ethics** was created to support and recognize this as one of Conoco's four core values. This award recognizes individuals or groups that make significant and sustainable contributions to this core value.

The award is designed to inspire others by recognizing extraordinary examples of individual and/or group leadership that demonstrates on an ongoing basis, sustainable excellence in personal and business conduct. The people recognized are role models whose behavior embodies what Conoco stands for both internally and externally.

## Definition / Judging Criteria

Living up to Conoco's core values in everything we do, individually and as a company, is fundamental to Conoco's success. Conoco must conduct its business with the highest ethical standards. As our activities grow and extend into new areas of the world, we are subject to an ever-widening variety of laws, customs and regulations. We need to be flexible and innovative, and at the same time absolutely unwavering in doing what is right, ethically and legally, so that we may enhance our corporate image, and still gain competitive advantage and increase shareholder value.

Conoco's business conduct guide, *Doing the Right Thing,* provides a summary of the company's policies and standards, and of significant laws relating to our business. Every employee is personally responsible for compliance with those laws and standards. However, this award is designed to recognize those individuals who go beyond simply complying with company policies or the applicable laws.

It is designed to recognize those individuals who seek to change the actions, attitudes or opinions of others with regard to what constitutes ethical behavior, both internally and externally. This may be done through the role modeling of a significantly higher standard of ethical conduct; through the implementation of policies and practices that drive our actions, or the actions of others externally, beyond the minimally acceptable standard or customary behavior; or through decision making that demonstrates that "doing the right thing" from an ethical perspective increases shareholder value.

Nominations should represent extraordinary behavior and will be judged according to specific criteria described below.

1. The significance of the achievement, effort or behavior. Significant improvement above the minimum required standard for ethical conduct; linkage to business objectives and implementation of policy and standards; and/or successful performance in spite of difficult and challenging circumstances such as location, language, culture and/or alignment with and cooperation between Conoco and an external party.

2. The degree of innovation/creativity displayed. Proactive assessment of and response to a need; implementation of new approaches to address ethical business conduct.

3. The degree or extent of employee involvement or support with respect to the higher standard or expectation role modeled or implemented. A work environment exists that encourages employees to conduct themselves ethically at all levels; employees recognize the value of strong ethical behavior and are accountable for their conduct; employees are actively involved in the administration of company standards and training others; and/or rewards and recognition programs reinforce the desired behavior at all levels across the company.

4. The leadership qualities exhibited in challenging norms or customary practices. Persistence in implementing improvement programs or new approaches that lead to outstanding ethical performance.

5. The impact on the company's image/value; internally (with employees) and/or externally (with stakeholders such as partners, governments, suppliers, customers, and communities) in a way that creates shareholder value over time.

## Eligibility

Nominees for this award may be an individual employee (regular or temporary), a team, an entire work unit or retiree of Conoco, for leadership or conduct while in Conoco service in the year of nomination. Contractors may be included in team or work unit awards. There may be multiple recipients each year, dependent upon the number and quality of nominations received. An organization's size or a person's position within the company is not a deciding factor.

## The Award

The President's Award for Business Ethics will be presented annually to award recipients or their representatives at a special recognition ceremony. This award will reflect a unique and globally symbolic representation of ethics and will be consistent in stature with that of other President's Awards. The award will remain with the group or individual. Any additional forms of recognition will be left to the discretion of the business units.

## Selection Team

Conoco Leadership Center—Legal and Finance are jointly responsible for coordinating the selection process to determine award recipients. Input on selection team membership will be solicited from multiple sources, with final selection of the team made by the president and CEO. The Selection Team will be vested with the power to select a winner(s) and other finalists. The team's decision will be reviewed and endorsed by the President and CEO.

The Selection Team will consist of employees who are recognized as credible role models and able to provide an objective assessment. Team makeup will reflect a broad and global cross-section of the organization. Diversity of thinking styles, beliefs, cultures and backgrounds will be represented, as well as different salary grade, gender, ethnic and business perspectives.

To insure new perspective while maintaining continuity, we expect about one-third of the team's membership to transition in any given year. About one-third of the team will be comprised of former recipients of the award.

In addition to employees, global external resources will be invited to participate on the team to provide additional perspectives.

---

## Nomination

Each year Conoco's President and CEO will send a communication to all employees inviting nominations. The communications will be combined with nomination requests for the other three Conoco core values.

Nominations shall be submitted using **this on-line form,** or follow the format described below:

- The name, address, phone number and e-mail of the person submitting the nomination and responsible for providing any additional information if necessary.
- The name of the individual(s) being nominated. Indicate the name of the nominated team or work group if applicable.
- REASON/RESULTS—briefly describe WHAT was accomplished. Include details of any measures or impact of the behavior or activity involved to the extent possible, the drivers and the significance of the accomplishment.
- STRATEGY AND TACTICS—briefly describe HOW the results were achieved. What obstacles had to be overcome? What new or innovative tools or processes were used?
- PEOPLE—describe WHO was involved in this achievement and why they made a difference. Describe the leadership criteria exhibited and the degree of teamwork and networking that was necessary.

Nominations should consist of no more than three pages, including a brief introductory summary. Clear and concise nominations are encouraged. The Selection Team will make judgments based upon "substance" of the achievement, not form or length of the nomination.

---

## The Selection Process

The Selection Team met at Conoco's corporate campus in Houston in December 1999. The team had been chosen by the president, after input from a variety of sources. After introductions, the team members heard comments on the importance of the process by one of the champions of the Ethics Award and a member of the president's top management team, Bob Goldman, Senior Vice President for Finance and CFO. The meeting facilitator then presented the ground rules for the deliberations, and the discussion began. A Conoco employee selector, called a validator, had been assigned by the team chair to do a workup of each nominee before the meeting. Each validator gave a ten-minute summary of this background information on his/her nominee to the group. The validator then placed that nominee into one of three categories: outstanding, good, or weak. The "outstanding" nominees were to constitute an initial short list of potential award winners, though other candidates could be added to this list by the committee. After each validator's presentation the selectors asked questions and discussed the nominee, but no comparative rankings were made by the committee at this phase of the discussion.

## Presentation of the Nominees by the Validators

Twelve nomination forms had been submitted by employees, with one nominee receiving two separate nominations. After each nominee was described to the committee by a validator, committee members were allowed to ask for clarifications regarding the facts presented or to add facts that had not been mentioned. Then the validator was asked to rank the nomination as "outstanding," "average," or "weak" in order to develop a short list so the relative strengths of the nominees could be discussed.

### (1) Patrick R. Defoe, Asset Manager, Grand Isle, Louisiana

The first nomination presented was Patrick R. Defoe, Asset Manager, Grand Isle, Gulf Coast & Mid-Continent Business Unit, Lafayette, Louisiana. "Patrick Defoe is an example of ethical leadership in a very unexciting business unit," his validator began.

The Grand Isle asset (50+ platforms and associated pipelines situated in the Gulf of Mexico) was a mature field, destined to be sold off within several years. The reservoir was depleting, making the property no longer internally competitive for development funding. That information gets around, and the tendency is for everyone involved, from the bottom to the top, to get lax on dotting the i's and crossing the t's. Everyone is worried about his/her own future with the company. Especially toward the end, as people begin transferring out or retiring, it's difficult to uphold the value of the asset for sale. Patrick would not let that happen. He let people know that there was work to be done and that it would be done according to Conoco standards. His persistent and sustained leadership approach over a six-year period turned around the performance of Grand Isle in every respect. He introduced new programs in vendor convergence, alliance contracting, and a proactive maintenance, and began to actively manage the unit's relationships with regulatory bodies such as the Minerals Management Service.

He would not tolerate ethical or other core value lapses from employees or from contractors. When computer equipment on some of the platforms was missing, phones were stolen, and employees cars were vandalized, he followed up with a thorough investigation rather than looking the other way. These could have been considered minor incidents since the monetary value was small and the unit would soon be sold. Patrick felt business ethics involved the small things as well as the big things. When there were allegations of environmental misconduct and unethical behavior involving documents, he called in Legal/Security and gave them a free hand to investigate no matter who was involved. As it turned out, both allegations were essentially unfounded, but he implemented the minor changes recommended by the investigators.

Pat Defoe motivated his people to deliver, and they did in terms of costs per barrel, safety, and environmental stewardship. As the description on the nomination form indicates, platform fires decreased from 17 in 1996 to none in 1999, and incidents of regulatory noncompliance dropped from 42 to 2 in the last year. The continuous improvement in the asset's performance was crucial to the successful sale which realized some $47M for the company's bottom line.

"How did he keep his employees motivated when they knew the property was up for sale?" one selector asked. "Usually employees just want to retire or get transferred out and leave the problems to someone else."

"He took it upon himself to actively network for other employment opportunities throughout Conoco," replied the validator. "While getting rid of an asset of this size inevitably results in some layoffs, he found places throughout Conoco, in Downstream, Natural Gas and Gas Pipelines and in Venezuela, Dubai, Indonesia, and U.S. Upstream for high-performing individuals, while at the same time maintaining the quality of work at Grand Isle. He carved out several 'win-win' solutions for Conoco. I can close by saying that this is a strong nomination. Because of his good work, Pat has been put in charge of assimilating an acquisition in Canada."

"A good example of the fact that no good deed goes unpunished!" one of the outside selectors noted.

## (2) Georgian LPG Terminal Project Team, Georgia and Russia

The next nomination presented was the Georgian LPG Terminal Project Team. The team members included David Huber, Lead, Conoco Energy Ventures, Istanbul & Batumi; Roy Mills, Finance, London & Batumi; Harry Crofton, Development Engineering, London; Mikhail Gordin, Supply Logistics, Moscow; Asuman Yazici, Marketing Manager, Istanbul; Fiona Braid, Legal, London; and Pat Cook, Human Resources, London. "This nomination represents ethical conduct in very difficult circumstances by employees some of whom were fairly new in their positions with Conoco," the validator began.

It is an Indiana Jones story. You arrive at the airport in an exotic regional capital with a briefcase full of $100 dollar bills and you have to open a bank account, find a hotel room, and start doing business there.

Conoco saw an opportunity to become the first western oil company to establish offices and a hydrocarbon operation in Batumi by refurbishing a liquefied petroleum gas terminal there for transshipment and sale of LPG gas in Turkey and the eastern Mediterranean. The idea was to buy the product in Russia and ship it by rail to the terminal. This was Conoco's first venture into the area so it was critical that the team set the proper ethical tone for future business and that all employees, expatriate and native, uphold the Conoco values. The target was to have the first trainload of gas arrive at the terminal just as the repairs were completed. They were financing the remedial work on the terminal; purchasing the LPG; arranging for transportation through customs in Russia, Azerbaijan, and Georgia; making terminal arrangements in Adjaria; and reselling the product in Turkey. Roy Mills was overseeing the transfer of funds that had to be coordinated with the rebuilding of the terminal by a Turkish contractor based on engineering work monitored by Harry Crofton. Mikhail Gordin, who at that time was based in Moscow, was scouring the country to secure a supply of natural gas and negotiating a transportation agreement with both a freight forwarder and the local refinery management. There were many setbacks at both ends, frequently created by pressure to sweeten deals and alter scheduled work plans. Though bribes and kickbacks are illegal in these areas, many companies who operate there accept them as distasteful necessities because the legal infrastructure is often insufficient to stop such practices. There was a lot of pressure on the team members to go along with these types of payments in order to keep the project on schedule. By their refusal to make any "extraordinary" payments and their constant reminder to local employees, suppliers, and local customs and tax officials that business would have to be done according to Conoco standards or not at all, the project now operates successfully without constant harassment for such payments.

David Huber, the team lead, used his persistence and experience of working in Russia to convince the local government of Adjaria that LPG terminalling and transportation via Batumi would be an attractive business opportunity. The nominator points out that through his vision setting and understanding of the cultural differences and language barriers, David was able to assemble a multinational, multi-lingual team capable of working across all of the countries involved: Mikhail who was responsible for finding the gas and transporting it through customs in Russia, Azerbaijan, and Georgia; David and Harry who made the terminal arrangements workable in Adjaria; and resale of the product in Turkey by Asuman. It is also important to mention the financial, legal, and human resources services provided by Roy, Fiona and Pat.

There was one other positive aspect of this story. In order for governments and businesses to understand the Conoco way of doing business, it was crucial to hire local employees who would adhere to Conoco values that ran contrary to some local practices. In an area where personal references are practically worthless, Human Resources, through Pat Cook, checked all references and used a special interview process to vet all new hires. Integrity was a prime concern and a killer factor in hiring. Team members reinforced this concern through advice regarding expected behavior, auditing, and recognition. In addition, in order to assure that good conduct was rewarded by salary schedules appropriate to the region, the team sought salary advice from the United Nations Development Program, a first for an energy company. The UNDP praised the company's treatment of employees in the region. Overall, I think this is a strong nomination.

"What worries me about this situation is that we would be rewarding employees for doing what was expected of them," objected a selector. "The company policy is clear about not paying bribes. These guys did what they were supposed to do."

"Were there any extra pressures from within the company," asked one of the outside selectors, "other than the usual concern to meet targets with a profitable project? That might make their behavior extraordinary. Remember, the guidelines talk about 'overcoming obstacles'." (See Exhibit 3.)

Well, these employees were relatively new in these particular jobs and new to that area, so even a failure caused by a conflict of Conoco's ethical practices with local practices could have been perceived as more serious than for a more experienced person. In a company like ours that really stands behind its values, failure on those grounds would have been accepted as the right way to do business, but the perception of danger might still be there for newer employees. From a business standpoint, however, there were no more than the usual pressures to succeed.

"There was no pressure directing them to violate the company's ethical standards, but there was extra pressure," another selector said. "Remember that our primary project in the region had already gone under, so the LPG terminal was our only active effort. We needed the terminal to succeed in order to have a platform from which to launch other projects. The team members knew that if they failed, Conoco would likely pull out of the region entirely."

# EXHIBIT 3
# ORGANIZATIONAL STRUCTURES THAT BLOCK ETHICAL ACTION

Note: This exhibit is not a Conoco document but is included by the authors to facilitate case discussion.

## Are Illegal and Unethical Activities Common in the Workplace?

The 2000 National Business Ethics Survey (NBES'00) conducted by the Ethics Resource Center, showed that in comparison to their 1994 survey data, companies are doing more in terms of their ethics programs—more have written standards, ethics training programs, and means for employees to get ethics advice. Many ethics indicators have improved, and a majority of employees are positive about ethics in their organizations. Many employees believe that their supervisors and organizational leaders talk about and model ethical behavior at work. Interestingly, there are relatively few differences in the ethics perceptions of employees in the government, for-profit, and non-profit sectors.

In a 1997 survey (EOAS'97) conducted by the Ethics Officer Association and the American Society of Chartered Life Underwriters and Chartered Financial Consultants, 48% of American workers admitted to illegal or unethical actions in the previous year.

The NBES'00 reported that 33% of American workers observed behaviors that violated either their organization's ethics standards or the law. [This report was based on a nationally representative telephone survey of fifteen hundred U.S. employees conducted between November 1999 and February 2000.]

A 1999 survey (KPMGS'99) conducted by KPMG LLP, a professional services firm, indicated that greater than 75% of U.S. workers surveyed had observed violations of the law or company standards in the previous twelve months. Nearly 50% said their company "would significantly lose public trust" if the observed infraction had been reported by the news media. [This report is based on questionnaires sent to the homes of 3,075 randomly selected U.S. working adults in October and November, 1999; 2,390 completed questionnaires were returned, for a response rate of 78%.]

## What are the Most Common Illegal and Unethical Activities?

The top five types of unethical/illegal activities in the EOAS'97 were:

1. cutting corners on quality control,
2. covering up incidents,
3. abusing or lying about sick days,
4. deceiving or lying to customers,
5. putting inappropriate pressure on others.

Others mentioned included cheating on an expense account, discriminating against co-workers, paying or accepting kickbacks, secretly forging signatures, trading sex for sales, and ignoring violations of environmental laws.

The five types of misconduct observed most frequently according to the NBES'00 were:

1. lying,
2. withholding needed information,
3. abusive or intimidating behavior toward employees,
4. misreporting actual time or hours worked, and
5. discrimination.

Common infractions cited in the KPMGS'99 were sexual harassment and employment discrimination, while other offenses mentioned included deceptive sales practices, unsafe working conditions, and environmental breaches.

## What are the Factors That Lead to Illegal and Unethical Activities in the Workplace?

The top ten factors that workers reported in EOAS'97 as triggering their unethical activities are: balancing work and family, poor internal communications, poor leadership, work hours and workload, lack of management support, need to meet sales, budget or profit goals, little or no recognition of achievements, company politics, personal financial worries, and insufficient resources.

Mid-level managers most often reported a high level of pressure to act unethically or illegally (20%). Employees of large companies cited such pressure more often than those at small businesses (21% versus 14%). High levels of pressure were reported more often by high school graduates than by college graduates (21% versus 13%).

The NBES'00 indicated that one in eight employees felt pressure to compromise their organizations' ethics standards. Almost two-thirds who feel this pressure attribute it to internal sources—supervisor, top management, and coworkers. Employees with longer tenure in their organizations felt more pressure to compromise their organizations' ethics standards. Employees who felt this pressure to compromise observe more misconduct in the workplace.

The KPMGS'99 reported that nearly three-fourths of the respondents blamed cynicism and low morale for employee misconduct. Some 55 percent of respondents said their CEO was unapproachable if an employee needed to deliver bad news; 61 percent thought their company would not discipline individuals guilty of an ethical infraction.

## An Organizational Focus Is as Important for Understanding Ethical Behavior as an Individual Focus

Since many of the causes cited as triggering unethical behavior are organizational factors, an organizational focus is as important as an individual focus in understanding the obstacles to ethical behavior. By focusing on structure, it is possible to identify certain common features of business organizations that act as organizational blocks to ethical behavior. These ways of organizing business activity can make it difficult for individuals to act in an ethical way, even if the corporation's ethics code requires ethical behavior. James A. Waters identifies seven such blocks to ethical action ("Catch 22; Corporate Morality as an Organizational Phenomenon," *Organizational Dynamics*, Spring 1978. Reprinted in Donaldson & Werhane, *Ethical Issues in Business,* 3rd Edition, 1988):

(a.) Strong role models who follow unethical practices make it difficult for new employees trained by them to imagine how the assigned tasks could be done without engaging in unethical practices. Corporations must pay careful attention to the messages that new employees get during their training about the importance of following the firm's ethics code.

(b.) The strict line of command followed in many organizations makes it difficult for individuals down the chain to resist an immediate supervisor's order to do something unethical. The employee must assume that the order has come from higher up the chain and represents company policy. If there are no channels of communication for questioning the ethics of an action without going to the higher-ups who presumably originated the order, the employee is unlikely to risk retribution by going above his/her supervisor's head. Thus, compliance in unethical activities can often be enforced by lower-level supervisors without the higher company officials ever knowing about it.

(c.) The separation of policy decisions from their implementation can be a strong block to ethical action. In most organizations, policy is set by upper management without discussion with lower-level employees. Lower-level employees may then be forced to resort to unethical activities in order to carry out unreasonable policies or goals set by the top management or risk losing their jobs.

(d.) The division of work necessary to accomplish the goals of large organizations also makes reporting unethical activities difficult. Employees in one channel do not see it as their responsibility to report wrongdoing in other channels nor do they usually have enough information about what is going on throughout the organization to be certain that the activities are unethical.

(e.) Task group cohesiveness can frustrate even well-structured internal reporting procedures. Members of a work group who are engaged in unethical activities will exert strong pressure on every member to be loyal to the group rather than report the activities to the company.

(f.) Loyalty to the company can lead employees to protect wrongdoers from outside intervention by the law or adverse public opinion. Employees can avoid investigating reported unethical activities out of fear that word will get out that wrongdoing has occurred.

(g.) Another organizational block is constituted by ambiguity about priorities. Corporate ethics codes may not make it clear to employees how conflicts between performance criteria and ethical criteria should be resolved. Companies may reward employees only on the basis of the "hard" measurable criteria of meeting sales goals or profit projections, with no consideration given to the means used to achieve these ends.

Two further blocks that Waters does not mention are time pressure and inadequate resources. Time pressure may make unethical shortcuts seem like the most expedient solution to a workload that cannot be completed in the time permitted. Inadequate resources to complete the job with ethical means may also pressure employees into unethical shortcuts. Overcoming these organizational blocks in meeting the expected standards of behavior would qualify as "extraordinary" and worthy of recognition.

### (3) Eric Johnson, Excel Paralubes, Lake Charles, Louisiana

"This may not be as dramatic a story," began the validator, "But it represents behavior that deserves recognition just as well. It involves day-to-day ethical leadership that set the tone for the employees of one of our joint ventures. EXCEL Paralubes is an effort to leverage technology and personnel from Conoco and Pennzoil in the creation of a product and profits that neither organization could realize alone. Conoco is the managing partner in the venture, which is sited next to the Conoco facility in Lake Charles." The validator continued:

> The nomination came from a Conoco manager working as the Organizational Development Coordinator for Petrozuata Upgrader, another joint venture in Venezuela. The nominator had been part of the EXCEL startup and knew that EXCEL had developed innovative work processes that had contributed to the success of EXCEL and would be readily adaptable to help with organizational development in Petrozuata. He asked Eric to share them with Petrozuata. Eric responded that he would be happy to help but that certain of these processes represented a competitive advantage to the EXCEL joint venture. Though these processes would certainly add to the bottom line at Conoco through its Venezuela venture, they could not be given out in fairness to the joint venture partner, Pennzoil. This response from a loyal Conoco employee who was conscious of his ethical and legal obligations to his joint venture so impressed the nominator that he submitted Eric for the award. The nominator also stated that, following Eric Johnson's leadership in this area, he has conveyed this standard of conduct to his peers at Petrozuata so that they are aware of their obligation to protect not only Conoco's interests but those of their joint venture partners as well.
>
> As I looked into Eric's activities at EXCEL, I was more and more impressed that this was not an isolated incident and that Eric was modeling ethical conduct crucial to the success of Conoco joint ventures. If we are the managing partner in the venture, the other partner needs to be confident that the Conoco employees in charge will not show any favoritism to Conoco in cost sharing. And to hear tell from the EXCEL and Conoco people on the site, Eric is fair to a fault. The EXCEL operation is right next to the Conoco plant in Lake Charles, Louisiana, and the two plants jointly use some of the facility. Eric has gotten flak from his counterparts at the Conoco plant for not cutting them any slack on sharing costs for these joint facilities. They would rather not have these costs show up in their budgets, but he reminds them that he is wearing his EXCEL hat and needs to look out for the interests of EXCEL. On one occasion, for example, he made Conoco pay for its share of grading the road which borders both plant sites. While that may seem unimportant, it sets a tone for all of the Conoco employees lent to the venture and has given Pennzoil such confidence in the fairness of the operation that they are planning additional ventures with Conoco. I think this nomination is another strong one.

"But again, isn't this conduct that we expect of all employees? Does it arise to an award level?" asked a selector.

"Well," the validator replied, "you need to realize that his long-term career is with Conoco and that most managers after several years with the joint venture return to work with their parent company. By upholding these standards he is risking burning some bridges with managers at Conoco that he might be working for or with in the future."

"We also have to consider that joint ventures of this kind are important to a company the size of Conoco, and we haven't been doing them for that long," another selector added. "We need models for how to make those ventures work, and an award might help to get the message out as to our company's expectations."

"When Conoco, for competitive reasons, elected to include convenience stores in our retail stations," the validator began, "the company found itself with a whole new kind of employee."

Instead of the salaried engineers, managers and support staff who make up most of the work force, we were responsible for recruiting, training, motivating, and monitoring a group of not very highly paid hourly workers who were our retail face to the public. In addition, these not very highly paid workers were surrounded by all kinds [of] temptations in the form of merchandise and cash, in a situation where direct supervision was too costly. Looking at this problem, Terry decided that there were two main options. One was to assume that a small percentage of employees were going to steal and concentrate on catching and punishing them. The other was to assume that the great majority of employees were honest and that a program that spent time and money recognizing their honesty in the face of temptation would motivate them to continue their good conduct. Such a program could convert or drive out the bad actors as well.

Terry decided to emphasize "keeping honest people honest." The program was designed to "catch people being honest and reward them for it." The first step was a strong training program for new employees that began with a unit that explained all the ways that employees can steal from a convenience store. Employees who expect to steal were thereby warned that the company knew all of their methods and most of the dropouts occurred in this early phase of the training. Honest employees understood what the temptations were and were taught how to avoid them. They understood that the company uses extensive control measures and that one of the purposes of these was to "catch them doing something right." Once on the job, the employees were continually motivated to be honest with visits by mystery shoppers who rewarded them on the spot for good behavior.

A second phase of the program involved systemized operational practices designed to decrease the opportunity for theft to occur. There are extensive control measures to manage inventory and track sales through scanning technology and regular and surprise audits. Security cameras have been installed in virtually all stores within the last two years. Honest employees were encouraged to be honest by knowing that dishonest behavior would be caught and punished. But the emphasis even in the audits was to reward people whose inventory and cash are all properly accounted for rather than focusing on the threat which controls pose to those who do wrong. The desire to accurately measure inventory and control losses was the catalyst in the decision to employ new and innovative scanning technology. The data resulting from this Loss Control Program has also proved valuable in the development of trend reports and standardized operations reports that can highlight loss control problems before they become critical.

The results of this approach to managing retail sales have been significant. While the standard rate of losses in the industry is 2% to 4% of gross revenue per year, Conoco's loss percentage has averaged 1.13% over the past three years. This difference translates into additional revenues of $1.5MM and $2.5MM per annum over the past two years. The turnover rate for employees is also significantly lower than the industry average, which contributes to lower recruitment and training costs.

In his position as Director of Security in Retail Operations, Terry was the sole employee in the retail sector assigned to Loss Control. His work designing and selling this program throughout the sector resulted in a function-wide commitment to the Retail Loss Control Program at all levels. Because of his efforts, loss control focused not on fixing problems by firing dishonest employees but on training personnel to recognize the importance of honesty and on implementing sustainable processes to prevent problems from occurring. All in all, I think this nomination warrants serious consideration.

## (5) Raymond S. Marchand, Upstream Aame, Damascus, Syria

"Raymond Marchand is a unique individual," the validator began.

Born a French-Algerian, Raymond has translated his dual nationality into a unique understanding of how to preserve Conoco values in some of the most complex and challenging business cultures in the world. As a young man he fought the Algerians as a member of the French Foreign Legion's "Blackfoot" brigade, a group that planned to parachute into Paris to assassinate French President De Gaulle for granting Algerian independence. After his military service, Raymond began working for Conoco as a laborer in the 1960s and quickly advanced into management responsibility. He has been in charge of the company's operations in Chad, Egypt, The Congo, Somalia, Angola, and Nigeria, and is now heading operations in Syria. His leadership in doing business the Conoco way or not doing business at all involved relationships both outside and inside the company. By his own example he established a clear policy of integrity in all dealings with government officials and contractors, and taught both native and expatriate employees that requests for "exceptional" payments could be refused continually without insulting the person making the request.

Raymond is most masterful in difficult business environments. In Somalia the U.S. government employed his experience in negotiating in a corrupt environment without compromising his standards. As the situation there deteriorated, Raymond was forced to leave the country to the sound of gunfire. In Nigeria his high ethical standards and personal negotiating style changed the paradigm of what was acceptable business conduct for Conoco's Nigerian employees, our Nigerian indigenous partners, and our Nigerian government contacts. His approach took the risk of losing business opportunities. The respect he garnered for his way of operating, however, gained opportunities for Conoco, especially as a new government under President Obasanjo made the ideal of integrity fashionable in that country.

Nigeria was a particularly challenging environment because 95% of the Conoco workforce was native born and had grown up in an atmosphere in which companies bought their way into whatever situation they wanted to be in. Marchand taught the whole organization from top to bottom that business could be conducted without such payments. His alternative to bribes was establishing relationships based on trust and dependability, an approach that requires spending the time to build personal relationships. Actions speak louder than words in establishing trust, and as his nominator put it, "You can see his heart behind everything he says and does." With the company's indigenous partners he was successful in resolving contractual problems and educating them about Conoco's core values, especially ethical behavior. In doing so he earned not only their respect but a wider recognition within the business community and the government that Conoco's integrity is second to none in Nigeria.

Because of his leadership, many of our operating costs have been lowered by newly empowered, bright young native Nigerian employees. Throughout Nigeria, I am told, all the Conoco employees respond to requests for "extraordinary" payments with Marchand's characteristic smile, two raised and waving hands, and the phrase "No can do!" delivered in a loud friendly voice. This behavior has become so standard that most people do not even request payments from Conoco employees.

Inside the company, Marchand has shown an equally high level of integrity. Whenever accusations have surfaced about irregularities in his operations, he has immediately requested a full company investigation of the matter and has ensured the full cooperation of all employees in his shop. When notified that he was being posted to Syria, he requested a meeting with a management committee from Auditing and Legal Affairs to map out strategies for dealing with the business environment in that country. I think his career achievements set a standard against which future award nominations can be measured.

"That mention of career achievement raises some interesting points regarding the award criteria," observed an outside selector. "Should the President's Ethics Award recognize only heroic ethical conduct which goes beyond the standard expected of every employee, or should employees be rewarded for meeting the expected standards? And if employees are recognized for meeting the expected standard, should this be only for consistent behavior over time (a lifetime of ethical action), or for behavior in difficult circumstances (pressures to meet other performance criteria)? Or would the company's objectives be furthered in giving awards sometimes for behavior which shows how the standards can be followed in ordinary circumstances (a good example, or 'Charlie Brown' award)?"

"It seems that we have examples of all of these possibilities in this group of nominees," another selector said. "In giving this first award, the company will be setting some kind of a standard for future nominations, though an evolution of the standards is certainly possible. But I think it is important to keep in mind that our decision may encourage some and discourage other types of nominations from being submitted in the future."

"We might want to consider giving more than one award this first year, since we are reviewing conduct from several prior years rather than one prior year," one selector said.

"It is interesting," another selector noted, "that we have some real diversity among the nominees. We have overseas and domestic. We have upstream (exploration and production), midstream (transportation and refining), and downstream (retailing). We have career nominations and specific project nominations, and we have individuals and a team. The only kind of nomination missing is for a single action which was unique enough, had such important consequences, or was done under such difficult circumstances that it was significant enough for a nomination."

## Making the Decision

The morning passed quickly as the nominees were presented. "These five nominees have made the short list based on the validators' evaluations," the facilitator said as she stood up to indicate that the descriptive phase of the work was concluded. "But any of the others can be considered as we begin to make judgments this afternoon. Archie [President Dunham] considers this award to be important for Conoco. We have a real task ahead of us. Steve has promised us an excellent lunch before we decide who to recommend for the first President's Award for Business Ethics."

*Questions*

1. Assess Conoco's core values as they relate to the President's Award for Business Ethics.
2. Evaluate the criteria used for the President's Award for Business Ethics.
3. Choose a winner for the Conoco Business Ethics Award from the five nominees. Defend your selection.

# Appendix A

# Company Codes of Ethics

## Lockheed Martin: Code of Ethics and Business Conduct*

This booklet, *Setting the Standard*, has been adopted by the Lockheed Martin Board of Directors as our company's Code of Ethics and Business Conduct. It summarizes the principles that guide our actions in the global marketplace as we strive to be the world's finest technology and systems enterprise. Our Code applies to all Lockheed Martin employees, members of the Board of Directors, agents, consultants, contract labor, or others, when they are representing or acting for the corporation. We expect our contractors and suppliers to be guided by these standards as well. Our Code promotes not only "doing things right," but also "doing the right things" to maintain our personal and institutional integrity.

At Lockheed Martin, we believe that ethical conduct requires more than simply complying with the laws, rules, and regulations that govern our business. We are a company that values teamwork, sets team goals, assumes collective accountability for actions, embraces diversity, and shares leadership. We are committed to excellence and pursue superior performance in every activity. However, it is the personal integrity of each of our employees and their commitment to the highest standards of personal and professional conduct that underlie the ethical culture of Lockheed Martin.

While we remain sensitive to the diverse social and cultural settings in which we conduct our business, Lockheed Martin aims to *set the standard* for ethical conduct at all of our locations throughout the world. We will achieve this through behavior in accordance with six principles: Honesty, Integrity, Respect, Trust, Responsibility, and Citizenship.

**Honesty:** to be truthful in all our endeavors; to be honest and forthright with one another and with our customers, communities, suppliers, and shareholders.

**Integrity:** to say what we mean, to deliver what we promise, to fulfill our commitments, and to stand for what is right.

**Respect:** to treat one another with dignity and fairness, appreciating the diversity of our work force and the uniqueness of each employee.

**Trust:** to build confidence through teamwork and open, candid communication.

**Responsibility:** to take responsibility for our actions, and to speak up—without fear of retribution—and report concerns in the workplace, including violations of laws, regulations and company policies, and seek clarification and guidance whenever there is doubt.

*Courtesy of Lockheed Martin/www.lockheedmartin.com ©2003 Lockheed Martin Corporation

**Citizenship:** to obey all the laws of the United States and other countries in which we do business, and to do our part to make the communities in which we live and work better.

There are numerous resources available to assist you in meeting the challenge of performing your duties and responsibilities. If you are faced with an ethical dilemma, your supervisor is usually the best source of information and guidance. Additionally, the Human Resources, Legal, Procurement, Contracts, Information Services, Energy Environment Safety & Health, Finance and Security organizations as well as Ethics Officers are available to assist you whenever necessary. Corporate Policy Statements and local policies and procedures that provide details pertinent to many of the provisions of the Code can be accessed via the Lockheed Martin Information Network (http://pageone.global.lmco.com) or obtained from your supervisor. Although your own common sense and good judgment should be your first guide to appropriate conduct, do not hesitate to use these additional resources whenever clarification is necessary.

We are proud of our employees and the important role our corporation plays in our communities, our industry, and in the national security of the United States and its allies. Thank you for doing your part to create and maintain an ethical work environment . . . and for *Setting the Standard.*

**VANCE D. COFFMAN   ROBERT J. STEVENS**
Chairman and President and
Chief Executive Officer Chief Operating Officer
March 2003

## Our Commitments

*For our employees* we are committed to honesty, just management, fairness, providing a safe and healthy environment free from the fear of retribution, and respecting the dignity due everyone.

*For our customers* we are committed to produce reliable products and services, delivered on time, at a fair price.

*For the communities* in which we live and work we are committed to observe sound environmental business practices and to act as concerned and responsible neighbors, reflecting all aspects of good citizenship.

*For our shareholders* we are committed to pursuing profitable growth, without taking undue risk, to exercising financial discipline in the deployment of our assets and resources, and to making accurate, timely, and clear disclosures in all public reports and communications.

*For our suppliers and partners* we are committed to fair competition and the sense of responsibility required of a good customer and teammate.

*We are committed to ethical behavior in all that we do.*

## Obey the Law

We will conduct our business in accordance with all applicable laws and regulations. The laws and regulations related to government contracting are far-reaching and complex, thus placing responsibilities on Lockheed Martin beyond those faced by companies without government customers. Compliance with the law does not comprise our entire ethical responsibility. Rather, it is a minimum, absolutely essential condition for performance of our duties.

*We will conduct our business in accordance with all applicable laws and regulations.*

## Promote a Positive Work Environment

All employees want and deserve a workplace where they feel respected, satisfied, and appreciated. As a global enterprise, we respect cultural diversity and recognize that the various countries in which we do business may have different legal provisions pertaining to the workplace. As such, we will adhere to the limitations specified by law in all of our locations, and further, we will not tolerate harassment or discrimination of any kind—especially involving age, sex, ancestry, color, disability, national origin, race, religion, United States military veteran's status, sexual orientation, marital status, or family structure.

Providing an environment that supports honesty, integrity, respect, trust, responsibility, and citizenship permits us the opportunity to achieve excellence in our workplace. While everyone who works for the company must contribute to the creation and maintenance of such an environment, our executives and management personnel assume special responsibility for fostering a work environment that is free from the fear of retribution and will bring out the best in all of us. Supervisors must be careful in words and conduct to avoid placing, or seeming to place, pressure on subordinates that could cause them to deviate from acceptable ethical behavior.

## Work Safely: Protect Yourself, Your Fellow Employees, and the World We Live in

We are committed to providing a drug-free, safe, and healthy work environment, and to observe environmentally sound business practices throughout the world. We will strive, at a minimum, to do no harm and where possible, to make the communities in which we work a better place to live. Each of us is responsible for compliance with environmental, health, and safety laws and regulations. Observe posted warnings and regulations. Report immediately to the appropriate management any accident or injury sustained on the job, or any environmental or safety concern you may have.

*We are committed to providing a drug-free, safe, and healthy work environment.*

## Keep Accurate and Complete Records

We must maintain accurate and complete company records. Transactions between the company and outside individuals and organizations must be promptly and accurately entered in our books in accordance with generally accepted accounting practices and principles in the United States. No one should rationalize or even consider misrepresenting facts or falsifying records. It will not be tolerated and will result in disciplinary action.

*No one should rationalize or even consider misrepresenting facts or falsifying records.*

## Make Accurate Public Disclosures

We must assure that all disclosures made in all periodic reports and documents filed with the Securities and Exchange Commission, and other public communications by the corporation, are full, fair, accurate, timely, and understandable. This obligation applies to all employees, including all financial executives, with any responsibility for the preparation of such reports, including drafting, reviewing, and signing or certifying the information contained therein. This requires operating in an environment of open communication, while not compromising proprietary and confidentiality concerns.

If you have concerns about any aspect of our financial disclosures, you should talk to your manager, the Finance organization, the Legal Department, or the Ethics Office. Any employee who is contacted by another employee expressing concerns about questionable accounting or auditing matters must immediately report those concerns to the Ethics Office.

*We are committed to full, fair, accurate, timely and understandable disclosure in all public communications.*

## Record Costs Properly

Employees and their supervisors are responsible for ensuring that labor and material costs are accurately recorded and charged on the company's records. These costs include, but are not limited to, normal contract work, work related to independent research and development, and bid and proposal activities.

*Employees and their supervisors are responsible for . . . the company's records.*

## Strictly Adhere to All Antitrust Laws

Antitrust is a blanket term for laws that protect the free enterprise system and promote open and fair competition. Such laws exist in the United States, the European Union, and in many other countries where the company does business. These laws deal with agreements and practices "in restraint of trade" such as price fixing and boycotting suppliers or customers, for example. They also bar pricing intended to run a competitor out of business; disparaging, misrepresenting, or harassing a competitor; stealing trade secrets; bribery; and kickbacks.

Antitrust laws are vigorously enforced. Violations may result in severe penalties such as forced sales of parts of businesses and significant fines against the company. There may also be sanctions against individual employees, including substantial fines and prison sentences. These laws also apply to international operations and transactions related to imports into and exports from the countries in which we do business. Employees involved in any dealings with competitors are expected to know that U.S. and other countries' antitrust laws may apply to their activities and to consult with the Legal Department prior to negotiating with or entering into any arrangement with a competitor.

### Know and Follow the Law When Involved in International Business

Corruption erodes confidence in the marketplace, undermines democracy, distorts economic and social development, and hurts everyone who depends on trust and transparency in the transaction of business. The company is committed to conduct its activities free from the unfair influence of bribery and to foster anti-corruption awareness among its employees and business relations throughout the world. There are several laws that govern these transactions:

- The Foreign Corrupt Practices Act (FCPA) is a United States law that prohibits corruptly giving, offering or promising anything of value to foreign officials or foreign political parties, officials or candidates, for the purpose of influencing them to misuse their official capacity to obtain, keep, or direct business or to gain any improper advantage. In addition, the FCPA prohibits knowingly falsifying a company's books and records or knowingly circumventing or failing to imple-

ment accounting controls. Employees involved in international operations must be familiar with the FCPA and with similar laws that govern our operations in other countries in which we do business.

- The International Traffic in Arms Regulations (ITAR) is a United States law that regulates the international transfers of equipment or technology that may contain prior approval, licensing, and reporting requirements. Employees involved in international operations must also be familiar with the ITAR.

- Additionally, it is illegal to enter into an agreement to refuse to deal with potential or actual customers or suppliers, or otherwise to engage in or support restrictive international trade practices or boycotts. It is always important that employees conducting international business know and abide by the laws of the United States and the countries that are involved in the activities or transactions.

These laws govern the conduct of Lockheed Martin employees throughout the world. If you participate in these business activities, you should know, understand, and strictly comply with these laws and regulations. If you are not familiar with these rules, consult with your supervisor, Business Development organization and the Legal Department prior to negotiating any foreign transaction.

### Follow the Law and Use Common Sense in Political Contributions and Activities

Lockheed Martin encourages its employees to become involved in civic affairs and to participate in the political process. Employees must understand, however, that their involvement and participation must be on an individual basis, on their own time, and at their own expense. In the United States, federal law prohibits corporations from donating corporate funds, goods, or services, directly or indirectly, to candidates for federal offices—this includes employees' work time. Local and state laws also govern political contributions and activities as they apply to their respective jurisdictions, and similar laws exist in other countries.

## Carefully Bid, Negotiate, and Perform Contracts

We must comply with the laws and regulations that pertain to the acquisition of goods and services by our customers. We will compete fairly and ethically for all business opportunities. In circumstances where there is reason to believe that the release or receipt of non-public information is unauthorized, do not attempt to obtain and do not accept such information from any source.

Appropriate steps should be taken to recognize and avoid organizational conflicts in which one business unit's activities may preclude the pursuit of a related activity by another company business unit.

If you are involved in proposals, bid preparations, or contract negotiations, you must be certain that all statements, communications, and representations to prospective customers are accurate and truthful. Once awarded, all contracts must be performed in compliance with specifications, requirements, and clauses.

## Avoid Illegal and Questionable Gifts or Favors

The sale of Lockheed Martin products and services should always be free from even the perception that favorable treatment was sought, received, or given in exchange for the furnishing or receipt of business courtesies. Employees will neither give nor accept business courtesies that constitute, or could be reasonably perceived as constituting, unfair business inducements or that would violate law, regulation or policies of the company or customer, or could cause embarrassment to or reflect negatively on the company's reputation. Although customs and practices may differ among the many marketplaces in which we conduct our business, our policies in this regard are substantially similar within the United States and elsewhere throughout the world. As a matter of respect for the rich and diverse customs practiced among our business relations internationally, permissive conduct may differ somewhat in accordance with applicable policy or upon guidance from the business unit's Ethics Officer and Legal Department.

## Gifts, Gratuities, and Business Courtesies to U.S., State, and Local Government Employees

Federal, state and local government departments and agencies are governed by laws and regulations concerning acceptance by their employees of entertainment, meals, gifts, gratuities, and other things of value from firms and persons with whom those government departments and agencies do business or over whom they have regulatory authority. It is the policy of Lockheed Martin to comply strictly with those laws and regulations.

### Federal Executive Branch Employees

Lockheed Martin employees are prohibited from giving anything of value to federal Executive Branch employees, except as follows:

- Lockheed Martin advertising or promotional items of little intrinsic value (generally $10.00 or less) such as a coffee mug, calendar, or similar item displaying the company logo;
- Modest refreshments such as soft drinks, coffee, and donuts on an occasional basis in connection with business activities; or
- Business-related meals and local transportation having an aggregate value of $20.00 or less per occasion, provided such items do not in aggregate exceed $50.00 in a calendar year. Although it is the responsibility of the government employee to track and monitor these thresholds, no Lockheed Martin employee shall knowingly provide meals and/or transportation exceeding the $20.00 individual or $50.00 annual limit.

Certain other exceptions regarding widely attended gatherings and business activities outside U.S. borders are detailed in company policy.

### Federal Legislative and Judiciary Branches, and State and Local Government Employees

Employees of the federal Legislative and Judiciary Branches and employees of state and local government departments or agencies are subject to a wide variety of different laws and regulations. These laws and regulations and Corporate Policy Statements pertaining to them must be consulted prior to offering such employees anything of value.

## Business Courtesies to Non-Government Persons

### Meals, Refreshments and Entertainment

It is an acceptable practice for Lockheed Martin employees to provide meals, refreshments, entertainment, and other business courtesies of reasonable value to non-government persons in support of business activities, provided:

■ The practice does not violate any law or regulation or the standards of conduct of the recipient's organization. It is the offeror's responsibility to inquire about prohibitions or limitations of the recipient's organization before offering any business courtesy; and

■ The business courtesy must be consistent with marketplace practices, infrequent in nature, and may not be lavish or extravagant. While it is difficult to define "lavish or extravagant" by means of a specific dollar amount, a common sense determination should be made consistent with reasonable marketplace practices.

### Gifts

Lockheed Martin employees are prohibited from offering or giving tangible gifts (including tickets to sporting, recreational, or other events) having a market value of $100.00 or more, to a person or entity with which the company does or seeks to do business, unless specifically approved by his or her supervisor, and the business unit's Ethics Officer or the Corporate Office of Ethics and Business Conduct.

## Business Courtesies to Foreign Government Personnel and Public Officials

The company may be restricted from giving meals, gifts, gratuities, entertainment, or other things of value to personnel of foreign governments and foreign public officials by the Foreign Corrupt Practices Act and by laws of other countries. Employees must obtain prior Legal Department approval where the hospitality (i.e., meal, gift, gratuity, entertainment or other thing of value) to be given is not clearly permissible under the Hospitality Guidelines and Matrix maintained by the Legal Department.

*Employees must discuss such situations with Legal Counsel . . .*

## Business Courtesies to Lockheed Martin Employees

### Meals, Refreshments and Entertainment

Although an employee may not use his or her position at Lockheed Martin to foster obtaining business courtesies, it is permissible to accept unsolicited meals, refreshments, entertainment, and other business courtesies on an occasional basis, provided:

■ The acceptance will foster goodwill and successful business relations;

■ The courtesies are not lavish or extravagant under the circumstances;

■ The courtesies are not frequent and do not reflect a pattern or the appearance of a pattern of frequent acceptance of courtesies from the same entities or persons; and

■ The employee accepting the courtesies would feel comfortable about discussing the courtesies with his or her manager or coworker, or having the courtesies known by the public.

It is the personal responsibility of each employee to ensure that his or her acceptance of such meals, refreshments, or entertainment is proper and could not reasonably be construed in any way as an attempt by the offering party to secure favorable treatment.

*It is the personal responsibility of each employee . . .*

## Gifts

Lockheed Martin employees are not permitted to accept compensation, honoraria, funds or monetary instruments in any form or amount, or any tangible gift (including tickets to sporting, recreational, or other events) that has a market value of $100.00 or more, from any entity, representatives of any entity, or any person that does or seeks to do business with the company, unless approved by his or her supervisor, and the business unit's Ethics Officer or the Corporate Office of Ethics and Business Conduct. Solicitation of gifts is always prohibited. If you have any questions about the propriety of a gift, gratuity, or item of value, contact your supervisor, Ethics Officer or the Corporate Office of Ethics and Business Conduct for guidance.

## Gifts to Lockheed Martin Employees Who Procure Goods or Services

If you buy goods or services for Lockheed Martin or are involved in the procurement process, you must treat all suppliers uniformly and fairly. In deciding among competing suppliers, you must objectively and impartially weigh all facts and avoid even the appearance of favoritism. For this reason, gifts from suppliers or vendors must not be accepted, except advertising or promotional items of nominal value such as a pen, key chain, water bottle, visor, cup or glass or similar items displaying a company's logo. Established routines and procedures should be followed in the procurement of all goods and services.

## *Steer Clear of Conflicts of Interest*

Playing favorites or having conflicts of interest—in practice or appearance—runs counter to the fair treatment to which we are all entitled. Avoid any relationship, influence, or activity that might impair, or even appear to impair, your ability to make objective and fair decisions when performing your job. A conflict of interest occurs whenever an individual's private interest interferes with the interest of the corporation. We owe a duty to Lockheed Martin to advance its legitimate interests when the opportunity to do so arises. You should never use company property or information for personal gain, or take for yourself personally any opportunity that is discovered through your company position.

## *Here are Some Ways a Conflict of Interest Could Arise:*

- Employment by a competitor or potential competitor, regardless of the nature of the employment, while employed by Lockheed Martin.

- Acceptance of gifts, payment, or services from those seeking to do business with Lockheed Martin.

- Placement of business with a firm owned or controlled by a Lockheed Martin employee or his/her family.

- Ownership of, or substantial interest in, a company that is a competitor or a supplier.

- Acting as a consultant to a Lockheed Martin customer or supplier.

- Having a personal interest or potential for gain in any company transaction.

Any situation, transaction, or relationship that might give rise to an actual or potential conflict of interest must be disclosed in writing to your supervisor and the Ethics Office.

*When in doubt, share the facts of the situation with your supervisor, Legal Department, or Ethics Officer.*

## *Know the Rules About Employing Former Government Officials*

There are extensive conflict of interest laws and regulations regarding the employment or use of former military and civilian government personnel. These rules extend to contact or negotiations with current government employees to discuss their potential employment by the company or their use as consultants or subcontractors. Conflict of interest laws and regulations must be fully and carefully observed. When in doubt, consult corporate and company policies and procedures, and seek the advice of your Legal Department, Human Resources, or Ethics Officer.

## Maintain the Integrity of Consultants, Agents, and Representatives

Business integrity is a key standard for the selection and retention of those who represent Lockheed Martin. Agents, representatives, or consultants must certify their willingness to comply with the company's policies and procedures and must never be retained to circumvent our values and principles. Paying bribes or kickbacks, engaging in industrial espionage, obtaining the proprietary data of a third party without authority, or gaining inside information or influence are just a few examples of what could give us an unfair competitive advantage in a government procurement and could result in violations of law.

## Protect Proprietary Information

Proprietary company information may not be disclosed to anyone without proper authorization. Keep proprietary documents protected and secure. In the course of normal business activities, suppliers, customers, and competitors may sometimes divulge to you information that is proprietary to their business. Respect these confidences.

*Keep proprietary documents protected and secure.*

## Obtain and Use Company and Customer Assets Wisely

Proper use of company and customer property, electronic communication systems, information resources, material, facilities, and equipment is your responsibility. Use and maintain these assets with the utmost care and respect, guarding against waste and abuse, and never borrow or remove them from company property without management's permission. Be cost-conscious and alert to opportunities for improving performance while reducing costs. While these assets are intended to be used for the conduct of Lockheed Martin's business, it is recog-

nized that occasional personal use by employees may occur without adversely affecting the interests of the company. Personal use of company assets must always be in accordance with corporate and company policy—consult your supervisor for appropriate guidance and permission.

All employees are responsible for complying with the requirements of software copyright licenses related to software packages used in fulfilling job requirements.

## Do Not Engage in Speculative or Insider Trading

In our role as a multinational corporation and a publicly owned company, we must always be alert to and comply with the securities laws and regulations of the United States and other countries.

*. . . we must always be alert . . .*

It is against the law for employees to buy or sell company stock based on material, non-public "insider" information about or involving the company. Play it safe. Don't speculate in the securities of Lockheed Martin when you are aware of information affecting the company's business that has not been publicly released or in situations where trading would call your judgment into question. This includes all varieties of stock trading such as options, puts and calls, straddles, selling short, etc. Two simple rules can help protect you in this area: (1) Don't use non-public information for personal gain. (2) Don't pass along such information to someone else who has no need to know.

This guidance also applies to the securities of other companies (suppliers, vendors, subcontractors, etc.) for which you receive information in the course of your employment at Lockheed Martin.

## For More Information:

In order to support a comprehensive Ethics and Business Conduct Program, Lockheed Martin has developed education and communication programs in many subject areas. These programs have been developed to provide employees with job-specific information to raise their level of awareness and sensitivity to key issues.

Interactive Multimedia Training Modules are available on the following topics:

Antiboycott International Consultants

Antitrust Compliance Kickbacks & Gratuities

Computing Information Resources Labor Charging

Information Protection Material Costs

Diversity Organizational Conflicts of Interest

Domestic Consultants Political Activities

Drug Free Workplace Procurement

Energy, Environment, Safety Procurement Integrity and Health Product Substitution

Ex-Government Employees Protecting Classified Information

Export Control Record Retention

Foreign Corrupt Practices Act Security

Government Property Sensitive Information Protection

Harassment in the Workplace Truth in Negotiations Act

Insider Trading

The current list of Interactive Multimedia Compliance Training Modules and Corporate Policy Statements relating to the above topics and others can be accessed via the Lockheed Martin Information Network at http://pageone.global.lmco.com/ or obtained from your supervisor. A compliance-training module is not available for Antiboycott, Political Activities, and Vendor Contacts, but is available via QWIZARD. The compliance training URL is http://ethics.corp.lmco.com/ethics/comp_train.html The Corporate Policy URL is http://policy.global.lmco.com/p3/index.html

**WARNING SIGNS—*YOU'RE ON THIN ETHICAL ICE WHEN YOU HEAR* . . .**

"Well, maybe just this once . . ."

"No one will ever know . . ."

"It doesn't matter how it gets done as long as it gets done."

"It sounds too good to be true."

"Everyone does it."

"Shred that document."

"We can hide it."

"No one will get hurt."

"What's in it for me?"

"This will destroy the competition."

"We didn't have this conversation."

*You can probably think of many more phrases that raise warning flags. If you find yourself using any of these expressions, take the Quick Quiz . . . and make sure you are on solid ethical ground.*

### *Quick Quiz—When in Doubt, Ask Yourself . . .*

1. Are my actions legal?
2. Am I being fair and honest?
3. Will my action stand the test of time?
4. How will I feel about myself afterwards?
5. How will it look in the newspaper?
6. Will I sleep soundly tonight?
7. What would I tell my child to do?
8. How would I feel if my family, friends, and neighbors knew what I was doing?

*If you are still not sure what to do, ask . . . and keep asking until you are certain you are doing the right thing.*

### *Our Goal: An Ethical Work Environment*

We have established the Office of Ethics and Business Conduct to underscore our commitment to ethical conduct throughout our company.

The Vice President–Ethics and Business Conduct reports directly to the Executive Office and the Audit and Ethics Committee of the Board of Directors, and oversees a vigorous corporate wide effort to promote a positive, ethical work environment for all employees. Our Ethics Officers operate confidential Ethics HelpLines at each operating company, as well as at the corporate level. You are urged to use these resources whenever you have a question or concern that cannot be readily addressed within your work group or through your supervisor.

*Ethics and Integrity are Fundamental to Mission Success.*

## Accountability

Each of us is responsible for adherence to the standards of conduct set forth in this Code and for raising questions if we are concerned that these standards are not being met. Violations of the Code are cause for corrective action, which may result in disciplinary action up to and including discharge.

*We are all accountable for adherence to the Code of Conduct.*

## How to Contact the Audit and Ethics Committee

The Audit and Ethics Committee of the Lockheed Martin Board of Directors has created a process by which employees may transmit complaints about accounting, internal controls, or auditing matters to the Committee, and for the confidential or anonymous submission of concerns regarding questionable accounting or auditing matters. If you wish to raise a question or concern to the Audit and Ethics Committee, you may do so by contacting the Office of Ethics and Business Conduct at Corporate Headquarters. Your concern will be communicated to the Chair of the Audit and Ethics Committee of the Board.

## 1: Contact the Ethics Office

You are encouraged to contact the Office of Ethics and Business Conduct to discuss any ethics question or concern, to report a violation of the Code, or for information on how to contact your local Ethics Officer. You can reach the Office of Ethics and Business Conduct through any of the following confidential means of communication:

Call: 800-LM ETHICS

Domestic: 800-563-8442

International: 800-5638-4427

For the Hearing or Speech Impaired: 800-441-7457

Fax: 301-897-6442

Internet E-Mail: corporate.ethics@lmco.com

*Note: Caller ID is not used on ethics phone numbers.*

Write: Office of Ethics and Business Conduct
Lockheed Martin Corporation
P.O. Box 34143
Bethesda, MD 20827-0143

## When You Contact Your Company Ethics Officer or the Office of Ethics and Business Conduct at Corporate Headquarters:

- You will be treated with dignity and respect.
- Your communication will be kept confidential to the greatest extent possible.
- Your concerns will be seriously addressed and, if not resolved at the time you call, you will be informed of the outcome.
- You need not identify yourself.

Remember, there's never a penalty for using the Ethics HelpLine in good faith. People in a position of authority can't stop you; if they try, they're subject to disciplinary action up to and including dismissal. Lockheed Martin will not tolerate retribution against employees who raise concerns to any source.

# HCA—The Hospital Corporation of America Code of Conduct*

## Mission and Values Statement

Above all else, we are committed to the care and improvement of human life. In recognition of this commitment, we will strive to deliver high quality, cost-effective healthcare in the communities we serve.

In pursuit of our mission, we believe the following value statements are essential and timeless:

- *We recognize and affirm the unique and intrinsic worth of each individual.*
- *We treat all those we serve with compassion and kindness.*
- *We act with absolute honesty, integrity and fairness in the way we conduct our business and the way we live our lives.*
- *We trust our colleagues as valuable members of our healthcare team and pledge to treat one another with loyalty, respect, and dignity.*

## Purpose of Our Code of Conduct

Our Code of Conduct provides guidance to all HCA colleagues and assists us in carrying out our daily activities within appropriate ethical and legal standards. These obligations apply to our relationships with patients, affiliated physicians, third-party payers, subcontractors, independent contractors, vendors, consultants, and one another.

The Code is a critical component of our overall Ethics and Compliance Program. We have developed the Code to ensure we meet our ethical standards and comply with applicable laws and regulations.

The Code is intended to be comprehensive and easily understood. In some instances, the Code deals fully with the subject covered. In many cases, however, the subject discussed has so much complexity

*This Code of Conduct is effective April 15, 2003. Reprinted with permission of HCA—The Hospital Corporation of America. http://hcahealthcare. com

(Note: All references to "HCA" or the "organization" in this Code of Conduct refer to HCA Inc. and/or its affiliates, as applicable.)

that additional guidance is necessary for those directly involved with the particular area to have sufficient direction. To provide additional guidance, we have developed a comprehensive set of compliance policies and procedures which may be accessed on the Ethics and Compliance site of our Intranet, as well as our external web site at www.hcahealthcare.com. Those policies expand upon or supplement many of the principles articulated in this Code of Conduct.

Though we promote the concept of management autonomy at local facilities in order to meet local needs, the standards set forth in the Code are mandatory and must be followed. A separate Code of Conduct has been developed for our facilities outside the United States.

## Code of Ethics for Senior Financial Officers and the Chief Executive Officer

Under the Sarbanes-Oxley Act of 2002 and related Securities and Exchange Commission (SEC) rules, the Company is required to disclose whether it has adopted a written Code of Ethics for its Senior Financial Officers and the Chief Executive Officer (CEO). Any amendments to, or implicit or explicit waiver of, the Code of Ethics for Senior Financial Officers and the CEO must be publicly disclosed as required by SEC rules. "Senior Financial Officers" include, but are not limited to, facility, Division and Group Chief Financial Officers (CFOs) and controllers, and Corporate officers with financial accounting and reporting responsibilities, including the Controller and principal accounting officer. The Code must be reasonably designed to deter wrongdoing and to promote: honest and ethical conduct, including the ethical handling of actual or apparent conflicts of interest between personal and professional relationships; full, fair, accurate, timely and understandable SEC filings and submissions and other public communications by the Company; compliance with applicable governmental laws, rules and regulations; prompt internal reporting of violations of the Code; and accountability for adherence to the Code.

The CEO and all Senior Financial Officers are bound by all provisions of this Code of Conduct and particularly those provisions relating to ethical conduct, conflicts of interest, compliance with law, and internal reporting of violations of the Code. The CEO and all Senior Financial Officers also have responsibility for full, fair, accurate, timely and understandable disclosure in the periodic reports and submissions filed by the Company with the SEC as well as in other public communications made by the Company ("Public Communications"). Accordingly, it is the responsibility of the CEO and each Senior Financial Officer promptly to bring to the attention of the internal working group responsible for the review of the Company's periodic SEC reports ("Disclosure Committee") any information of which he or she may become aware that materially affects the disclosures made by the Company in its Public Communications.

The CEO and each Senior Financial Officer also shall bring promptly to the attention of the Disclosure Committee any information he or she may have concerning significant deficiencies in the design or operation of internal controls which could adversely affect the company's ability to record, process, summarize and report financial data; or any fraud, whether or not material, that involves management or other employees who have a significant role in the Company's financial reporting, disclosures or internal controls.

The Corporate Ethics and Compliance Steering Committee shall determine appropriate actions to be taken in the event of violations of the Code by the CEO and the Company's Senior Financial Officers. Such actions shall be reasonably designed to deter wrongdoing and to promote accountability for adherence to the Code.

In determining what action is appropriate in a particular case, the Corporate Ethics and Compliance Steering Committee shall take into account all relevant information, including the nature and severity of the violation, whether the violation was a single occurrence or repeated occurrences, whether the violation appears to have been intentional or inadvertent, whether the individual in question had been advised prior to the violation as to the proper course of action and whether or not the individual in question had committed other violations in the past. The Corporate Ethics and Compliance Steering Committee must report periodically any actions taken pursuant to this paragraph to the Ethics and Compliance Committee of the Board of Directors.

Any waiver of or amendments to the Code of Ethics for Senior Financial Officers and the CEO must be approved by the Ethics and Compliance Committee of the Company's Board of Directors.

## Leadership Responsibilities

While all HCA colleagues are obligated to follow our Code, we expect our leaders to set the example, to be in every respect a model. We expect everyone in the organization with supervisory responsibility to exercise that responsibility in a manner that is kind, sensitive, thoughtful, and respectful. We expect each supervisor to create an environment where all team members feel free to raise concerns and propose ideas. We also expect that they will ensure those on their team have sufficient information to comply with laws, regulations, and policies, as well as the resources to resolve ethical dilemmas. They must help to create a culture within HCA which promotes the highest standards of ethics and compliance. This culture must encourage everyone in the organization to share concerns when they arise. We must never sacrifice ethical and compliant behavior in the pursuit of business objectives.

Specific guidance for leaders throughout the organization regarding their responsibilities under our Ethics and Compliance Program is included in a supplement for leaders to this Code. Leaders at all levels of the organization should use that guidance to most effectively incorporate ethics and compliance into all aspects of our organization.

## Our Fundamental Commitment to Stakeholders*

We affirm the following commitments to HCA stakeholders:

---

*The term "stakeholder" refers to those groups of individuals to whom an institution sees itself as having obligations.

*To our patients:* We are committed to providing quality care that is sensitive, compassionate, promptly delivered, and cost-effective.

*To our HCA colleagues:* We are committed to a work setting which treats all colleagues with fairness, dignity, and respect, and affords them an opportunity to grow, to develop professionally, and to work in a team environment in which all ideas are considered.

*To our affiliated physicians:* We are committed to providing a work environment which has excellent facilities, modern equipment, and outstanding professional support.

*To our third-party payers:* We are committed to dealing with our third-party payers in a way that demonstrates our commitment to contractual obligations and reflects our shared concern for quality healthcare and bringing efficiency and cost effectiveness to healthcare. We encourage our private third-party payers to adopt their own set of comparable ethical principles to explicitly recognize their obligations to patients as well as the need for fairness in dealing with providers.

*To our regulators:* We are committed to an environment in which compliance with rules, regulations, and sound business practices is woven into the corporate culture. We accept the responsibility to aggressively self-govern and monitor adherence to the requirements of law and to our Code of Conduct.

*To our joint venture partners:* We are committed to fully performing our responsibilities to manage our jointly owned facilities in a manner that reflects the mission and values of each of our organizations.

*To the communities we serve:* We are committed to understanding the particular needs of the communities we serve and providing these communities quality, cost-effective healthcare. We realize as an organization that we have a responsibility to help those in need. We proudly support charitable contributions and events in the communities we serve in an effort to promote good will and further good causes.

*To our suppliers:* We are committed to fair competition among prospective suppliers and the sense of responsibility required of a good customer. We encourage our suppliers to adopt their own set of comparable ethical principles.

*To our volunteers:* The concept of voluntary assistance to the needs of patients and their families is an integral part of the fabric of healthcare. We are committed to ensuring that our volunteers feel a sense of meaningfulness from their volunteer work and receive recognition for their volunteer efforts.

*To our shareholders:* We are committed to the highest standards of professional management, which we are certain can create unique efficiencies and innovative healthcare approaches and thus ensure favorable returns on our shareholders' investments over the long term.

## Our Patients

### Patient Care and Rights

Our mission is to provide high quality, cost-effective healthcare to all of our patients. We treat all patients with warmth, respect, and dignity and provide care that is both necessary and appropriate. We make no distinction in the availability of services; the admission, transfer or discharge of patients; or in the care we provide based on age, gender, disability, race, color, religion, or national origin.

Each patient is provided with a written statement of patient rights and a notice of privacy practices. These statements include the rights of a patient to make decisions regarding medical care and a patient's rights related to his or her health information maintained by the facility. Such statements conform to all applicable state and federal laws, including but not limited to the Health Insurance Portability and Accountability Act of 1996 (hereinafter referred to as HIPAA).

We seek to involve patients in all aspects of their care, including giving consent for treatment and making healthcare decisions, which may include managing pain effectively, foregoing or withdrawing treatment, and, as appropriate, care at the end of life. As applicable, each patient or patient representative is provided with a clear explanation of care including, but not limited to, diagnosis, treatment plan, right to refuse or accept care, care decision dilemmas, advance directive options, estimates of treatment costs, organ donation and procurement, and an explanation of the risks, benefits, and alternatives associated with available treatment options. Patients have the right to request transfers to other facilities. In such cases, the patient is given an explanation of the benefits, risks, and alternatives of the transfer.

Patients are provided information regarding their right to make advance directives. Patient advance directives or resuscitative measures are honored within the limits of the law and our organization's mission, philosophy, values, and capabilities. In the promotion and protection of each patient's rights, each patient and his or her representatives are accorded appropriate confidentiality, privacy, security and protective services, opportunity for resolution of complaints, and pastoral care or spiritual care.

Patients are treated in a manner that preserves their dignity, autonomy, self-esteem, civil rights, and involvement in their own care. HCA facilities maintain processes to support patient rights in a collaborative manner which involves the facility leaders and others. These structures are based on policies and procedures, which make up the framework addressing both patient care and organizational ethics issues. These structures include informing each patient or, when appropriate, the patient's representative of the patient's rights in advance of furnishing or discontinuing care. Patients and, when appropriate, their families are informed about the outcomes of care, including unanticipated outcomes. Additionally, patients are involved as clinically appropriate in resolving dilemmas about care decisions. Additionally, facilities maintain processes for prompt resolution of patient grievances which include informing patients of whom to contact regarding grievances and informing patients regarding the grievance resolution. HCA facilities maintain an ongoing, proactive patient safety effort for the identification of risk to patient safety and the prevention, reporting and reduction of healthcare errors. HCA colleagues receive training about patient rights in order to clearly understand their role in supporting them.

We strive to provide health education, health promotion, and illness-prevention programs as part of our efforts to improve the quality of life of our patients and our communities.

## Patient Information

We collect information about the patient's medical condition, history, medication, and family illnesses to provide quality care. We realize the sensitive nature of this information and are committed to maintaining its confidentiality. Consistent with HIPAA, we do not use, disclose or discuss patient-specific information with others unless it is necessary to serve the patient or required by law.

HCA colleagues must never use or disclose confidential information that violates the privacy rights of our patients. In accordance with our appropriate access and privacy policies and procedures, which reflect HIPAA requirements, no HCA colleague, affiliated physician, or other healthcare partner has a right to any patient information other than that necessary to perform his or her job.

Subject only to emergency exceptions, patients can expect their privacy will be protected and patient specific information will be released only to persons authorized by law or by the patient's written authorization.

## *Legal and Regulatory Compliance*

HCA provides varied healthcare services in many states. These services are provided pursuant to appropriate federal, state, and local laws and regulations, and the conditions of participation for Federal healthcare programs. Such laws, regulations, and conditions of participation may include, but are not limited to, subjects such as certificates of need, licenses, permits, accreditation, access to treatment, consent to treatment, medical record-keeping, access to medical records and confidentiality, patients' rights, clinical research, end-of-life care decision-making, medical staff membership and clinical privileges, corporate practice of medicine restrictions, and Medicare and Medicaid program requirements. The organization is subject to numerous other laws in addition to these healthcare laws, regulations, and the conditions of participation.

We have developed policies and procedures to address many legal and regulatory requirements. However, it is impractical to develop policies and procedures that encompass the full body of applicable law and regulation. Obviously, those laws and regulations not covered in organization policies and procedures must be followed. There is a range of expertise within the organization, including operations counsel and numerous functional experts (*i.e.,* Responsible Executives), who should be consulted for advice concerning human resources, legal, regulatory, and the conditions of participation requirements.

Anyone aware of violations or suspected violations of laws, regulations, the conditions of participation, or Company policies and procedures must report them immediately to a supervisor or member of management, the Facility Human Resources Manager, the Facility Ethics and Compliance Officer, the Ethics Line, or the Corporate Ethics and Compliance Officer.

### Coding and Billing for Services

We have implemented policies, procedures and systems to facilitate accurate billing to government payers, commercial insurance payers, and patients. These policies, procedures, and systems conform to pertinent federal and state laws and regulations. We prohibit any colleague or agent of HCA from knowingly presenting or causing to be presented claims for payment or approval which are false, fictitious, or fraudulent.

In support of accurate billing, medical records must provide reliable documentation of the services we render. It is important that all individuals who contribute to medical records provide accurate information and do not destroy any information considered part of the official medical record.

Accurate and timely documentation also depends on the diligence and attention of physicians who treat patients in our facilities. We expect those physicians to provide us with complete and accurate information in a timely manner. Any subcontractors engaged to perform billing or coding services are expected to have the necessary skills, quality control processes, systems, and appropriate procedures to ensure all billings for government and commercial insurance programs are accurate and complete. HCA requires such entities to have their own ethics and compliance programs and code of conduct or to adopt HCA's code as their own. In addition, third-party billing entities, contractors, and preferred vendors under contract consideration must be approved consistent with the corporate policy on this subject.

For coding questions in a hospital or ambulatory surgery center contact the Coding Helpline at 1-800-537-1666. For questions regarding Health Information Management Services (HIMS) Policies and Procedures, contact the HIMS P & P Helpline at 1-800-690-0919 or e-mail at: HIMS P&P Helpline. For billing questions in a hospital, contact the Billing Helpline at 1-888-735-3669. For billing or coding questions in HCA Physician Services, call 1-800-373-5620, option 1.

### Cost Reports

We are required by federal and state laws and regulations to submit certain reports of our operating costs and statistics. We comply with federal and state laws, regulations, and guidelines relating to all cost reports.

These laws, regulations, and guidelines define what costs are allowable and outline the appropriate methodologies to claim reimbursement for the cost of services provided to program beneficiaries. Several HCA policies address cost report compliance and articulate our commitment to: maintain and distribute a Reimbursement Manual to Reimbursement Department personnel that includes corporate and departmental policies and procedures; provide effective and timely education and training programs for Reimbursement Department personnel regarding federal and state laws, regulations and guidelines, and corporate policies; maintain a standardized workpaper package to provide consistency in the preparation, organization, presentation, and review of cost reports; apply a uniform cost report review process; identify and exclude non-allowable costs; adhere to documentation standards; and use transmittal letters to report protested items and make other appropriate disclosures. Additionally, we submit our cost report process to internal audits and maintain a peer review process.

All issues related to the preparation, submission and settlement of cost reports must be performed by or coordinated with our Reimbursement Department.

## Emergency Treatment

We follow the Emergency Medical Treatment and Active Labor Act ("EMTALA") in providing an emergency medical screening examination and necessary stabilization to all patients, regardless of ability to pay. Provided we have the capacity and capability, anyone with an emergency medical condition is treated.

In an emergency situation or if the patient is in labor, we will not delay the medical screening and necessary stabilizing treatment in order to seek financial and demographic information. We do not admit, discharge, or transfer patients with emergency medical conditions simply based on their ability or inability to pay.

Patients with emergency medical conditions are only transferred to another facility at the patient's request or if the patient's medical needs cannot be met at the HCA facility (*e.g.*, we do not have the capacity or capability) and appropriate care is knowingly available at another facility. Patients are only transferred in strict compliance with state and federal EMTALA regulatory and statutory requirements.

## Surveys

From time-to-time, government agencies and other entities conduct surveys in our facilities. We respond with openness and accurate information. In preparation for or during a survey or inspection, HCA colleagues must never conceal, destroy, or alter any documents; lie; or make misleading statements to the agency representative.

Colleagues also must never attempt to cause another colleague to fail to provide accurate information or obstruct, mislead, or delay the communication of information or records relating to a possible violation of law.

## Accreditation

In preparation for, during and after surveys, HCA colleagues deal with all accrediting bodies in a direct, open and honest manner. No action should ever be taken in relationships with accrediting bodies that would mislead the accreditor or its survey teams, either directly or indirectly.

The scope of matters related to accreditation of various bodies is extremely significant and broader than the scope of this Code of Conduct. The purpose of our Code of Conduct is to provide general guidance on subjects of wide interest within the organization. Accrediting bodies may address issues of both wide and somewhat more focused interest.

## Business Information and Information Systems

### Accuracy, Retention, and Disposal of Documents and Records

Each HCA colleague is responsible for the integrity and accuracy of our organization's documents and records, not only to comply with regulatory and legal requirements but also to ensure records are available to support our business practices and actions. No one may alter or falsify information on any record or document. Records must never be destroyed in an effort to deny governmental authorities that which may be relevant to a government investigation.

Medical and business documents and records are retained in accordance with the law and our record retention policy, which includes comprehensive retention schedules. Medical and business documents include paper documents such as letters and memos, computer-based information such as e-mail or computer files on disk or tape, and any other medium that contains information about the organization or its business activities.

It is important to retain and destroy records only according to our policy. HCA colleagues must not tamper with records. Additionally, no one may remove or destroy records prior to the specified date without first obtaining permission as outlined in the Company records management policy.

## Information Security and Confidentiality

Confidential information about our organization's strategies and operations is a valuable asset. Although HCA colleagues may use confidential information to perform their jobs, it must not be shared with others unless the individuals and/or entities have a legitimate need to know the information in order to perform their specific job duties or carry out a contractual business relationship. In addition, these individuals and/or entities must have agreed to maintain the confidentiality of the information. Confidential information includes personnel data maintained by the organization; patient lists and clinical information; patient financial information; passwords; pricing and cost data; information pertaining to acquisitions, divestitures, affiliations and mergers; financial data; details regarding federal, state, and local tax examinations of the organization or its joint venture partners; research data; strategic plans; marketing strategies and techniques; supplier and subcontractor information; and proprietary computer software. In order to maintain the confidentiality and integrity of patient and confidential information, such information should be sent through the Internet only in accordance with information security policies and standards, which require, among other things, that the individual and/ or entity be validated and the information be encrypted.

We exercise due care and due diligence in maintaining the confidentiality, availability and integrity of information assets the Company owns or of which it is the custodian. Because so much of our clinical and business information is generated and contained within our computer systems, it is essential that each HCA colleague protect our computer systems and the information contained in them by not sharing passwords and by reviewing and adhering to our information security policies and guidance.

If an individual's employment or contractual relationship with HCA ends for any reason, the individual is still bound to maintain the confidentiality of information viewed, received or used during the employment or contractual business relationship with HCA. This provision does not restrict the right of a colleague to disclose, if he or she wishes, information about his or her own compensation, benefits, or terms and conditions of employment.

## Electronic Media

All communications systems, including but not limited to electronic mail, Intranet, Internet access, telephones, and voice mail, are the property of the organization and are to be used primarily for business purposes in accordance with electronic communications policies and standards. Limited reasonable personal use of HCA communications systems is permitted; however, users should assume these communications are not private.

Users of computer and telephonic systems should presume no expectation of privacy in anything they create, store, send, or receive on the computer and telephonic systems, and the Company reserves the right to monitor and/or access communications usage and content consistent with Company policies and procedures.

Colleagues may not use internal communication channels or access to the Internet at work to post, store, transmit, download, or distribute any threatening materials; knowingly, recklessly, or maliciously false materials; obscene materials; or anything constituting or encouraging a criminal offense, giving rise to civil liability, or otherwise violating any laws. Additionally, these channels of communication may not be used to send chain letters, personal broadcast messages, or copyrighted documents that are not authorized for reproduction.

Colleagues who abuse our communications systems or use them excessively for nonbusiness purposes may lose these privileges and be subject to disciplinary action.

## Financial Reporting and Records

We have established and maintain a high standard of accuracy and completeness in documenting, maintaining, and reporting financial information. This information serves as a basis for managing our business and is important in meeting our obligations to patients, colleagues, shareholders, suppliers, and others. It is also necessary for compliance with tax and financial reporting requirements.

All financial information must reflect actual transactions and conform to generally-accepted accounting principles. All funds or assets must be properly recorded in the books and records of the Company. HCA maintains a system of internal controls to provide reasonable assurances that all transactions are executed in accordance with management's authorization and are recorded in a proper manner so as to maintain accountability of the organization's assets.

We diligently seek to comply with all applicable auditing, accounting and financial disclosure laws, including but not limited to the Securities Exchange Act of 1934 and the Sarbanes-Oxley Act of 2002. Senior financial officers receive training and guidance regarding auditing, accounting and financial disclosure relevant to their job responsibilities. They are also provided the opportunity to discuss issues of concern with the Board of Directors' Audit Committee. Anyone having concerns regarding questionable accounting or auditing matters should report such matters to the Board of Directors' Audit Committee by calling the HCA Ethics Line (1-800-455-1996).

## Workplace Conduct and Employment Practices

### Conflict of Interest

A conflict of interest may occur if an HCA colleague's outside activities, personal financial interests, or other personal interests influence or appear to influence his or her ability to make objective decisions in the course of the colleague's job responsibilities. A conflict of interest may also exist if the demands of any outside activities hinder or distract a colleague from the performance of his or her job or cause the individual to use HCA resources for other than HCA purposes. HCA colleagues are obligated to ensure they remain free of conflicts of interest in the performance of their responsibilities at HCA. If colleagues have any question about whether an outside activity or personal interest might constitute a conflict of interest, they must obtain the approval of their supervisor before pursuing the activity or obtaining or retaining the interest. Clinical decisions will be made without regard to compensation or financial risk to HCA leaders, managers, clinical staff, or licensed, independent practitioners.

No waiver of this conflict of interest provision may be granted to an Executive Officer (*i.e.*, an officer subject to Section 16 of the Securities Exchange Act of 1934) unless approved in advance by the Ethics and Compliance Committee of the Company's Board of Directors.

### Controlled Substances

Some of our colleagues routinely have access to prescription drugs, controlled substances, and other medical supplies. Many of these substances are governed and monitored by specific regulatory organizations and must be administered by physician order only. Prescription and controlled medications and supplies must be handled properly and only by authorized individuals to minimize risks to us and to patients. If one becomes aware of inadequate security of drugs or controlled substances or the diversion of drugs from the organization, the incident must be reported immediately.

### Copyrights

HCA colleagues may only use copyrighted materials pursuant to the organization's policy on such matters.

### Diversity and Equal Employment Opportunity

Our colleagues provide us with a wide complement of talents which contribute greatly to our success. We are committed to providing an equal opportunity work environment where everyone is treated with fairness, dignity, and respect. We comply with all laws, regulations, and policies related to non-discrimination in all of our personnel actions. Such actions include hiring, staff reductions, transfers, terminations, evaluations, recruiting, compensation, corrective action, discipline, and promotions.

No one shall discriminate against any individual with regard to race, color, religion, sex, national origin, age, disability, sexual orientation, or status as a Vietnam-era or special disabled veteran with respect to any offer, or term or condition, of employment. We make reasonable accommodations to the known physical and mental limitations of otherwise qualified individuals with disabilities.

## Harassment and Workplace Violence

Each HCA colleague has the right to work in an environment free of harassment and disruptive behavior. We do not tolerate harassment by anyone based on the diverse characteristics or cultural backgrounds of those who work with us. Degrading or humiliating jokes, slurs, intimidation, or other harassing conduct is not acceptable in our workplace.

Sexual harassment is prohibited. This prohibition includes unwelcome sexual advances or requests for sexual favors in conjunction with employment decisions. Moreover, verbal or physical conduct of a sexual nature that interferes with an individual's work performance or creates an intimidating, hostile, or offensive work environment has no place at HCA.

Harassment also includes incidents of workplace violence. Workplace violence includes robbery and other commercial crimes, stalking, violence directed at the employer, terrorism, and hate crimes committed by current or former colleagues. Colleagues who observe or experience any form of harassment or violence should report the incident to their supervisor, the Human Resources Department, a member of management, the Facility Ethics and Compliance Officer, or the Ethics Line.

## Health and Safety

All HCA facilities comply with all government regulations and rules, HCA policies, and required facility practices that promote the protection of workplace health and safety. Our policies have been developed to protect our colleagues from potential workplace hazards. Colleagues must become familiar with and understand how these policies apply to their specific job responsibilities and seek advice from their supervisor or the Safety Officer whenever they have a question or concern. It is important that each colleague immediately advise his or her supervisor or the Safety Officer of any serious workplace injury or any situation presenting a danger of injury so timely corrective action may be taken to resolve the issue.

## Hiring of Former and Current Government and Fiscal Intermediary Employees

The recruitment and employment of former or current U.S. government employees may be impacted by regulations concerning conflicts of interest. Hiring employees directly from a fiscal intermediary requires certain regulatory notifications. Colleagues should consult with the Corporate Human Resources Department or the Legal Department regarding such recruitment and hiring.

## Insider Information and Securities Trading

In the course of colleagues' employment with HCA, they may become aware of non-public information about HCA material to an investor's decision to buy or sell the organization's securities. Non-public, material information may include plans for mergers, marketing strategy, financial results, or other business dealings.

Colleagues may not discuss this type of information with anyone outside of the organization. Within the organization, colleagues should discuss this information on a strictly "need to know" basis only with other colleagues who require this information to perform their jobs.

Securities law and HCA policy prohibit individuals from trading in the marketable securities of a publicly held organization or influencing others to trade in such securities on the basis of non-public, material information. These restrictions are meant to ensure the general public has complete and timely information on which to base investment decisions.

If an HCA colleague obtains access to non-public, material information about the organization or any other company while performing his or her job, the colleague may not use that information to buy, sell, or retain securities of HCA or that other company. Even if he or she does not buy or sell securities based on what he or she knows, discussing the information with others, such as family members, friends, vendors, suppliers, and other outside acquaintances, is prohibited until the information is considered to be public. Information is considered to be public two days after a general release of the information to the media.

## Interactions with Physicians

Federal and state laws and regulations govern the relationship between hospitals and physicians who may refer patients to the facilities. The applicable federal laws include the Anti-Kickback Law and the Stark Law.

It is important that those colleagues who interact with physicians, particularly regarding making payments to physicians for services rendered, leasing space, recruiting physicians to the community, and arranging for physicians to serve in leadership positions in facilities, are aware of the requirements of the laws, regulations, and policies that address relationships between facilities and physicians.

If relationships with physicians are properly structured, but not diligently administered, failure to administer the arrangements as agreed may result in violations of the law. Any business arrangement with a physician must be structured to ensure compliance with legal requirements, our policies and procedures and with any operational guidance that has been issued. Most arrangements must be in writing and approved by the Legal Department.

Keeping in mind that it is essential to be familiar with the laws, regulations, and policies that govern our interactions with physicians, two overarching principles govern our interactions with physicians:

*We do not pay for referrals.* We accept patient referrals and admissions based solely on the patient's medical needs and our ability to render the needed services. We do not pay or offer to pay anyone—colleagues, physicians, or other persons or entities—for referral of patients.

*We do not accept payments for referrals we make.* No HCA colleague or any other person acting on behalf of the organization is permitted to solicit or receive anything of value, directly or indirectly, in exchange for the referral of patients. Similarly, when making patient referrals to another healthcare provider, we do not take into account the volume or value of referrals that the provider has made (or may make) to us.

## License and Certification Renewals

Colleagues, individuals retained as independent contractors, and privileged practitioners in positions which require professional licenses, certifications, or other credentials are responsible for maintaining the current status of their credentials and shall comply at all times with federal and state requirements applicable to their respective disciplines. To assure compliance, HCA may require evidence of the individual having a current license or credential status.

HCA does not allow any colleague, independent contractor or privileged practitioner to work without valid, current licenses or credentials.

## Personal Use of HCA Resources

It is the responsibility of each HCA colleague to preserve our organization's assets including time, materials, supplies, equipment, and information. Organization assets are to be maintained for business-related purposes.

As a general rule, the personal use of any HCA asset without prior supervisory approval is prohibited. The occasional use of items, such as copying facilities or telephones, where the cost to HCA is insignificant, is permissible. Any community or charitable use of organization resources must be approved in advance by one's supervisor. Any use of organization resources for personal financial gain unrelated to the organization's business is prohibited.

## Relationships Among HCA Colleagues

In the normal day-to-day functions of an organization like HCA, there are issues that arise which relate to how people in the organization deal with one another. It is impossible to foresee all of these, and many do not require explicit treatment in a document like this. A few routinely arise, however. One involves gift giving among colleagues for certain occasions. While we wish to avoid any strict rules, no one should ever feel compelled to give a gift to anyone, and any gifts offered or received should be appropriate to the circumstances. A lavish gift to anyone in a supervisory role would clearly violate organization policy.

Another situation, which routinely arises, is a fund-raising or similar effort undertaken by individual colleagues, in which no one should ever be compelled to participate. Similarly, when the Company or a facility determines to support charitable organizations such as the United Way, no colleague should be compelled to contribute to the charitable organization, nor should there be any workplace consequences of such non-participation.

## Relationships with Subcontractors and Suppliers

We must manage our subcontractor and supplier relationships in a fair and reasonable manner, free from conflicts of interest and consistent with all applicable laws and good business practices. We promote competitive procurement to the maximum extent practicable. Our selection of subcontractors, suppliers, and vendors will be made on the basis of objective criteria including quality, technical excellence, price, delivery, adherence to schedules, service, and maintenance of adequate sources of supply. Our purchasing decisions will be made on the supplier's ability to meet our needs, and not on personal relationships and friendships. We employ the highest ethical standards in business practices in source selection, negotiation, determination of contract awards, and the administration of all purchasing activities. We do not communicate to a third-party confidential information given to us by our suppliers unless directed in writing to do so by the supplier. We do not disclose contract pricing and information to any outside parties. (The subject of Business Courtesies, which might be offered by or to subcontractors or suppliers, is discussed on pages 26 to 29 of this Code.)

## Research, Investigations, and Clinical Trials

We follow high ethical standards and comply with federal and state laws and regulations in any research, investigations and clinical trials conducted by our physicians and professional staff. We do not tolerate intentional research misconduct. Research misconduct includes making up or changing results or copying results from other studies without performing the clinical investigation or research. Our hospitals protect the patients and respect their rights during research, investigations, and clinical trials.

All patients asked to participate in a clinical investigation or research project are given a full explanation of alternative services that might prove beneficial to them. They are also fully informed of potential discomforts and are given a full explanation of the risks, expected benefits, and alternatives. The patients are fully informed of the procedures to be followed, especially those that are experimental in nature.

Refusal of a patient to participate in a research study will not compromise his or her access to services. Patient informed consent to participate in clinical investigations or research is documented and retained pursuant to Company and hospital policies.

Any HCA facility or colleague applying for or performing research of any type is responsible for maintaining the highest ethical standards in any written or oral communications regarding the research project as well as following appropriate research guidelines. As in all accounting and financial record-keeping, our policy is to submit only true, accurate, and complete costs related to research grants. Any HCA facility or colleague engaging in human subject research must do so in conjunction with an Institutional Review Board (IRB) and consistent with Company policies regarding human subject research and IRBs.

## Ineligible Persons

We do not contract with, employ, or bill for services rendered by an individual or entity that is excluded or ineligible to participate in Federal healthcare programs; suspended or debarred from Federal government contracts; or has been convicted of a criminal offense related to the provision of healthcare items or services and has not been reinstated in a Federal healthcare program after a period of exclusion, suspension, debarment, or ineligibility, provided that we are aware of such criminal offense. We routinely search the Department of Health and Human Services' Office of Inspector General and General Services Administration's lists of such excluded and ineligible persons. A number of Company policies address the procedures for timely and thorough review of such lists and appropriate enforcement actions.

Colleagues, vendors, and privileged practitioners at one or more HCA facilities are required to report to us if they become excluded, debarred, or ineligible to participate in Federal healthcare programs; or have been convicted of a criminal offense related to the provision of healthcare items or services.

## Substance Abuse and Mental Acuity

To protect the interests of our colleagues and patients, we are committed to an alcohol and drug-free work environment. All colleagues must report for work free of the influence of alcohol and illegal drugs. Reporting to work under the influence of any illegal drug or alcohol; having an illegal drug in a colleague's system; or using, possessing, or selling illegal drugs while on HCA work time or property may result in immediate termination. We may use drug testing as a means of enforcing this policy.

It is also recognized individuals may be taking prescription or over-the-counter drugs, which could impair judgment or other skills required in job performance. Colleagues with questions about the effect of such medication on their performance or who observe an individual who appears to be impaired in the performance of his or her job must immediately consult with their supervisor.

## Marketing Practices

### Antitrust

Antitrust laws are designed to create a level playing field in the marketplace and to promote fair competition.

These laws could be violated by discussing HCA business with a competitor, such as how our prices are set, disclosing the terms of supplier relationships, allocating markets among competitors, or agreeing with a competitor to refuse to deal with a supplier. Our competitors are other health systems and facilities in markets where we operate.

At trade association meetings, colleagues must be alert to potential situations where it may not be appropriate to participate in discussions regarding prohibited subjects with competitors. Prohibited subjects include any aspect of pricing, our services in the market, key costs such as labor costs, and marketing plans. If a competitor raises a prohibited subject, colleagues must end the conversation immediately. Colleagues must document their refusal to participate in the conversation by requesting their objection be reflected in the meeting minutes and notify the Legal Department of the incident.

In general, colleagues avoid discussing sensitive topics with competitors or suppliers, unless they are proceeding with the advice of the Legal Department. Colleagues also must not provide any information in response to an oral or written inquiry concerning an antitrust matter without first consulting the Legal Department.

### Gathering Information about Competitors

It is not unusual to obtain public information about other organizations, including our competitors, through legal and ethical means such as public documents, public presentations, journal and magazine articles, and other published and spoken information. However, colleagues should avoid seeking or receiving information about a competitor through other non-public means if they know or have reason to believe the information is proprietary or confidential. For example, a colleague should not seek proprietary or confidential information when doing so would require anyone to violate a contractual agreement, such as a confidentiality agreement with a prior employer.

## Marketing and Advertising

We may use marketing and advertising activities to educate the public, provide information to the community, increase awareness of our services, and to recruit colleagues. We present only truthful, fully informative, and non-deceptive information in these materials and announcements.

## Foreign Corrupt Practices Act

The United States Foreign Corrupt Practices Act (FCPA) requires us to exercise care in our dealings with foreign government officials, employees, or representatives; and members of their families. The FCPA prohibits providing anything of value to any of these individuals for the purpose of obtaining or retaining business. Under the FCPA, HCA is responsible for the actions of its agents and representatives. Before offering anything of value to foreign government officials, employees or representatives or a member of their family, an HCA colleague must obtain advice from the Corporate Ethics and Compliance Department or the Legal Department.

## *Environmental Compliance*

It is our policy to comply with all environmental laws and regulations as they relate to our organization's operations. We act to preserve our natural resources to the full extent reasonably possible. We comply with all environmental laws and operate each of our facilities with the necessary permits, approvals, and controls. We diligently employ the proper procedures to provide a good environment of care and to prevent pollution.

In helping HCA comply with these laws and regulations, all HCA colleagues must understand how job duties may impact the environment, adhere to all requirements for the proper handling of hazardous materials, and immediately alert supervisors

to any situation regarding the discharge of a hazardous substance, improper disposal of hazardous and medical waste, or any situation which may be potentially damaging to the environment.

## *Business Courtesies*

### General

This part of the Code of Conduct should not be considered in any way as an encouragement to make, solicit, or receive any type of entertainment or gift. For clarity purposes, please note that these limitations govern activities with those outside of HCA. This section does not pertain to actions between HCA and its colleagues or actions among HCA colleagues themselves. (See "Relationships Among HCA Colleagues" on page 22.)

### Receiving Business Courtesies

We recognize there will be times when a current or potential business associate, including a potential referral source, may extend an invitation to attend a social event in order to further develop a business relationship.

An HCA colleague may accept such invitations, provided: (1) the cost associated with such an event is reasonable and appropriate, which, as a general rule, means the cost will not exceed $100.00 per person; (2) no expense is incurred for any travel costs (other than in a vehicle owned privately or by the host entity) or overnight lodging; and (3) such events are infrequent. The limitations of this section do not apply to business meetings at which food (including meals) may be provided. Prior to accepting invitations to training and educational opportunities that include travel and overnight accommodations at reduced or no cost to a colleague or HCA, consult our policies and seek appropriate approvals.

HCA colleagues may accept gifts with a total value of $50.00 or less in any one year from any individual or organization who has a business relationship with HCA. For purposes of this paragraph, physicians practicing in HCA facilities are considered to have such a relationship. Perishable or consumable gifts given to a department or group are not subject to any specific limitation. HCA colleagues may accept gift certificates, but may never accept cash or financial instruments (*e.g.*, checks, stocks). Finally, under no circumstances may an HCA colleague solicit a gift.

This section does not limit HCA facilities from accepting gifts, provided they are used and accounted for appropriately.

## Extending Business Courtesies to Non-referral Sources

No portion of this section, "Extending Business Courtesies to Non-referral Sources," applies to any individual who makes, or is in a position to make, referrals to an HCA facility. Such business courtesies are addressed in the *Extending Business Courtesies to Possible Referral Sources* section of this Code and Company policies.

There may be times when a colleague wishes to extend to a current or potential business associate (other than someone who may be in a position to make a patient referral) an invitation to attend a social event (*e.g.*, reception, meal, sporting event, or theatrical event) to further or develop a business relationship. The purpose of the entertainment must never be to induce any favorable business action. During these events, topics of a business nature must be discussed and the host must be present. These events must not include expenses paid for any travel costs (other than in a vehicle owned privately or by the host entity) or overnight lodging. The cost associated with such an event must be reasonable and appropriate. As a general rule, this means the cost will not exceed $100.00 per person. Moreover, such business entertainment with respect to any particular individual must be infrequent, which, as a general rule, means not more than four times per year. Consult Company policy for events that are expected to exceed $100 or were not expected to but inadvertently do exceed $100. That policy requires establishing the business necessity and appropriateness of the proposed entertainment. The organization will under no circumstances sanction participation in any business entertainment that might be considered lavish. Departures from the $100.00 guideline are highly discouraged.

Also, HCA facilities may routinely sponsor events with a legitimate business purpose (*e.g.*, hospital board meetings or retreats). Provided that such events are for business purposes, reasonable and appropriate meals and entertainment may be offered. In addition, transportation and lodging can be paid for. However, all elements of such events, including these courtesy elements, must be consistent with the corporate policy on such events.

It is critical to avoid the appearance of impropriety when giving gifts to individuals who do business or are seeking to do business with HCA. We will never use gifts or other incentives to improperly influence relationships or business outcomes. Gifts to business associates who are not government employees must not exceed $50.00 per year per recipient. Any gifts to Medicare or Medicaid beneficiaries must not exceed $10.00 per item nor total more than $50.00 per year per recipient. An HCA colleague or facility may give gift certificates, but may never give cash or financial instruments (*e.g.*, checks, stocks). The corporate policy on business courtesies permits occasional exceptions to the $50 limit to recognize the efforts of those who have spent meaningful amounts of volunteer time on behalf of HCA.

U.S. Federal and state governments have strict rules and laws regarding gifts, meals, and other business courtesies for their employees. HCA does not provide any gifts, entertainment, meals, or anything else of value to any employee of the Executive Branch of the Federal government, except for minor refreshments in connection with business discussions or promotional items with the HCA or facility logo valued at no more than $10.00. With regard to gifts, meals, and other business courtesies involving any other category of government official or employee, colleagues must determine the particular rules applying to any such person and carefully follow them.

## Extending Business Courtesies to Possible Referral Sources

Any entertainment or gift involving physicians or other persons who are in a position to refer patients to our healthcare facilities must be undertaken in accordance with corporate policies, which have been developed consistent with federal laws, regulations, and rules regarding these practices. HCA colleagues must consult Company policies prior to extending any business courtesy to a potential referral source.

## Government Relations and Political Activities

The organization and its representatives comply with all federal, state, and local laws governing participation in government relations and political activities. Additionally, HCA funds or resources are not contributed directly to individual political campaigns, political parties, or other organizations which intend to use the funds primarily for political campaign objectives. Organization resources include financial and non-financial donations such as using work time and telephones to solicit for a political cause or candidate or the loaning of HCA property for use in the political campaign. The conduct of any political action committee is to be consistent with relevant laws and regulations. In addition, political action committees associated with the organization select candidates to support based on the overall ability of the candidate to render meaningful public service. The organization does not select candidates to support as a reflection of expected support of the candidate on any specific issue.

The organization engages in public policy debate only in a limited number of instances where it has special expertise that can inform the public policy formulation process. When the organization is directly impacted by public policy decisions, it may provide relevant, factual information about the impact of such decisions on the private sector. In articulating positions, the organization only takes positions that it believes can be shown to be in the larger public interest. The organization encourages trade associations with which it is associated to do the same.

It is important to separate personal and corporate political activities in order to comply with the appropriate rules and regulations relating to lobbying or attempting to influence government officials. No use of corporate resources, including e-mail, is appropriate for personally engaging in political activity. A colleague may, of course, participate in the political process on his or her own time and at his or her own expense. While doing so, it is important HCA colleagues not give the impression they are speaking on behalf of or representing HCA in these activities. Colleagues cannot seek to be reimbursed by HCA for any personal contributions for such purposes.

At times, HCA may ask colleagues to make personal contact with government officials or to write letters to present our position on specific issues. In addition, it is a part of the role of some HCA management to interface on a regular basis with government officials. If a colleague is making these communications on behalf of the organization, he or she must be certain to be familiar with any regulatory constraints and observe them. Guidance is always available from the Corporate Government Relations and Legal Departments as necessary.

## The Company's Ethics and Compliance Program

### Program Structure

The Ethics and Compliance Program is intended to demonstrate in the clearest possible terms the absolute commitment of the organization to the highest standards of ethics and compliance. The elements of the program include setting standards (the Code and Policies and Procedures), communicating the standards, providing a mechanism for reporting potential exceptions, monitoring and auditing, and maintaining an organizational structure that supports the furtherance of the program. Each of these elements is detailed below.

These elements are supported at all levels of the organization. Providing direction, guidance and oversight are the Ethics and Compliance Committee of the Board of Directors; the Corporate Ethics and Compliance Steering Committee consisting of senior management; and the Corporate Ethics and Compliance Policy Committee consisting of senior management and three facility CEOs.

The Senior Vice President for Ethics, Compliance

and Corporate Responsibility, who serves as the Corporate Ethics and Compliance Officer, and the Ethics and Compliance Department are responsible for the day-to-day direction and implementation of the Ethics and Compliance Program. This includes developing resources (including policies and procedures, training programs, and communication tools) for and providing support (including operating the Ethics Line, conducting program assessment, and providing advice) to Facility Ethics and Compliance Officers (ECOs) and others.

Responsible Executives are individuals in the Corporate Office who have expertise in various areas of compliance risk and who are called upon in their areas of expertise to lead policy and training development efforts, conduct monitoring and auditing as appropriate, and provide advice.

Playing a key role in ensuring the successful implementation or our Ethics and Compliance Program, Facility ECOs are responsible for distributing standards, ensuring training is conducted, conducting monitoring and responding to audits, investigating and resolving Ethics Line cases, and otherwise administering the Ethics and Compliance Program in their facilities. Hospital ECOs are also expected to establish and maintain a Facility Ethics and Compliance Committee (FECC) to assist them in these efforts. Some Divisions have appointed Division ECOs. Those individuals assist in directing and assessing the Ethics and Compliance Program for their divisions.

Another important resource that may be able to address issues arising out of this Code of Conduct is the Human Resources Manager. Human Resources Managers are highly knowledgeable about many of the compliance risk areas described in this Code of Conduct that pertain to employment and the workplace and are responsible for ensuring compliance with various employment laws. If a concern relates to specific details of an individual's work situation, rather than larger issues of organizational ethics and compliance, the Human Resources Manager is the most appropriate person to contact. In that we promote the concept of management autonomy at local facilities, every effort should be made to resolve workplace conduct and employment practice issues through the individual's supervisor and the Human

Resources Manager at the local facility. Experience has shown that this is an effective and productive way to deal promptly with these matters. Some Divisions have appointed Division Human Resources Managers who assist in investigating and resolving Ethics Line cases and workplace conduct and employment practices issues.

All of these individuals or groups are prepared to support HCA colleagues in meeting the standards set forth in this Code. Membership lists for each of the Corporate entities and the Facility ECOs can be found at the Ethics and Compliance site on the organization's Intranet.

## Corporate Integrity Agreement

In conjunction with settling a federal investigation, on January 25, 2001, HCA entered into a Corporate Integrity Agreement (CIA) with the U.S. Department of Health and Human Services' Office of Inspector General. The CIA, which will be in effect for 8 years, requires us to maintain our Ethics and Compliance Program, report certain potential violations of Federal healthcare program laws to the government, subject certain aspects of our Ethics and Compliance Program to internal and external audits, and submit reports to the Federal government regarding our Program. The full text of the CIA and accompanying information is available on our Intranet and Internet sites.

## Setting Standards

With respect to our Ethics and Compliance Program, we set standards through this Code of Conduct, ethics and compliance policies and procedures and, occasionally, through other guidance mechanisms, such as Compliance Alerts and advisory memoranda. It is the responsibility of each individual to be aware of those policies and procedures that pertain to his or her work and to follow those policies and procedures.

## Training and Communication

Comprehensive training and education has been developed to ensure that colleagues throughout the organization are aware of the standards that apply to them. Code of Conduct training is conducted at the time an individual joins the organization and annually for all colleagues. Compliance training in areas of compliance risk (*e.g.,* billing, coding, cost reports) is required of certain individuals. Company policies outline the training requirements. All ethics and compliance training is required to be recorded in the Company's Learning Management System (LMS). Through the LMS, system administrators and ECOs track colleagues' compliance with their training requirements and report such information as necessary.

Many resources regarding our program are available to all HCA colleagues on our Intranet and to the general public on the Internet. We encourage all colleagues to frequently visit both sites.

## Resources for Guidance and Reporting Concerns

To obtain guidance on an ethics or compliance issue or to report a concern, individuals may choose from several options. We encourage the resolution of issues, including human resources-related issues (*e.g.,* payroll, fair treatment and disciplinary issues), at a local level. Colleagues should use the human resources-related problem solving procedure at their facility to resolve such issues. It is an expected good practice, when one is comfortable with it and think it appropriate under the circumstances, to raise concerns first with one's supervisor. If this is uncomfortable or inappropriate, the individual may discuss the situation with the Facility Human Resources Manager, the Facility ECO, or another member of management at the facility or in the organization. Individuals are always free to contact the Ethics Line at 1-800-455-1996.

HCA makes every effort to maintain, within the limits of the law, the confidentiality of the identity of any individual who reports concerns or possible misconduct. There is no retribution or discipline for anyone who reports a concern in good faith. Any colleague who deliberately makes a false accusation with the purpose of harming or retaliating against another colleague is subject to discipline.

## Personal Obligation to Report

We are committed to ethical and legal conduct that is compliant with all relevant laws and regulations and to correcting wrongdoing wherever it may occur in the organization. Each colleague has an individual responsibility for reporting any activity by any colleague, physician, subcontractor, or vendor that appears to violate applicable laws, rules, regulations, accreditation standards, standards of medical practice, Federal healthcare conditions of participation, or this Code. If a matter that poses serious compliance risk to the organization or that involves a serious issue of medical necessity, clinical outcomes or patient safety is reported locally, and if the reporting individual doubts that the issue has been given sufficient or appropriate attention, the individual should report the matter to higher levels of management or the Ethics Line until satisfied that the full importance of the matter has been recognized.

## Internal Investigations of Reports

We are committed to investigating all reported concerns promptly and confidentially to the extent possible. The Corporate Ethics and Compliance Officer coordinates any findings from corporate-led investigations and immediately recommends corrective action or changes that need to be made. We expect all colleagues to cooperate with investigation efforts.

## Corrective Action

Where an internal investigation substantiates a reported violation, it is the policy of the organization to initiate corrective action, including, as appropriate, making prompt restitution of any overpayment amounts, notifying the appropriate governmental agency, instituting whatever disciplinary action is necessary, and implementing systemic changes to prevent a similar violation from recurring in the future.

## Discipline

All violators of the Code will be subject to disciplinary action. The precise discipline utilized will depend on the nature, severity, and frequency of the violation and may result in any or all of the following disciplinary actions:

- *Oral warning;*
- *Written warning;*
- *Written reprimand;*
- *Suspension;*
- *Termination; and/or*
- *Restitution.*

## Measuring Program Effectiveness

We are committed to assessing the effectiveness of our Ethics and Compliance Program through various efforts.

Much of this effort is provided by the Internal Audit & Consulting Services Department, which routinely conducts internal audits of issues that have regulatory or compliance implications. Responsible Executives routinely undertake monitoring efforts in support of policies and compliance in general. Facilities conduct self-monitoring, and the Ethics and Compliance Department conducts reviews of hospital ethics and compliance programs designed to assess facility implementation of the Code, policies and procedures, Ethics Line and related investigations, and monitoring efforts. These compliance process reviews permit the Ethics and Compliance Department to identify and share best practices.

Most of these methods of assessment result in reports of findings by the reviewers and corrective action plans by the facilities that are reviewed. Through these reviews, we are continuously assessing the effectiveness of the Program and finding ways to improve it.

## Acknowledgment Process

HCA requires all colleagues to sign an acknowledgment confirming they have received the Code, understand it represents mandatory policies of HCA and agree to abide by it. New colleagues are required to sign this acknowledgment as a condition of employment. Each HCA colleague is also required to participate in annual Code of Conduct training, and records of such training must be retained by each facility.

Adherence to and support of HCA's Code of Conduct and participation in related activities and training is considered in decisions regarding hiring, promotion, and compensation for all candidates and colleagues. New colleagues must receive Code of Conduct training within 30 days of employment.

HCA-The Healthcare Company
One Park Plaza
Nashville, Tennessee 37203
(615) 344-9551
www.hcahealthcare.com
© HCA Inc. 2003

# Appendix B

# The Caux Round Table Business Principles of Ethics

## Principle 1. The Responsibilities of Businesses: Beyond Shareholders Toward Stakeholders

The value of a business to society is the wealth and employment it creates and the marketable products and services it provides to consumers at a reasonable price commensurate with quality. To create such value, a business must maintain its own economic health and viability, but survival is not a sufficient goal.

Businesses have a role to play in improving the lives of all their customers, employees, and shareholders by sharing with them the wealth they have created. Suppliers and competitors as well should expect businesses to honor their obligations in a spirit of honesty and fairness. As responsible citizens of the local, national, regional, and global communities in which they operate, businesses share a part in shaping the future of those communities.

## Principle 2. The Economic and Social Impact of Business: Toward Innovation, Justice, and World Community

Businesses established in foreign countries to develop, produce, or sell should also contribute to the social advancement of those countries by creating productive employment and helping to raise the purchasing power of their citizens. Businesses also should contribute to human rights, education, welfare, and vitalization of the countries in which they operate.

Businesses should contribute to economic and social development not only in the countries in which they operate, but also in the world community at large, through effective and prudent use of resources, free and fair competition, and emphasis upon innovation in technology, production methods, marketing, and communications.

## Principle 3. Business Behavior: Beyond the Letter of Law Toward a Spirit of Trust

Accepting the legitimacy of trade secrets, businesses should recognize that sincerity, candor, truthfulness, the keeping of promises, and transparency contribute not only to their own credibility and stability but also to the smoothness and efficiency of business transactions, particularly on the international level.

## Principle 4. Respect for Rules

To avoid trade frictions and to promote freer trade, equal conditions for competition, and fair and equitable treatment for all participants, businesses should respect international and domestic rules. In addition, they should recognize that some behavior, although legal, may still have adverse consequences.

## Principle 5. Support for Multilateral Trade

Businesses should support the multilateral trade systems of the GATT/World Trade Organization and similar international agreements. They should cooperate in efforts to promote the progressive and judicious liberalization of trade, and to relax those domestic measures that unreasonably hinder global commerce, while giving due respect to national policy objectives.

Source: Reprinted with permission from *Business Ethics*, P.O. Box 8439, Minneapolis, MN (612) 879-0695.

## Principle 6. Respect for the Environment

A business should protect and, where possible, improve the environment, promote sustainable development, and prevent the wasteful use of natural resources.

## Principle 7. Avoidance of Illicit Operations

A business should not participate in or condone bribery, money laundering, or other corrupt practices; indeed, it should seek cooperation with others to eliminate them. It should not trade in arms or other materials used for terrorist activities, drug traffic, or other organized crime.

## Principle 8. Customers

We believe in treating all customers with dignity, irrespective of whether they purchase our products and services directly from us or otherwise acquire them in the market. We therefore have a responsibility to:

- provide our customers with the highest quality products and services consistent with their requirements;
- treat our customers fairly in all aspects of our business transactions, including a high level of service and remedies for their dissatisfaction;
- make every effort to ensure that the health and safety of our customers, as well as the quality of their environment, will be sustained or enhanced by our products and services;
- assure respect for human dignity in products offered, marketing, and advertising; and
- respect the integrity of the culture of our customers.

## Principle 9. Employees

We believe in the dignity of every employee and in taking employee interests seriously. We therefore have a responsibility to:

- provide jobs and compensation that improve workers' living conditions;
- provide working conditions that respect each employee's health and dignity;
- be honest in communications with employees and open in sharing information, limited only by legal and competitive restraints;
- listen to and, where possible, act on employee suggestions, ideas, requests, and complaints;
- engage in good faith negotiations when conflict arises;
- avoid discriminatory practices and guarantee equal treatment and opportunity in areas such as gender, age, race, and religion;
- promote in the business itself the employment of differently abled people in places of work where they can be genuinely useful;
- protect employees from avoidable injury and illness in the workplace;
- encourage and assist employees in developing relevant and transferable skills and knowledge; and
- be sensitive to serious unemployment problems frequently associated with business decisions, and work with governments, employee groups, other agencies and each other in addressing these dislocations.

## Principle 10. Owners/Investors

We believe in honoring the trust our investors place in us. We therefore have a responsibility to:

- apply professional and diligent management in order to secure a fair and competitive return on our owners' investment;
- disclose relevant information to owners/investors subject only to legal requirements and competitive constraints;
- conserve, protect, and increase the owners/investors' assets; and
- respect owners/investors' requests, suggestions, complaints, and formal resolutions.

## Principle 11. Suppliers

Our relationship with suppliers and subcontractors must be based on mutual respect. We therefore have a responsibility to:

- seek fairness and truthfulness in all of our activities, including pricing, licensing, and rights to sell;
- ensure that our business activities are free from coercion and unnecessary litigation;
- foster long-term stability in the supplier relationship in return for value, quality, competitiveness, and reliability;
- share information with suppliers and integrate them into our planning processes;
- pay suppliers on time and in accordance with agreed terms of trade; and
- seek, encourage, and prefer suppliers and subcontractors whose employment practices respect human dignity.

## Principle 12. Competitors

We believe that fair economic competition is one of the basic requirements for increasing the wealth of nations and, ultimately, for making possible the just distribution of goods and services. We therefore have a responsibility to:

- foster open markets for trade and investment;
- promote competitive behavior that is socially and environmentally beneficial and demonstrates mutual respect among competitors;
- refrain from either seeking or participating in questionable payments of favors to secure competitive advantages;
- respect both tangible and intellectual property rights; and

- refuse to acquire commercial information by dishonest or unethical means, such as industrial espionage.

## Principle 13. Communities

We believe that as global corporate citizens, we can contribute to such forces of reform and human rights as are at work in the communities in which we operate. We therefore have a responsibility in those communities to:

- respect human rights and democratic institutions, and promote them wherever practicable;
- recognize government's legitimate obligation to the society at large and support public policies and practices that promote human development through harmonious relations between business and other segments of society;
- collaborate with those forces in the community dedicated to raising standards of health, education, workplace safety, and economic well-being;
- promote and stimulate sustainable development and play a leading role in preserving and enhancing the physical environment and conserving the earth's resources;
- support peace, security, diversity, and social integration;
- respect the integrity of local cultures; and
- be a good corporate citizen through charitable donations, educational and cultural contributions, and employee participation in community and civic affairs.

# Endnotes

Chapter 1

1. Eric Hellweg, "Mopping Up After Merrill Lynch, *Business2.com,* Sept. 10, 2002, www.business2.com.
2. "Golin/Harris Trust Survey Finds 69 Percent of Americans Say 'I Just Don't Know Whom to Trust Anymore'," PRNewswire, Feb. 26, 2002, via AmericaOnline.
3. Paul W. Taylor, *Principles of Ethics: An Introduction to Ethics,* 2d ed. (Encino, Calif.: Dickenson, 1975), p. 1.
4. Adapted and reproduced from *The American Heritage Dictionary of the English Language,* 3d ed. Copyright © 1996 by Houghton Mifflin Company.
5. Wroe Alderson, *Dynamic Marketing Behavior* (Homewood, Ill.: Irwin, 1965), p. 320.
6. The Ethics Resource Center, *2000 National Business Ethics Survey: How Employees Perceive Ethics at Work* (Washington, D.C.: Ethics Resource Center, 2000), pp. 4, 28, 29.
7. "Metabolife Probe Launched," CNN, Aug. 15, 2002, www.cnn.com/2002/HEALTH/ diet.fitness/08/15/ephedra.investigatio/index.html.
8. Julie Creswell, "Will Martha Walk?" *Fortune,* Nov. 25, 2002, pp. 121–124; Shelley Emling, "Martha Stewart Indicted on Fraud," *Austin American-Statesman,* June 5, 2003, www.statesman.com; Constance L. Hays, "Stiff Sentence for ImClone Founder," *Austin American-Statesman,* June 11, 2003, www.statesman.com.
9. Greg Farrell, "Hunt Is on for Notebook that Scrushy Denies Exists," *USA Today,* June 12, 2003, p. B1.
10. Jeffrey M. Jones, "Effects of Year's Scandals Evident in Honesty and Ethics Ratings," Gallup Organization, press release, Dec. 4, 2002, www.gallup.com/poll/releases/pr021204.asp.
11. Charles Piller, "Bell Labs Says Its Physicist Faked Groundbreaking Data," *Austin American-Statesman,* Sep. 26, 2002, www.austin360.com/statesman/.
12. Keith H. Hammonds, "Harry Kraemer's Moment of Truth," *Fast Company,* Nov. 2002, www.fastcompany.com/online/64/kraemer.html.
13. Archie B. Carroll, *Business and Society: Ethics and Stakeholder Management* (Cincinnati, Ohio: South-Western, 1989), pp. 225–227.
14. Alan R. Yuspeh, "Development of Corporate Compliance Programs: Lessons Learned from the DII Experience," in *Corporate Crime in America: Strengthening the "Good Citizenship" Corporation* (Washington, D.C.: U.S. Sentencing Commission, 1995), pp. 71–79.
15. Eleanor Hill, "Coordinating Enforcement Under the Department of Defense Voluntary Disclosure Program," in *Corporate Crime in America: Strengthening the "Good Citizenship" Corporation* (Washington, D.C.: U.S. Sentencing Commission, 1995), pp. 287–294.
16. "Huffing and Puffing in Washington: Can Clinton's Plan Curb Teen Smoking?" *Consumer Reports,* 60 (Oct. 1995): 637.
17. Arthur Levitt, with Paula Dwyer, *Take on the Street* (New York: Pantheon Books, 2002).
18. Hill, "Coordinating Enforcement Under the Department of Defense Voluntary Disclosure Program."
19. Richard P. Conaboy, "Corporate Crime in America: Strengthening the Good Citizen Corporation," in *Corporate Crime in America: Strengthening the "Good Citizenship" Corporation* (Washington, D.C.: U.S. Sentencing Commission, 1995), pp. 1–2.

20. *United States Code Service* (Lawyers Edition), 18 U.S.C.S. Appendix, Sentencing Guidelines for the United States Courts (Rochester, N.Y.: Lawyers Cooperative Publishing, 1995), § 8A.1.

21. Anthony Bianco, William Symonds, and Nanette Byrnes, "The Rise and Fall of Dennis Kozlowski," *Business Week,* Dec. 17, 2002, pp. 65–77.

22. "WorldCom CEO Slaps Arthur Andersen," CNN, July 8, 2002, www.cnn.com.

23. "Fraud Inc.," CNN/Money, http://money.cnn.com/news/specials/corruption/ (accessed Feb. 5, 2002); "SEC Formalizes Investigation into Halliburton Accounting," *Wall Street Journal,* Dec. 20, 2002, http://online.wsj.com.

24. Gary Langer, "Confidence in Business: Was Low and Still Is," ABC News, July 1, 2002, http://abcnews.com.

25. "Corporate Reform Bill Passed," CNN, July 25, 2002, www.cnn.com.

26. "Keeping an Eye on Corporate America," *Fortune,* Nov. 25, 2002, pp. 44–46.

27. Avi Shafran, "Aaron Feuerstein: Bankrupt and Wealthy," aish.com, June 30, 2002, www.aish.com/societyWork/work/Aaron_Feuerstein_Bankrupt_and__Wealthy.asp.

28. Bernard J. Jaworski and Ajay K. Kohli, "Market Orientation: Antecedents and Consequences," *Journal of Marketing,* 57 (July 1993): 53–70.

29. Terry W. Loe, "The Role of Ethical Climate in Developing Trust, Market Orientation and Commitment to Quality," unpublished Ph.D. dissertation, University of Memphis, 1996.

30. The Ethics Resource Center, *2000 National Business Ethics Survey,* p. 5.

31. John Galvin, "The New Business Ethics," *SmartBusinessMag.com,* June 2000, p. 99.

32. Galvin, "The New Business Ethics," p. 97.

33. David Rynecki, "Here Are 8 Easy Ways to Lose Your Shirt in Stocks," *USA Today,* June 26, 1998, p. 3B.

34. "Trend Watch," *Business Ethics,* Mar./Apr. 2000, p. 8.

35. "Today's Briefing," *Commercial Appeal,* Oct. 12, 2000, p. C1.

36. Loe, "The Role of Ethical Climate."

37. O. C. Ferrell, Isabelle Maignan, and Terry W. Loe, "The Relationship Between Corporate Citizenship and Competitive Advantage," in *"Rights, Relationships, and Responsibilities,"* edited by O. C. Ferrell, Lou Pelton, and Sheb L. True (Kennesaw, GA: Kennesaw State University, 2003).

38. S. B. Graves and S. A. Waddock, "Institutional Owners and Corporate Social Performance: Maybe Not So Myopic After All," *Proceedings of the International Association for Business and Society,* San Diego, 1993; and S. Waddock and S. Graves, "The Corporate Social Performance–Financial Performance Link," *Strategic Management Journal,* 18 (1997): 303–319.

39. Melissa A. Baucus and David A. Baucus, "Paying the Payer: An Empirical Examination of Longer Term Financial Consequences of Illegal Corporate Behavior," *Academy of Management Journal* (1997): 129–151.

40. Kurt Eichenwald and N. R. Kleinfeld, "At Columbia/HCA, Scandal Hurts," *Commercial Appeal,* Dec. 21, 1997, pp. C1, C3.

41. Julia Flynn, "Did Sears Take Other Customers for a Ride?" *Business Week,* Aug. 3, 1992, pp. 24–25; Harriet Johnson Brackey, "Auto Repair Rip-Offs Bane of Consumer," *USA Today,* July 15, 1992.

42. Chris Welles, "What Led Beech-Nut Down the Road to Disgrace?" *Business Week,* Feb. 22, 1988, pp. 124–128.

43. Galvin, "The New Business Ethics."

44. Curtis C. Verschoor, "A Study of the Link Between a Corporation's Financial Performance and Its Commitment to Ethics," *Journal of Business Ethics,* 17 (Oct. 1998): 1509.

*Chapter 2*

1. "Bristol-Myers Squibb Subject to SEC Probe," CNN, July 11, 2002, www.cnn.com.
2. Debbie Thorne, O. C. Ferrell, and Linda Ferrell, *Business and Society* (Boston: Houghton Mifflin, 2003), pp. 64–65.
3. "Enron 101," *BizEd*, May/June 2002, pp. 40–46.
4. Isabelle Maignan, O. C. Ferrell, and Linda Ferrell, "Managing Corporate Social Responsibility: How to Nurture Stakeholders' Confidence," working paper, Colorado State University, 2003, pp. 3–5.
5. Maignan, Ferrell, and Ferrell, "Managing Corporate Social Responsibility."
6. Maignan, Ferrell, and Ferrell, "Managing Corporate Social Responsibility."
7. Thorne, Ferrell, and Ferrell, *Business and Society.*
8. Theodore Levitt, *The Marketing Imagination* (New York: The Free Press, 1983).
9. Norman Bowie, "Empowering People As an End for Business," in *People in Corporations: Ethical Responsibilities and Corporate Effectiveness,* edited by Georges Enderle, Brenda Almond, and Antonio Argandona (Dordrecht, The Netherlands: Kluwer Academic Press, 1990), pp. 105–112.
10. "Business Leaders, Politicians and Academics Dub Corporate Irresponsibility 'An Attack on America from Within'," Business Wire, Nov. 7, 2002, via America Online.
11. Isabelle Maignan and O. C. Ferrell, "Corporate Social Responsibility: Toward a Marketing Conceptualization," *Journal of the Academy of Marketing Science,* forthcoming 2004.
12. Maignan and Ferrell, "Corporate Social Responsibility."
13. Maignan and Ferrell, "Corporate Social Responsibility."
14. Maignan and Ferrell, "Corporate Social Responsibility."
15. Maignan and Ferrell, "Corporate Social Responsibility."
16. Vernon R. Loucks Jr., "A CEO Looks at Ethics," *Business Horizons,* 30 (Mar.–Apr. 1987): 4.
17. James Bandler, "Two Big Film Makers Strive to Crush Renegade Recycler," *Wall Street Journal,* Dec. 4, 2002, http://online.wsj.com.
18. Eric H. Beversluis, "Is There No Such Thing As Business Ethics?" *Journal of Business Ethics,* 6 (Feb. 1987): 81–88. Reprinted by permission of Kluwer Academic Publishers, Dordrecht, Holland.
19. Beversluis, "Is There No Such Thing As Business Ethics?", p. 82.
20. Emily Nelson and Laurie P. Cohen, "Why Grubman Was So Keen to Get His Twins into the Y," *Wall Street Journal,* Nov. 15, 2002, http://online.wsj.com.
21. John Byrne, "Fall from Grace," *Business Week,* Aug. 12, 2002, pp. 50–56.
22. Jenny Summerour, "Bribery Game," *Progressive Grocer,* Jan. 2000, p. 43.
23. William T. Neese, O. C. Ferrell, and Linda Ferrell, "An Analysis of Mail and Wire Fraud Cases Related to Marketing Communication: Implications for Corporate Citizenship," working paper, 2003.
24. "Snapshot," *USA Today,* Oct. 3, 2002.
25. Paul Davidson, "AOL Investigators Face Complex Task," *USA Today,* Sep. 4, 2002, p. 6B.
26. Matt Kranz, "More Earnings Restatements on Way," *USA Today,* Oct. 25, 2002, p. 3B.
27. Nicole Bullock, "Qwest's Credit Ratings Reflect Risks Despite Recent Debt Swap," *Wall Street Journal,* Dec. 30, 2002, p. B4.
28. Cassell Bryan-Low, "Accounting Firms Face Backlash over the Tax Shelters They Sold," *Wall Street Journal,* Feb. 7, 2003, http://online.wsj.com.
29. Bryan-Low, "Accounting Firms Face Backlash."
30. "WorldCom Finds Another $3.3B in Errors," CNN, Aug. 8, 2002, www.cnn.com/2002/BUSINESS/asia/08/08/US.worldcom.biz/index.html.
31. Jeff Bater, "FTC Says Companies Falsely Claim Cellphone Patches Provide Protection," *Wall Street Journal,* Feb. 21, 2002, http://online.wsj.com.

32. Archie B. Carroll, *Business and Society: Ethics and Stakeholder Management* (Cincinnati, Ohio: South-Western, 1989), pp. 228–230.

33. "Mott's Will Rewrite Some Labels Blamed for Misleading People," *Wall Street Journal,* Aug. 2, 2000, p. B7.

34. "AT&T Settles Lawsuit Against Reseller Accused of Slamming," *Business Wire,* via America Online, May 26, 1998.

35. Neese, Ferrell, and Ferrell, "An Analysis of Mail and Wire Fraud Cases Related to Marketing Communication."

36. "Retail Theft and Inventory Shrinkage," What You Need to Know about . . . Retail Industry, http://retailindustry.about.com/library/weekly/02/aa021126a.htm (accessed Feb. 6, 2003).

37. "Prosecutor Recommends Probation for Actress Winona Ryder," CNN.com, Dec. 3, 2002.

38. Daryl Koehn, "Consumer Fraud: The Hidden Threat," University of St. Thomas, www.stthom.edu/cbes/commentary/HBJCONFRAUD.html (accessed Feb. 6, 2003).

39. Bureau of the Census, *Statistical Abstract of the United States, 2001* (Washington, D.C.: Government Printing Office, 2002), p. 17.

40. "U.S. Equal Employment Opportunity Commission: An Overview," U.S. Equal Employment Opportunity Commission, www.eeoc.gov/overview.html (accessed Feb. 4, 2003).

41. Peter Brimelow, "Is Sexual Harassment Getting Worse?" *Forbes,* Apr. 19, 1999.

42. Randall Smith, "Salomon Must Pay $3.2 Million to Broker over Sex-Bias Case," *Wall Street Journal,* Dec. 17, 2002, http://online.wsj.com.

43. "$3.5 Million Settlement in Woolworth Age Discrimination Case," CNN.com, Nov. 15, 2002, www.cnn.com.

44. Sue Shellenberger, "Work & Family," *Wall Street Journal,* May 23, 2001, p. B1.

45. "What Is Affirmative Action," HR Content Library, Oct. 12, 2001, www.hrnext.com/content/view.cfm?articles_id=2007&subs_id=32.

46. "What Affirmative Action Is (and What It Is Not)," National Partnership for Women & Families, www.nationalpartnership.org/content.cfm?L1=202&DBT=Documents&NewsItemID=289&HeaderTitle=Affirmative%20Action, (accessed Feb. 4, 2003).

47. "What Is Affirmative Action."

48. "What Affirmative Action Is (and What It Is Not)."

49. "What Affirmative Action Is (and What It Is Not)"; Thorne, Ferrell, and Ferrell, *Business and Society,* pp. 255–259.

50. "Fords Finance Unit Is Accused of Charging Higher Rates to Blacks," *Wall Street Journal,* Nov. 2, 2000, p. B20.

51. Quoted in John Galvin, "The New Business Ethics," *SmartBusinessMag.com,* June 2000, p. 86.

52. Galvin, "The New Business Ethics," p. 97.

53. "Sonera Executive Is Arrested in a Widening Privacy Probe," *Wall Street Journal,* Nov. 22, 2002, http://online.wsj.com.

54. "Privacy (Employee)," Business for Social Responsibility, www.bsr.org/ (accessed Feb. 6, 2003).

55. Jeffrey Pfeffer, "Why Spy?" *Business2.com,* Feb. 2003, www.business2.com/articles/mag/0,1640,46179,00.html?cnn=yes.

56. Galvin, "The New Business Ethics," p. 97.

57. "Ethical Issues in the Employer–Employee Relationship," Society of Financial Service Professionals, www.financialpro.org/press/Ethics/es2000/Ethics_Survey_2000_Report_FINAL.cfm (accessed Feb. 6, 2003).

58. Stephenie Steitzer, "Commercial Web Sites Cut Back on Collections of Personal Data," *Wall Street Journal,* Mar. 28, 2002, http://online.wsj.com.

59. Margaret Littman, "How Marketers Track Underage Consumers," *Marketing News,* May 8, 2000, pp. 4, 7.

60. Eve M. Caudill and Patrick E. Murphy, "Consumer Online Privacy: Legal and Ethical Issues," *Journal of Public Policy & Marketing,* 19 (Spring 2000): 7.

61. Galvin, "The New Business Ethics," p. 98.

62. Steitzer, "Commercial Web Sites Cut Back on Collections of Personal Data."

63. Anna Wilde Mathews, "Copyrights on Web Content Are Backed," *Wall Street Journal,* Oct. 27, 2000, p. B10.

64. "Today's Briefing," *Commercial Appeal,* Nov. 15, 2000, p. C1.

65. "Danger on the Highway: Bridgestone/Firestone's Tire Recall," in William M. Pride and O. C. Ferrell, *Marketing: Concepts and Strategies,* 12th ed. (Boston: Houghton Mifflin, 2003), pp. 108–110.

## Chapter 3

1. "Leading the Way: Profiles of Some of the '100 Best Corporate Citizens' for 2002," *Business Ethics,* May 16, 2002, www.business-ethics.com/newpage.htm.

2. Archie B. Carroll, "The Pyramid of Corporate Social Responsibility: Toward the Moral Management of Organizational Stakeholders," *Business Horizons* 34 (July–Aug. 1991): 42.

3. Isabelle Maignan, O. C. Ferrell, and G. Tomas M. Hult, "Corporate Citizenship: Cultural Antecedents and Business Benefits," *Journal of the Academy of Marketing Science,* 27 (Fall 1999): 457.

4. Herman Miller, www.hermanmiller.com (accessed Jan. 13, 2003).

5. Sandra Waddock, "Comment: Fluff Is Not Enough—Managing Responsibility for Corporate Citizenship," *Ethical Corporation,* Mar. 18, 2002, www.ethicalcorp.com/content.asp?ContentID=47.

6. "Enron 101," *BizEd,* May/June 2002, pp. 40–46.

7. William M. Pride and O. C. Ferrell, *Marketing: Concepts and Strategies,* 12th ed. (Boston: Houghton Mifflin, 2003), p. 87.

8. Gregory L. White, "Russian Maneuvers Are Making Palladium Ever More Precious," *Wall Street Journal,* Mar. 6, 2000, pp. A1, A14.

9. David Armstrong and Ann Zimmerman, "Suit Claims Eckerd Overcharged for Drugs," *Wall Street Journal,* Feb. 4, 2002, p. B2.

10. Ron Winslow, "One Patient, 34 Days in the Hospital, a Bill for $5.2 Million," *Wall Street Journal,* Aug. 2, 2001, pp. A1, A16.

11. Michael Arndt, Wendy Zellner, and Peter Coy, "Too Much Corporate Power," *Business Week,* Sept. 11, 2000, p. 149.

12. "Drug Firms Agree to Settle Lawsuit over Cardizem," *Wall Street Journal,* Jan. 28, 2003, p. A1.

13. Stephen Scheibal, "Civic Group Takes Issue with Chain Bookstore," *Austin American-Statesman,* Dec. 11, 2002, www.austin360.com/statesman/.

14. Gary Martin, "Clear Channel Accused of Stifling Competition, Bullying Musicians," *Austin American-Statesman,* Jan. 31, 2003, www.austin360.com/statesman/; Yochi J. Dreazen and Joe Flint, "FCC Eases Media-Ownership Caps, Clearing the Way for New Mergers," *Wall Street Journal,* June 3, 2003, http://online.wsj.com.

15. Gregory T. Gundlach, "Price Predation: Legal Limits and Antitrust Considerations," *Journal of Public Policy & Marketing,* 14 (Fall 1995): 278.

16. Quoted in "Software Publishers Association Applauds Department of Justice Antitrust Competition Action; Department Acts in Support of Software Industry Competition Principles," PRNewswire.com, May 18, 1998.

17. "Store Files Antitrust Lawsuit Against Microsoft," PRNewswire.com, May 18, 1998.

18. Don Clark, Mark Wigfield, Nick Wingfield, and Rebecca Buckman, "Judge Approves Most of Pact, in Legal Victory for Microsoft," *Wall Street Journal,* Nov. 1, 2002, http://online.wsj.com; Kim Peterson, Brier Dudley, and Bradley Meacham, "Microsoft Settles with California for $1 Billion," *Seattle Times,* Jan. 11, 2003, pp. A1, A10.

19. Shane W. Robinson, "Corporate Espionage 101," SANS Institute, Feb. 15, 2002, http://rr.sans.org/social/espionage.php.

20. Matthew G. Nelson, "Wireless Goal: Don't Get Whacked," *Information Week,* July 9, 2001, www.informationweek.com/story/IWK20010705S0013.

21. Robinson, "Corporate Espionage 101."

22. Devin Leonard, "The Curse of Pooh," *Fortune,* Jan. 20, 2003, pp. 85–92.

23. "A Child Shall Lead the Way: Marketing to Youths," *Credit Union Executive,* May–June 1993, pp. 6–8.

24. "Federal Web Sites Ignore Children's Privacy Law," *Commercial Appeal,* Oct. 7, 2000, p. A7.

25. Otto Krusius, "From Out of the Mouses of Babes," *Kiplinger's,* Nov. 2000, p. 32.

26. Bureau of Labor Statistics, "Highlights of Women's Earnings in 2001," U.S. Department of Labor, May 2002, available at /www.bls.gov/cps/cpswom2002.pdf

27. "Jury Finds Wal-Mart Guilty of Forcing Unpaid Overtime," *Wall Street Journal,* Dec. 20, 2002, http://online.wsj.com.

28. Arndt, Zellner, and Coy, "Too Much Corporate Power," p. 150.

29. Dave Bryan, "Royal Caribbean Guards Against Pollution," *USA Today,* www.usatoday.com/life/travel /lt092.htm (accessed Oct. 13, 2000).

30. John Yaukey, "Discarded Computers Create Waste Problem," *USA Today,* www.usatoday.com/news/ndsmonl4.htm (accessed Oct. 13, 2000).

31. Andrew Park, "Stemming the Tide of Tech Trash," *Business Week,* Oct. 7, 2002, pp. 36A–36F.

32. Win Swenson, "The Organizational Guidelines' 'Carrot and Stick' Philosophy, and Their Focus on 'Effective' Compliance," in *Corporate Crime in America: Strengthening the "Good Citizenship" Corporation* (Washington, D.C.: U.S. Sentencing Commission, 1995), pp. 17–26.

33. *United States Code Service* (Lawyers Edition), 18 U.S.C.S. Appendix, Sentencing Guidelines for the United States Courts (Rochester, N.Y.: Lawyers Cooperative Publishing, 1995), § 8A.1.

34. "Corporate Reform Bill Passed," CNN, July 25, 2002, www.cnn.com.

35. Penelope Patsuris, "The Corporate Scandal Sheet," *Forbes,* Aug. 26, 2002, www.forbes.com/home/2002/07/25/accountingtracker.html

36. Nelson D. Schwartz, "The Looting of Kmart, Part 2," *Fortune,* Feb. 17, 2003, p. 30; Elliot Blair Smith, "Probe: Former Kmart CEO 'Grossly Derelict'," *USA Today,* Jan. 27, 2003, p. B1.

37. David McHugh, "Business Wants to Restore Public Trust," America Online, Jan. 28, 2003.

38. McHugh, "Business Wants to Restore Public Trust"; "Post-Enron Restatements Hit Record," MSNBC, Jan. 21, 2003, www.msnbc.com.

39. Ingrid Murro Botero, "Charitable Giving Has 4 Big Benefits," *Business Journal of Phoenix,* Jan. 1, 1999, www.bizjournals.com/phoenix/stories/1999/01/ 04/smallb3.html.

40. Gardiner Harris and Michael Waldholz, "Merck & Co. Will Pledge $100 Million of Vaccines to World's Poorest Children," *Wall Street Journal,* Mar. 2, 2000, p. B2.

41. "The Merck Mectizan Donation Program," Merck, www.merck.com/about/cr/policies_performance/social/mectizan_donation.html (accessed Jan. 10, 2003).

42. "Cisco Systems to Provide Technology Assistance for Non-Profit Community Organizations in Massachusetts, New Hampshire," Cisco, press release, Oct. 4, 2000, http://newsroom.cisco.com/dlls/fspnisapi20f1.html.

43. Lawrence Ulrich, "The New Green Machines," *Money,* 32 (July 2003): 117–119.

44. "Leading the Way: Profiles of Some of the '100 Best Corporate Citizens'."

45. "Charity Holds Its Own in Tough Times," American Association of Fundraising Counsel, press release, June 23, 2003, www.aafrc.org/press_releases/.

46. "Leading the Way: Profiles of Some of the '100 Best Corporate Citizens'."

47. Tom Klusmann, "The 100 Best Corporate Citizens," *Business Ethics,* Mar.–Apr. 2000, p. 13.

48. "Leading the Way: Profiles of Some of the '100 Best Corporate Citizens'."

49. "HP Philanthropy," Hewlett-Packard, http://grants.hp.com/ (accessed Jan. 10, 2003).

50. "McDonald's Employees Honor Ray Kroc's Birthday by Giving Back to Communities Nationwide," PRNewswire.com (accessed Oct. 13, 2000).

51. G. A. Steiner and J. F. Steiner, *Business, Government, and Society* (New York: Random House, 1988).

52. Milton Friedman, "Social Responsibility of Business Is to Increase Its Profits," *New York Times Magazine,* Sept. 13, 1970, pp. 122–126.

53. 1997 Cone/Roper Cause-Related Marketing Trends in "Does It Pay to Be Ethical?" *Business Ethics,* Mar.–Apr. 1997, p. 15.

54. Isabelle Maignan, "Antecedents and Benefits of Corporate Citizenship: A Comparison of U.S. and French Businesses," unpublished Ph.D. dissertation, University of Memphis, 1997.

55. Excerpted from R. Edward Freeman and Daniel R. Gilbert Jr., *Corporate Strategy and the Search for Ethics* (Englewood Cliffs, N.J.: Prentice-Hall, 1988), pp. 7, 90, 105. Reprinted by permission.

## Chapter 4

1. Thomas M. Jones, "Ethical Decision Making by Individuals in Organizations: An Issue-Contingent Model," *Academy of Management Review,* 16 (Feb. 1991): 366–395; O. C. Ferrell and Larry G. Gresham, "A Contingency Framework for Understanding Ethical Decision Making in Marketing," *Journal of Marketing,* 49 (Summer 1985): 87–96; O. C. Ferrell, Larry G. Gresham, and John Fraedrich, "A Synthesis of Ethical Decision Models for Marketing," *Journal of Macromarketing,* 9 (Fall 1989): 55–64; Shelby D. Hunt and Scott Vitell, "A General Theory of Marketing Ethics," *Journal of Macromarketing,* 6 (Spring 1986): 5–16; William A. Kahn, "Toward an Agenda for Business Ethics Research," *Academy of Management Review,* 15 (Apr. 1990): 311–328; Linda K. Trevino, "Ethical Decision Making in Organizations: A Person-Situation Interactionist Model," *Academy of Management Review,* 11 (Mar. 1986): 601–617.

2. Jones, "Ethical Decision Making," pp. 367, 372.

3. Donald P. Robin, R. Eric Reidenbach, and P. J. Forrest, "The Perceived Importance of an Ethical Issue As an Influence on the Ethical Decision-Making of Ad Managers," *Journal of Business Research,* 35 (Jan. 1996): 17.

4. "Lead Attorneys in Enron Shareholder Litigation: Wall St. Banks Operated Giant Ponzi Scheme," Corporate Governance Fund Report, Aug. 14, 2002, www.cgfreport.com/NewsFlashMilberg.htm.

5. "Ponzi Schemes," U.S. Securities & Exchange Commission, www.sec.gov/answers/ponzi.htm (accessed Feb. 13, 2003).

6. Roselie McDevitt and Joan Van Hise, "Influences in Ethical Dilemmas of Increasing Intensity," *Journal of Business Ethics,* 40 (Oct. 2002): 261–274.

7. Anusorn Singhapakdi, Scott J. Vitell, and George R. Franke, "Antecedents, Consequences, and Mediating Effects of Perceived Moral Intensity and Personal Moral Philosophies," *Journal of the Academy of Marketing Science,* 27 (Winter 1999): 19.

8. Robin, Reidenbach, and Forrest, "The Perceived Importance."

9. Singhapakdi, Vitell, and Franke, "Antecedents."

10. Robin, Reidenbach, and Forrest, "The Perceived Importance."

11. Robin, Reidenbach, and Forrest, "The Perceived Importance," p. 17.

12. Jerry Markon, "Former Executive of Adelphia Plans to Plead Guilty," *Wall Street Journal,* Nov. 14, 2002, p. A5.

13. Joseph W. Weiss, *Ethics: A Managerial Stakeholder Approach* (Belmont, CA: Wadsworth, 1994), p. 13.

14. O. C. Ferrell and Linda Ferrell, "Role of Ethical Leadership in Organizational Performance," *Journal of Management Systems,* 13 (2001): 64–78.

15. Richard T. DeGeorge, *Business Ethics,* 3d ed. (New York: Macmillan, 1990), pp. 14, 26–27, 40, 63, 79–90, 83–85, 105–108, 160–178.

16. James Weber and Julie E. Seger, "Influences upon Organizational Ethical Subclimates: A Replication Study of a Single Firm at Two Points in Time," *Journal of Business Ethics,* 41 (Nov. 2002): 69–84.

17. Sean Valentine, Lynn Godkin, and Margaret Lucero, "Ethical Context, Organizational Commitment, and Person-Organization Fit," *Journal of Business Ethics,* 41 (Dec., 2002): 349–360.

18. Bruce H. Drake, Mark Meckler, and Debra Stephens, "Transitional Ethics: Responsibilities of Supervisors for Supporting Employee Development," *Journal of Business Ethics,* 38 (June 2002): 141–155.

19. Ferrell and Gresham, "A Contingency Framework," pp. 87–96.

20. Nick Wingfield, "DoubleClick Moves to Appoint Panel for Privacy Issues," *Wall Street Journal,* May 17, 2000, p. B10.

21. Adapted from Debbie Thorne, O. C. Ferrell, and Linda Ferrell, *Business and Society: A Strategic Approach to Corporate Citizenship* (Boston: Houghton Mifflin, 2003), pp. 169–193.

22. Markon, "Former Executive of Adelphia Plans to Plead Guilty."

23. Darryl Reed, "Corporate Governance Reforms in Developing Countries," *Journal of Business Ethics,* 37 (May 2002): 223–247.

24. Bryan W. Husted and Carlos Serrano, "Corporate Governance in Mexico," *Journal of Business Ethics,* 37 (May 2002): 337–348.

25. Maria Maher and Thomas Anderson, *Corporate Governance: Effects on Firm Performance and Economic Growth* (Paris: Organisation for Economic Co-operation and Development, 1999).

26. A. Demb and F. F. Neubauer, *The Corporate Board: Confronting the Paradoxes* (Oxford: Oxford University Press, 1992).

27. Joshua Chaffin, "Piper to Pay 32.5 Million to Join Global Settlement, *Financial Times,* Dec. 31, 2002, p. 14.

28. Maher and Anderson, *Corporate Governance.*

29. Organisation for Economic Co-operation and Development, *The OECD Principles of Corporate Governance* (Paris: Organisation for Economic Co-operation and Development, 1999).

30. Louis Lavelle, "The Best & Worst Boards," *Business Week,* Oct. 7, 2002, pp. 104–114.

31. Andrew Backover, "Overseer Confident WorldCom Will Come Back," *USA Today,* Dec. 31, 2002, p. 8A.

32. Melvin A. Eisenberg, "Corporate Governance: The Board of Directors and Internal Control," *Cordoza Law Review,* 19 (Sept./Nov. 1997): 237.

33. Matt Krantz, "Web of Board Members Ties Together Corporate America," *USA Today,* Nov. 23, 2002, pp. 1B–3B.

34. Krantz, "Web of Board Members Ties Together Corporate America."

35. Lavelle, "The Best & Worst Boards."

36. John A. Byrne, with Louis Lavelle, Nanette Byrnes, Marcia Vickers, and Amy Borrus, "How to Fix Corporate Governance," *Business Week,* May 6, 2002, pp. 69–78.

37. "How Business Rates: By the Numbers," *Business Week,* Sep. 11, 2000, pp. 148–149.

38. Michael Arndt, Wendy Zellner, and Peter Coy, "Too Much Corporate Power," *Business Week,* Sep. 11, 2000, p. 154.

39. Graef Crystal, "Conseco Pays Dearly to Rid Itself of Failing Chief," *Commercial Appeal,* May 16, 2000, p. B6.

40. Sarah Anderson, John Cavanagh, Ralph Estes, Chuck Collins, and Chris Hartman, *A Decade of Executive Excess: The 1990s Sixth Annual Executive Compensation Survey* (Boston, MA: United for a Fair Economy, 1999).

41. Louis Lavelle, "CEO Pay, The More Things Change . . . ," *Business Week,* Oct. 16, 2000, pp. 106–108.

42. Louis Lavelle, with Frederick F. Jespersen and Michael Arndt, "Executive Pay," *Business Week,* Apr. 15, 2002, www.businessweek.com/magazine/content/02_15/b3778012.htm.

43. Lavelle, "The Best & Worst Boards."

44. Gary Strauss, "America's Corporate Meltdown," *USA Today,* June 27, 2002, pp. 1A, 2A.

45. Phyllis Plitch, "Firms with Governance Disclosure See Higher Returns—Study," *Wall Street Journal,* Mar. 31, 2003, http://online.wsj.com/.

## Chapter 5

1. James R. Rest, *Moral Development Advances in Research and Theory* (New York: Praeger, 1986), p. 1.

2. "Business Leaders, Politicians and Academics Dub Corporate Irresponsibility 'An Attack on America from Within'," Business Wire, Nov. 7, 2002, via America Online.

3. Abhijit Biswas, Jane W. Licata, Daryl McKee, Chris Pullig, and Christopher Daughtridge, "The Recycling Cycle: An Empirical Examination of Consumer Waste Recycling and Recycling Shopping Behaviors," *Journal of Public Policy & Marketing,* 19 (Spring 2000): 93.

4. Charles Gasparino, "Grubman Informed Weill of AT&T Meetings," *Wall Street Journal,* Nov. 15, 2002, pp. C1, C13.

5. "Court Says Businesses Liable for Harassing on the Job," *Commercial Appeal,* June 27, 1998, p. A1.

6. Richard Brandt, *Ethical Theory* (Englewood Cliffs, N.J.: Prentice-Hall, 1959), pp. 253–254.

7. J. J. C. Smart and B. Williams, *Utilitarianism: For and Against* (Cambridge, England: Cambridge University Press, 1973), p. 4.

8. C. E. Harris Jr., *Applying Moral Theories* (Belmont, Calif.: Wadsworth, 1986), pp. 127–128.

9. Penelope Patsuris, "The Corporate Accounting Scandal Sheet," *Forbes,* Aug. 26, 2002, www.forbes.com/2002/07/25/accountingtracker.html; Debra Solomon, "Adelphia Plans to Dismiss Deloitte," *Wall Street Journal,* June 10, 2002, p. A3.

10. Immanuel Kant, "Fundamental Principles of the Metaphysics of Morals," in *Problems of Moral Philosophy: An Introduction,* 2d ed., ed. Paul W. Taylor (Encino, Calif.: Dickenson, 1972), p. 229.

11. Example adapted from Harris, *Applying Moral Theories,* pp. 128–129.

12. Gerald F. Cavanaugh, Dennis J. Moberg, and Manuel Velasquez, "The Ethics of Organizational Politics," *Academy of Management Review,* 6 (July 1981): 363–374; the U.S. Bill of Rights, www.law.cornell.edu/constitution/constitution.billofrights.html (accessed Feb. 17, 2003).

13. Marie Brenner, "The Man Who Knew Too Much," *Vanity Fair,* May 1996, available at www.jeffreywigand.com/insider/vanityfair.html (accessed Feb. 17, 2003).

14. Norman E. Bowie and Thomas W. Dunfee, "Confronting Morality in Markets," *Journal of Business Ethics,* 38 (Jul. 2002): 381–393.

15. Kant, "Fundamental Principles," p. 229.

16. Thomas E. Weber, "To Opt In or Opt Out: That Is the Question When Mulling Privacy," *Wall Street Journal,* Oct. 23, 2000, p. B1.

17. Manuel G. Velasquez, *Business Ethics Concepts and Cases,* 4th ed. (Upper Saddle River, N.J.: Prentice-Hall, 1998), pp. 132–133.

18. Velasquez, *Business Ethics Concepts and Cases.*

19. Ian Maitland, "Virtuous Markets: The Market As School of the Virtues," *Business Ethics Quarterly,* Jan. 1997, p. 97.

20. Surendra Arjoon, "Virtue Theory As a Dynamic Theory of Business," *Journal of Business Ethics,* 28 (May 2000): 159.

21. Maitland, "Virtuous Markets," p. 97.

22. Stefanie E. Naumann and Nathan Bennett, "A Case for Procedural Justice Climate: Development and Test of a Multilevel Model," *Academy of Management Journal,* 43 (Oct. 2000): 881–889.

23. Joel Brockner, "Making Sense of Procedural Fairness: How High Procedural Fairness Can Reduce or Heighten the Influence of Outcome Favorability," *Academy of Management Review,* 27 (Jan. 2002): 58–76.

24. "Wainwright Bank and Trust Company Award for Social Justice Inside and Out," *Business Ethics,* Nov./Dec. 1998, p. 11.

25. John Fraedrich and O. C. Ferrell, "Cognitive Consistency of Marketing Managers in Ethical Situations," *Journal of the Academy of Marketing Science,* 20 (Summer 1992): 245–252.

26. Manuel Velasquez, Claire Andre, Thomas Shanks, S. J., and Michael J. Meyer, "Thinking Ethically: A Framework for Moral Decision Making," *Issues in Ethics* (Winter 1996): 2–5.

27. Leslie Cauley, "AT&T to Offer Hard-Core Adult Movies in Drive for Digital-Cable Subscribers," *Wall Street Journal,* May 31, 2000, p. B16.

28. Lawrence Kohlberg, "Stage and Sequence: The Cognitive Developmental Approach to Socialization," in *Handbook of Socialization Theory and Research,* ed. D. A. Goslin (Chicago: Rand McNally, 1969), pp. 347–480.

29. Kohlberg, "Stage and Sequence."

30. Adapted from Kohlberg, "Stage and Sequence."

31. Harvey S. James Jr., "Reinforcing Ethical Decision Making Through Organizational Structure," *Journal of Business Ethics,* 28 (Nov. 2000): 45.

32. Clare M. Pennino, "Is Decision Style Related to Moral Development Among Managers in the U.S.?" *Journal of Business Ethics,* 41 (Dec. 2002): 337–347.

33. The Ethics Resource Center, *2000 National Business Ethics Survey: How Employees Perceive Ethics at Work* (Washington D.C.: Ethics Resource Center, 2000), p. 20.

34. George Izzo, "Compulsory Ethics Education and the Cognitive Moral Development of Salespeople: A Quasi-Experimental Assessment," *Journal of Business Ethics,* 28 (Dec. 2000): 223.

35. Jeffrey M. Jones, "Effects of Year's Scandals Evident in Honest and Ethics Ratings," The Gallup Organization, Dec. 4, 2002, www.gallup.com/poll/releases/pr021204.asp.

36. Edward Soule, "Managerial Moral Strategies—In Search of a Few Good Principles," *Academy of Management Review,* 27 (Jan. 2002): 114–124.

*Chapter 6*

1. "Fourth Quarter Scores," American Customer Satisfaction Index, Feb. 18, 2003, www.theacsi.org/fourth_quarter.htm.

2. Richard L. Daft, *Organizational Theory and Design* (St. Paul, MN.: West Publishing, 1983), p. 482.

3. Stanley M. Davis, quoted in Alyse Lynn Booth, "Who Are We?" *Public Relations Journal*, July 1985, pp. 13–18.

4. T. E. Deal and A. A. Kennedy, *Corporate Culture: Rites and Rituals of Corporate Life* (Reading, MA: Addison Wesley, 1982), p. 4.

5. G. Hofstede, "Culture's Consequences: International Differences," in *Work-Related Values* (Beverly Hills, CA: Sage Publications, 1980), p. 25.

6. N. M. Tichy, "Managing Change Strategically: The Technical, Political and Cultural Keys," *Organizational Dynamics*, Autumn 1982, pp. 59–80.

7. J. W. Lorsch, "Managing Culture: The Invisible Barrier to Strategic Change," *California Management Review*, 28 (Winter 1986): 95–109.

8. "Transforming Our Culture: The Values for Success," Mutual of Omaha, www.careerlink.org/emp/mut/corp.htm (accessed Feb. 19, 2003).

9. William Clay Ford Jr., "A Message from the Chairman," Ford Motor Company, www.ford.com/en/ourCompany/corporateCitizenship/ourLearningJourney/message . . . (accessed Feb. 19, 2003).

10. Chip Cummins, "Workers Wear Feelings on Their Hard Hats and Show True Colors," *Wall Street Journal*, Nov. 7, 2000, p. A1.

11. N. K. Sethia and M. A. Von Glinow, "Arriving at Four Cultures by Managing the Reward System," in *Gaining Control of the Corporate Culture* (San Francisco: Jossey-Bass, 1985), p. 409.

12. Marjorie Kelly and Tom Klusmann, "Is IBM Still Socially Responsible?" *Business Ethics*, July/Aug. 2000, pp. 4–5.

13. "Southwest Airlines Fact Sheet," Southwest Airlines, Feb. 18, 2003, www.southwest.com/about_swa/press/factsheet.html.

14. Barbara Whitaker, "UPS Program Softens Managers' Hearts," *Commercial Appeal*, July 30, 2000, p. E2.

15. Paul Beckett and Ron Lieber, "Visa, MasterCard May Face Over $500 Million in Refunds," *Wall Street Journal*, Feb. 10, 2003, http://online.wsj.com.

16. "Thomas Weisel Settles Suit, Agrees to Pay $12.5 Million," *Wall Street Journal*, Feb. 12, 2003, http://online.wsj.com.

17. "Starbucks Mission Statement," Starbucks, www.starbucks.com/aboutus/environment.asp (accessed Feb. 19, 2003).

18. Peter Asmus, with Sandra Waddock and Samuel Graves, "100 Best Corporate Citizens of 2003," *Business Ethics*, Spring 2003, p. 8; "Leading the Way: Profiles of Some of the '100 Best Corporate Citizens' for 2002," *Business Ethics*, May 16, 2002, www.business-ethics.com/newpage.htm; "Press Release," Starbucks, Feb. 18, 2003, www.starbucks.com/aboutus/pressdesc.asp?id=295.

19. "CSFB Reportedly Erased Key Files," MSNBC.com, Feb. 13, 2003, www.msnbc.com/news/872288.asp.

20. Isabelle Maignan, O. C. Ferrell, and Thomas Hult, "Corporate Citizenship, Cultural Antecedents and Business Benefit," *Journal of the Academy of Marketing Science*, 27 (October 1999): 455–469.

21. R. Eric Reidenbach and Donald P. Robin, *Ethics and Profits* (Englewood Cliffs, NJ: Prentice-Hall, 1989), p. 92.

22. Reidenbach and Robin, *Ethics and Profits*.

23. "Small Virtues: Entrepreneurs Are More Ethical," *Business Week Online*, Mar. 8, 2000, www.businessweek.com/smallbiz/0003/ ib3670029.htm?scriptFramed.

24. Constance E. Bagley, "The Ethical Leader's Decision Tree," *Harvard Business Review*, Feb. 2003, p. 18.

25. John Byrne, "How Al Dunlap Self-Destructed," *Business Week*, July 6, 1998, pp. 44–45.

26. "Sunbeam Ex-CEO 'Chainsaw Al' Dunlap Settles SEC Case," Securities Class Action Clearinghouse, Stanford Law School, press release, Sep. 4, 2002, http://securities.stanford.edu/news-archive/2002/20020904_Settlement03_Roland.htm.

27. Daniel J. Brass, Kenneth D. Butterfield, and Bruce C. Skaggs, "Relationship and Unethical Behavior: A Social Science Perspective," *Academy of Management Review*, 23 (Jan. 1998): 14–31.

28. Andrew Kupfor, "Mike Armstrong's AT&T: Will the Pieces Come Together," *Fortune*, Apr. 26, 1999, p. 89.

29. Daniel Goleman, "Leadership That Gets Results," *Harvard Business Review*, Mar.–Apr. 2000, pp. 78–90.

30. J. M. Burns, *Leadership* (New York: Harper and Row, 1985).

31. Royston Greenwood, Roy Suddaby, and C. R. Hinings, "Theorizing Change: The Role of Professional Associations in the Transformation of Institutionalized Fields," *Academy of Management Journal*, 45 (Jan. 2002): 58–80.

32. "WorldCom Chief Outlines Initial Turnaround Strategy," *Wall Street Journal*, Jan. 14, 2003, http://online.wsj.com.

33. John R. P. French and Bertram Ravin, "The Bases of Social Power," in *Group Dynamics: Research and Theory*, ed. Dorwin Cartwright (Evanston, IL: Row, Peterson, 1962), pp. 607–623.

34. Lyman W. Porter, "Job Attitudes in Management: II. Perceived Importance of Needs As a Foundation of Job Level," *Journal of Applied Psychology*, 47 (Apr. 1963): 141–148.

35. Clayton Alderfer, *Existence, Relatedness, and Growth* (New York: Free Press, 1972), pp. 42–44.

36. Louis P. White and Long W. Lam, "A Proposed Infrastructural Model for the Establishment of Organizational Ethical Systems," *Journal of Business Ethics*, 28 (Nov. 1, 2000): 35–42.

37. Gary Edmondson, Kate Carlisle, Inka Resch, Karen Anhalt, and Heidi Dawley, "Human Bondage," *Business Week*, Nov. 27, 2000, pp. 147–160.

38. "Today's Briefing," *Commercial Appeal*, Sept. 5, 2000, p. B4.

39. Michael Hirsh and Kenneth Klee, "Ubiquity and Its Burdens." *Newsweek*, Jan. 24, 2000, http://newsweek.com/nw-srv/ printed/int/sr/a54645-2000jan24.htm.

40. Gael McDonald, "Business Ethics: Practical Proposals for Organizations," *Journal of Business Ethics*, 25 (May 2000): 179.

41. Michael Connor, "Philip Morris: More Spent on Health Ads," *Yahoo! News*, May 23, 2000, http://dailynews.yahoo.com/h/nm/2000523/bs/tobacco_engle_1.html; "Philip Morris U.S.A. Expresses Confidence in Its Youth Smoking Prevention Advertising Based on Extensive Research Findings," Business Wire, May 29, 2002, via www.findarticles.com.

## Chapter 7

1. "About Merck: Mission Statement," Merck & Co., www.merck.com/about/mission.html (accessed Feb. 19, 2003).

2. "A Guide to Corporate Scandals," MSNBC.com, www.msnbc.com/news/wld/business/brill/Corporate Scandal_DW.asp (accessed Feb. 26, 2003).

3. Bob Lewis, "Survival Guide: The Moral Compass—Corporations Aren't Moral Agents, Creating Interesting Dilemmas for Business Leaders," *InfoWorld*, Mar. 11, 2002, via www.findarticles.com.

4. Rogene A. Buchholz and Sandra B. Rosenthal, *Business Ethics* (Upper Saddle River, N.J.: Prentice-Hall, 1998), p. 171.

5. Marjorie Kelly, "14th Annual Business Ethics Awards," *Business Ethics,* Fall 2002, pp. 10–13.

6. John Fraedrich and O. C. Ferrell, "Cognitive Consistency of Marketing Managers in Ethical Situations," *Journal of the Academy of Marketing Science,* 20 (Summer 1992): 243–252.

7. "Ex-Tyco CFO Indicted for Tax Evasion," CNN/Money, Feb. 19, 2003, http://money.cnn.com/.

8. O. C. Ferrell and Linda Ferrell, "Role of Ethical Leadership Organizational Performance," *Journal of Management Systems,* 13 (2001): 64–78.

9. "A Guide to Corporate Scandals."

10. Catherine Valenti, "Ethical Culture: Is the Enron Saga a Sign That Ethics in the Workplace Are Disappearing?" ABCNews.com, Feb. 21, 2002, http://abcnews.go.com/sections/business/DailyNews/corporate_ethics_020221.html.

11. O. C. Ferrell and K. Mark Weaver, "Ethical Beliefs of Marketing Managers," *Journal of Marketing,* 42 (July 1978): 69–73.

12. Michael S. James, "What Is Ethical? Politics, Circumstances, Excuses Can Blur What Is Right," ABCNews.com, Feb. 21, 2002, http://abcnews.go.com/sections/us/Daily News/personal_ethics020221.html.

13. The Ethics Resource Center, *2000 National Business Ethics Survey: How Employees Perceive Ethics at Work* (Washington, D.C.: Ethics Resource Center, 2000), p. 55.

14. Terry W. Loe and O. C. Ferrell, "Ethical Climate's Relationship to Trust, Market Orientation and Commitment to Quality: A Single Firm Study," *Academy of Marketing Science Proceedings,* May 1997, pp. 211–215.

15. Stephen R. Covey, "Is Your Company's Bottom Line Taking a Hit?" *PR Newswire,* May 29, 1998.

16. Vikki Kratz, "Don't Be Shy," *Business Ethics,* Jan./Feb. 1996, p. 15.

17. Robert Galford and Anne Seibold Drapeau, "The Enemies of Trust," *Harvard Business Review,* Feb. 2003, pp. 88–94.

18. Margaret H. Cunningham and O. C. Ferrell, "Ethical Decision-Making Behavior in Marketing Research," working paper, School of Business, Queen's University, Kingston, Ontario, 2003.

19. "Snapshot: How Employees Make Workers Happy," *USA Today,* June 14, 2000.

20. "Reeve's Ad Touches a Nerve," *Commercial Appeal,* February 2, 2000, p. A6.

21. E. Sutherland and D. R. Cressey, *Principles of Criminology,* 8th ed. (Chicago: Lippincott, 1970), p. 114.

22. O. C. Ferrell and Larry G. Gresham, "A Contingency Framework for Understanding Ethical Decision Making in Marketing," *Journal of Marketing,* 49 (Summer 1985): 90–91.

23. Edward Wong, "Shuttle Insulator Admits to Shortcuts," *Austin American-Statesman,* Feb. 18, 2003, http://austin360.com/statesman.

24. James S. Bowman, "Managerial Ethics in Business and Government," *Business Horizons,* 19 (October 1976): 48–54; William C. Frederick and James Weber, "The Value of Corporate Managers and Their Critics: An Empirical Description and Normative Implications," in *Research in Corporate Social Performance and Social Responsibility,* ed. William C. Frederick and Lee E. Preston (Greenwich, CT: JAI Press, 1987), pp. 149–150; Linda K. Trevino and Stuart Youngblood, "Bad Apples in Bad Barrels: A Causal Analysis of Ethical Decision Making Behavior," *Journal of Applied Psychology,* 75 (Aug. 1990): 38.

25. Richard Lacavo and Amanda Ripley, "Persons of the Year 2002—Cynthia Cooper, Coleen Rowley, and Sherron Watkins," *Time,* Dec. 22, 2002, www.time.com/personoftheyear/2002.

26. John W. Schoen, "Split CEO–Chairman Job, Says Panel," MSNBC.com, Jan. 9, 2003, www.msnbc.com/news/857171.asp.

27. Jathon Sapsford and Paul Beckett, "The Complex Goals and Unseen Cost of Whistle-Blowing," *Wall Street Journal,* Nov. 25, 2002, pp. A1, A10.

28. "Today's Briefing," *Commercial Appeal,* Mar. 2, 2000, p. C1.

29. Paula Dwyer and Dan Carney, with Amy Borrus, Lorraine Woellert, and Christopher Palmeri, "Year of the Whistleblower," *Business Week,* Dec. 16, 2002, pp. 106–110.

30. Stephanie Armour, "More Companies Urge Workers to Blow the Whistle," *USA Today,* Dec. 16, 2002, p. B1.

31. The Ethics Resource Center, *2000 National Business Ethics Survey,* pp. 42, 43, 46, 51.

32. *2000 National Business Ethics Survey,* p. 45.

33. Maynard M. Dolecheck and Carolyn C. Dolecheck, "Ethics: Take It from the Top," *Business,* Jan./Mar. 1989, pp. 12–18.

34. "Wal-Mart Sweatshops in Honduras," National Labor Committee, www.nlcnet.org/walmart/honwal.htm (accessed Feb. 19, 2003).

35. Nicholas Stein, "America's Most Admired Companies," *Fortune,* Mar. 3, 2003, pp. 81–94.

36. *2000 National Business Ethics Survey,* p. 30.

37. "A Guide to Corporate Scandals."

38. Jeffrey L. Seglin, "Forewarned Is Forearmed? Not Always," *New York Times,* Feb. 16, 2003, www.nytimes.com/2003/02/16/business/yourmoney/16ETHI.html; Barbara Ley Toffler, *Final Accounting: Ambition, Greed and the Fall of Arthur Andersen* (New York: Broadway Books, 2003).

39. Nicole Harris, "Spam That You Might Not Delete," *Business Week,* June 15, 1998, p. 116.

40. Stephen Hunt, "Suspect in Utah Diet-Product Fraud Case to Take Back His Guilty Pleas," *Salt Lake Tribune,* Nov. 28, 1999.

41. *2000 National Business Ethics Survey,* p. 30.

42. *2000 National Business Ethics Survey,* p. 30.

43. Wong, "Shuttle Insulator Admits to Shortcuts."

44. Patricia Casey Douglas, Ronald A. Davidson, Bill N. Schwartz, "The Effect of Organizational Culture and Ethical Orientation on Accountants' Ethical Judgments," *Journal of Business Ethics,* 34 (Nov. 2001): 101–122.

45. "FTC Says Violent Products Aimed at Children," *Commercial Appeal,* Sept. 12, 2000, pp. A1, A2.

46. Kalpa Srinivasan, "FTC: Show Industry Marketed Violence," Yahoo! News, Sept. 10, 2000, http://dailynews.yahoo.com/h/ap/2000910/pl/ entertainment_violence_3.html.

47. Frederick and Weber, "The Value of Corporate Managers," pp. 149–150.

48. Rebecca Smith and Alexei Barrionuevo, "Dynegy Ex-Trader Is Indicted on Criminal-Fraud Charges, *Wall Street Journal,* Jan. 28, 2003, http://online.wsj.com.

49. Gene R. Laczniak and Patrick E. Murphy, *Ethical Marketing Decisions: The Higher Road* (Boston: Allyn & Bacon, 1993), p. 14.

## Chapter 8

1. "SEC Chief Donaldson Pushes Ethics," MSNBC News, Feb. 28, 2003, www.msnbc.com/news/878994.asp.

2. "62% of Americans Tell CEOs 'You're Not Doing Enough to Restore Trust and Confidence in American Business,'" Golin/Harris International, press release, June 20, 2002 www.golinharris.com/news/releases.asp?ID=3788.

3. Linda K. Trevino and Stuart Youngblood, "Bad Apples in Bad Barrels: Causal Analysis of Ethical Decision Making Behavior," *Journal of Applied Psychology,* 75 (Aug. 1990): 378–385.

4. Kara Wetzel, "SEC Files Complaint Against ClearOne," *Wall Street Journal,* Jan. 15, 2003, http://online.wsj.com/.

5. Trevino and Youngblood, "Bad Apples in Bad Barrels."

6. "AmericaEconomia Annual Survey Reveals Ethical Behavior of Businesses and Executives in Latin America," *AmericaEconomia*, Dec. 19, 2002 via www.prnewswire.com.

7. Constance E. Bagley, "The Ethical Leader's Decision Tree," *Harvard Business Review*, Feb. 2003, pp. 18–19.

8. "Ex-Tyco CFO Indicted for Tax Evasion," CNN/Money, Feb. 19, 2003, http://money.cnn.com/; "A Guide to Corporate Scandals," MSNBC.com, www.msnbc.com/news/wld/business/brill/Corporate Scandal_DW.asp (accessed Feb. 26, 2003).

9. "Fast Fact," *Fast Company*, Sept. 2000, p. 96.

10. Merck & Co., Inc., 1999 Annual Report, p. 29.

11. "Fast Fact."

12. Gary R. Weaver and Linda K. Trevino, "Compliance and Values Oriented Ethics Programs: Influences on Employees' Attitudes and Behavior," *Business Ethics Quarterly*, 9 (Apr. 1999): 315–335.

13. Peter R. Kendicki, "The Options Available in Ethics Programs," *National Underwriter*, Nov. 12, 2001, pp. 57–58.

14. Ethics Resource Center, *The Ethics Resource Center's 2000 National Business Ethics Survey: How Employees Perceive Ethics at Work* (Washington D.C.: Ethics Resource Center, 2000), p. 16.

15. Mark S. Schwartz, "A Code of Ethics for Corporate Code of Ethics," *Journal of Business Ethics*, 41 (Nov. 2002): 37.

16. Schwartz, "A Code of Ethics for Corporate Code of Ethics."

17. "2002 Fidelity Investments Code of Ethics Summary," Fidelity Investments, http://personal.fidelity.com/myfidelity/InsideFidelity/index.html (accessed Mar. 3, 2003).

18. "TI Recognized As an Ethics Benchmark," www.ti.com/corp/docs/company/citizen/ethics/benchmark.shtml (accessed Feb. 25, 2003). Courtesy Texas Instruments, Inc.

19. "Ethics Is the Cornerstone of TI," www.ti.com/corp/docs/company/citizen/ethics/brochure/index.shtml (accessed Feb. 25, 2003). Courtesy Texas Instruments, Inc.

20. "The TI Ethics Quick Test," www.ti.com/corp/docs/company/citizen/ethics/quicktest.shtml (accessed Feb. 25, 2003). Courtesy Texas Instruments, Inc.

21. Ethics Resource Center, *2000 National Business Ethics Survey*, p. 22.

22. Allynda Wheat, "Keeping an Eye on Corporate America," *Fortune*, Nov. 25, 2002, pp. 44–45.

23. Wheat, "Keeping an Eye on Corporate America."

24. "Top Corporate Ethics Officers Tell Conference Board That More Business Ethics Scandals Are Ahead; Survey Conducted at Conference Board Business Ethics Conference," PR Newswire, June 17, 2002, via www.findarticles.com.

25. "Eye on Europe," *Business Ethics*, May/June and July/Aug. 2002, p. 9.

26. Ethics Resource Center, p. 18.

27. "Ethics, Compliance, and Corporate Responsibility," HCA Healthcare, http://ec.hcahealthcare.com (accessed Mar. 3, 2003).

28. O. C. Ferrell and Larry Gresham, "A Contingency Framework for Understanding Ethical Decision Making in Marketing," *Journal of Marketing*, 49 (Summer 1985): 87–96.

29. Diane E. Kirrane, "Managing Values: A Systematic Approach to Business Ethics," *Training and Development Journal*, 1 (Nov. 1990): 53–60.

30. "Ethics and Business Conduct," www.boeing.com/companyoffices/aboutus/ethics/index.htm (accessed Feb. 25, 2003). Courtesy of Boeing Business Services Company.

31. Debbie Thorne LeClair and Linda Ferrell, "Innovation in Experiential Business Ethics Training," *Journal of Business Ethics*, 23 (Feb. 2000): 313–322.

32. "Top Corporate Ethics Officers Tell Conference Board That More Business Ethics Scandals Are Ahead."

33. "Top Corporate Ethics Officers Tell Conference Board That More Business Ethics Scandals Are Ahead."

34. Janet Wiscombe, "Don't Fear Whistle-Blowers: with HR's Help, Principled Whistle-Blowers Can Be a Company's Salvation," *Workforce,* July 2002 via www.findarticles.com.

35. Mael Kaptein, "Guidelines for the Development of an Ethics Safety Net," *Journal of Business Ethics,* 41 (Dec. 2002): p. 217.

36. Wiscombe, "Don't Fear Whistle-Blowers."

37. Ethics Resource Center, p. 7.

38. Curt S. Jordan, "Lessons in Organizational Compliance: A Survey of Government-Imposed Compliance Programs," *Preventive Law Reporter,* Winter 1994, p. 7.

39. Lori T. Martens and Kristen Day, "Five Common Mistakes in Designing and Implementing a Business Ethics Program," *Business and Society Review,* 104 (Summer 1999): 163–170.

40. Anne C. Mulkern, "Auditors Smelled Trouble," *Denver Post,* Oct. 2, 2002, p. A1.

## Chapter 9

1. John Rosthorn, "Business Ethics Auditing—More Than a Stakeholder's Toy," *Journal of Business Ethics,* 27 (Sept. 2000) 9–19.

2. Debbie McAlister, O. C. Ferrell, and Linda Ferrell, *Business and Society: A Strategic Approach to Corporate Citizenship,* 2d ed. (Boston: Houghton Mifflin, 2005).

3. Rosthorn, "Business Ethics Auditing."

4. "Environmental and Social Report," British Petroleum, www.bp.com/environ_social/ guide_environ_social/... (accessed Mar. 17, 2003).

5. "Accountability," Business for Social Responsibility, www.bsr.org/BSRResources/ WhitePaperDetail.cfm?DocumentID=259 (accessed Feb. 13, 2003).

6. "Bristol-Myers Restates Profit, Sales over Inventory Debacle," *Wall Street Journal,* Mar. 10, 2003, http://online.wsj.com; "Peter Dolan: Bristol-Myers Squibb," in "The Worst Managers," *Business Week,* Jan. 13, 2003, p. 80.

7. "Why Count Social Performance," in *Building Corporate Accountability: The Emerging Practices in Social and Ethical Accounting, Auditing and Reporting,* ed. Simon Zadek, Peter Pruzan, and Richard Evans (London: Earthscan Publications Ltd., 1997), pp. 12–34.

8. Kevin J. Sobnosky, "The Value-Added Benefits of Environmental Auditing," *Environmental Quality Management,* 9 (Winter 1999): 25–32.

9. "Accountability," Business for Social Responsibility.

10. Trey Buchholz, "Auditing Social Responsibility Reports: The Application of Financial Auditing Standards," Colorado State University, professional paper, Nov. 28, 2000, p. 3.

11. "Accountability," Business for Social Responsibility.

12. Nicholas Stein, "America's Most Admired Companies," *Fortune,* Mar. 3, 2003, p. 81.

13. Wendy Zellner, "No Way to Treat a Lady?" *Business Week,* Mar. 3, 2003, pp. 63–66.

14. John Pearce, *Measuring Social Wealth* (London: New Economics Foundation, 1996) as reported in Warren Dow and Roy Crowe, *What Social Auditing Can Do for Voluntary Organizations* (Vancouver: Volunteer Vancouver, July 1999), p. 8.

15. Mark Maremont, "Tyco Holders Reject Proposal to Reincorporate in the U.S.," *Wall Street Journal,* Mar. 7, 2003, http://online.wsj.com.

16. Dennis K. Berman, "Qwest Spends Top Dollar to Defend Its Accounting," *Wall Street Journal,* Mar. 10, 2003, http://online.wsj.com.

17. "The Effect of Published Reports of Unethical Conduct on Stock Prices," reported in "Business Ethics," Business for Social Responsibility, www.bsr.org/BSRResources/White PaperDetail.cfm?DocumentID=270 (accessed Mar. 5, 2003).

18. Ronald Alsop, "Scandal-Filled Year Takes Toll on Firms' Good Names," *Wall Street Journal,* Feb. 12, 2003, http://online.wsj.com.

19. "U.S. Companies Risk Reputations and Finances Due to Broadening Public Concern with All Forms of Corporate Behavior," PRNewswire, Aug. 19, 2002, via www.findarticles.com.

20. Penelope Patsuris, "The Corporate Accounting Scandal Sheet," *Forbes,* Aug. 26, 2002, www.forbes.com/2002/07/25/accountingtracker.html.

21. Warren Dow and Roy Crowe, *What Social Auditing Can Do for Voluntary Organizations* (Vancouver: Volunteer Vancouver, July 1999), pp. 15–18.

22. Peter Raynard, "Coming Together: A Review of Contemporary Approaches to Social Accounting, Auditing and Reporting in Non-Profit Organizations," *Journal of Business Ethics,* 17 (Oct. 1998): 1471–1479.

23. Tracy Swift and Nicole Dando, "From Methods to Ideologies: Closing the Assurance Expectations Gap in Social and Ethical Accounting," *Journal of Corporate Citizenship,* Winter 2002, pp. 81–90.

24. "What Is Corporate Social Responsibility?" Vasin, Heyn & Company, www.vhcoaudit.com/SRAarticles/WhatIsCSR.htm (accessed Feb. 13, 2003).

25. The methodology in this section was adapted from McAlister, Ferrell, and Ferrell, *Business and Society.*

26. "Accountability," Business for Social Responsibility.

27. Johann Mouton, "Chris Hani Baragwanath Hospital Ethics Audit," Ethics Institute of South Africa, 2001, available at www.ethicsa.org/report_CHB.html.

28. "Verification," Business for Social Responsibility, www.bsr.org/BSRResources/WhitePaperDetail.cfm?DocumentID=440 (accessed Feb. 13, 2003).

29. "Ethical Statement," Social Audit, SocialAudit.org, www.socialaudit.org/pages/ethical.htm (accessed Mar. 4, 2003).

30. "Niagara Mohawk, A National Grid Company," Better Business Bureau, www.bbb.org/torchaward/niagara.asp (accessed Mar. 17, 2003).

31. "Verification," Business for Social Responsibility.

32. "Verification," Business for Social Responsibility.

33. "Ethical Statement," Social Audit.

34. "Ethics, Compliance & Corporate Responsibility: Introduction," HCA Healthcare, http://ec.hcahealthcare.com (accessed Feb. 17, 2003).

35. "Verification," Business for Social Responsibility.

36. Joseph B. White, "Ford President Faces Inquiry over Ad-Related Directive," *Wall Street Journal,* Mar. 10, 2003, http://online.wsj.com.

37. Buchholz, "Auditing Social Responsibility Reports," p. 15.

38. Mouton, "Chris Hani Baragwanath Hospital Ethics Audit."

39. "Verification," Business for Social Responsibility.

40. "Introduction to Corporate Social Responsibility," Business for Social Responsibility, www.bsr.org/BSRResources/WhitePaperDetail.cfm?DocumentID=138 (accessed Mar. 5, 2003).

41. Mouton, "Chris Hani Baragwanath Hospital Ethics Audit."

42. "Introduction to Corporate Social Responsibility," Business for Social Responsibility.

43. Andrew Countryman, "SEC: HealthSouth Earnings Overstated by $1.4 Billion," *Austin American-Statesman,* Mar. 20, 2003, http://austin360.com/statesman/; Carrick Mollenkamp and Chad Terhune, "HealthSouth Says Its Auditor Has Found Big Mistatements," *Wall Street Journal,* July 8, 2003, http://online.wsj.com.

44. "Accountability," Business for Social Responsibility.

45. "Accountability," Business for Social Responsibility.

46. Ethics Officer Association, www.eoa.org (accessed Mar. 5, 2003).
47. "Accountability," Business for Social Responsibility.
48. "Verification," Business for Social Responsibility.
49. "Verification," Business for Social Responsibility.
50. "Environmental and Social Report," British Petroleum.
51. Swift and Dando, "From Methods to Ideologies," p. 81.
52. Buchholz, "Auditing Social Responsibility Reports," pp. 16–18.
53. Buchholz, "Auditing Social Responsibility Reports," pp. 19–20.
54. "Accountability," Business for Social Responsibility.
55. Buchholz, "Auditing Social Responsibility Reports," pp. 19–20.
56. Mouton, "Chris Hani Baragwanath Hospital Ethics Audit."
57. *KPMG International Survey of Corporate Sustainability Reporting 2002* (Amsterdam: University Amsterdam, 2002), www.kpmg.com.
58. Sandra Waddock and Neil Smith, "Corporate Responsibility Audits: Doing Well by Doing Good," *Sloan Management Review,* 41 (Winter 2000): 75–83.
59. Buchholz, "Auditing Social Responsibility Reports," p. 1.
60. Waddock and Smith, "Corporate Responsibility Audits."
61. Buchholz, "Auditing Social Responsibility Reports," p. 1.
62. Waddock and Smith, "Corporate Responsibility Audits."
63. J. C. Collins and J. I. Porras, *Built to Last: Successful Habits of Visionary Companies* (New York: Harper Collins, 1997).
64. Waddock and Smith, "Corporate Responsibility Audits."

## Chapter 10

1. Alan K. Reichert, Marion S. Webb, and Edward G. Thomas, "Corporate Support for Ethical and Environmental Policies: A Financial Management Perspective," *Journal of Business Ethics,* 25 (May 2000): 54.
2. Neil King Jr., "WTO Panel Rules Against Law on U.S. Punitive Import Duties," *Wall Street Journal,* June 18, 2002, p. A2.
3. Michael D. White, *Short Course in International Marketing Blunders* (Novato, Calif.: World Trade Press, 2002).
4. White, *Short Course in International Marketing Blunders.*
5. David A. Ricks, *Big Business Blunders: Mistakes in Multinational Marketing* (Homewood, Ill.: Dow-Jones Irwin, 1983), pp. 83–84.
6. O. C. Ferrell and Geoffrey Hirt, *Business: A Changing World* (Burr Ridge, Ill.: Irwin/McGraw-Hill, 2000), p. 257.
7. Tibbett L. Speer, "Avoid Gift Blunders in Asian Locales," *USA Today,* Apr. 25, 2000, www.usatoday.com/life/travel/business/1999/t0316bt2.htm.
8. Jim Carlton, "Stymied in Alaska, Oil Producers Flock to a New Frontier," *Wall Street Journal,* Sept. 4, 2002, pp. A1, A15.
9. Michael Williams, "Many Japanese Banks Ran Amok While Led by Former Regulators," *Wall Street Journal,* Jan. 19, 1996, pp. A1, A9.
10. Andrew Singer, "General Motors: Ethics Increasingly Means Social Responsibility Too," *Ethikos,* May/June 2000, pp. 9, 11–13.
11. Edward Alden, "Multinationals in Labour Pledge . . . ," *Financial Times,* July 28, 2000, www.globalarchive.ft.com/search-components/ index.jsp.
12. O. C. Ferrell, Thomas N. Ingram, and Raymond W. LaForge, "Initiating Structure for Legal and Ethical Decisions in a Global Sales Organization," *Industrial Marketing Management,* Nov. 2000, pp. 1–10.

13. Rachel Emma Silverman, "Here's the Retirement Jack Welch Built: $1.4 Million a Month," *Wall Street Journal*, Oct. 31, 2002, pp. A1, A15.

14. Peter Waldman, "Unocal to Face Trial over Link to Forced Labor," *Wall Street Journal*, June 13, 2002, pp. B1, B3.

15. "Ethics in the Global Market," Texas Instruments, www.ti.com/corp/docs/company/citizen/ethics/market.shtml (accessed Mar. 7, 2003).

16. Business for Social Responsibility, www.bsr.org (accessed Mar. 7, 2003).

17. Stephen Power, "Update Needed for Tire Rules, Activists Argue," *Wall Street Journal*, Sept. 8, 2000, p. B4; Tom Sharp, "Tiremaker Admits Mislabels," *Commercial Appeal*, Aug. 29, 2000, pp. B5, B10; Devone Spurgeon, "State Farm Researcher's Sleuthing Helped Prompt Firestone Recall," *Wall Street Journal*, Sept. 1, 2000, p. B6; Joseph White and Stephen Power, "Federal Regulator Won't Probe Safety of Ford Explorer," *Wall Street Journal*, Feb. 13, 2002, p. A4.

18. Rebecca Santana, "Women Entrepreneurs Take on Russia," *MSNBC*, Sept. 4, 1999, www.msnbc.com/news/420132.asp.

19. "Bottom-Line Ethics," *Christian Science Monitor*, Apr. 3, 2000, p. 8, www.csmonitor.com/durable/2000/04/03/p8sl.htm.

20. "Children's Rights: Child Labor," Human Rights Watch, www.hrw.org/children/labor.htm (accessed Mar. 7, 2003).

21. Matthew L. Kish, "Human Rights and Business: Profiting from Observing Human Rights," *Ethics in Economics*, nos. 1 and 2, 1998.

22. Brandon Mitchener and Dan Bilefsky, "EU Fines Brewers, Other Companies for Price Fixing," *Wall Street Journal*, Dec. 6, 2001, p. A17.

23. David Fairlamb and Gail Edmondson, "Has the Euro Unleashed a Wave of Price-Gouging?" *Business Week*, Sept. 16, 2002, p. 4.

24. Peter Fritsch, "A Cement Titan in Mexico Thrives by Selling to Poor," *Wall Street Journal*, Apr. 22, 2002, pp. A1, A11.

25. www.prnewswire.com/cgi-bin/stories.pl?ACCT=104&STORY=/. . ./0000889557&EDATE (accessed May 8, 2000).

26. Geoff Winestock and Neil King Jr., "EU Aims at White House in Retaliation to Steel Tariffs," *Wall Street Journal*, Mar. 22, 2002, p. A2.

27. "Russian, Chinese, Taiwanese and S. Korean Companies Widely Seen Using Bribes in Developing Countries," Transparency International, press release, May 14, 2002, http://www.transparency.org/pressreleases_archive/2002/2002.05.14.bpi.en.html.

28. Skip Kaltenhauser, "Bribery Is Being Outlawed Worldwide," *Business Ethics*, May–June 1998, p. 11.

29. "Transparency International Bribe Payer's Survey 1999," Transparency International, Jan. 20, 2000, www.transparency.org/cpi/1999/bps.html.

30. "Genetic Engineering Hot New Topic in Shareholder Resolutions," *Business Ethics*, March/April 2000, p. 22.

31. Francesca Lyman, "Should Gene Foods Be Labeled?" *MSNBC*, Sept. 15, 1999, www.msnbc.com/news/312001.asp.

32. "Snapshot: U.S. Cigarette Exports," *USA Today*, www.usatoday.com/snapshot/money/msnap078.htm (accessed Mar. 7, 2003).

33. "Nestlé Infant Formula: The Consequences of Spurning the Public Image," in *Marketing Mistakes*, 3d ed., ed. Robert F. Hartley (Columbus, Ohio: Grid Publishing, 1986), pp. 47–61; "Nestlé and the Role of Infant Formula in Developing Countries: The Resolution of a Conflict," a series of reports, articles, and press releases provided by Nestlé Coordination Center for Nutrition, Inc., 1984.

34. Thomas M. Burton and Jill Carroll, "ConAgra Recalls Beef Products After at Least 16 People Become Ill," *Wall Street Journal*, July 22, 2002, p. B6.

35. Thomas M. Burton, "Baxter Devices Probed on Links with 10 Deaths," *Wall Street Journal,* Sept. 4, 2001, p. B2.

36. Betsy McKay, "PepsiCo Challenges Itself to Concoct Healthier Snacks," *Wall Street Journal,* Sept. 23, 2002, pp. A1, A10.

37. Delphi Automotive Systems Corporation 1999 Annual Report, p. 17.

38. Aaron Bernstein, Michael Arndt, Wendy Zellner, and Peter Coy, "Too Much Corporate Power," *Business Week,* Sept. 11, 2000, p. 150.

39. "Mexico City Takes Action Against Polluters," Reuters Newswire, May 31, 1998, via America Online.

40. "Greenpeace Warns Israel to Stop Sea Dumping," Reuters Newswire, June 5, 1998 via America Online.

41. "Australia May Be Worst Air Polluter," Associated Press Newswire, June 1, 1998, via America Online.

42. Mylene Mangalindan, "Users Flame New Yahoo Privacy Plan," *Wall Street Journal,* Apr. 8, 2002, p. A16.

43. Julia Angwin and Nichole Harris, "Order to Open Instant Messages May Not Matter," *Wall Street Journal,* Sept. 18, 2000, pp. A1, B8.

44. "Study: Internet Fraud Cost $18 Million," CNN, Apr. 11, 2002, www.cnn.com.

45. "In the News—April 2000," BSR, www.bsr.org/resourcecenter/news/news_output.asp?newsDT=2000-04&hTID=266 (accessed Aug. 22, 2000).

46. Cory Johnson, "Day Trading Defined," *Industry Standard,* May 13, 2000, www.thestandard.com/article/display/0%2C1151%2C12608%2C00.html.

47. Ruth Simon, "Day Trading Scrutiny Expands," *Wall Street Journal,* Aug. 25, 1999, p. C11.

48. Geri Smith, "Mexico: Zedillo Has to Sweep the Banks Clean," *Business Week Online,* June 1, 1998, www.businessweekonline.com.

49. Andrew Higgins, Alan S. Cullison, Michael Allen, and Paul Beckett, "Shell Games," *Wall Street Journal,* Aug. 26, 1999, pp. A1, A11; Andrew Higgins, Paul Beckett, and Ann Davis, "Off Duties," *Wall Street Journal,* Sept. 15, 1999, pp. A1, A17; Steve LeVine, Paul Beckett, and Andrew Higgins, "Moscow Bank Called Main Player in Russian Laundering Scheme," *Wall Street Journal,* Sept. 15, 1999, B10; Erik Portanger, "Barclays Closing Some Russian Accounts," *Wall Street Journal,* Sept. 16, 1999, p. A25; Glenn Simpson and Paul Beckett, "Money-Laundering Rules to Include Securities Firms," *Wall Street Journal,* Nov. 21, 2001, p. A2.

50. Lola Nayar, "India Is Fighting 40 Basmati Patent Cases in 25 Countries," Rediff.com, Aug. 24, 2001, www.rediff.com/money/2001/aug/24rice.htm.

51. Jefferson Graham, "Napster Ordered to Shut Down," *USA Today,* July 2, 2000, www.usatoday.com/life/music/music208.htm; "Napster Brief Denies Wrongdoing," *USA Today,* July 27, 2000, www.usatoday.com/life/cyber/tech/review/crh283.htm; "Napster Wins Respite from Shutdown Order," *USA Today,* July 29, 2000, www.usatoday.com/life/cyber/tech/review/crh356.htm; "Napster Among Top 50 Web Sites," *USA Today,* Aug. 23, 2000, www.usatoday.com/life/cyber/tech/review/crh438.htm.

52. Greg Brosman, "Guatemalan Counterfeit Law Fuels Illegal Industry," *Yahoo! Finance,* July 28, 2000, http://biz.yahoo.com/rf/000728/n28384015 .html.

53. Mrinalini Datta, "Unilever, Others Lose Millions in India to Copycats," Bloomberg.com, Sept. 7, 2000, http://...fgcgi.cgi?ptitle=All%20Columns&touch =1&s1-blk&tp=ad_topright_bbco&T-markets =fgcgi_.

54. "'One World, One Forest'; The World Trade Organization," American Lands Alliance, www.americanlands.org/forestweb/world.htm (accessed Mar. 7, 2003).

# Index